PC W⊕RLD Q&A® BIBLE

INSTANT REFERENCE CARD

BASICS: Q&A 4.0

What to do: The Main menu gives you access to Q&A's five components — word processor Write, and database components File, Report, Utilities, and the Intelligent Assistant. You select a menu option by typing the letter preceding it, by moving the cursor to the option and pressing <Enter>, or by clicking on the option with the mouse. Most instructions require <Enter> for completion.

Q&A OVERALL

Return to previous option	<Esc>
Continue/proceed	<F10> (sometimes <Enter>)
Get help	<F1>
Exit to DOS	<Esc> to Main menu, x

USING Q&A WRITE

Create new file	Write, Type/Edit
Get existing file	Write, Get, type filename, <Enter>
Clear memory for new file	Write, Clear
Save file	<Shift><F8>, type filename, <Enter>
Save file to ASCII	<Ctrl><F8>, type filename, <Enter>
Undo/restore text	<Shift><F7>
List all files and open one	Write, Get, erase filename defaults, <Enter>, move cursor to filename, <F10>

• Getting Around

Move left/right one character	<Cursor Left>/<Cursor Right>
Move up/down one line	<Cursor Up>/<Cursor Down>
Go to beginning/end of line	<Home>/<End>
Go to top/bottom of screen	<Home>/<End> twice
Go to top/bottom of page	<Home>/<End> three times
Go to beginning/end of document	<Home>/<End> four times
Go to page or line number	<Ctrl><F7> type page/line number
Scroll up/down	<F9>/<Shift><F9>
Search and replace	<F7>

• Manipulating Text

Delete character	<Backspace> or <Delete>
Delete line	<Shift><F4>
Delete to end of line	<Ctrl><F4>
Delete word	<F4>

Note: To work with text as a block, place the cursor on the first character, then select a function from the list below.

Copy block	<F5>, select block, <F10>, move cursor to new location, <F10>
Copy block to file	<Ctrl><F5>, select block, type filename, <Enter>
Move block	<Shift><F5>, select block, <F10>, move cursor to new location, <F10>
Move block to file	<Alt><F5>, select block, type filename, <Enter>
Delete block	<F3>, select block, <F10>
Print block	<Ctrl><F7>, select block, <F10>

Tip: The following commands access many of Write's features.

Text enhancement choices	<Shift><F6>
Editing options	<F8>
List fields for merge	<Alt><F7>

USING Q&A FILE

Create new file	File, Design file, Design a new file, type filename, <Enter>
Redesign existing file	File, Design file, Redesign a file, type filename, <Enter>
Save file	<Shift><F10>
Go to another menu or spec	<Shift><F9>
Import/export file	File, Utilities, Import data/Export data

• Getting Around

Go to next record	<F10>
Go to last record	<F9>
Go to next field	<Cursor Up> or <Cursor Down> or <Tab> or <Shift><Tab>
Go to beginning/end of field	<Home>/<End>
Go to top/bottom of page	<Home>/<End> twice
Go to beginning/end of form	<Home>/<End> three times
Go to beginning/end of file	<Ctrl><Home>/<Ctrl><End>
Go to previous page of form	<Page Up>
Go to next page of form	<Page Down>

• Manipulating Data

Add new records	File, Add Data, type filename, <Enter>, type data, <F10>
Add data from Update mode	<Ctrl><F6>
Delete character	<Backspace> or <Delete>
Delete word	<F4>
Delete line	<Shift><F4>
Delete record	<F3>
Insert current date/time	<Ctrl><F5>/<Alt><F5>

• Retrieve/Sort Records

Search from Main menu	File, Search/Update, type filename, <Enter>, fill in retrieve specs, <F10>
Search from within database	<F7>, fill in retrieve specs, <F10>
Sort from Main menu	File, Search/Update, type filename, <Enter>, <F8>, type sort spec, <F10>
Sort from within database	<F7>, <F8>, type sort spec, <F10>

Tip: To save retrieve specs or sort specs, fill in the requirements, <Shift><F8>, type spec name, <Enter>. To retrieve saved specs, <Alt><F8>, select spec name, <Enter>, <F10>.

• Design a New Form

Create field	From Design/Redesign file, type field
Create fixed-length field	
Create title	
Insert blank line	
Editing options	
Insert/overtype	

• Form and Table Views

Display Table View	
Return to Form View	
Redefine Table View	<Shift><F6>, type sequence, <F10>
Edit Mode in Table View	<F5>
Exit Edit Mode in Table View	<F10>
Expand field length	<F6>
List restricted values	<Alt><F7>

• Print

Print one record	<F2>, set Print Options, <F10>
Print all records	<Ctrl><F2>, set Print Options, <F10>
Design free-form or coordinate print spec	File, Print, type filename, <Enter>, Design/Redesign a Spec, type spec name, <Enter>, retrieve specs, <F10>, field specs, <F10>, <F10>

Tip: Use Help to determine what parameters to use in setting up a print spec.

D1518966

USING Q&A REPORT

For printing simple reports or preprinted forms, use File's free-form or coordinate printing options (see previous page).

Use Q&A's report function for producing more complex columnar or cross-tab reports. Press <F1> for guidelines to help in filling out report specifications.

• Designing Reports

Design columnar report	Report, Design/Redesign report, type filename, <Enter>, type report name, <Enter>, choose Columnar report, fill in retrieve specs, <F10>, fill in Column/Sort specs, <F10>, fill in Print options, <F10>
Design cross-tab report	Report, Design/Redesign report, type filename, <Enter>, type report name, <Enter>, choose Cross tab report, fill in retrieve specs, <F10>, fill in Cross tab specs, <F10>, fill in Print options, <F10>
Change page size, margins	From Print options, <F8> for Define page
Redesign report	Report, Design/Redesign report, type filename, <Enter>, type report name, <Enter>, fill in retrieve specs, <F10>, fill in Column/Sort or Cross tab specs, <F10>, fill in Print options, <F10>
Create derived column	From Column/Sort spec or Cross tab spec, <F8>, fill in Derived column specs, <F10>, fill in Print options, <F10>
Sort Columnar Report	On Column/Sort spec, select fields to be sorted, after field ID type AS (ascending sort), DS (descending sort), YS (ascending by year), or MS (ascending by month)

Tip: Sort Columnar reports when you intend to use a field for control breaks (for such tasks as calculating totals and subtotals as key values change).

• Print Report

Print from Column/Sort spec	<F10>, fill in Print options, <F10>
Print from Cross tab spec	<F10>, fill in Print options, <F10>
Print from Main menu	Report, Print, type filename, <Enter>, type report name, <Enter>, press <Enter> for no changes
Change report headers/footers	From Print options, <F8>, <Tab> to Header or Footer, type header or footer text, <F10>

• Report Global Options

Set standard column width	Report, Set global options, type filename, <Enter>, Column global options, set column heading/widths, type new heading or widths, <F10>
Set columnar format or defaults	Report, Set global options, type filename, <Enter>, Columnar global options, select and set options, <F10>
Set Cross-tab column/row heads, format, or defaults	Report, Set global options, type filename, <Enter>, Cross tab global options, select and set options, <F10>

USING Q&A UTILITIES

Use the Main menu's Utilities to define standards for Q&A as a whole. For tasks that relate only to databases, look at File Utilities, and for word processing tasks, Write Utilities.

• Printer Tasks

Install printer	Utilities, Install printer, choose printer, set/select printer port, model and mode, <F10>
Install font description files	Utilities, Modify font file, follow directions

• Miscellaneous Tasks

DOS list, rename, delete, or copy	Utilities, DOS file facilities, choose utility, when done press <F10>
Change default directory	Utilities, Set global options, <Tab> to directory, retype name, <F10>
Modify Main menu	Utilities, Alternate programs, type program name, <Tab>, type menu selection, <F10>

USING Q&A INTELLIGENT ASSISTANT

The Assistant menu contains two tools that enable you to retrieve data from a database using simple instructions: the Query Guide and the Intelligent Assistant (IA). The Query Guide provides a structured, menu-driven way to query the database that is time-consuming but well suited to beginners. The IA is more free-form, requiring you to type queries in sentences using a special syntax and vocabulary. You can expand its vocabulary as your querying needs increase.

Display quick introduction	Assistant, Get acquainted
Retrieve data using Query Guide	Assistant, Query Guide, type filename, <Enter>, follow directions
Retrieve data using IA	Assistant, Ask me to do something, type filename, <Enter>, type request, <Enter>, <Enter> to verify question
Print results of query	<F2><F10>
Define synonym	From request screen, type "Define Synonym" or press <F8>, select word function, <Enter>, type synonym, <F10>
List vocabulary	From request screen, <F6>, select type of vocabulary, <Enter>, <Esc>

Tip: To enable Q&A to answer your queries more efficiently, you can first define the contents of the fields in your database.

Describe your database to IA	Assistant, Teach me about your database, go through options 1 to 6 of Basic Lessons menu
Describe your database to Query Guide	Assistant, Teach Query Guide, follow directions as they are presented

• Special Vocabulary

Tip: Use the following terms to define the elements you want a report to show.

Suppress identifying columns	WNIC – with no identification columns
Do not print restricted columns	WNRC – with no restriction columns
Print specified columns only	WNEC – with no extra columns

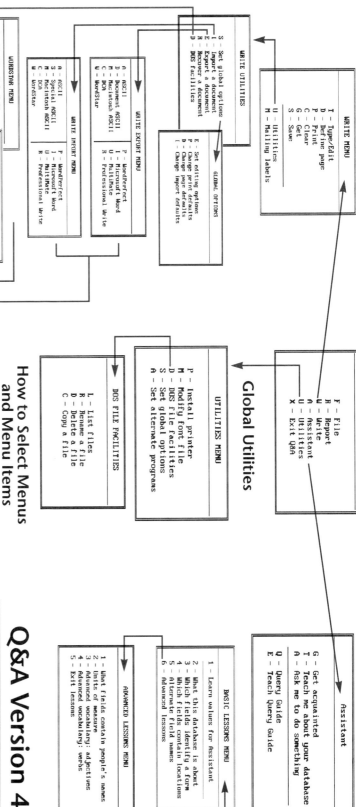

Word Processor

WRITE MENU
- T – Type/Edit
- D – Define page
- P – Print
- C – Clear
- G – Get
- S – Save
- U – Utilities
- M – Mailing labels

WRITE UTILITIES
- S – Set global options
- I – Import a document
- E – Export a document
- R – Recover a document
- D – DOS facilities

GLOBAL OPTIONS
- E – Set editing options
- M – Change print defaults
- D – Change page defaults
- I – Change import defaults

WRITE IMPORT MENU
- P – WordPerfect
- I – Microsoft Word
- U – MultiMate
- D – DCA
- R – Professional Write

WRITE EXPORT MENU
- A – ASCII
- S – Special ASCII
- M – Macintosh ASCII
- C – DCA
- U – WordStar

WORDSTAR MENU
- 1 – WordStar 3.3, 3.31
- 2 – WordStar 3.45
- 3 – WordStar 4.0
- 4 – WordStar 5.0
- 5 – WordStar 5.5

MICROSOFT WORD MENU
- 1 – Microsoft Word 3.0,3.1
- 2 – Microsoft Word 4.0
- 3 – Microsoft Word 5.0

PROFESSIONAL WRITE
- 1 – PFS:Write Version C
- 2 – Professional Write 1.0
- 3 – PFS:First Choice 1.0
- 4 – PFS:First Choice 2.0
- 5 – Pro Write 2.0, 2.1

MULTIMATE MENU
- 1 – MultiMate 3.3
- 2 – MultiMate Adv. 3.6
- 3 – MultiMate Adv. II 3.7
- 4 – MultiMate 4

WORDPERFECT MENU
- 1 – WordPerfect 5.0
- 2 – WordPerfect 5.1

DOS FACILITIES
- L – List files
- R – Rename a document
- D – Delete a document
- C – Copy a document

Global Utilities

UTILITIES MENU
- P – Install printer
- M – Modify font file
- D – DOS file facilities
- S – Set global options
- A – Set alternate programs

DOS FILE FACILITIES
- L – List files
- R – Rename a file
- D – Delete a file
- C – Copy a file

Q&A MAIN MENU
- F – File
- R – Report
- W – Write
- A – Assistant
- U – Utilities
- X – Exit Q&A

Assistant

Assistant
- G – Get acquainted
- T – Teach me about your database
- A – Ask me to do something
- Q – Query Guide
- E – Teach Query Guide

BASIC LESSONS MENU
- 1 – Learn values for Assistant
- 2 – What this database is about
- 3 – Which fields identify a form
- 4 – Which fields contain locations
- 5 – Alternate field names
- 6 – Advanced lessons

ADVANCED LESSONS MENU
- 1 – What fields contain people's names
- 2 – Units of measure
- 3 – Advanced vocabulary: adjectives
- 4 – Advanced vocabulary: verbs
- 5 – Exit lessons

How to Select Menus and Menu Items

Preset Method: Highlight the item on the menu by pressing the letter of the item, the number of the item (its relative position on the menu), or by using your cursor keys. Then press **<Enter>**.

Automatic Execution: Allows you to choose the menu item without pressing **<Enter>**.

1. Select Utilities from the Q&A Main menu.
2. Select Set Global Options from the Utilities menu.
3. At the Set Global Defaults screen, change "Automatic Execution" from No to Yes.
4. Press **<F10>** to save your new setting.

You can now choose any menu item simply by pressing its letter or the number that corresponds to its relative position on the menu.

Q&A Version 4.0
Menu System
by Thomas J. Marcellus

Showing the Five Modules:

- **FILE** (Database Manager)
- **REPORT** (Report Generator)
- **WRITE** (Word Processor — Mail Merge and Mailing Labels)
- **ASSISTANT** (Intelligent Assistant and Query Guide)
- **UTILITIES** (Global presets and DOS file Operations)

Press **<F1>** at any menu for information on the selections.

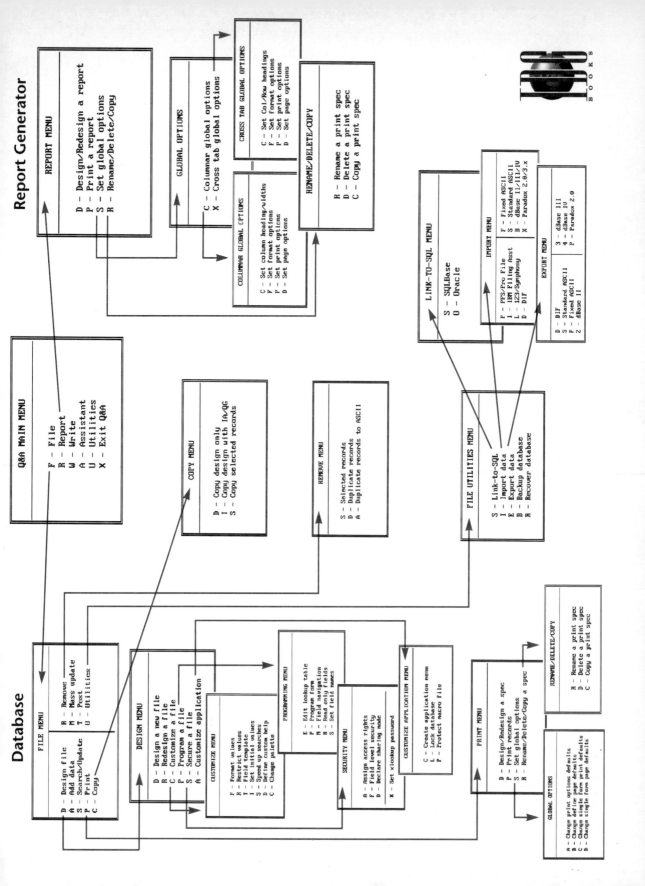

PC W🌐RLD

Q&A® BIBLE

EXPERT INSTRUCTION, TIPS & APPLICATIONS

By Thomas J. Marcellus

Technical Editor,
The Quick Answer, Q&A Journal

Special Preface by
Gordon Eubanks, Jr.
President, Symantec Corp.

IDG Books Worldwide, Inc.
An International Data Group Company
San Mateo, California 94402

PC World Q&A Bible

Published by
IDG Books Worldwide, Inc.
An International Data Group Company
155 Bovet Road, Suite 730
San Mateo, CA 94402
415-358-1250

Library of Congress Catalog Card No.: 90-084495

ISBN 1-878058-03-7

Printed in the United States of America

10 9 8 7 6 5 4 3 2 1

Project Manager: Janna Custer, Senior Editor
Editor-in-Chief: Michael E. McCarthy
Production Manager: Lana Olson
Technical review by Dr. Charles W.M. Restivo
Edited by Christine Strehlo, Eric Lach, and Jennifer Foster
Proofreading by Caroline Craig
Interior design by Peppy White
Production by University Graphics, Palo Alto, California

Distributed in the United States by IDG Books Worldwide, Inc.
Distributed in Canada by Macmillan of Canada, a Division of Canada Publishing Corporation.

For information on translations and availability in other countries, contact IDG Books Worldwide.

For sales inquiries and special prices for bulk quantities, write to the address above or call IDG Books Worldwide at 415-358-1250.

Dedication

To Mom & Dad, on your Golden Anniversary, 1991

Acknowledgements

Special thanks to Mark Winn for introducing me to the PC under duress many years ago, to Bob "Baba Ramdos" Gramcko for bringing Q&A to my attention, to Sam Taylor for suggesting I do a book on it, to Lisa Goldstone and Beth Nagengast at Symantec for their enthusiastic cooperation, and to the crack Q&A 4.0 programming team whose ingenuity and hard work have produced a great champion.

The publishers would like to give special thanks to Bill Murphy, without whom this book would not have been possible.

About IDG Books Worldwide

Welcome to the world of IDG Books Worldwide.

International Data Group (IDG) is the world's leading publisher of computer periodicals, with more than 150 weekly and monthly newpapers and magazines reaching 25 million readers in more than 40 countries. If you use personal computers, IDG Books is committed to publishing quality books that meet your needs. We rely on our extensive network of publications — including such leading periodicals as *ComputerWorld, InfoWorld, MacWorld, PC World, Portable Computing, Publish, Network World, SunWorld, AmigaWorld,* and *GamePro* — to help us make informed and timely decisions in creating useful computer books that meet your needs.

Every IDG book strives to bring extra value and skill-building instruction to the reader. Our books are written by experts, with the backing of IDG periodicals, and with careful thought devoted to issues such as audience, interior design, use of icons, and illustrations. Our editorial staff is a careful mix of high-tech journalists and experienced book people. Our close contact with the makers of computer products helps ensure accuracy and thorough coverage. Our heavy use of personal computers at every step in production means we can deliver books in the most timely manner.

We are delivering books of high quality at competitive prices, on topics customers want. At IDG, we believe in quality, and we have been delivering quality for 25 years. You'll find no better book on a subject than an IDG book.

Jonathan Sacks
President
IDG Books Worldwide, Inc.

International Data Group's publications include: ARGENTINA'S Computerworld Argentina; ASIA'S Computerworld Hong Kong. Computerworld Southeast Asia, Computerworld Malaysia. Computerworld Singapore, Infoworld Hong Kong, Infoworld SE Asia; AUSTRALIA'S Computerworld Australia, PC World, Macworld, Lotus, Publish!; AUSTRIA'S Computerwelt Oestereich; BRAZIL'S DataNews, PC Mundo, Automacao & Industria; BULGARIA'S Computer Magazine Bulgaria, Computerworld Bulgaria; CANADA'S ComputerData, Direct Access, Graduate CW, Macworld; CHILE'S Informatica, Computacion Personal; COLUMBIA'S Computerworld Columbia; CZECHOSLOVAKIA'S ComputerWorld Czechoslovakia, PC World; DENMARK'S CAD/CAM WORLD, Computerworld Danmark, PC World, Macworld, Unix World, PC LAN World, Communications World; FINLAND'S Mikro PC, Tietoviikko; FRANCE'S Le Mond Informatique, Distributique, InfoPC, Telecoms International; GERMANY'S AmigaWelt, Computerwoche, Information Management, PC Woche, PC Welt, Unix Welt, Macwelt RD; GREECE'S Computerworld, PC World, Macworld; HUNGARY'S Computerworld SZT, Mikrovilag; INDIA'S Computers & Communications; ISRAEL'S People & Computers; ITALY'S Computerworld Italia, PC World Italia; JAPAN'S Computerworld Japan, Macworld, SunWorld Journal; KOREA'S Computerworld, PC World; MEXICO'S Computerworld Mexico, PC Journal; THE NETHERLAND'S Computerworld Netherlands, PC World, AmigaWorld; NEW ZEALAND'S Computerworld New Zealand, PC World New Zealand; NIGERIA'S PC World Africa; NORWAY'S Computerworld Norge, PC World Norge CAD/CAM, Macworld Norge; PEOPLE'S REPUBLIC OF CHINA'S China Computerworld, China Computerworld Monthly; PHILLIPPINE'S Computerworld Phillippines, PC Digest/PC World; POLAND'S Komputers Magazine, Computerworld; ROMANIA'S Infoclub; SPAIN'S CIM World, Communicaciones World, Computerworld Espana, PC World, AmigaWorld; SWEDEN'S ComputerSweden, PC/Nyhetherna, Mikrodatorn, PC World, Macworld; SWITZERLAND'S Computerworld Schweiz, Macworld; TAIWAN'S Computerworld Taiwan, PC World, Publish; THAILAND'S Computerworld; TURKEY'S Computerworld Monitor, PC World/Turkiye; UNITED KINGDOM'S Graduate Computerworld, PC Business World, ICL Today, Lotus UK, Macworld UK; UNITED STATES' AmigaWorld, A+, CIO, Computerworld, Digital News, Federal Computer Week, GamePro, InfoWorld, Lotus, Macworld, Network World, NextWorld, PC Games, PC World, Portable Office, PC Letter, Publish!, Run, SunWorld Journal; USSR'S MIR PC, Computerworld, Computer Express, Network, Manager Magazine; VENEZUELA'S Computerworld Venezuela, Micro Computerworld; YUGOSLAVIA'S Moj Mikro

Contents

Chapter 2:
Write — Your Full-Featured Word Processor 43

Chapter 3:
File — The Workhorse Database Manager 153

Chapter 4:
Advanced Database Design and Procedures 243

Chapter 5: Mail Merge and Mailing Labels 351

Chapter 6:
Report — The Information Generator 379

Chapter 7: Q&A's English-Language Interface 465

Chapter 8:
Q&A Macros and Custom Application Menus 527

Chapter 9: Utilities — The Q&A Toolkit..................577

Chapter 10: Business Applications in Q&A.............631

Chapter 11:
Using & Customizing Your Free Disk Applications........687

Foreword

Q&A's remarkable success in recent years is largely due to the support of the community of Q&A enthusiasts who have contributed to the improvement of the product through their imaginative technical ideas, suggestions, and tailored solutions.

Version 4.0, the culmination of that community's efforts to get the most from Q&A, is an exciting, innovative product that breaks important new ground in meeting the wide-ranging automation needs of today's businesses. Offering an even greater level of power without sacrificing any of the ease of use that has made Q&A the number-one-rated and top-selling file manager and word processor, Q&A version 4.0 is, we're confident, the only database you'll ever need.

Tom Marcellus's *PC World Q&A Bible* is a key reference guide to have on your shelf. An important book both for Symantec and the Q&A user community, it delves deeply into the tremendous power of Q&A on a real-world applications level, demonstrating techniques that harness that power even if you have no previous programming or software experience.

With its step-by-step approach to building sophisticated interactive business applications by drawing on Q&A's enhanced features and capabilities, *PC World Q&A Bible* shows you how to automate your business yourself — painlessly and intelligently. If you've been using Q&A 3.0, you'll find all the fantastic new version 4.0 tools explored here, enabling you to further boost your existing data management, mail-merge, and reporting productivity. If you're brand new to Q&A, this book will move you through all the basics quickly, and then on to the stimulating realm of advanced techniques.

PC World Q&A Bible offers a unique approach to tapping the potential of Q&A because it takes advantage of the experience and insight of a veteran Q&A consultant and applications developer. Tom Marcellus has created scores of automation solutions for a wide variety of business types and sizes. So whether Q&A is your first file manager, or you're a professional software developer who needs a time-saving alternative that makes it easy to build fully customized applications for your clients, this book will help you get the most from our award-winning integrated package.

At Symantec we've listened carefully to our user community to ensure that your experience with Q&A is a rewarding one. Explore Q&A 4.0, enjoy its ease and flexibility, use it to meet all your word processing, data management, and information requirements. And use this book as your guide in designing the specific applications you'll need to bring the indispensable power of automation to your business.

— Gordon Eubanks, Jr.
President and CEO
Symantec Corporation

xviii

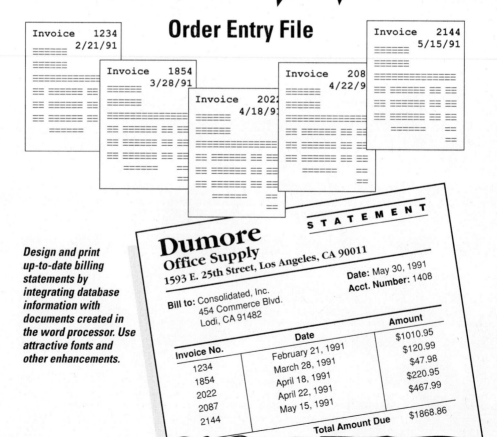

APPLICATION MENU

1 - Order Entry
2 - Add New Customer
3 - Add New Stock No.
4 - Table Vu Inventory
5 - Outstanding POs
6 - Close POs
7 - Post Cash Received
8 - Update Inventory
9 - Print Statements

Design custom application menus to configure Q&A to your exact data entry and processing needs.

Customer File

Acct# 12344
Smith & Smith Inc.

Acct# 3411
The Barnes Company

Acct# 1408
Consolidated Inc.
454 Commerce Bl.
Lodi CA 91482
Limit $2000.00
Type Retail

Inventory File

Stk# RJ34C Paper Tray
Cost $3.50 **Price** $8.00

Stk# B255X Office Chair
Cost $37.00 **Price** $69.00

Stk# X355 Utility Table
Cost $12.50 **Price** $37.95
On Hand 17 **On Order** 30

Use your Q&A databases interactively. Information from one file can be retrieved into another file at your command. And you can "Post" values between different files.

Update your inventory from sales, or process and print your monthly billing statements with the press of a key.

Order Entry File

Invoice 1234 2/21/91
Invoice 1854 3/28/91
Invoice 2022 4/18/91
Invoice 2087 4/22/91
Invoice 2144 5/15/91

Design and print up-to-date billing statements by integrating database information with documents created in the word processor. Use attractive fonts and other enhancements.

S T A T E M E N T

Dumore
Office Supply
1593 E. 25th Street, Los Angeles, CA 90011

Date: May 30, 1991
Acct. Number: 1408

Bill to: Consolidated, Inc.
454 Commerce Blvd.
Lodi, CA 91482

Invoice No.	Date	Amount
1234	February 21, 1991	$1010.95
1854	March 28, 1991	$120.99
2022	April 18, 1991	$47.98
2087	April 22, 1991	$220.95
2144	May 15, 1991	$467.99
	Total Amount Due	$1868.86

Introduction

Since the first version of Q&A, released by Symantec in 1985, Q&A has justifiably built itself a reputation for giving you easy access to your information in its database report and word processing modules. Now Symantec has improved on that reputation by adding myriad improvements to Q&A with release 4.0 in May 1991.

Q&A 4.0 can do it all, whether your goal is to store names and addresses of customers to merge with personalized form letters and mailing labels; to maintain information on inventory items, equipment, real estate, insurance policies, and sales prospecting; or to use an integrated system to automate your company's day-to-day business activities, from purchasing to payroll.

There's one catch, however. In order to *really* explore the depth and potential of Q&A 4.0 you'll need this book. Why? Because here you'll find not only the basics, but also the techniques you need to create sophisticated applications — techniques complemented by a wealth of inside tips and tricks on how to approach, design, and fine-tune your Q&A applications to meet your exact needs.

I am currently technical editor of *The Quick Answer,* which provides tricks, tips and application ideas for Q&A users. I am also a business consultant specializing in Q&A, and have more than five years of real-world experience in customizing Q&A for business clients.

This means that I've got a good handle on the types of applications business people want, as well as what they need their existing Q&A applications to do for them but don't know how to make the product deliver. I know that Q&A users as a group are not really using the software to its fullest advantage, and it seems to me that it's time users of the product were offered a book that explores the basics as well as the expanded role the more sophisticated Q&A features play in practical applications.

This book shows you how to do it all with Q&A: expert word processing, comprehensive database file management, sophisticated mail-merge, exceptional reporting, and more. This book is your complete guide to the features and techniques you can use to harness the full power of Q&A to fill all your automation needs.

Who Can Use This Book

I call this book the *Q&A Bible* because I've tried to make it complete and useful for everyone from beginners to advanced users. It's the one book you'll need no matter where on the Q&A learning curve you are right now.

• If you're contemplating purchasing Q&A, use this book to familiarize yourself with the software and discover how Q&A can help you meet your business automation needs.

• If you've recently purchased Q&A and are looking for ideas and assistance with specific applications for your home or office, this is the book for you. Even if you've never before worked with a word processor or have no inkling of what a database actually is or does, you'll find the answers here, as well as specific examples to help you put Q&A to work for you right now.

• If you're already experienced with Q&A, use this book to find out what new features version 4.0 has to offer and to explore advanced database design, programming, reporting, and integration techniques in order to improve your existing applications and design valuable new ones.

• If you're a business owner or manager seeking real know-how and clear, comprehensive examples in order to rapidly build database, report, and mail-merge applications to manage and expand your operations, you've come to the right place.

• And if you're a software developer who thinks that only a relational database product can satisfy your clients' needs, find out here how you may be able to get everything you need in Q&A — for hundreds of dollars less, in a fraction of the time, and *without* a steep learning curve for you or your clients.

• If you're already an experienced Q&A user shopping for tips and tricks to beef up your applications, you can use the material on advanced database design and programming in Chapter 4, the information on advanced power tools in Chapter 12, and also Chapter 10, where the focus is on making your applications interactive.

Note: You can use this book with version 3.0, but keep in mind that some of the menu options will differ, as will a number of the procedures and exercises discussed in the text. Even though version 3.0 and the new version 4.0 look and feel similar throughout most of the program, there will be places in this book where you will not be able to accomplish the objective under discussion with the older version.

As you read the book you'll learn how to think and work creatively with Q&A so that no matter what types of applications you need — modest or advanced — you'll be equipped to tackle them rapidly and with a great deal of personal satisfaction.

To that end, included with this book is a valuable Q&A application diskette. Containing ten fully designed business databases and a variety of ready-to-use report formats, as well as several additional files, it represents more than 100 hours of expert development time.

What Q&A Is

While today's more advanced word processing programs do offer limited database functions, such as the capability to store and retrieve name and address lists for merging into documents, they're document-oriented and tend to be awkward file managers. Further, they can't provide you with reports on what's in your files.

And database management programs, which are designed to accumulate and manipulate data, are not very adept at rigorous text-related tasks.

Because of these limitations and the business world's demand for *both* types of programs, *integrated* software packages have become increasingly popular. Combining two or more software functions such as word processing and data file management under a single consistent user interface, these products have ushered in a new era in computing convenience.

The leader in this class of integrated software — with both an award-winning database and a full-featured word processor — is Symantec Corporation's Q&A. Exceptionally easy to work with, yet powerful enough to satisfy the information and processing needs of even large corporations, Q&A is today's top-rated and best-selling integrated word processor and file manager.

(Here's proof: Since 1988, Q&A has been named the number one Flat File Database by *PC Week* (1989), *Software Digest* (1988), *LAN Times* (1989), and *InfoWorld* (1988). It also has received *PC Magazine's* 1988 Award for Technical

Excellence and also the April 1988 Editor's Choice award; *InfoWorld* rated it 1989 Best Buy in Its Class; *Software Digest* rated Q&A the number one Simplified Word Processor in July 1989; Software Publishers Association rated Q&A the Best Business Application: Numeric or Data Oriented, Best Multi-User Product, and Best Multi-function Program in 1989; and *PC World* gave it its October 1990 Readers Choice award.)

What Can Q&A Do?

Q&A is divided into several modules: database, word processing, report generator, utilities, Intelligent Assistant, and custom application menus, each with unique capabilities and unexpected power that can help you do your job quickly and efficiently. Here is a summary of the features in each module.

Database Power

Although one of Q&A's strengths is query simplicity, query simplicity isn't of much practical value if the product itself is limited by the types of information it can handle, the size and volume of records it can manage, or by restrictions placed on your database design options. You'll find that Q&A is every bit as versatile in accommodating your custom design requirements as it is adept at manipulating even extremely large data files.

Q&A is outstanding for the following types of database management applications:

- Personnel, insurance, medical, student, and activity records.

- Lists of clients, contacts, suppliers, and customers, with all their particulars, and tracking office supplies, services contracts, and the like.

- Maintaining schedules of appointments and meetings and expense and travel reports.

- Simple financial records, such as checkbook and savings account balances, asset and liability records, personal financial records.

- More sophisticated financial record-keeping such as commercial accounts payable, accounts receivable, and monthly billings.

- Routine business order-processing tasks such as invoicing, purchase orders, and sales orders.

- Interactive applications such as order-processing systems for which you need to look up information or update records in one file based on information in other files.

- Creating stand-alone applications, complete with custom menu systems, that you can then sell to others.

In Chapters 3, 4, 10, 11, and 12 you will learn to use Q&A for some of the above applications as well as to design and redesign new database forms to manage order processing, customer, employee, and inventory information.

Word Processing Power

Q&A's word processor, called "Write," is full-featured and integrates completely with the File module. The Write module can be used as a stand-alone word processor (and in fact can be purchased separately) for composing, formatting, and printing letters, articles, contracts, memos — anything for which you would use a typewriter. But it also includes features that go far beyond even the most sophisticated electronic typewriters.

Q&A's word processing module is ideal for:

- Business correspondence, memos, outlines, policy and training manuals, contracts, and proposals.

- Advertising, announcements, and other types of mass mailings where you want your promotional materials personally addressed to specific persons and firms.

- Producing address labels for shipping and mailing (these operations require some database interaction).

- Articles, term papers, books, and research reports that do not require extensive indexes and footnotes.

Write's capabilities will be discussed in detail in Chapter 2.

Report Generator

Creating simple or sophisticated reports in Q&A is a snap. You simply tell Q&A which columns of the report you want the information in, how you want it to appear when printed, and whether you want the report to include totals, subtotals, and so on. Producing a report on information in a Q&A database can be as easy as typing 1, 2, and 3 into the three fields you want to see as columns in the report. Both standard columnar and cross-tabulated summary report formats are available.

In Chapter 6 you'll learn how to design and print a variety of reports that will tell you everything you could possibly want to know about what's in your records and files.

Intelligent Assistant

Q&A is the only database product on the market that allows you to query and manipulate your data through natural-language commands. To you and me, this means plain *English*.

Also in the Assistant module you'll find Q&A's exciting new Query Guide. You can use the Query Guide (QG) instead of the Intelligent Assistant to build your queries and reports a step at a time.

The Intelligent Assistant and its Query Guide are options you can use or not, depending on the level of skill possessed by those using your system and their familiarity with Q&A. It has some drawbacks or trade-offs. In Chapter 7 I'll show you how to get the most from it and how to decide whether to use it at all.

Help

Most software products offer some form of on-screen help feature to assist when you become confused or uncertain as to how to proceed. Q&A furnishes *context-sensitive* help — information that pertains to what you are working on at the moment.

You can also create *custom* help screens for your Q&A databases to assist data entry people, placing the screens strategically so that if an error is made during data entry your help screen will pop up to give the operator information more specific than that offered by Q&A's built-in help.

Help and creating custom help screens will be covered in greater detail in Chapter 4.

Utilities

You'll need to use the Q&A utilities if you need to import data or documents from other programs (such as dBASE, Paradox, Lotus 1-2-3, Professional File, ASCII, WordPerfect, Microsoft Word, MultiMate, and WordStar), export from Q&A to other formats, or recover database or document files that have been damaged by power interruptions or disk problems. You'll learn all about how to make optimal use of these various utilities as we proceed through the book.

Custom Applications in Q&A

An especially attractive advantage of Q&A is the complete freedom you have to design powerful custom applications. Version 4.0 added an even greater level of flexibility with the addition of several new features, including the capability to create custom application menus to launch procedures and operations tailored to the way you work with Q&A.

Of course, this doesn't mean that Q&A will design your applications for you. Only you can do that. But your efforts, guided by Q&A's excellent help facilities and built-in error-trapping, will pay off. The illustration at the beginning of this introduction is one example of the unexpected power of Q&A.

I'll show you how to customize Q&A for your applications as we go along, but especially in Chapters 8, 10, and 11.

What's New in Q&A 4.0?

Myriad improvements were added to Q&A with the May 1991 upgrade release. Below is a brief summary of these improvements. (A *complete* rundown of *all* the new Q&A 4.0 features, along with specific chapter references, can be found in Appendix A).

The Database

- Batch Posting enables users to post values to selected *external* database fields, enabling you to retrieve as well as write information to databases other than the one in which you're working.

- You can store and reuse database query, sorting, mass update, posting, merge, import, export, and table view specifications, eliminating the need to retype complex parameters. Also, you can now edit database records while in the table view.

- Updates to Q&A's Import/Export feature allow conversion to and from the latest dBASE and Paradox releases, and import conversion for Lotus 1-2-3 2.2 and Professional File 2.0.

- Automatic lookups to multiple external database fields can be accomplished with a single command; direct external lookup to dBASE II, III, and IV files is now possible as well.

- Field templates speed up and control the entry of values, such as telephone and Social Security numbers.

- Pop-up lists enable you to fill in fields by selecting restricted values.

- New forced lowercase and initial capitalization text-formatting types make data input easier and consistent.

- Application development tools are far more sophisticated: custom menus can be created; macros can be named and locked into specific Q&A applications, and macro files can be protected; database operations can be locked, and access to file information can be restricted at the field level with read-only and hidden fields; complete stand-alone applications that don't even look like Q&A can be designed and even sold to third parties without a license.

- Records can be queried and retrieved using optional programming functions.

- New database utilities help you find and delete duplicate records, and print optional programming statements for easy program editing.

- A host of new and improved programming features are included for you to use at your option. You can still do wonders with Q&A with absolutely no programming.

- A field editor allows you to comfortably view and edit lengthy programming statements and expand text field size up to 32K (16 pages) during data entry.

- Q&A's mail-merge feature is more versatile; programming functions and multifile lookup can now be used in advanced mail-merge applications.

- Links to Oracle and Gupta SQL servers are available.

Report Generator

- New cross-tabulated report capabilities enable you to see spreadsheet-like summaries and relationships between collections of database information.

- Report Preview enables you to view reports on-screen in what-you-see-is-what-you-get (WYSIWYG) format before sending them to the printer.

- Line spacing and split-record control are now user-selectable.

- Printing is enhanced — use bold, italics, and fonts anywhere in your forms and reports.

- Standard deviation and variance in reports can be specified.

- Conditional logic is available in report-derived columns.

Word Processing

- WYSIWYG support on the document screen is improved.

- Page preview enables you to see exactly what the document will look like before printing.

- Hyphenation is made easier.

- A 660,000-word thesaurus is built in.

- Optional mail-merge programming is provided — merge information from multiple databases; use formulas and calculations on multiple fields.

- Mailing-label printing is improved — multiple labels can be printed, and greater support for Avery labels is provided.

- Text can be formatted in all uppercase, lowercase, or initial caps.

- Document conversion is enhanced to support conversion to and from the most popular word processing programs, including WordPerfect, Microsoft Word, and WordStar.

- Support for scalable fonts is enhanced.

- Pagination and search/replace capabilities can be implemented across joined documents.

- Damaged documents can be recovered.

Intelligent Assistant

- A query guide assists in performing Intelligent Assistant operations.

- The Intelligent Assistant's vocabulary is expanded to speed execution of English-language commands.

Network

- Record-locking is automatic, and screen update is instantaneous.

- Network user group security features are built in, including seven levels of password protection.

General

- Q&A installs automatically on your hard disk.

- A mouse can be used to select items from menus and lists, and to navigate through documents and database forms.

- Improved memory management makes it easier to work with long documents and perform complex queries and reports.

- Printer support is improved.

- Macros can be run from pop-up lists and user-designed menus.

- Enhancements and other word-processing and file operations can be selected from convenient pop-up menus, eliminating the need to remember function key assignments.

- Custom 72-character descriptions of files can be created.

- A built-in support diagnostics window reports on your computer's configuration and status — you can get the important facts on your system by pressing **<Ctrl><F3>** from the Q&A Main menu.

Have any of these vigorous new features been added at the expense of Q&A's acclaimed ease of use? Not at all. Now you can simply do more with Q&A, and do it more simply.

For Users of Earlier Versions of Q&A

This book was written with Q&A version 4.0 in mind. The 4.0 version features not only enable you to do more with Q&A, but make Q&A even easier to use. So I encourage you to upgrade right away.

Symantec's upgrade policy is this: If you purchased your copy of Q&A *on or after* March 6, 1991, you're entitled to a free upgrade. If you purchased Q&A *before* March 6, 1991, the upgrade is yours for $85. Registered Q&A users should have received an upgrade announcement along with an order form from Symantec by May 31, 1991. If you didn't send in your registration card after purchasing Q&A, or should have received the upgrade offer but didn't, call Symantec's upgrade hotline at 800-228-4122, ext. 101.

If ordering your upgrade by mail, be sure to tell Symantec whether you want the program in 5.25- or 3.5-inch diskette format. You'll receive the 4.0 program along with the new documentation. Send your order to:

Symantec Corporation
10201 Torre Avenue
Cupertino, CA 95014-2132
Attn: Q&A Upgrade

The list price of Q&A 4.0 is $399, but it should be available from your local software store or mail-order house for under $300.

How to Use This Book

As I proceed through the book I'll be guiding you in creating a complete automated system. By the end of the book we'll have a typical company's (and perhaps yours, too) entire order-processing and information system in Q&A, including customer records, supplier data, purchase ordering, inventory control, sales invoicing, and even personnel records. But if you're not looking for Q&A to handle these particular types of applications for you, don't worry; we're simply using them to provide a practical framework within which to explore Q&A's features and application potential. As you observe the concepts and techniques in action along the way, you'll recognize how to make similar use of them in whatever types of applications you happen to be most interested.

By the time you've finished with the book you'll be a master, fully equipped to tackle virtually any application with Q&A.

 Note: This books goes far beyond the documentation that ships with Q&A. It includes the experience that I have picked up over the last 10 years as a general business consultant, the last five as an office automation and database consultant.

Each chapter (database management, word processing, and the like) also includes the tricks and tips that I have learned or gathered in my job as technical editor of *The Quick Answer*.

In Chapter 1 I'll help you **install** Q&A on your computer's hard disk and I'll customize Q&A for your particular brand of printer, and take you on a quick tour of Q&A's menu system and major features so you'll feel confident moving around inside the program.

In Chapter 2 we'll explore all the features of Q&A's easy-to-learn word processor, **Write**, and bring you up to speed on creating, revising, formatting, and printing documents.

In Chapter 3 I'll take you step by step through all the basics of designing data entry forms in the Q&A **File** module. You'll learn how to map out your database requirements, place information fields on your input forms, redesign your forms when the need arises, add new records to your files, and sort, retrieve, and update these records after they've been entered.

In Chapter 4 we'll employ advanced features and techniques to **customize** your databases for extra performance. Here you'll also learn how to make use of Q&A's powerful **file management** features to manipulate selected groups of database records. The sophisticated order entry database that we'll create here can also be found on the Applications disk supplied with this book.

In Chapter 5 I'll guide you through Q&A's celebrated **mail-merge** and **mailing label** facilities. You'll get all the basics and then discover a variety of techniques for creating the kinds of sophisticated applications that are sure to meet your toughest mail-merge requirements. The customer database that we'll customize here is also on the Applications disk.

In Chapter 6 I'll give you the know-how you need to produce all kinds of useful and good-looking **reports** from the information contained in your databases. Standard reports in Q&A are a snap to design once you've observed the process in action. Together, we'll also design several more complex multiple-file and derived-column reports, and a cross-tabulated summary report as well.

In Chapter 7 I'll tell you about the **Intelligent Assistant**, Q&A's unique interface that allows you to query and even change the information contained in your database files using ordinary English commands.

In Chapter 8 you'll learn how to create, save, and use **macros** — those productivity boosters you can use anywhere in Q&A to automate document handling and reduce the time spent performing routine database chores. Here you'll also learn how to create custom menus that alter the look and feel of Q&A to suit your preference. You'll find out how you can run your reports and data management procedures with a single keystroke.

In Chapter 9 I'll focus on the **Utilities** module, Q&A's handy toolkit for **importing** and **exporting** data and documents between Q&A and other software products. This chapter also shows you how to **secure** your database designs against unauthorized tampering, and use Q&A's other utilities as well.

In Chapter 10 I'll explore Q&A's **advanced applications** potential, creating a variety of databases leading to a robust business management system that draws on the wealth of facilities Q&A offers. You'll make your databases interactive, and exploit Q&A's complementary features to accomplish objectives appropriate to your own particular information and processing needs. The databases that we'll create here can also be found on the Applications disk that is supplied with this book.

In Chapter 11 I'll discuss the **Applications disk** supplied with this book that contains nine fully designed business databases and a variety of ready-to-use report formats, as well as several additional files. I'll tell you how to install the diskette files on your hard disk and use them to your best advantage.

Included in Chapter 11 is a **tutorial** that takes you through the system a step at a time. Once you've gotten a feel for how the database files and reports work, you can then use what you've learned in the preceding chapters to modify them to accommodate your exact data management and information requirements.

Chapter 12 is for truly advanced users. I'll tell you how to create a **window-like environment** for Q&A as well as a powerful **UPS manifesting system** and a complete monthly billing statement application.

Finally, in Chapter 13, I'll examine the essentials of installing and running Q&A in a **multiuser** environment, including how to create network user groups and set up password protection schemes to guard against unauthorized access to database information and operations.

Several appendixes are also included at the back of this book.

Appendix A is a comprehensive list of all of the **new features** of Q&A 4.0, divided by function.

In **Appendix B** I'll tell you how to use Q&A's **fax capabilities**, **serial port settings**, and **special printer options**, as well as troubleshooting common printer and font problems.

Appendix C contains a list of the **extended IBM graphics character set**, while **Appendix D** tells you how to use the **Symantec Bulletin Board System**, **Appendix E** lists the Q&A **program files**, and **Appendix F** tells you how to use Q&A with a **mouse**.

Appendix G covers Q&A's **QABACKUP** program, a handy little backup/restore utility that runs from its own DOS prompt, and **Appendix H** explains how to run Q&A under Windows 3.0.

Sample Files on Disk

The Applications disk supplied with this book contains ten fully designed business databases and a variety of ready-to-use report formats, as well as several additional files.

You'll find these database applications discussed in detail in Chapters 4, 5, 10, and 11. They'll go far in helping you quickly harness the application power of Q&A, enabling you to put this power to work for you right away. See Chapter 11 for details on how to modify these databases for your needs.

Filename	Description
README.DOC	Special instructions in ASCII document format on installing and using the Apps disk.
MENUMCRO.ASC	ASCII macro file containing custom menu structures and menu item macros.
INVOICE.DTF	Records and generates formal invoices you can send to customers. Retrieves information from external databases CUSTOMER.DTF, STOCK.DTF, and UPSRATES.DTF.
PO.DTF	Records and generates formal purchase orders you can send to suppliers for stock items. Retrieves information from external databases VENDOR.DTF and STOCK.DTF.
CUSTOMER.DTF	Records and maintains customer-related information such as name, address, phone, and credit limit.
VENDOR.DTF	Records and maintains supplier-related information such as company name, address, phone, salesperson, products supplied, and terms.
STOCK.DTF	Records and maintains product-related information such as stock numbers, descriptions, costs, prices, and quantities on hand. Uses VENDOR.DTF as lookup file.
EMPLOYEE.DTF	Records and maintains employee-related information such as name, address, position, hire date, pay rate, tax status code, emergency contact, and vacation and sick days.
RECEIVER.DTF	Records the receipt of stock items delivered from outside vendors, which are then posted to STOCK.DTF and PO.DTF. Uses both PO.DTF and STOCK.DTF to verify that PO number and stock number entered are valid.

Filename	Description
SHIPDATE.DTF	Records actual date orders were shipped. Dates are then posted to INVOICE.DTF.
REMIT.DTF	Where remittances received in payment of invoices are entered. They are then posted daily to INVOICE.DTF. Uses INVOICE.DTF as lookup file to validate invoice number entered.
UPSRATES.DTF	Functions as a dummy UPS shipping rates database. INVOICE.DTF programming retrieves UPS shipping charges from this file based on shipping point, delivery zone, and calculated total weight of items on invoice.

Icons

This book contains tips (both those documented by Q&A and those found nowhere else but here), warnings, reminders, and notes, as well as identifiers of new features of Q&A 4.0. These tips, warnings, and the like can be identified by icons next to the relevant text. You've already seen a few of these icons in this introduction. Here's what they'll look like and what they'll mean:

 New: These tell you that the feature being discussed is a new feature in Q&A; or, if not new, then vastly improved.

 Tip: The text next to this icon gives you shortcuts and ideas of the best way to do things. While these tips are mentioned in the Q&A documentation, I've expanded on them to make them clearer and more useful to you.

 Author's Tip: These ideas and shortcuts are not documented by Symantec. They have come from my own knowledge and experience and are designed to help you enhance your existing applications to get exactly the result you want.

Remember: These are basic concepts from elsewhere in the book that I'm reiterating here.

 Warning: This information is vital to the well being of your files! If you ignore it, you are likely to spend hours recreating your work.

 Note: This information isn't vital to your knowledge about a specific problem, but it is helpful.

Summary

Q&A continues to win high acclaim from the industry, and sales figures peg it as one of the most popular integrated software packages out there. It's especially pleasing to me to have this opportunity to give you the grand tour of what I consider to be the top gun of today's business-oriented integrated software packages.

About the Author

Tom Marcellus received his B.A. with honors in business administration from Eastern Michigan University in 1972. Since 1985 he has been a technical writer, editor, and business automation consultant specializing in microcomputer database management and information solutions for small- to medium-sized companies.

Tom has been a Q&A applications developer since version 2.0, and served on the Q&A 4.0 beta-testing team, closely following the new version's development since May of 1990. He is currently the editor of *The Quick Answer,* an independent monthly guide to Q&A expertise published by Pinnacle Publishing, Inc. of Federal Way, Washington.

Chapter 1
Starting Out Smart
With Q&A®

In this chapter you'll learn:

▶ Q&A's technical specifications.

▶ How to use Q&A's built-in help screens.

▶ How to install the Q&A program files on your hard disk.

▶ How to fine-tune Q&A for your system.

▶ How to create directories for your Q&A files.

▶ How to customize Q&A to work with your printer.

▶ How to use Q&A's menu system.

▶ How to choose which Q&A modules (Write, File, Report, Intelligent Assistant, and Utilities) are best suited to your tasks.

This chapter covers the basics of Q&A — what it is, how much memory is required to run it, how to install it, and how to use the menus — at the same time giving you good computer techniques that you can apply to other software packages as well.

Overview

Since the first version of Q&A was released by Symantec in 1985, the product has been designed as an integrated business application package suited for newcomers to the world of automation; yet the product is also tough enough to handle large and complex data management and information chores. Since version 1.0, Symantec has remained true to its commitment to easy access to your information. Entering data *into* the computer is one thing. But to painlessly manipulate, retrieve, and make sense of it all later is quite another. Q&A excels at both.

The very name of the product, an abbreviation of "Question and Answer," underscores the software maker's continued emphasis on the simplicity of *querying,* or asking questions about what's in the database.

For example, you might need to know which of your customers are located in California and view the answer in a report sorted by customer name. All database products provide the means to perform a simple query like this, but Q&A makes it exceptionally easy. Moreover, using Q&A's unique Intelligent Assistant module, you can simply type: "List CA customers in alphabetical order," and Q&A will give you the answer.

Q&A: A Flat-File Database...

Q&A is what is often referred to as a *flat-file* database manager. I'll explain. *Relational* databases (such as Paradox and dBASE) store their database information in two-dimensional tables (in rows and columns, like a spreadsheet) and such programs can work with two or more files at the same time through links established by common fields and various programming procedures.

Such an arrangement allows, for example, the data in one file to be automatically updated when a change to related fields in a separate database are made. Therefore, if you had a customer file and an invoice file, you could set up a relationship so that when the customer's address is changed in the customer file, that change will be automatically reflected in all the invoices on file for that particular customer. Establishing such relational links, however, can be complicated, and typically requires extensive database know-how and programming expertise.

A flat filer does not possess the facilities for programming such cross-file links as above, although it can rival its high-end relational counterparts in a number of other ways.

...With Relational Features

A Q&A database, for example, can be quickly programmed to retrieve data from an external database and place that data into the current data entry form — a powerful capability for a nonrelational database product. For example, when creating an invoice, you can have the customer's name and complete address from the customer file automatically looked up and typed in; likewise, you can have an ordered item's description and price looked up and typed into the invoice when you enter the part number.

In the area of posting or copying values from one database to another, Q&A has advanced far ahead of any other flat filer. The posting feature available in version 4.0 enables you to link fields common to two databases and replace, add to, subtract, multiply, or divide values in one database's records to or from the corresponding field values in the other database. This new feature makes important operations such as updating inventory records from invoice line items, and even accounting operations, possible.

These two features taken together — decidedly *untypical* of flat-file database packages — bring to Q&A users the functional benefits of two of the main reasons why people often decide in favor of the more complex relational databases.

Look at it this way: if a flat filer is far easier to work with, offers more database and report flexibility than you are ever likely to need, can emulate the most desirable features of a relational product, and offers built-in word processing with spelling checker, thesaurus, automatic mail-merge and mailing label facilities — *and these are the capabilities you need* — then what's the point in spending several hundred dollars more on a complicated software package only to face a steeper learning curve? And after all that, you may use only 10 percent of the product's capabilities.

Today's Q&A represents an advance in software capability that goes far beyond the simple word processor and flat-file database manager of previous years. And it does so without sacrificing the ease of use for which flat-file database management systems are well known. Combining power and versatility with a remarkably short learning curve, Q&A has become the solution of choice for both small businesses and corporate giants who need to get their computer applications up and running in a hurry.

Database Power

A database is a file — a collection of many records. Each record, in turn, is a collection of information about a particular subject. One could have a database of customers, including their names, addresses, and phone numbers; a database of component parts, products, used cars, books, insurance policies, geographical locations, suppliers, invoices, purchase orders, and so forth.

For example, a form for a database of inventory items would contain information blanks (called "fields") for storing the part number, description, price, and any additional particulars. Each individual record in that database will contain these same fields. Only the information in the fields will vary.

The three major elements of any database are the fields placed into the form during the database design phase, the individual database records with the information entered into those fields, and the file as a whole. In Q&A, designing a database can be as easy as typing this on the screen:

```
Company:

Street:

City:          State:          Zip:
```

then pressing a few keys, and then entering your information. Table 1-1 summarizes Q&A design limits with respect to the maximum number of fields in a record, records in a database, and maximum file size.

Table 1-1
Q&A File Limits

Screen pages per form (record)	10
Fields per record	2,045
Fields per screen page	248
Characters per record	64,512
Characters per field	32,768
Number of records per file	16 million
File size	1,024 megabytes

A single Q&A database can manage up to 2,045 different items per record and up to 16 million individual records per database file. There is no upper limit on the number of different databases you can have. All limits, of course, are subject to available space on your hard disk.

As you can see, Q&A is very generous when it comes to the size of a data file, the number of records it can contain, and the maximum size of each record in the database. Referring to Q&A as a "powerful" database manager is something of an understatement. Many databases — even some of the expensive high-end products — permit no more than a few hundred fields per record; Q&A gives you more than 2,000. Where some limit you to only a few screen pages per record, Q&A allows you to use up to 10.

You can specify up to 115 indexes per file (to speed searches and other database operations) and up to 512 sorting levels. Seven information types are supported (text, numeric, money, date, time, yes/no, and keyword). Q&A's decimal accuracy stretches to 15 digits, and you can do arithmetic on date and time information. You can add speed and flexibility to your data entry with optional easy-to-learn programming commands. Q&A can look up and return information from other Q&A and dBASE databases, as well as copy values from one database file to another on a field-to-field basis, performing arithmetic operations on the data along the way.

Reports with up to 50 columns and 50 sorting levels are supported, and you can save up to 200 different report designs per database. If you need to work between other database or word processing programs, you'll find Q&A's import/export facilities unrivaled. And full record-locking and multilevel password support makes Q&A an excellent choice for applications shared across networks.

You can even create individualized application menus, help screens, and macros to fully customize Q&A to accommodate your own preferences and processing requirements.

That's *power!* — and Q&A has a great many other remarkable features you'll come to know and appreciate as we move through this book.

Word Processing Power

Write can accommodate 80-page or longer documents (depending on computer memory) with headers, footers, up to nine different fonts per document, and all the text manipulation and enhancement features you're likely to ever need. All printer makes and models are supported, and the new page preview feature available in all the modules lets you see exactly what your output will look like before using even a single sheet of paper.

A 100,000-word spelling checker is built right in along with a 640,000-word thesaurus to help you in the creation of your documents. And Q&A brings considerable ease and flexibility to defining page characteristics and applying attractive fonts and other text enhancements to your compositions.

Companies that need to merge information from their databases with documents created in the word processor will find Q&A especially robust, yet still extremely easy to use. You simply type your letter and tell Q&A where to place the variable database information in the document.

For example, if you want to send a personalized thank-you letter to everyone who purchased something from your company during the past week, you simply compose the letter in the word processor, telling Q&A where you'd like the customer's name, address, and any other database information to appear; Q&A does the rest of the work for you. Both the letter and your merge instructions can then be saved to be used again and again.

The same capabilities are available for mailing labels as well. More than 50 of the most popular label formats are supported — including predesigned formats for videotapes and audio cassettes — and you can design your own custom labels in a matter of minutes.

If you'd like to get fancy, Q&A now offers the ability to add optional *programming* to your mail-merge operations, increasing both the sophistication and flexibility available to you in your mailing campaigns.

Report Generator

Q&A can produce simple or sophisticated reports easily. You can even include in your Q&A reports information not in the database by using the external database lookup feature, enabling you to produce reports revealing relationships between information contained in two or more separate files such as invoice and customer.

You can add derived columns to your reports — columns that get their information from one or more other columns to give you new (derived) information that is not, by itself, contained in the database.

In the chapters to come you'll learn how to design and print a variety of reports that will tell you everything you could possibly want to know about what's in your records and files.

Intelligent Assistant

Q&A is the only database product to let you query and manipulate your data through English-language commands. Q&A's Intelligent Assistant module requires you to proceed through a series of elementary steps designed to teach the Assistant about your database and any special words you'll be using to ask questions about it.

In a customer database with addresses, phone numbers, and names of contacts, for example, you would want the Assistant to know that the word "customer" might also be expressed by a user as "client" or "company" or "firm" (or all four). Then you could ask the Assistant: "Which clients are in the 408 area code?" "Get me the phone number and buyer at Delta Systems," "What's the address of Johnson Paper Supply?" or "Change the buyer's name at Johnson Electronics to Bill Sweeney." You can generate entire reports using Q&A's Intelligent Assistant, have individual records brought up for you to view or update, and even change all the records in an entire file at one time using ordinary English phrasing, such as "Increase all the credit limits by $1,000.00."

Along with the Intelligent Assistant (IA) is the new Query Guide. You can use the Query Guide (QG) instead of the IA to build your queries and reports a step at a time. Rather than having to type your requests in sentences, you simply give the QG a general idea of what you want to do, and the Guide will offer you a series of plain English options that help you narrow down the request until it can produce exactly what you want. With no typing or computer experience, you can sit comfortably and simply respond to the Query Guide's questions, and the answer you need will be on the screen in no time!

The Intelligent Assistant and its Query Guide are options you can implement or not, depending on the level of skill possessed by those using your system and their familiarity with Q&A. It has some drawbacks or trade-offs, mostly to do with time and memory. In this book I'll show you how to get the most from it and to decide whether to use it.

Help

Q&A's help key, **<F1>**, activates Help no matter where you are in the program for more information to guide you along. Q&A is well-known for the clarity and comprehensiveness of its help screens.

In addition to providing you with a selection and explanations of the options available to you at any particular point in the program, Q&A's help screens give you the page number references in the manuals where you can go for more detailed information about what you're trying to achieve. Get familiar with using these help screens early in your relationship with Q&A and you'll find that in most cases you won't need to refer to the manuals at all. That's how good Q&A's help system is.

You can also create *custom* help screens for your Q&A databases. For example, you might want to inform your operator (someone on your staff, a temp, or even yourself) that the data entered must be within a certain range of preselected values, for example, and actually display that value range on screen. You'll discover a variety of uses for these custom help screens. They're extremely easy to create in Q&A, and I'll give you plenty of ideas on where and how to use them in Chapter 4.

Utilities

Utilities are those special facilities of a software program that allow you to improve the value and performance of your system. You may need to import data or documents from other programs, or export these from Q&A to other formats. Q&A supports a wide variety of import/export formats that you can choose from, including dBASE, Paradox, Lotus 1-2-3, Professional File, ASCII, WordPerfect, Microsoft Word, Multimate, Wordstar, and more. No matter the format of any data or documents you now have, chances are that Q&A has the tools you'll need to work with them.

Q&A also allows you to work with your DOS directories and files without leaving the program. Q&A's List Manager is especially useful in moving, renaming, copying, and deleting files in any directory. Version 4.0 includes the capability to give your Q&A filenames 72-character descriptions (making them easier to locate and identify), a real improvement over MS-DOS, which gives you a maximum of 11 characters to work with.

With Q&A's utilities you can also establish presets to apply to all the work you do in the program. You can standardize page and printing characteristics for your documents and reports, select from a variety of editing options, establish default document and data directories, launch other programs from inside Q&A, and even modify and create font files.

Other powerful Q&A utilities enable you to recover database or document files that have been damaged by power interruptions or disk problems. You'll learn all about how to make optimal use of these various utilities as we proceed through the book.

Custom Applications in Q&A

This doesn't mean that Q&A will design your databases and reports for you. Only you can do that. But you don't have to be an expert or even computer-savvy to do it. You simply decide what it is you want Q&A to do for you and, with the program's rich variety of tools, built-in help facilities, and sensible safeguards, go ahead and do it.

You'll be amazed at how smart Q&A is and the ease with which you can create and run your applications after only a little practice. Whether you have mostly word processing projects in mind, primarily database file management needs, or applications involving the use of both, Q&A will help you make the most of them.

Setting Up and Starting Out

Q&A 4.0's automatic installation program will have you up and running in no time. You'll use this utility to copy the Q&A program files from the master diskettes to your computer's hard disk. The installation procedure is essentially the same whether you're installing Q&A for the first time or upgrading from an earlier version of Q&A.

Q&A stores your various computer, printer, and monitor configuration details as well so it will always know how best to work with your system.

Once you have the program files copied to your computer's hard disk and Q&A is running, you can then install your printer or printers. The word "install" is used here in the sense of letting Q&A know what kinds of printers you're using with your system and how they're physically connected to your computer.

Q&A allows you to have up to five different printers, or printer modes (draft and letter-quality printing, for example), installed at a time, and you'll be able to use any one of them by selecting them with a keystroke or two. The program supports most every printer on the market, from office typewriters with built-in computer interface ports, all the way up to today's most sophisticated Postscript laser printers. And it's highly unlikely that your printer is so new, old, or exotic that Q&A won't be able to work with it efficiently.

System Requirements

Q&A for DOS requires an IBM PC/XT/AT, PS2, or compatible computer with a recommended minimum of 640K of RAM are required for DOS 4.0 and network use (I run Q&A with 525K and have never gotten a lack-of-memory message).

Your computer's operating system needs to be MS-DOS or PC-DOS version 2.1 or later; DOS 3.1 or later is required for network use, and DOS 3.3 or later is required for PS/2 computers.

If you'll be using Q&A on a network, each local computer will need at least 484K of RAM.

You'll also need a hard disk drive and, of course, a monitor. And if you plan to make use of Q&A 4.0's WYSIWYG page preview features, you'll need a graphics display adapter installed in your computer.

If your computer has expanded memory of the type that meets the Lotus-Intel-Microsoft (LIM) Expanded Memory Specification (EMS) version 4.0, Q&A can make use of it (EMS is required for linking to SQL). Any available expanded memory will be used by Q&A during sorting and similar database procedures, and to hold documents in memory that are too large to fit in available conventional memory. With 640K of conventional RAM available, Q&A can hold a document of about 80 single-spaced pages in memory.

If you have a Microsoft-compatible mouse attached to your computer, you can use it to make selections from menus and lists and to navigate around documents and database forms. Q&A 4.0 automatically recognizes the presence of a pointing device so long as your CONFIG.SYS file contains the appropriate device driver.

Hard Disk Caching

A disk cache is an area of RAM set aside to store data and program instructions frequently accessed from your computer's hard disk, and can considerably improve the speed of disk-intensive tasks, especially database procedures. Disk-caching utilities aren't expensive, and can be configured to make use of any extra memory your computer has (conventional, expanded, or extended) to cut down on both the time and frequency of disk accesses and thus further speed your processing tasks. If your computer has some additional unallocated memory, and you plan to use Q&A for serious database management, a disk cache utility can be well worth the small investment.

Installing Q&A on Your Computer's Hard Disk

New: Installing Q&A 4.0 in your computer is a quick and painless process. You must use the installation utility supplied with the program because the files are packed to conserve floppy disk space and must be unpacked by the utility to be copied to your hard disk.

Warning: If you're upgrading from an earlier version of Q&A, existing printer settings will be lost! Be sure to make a note of the types of printers you have installed at the Printer Selection screen before installing the 4.0 upgrade. Although Q&A 4.0 does not automatically upgrade printer files from earlier versions, you can select 4.0 printer files during upgrade installation, or upgrade your current printer file to 4.0 format using the QAFONT utility discussed in Chapter 9. This is not a concern if you're installing Q&A for the first time.

Secondly, if you have pre-4.0 Q&A databases containing XLOOKUP commands, or use macros to open database files, start Q&A 4.0 after upgrade installation and immediately access (open) all affected files in Add Data of Search?Update mode. This enables Q&A to upgrade the files to 4.0 format and ensures that external and macros won't be halted during execution. Once a database has been upgraded to 4.0, it cannot be used with an earlier version of Q&A.

Finally, since some of the menus in Q&A 4.0 have changed, you may need to edit or redefine any existing macros you have that make selections from, or cross, menus. Refer to the Q&A menu map on the tear-out reference card supplied with this book. After installing the 4.0 upgrade., loading Q&A, and opening your data files one by one (to allow Q&A to upgrade them), test your macros to be sure they're working properly. See Chapter 8 for details on how to create, use, and edit macros.

Upgrading to 4.0 from an earlier version of Q&A will not affect your existing QA..CFG file (where global options, default directories, and alternate Main menu programs information is stored); nor will the upgrade affect any personal spelling dictionary or macro files you've created.

To install the program you'll need about three megabytes of free hard disk space. The installation procedure will tell you exactly how much hard disk space you'll need, and how much is available on the selected drive. The procedure is the same whether you're installing Q&A for the first time or upgrading to version 4.0 from an earlier version, except as noted below.

1. Check that the write-protect notch on the right edge of each Q&A master disk is covered with a tab. This makes the disks "read-only" so they can't be accidentally written on or erased. If you're using 3½-inch disks, slide the disk lock tabs to the top of the disks.

2. Switch on your computer, and move to a DOS prompt (usually C:\).

3. Place the Installation/Program Disk #1 in floppy drive A and close the drive door. At the DOS prompt, type **a:install** and press **<Enter>**. A screen welcomes you to the installation utility for Q&A version 4.0, and advises you that the installation program can be used to:

    • Install Q&A for the first time;

    • Upgrade an existing copy of Q&A; or

    • Copy selected program files, font files, sample databases, and Q&A utilities. Several sample databases, are supplied with the program.

 Note: if the install program won't run, try loading it with **a:install -m** for a monochrome monitor, or **a:install -c** for a color monitor. Be sure to leave a space before the **-m** or **-c**.

    Press **<Enter>** to continue with the installation. During the installation process you can press **<Esc>** to back up to a previous screen, or press **<Alt><X>** to terminate the installation and exit to the DOS operating system.

4. The next screen displays all the available drives on your computer, and asks you to select the drive from which Q&A is being installed. If you're installing Q&A from the A: drive, be sure the A: is highlighted, and press **<Enter>**. Otherwise, use your cursor keys to highlight the appropriate drive, and then press **<Enter>**. If your computer has more drives than those displayed, use your cursor keys to scroll down to bring the remaining drive letters into view, highlight the one from which you want to install Q&A, and press **<Enter>**.

5. The next screen asks you to select the destination (target) drive letter — the drive where you want to install the Q&A 4.0 program files. Highlight the appropriate drive (C:, D:, or E:, for example) with your cursor keys, and press **<Enter>**.

6. The Q&A installation utility now scans the target drive you selected for other copies of the Q&A program files, and displays a list of directories, if any, where existing copies of Q&A program files are currently installed.

   a. If you're upgrading to version 4.0 from an earlier version of Q&A, highlight the drive and directory shown, and press **<Enter>**. The installation program will let you know that you're about to overwrite existing Q&A program files, and ask if you'd like to back up those files before proceeding. If you answer "Yes," a BACKUPQA subdirectory will be created, and your existing program and printer files will be copied there (this is just a safeguard on the off chance that anything should go wrong during installation). Any database, document, or macro files already in the directory will not be affected.

   b. If you're installing Q&A for the first time, press **<Enter>** and the program will offer to create a Q&A directory for you. If you selected C: as your target drive, for example, the drive and directory **C:\QA** will be suggested. You can accept this directory, or type in a different one. When you press **<Enter>**, the new directory for your Q&A program files will be created for you.

7. Now that your target drive and directory have been established, you'll be asked whether you wish a Complete or Selective installation. A box in the lower right corner of the screen tells you how many kilobytes you need to install the entire program, and how much unused disk space is available on your target drive. If you don't have enough space on the target drive, you'll have to free some by exiting to DOS and deleting some files, or backing up with the **<Esc>** key and selecting another target drive (if your hard disk has several partitions such as C: and D:).

   a. If you're installing Q&A for the first time, upgrading to version 4.0, or reinstalling the entire program, select Complete installation, press **<Enter>**, and go to step 8 below. The old Q&A program files will be erased and the new 4.0 files copied over, but any existing database, document, or other files will not be affected.

   Warning: If you've created any custom mailing labels in an earlier version, the installation utility asks if you want them upgraded. Select Yes to have them upgraded. If you select No, you'll lose your custom label specifications.

   b. If you've already installed version 4.0, and want only to install specific program, font, tutorial, or utility files, highlight Selective installation and press **<Enter>**. Q&A will ask you what kind of files to install, and after you've made your selection the files will display in a scrollable window. Highlight the files you want to selectively install and press the space bar to tag them. Press **<Enter>** to install the

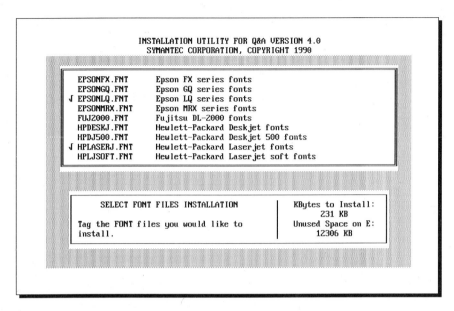

```
                INSTALLATION UTILITY FOR Q&A VERSION 4.0
                   SYMANTEC CORPORATION, COPYRIGHT 1990

        EPSONFX.FNT       Epson FX series fonts
        EPSONGQ.FNT       Epson GQ series fonts
      √ EPSONLQ.FNT       Epson LQ series fonts
        EPSONMRX.FNT      Epson MRX series fonts
        FUJ2000.FNT       Fujitsu DL-2000 fonts
        HPDESKJ.FNT       Hewlett-Packard Deskjet fonts
        HPDJ500.FNT       Hewlett-Packard Deskjet 500 fonts
      √ HPLASERJ.FNT      Hewlett-Packard Laserjet fonts
        HPLJSOFT.FNT      Hewlett-Packard Laserjet soft fonts



         SELECT FONT FILES INSTALLATION     │  KBytes to Install:
                                            │      231 KB
      Tag the FONT files you would like to  │  Unused Space on E:
      install.                              │      12306 KB
```

Figure 1-1: The Font Description File Screen. Highlight the printer files that correspond to the printers you plan to use with Q&A, and press the space bar to tag them for installation. Pressing the space bar once tags the file. Pressing the space bar again untags the file. You can press **<F3>** to tag all the files shown, or **<F4>** to untag them all. The box in the lower right corner of the screen indicates the size of the tagged files and the available space on your hard disk. Press **<Enter>** when you're ready to install the tagged files.

tagged files, and you'll be prompted to insert the appropriate Q&A 4.0 master diskette into the specified source drive (Appendix E contains a listing of all the Q&A program files along with brief descriptions).

8. If you've selected Complete installation, the utility will proceed to copy the files from the Master Program disks to your hard drive. You'll be prompted to place disk #2, then disk #3, and so forth, into the specified floppy drive as the program files are copied over.

9. When the installation of the program files is completed, press **<Enter>** to install optional files. First up are the font description files for the printers Q&A supports. When the list of font description files displays (see Figure 1-1), highlight the files to install, tag them with the space bar, and then press **<Enter>** to copy them to your hard drive. You can install the tutorial files (should you wish to run the Q&A tutorial later) and the utility files in the same manner (see the Optional Files section below for more information).

10. After you've installed any optional files, the program will ask your permission to check your computer's CONFIG.SYS file to make sure it contains the statements Files=20 and Buffers=10. Answer "Yes" unless you're sure your CONFIG.SYS file contains statements for at least 20 files and 10 buffers. The utility won't modify an existing CONFIG.SYS that meets these minimum requirements, but it will increase the files and buffers if necessary (without affecting any other CONFIG.SYS statements), or create the CONFIG.SYS file in your root directory if one doesn't already exist. If your CONFIG.SYS file has been created or updated by the installation program, you'll need to reboot your computer after exiting to DOS to load the new configuration into memory. At any DOS prompt, just press the **<Alt><Ctrl>** and **<Del>** keys simultaneously to reboot the computer.

Optional Files

These files are not critical to running Q&A. However, most can certainly contribute to your enjoyment of the program and should only be left off your hard disk if you just don't have enough room.

Font Description Files

The font description printer files supplied with Q&A are not the printer fonts themselves, but contain the codes necessary for Q&A to work with your printer and for any fonts you use with that printer. You'll be able to tell which font description file you need to install by looking at the eight-character filename and the make and model of printer that follows it (see Figure 1-1). If you can't decide among several choices, tag and install the most likely ones. You can later delete from your hard disk the ones you don't use.

If you can't find the right font description file for your printer, check your printer's manual to find out if your model emulates another printer. Many printers emulate certain Epson, IBM, or Hewlett-Packard models, and if yours does, you can use Q&A's font description file for that model.

If your printer is a brand-new model, it may be too early for the font description file to be included in the Q&A release you purchased. In this case it's likely that either Symantec or the printer manufacturer will have the printer driver (font description file) you need. If you have a modem, you can check the Symantec bulletin board system or the Symantec forum on CompuServe and download the printer driver if it's there (see Appendix D for information on how to use the Symantec bulletin board system). Or, you can phone Symantec Product Support. They'll send you the font description file you need free of charge if they have it available. If they don't, they'll surely be able to offer a satisfactory alternative.

Tutorial Files

If you plan on using the tutorial guide that comes with Q&A version 4.0, you'll need to install the tutorial files. The tutorial includes a sample database file (WRIGHT.DTF) and mail-merge letter, and allows you to familiarize yourself with many of the basic features of the product. After using the tutorial, you'll have to re-install these files if someone else wants to go through the practice lessons. You can use the selective installation procedure to do this.

Utility Files

Q&A 4.0 comes with a variety of utility files that may come in handy later on. You can install them during the initial complete installation, or selectively install them later as you need them.

QABACKUP.EXE enables you to back up database files that are too large to fit on a single disk. It's easier to use than DOS's Backup utility. More on this in Appendix G.

HIMEM.SYS is an extended memory driver. If your computer has extended memory (any RAM above 640 kilobytes), an 80386 or higher CPU, and is using DOS 3.0 or higher, you can install HIMEM.SYS to convert your extended memory to the type of expanded memory Q&A can use. You don't need HIMEM.SYS if you are already using an expanded memory driver. HIMEM.SYS, a Microsoft product, comes bundled with Microsoft Windows and DOS 4.0 and higher, and you should use the version of HIMEM.SYS included with these products if you have them installed.

If you've installed and plan to use HIMEM.SYS with Q&A, you'll need to add a line to your CONFIG.SYS file. You can do this in Q&A's Write module:

1. Load Q&A (see the section following, "Starting Q&A").

2. Choose Write from the Main menu.

3. Choose Get from the Write menu, type in the path to your CONFIG.SYS file, including the filename, and press **<Enter>**. On most systems, the path will be: **C: \CONFIG.SYS**.

4. Press **<Enter>** for ASCII at the Import Document menu.

5. Add the device driver command to the end of the file, being sure to specify the complete path to where HIMEM.SYS is located. For example: **DEVICE=C:\QA\HIMEM.SYS**.

6. Press **<Ctrl><F8>** to save the modified CONFIG.SYS file to ASCII format, exit Q&A to DOS, and reboot your computer. You can view or print this document file using the Write word processor.

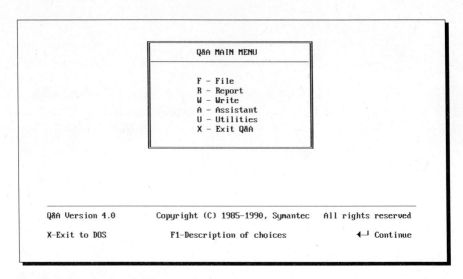

```
                    Q&A MAIN MENU

                  F - File
                  R - Report
                  W - Write
                  A - Assistant
                  U - Utilities
                  X - Exit Q&A


    Q&A Version 4.0      Copyright (C) 1985-1990, Symantec   All rights reserved

    X-Exit to DOS          F1-Description of choices          ←┘ Continue
```

Figure 1-2: The Q&A Main Menu.

QAFONT.EXE enables you to upgrade older Q&A font description files to version 4.0 format or to create a Q&A font description file from a selected soft font file. All the popular HP LaserJet-compatible soft fonts are supported. You can create new font description files for these fonts, or append new descriptions to existing font description files. More on this in Chapter 9.

Your Q&A version 4.0 package may contain additional files that were not included in the product at the time of this writing.

Ready-to-Use Database Files

Q&A 4.0 comes with a variety of predesigned database templates (data entry forms) that you can install and begin using right away. If you install them and later decide you don't need them, you can delete them by using Q&A's DOS Utilities. Appendix E contains a list and brief descriptions of these sample databases.

Starting Q&A

1. Be sure you are in the directory where you installed Q&A. If you installed the program on the C: drive in the QA directory, type **CD\QA** and press **<Enter>**.

2. From the DOS prompt type **QA** (*not* Q&A) and press **<Enter>**. If the Q&A Main menu appears after a few seconds and looks good, you're in business (see Figure 1-2). But if the Main menu doesn't come up after a

brief period, or if the menu doesn't look right or is hard to read, see the following section, "Correcting for Type of Monitor."

Correcting for Type of Monitor

Q&A is normally able to configure itself automatically for the type of monitor your system has, but some monitors require a special start-up setting. If Q&A doesn't load properly or loads but looks awful on the screen, you may need to include one of these special switches along with the QA command that loads the program. Once you load Q&A with this switch, Q&A will remember it and you won't have to use the switch again.

If your system's monitor displays color, try loading Q&A with the following command:

qa -scc <Enter> (Be sure to leave a space between **qa** and the dash.)

If you have a monochrome monitor (green or amber against a black background), try:

qa -smc -a <Enter>

And if that doesn't work, try:

qa -smm <Enter>

Tip: On a Compaq computer, make sure the monitor intensity is turned up sufficiently.

With a composite monitor, or if the above switches don't help, load Q&A by typing:

qa -a <Enter>

Use the following switches for these display systems:

NEC Multispeed	qa -st
ATT 6300 with mono display	qa -smc
Any PS/2 with mono display	qa -smc -a
Toshiba 1100 & 3100	qa -smc
or	qa -smc -a
Zenith laptops	qa -a
Compaqs with color displays	qa -scc
LCD display computers	qa -a
or	qa -st

Once you've determined that Q&A is on your system and working properly, you can change your startup batch file to include Q&A so it can be automatically loaded every time the computer is turned on.

Automatically Loading Q&A at System Start-Up

You can have Q&A automatically loaded each time you start your computer by creating an AUTOEXEC.BAT file in your root directory. The filename stands for "AUTOmatic EXECution BATch" file. A batch file is a DOS file that contains one or more commands written in batch (group) form. DOS looks for an AUTOEXEC.BAT file right after it finds and loads your CONFIG.SYS file.

If you're starting your programs from a DOS shell or menu program that displays automatically after you've turned on or rebooted your computer, then you've already got an AUTOEXEC.BAT file and won't need to create one. Consult that program's reference manual for information on how to launch a program from it, and follow the steps to add Q&A to its menu of selections. See Appendix H if you'll be running Q&A under Windows 3.0.

Should you want to see if you already have an AUTOEXEC.BAT file and, if so, what's in it, go to the root directory and, at the DOS prompt, type **autoexec.bat** and press **<Enter>**. If the file exists DOS will display its contents on the screen. Otherwise you'll get a "File not found" message.

If the file is there and you don't know how to modify it, better get someone who does. You can use the DOS EDLIN program, or your Q&A Write word processor to modify a DOS batch file such as AUTOEXEC.BAT, but you need to know what you're doing. Your DOS manual can show you how.

If you don't have an AUTOEXEC.BAT file and want to create one to load Q&A automatically at start-up, follow these steps:

1. At the DOS prompt in the root directory type **copy con autoexec.bat** and press **<Enter>**. This command tells DOS to copy what you type from the keyboard ("CONsole") into the AUTOEXEC.BAT file.

Skip the next two steps and go to step 4 if your computer has a built-in clock that keeps the time and date automatically.

2. Type **date** and press **<Enter>**.

3. Type **time** and press **<Enter>**.

4. Type **path=c:\;c:\dos;c:\qa** and press **<Enter>**. This is called a "path statement" and will enable you to run DOS commands from the QA subdirectory. This statement presumes that your root directory is on C: and that your DOS files are in a subdirectory (of the root directory) that is named DOS.

5. Type **prompt=pg** and press **<Enter>**. This tells DOS to always let you know what directory you're in. When you're in the QA subdirectory, for example, instead of merely a C:> prompt showing, you'll see a

C:\QA> prompt, indicating you're in the QA subdirectory of the root directory of drive C:.

6. Type **cd qa** and press **<Enter>** to tell DOS to change to the QA subdirectory.

7. Type **qa**, and then press **<Ctrl><Z>** and then **<Enter>** to copy these lines into the AUTOEXEC.BAT file. (After typing the letters **qa**, you hold down the **<Ctrl>** key while pressing the **Z** key. You then let up on these keys and press **<Enter>**.)

8. Now press the **<Alt><Ctrl>** and **<Del>** keys simultaneously to reboot the computer. Q&A should now load automatically.

Other Start-Up Options

You can have Q&A load a macro buffer larger than the default 3K at start-up, and also a macro that will execute as soon as the main program is loaded. For more on these advanced start-up options, see Chapter 8.

If you want to start Q&A and open a data file at the same time, use the command **qa** *filename* to load the program. Starting Q&A with the command **qa invoice**, for example, loads Q&A and opens the invoice file if you have one.

In addition, you can easily create several different configurations of Q&A to suit your preferences, and select which configuration you want to load with the program. This enables you to start Q&A with different default setups, different printers, an alternate Main menu, or an alternate custom menu system, for example. Chapter 9 has more information on how to do this.

Printer Installation

During printer installation, remember that you can press the **<F1>** key for help with any phase of the process.

1. Load Q&A.

2. From the Main menu select **U** for Utilities and press **<Enter>**.

3. At the Utilities menu select **P <Enter>** to install your printer.

4. At the Printer Selection screen shown in Figure 1-3, select a printer A through E and press **<Enter>**. You can install up to five printers (printer models, or printer modes such as draft and letter quality, or a combination of both, so long as the total of models plus modes is five or less). If

```
                        PRINTER SELECTION
                        =================

    A "Q&A PRINTER" is a combination of a PORT and a specific PRINTER MODEL
    and MODE (e.g. draft or letter).  Press F1 if you want more explanation.

    Highlight the Q&A PRINTER you want to install by pressing ↑ or ↓, then
    press ◄─┘ .

    ┌─────────────────────┬─────────┬──────────────────────────────────┐
    │ Q&A PRINTER         │  PORT   │ PRINTER MODEL AND MODE           │
    ├─────────────────────┼─────────┼──────────────────────────────────┤
    │ Printer A  (PtrA)   │  LPT1   │ Epson LQ-2500                    │
    │ Printer B  (PtrB)   │  LPT1   │ HP LaserJet II (Portrait)        │
    │ Printer C  (PtrC)   │  LPT1   │ HP LaserJet II (Landscape)       │
    │ Printer D  (PtrD)   │  COM1   │ Basic (Vanilla) Printer          │
    │ Printer E  (PtrE)   │  COM2   │ Basic (Vanilla) Printer          │
    └─────────────────────┴─────────┴──────────────────────────────────┘
```

Figure 1-3: The Printer Selection Screen. It shows two printers already installed, with two modes installed for the second printer (the LaserJet).

you're installing a printer for the first time, highlight the Printer A selection and press **<Enter>**.

This will bring you to the Port Selection screen. LPT and COM refer to the different types of ports to which a printer can be physically attached to your computer. LPT ports are parallel ports, and COM ports are serial ports. Check your printer manual to determine whether your printer requires a parallel or serial connection. You'll also need to determine if your computer has more than one parallel or serial port if you plan to install your printers at ports other than LPT1 or COM1. LPT1 is correct for most printer installations.

You can also select File as a "port." This will direct your output to a disk file instead of to your printer, where Q&A will save it for you with any enhancements and special formatting characteristics intact.

5. At the Printer Port Selection screen (see Figure 1-4), use your cursor keys to highlight the printer port you want and press **<Enter>**.

6. When the list of printer manufacturers appears, highlight the manufacturer of your printer by using the space bar or cursor keys and press **<Enter>**. Press **<PgDn>** to view additional manufacturers (see Figure 1-5).

7. At the list of printers for that manufacturer, highlight the model and printer mode you're installing and press **<Enter>**. Press **<PgDn>** for more models and modes.

```
                          PORT SELECTION
                          =============

      Highlight the PORT you wish to assign to the Q&A PRINTER by pressing
      ↑ and ↓.  Press ←┘ to select the highlighted PORT.

      ┌─────────────────────┬─────────┬────────────────────────────────┐
      │ Q&A PRINTER         │ PORT    │ PRINTER MODEL AND MODE         │
      ├─────────────────────┼─────────┼────────────────────────────────┤
      │ Printer A  (PtrA)   │ LPT1    │ Epson LQ-2500                  │
      │                     │ LPT2    │                                │
      │                     │ LPT3    │                                │
      │                     │ COM1    │                                │
      │                     │ COM2    │                                │
      │                     │ FILE    │                                │
      │                     │         │                                │
      └─────────────────────┴─────────┴────────────────────────────────┘
```

Figure 1-4: The Printer Port Selection Screen. The usual port for printer installation is LPT1.

```
                    LIST OF PRINTER MANUFACTURERS
      ┌───────────────────────────────────────────────────────────────┐
        Basic (Vanilla)        Cordata            IBM
        Adler                  CPT                IDS
        Alps                   DaisyWriter        Juki
        AMT                    Dataproducts       Kyocera
        Anadex                 Datasouth          Mannesmann Tally
        Apple                  Diablo             NEC
        AST                    Diconix            Okidata
        AT&T                   Digital            Olivetti
        Brother                DTC                Olympia
        BusinessLand           Epson              Output Technology
        C. Itoh                Fortis             Panasonic
        Canon                  Fujitsu            PaperJet
        Citizen                Gemini             PMC
        Comrex                 Hewlett Packard    Primage
      └───────────────────────────────────────────────────────────────┘
      ┌───┐     Press ↑ ↓ ← → or the space bar to select your    ┌────┐
      │   │             printer's manufacturer, then press ←┘     │PgDn│
      └───┘                                                        └────┘
```

Figure 1-5: Sample Screen from Q&A Version 4.0's Printer Manufacturer List.

If your particular printer model isn't on Q&A's list you may be able to install it as another printer model which yours emulates. Many printers emulate Epson, IBM, or Hewlett-Packard models. A Panasonic KXP-1124, for example, can emulate either an Epson LQ-2500 or an IBM Proprinter X24, and can be installed in Q&A as either one. Check your printer manual for the models that yours emulates. It may be necessary to set switches on the printer to get the emulation mode you need.

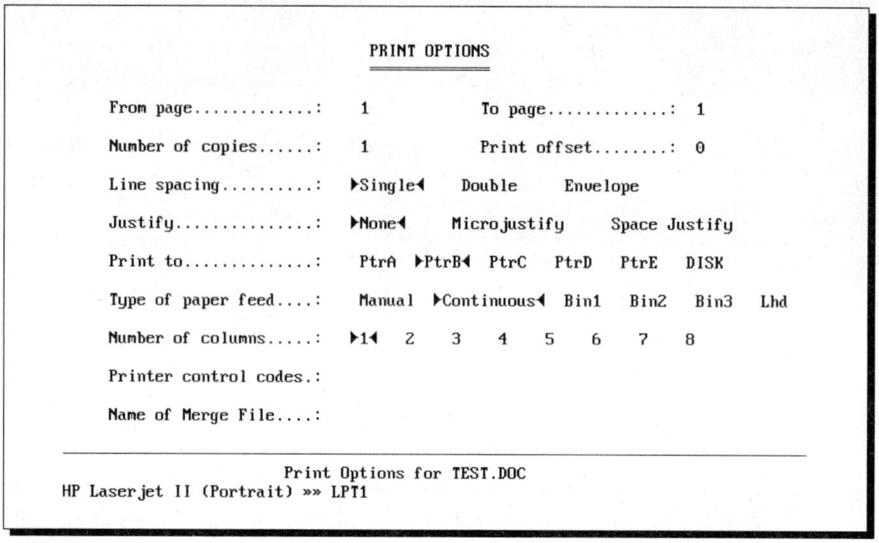

```
                        PRINT OPTIONS
                        ============

    From page............:   1          To page............:   1

    Number of copies......:  1          Print offset........:   0

    Line spacing.........:  ▶Single◀    Double      Envelope

    Justify..............:  ▶None◀      Microjustify     Space Justify

    Print to.............:   PtrA ▶PtrB◀ PtrC   PtrD   PtrE   DISK

    Type of paper feed....:  Manual ▶Continuous◀  Bin1    Bin2    Bin3    Lhd

    Number of columns.....:  ▶1◀  2    3    4    5    6    7    8

    Printer control codes.:

    Name of Merge File....:
    _____
                     Print Options for TEST.DOC
    HP Laserjet II (Portrait) »» LPT1
```

Figure 1-6: Q&A 4.0's Word Processor Print Options Screen. It shows the five available printer selections (on the "Print to" line). PtrA through PtrE correspond to the printers installed at the Printer Selection screen. The highlight is on PtrB, which in this case is a LaserJet II in portrait mode, connected to LPT1.

8. If you're installing a standard brand of printer, you can press **<F10>** now to confirm your printer installation. If you need to select any special printer options, are having printer problems, are installing a serial printer, or want to set up special cut-sheet feeder options, press **<F8>** for the Special Printer Options screen and see Appendix B for further information.

9. After your first printer is installed Q&A will ask if you'd like to install another. If so, repeat the procedure from step 4 above for installing additional printers or printer modes.

Remember, if your printer has several modes (draft and letter quality on dot matrix printers, or portrait and landscape orientation on laser printers, for example), you can install each of the alternate modes as a printer and thereby select the mode you want from Q&A's Print Options screen at printing time with just a couple of keystrokes (see Figure 1-6).

If you're installing an HP LaserJet II, IIP, IID, or III, for example, you can install the following five modes: Portrait, Landscape, Legal Portrait, Legal Landscape, and Envelope.

Also, you can install any or all of your printers and modes (up to five total) on a single port (LPT1, for instance). If your computer has only this one port, but you have two printers, you can use an external A/B switch box to manually switch between the two physical printers.

Q&A and Printer Fonts

Q&A supports an exceptionally wide range of printers as well as the special effects these printers are able to produce. Laser, ink-jet, and most modern dot matrix printers can all produce a variety of special printing effects such as bold, italic, underline, expanded text, condensed, and proportional spacing, for example. And you can really dress up your Q&A documents using these special printer and font capabilities.

Q&A's font and laser printer support, which includes PostScript, allows you to create near-typeset-quality documents quickly and easily. Font description files — different from the fonts themselves — are supplied with Q&A. These files contain information about your fonts that Q&A requires when printing your documents.

You must have your own actual fonts, however, because fonts are not supplied with Q&A. A variety of fonts may be built right into your printer, or you may either have plug-in font cartridges or the type of fonts that you load into memory or download to the printer prior to starting Q&A ("downloadable soft fonts").

But all this is getting a little ahead of things. Before your fonts are of any real value when working with Q&A, you'll need to know how to create documents in which to use them. This procedure is discussed in Chapter 2, which covers Write, Q&A's word processor. That's where you'll find out all about fonts, how to install them, and how they can be used in Q&A documents.

Q&A'S Congenial Menu System _____

Q&A is a menu-driven program with on-screen displays for selecting the exact program action or option you want by any of several easy methods. The menu system is tiled: when you select from a menu a particular operation you wish to do in Q&A, a submenu often appears asking you to further define your task, perhaps by making yet another menu selection or typing in the name of the file with which you want to work.

You won't need to memorize any commands at all to make your menu selections, and you don't have to worry about getting lost. Pressing the **<Esc>**

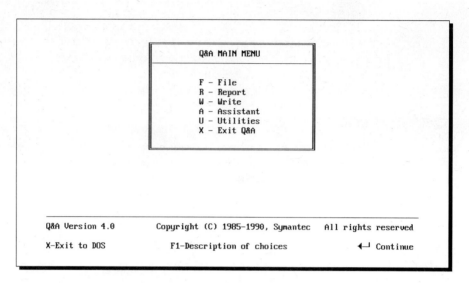

```
                        Q&A MAIN MENU

                        F - File
                        R - Report
                        W - Write
                        A - Assistant
                        U - Utilities
                        X - Exit Q&A




    Q&A Version 4.0      Copyright (C) 1985-1990, Symantec   All rights reserved

    X-Exit to DOS            F1-Description of choices           ↵ Continue
```

Figure 1-7: The Q&A Main Menu.

key from anywhere in the program will always lead you back to Q&A's
Main menu.

In this final section of the chapter I'll take you on a tour of the menu system
and briefly describe what the menu selections lead to and how they're used. I'll
also look at a few of the screens associated with Q&A's major program options,
as well as pause here and there to show you how to fine-tune the way in
which Q&A works for you.

If you're a quick study, experienced with software programs in general, and
wish to jump ahead of the class for a little solo experimentation, use this
chapter to familiarize yourself with the program's structure. (The organization of
Q&A's menu system is depicted graphically at the end of this chapter, and also
on the tear-out reference card in the front of the book.)

On the other hand, if you're brand new to Q&A or inexperienced with
computers or software programs, this will be your initial product orientation.
When you've finished this chapter you should feel comfortable moving around
inside the program and be ready to explore the features that make Q&A the
application workhorse it is.

The Q&A Main Menu

Each time you load Q&A, the first thing you'll see on screen will be the Main
menu (see Figure 1-7). From here you can select any of five major operations,
representing the five Q&A modules: File, Report, Write, Assistant, and Utilities.

You can also press **X** to exit Q&A and return to your operating system (DOS) or shell program.

Warning: Don't ever exit Q&A without first returning to the Main menu and pressing **X** — this could damage any files that are still open.

Several methods are available for you to make your selection at any Q&A menu.

1. You can use your cursor keys (sometimes referred to as navigation keys) to highlight the selection you want and then press **<Enter>**. On some keyboards the cursor keys are located on the numeric keypad and are used with "NumLock" off. On enhanced keyboards the cursor keys are isolated from the rest of the keys on the keyboard.

2. If you're using a mouse with Q&A, you can point to the menu selection you want and click on the mouse. Clicking it a second time invokes that menu selection. Clicking the mouse from outside any menu box is the equivalent of pressing **<Esc>** on the keyboard.

3. You can press the number that corresponds to the selection's relative position (from top to bottom) on the menu; doing so will highlight the selection. Press **<Enter>**. Where a menu contains more than nine items, however, you can select only through the first nine in this manner.

4. You can press the letter of the selection to highlight it, and then press **<Enter>**.

5. Or you can configure Q&A so that all you'll have to do is press the letter or number that corresponds to the desired selection in order to invoke that selection without having to press **<Enter>**.

Here's how you set up Q&A to use this fifth menu item selection option.

   a. From the Q&A Main menu press **U** for Utilities and press **<Enter>**. This will take you to the Utilities menu (see Figure 1-8).

   b. At the Utilities menu press **S** for Set Global Defaults, and then press **<Enter>**. This will take you to the Set Global Defaults screen shown in Figure 1-9.

   c. At the Set Global Defaults screen press the down arrow cursor key three times to get to the "Automatic Execution" line (no need at this point to pay any attention to the other items on the screen).

   d. Change the "Automatic Execution" default setting from "No" to "Yes" by pressing your left arrow cursor key once.

   e. Now press **<F10>** to save this change. Q&A will always remember this setting unless you change it back again.

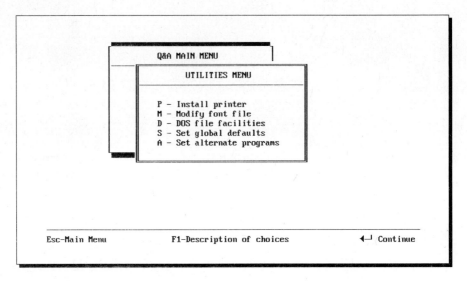

Figure 1-8: The Q&A Utilities Menu.

You should now be back at the Utilities menu. Press the **<Esc>** key once to return to the Main menu.

Remember: Pressing the **<Esc>** key in Q&A always moves you back toward the Main menu from wherever you are in the program.

To test this new automatic execution option, just press the letter **U** from the Main menu, or point to it and click the mouse. This should take you to the Utilities menu again without having to press the **<Enter>** key.

Now, because the Set Global Defaults option is the fourth choice down on the Utilities menu and also begins with an "S," you can invoke this selection either by pressing the number **4** or the letter **S.**

Try it. Your keypress or mouse click should take you once again to the Set Default Directories screen. Now press **<Esc>** twice to return to the Q&A Main menu.

That's how simple it will be for you to maneuver to any Q&A menu, or to return to the Main menu from wherever you are in the program.

Setting Your Q&A Default Directories

Since you've now taken a trip to Q&A's Set Global Defaults screen and survived to tell about it, let's return there again to establish another few defaults.

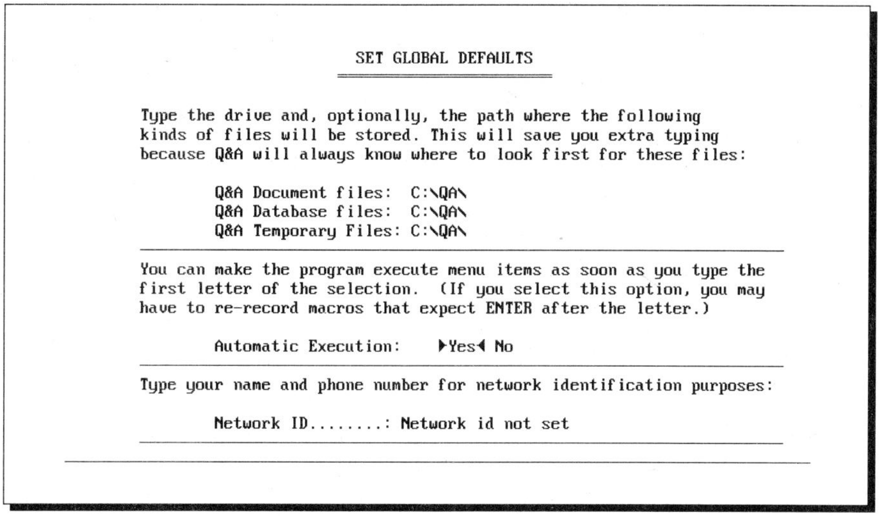

```
                    SET GLOBAL DEFAULTS
                    ═══════════════════

    Type the drive and, optionally, the path where the following
    kinds of files will be stored. This will save you extra typing
    because Q&A will always know where to look first for these files:

            Q&A Document files:  C:\QA\
            Q&A Database files:  C:\QA\
            Q&A Temporary Files: C:\QA\

    You can make the program execute menu items as soon as you type the
    first letter of the selection.  (If you select this option, you may
    have to re-record macros that expect ENTER after the letter.)

            Automatic Execution:    ▶Yes◀ No

    Type your name and phone number for network identification purposes:

            Network ID........: Network id not set
```

Figure 1-9: The Set Global Defaults Screen.

Q&A and you are concerned mainly with managing four types of files:

- Q&A's own *program* files — the files copied to your computer's hard disk during the installation process. These contain the software instructions that tell the computer what to do, along with any configuration files that Q&A needs to refer to for information about your system. (Q&A takes care of these without your involvement.)

- *Temporary* files — Q&A may need to create and use certain files during sorting and other database operations. You won't ever see these files because Q&A creates them automatically and then deletes them when the operation for which they were required has been completed.

- Your *document* files — letters, memos, and articles that you type, edit, and print in the word processor, as well as macro files.

- Your *database* files — customer lists, invoices, employee files, and any others that you create, add to, and update in Q&A's database (File) module.

You'll recall that when we installed the Q&A program files on your hard drive a special QA directory was created for them. What we want to do now is create two *additional* directories: one for your documents, and another for your database files. If we do this, Q&A will always know where to look for

```
Root Directory C:\
─────────────
            ↦Command.com
            ↦Config.sys
            ↦Autoexec.bat
                        ─DOS Directory C:\DOS\
                                ↦DOS file
                                ↦DOS file
                                ↦DOS file
                                ↦Etc.

                        ─QA Directory C:\QA\
                        ↦Q&A program file
                        ↦Q&A program file
                        ↦Etc.
                                ─Q&A Documents Directory C:\QA\DOCS\
                                        ↦Letter
                                        ↦Memo
                                        ↦Article

                                ─Q&A Data Directory C:\QA\DATA\
                                        ↦Customers
                                        ↦Invoices
                                        ↦Employees
```

Figure 1-10: Directory Structure for Q&A Files.

these files first and, since down the road a piece you may have created and saved literally dozens or even hundreds of files, keeping these different types of files in their own directories will enable Q&A (and you!) to find and retrieve them faster.

Besides, it's just good disk management to store different types of files in their own directories. When it comes time to back them up, it will be more convenient and efficient to concentrate on backing up your *created* database and document files first. And if these are in their own directories, the process of backing them up will be greatly simplified.

Figure 1-10 shows what your directory structure will look like once you've added new subdirectories for your document and data files.

Notice how the DOS and QA directories branch off the main or root directory. These are technically *sub*directories of the root directory.

Notice also how the Q&A documents and data directories branch off from the QA directory. It's like an upside-down tree. The root directory represents the trunk; the QA directory is a branch attached to that trunk; and the two Q&A subdirectories are branches of *that* branch.

To create your DOCS and DATA subdirectories to branch off the QA directory (assuming you created the QA directory C:\QA when installing Q&A), exit Q&A through the Main menu, and:

1. Go to the QA directory. If you're in the root directory, type **cd qa** and **<Enter>**.

2. From the QA directory, type **md docs <Enter>**, and then **md data <Enter>**.

New: You should also create a subdirectory at this time for temporary files created by Q&A during certain database operations. Type **md temp <Enter>** to create this third subdirectory. If your databases will be large, and your hard drive includes a partition that you're not using, such as D: or E:, you can create your TEMP directory there, thus giving Q&A lots of space for the temporary files it may need to create during certain database operations, thereby increasing its execution speed.

3. Now type **cd\qa <Enter>** to change back to the QA directory and type **qa <Enter>** to load the Q&A program.

From Q&A:

4. Press **U** for the Utilities menu.

5. At the Utilities menu press **S** for Set Global Defaults. This will take you to the Set Global Defaults screen again.

6. On the "Q&A Document Files" line type **c:\qa\docs**.

On the "Q&A Database Files" line type **c:\qa\data**. On the "Q&A Temporary Files" line type **c:\qa\temp**.

You can specify that your files be stored on other drives and in other directories. For example, you might want to store your document files on a floppy disk in drive A:, in which case you'd type **a:** on the "Q&A Document Files" line. Q&A would then prompt you to insert the disk in the drive when working with document files in the Write module.

Or, you may want to keep your database files on another hard drive partition. As long as you specify the pathname of the files at this screen, Q&A will always know where to look for them first.

Advanced users can create multiple Q&A configurations, with different default directories assigned to each configuration. More on this in Chapter 9.

7. When you're done setting your default directories, press **<F10>** to save the settings and **<Esc>** back to the Main menu.

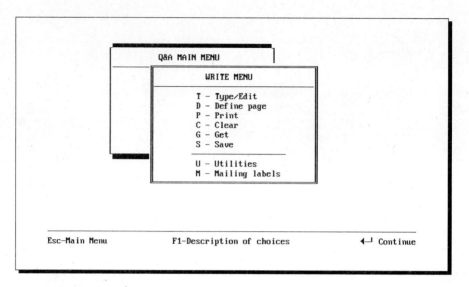

Figure 1-11: The Write Menu with Its Options.

You're now in business. Whenever you set about creating, changing, or retrieving a document or database file, Q&A will always present the preset directory for you to type in the name of the file you want. And when you tell Q&A to search for a file, it will know which directory to search first.

You can even go a step or two further, especially with your new Q&A DOCS directory. If your documents will consist of different types of correspondence, such as letters and memos, you can create subdirectories in DOS that branch off the C:\QA\DOCS directory, perhaps naming these directories C:\QA\DOCS\LETTERS\, C:\QA\DOCS\FORMLTRS\ and C:\QA\DOCS\MEMOS\. This way, if your form letters are your most sacred documents and you're editing them frequently, you can simply go to the FORMLTRS directory from inside the program and tell Q&A, with just a few keystrokes, to make a backup copy of all your form letters onto a floppy disk in drive A:.

You'll find out how to use Q&A's List Manager to search for, copy, delete, and rename your files in Chapter 9 on Utilities.

The Write Menu

Although the word processing module isn't the first option on Q&A's Main menu, it's likely to be the module you'll want to start with. So let's take a look at the Write menu first. Press **W** for Write (see Figure 1-11).

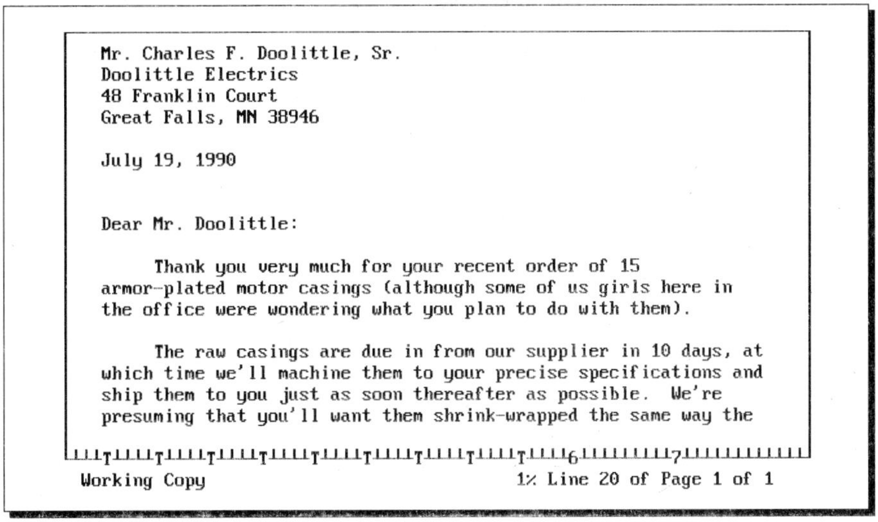

```
┌─────────────────────────────────────────────────────────────┐
│  ┌──────────────────────────────────────────────────────┐   │
│  │  Mr. Charles F. Doolittle, Sr.                        │   │
│  │  Doolittle Electrics                                  │   │
│  │  48 Franklin Court                                    │   │
│  │  Great Falls, MN 38946                                │   │
│  │                                                       │   │
│  │  July 19, 1990                                        │   │
│  │                                                       │   │
│  │                                                       │   │
│  │  Dear Mr. Doolittle:                                  │   │
│  │                                                       │   │
│  │      Thank you very much for your recent order of 15  │   │
│  │  armor-plated motor casings (although some of us girls here in │
│  │  the office were wondering what you plan to do with them). │
│  │                                                       │   │
│  │      The raw casings are due in from our supplier in 10 days, at │
│  │  which time we'll machine them to your precise specifications and │
│  │  ship them to you just as soon thereafter as possible.  We're │
│  │  presuming that you'll want them shrink-wrapped the same way the │
│  └──────────────────────────────────────────────────────┘   │
│  ∟∟⊥T∟∟∟⊥T∟∟∟⊥T∟∟∟⊥T∟∟∟⊥T∟∟∟⊥T∟∟∟⊥T∟∟∟⊥T∟∟∟⊥6∟∟∟∟∟∟∟7∟∟∟∟∟∟∟│
│  Working Copy                          1% Line 20 of Page 1 of 1 │
└─────────────────────────────────────────────────────────────┘
```

Figure 1-12: The First Screen Page of a Letter Composed in Q&A's Word Processor.

Notice that a portion of the Q&A Main menu is still visible behind the Write menu. Some menus in Q&A are four levels deep. But no matter how deep into the menu system you go, you'll always be able see a portion of the previous menu or menus displayed behind the current one.

The selections available from the Write menu are: Type/Edit, Define Page, Print, Clear, Get, Save, Utilities (for word processing activities), and Mailing labels. You'll learn much more about these selections in the next chapter. Briefly, here's what they do:

Type/Edit: This selection takes you to Q&A's Type/Edit screen (also referred to as "the editor") where you'll compose, revise, add enhancements to, and print your word processing documents. Figure 1-12 shows the first screen page of a sample letter. A "screen page" is equivalent to about one-third of an actual 8½-by-11-inch printed page.

Define page: Whenever you prepare to type a letter in an ordinary typewriter, you decide on the size of paper to use, the free white space (margins) you want to leave around the edges of the sheet, and, if the typewriter can accommodate different print wheels or type balls, the size of the characters you want to print. When you begin working in the word processor, you'll make the same decisions. The Define Page screen enables you to set these page characteristics for each document. You can also designate default page characteristics for all your documents so that Q&A will know in advance how you want your pages to look.

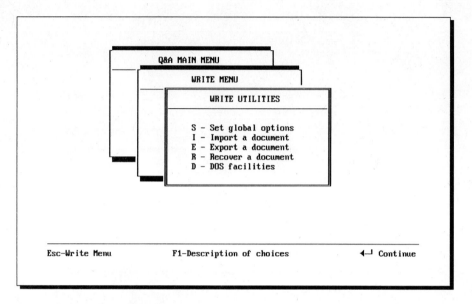

Figure 1-13: The Write Utilities Menu.

Print: Selecting Print from the Write menu takes you to the Print Options screen (shown in Figure 1-6), from which you can choose a variety of printing alternatives. You can select the pages you want printed, how many copies, the line spacing you want, whether or not you want your text justified, the printer or printer mode you wish Q&A to use (if you've installed more than one), the type of paper feed, number of columns, any printer control codes you want Q&A to send to your printer, and the name of the merge file if you're merging database information into your document. Like the Define Page screen, you can set blanket printing options to apply to all your documents.

Clear: The Clear option from the Write menu enables you to release a current document from memory so you can load a different document or start a new one. Clearing a document has no affect on the version that may already be stored on your disk. Clear can also be used to cancel any changes made to the document during the current editing session.

Get: The Get selection allows you to retrieve a document already stored on disk and bring it onto the Type/Edit screen for editing or printing. When you select Get, Q&A pops up a box and prompts you to type in the name of the document you wish to retrieve.

Save: The Save option from the Write menu is used to save to disk the document currently in memory. There must be a document in the editor to use this option or Q&A will give you an error message.

Utilities: Figure 1-13 shows the Write Utilities menu branching off from the Write menu (the Write menu, similarly, branches off from the Main menu) and the options available to you here.

Set global options: This selection takes you to another menu from which you can customize your editing, and page and printing options for all your *new* Q&A documents. When you create *global* settings you're telling Q&A to make these the defaults for all documents you create from this point forward. When Q&A saves a document it also stores the various options associated with it at the time you saved it. So later, when you Get a document, it won't be affected by any changes to global defaults that were made since it was saved.

Import/Export a document: You can import documents into Q&A from a variety of popular word processing programs, and export documents from Q&A to these other programs as well. Q&A takes care of the conversion for you, and maintains the formatting and enhancements in the original document.

Recover a document: Computer files can become damaged by sudden power interruptions. Q&A enables you to restore such documents.

DOS facilities: You may need to copy, rename, move, or delete one or more documents that are stored on disk. Q&A provides the facilities for you to do this easily and quickly, without leaving the program.

Mailing labels: Q&A's powerful mailing label feature lets you select from a wide variety of standard predefined label formats, or create your own. Figure 1-14 shows the screen Q&A displays when you select the Mailing labels option from the Write menu. Defining labels and merging database information into them (such as names and addresses from a customer file) is not difficult — you'll see how it's done in Chapter 5.

The File Menu

A database file is quite different from a document file created in the Write module. Document files — one file per document — tend to be small in comparison to database files, which can contain hundreds, thousands, or even millions of individual records. The File module is where you'll do all your database-related operations. Pressing **F** from the Q&A Main menu takes you to the File menu shown in Figure 1-15. From here you can select the type of database task you want Q&A to perform from the nine available options. For details on how to use these various options available from the File menu see Chapters 3 and 4.

Design file: Select this option when you want to create a new data entry form or redesign or add custom features to an existing one. Information (records) is entered into the database through the "form," and it's the form you create and

```
                        LIST OF MAILING LABELS

    ▓▓▓▓▓▓▓▓▓▓▓▓▓▓▓▓▓▓▓▓         Avery 5197 4" x 1 1/2" HP II
    Avery 5160 2 5/8" x 1" HP   Avery 5260 2 5/8" x 1" HP
    Avery 5160 2 5/8" x 1" HP II Avery 5260 2 5/8" x 1" HP II
    Avery 5161 4" x 1" HP        Avery 5261 4" x 1" HP
    Avery 5161 4" x 1" HP II     Avery 5261 4" x 1" HP II
    Avery 5162 2 3/4" x 2 3/4" HP  Avery 5262 4" x 1 1/2" HP
    Avery 5162 2 3/4" x 2 3/4" HPII Avery 5262 4" x 1 1/2" HP II
    Avery 5163 4" x 2" HP        Pin fed 2 1/2" x 15/16" - 3 up
    Avery 5163 4" x 2" HP II     Pin fed 3 1/2" x 1 7/16" - 1 up
    Avery 5164 4" x 3 3/8 HP     Pin fed 3 1/2" x 15/16" - 1 up
    Avery 5164 4" x 3 3/8 HP II  Pin fed 3" x 15/16" - 4 up
    Avery 5196 2 3/4" x 2 3/4" HP  Pin fed 3.3" x 15/16" - 4 up
    Avery 5196 2 3/4" x 2 3/4" HPII Pin fed 4 1/2" x 3" - 1 up
    Avery 5197 4" x 1 1/2" HP    Pin fed 4" x  15/16" - 2 up

                                    ┌─────────────────────────┐
                                    │ Press PgDn for more     │
                                    └─────────────────────────┘

            Enter name:_____
```

Figure 1-14: Q&A's Mailing Label Selection Screen. Here you select a predefined label or assign a name to a unique label format you wish to create.

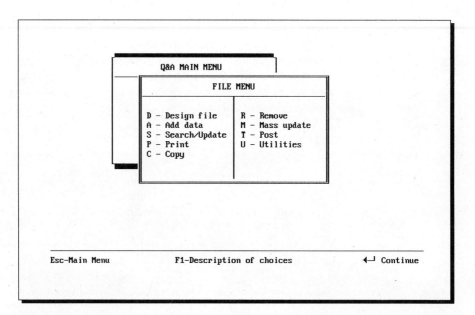

Figure 1-15: The File Menu.

customize when designing your database. Selecting Design file takes you to a submenu with the following additional choices:

- Design a new file: Lay out the form design for your database on screen by typing descriptive labels for your information fields. (See Figure 1-16 for an example of a database form for inventory items.) Details on how to create data entry forms are in Chapter 3.

- Redesign a file: Change the layout of an existing form; add, move, edit, or delete information fields. See Chapter 3.

- Customize a file: Add features to your database such as special information type fields (money, dates, or numbers), restrictions on what can be entered, initial information for all records, faster search capabilities, and custom help screens; select the color or appearance attributes of your data entry form. See Chapter 4.

- Program a file: Create or edit a table that contains information you'll frequently need during data entry; add programming statements to your database to make data entry easier, faster, and less error prone; prevent the information in specified fields from being changed; assign alternate names to your information fields so you can easily refer to them in programming statements and mail-merge operations. See Chapter 4.

- Secure a file: Create network user groups, assign access rights and passwords, and add other security features to your database to protect it from unauthorized viewing or tampering in a multiuser environment. See Chapter 13.

- Customize an application: Create special custom menus that help you work with Q&A the way you want to; prevent others from changing the design and custom features of your database, or from running procedures that could affect the information in your records. See Chapters 8 and 9.

Add data: You'll select this option from the File menu whenever you want to add new records to your database. For example, if someone purchased an item from your company for the first time, you'd want to add his name, address, and other information to the customer file if you were maintaining such records. See Chapter 3.

Search/Update: You use Search/Update to view records already in the database, and to change the information in those records. If an existing customer changed his address, for instance, you'd use Search/Update to locate the record and enter the address change. See Chapter 3.

```
                    INVENTORY ITEMS DATABASE


   PART NUMBER: XKP-44012      DESCRIPTION: 24 Gauge Spindle Wire Pack

   DATE ADDED: June 5, 1990    SOURCE: Alliance Electronics, Inc.

   COST: $17.25    RETAIL: $37.50    WHOLESALE: $28.95

   QTY ON HAND:   34
     SOLD TODAY:   5
   SOLD TO DATE: 245                  ┌─────Application Notes─────┐
   REORDER LEVEL:  15                 │ Recommended for all static wound motors.
     REORDER QTY:  50                 │ For use on B and C series Dorker motors.
                                      │ Will fuse under extreme RPM/heat loads.
                                      │ Use P/N XKP-30022 for heavy soldering
                                      │ applications.

STOCK.DTF       New form 2   of 2       Total Forms: 689       Page 1 of 1

Esc-Exit    F1-How to add   F3-Delete form   F7-Search   F8-Calc   F10-Continue
```

Figure 1-16: A Sample Database Record for an Inventory Item. The field labels are the phrases ending in colons. The items that follow the colons are the values (information) typed into the record during data entry.

Print: You can print out your forms as they appear on screen, or quickly design printing specifications that tell Q&A which fields to print, and where on the page to print them. When you select Print from the File menu, the Print submenu displays for you to further define your task. See Chapter 3.

Copy: You can make an exact copy of your database design, or select a group of records to copy to another file. See Chapter 4.

Remove: You may need to remove outdated or duplicate records from your database. The Remove menu offers you several options. See Chapter 4.

Mass update: When you want to change the information in an entire group of database records, such as raising the prices of all your products by 5 percent, Mass update offers you a fast and easy method of doing it. See Chapter 4.

Post: A powerful Q&A 4.0 feature that enables you to copy information from one database to another. For example, you can post quantities of items sold on invoices to the inventory database, and thus maintain up-to-date inventory balances. See Chapters 4 and 10.

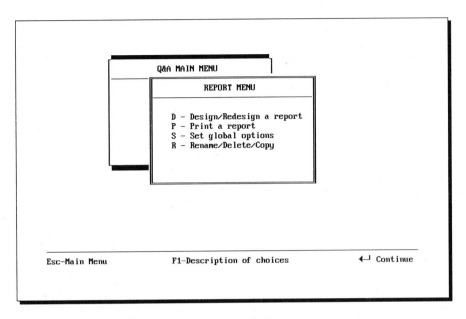

Figure 1-17: The Report Menu.

Utilities: The Utilities submenu provides tools for exchanging data between Q&A and other popular database programs, backing up your databases, recovering data files damaged by a power loss, and linking to databases stored on SQL servers. See Chapters 4 and 9.

The Report Menu

In Q&A you can design reports — simple or complex — from the information contained in your databases. Reports organize the information you want to see and present it in formats (rows and columns) that can be easily read and understood, providing you with the opportunity not only to view your data, but also to see relationships, totals, and the results of various calculations. A report can be as simple as a list of your suppliers' telephone numbers, or as complex as a complete physical inventory analysis with subtotals by categories of parts, percentages, valuations at cost, and so forth. Chapter 6 tells you all about how to design reports in Q&A.

When you select Report from Q&A's Main menu, you are taken to the Report menu. Figure 1-17 shows the options available here.

Design/Redesign a report: This option allows you to design a new report or modify the specifications of an existing one (Q&A saves your report designs). A report design is tied to a specific database, although you can have Q&A look up information from other files to include in your reports. When you select Design/Redesign a report, Q&A asks you to enter the name of the database you wish to use for your report. After that Q&A displays a list of the existing report designs for that file, if any. You can select an existing report to modify, or type in a name for the new report you wish to design.

Print a report: Use this option when you wish to print a report that has already been designed. Before actually running the report Q&A will always give you the opportunity to make temporary changes to your report design.

Set global options: You can set format, page, and printing options for all your new reports just as you can set similar global options for documents in the Write module. You can also standardize column headings and widths for all your reports. Changing the Report global options has no affect on existing report designs, just those you create from that point forward.

Rename/Delete/Copy: Q&A lets you change the names of your existing reports, delete complete report designs, and copy the specifications of any report in order to use those existing designs to quickly create new reports.

The Intelligent Assistant

By selecting Assistant from the Main menu you can access Q&A's unique English-language interface, the Intelligent Assistant. From here, using English commands, you can obtain information from your databases, generate reports, and add, change, or delete information from your Q&A databases, all without having to know the more formal procedures of the File and Report modules.

You'll be able to type in questions and commands such as, "Which part numbers show less than five in stock?" or "List the invoices with a balance due greater than $20.00," or "Get me the salesman's name and fax number at Miller Office Supplies."

The Intelligent Assistant (IA) has a built-in vocabulary of more than 600 words, and it can do arithmetic and give you the current date and time. If it doesn't recognize special terms you wish to use in your questions and commands, it's a snap to teach it.

Use the Intelligent Assistant to:

- Quickly generate one-time reports.

- Locate, sort, and view single forms and groups of forms.

- Get a blank database form to fill in.

- Change information in one form, a select group of forms, or all the forms in the database.

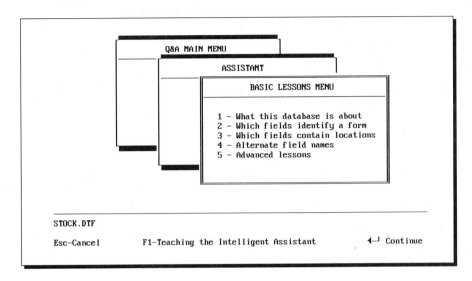

Figure 1-18: The Intelligent Assistant's Basic Lessons Menu.

- Ask who, what, when, how many, and yes/no questions about the database.

- Do calculations and get the current date and time.

- Ask follow-up questions.

To get the IA prepared and ready to respond to your questions, you'll first need to create a database and add some records to it. (Several databases are included on the free Applications Disk located in the back of this book.) Then, when you access the IA for the first time and confirm that you wish to use it, it will ask you a series of mostly fill-in-the-blanks type questions at the Basic Lessons menu (see Figure 1-18).

From this menu you'll teach the IA what your database is about, which fields in the database should always be included in reports, which fields contain locations (addresses, cities, states, zips), and any synonyms you may use to describe what you want the IA to prepare, get, or carry out for you.

The Advanced Lessons menu (not shown) prompts you to tell the Assistant which fields in your database contain people's names, and what units of measure (ounces or inches, for example) are used in certain fields. Here, as well, you'll be able to teach the IA about any special verbs and adjectives you might use when asking questions or giving commands. The better you and the IA understand one another from the beginning, the easier it will be to have your wishes carried out using the language in a way that comes most natural to you.

The process of teaching the IA is both fun and rewarding (you'll learn some things yourself!), and it only needs to be done once for each database.

Also in the Assistant module you'll find Q&A version 4.0's exciting new Query Guide. Rather than typing your requests in sentences, you simply give the Guide a general idea of the kind of operation you want to perform, and the Guide will lead you smartly through the process of building your query or report.

You'll find out all about how to set up and use both the Intelligent Assistant and the Query Guide in Chapter 7.

The Utilities Menu

We've already had a little experience with the Utilities menu. Earlier in this chapter we used the Set Global Options screen to designate the default directories for our Q&A document and database files, and covered the Install printer procedure as well. See Figure 1-8 for the other utilities options available at this menu.

Install printer: Whenever you wish to install an additional printer or printer mode, uninstall a printer or mode, change a printer port, change the order in which your printers appear on Q&A's Print Options screens, or set up special printer options, select Install printer from the Utilities menu.

Modify font file: For experienced Q&A users only! Select this to create or modify a font description file. The procedure is covered in Chapter 9.

DOS file facilities: Use this menu selection to see what files are stored on your disk, change the name of or move a Q&A document or database file, delete files that are no longer useful, or make back-up copies of valuable files. These procedures are covered in detail in Chapter 9.

Set global options: You can set or change the default directories for your document and database files, turn automatic execution of menu items "on" (both of which we did earlier in this chapter), and enter your Network ID if you're using Q&A on a network.

Set alternate programs: You can install up to six alternate DOS programs or Q&A macros right on your Q&A Main menu. If you use other software programs besides Q&A, you can launch them directly from the Main menu, and be returned to Q&A when you've exited from them. If you have routine chores assigned to macros, you can place these on the Main menu as well, and launch them with a single keystroke. See Chapters 8 and 9 for the details.

Summary

The tasks Q&A's utilities can perform for you will all be discussed in greater detail later in this book. You'll discover that Q&A offers a veritable wealth of tools to enhance your system, improve its value and performance, and increase the ease with which you can get even seemingly complex chores done with very little time and practically no effort at all.

To help you understand Q&A's overall menu structure and thus ease moving around from menu to menu, the tear-out card in the front of this book provides a detailed outline of how each menu item relates to others. Now that you have a feel for moving around Q&A, you're ready to tackle the first module, Write, which is discussed in Chapter 2.

Chapter 2
Write — Your Full-Featured Word Processor

In this chapter you'll learn how to:

▶ Type with Q&A's easy-to-learn word processor.

▶ Create, revise, and store all kinds of documents.

▶ Use Write's advanced editing features to manipulate whole documents or portions of them.

▶ Format your documents for page size and margins.

▶ Spell-check your documents and use the built-in thesaurus.

▶ Search your documents for special words, word strings, codes, and symbols to change, replace, or delete them.

▶ Print your documents.

▶ Enhance the appearance of your documents with fonts and other special features and effects.

▶ Harness your printer's full range of capabilities.

This chapter will cover Q&A's word processor from A to Z, from beginning to end, including tips undocumented by Q&A that will make it easier for you to use the unexpectedly powerful word processing package.

The first part of the chapter covers the basics — from selecting Write at the Q&A Main menu through creating a document, saving it, and printing it, as well as retrieving a previously saved document and clearing the screen of any current document.

The second part of this chapter shows you how to use the more advanced features to format, manipulate, and enhance your documents. This section will also cover methods of forcing your printer to give you the output you need.

Overview

Write is Q&A's word processing module. You can use it to compose, revise, manipulate, format, print, and save anything from memos, letters, and legal documents to articles, term papers and book-length manuscripts. The Write module is a good place to begin using Q&A because it familiarizes you with many of the basics that you'll need to know when you move on to the File and Report modules.

Whatever you may have been doing with a typewriter, Write can do it faster and with far better results. Write lets you move paragraphs around, insert other documents into the document on which you're working, and check your spelling. It provides you with synonyms from its built-in thesaurus and allows you to change the layout of your documents whenever you want. Depending on the capabilities of your printer, Write has the tools to help you enhance the appearance of your documents with special printer effects and fonts.

What's more, you can use Write with Q&A's File module to automatically create professional mail-merge documents such as personally addressed letters, announcements, or billing statements — any type of document that must be sent to many different addresses.

I'll begin this chapter by familiarizing you with the basics of typing and editing simple letters in Write. You'll need to install your printer in Q&A if you haven't already done so (see Chapter 1).

Once you've got the hang of entering plain text in Write and are comfortable with the Type/Edit screen (also referred to as "the editor"), I'll move on to more advanced editing, formatting, enhancing, saving, and printing, and to the extensive variety of additional Write features you can call upon at any time to help you perform masterful feats with your documents. Conversion of documents between Q&A and other word processing programs is covered in Chapter 9.

If all you need is a handy word processor to help you bang out your letters and other compositions, Q&A's Write is about as fast and easy to work with as they get. But behind its unassuming front end lies a rich assortment of powerful features that will help you make short work of even the most complex document handling chores. I'll show you how to use all of Write's features, one by one, in the following pages.

 Note: If at any time you find yourself confused or in trouble, just press **<Esc>** to back out of the operation. Pressing **<Esc>** will take you back toward the Main menu. Q&A always warns you if you're about to lose your document or any changes made to it, and tells you how to prevent that from happening. You can also press the **<F1>** help key to get on-line help.

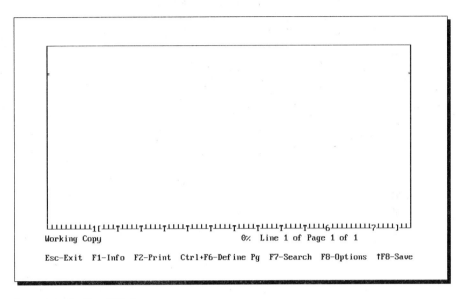

Figure 2-1: The Type/Edit Screen.

 Warning: Whatever you do, *never turn your computer off without first exiting the editor properly and at least returning to a menu.* Turning off your machine while files are still open can irreparably damage those files. You should exit Q&A by first pressing the **<Esc>** key to take you back to the Main menu, and then pressing **X** at the Main menu to bring you back to DOS. Then it's safe to cut the power.

Basic Word Processing Operations

Selecting Write from the Q&A Main menu takes you to the Write menu where you have eight choices: Type/Edit, Define page, Print, Clear, Get, Save, Utilities, and Mailing labels.

Select Type/Edit to bring up the word processing screen as shown in Figure 2-1.

Using the Cursor

At the Type/Edit screen, get a feel for moving the cursor around the screen. The cursor is your position marker; when you type a character, it will appear at the cursor position, and the cursor will advance to the next space awaiting your next keystroke. Use your cursor navigation keys (the up, down, left, and right arrows) to move the cursor first up, then down, then left, and then right. If you have an enhanced keyboard, it will have a separate bank of dedicated cursor keys. The cursor navigation keys on older keyboards are located on the numeric keypad, and are available when the Num Lock setting is off.

Notice that when you move the cursor to the right, and keep it going in that direction, it will suddenly appear at the left margin of the next line down. This is a demonstration of how Q&A automatically wraps from the end of one line to the beginning of the next.

Notice also that when you get the cursor moving vertically down the page, it just keeps on going for as long or as many times as you press the down arrow key.

Move the cursor down the blank page until you've passed the solid line that indicates the break between the first and second pages. Keep an eye on the status line at the bottom of the screen while you're doing this and you'll notice that the line numbers increase as the cursor moves down the page, and that when the cursor lands in the second page the page number on the status line changes from 1 to 2.

Now, with the cursor anywhere in page 2, hold down the **<Ctrl>** key and press the **<Home>** key. With no text on the screen you may have missed what just occurred. But if you check your status line you'll see that you're now back on line 1 of page 1. Pressing **<Ctrl><Home>** always moves the cursor to the first character of the document from no matter where in the document you are.

Next, press the **<Tab>** key a few times and notice how it moves the cursor to the right several characters at a time. Hold down the **<Shift>** key while pressing **<Tab>**, and the cursor moves back toward the left margin the same number of character columns per keystroke. Table 2-1 summarizes the keys and key combinations used to control cursor movement.

Entering Text

With your cursor at the left margin of the first line of page 1 (pressing **<Ctrl><Home>** will take the cursor there from wherever it is on the screen), type the lines of text in the next paragraph. Don't use the **<Enter>** key at the ends of the lines. If you make a mistake while typing the lines, use the **<Backspace>** key to erase the unwanted letters or word, and then continue.

```
Where was this snazzy word processing program last
month when I had to hammer out three major revisions
to that long contract for Mr. Dolittle?
```

Table 2-1
Moving the Cursor around the Type/Edit Screen

Key	Function
< ↔	One character to the left
< →	One character to the right
< ↑	One line up
< ↓	One line down
\<Ctrl\>\<→\>	Next word on the line
\<Ctrl\>\<↔\>	Previous word on the line

To move up through a document:

\<Home\>	First character of the line
\<Home\>\<Home\>	First character on the current screen
\<Home\>\<Home\>\<Home\>	First character of the document page
\<Home\>\<Home\>\<Home\>\<Home\>	First character of the document
\<Ctrl\>\<Home\>	First character of the document
\<PgUp\>	To the top of the previous screen
\<Ctrl\>\<PgUp\>	First character of previous page
\<F9\>	Scroll up

To move down through a document:

\<End\>	Last character of the line
\<End\>\<End\>	Last character on the current screen
\<End\>\<End\>\<End\>	Last character of the document page
\<End\>\<End\>\<End\>\<End\>	Last character of the document
\<Ctrl\>\<End\>	Last character of the document
\<PgDn\>	To the top of the next screen
\<Ctrl\>\<PgDn\>	First character of next page
\<Shift\>\<F9\>	Scroll down

To move the cursor to a specific line or page:

\<Ctrl\>\<F7\>	Enter line and/or a page number to go to

Did you notice how the sentence automatically wrapped at the end of the first and second lines? You didn't have to press the **<Enter>** key.

Insert Versus Overtype Mode

Q&A is preset to overtype mode, meaning it will type right over and erase any text that gets in the way of the cursor as you're typing along. The **<Insert>** or **<Ins>** key on your keyboard is a toggle switch that turns insert mode on and then off again when you press it a second time. If you've changed your editing default (more on this later) to make insert the default typing mode, then pressing **<Ins>** while on the Type/Edit screen the first time will toggle you into typeover mode.

The status line at the bottom of the screen will tell you when insert is on, and so will the cursor. It blossoms in size to occupy an entire character cell when in insert mode.

When you're typing additional text into existing text lines, insert mode is the way to go. But if you're typing corrections over material that you no longer want, the default typeover mode will serve you better.

Word Wrap

There's no need to press **<Enter>** or **<Return>** as you're typing. Should the last word be too long to fit on the line, Q&A Write automatically wraps it to the next line. This feature is especially convenient for fast typists and long documents. Simply type away and let Q&A worry about where to end the lines.

There's also a good reason why you should get out of habit of pressing **<Enter>** at the end of a normal text line. Besides being an unnecessary keystroke, it places an invisible "hard" carriage return at the end of the line, and then the text lines may not readjust properly should you later insert additional text above that point. When you let Q&A wrap words automatically, it places invisible "soft" carriage returns at the ends of the lines. Q&A can easily remove these soft returns if the lines need to be readjusted due to the addition or deletion of text.

At first, it can seem like a difficult habit to break if you're used to working on a typewriter that required you to press **<Return>** at the end of each line. But you'll get comfortable with it in no time.

Save your **<Enter>** key for the ends of paragraphs and for other lines you deliberately wish to keep short, such as name, address, and salutation lines at the beginning of letters.

Deleting and Inserting Words

Continuing with our exercise, let's change the words "word processing program" in your text to "word processor." If your keyboard is the enhanced type and has a separate bank of cursor keys, use these. Otherwise, be sure the Num Lock setting on your numeric keypad is turned off so that numbers won't be typed when you press the keys for cursor control.

1. Use your navigation (cursor) keys to position the cursor directly beneath the letter *w* in *word*.

2. Then press the **<Delete>** key (sometimes marked **<Del>**) until the words *word processing program* are all erased. Pressing **<Del>** erases the characters as well as the space they occupied. Holding the key down will speed up the deletion, but be careful not to overshoot and delete too much.

3. Now, with the cursor positioned to the right of the space immediately after the word *snazzy*, press the **<Ins>** key (so the cursor is large and bright) and type in the words *word processor.* You'll notice that the text to the right of where you typed these two words is shoved farther to the right and then wrapped as necessary.

When entering text, if you find that you frequently need to go back to previous lines to make corrections, you might prefer to work routinely in insert rather than typeover mode. In insert mode you can position the cursor over the first unwanted character or space and press **<Del>**, or position the cursor over the last unwanted character or space and press **<Backspace>** until all the unwanted characters to the left of the cursor have been erased. Since you're working in insert mode you can then simply type the corrected text without having to toggle the **<Ins>** key on and off.

Quantum Cursor Leaps and Text Deletion

Experiment with the **<Home>** and **<End>** keys to get a feel for moving the cursor more rapidly:

1. Position the cursor in the middle of the last line of text.

2. Press the **<Home>** key and notice how the cursor jumps to the first character of the same line.

3. Press the **<End>** key to move the cursor to the end of the same line.

4. Hold down the **<Ctrl>** key and press the left arrow key once to move the cursor to the beginning of the previous word. Then, holding down the **<Ctrl>** key, press the left arrow key *several* times. Notice how the cursor keeps moving to the first letters of the previous words on the line.

Deleting words, lines, and even entire paragraphs is also easy to do in Write.

Deleting a word: Place the cursor under the first letter of the word you want to delete and press **<F4>**. Q&A will delete the word and close up the space. Pressing **<F4>** when the cursor is positioned at a word, but *not* at its first letter, will delete from the cursor position to the end of the word, but not the trailing space.

Restoring text: Pressing **<Shift><F7>** restores any word, line, or block of text just deleted. This feature doesn't work, however, when you've used **<Del>**, **<Backspace>**, or the space bar to delete text character by character.

Deleting a line: Place the cursor anywhere on the line you want to delete and press **<Shift><F4>**. Restore the line just deleted by immediately pressing **<Shift><F7>**.

Deleting part of a line: Position the cursor just to the left of the text on the line you want to delete and press **<Ctrl><F4>**. The rest of the line to the right of the cursor will be zapped, while the text to the left of it will remain intact.

Deleting a block of text: Position the cursor at the beginning of the text you wish to delete. Press **<F3>** and the letter at the cursor position will be highlighted. Now, using the cursor keys, highlight all the text to be deleted. If you have several lines to delete, you can use the down arrow cursor key to highlight a line at a time. When you've highlighted all the text to be deleted, press **<F10>** to confirm. Pressing **<Shift><F7>** immediately after deleting a block of text, and before making any additional deletions, will undelete that same block of text, restoring it to the screen at the cursor position. Q&A will let you know if a block of text marked for deletion is too big to be restored.

Experiment by moving the cursor around the screen, and typing, revising, deleting, and restoring words, lines, and blocks of text. The more familiar you are with these tools the more productive your word processing will be. And remember that you can always press **<F1>** no matter where you are in your document for an on-screen reference of what the various function, navigation, and editing keys will do for you.

Saving Your Document

Do yourself a favor by saving your work often. Don't wait until you're on page 12 of a new document when a power failure hits and wipes out the entire day's work. Get into the habit of saving your current document to disk every 10 minutes or so. It only takes a few keystrokes, and it's better to be safe than sorry.

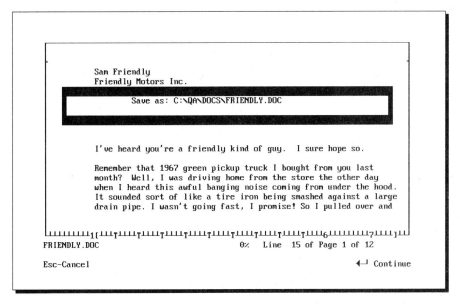

```
        Sam Friendly
        Friendly Motors Inc.

              Save as: C:\QA\DOCS\FRIENDLY.DOC


        I've heard you're a friendly kind of guy.  I sure hope so.

        Remember that 1967 green pickup truck I bought from you last
        month?  Well, I was driving home from the store the other day
        when I heard this awful banging noise coming from under the hood.
        It sounded sort of like a tire iron being smashed against a large
        drain pipe. I wasn't going fast, I promise! So I pulled over and
```
FRIENDLY.DOC   0%   Line 15 of Page 1 of 12

Esc-Cancel   ◄┘ Continue

Figure 2-2: Saving a Document from Inside the Editor. Q&A displays the path, and also the filename if the document has been saved with this name before. You can change the document name or path simply by typing over the existing line.

There are two ways to save a document in the editor: from the Type/Edit screen, and by using the Save option from the Write menu.

If you want to save the document while it's on screen:

1. Press **\<Shift>\<F8>**. A prompt will tell you to enter the name of the document after the pathname. If an earlier version of this same document was saved, Q&A will display the document name along with the pathname.

2. Type in the document name if you need to, or give it a new name by typing over the old one, and then press **\<Enter>**. Document names must follow the DOS convention of a maximum of eight characters, plus a period and three more characters if desired. If you've renamed the document, the earlier version (under the old name) will still be on disk (see Figure 2-2).

Q&A will save the entire document for you (not just the portion that's showing) and return you to the Type/Edit screen with the document still displayed.

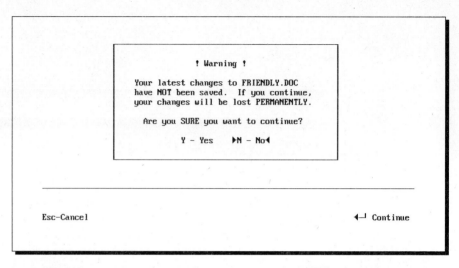

```
                          ! Warning !

            Your latest changes to FRIENDLY.DOC
            have NOT been saved.  If you continue,
            your changes will be lost PERMANENTLY.

            Are you SURE you want to continue?

                    Y - Yes    ▶N - No◀
```

Esc-Cancel   ◀─┘ Continue

Figure 2-3: Q&A's Warning Prompt. Q&A won't let you get away with losing a new document, or losing any changes made to a previously saved document, without some effort on your part.

If you prefer to save the document from the Write menu:

1. Press **<Esc>** once from the Type/Edit screen to go to the Write menu.

2. Select the Save option. A box will appear prompting you to enter the name of the document after the pathname. If an earlier version of this document was saved, Q&A will display the document name along with the pathname.

3. Type in the document name (if needed), or give it a new name by typing over the other old one, and then press **<Enter>**. If you've renamed the document, the earlier version (under the old filename) will still be on disk.

Even after you leave Type/Edit and return to the Write menu, Q&A will keep your document in the editor, waiting for you to return to work on it some more.

If you attempt to **<Esc>** past the Write menu without saving a document that has been modified in the current session, however, Q&A will warn you that your changes will be lost if you continue (see Figure 2-3). If you don't want to lose your changes, select "No" by typing the letter **N** (or press **<Enter>** if the No option is highlighted) and Q&A will return you to the Write menu. From there you can save the document, or press either **<Enter>** or **T** to return to the document still in the editor.

Although DOS limits your filenames to a maximum of eight characters plus an optional period and three more characters, Q&A enables you to create 70-character filename descriptions. You can write descriptive comments to attach to your document and data files at any Q&A List Manager screen, and you'll then be able to identify and select the exact file you want. See Chapter 9 for more on this useful feature.

Printing from the Type/Edit Screen

Printing a document from the Type/Edit screen is easy, and Write gives you a variety of printing options from which you can choose when you're ready to send your document to the printer. These options will be covered in detail later in this chapter. For now, let's simply print what you have on screen (anything) to round out the tutorial. This brief printing demonstration assumes that you installed your printer as Printer A in the previous chapter.

1. Be sure your printer is turned on, is on line, and has paper loaded.

2. With the document on screen, press **<F2>** to display the Print Options screen. Be sure PtrA on the "Print to" line is highlighted, and the "Page preview" option is set to "No."

3. Press **<F10>** to send the document to the printer. It should begin printing. If it doesn't, check the printer installation procedure in Chapter 1 again, and see the section "Printing in Write" further ahead in this chapter.

Elements of the Type/Edit Screen

There are a number of things to know about how Q&A displays the imaginary sheet of paper onto which you type your text.

First of all, your screen cannot show a whole vertical page, but only about a third of it at any one time. If you press the down-arrow cursor key and hold it, the screen will scroll to the bottom of the first page where a solid horizontal line will appear. If you pass this line with the cursor, the single solid line will turn into a double line, indicating that you've crossed the boundary from page 1 to page 2. So a standard-sized sheet of 8½-by-11-inch paper will actually consume three screen pages at 20 lines per screen page, for a total of 60 lines — more or less depending on your top and bottom margin settings.

Horizontally, or across the page, the standard display in Q&A shows a maximum of 78 columns or characters at one time. It makes no difference on the visible display whether your document has been formatted for narrow margins and small type — the display screen will only show 10 characters to the inch.

So remember that even though your *printer* may be capable of producing a wide range of characters-per-inch (often abbreviated *cpi*) including 10 cpi (pica), 12 cpi (elite), 15 and even 17 cpi (condensed), your display will only show the uniform 10 cpi.

Note: To see how the page will look with different characters-per-inch, use the Page Preview feature (located on the Print Options screen).

The Ruler Line

The ruler-like line running from left to right along the bottom of the screen indicates three things:

Margins: The left and right limits of the typing area of the page, which you can change, are indicated by the **[** and **]** symbols.

Tab stops: The **<Tab>** key on your keyboard is used to move the cursor or a line of text to the right more than a single space at a time. Tab stops (which you can change) are positioned along the ruler line as a series of "T"s.

Column positions: Each tick on the ruler line indicates one space or character position on the page. Each group of 10 ticks terminates in a number that tells you how far you are from the left edge of the sheet. The number 2 on the ruler line means 20 characters from the left edge, and so forth.

Cursor Position

When the Type/Edit screen first displays you'll see the cursor blinking in the correct position to start typing — at the left margin on the first line of the page. This left margin position corresponds to the **[** symbol just to the right of the "1" on the ruler line near the bottom of the screen. The "ghost cursor" on the ruler line follows the horizontal motion of the actual cursor as you type across the page and thus can be helpful if you need to count horizontal spaces or inches to align text in a column.

Edge of Sheet

Figure 2-1 shows the solid lines that surround the Type/Edit screen. These show the edges of a sheet of imaginary paper. You can't see the line that defines the bottom of the sheet because it's well below the current screen view. Write's default sheet size is the standard 8½-by-11-inch piece of paper with one-inch margins all around, except for a right margin that is slightly greater than an inch. If you prefer to work on your documents without these solid lines, you can turn them "off" at the Editing Options screen under Global Options.

Left/Right Margins

These set the limits on where you can start typing on the left, and the maximum length of your horizontal lines. Q&A automatically wraps a word to the next line if it won't fit on the preceding line.

Top/Bottom Margins

The top margin on the Type/Edit screen is shown by small double-ticks on the left and right sheet edges (see Figure 2-1). The margin at the bottom of the page is similarly marked, although you can't see it until the cursor is moved there.

The Status Line

This third from the last line at the bottom of the screen (see Figure 2-1) tells you a few things you might need to know about the document on which you're working:

- The title or name of your document (Q&A names a document "Working Copy" until you name and save it).

- The percentage of currently available memory your document is using (which in Figure 2-1 is 0 percent because no text has as yet been entered).

- The page and line numbers corresponding to the position of the cursor, along with the total number of pages in the document.

- Which special features are "on" at the cursor position (such as bold, italics, font, and insert mode).

The Message Line

Q&A uses this line (just below the status line) to display messages, warnings, or instructions as the situation calls for them during Type/Edit. In Figure 2-1 the message line is blank.

The Key Assignment Line

The function or "F" keys you are most likely to want to use are displayed along the bottom line of the screen. As in all Q&A modules, the function keys tell Q&A what you want to do, and are sometimes pressed while simultaneously holding down the **<Shift>**, **<Ctrl>**, or **<Alt>** key. For example, if the command you want to invoke is accessible by pressing **<Shift><F2>**, it means that you hold down the **<Shift>** key, press **<F2>**, and then let both keys go.

Table 2-2
Function Keys in Q&A Write

Function Key	Meaning
<F1>	Online, context-sensitive help.
<Alt><F1>	Thesaurus.
<Shift><F1>	Document spelling check.
<Ctrl><F1>	Word spelling check.
<F2>	Print document (takes you to the Print Options screen).
<Shift><F2>	Access Q&A's Macro menu (see Chapter 8).
<Ctrl><F2>	Print a block of text.
<F3>	Delete a block of cursor-highlighted text.
<Ctrl-F3>	Get a count of the words, lines, and paragraphs in the document.
<F4>	Delete the word at the cursor.
<Shift><F4>	Delete the line the cursor is on.
<Ctrl><F4>	Delete from the cursor position to the end of the line.
<F5>	Copy a block of text to another location in the document.
<Shift><F5>	Move a block of text to another location in the document.
<Ctrl><F5>	Copy a block of text to a new document.
<Alt><F5>	Move a block of text to a new document.
<F6>	Set a temporary left and/or right margin (indents), or clear a temporary margin.
<Shift><F6>	Select from available text enhancements such as bold, italics, superscript, or installed fonts, or return enhanced text to normal.
<Ctrl><F6>	Go to the Define Page screen to set margins, page length, width, numbering, and characters per inch.
<Alt><F6>	Place a soft hyphen at the cursor position.
<F7>	Define document search-and-replace criteria. Press <PgDn> after pressing <F7> for advanced search options.
<Alt><F7>	Display a list of available fields to include in a merge document.
<Shift><F7>	Restores text just deleted. Also used to make multiple copies of a block of text.
<Ctrl><F7>	Take the cursor to a specified page and/or line.
<F8>	Brings up a special Options menu to layout the page, retrieve a document, display a list of recent documents, do text block operations, embed printer commands in the document, or select other Write features.
<Shift><F8>	Save the document on the screen to disk.
<Ctrl><F8>	Save the document in ASCII format.
<F9>	Scroll down the document line by line.
<Shift><F9>	Scroll up the document line by line.
<Ctrl><F9>	Assign fonts for the current document.
<Alt><F9>	Do a calculation on a row or column of numbers.
<F10>	Tells Q&A to carry out a command.

Table 2-2 shows all the function key assignments for Write. Looking over the descriptions of what these various function key combinations do gives you a good idea of the operations available to you in the Write module. You can display an abbreviated table of these key assignments from the Type/Edit screen by pressing the Help key, **<F1>**.

Note: The commands also appear in the tear-out quick reference card in the back of this book.

Many of the operations initiated by function keys throughout Q&A are also available from the Options menu, activated by pressing **<F8>**. Thus it's not imperative that you remember which function keys do what. Write's Options menu, covered in the section "Advanced Type/Edit Operations," is especially helpful when using a mouse.

Optional WordStar Commands

A number of cursor movement and editing operations in Write can be performed by using an alternate set of commands which mimic those of the WordStar word processing program. Table 2-3 lists these optional commands. If you're a fast touch-typist, or find it easier to work on your documents without having to move your fingers away from the main keyboard area in order to reach the function keys, you may find these alternate **<Ctrl>***key* combinations more convenient while working with your documents.

You can create even more specialized **<Ctrl>***key* combinations for manipulating the cursor and text by using keyboard macros.

A macro is a stored recording of a number of actual keystrokes which you invoke when you wish Q&A to automatically execute, or "play back," those keystrokes (sort of like a player piano). For example, you might want to have a "Go to top of page" command. You can create a macro that will do this for you automatically when you press **<Ctrl>** and a key simultaneously. Chapter 8 tells you all about how to record, save, and invoke keyboard macros.

Using the Get Command to Retrieve a Document

You now know how to create, save, and print a document, but how do you retrieve one you've already saved? When you retrieve a document that was previously saved to disk, Write gives you a *copy* of that document and keeps the original safely stored away. The copy is identical to the version on disk until you revise the copy and save it back to disk under the same name. So if you accidentally lose or mess up the copy with which you are working, you can easily retrieve the version that was last saved to disk.

Table 2-3
Write's WordStar-like Key Combinations

Cursor movement key combinations:

Key	Action
<Ctrl><A>	To previous word
<Ctrl><S>	To previous character
<Ctrl><D>	To next character
<Ctrl><F>	To next word
<Ctrl><E>	To previous line
<Ctrl><X>	To next line
<Ctrl><R>	To first character of previous screen
<Ctrl><C>	To first character of next screen
<Ctrl><I>	Tab
<Ctrl><M>	Enter (Return)

Editing key combinations:

Key	Action
<Ctrl><G>	To delete character at the cursor position
<Ctrl><T>	To delete word at the cursor
<Ctrl><N>	To insert a new line
<Ctrl><Y>	To delete the line
<Ctrl><H>	Backspace
<Ctrl><V>	To toggle insert mode on and off

However, should you lose a document that has *never* been saved to disk, there's no way to retrieve it. That's why it's a good practice to frequently save both new and modified documents to disk as you're working on them.

What follows is the procedure for bringing a document on disk into the editor:

From the Write menu, press **G** (for Get). Q&A will ask you for the name of the document. Type in the name of the document you want to bring into the editor, and press **<Enter>**.

If you're working on a document, save it, do something else in Q&A, and then return to Write and retrieve by pressing **G**, the name of that last document will appear at the filename prompt so long as you haven't exited Q&A in the meantime.

If you've forgotten the name of the document, or want to see a list of all the documents in the *current* directory, press **<Enter>** with the document name left blank at the pathname prompt. At the list of files, use your cursor keys to highlight the document you want and press **<Enter>**. If it's a Q&A-compatible document it will be brought directly into the editor. You can give your documents descriptive 70-character names (in addition to the DOS filename) so that they can be located faster. See Chapter 9.

If you call up a list of files for the current directory and there are also additional directories branching off from the current directory, you'll see the names of the additional directories preceded by a "\" character at the top of the list of files. To look at the files in another directory, highlight the directory name and press **<Enter>**. If the document you want is now on the list, highlight it and press **<Enter>** to bring it into the editor.

If your document, database, and other files are all in the same directory, then some of the filenames you'll see on screen may not be document files. If you try to select a nondocument file (such as a database file), Write will tell you it's an unknown file format and will ask you to select from a menu of file formats. Should you continue this misadventure by selecting a file format, the file will be brought to the Type/Edit screen and may contain incomprehensible characters.

Keep in mind that you can work on only one document at a time. If you try to retrieve a document when another one with unsaved changes is already in the editor, Write will warn you and give you the chance to save the first one before retrieving the next one. When Write retrieves your document and brings it into the editor, the cursor will be positioned exactly where it was when you last saved it.

Instead of using the Get command on the Write menu to retrieve the document you want to work on, you can use the Options menu from inside the editor. From the blank Type/Edit screen, press **<F8>** and choose Documents. The names of the last 12 documents you've worked on will be displayed, and you can highlight the one you want and press **<Enter>** to bring it onto the Type/Edit screen. If the document you want isn't on the list, select Get a Document, type in its filename at the prompt, and press **<Enter>**.

Write can automatically read and get a number of document types including Q&A Write, pfs:Write, and IBM Writing Assistant. Q&A can also read Old WordStar (versions 3.3 and below), Lotus 1-2-3, and Symphony spreadsheets, as well as other formats that have been printed to disk, saved as text only, or saved in ASCII format. When Write detects one of these document formats as you're trying to bring it into the editor, you'll be presented with the Import Document menu (see Figure 2-4).

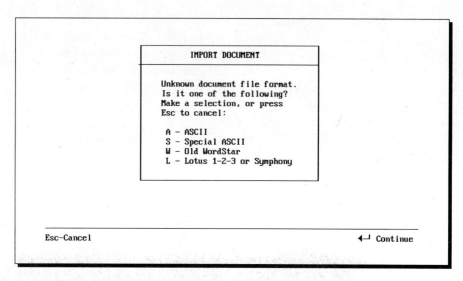

```
                    ┌─────────────────────────────────┐
                    │        IMPORT DOCUMENT          │
                    ├─────────────────────────────────┤
                    │                                 │
                    │   Unknown document file format. │
                    │   Is it one of the following?   │
                    │   Make a selection, or press    │
                    │   Esc to cancel:                │
                    │                                 │
                    │   A - ASCII                     │
                    │   S - Special ASCII             │
                    │   W - Old WordStar              │
                    │   L - Lotus 1-2-3 or Symphony   │
                    │                                 │
                    └─────────────────────────────────┘



     Esc-Cancel                                    ←┘ Continue
```

Figure 2-4: Write's Import Document Menu.

From this menu, selecting ASCII tells Q&A to import the document as a straight ASCII document with carriage returns placed where they already exist in the document. If you select Special ASCII, Write will import the document without carriage returns, giving you a document that will automatically word wrap in the editor and leave normal blank-line spaces at the ends of paragraphs. The Old WordStar selection imports this type of document directly with all enhancements intact.

If you choose Lotus 1-2-3 or Symphony from the Import Document menu, Write will display the Lotus range spec (see the discussion in Chapter 9 on integrating Lotus 1-2-3). When you've defined the range, Write will import it with a hard carriage return at the end of each spreadsheet row. Other document files from programs such as Multimate, WordPerfect, Microsoft Word, DCA, and later versions of WordStar must be converted by Q&A using the Import selection from the Write Utilities menu (more on this in Chapter 9).

Finally, if you want to retrieve an entire document to insert into the document already on the Type/Edit screen, see "Beyond the Basics" below on "Inserting an External Document Into the Current One."

The Clear Command

When you have finished with a document and want to start on another, you will have to use the Clear command on the Write menu. If the current document has not been saved to disk when you select Clear, Write will warn you that you'll lose it (or at least lose any changes made to it since it was last saved) if you continue. At this point you'll probably want to save the document before getting or starting another one.

Using the Clear command from the Write menu is the same as escaping from the Type/Edit screen from an unsaved document. If you answer "Yes" when Write asks if you want to continue without saving, the editor will be cleared, but you will lose that document, or at least any changes you made to it during the most recent editing session.

Define the Page

Q&A comes out of the box with certain convenient assumptions. It assumes you'll be using 8½-by-11-inch paper, one-inch margins all around, and prints to whatever printer you installed as "Printer A." But you can change any of these assumptions permanently or just for this session. You can also add headers and footers and change the characters-per-inch as well as many other things.

Before moving on to Write's more advanced Type/Edit features you should know how to format and print out a document. Write provides you with practically limitless options to get the precise document appearance you're after.

The fundamental steps involved in producing word-processing documents are:

1. Typing and editing the document to end up with the exact text and layout you want.

2. Telling Q&A how to structure the document pages by defining elements such as margins, page length, headers, and footers.

3. Selecting your printing options (assuming you've already installed your printer).

By now you should be familiar with how to type text and carry out the fundamental document-editing tasks such as inserting, replacing, and deleting letters, words, and lines. You might think that once your text is written the only thing left to do is to command Q&A to print it out. But you've been doing more than just typing text — you've been creating a *document.* And any document — whether it's a letter, memo, article, or book chapter — has to be properly formatted so that when printed out it *looks* like you would expect it to look. Here's where Write's Define Page screen comes into play.

The Define Page screen is where you set your page characteristics that will affect each page and thus the document as a whole.

If you look at a typewritten letter, or a page from a book or magazine, you'll notice two obvious characteristics. One is the physical page size — the dimensions of the sheet of paper on which the text is printed. Most business letters, for example, are printed on 8½-by-11-inch sheets of paper.

The second characteristic is the text image area. This is the portion of the entire sheet of paper taken up by the printed image. The free or empty spaces that surround this printed image are the margins.

When you define your document page in Write, you are telling Q&A what the physical dimensions of the sheet of paper are, how much blank space you want placed around the text image area, the density of printing you want (characters-per-inch, or *cpi*), and on which page you'd like to begin printing your page numbers and headers and footers.

When you set your page characteristics you are affecting both what you see on the Type/Edit screen and what Write will print out on paper. Different documents can have different page characteristics. You can change these settings at any time and for any document. And when you save your document, these characteristics are saved right along with it.

You can also create *default* page characteristics — defaults ensure that, barring any changes you make to individual document settings, Q&A will always set up your new documents to print with the same margins, page length, and any other default elements you set (see the "Write Utilities" section toward the end of this chapter). This comes in handy, for example, if you're regularly typing business letters that must conform to a standard format.

The Define Page Screen

The decision as to *when* to define the page characteristics for a document is entirely up to you. You can press **D** at the Write menu for the Define Page screen, and make your settings either just before you are about to start on your document, or when there is a document already in the editor. Regardless of whether you set defaults in this manner, you can also define characteristics on-the-fly — while working on your document in the editor you can press **<Ctrl><F6>** to define the page characteristics for that document. Or you can simply accept Write's default settings for new documents which assume a standard 8½-by-11-inch page with one-inch margins all around and 10-cpi printing, in which case you need not bother changing anything on the Define Page screen.

Some people prefer to focus their attention on typing the text for the document, putting off any page formatting considerations until later. On the other hand, some people would rather format their document pages before actually starting the type/edit process. Figure 2-5 shows Write's Define Page screen and its available options.

```
                            DEFINE PAGE
                            ==========


          Left margin: 10              Right margin : 68

          Top margin : 6              Bottom margin: 6

          Page width : 78              Page length  : 66

          Characters per inch............:  ▶10◀   12    15    17

          Begin header/footer on page #...:   1

          Begin page numbering with page #:   1


   _____

                    Page Options for Working Copy

    Esc-Cancel        F1-Info       F2-Print Options              F10-Continue
```

Figure 2-5: Q&A's Define Page Screen. It is used to tell Q&A the physical page dimensions, the size margins you want, the characters-per-inch in which the text will be printed, and where page numbering is to begin. Shown here are Write's defaults.

For all values you wish to set or change at the Define Page screen:

1. Move the cursor to the item you want to change.

2. To make your change:

- For all items *except* characters-per-inch, simply type in the new value and press **<Tab>** or **<Enter>** to move the cursor to the next value to be changed.

- For characters-per-inch, highlight your selection and then press **<Enter>**.

3. When you've entered all the new settings you want, press **<F10>** for Type/Edit screen.

Setting Your Page Size and Margins

Page length and top and bottom margins (*vertical* distances) can be defined in terms of inches, centimeters, or number of lines (Figure 2-6 illustrates the placement of such page elements). Ordinarily there are six vertical lines to the inch (the same as on most typewriters), and thus 66 lines to a standard 8½-by-11-inch sheet of paper (6 3 11 = 66). So if you wanted one-inch top and

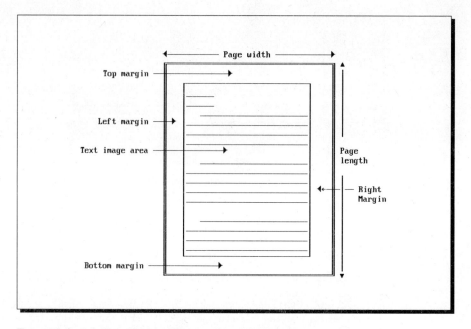

Figure 2-6: Sample Page Showing Margins, Page Width, and Page Length. Page (paper) dimensions are represented enclosed by the double-line box. Text image area is shown enclosed by the single-line box.

bottom margins on a standard sheet of paper, you would set these values as follows:

- Page length: 11" *or* 66 (lines).

- Top margin: 1" *or* 6 (lines).

- Bottom margin: 1" *or* 6 (lines).

When you specify inches be sure to type the inch symbol (") after the number or Q&A will think you're specifying lines. When specifying centimeters, follow the number with cm. Fractions of inches or centimeters can be entered in decimal form. For example, a top margin of 1¼ inches is specified by the decimal number 1.25. If you're specifying your top and bottom margins and page length in *lines* rather than inches, you can use only whole numbers and no decimals.

Your printer may not be capable of printing 66 lines on a sheet of 8½-by-11-inch paper. Laser printers, as well as other sheet-fed printers, have built-in minimum margin settings that must be taken into account. Consult your printer manual for more information.

Table 2-4
Maximum Page Widths by Paper Size and CPI

Your printer may have certain line-length limitations, so these are approximate values.

Page Size	10 cpi	12 cpi	15 cpi	17 cpi
8½" x 11"	85	102	128	145
8½" x 14"	85	102	128	145
15" x 11"	140	168	210	238
11" x 8½"	110	132	165	185
14" x 8½"	140	168	210	238

Page width and left and right margins (*horizontal* distances) can be defined in terms of either inches, centimeters, or character columns. A character column is the space taken up by a single character when using a monospaced font.

When defining these values in terms of inches or centimeters, you can use decimal numbers. Again, be sure to add the inch (") or **cm** indicator after the value so Q&A knows you mean inches or centimeters.

Left and right margin and page-width settings in *characters columns* can only be specified in whole numbers. With 10-pitch type there are 10 characters (or character *columns*) to the horizontal inch. Twelve-pitch type means 12 characters to the inch, and so forth. So if you wanted a one-inch left margin with 10-cpi printing, you could define your left margin as 10. Table 2-4 summarizes maximum page widths at various cpi settings and page sizes.

There are similarities and differences between *character columns* (for setting left/right margins and page widths), and *characters-per-inch* (for specifying the character density in which the document is to be printed).

Margin sizes, page width, and cpi settings in a document are all closely related — keep this fact in mind when working with the Define Page screen.

Warning: When you change the *characters-per-inch* value at the Define Page screen you are also changing the basis on which any *character column* values for left and right margins and page widths are computed by Q&A. In other words, left and right margins and page widths, *when specified in character columns*, are dependent on the document's current cpi setting.

A cpi setting of 10, for example, means that a left margin setting of 10 will result in a true one-inch margin. A cpi setting of 12, however, means that a left margin setting of 10 will result in a left margin of ten 12-cpi columns, or something *less* than an inch. If you've set your left and right margins in character columns, then changing your cpi value will affect these margins. For example, if you change your cpi to 15, and leave your left margin at 10, you'll wind up with a smaller left margin because that left margin setting of 10 no longer means one inch, but only *two-thirds* (10/15ths) of an inch.

If you've set your left and right margins or page width in inches, then changing your cpi will *not* affect these because an inch is an inch no matter the cpi print density you've specified.

Thus, to secure your left and right margins so that changes to the characters-per-inch setting won't affect them, specify these margins in inches rather than in character columns. Then, should you change your cpi setting, Q&A will reformat your document without changing the margin widths. An increase in the cpi setting at the Define Page screen will result in more characters being printed on a line, while decreasing the cpi will mean less characters printed per line.

When printing with proportional fonts (Times, Helvetica, etc.) set your left and right margins and page width in inches. If the document's regular font is proportional, Q&A converts any page dimensions expressed in columns into inches to ensure that the page's dimensions won't be affected by font changes.

You can mix inches and cpi alternatives when setting your page width and left and right margins. For example, you can set your left and right margins in character columns, but your page width in inches. Just remember that whenever these values are defined in character columns, *and you change your cpi setting*, the appearance of your whole page will be affected by the change.

Thus, it's a good idea to familiarize yourself with your printer's capabilities. Some printers (such as laser printers and other sheet-fed printers) cannot print 66 vertical lines on an 8½-by-11-inch sheet of paper and won't print the entire width of the page. Your printer may have built-in margins which, when added to the margins you've specified at the Define Page screen, may cause part of a single-page document to be forced onto a second page. Also, be sure that your margins aren't being overruled by manual settings at the printer's own control panel.

Your printer may not be capable of printing at one or more of Q&A's 10-, 12-, 15-, and 17-cpi settings. Check the operator's manual that came with your printer to determine its limitations with regard to margins, page sizes, and printing density.

Table 2-5
Write's Minimum and Maximum Page Widths
in Inches and Characters-per-Inch

Page Width	Inches	Columns			
		10cpi	12cpi	15cpi	17cpi
Minimum	1"	10	12	15	17
Maximum	14"	150	168	210	238

Table 2-6
Minimum and Maximum Page Lengths
in Inches and Lines

Page Length	Inches	Lines
Minimum	1"	6
Maximum	32"	192

New: If your printer isn't capable of printing at your 17-cpi setting, for example, Write will select the closest match within its own limits (see Tables 2-5 and 2-6).

Setting Characters-per-Inch

Many printers today will handle a variety of pitch densities (pitch density here refers to the number of characters-per-inch the printer is capable of producing on paper). Q&A gives you a choice of four of the most commonly supported pitches: pica (10 cpi), elite (12 cpi), and compressed (15 and 17 cpi). Some dot-matrix printers will even print at 20 cpi. The Hewlett-Packard LaserJet Line Printer pitch of 16.67 cpi corresponds roughly to Q&A's 17 cpi.

Author's Tip: Keep these points (undocumented by Q&A) in mind when defining your page dimensions, margins, and characters-per-inch:

- Page *length*, minus the sum of your top and bottom margins, determines your vertical text-image area.

- Page *width*, minus the sum of your left and right margins, determines the width of your text-image area.

- You can establish Define Page options defaults for all your new documents using Write's global options (explained in "Using Write's Advanced Features"), but you can override any or all of these global default settings on a per-document basis while the document is in the Write editor.

- Left/right margin and page-width settings in character columns are valid for fixed-space (mono-spaced) fonts only. If you are using proportional fonts in the document, get used to setting your margins and page width in *inches* because Write will convert these to inches where your regular font for the document is proportional. The character columns value is meaningless when the font will print a varying number of characters-per-inch of horizontal space.

- If your left and right margins and/or page width are set in character columns rather than inches, changing your pitch setting will affect these margins and page width, and your document may not look as good as you expected when it is printed.

- Define your left and right margins and page width in inches at the Define Page screen to secure them against changes to the cpi.

- The higher the cpi setting, the smaller (more condensed) your letters and words will look when the document is printed. In addition, when you use a high cpi setting, less of the document is displayed on the screen when you are working with it.

A normal display will show only up to 78-character columns no matter how many characters-per-inch you've selected at the Define Page screen. If your line length is set to a value higher than this, the right edge of your document will be off the screen until the cursor moves into that area. Then the left side of the document will go off-screen. If you want to see the entire width of the document as you're working on it, either increase your left and right margin values or reduce your cpi. You can always go back and change them when you're ready to print.

- If you need to work in terms of inches of *line length* on a standard sheet of 8½-by-11-inch paper, use the following formula with all settings in inches: Subtract your left margin from your page width, and then subtract the *line length* you want from that result. The difference will give you the proper right margin setting.

- Changing margin, page, or cpi settings while working on a document, and then immediately returning to it, forces Write to reformat the document according to your new settings. During this process the status message "formatting" will flash on the screen. It may take a moment or so depending on the length of the document. As soon as the reformatting is finished, you'll be returned to the Type/Edit screen. The ruler line at the bottom of the screen will have also been updated to reflect how much text will now fit on a line at the new settings.

- Saving the document will save all your Define Page settings along with it.

- The capabilities of your printer may determine how far you can go in setting your cpi, margins, page length and width from inside Q&A and seeing the correct results of these settings in your printed documents. As you're creating your document, Write formats it according to the current Define Page settings, *not necessarily* the printer. Knowing your printer's limitations regarding these items will help you select workable Define Page values so that what you see on the display will more closely represent what you get when you print the document.

Header/Footer Starting Page

Although shown on the Define Page screen, header/footer starting page is discussed in "Beyond the Basics" later in this chapter. Briefly, Q&A's Define Page screen enables you to select the page on which you want your header or footer to start appearing. Typing a "2" at this line means "Start printing the header, footer (or both) on page 2 of this document."

Starting Page Number

If you want page numbers printed on your document, you must create a header or footer while at the Type/Edit screen. A header or footer can be as simple as a sole character, such as the "#" sign, that tells Q&A where you want the page number placed.

Once this is done, you can use the Define Page screen to indicate the starting page for page numbers. Your initial document pages might include a title page and table of contents, and you may not want page numbers to show up on these. See the section on headers and footers to create page numbers for documents that are continuations (chapters, for example) of other Write documents. This differs from telling Q&A where to begin printing page numbers in the *current* document.

Printing in Write

Depending on the capabilities of your printer, anything you can create in Write, or import into Write, can be printed from Write. This includes correspondence, mail-merged documents, reports, forms, pictures, graphs, charts, database and spreadsheet data, envelope addresses, mailing labels, and more.

You tell Q&A how to print your document by filling in a form, much like the way in which you specified your page-formatting values at the Define Page screen above.

At the Define Page screen you established the dimensions (margins, width, length) of your document pages for the display screen as well as the printer.

At the Print Options screen (see Figure 2-7) you specify the additional information that Q&A needs to know before sending your document to the printer.

If your printer utilizes fonts (even PostScript) and you have these fonts, Q&A probably supports them for use in your documents. Installing font files, as well as embedding printer control codes in your documents to create special printing effects, will be discussed in detail later in this chapter under "Advanced Printing Techniques." Let's start with the basics here, so you'll know how to produce good-looking printed output from the Write module right away.

Before exploring Write's Print Options screen, there are a few things you should note:

- Your printer must be properly installed before you attempt to print any documents from Write (see Chapter 1 if you haven't yet installed your printer).

- Appendix B provides some troubleshooting tips for common printing problems.

- You can always use the Page Preview option to see what your document will look like *before* you send it to the printer.

- You can interrupt or cancel a printing operation at any time. Press **<Esc>** to cancel the printing job completely (your printer will continue to run until its buffer is cleared). Press **<F2>** if you want to change any of your Define Page or Print Options settings. If you make any changes on the Print Options screen and then press **<F10>** to resume printing, Q&A will start over at the beginning of the document.

If you have a document in the editor, you can reach the Print Options screen by pressing **<F2>** from the Type/Edit screen, or by selecting **P** (Print) from the Write menu. Write's default values, shown in Figure 2-7, will probably be right for you in most cases.

If you want to change the default settings for all your *new* documents, use "Change print defaults" on the Global Options menu under Write Utilities (more on this later in the chapter).

To change the settings on the Print Options screen for the current document:

1. Move the cursor to the field you want to change.

```
                        PRINT OPTIONS

    From page............:   1              To page............:  END

    Number of copies......:  1             Print offset........:  0

    Line spacing.........:  ▶Single◀   Double      Envelope

    Justify..............:   Yes  ▶No◀  Space justify

    Print to.............:  ▶PtrA◀  PtrB   PtrC   PtrD   PtrE   DISK

    Page preview.........:   Yes  ▶No◀

    Type of paper feed....:  Manual  ▶Continuous◀  Bin1   Bin2   Bin3   Lhd

    Number of columns.....:  ▶1◀   2    3    4    5    6    7    8

    Printer control codes.:

    Name of merge file....:
```

Figure 2-7: Write's Print Options Screen with Default Settings as Shown.

2. To make the change:

a. Type in the new value for any fields that require you to do so (From page, To page, Number of copies, Print offset, Name of merge file, and Printer control codes). Details on these settings are discussed below.

b. For any fields that require you simply to highlight your selection (Line spacing, Justify, Print to, Page preview, Type of paper feed, Number of columns) use the space bar or cursor keys to highlight your choice, and then press **<Enter>**.

3. Repeat these steps for any other values you want to change.

From Page/to Page

Use this feature to tell Q&A the *range* of pages you wish to print. Perhaps you've been editing one section of a long document and you only want to print the pages involved so they can be proofread. In such a case you would type in the starting page number you want to print (From page) and ending page number (To page). The preset value will print all pages in the document. To print a single page, type that page number in both fields.

You don't have to specify page-number printing in headers or footers to have Q&A count your document's pages. Q&A knows how many pages are in the document because it keeps track of them on the status line at the bottom of the Type/Edit screen. When you specify a page or page range to be printed, Q&A understands this to mean *status line* page numbers.

Number of Copies

How many copies of your document do you want printed? Q&A will let you print up to 99,999, but it's unlikely that you'd ever want to print that many unless you were running a month-long self-destruct test on your printer! The preset value is one copy.

If you want several copies, simply type in the number. If you want a lot of copies, consider printing a single one and then using the copy machine to run off the rest; copy machines are usually faster than printers. When you specify multiple copies of a document to be printed, Q&A will print all the pages (1, 2, 3, and so on) in the document first, and then go back and print the document again. This is also true if you've specified multiple copies of a range of pages to be printed.

Print Offset

Offset refers to the horizontal location where the first character of each line is to be printed. It positions the print head in relation to the left edge of the paper. During the course of the day you may print several kinds of documents, each of which requires an adjustment to the left margin. Instead of changing your document's left margin setting at the Define Page screen or physically repositioning the paper in the printer (if your printer permits this), you can simply type in a different offset value at the Print Options screen for each document.

The absolute offset distance is based on the cpi specified on the Define Page screen. If your document is set to print at 10 characters-per-inch, an offset value of 5 starts the printing a half-inch to the right of where it would normally start printing. A positive offset value starts the printing farther to the right, while a negative number (with a minus sign in front of it) entered here starts the printing that much farther to the left. Print Offset doesn't change your document margin settings as specified at the Define Page screen.

 Tip: Print Offset is a handy means of overriding an unworkable left margin setting *for the current printer and paper position* by adjusting the point at which the print head should start placing the ink.

Line Spacing

Here you've got three screen options: Single, Double, and Envelope. But by embedding printer control codes in your document (discussed in "Advanced Printing Techniques" in this chapter) or typing them on the Print Options screen (see the discussion of printer control codes in this chapter), you can set your line spacing to any value desired and have it affect the entire document or a portion of it. The single- and double-space settings at the Print Options screen work like a regular typewriter and apply to the entire document. Single-spacing is the preset value.

To *see* double- or triple-spaced lines while working on your document, press **<F8>** from the Type/Edit Screen to display the Options menu, select "Align Text," and then choose the spacing you want from the submenu. See "Line Spacing" in the "Advanced Type/Edit Operations" section in this chapter for more details.

Envelope is a special feature that allows you to capture the name and address from a letter you've just written and print it onto an envelope. To do this:

1. Create your letter on the Type/Edit screen.

2. Press **<F2>**, and at the Print Options screen select Envelope. Press **<F10>** and Q&A will ask you to place the envelope in the printer.

3. Line up the envelope with its top edge just below the print head, and press **<Enter>** at the prompt to print. The address will print centered on the envelope, eight lines down from the top edge and indented 3½ inches.

Q&A finds the name and address in the document by looking for the first line of text that starts at the left margin. It will ignore anything that's indented, such as your return address (which means that you *must* keep each line of your return address at least one space away from the left margin if you want this to work properly).

Write then checks to see if that first flush-left line is a date. Any line that ends with two or more digits is interpreted as a date and is ignored.

The first line of text that starts at the left margin and isn't a date is recognized by Write to be the first line of the address. Write will begin printing onto the envelope from there, and will print subsequent lines until it encounters a blank line (see Figure 2-8).

To print letters and envelopes with information from your database files (mail-merge), see Chapter 5.

Justification

New: Humans find it easy to justify. So does Q&A Write. Ordinarily, Write will print your documents with what is called a "ragged-right" (unjustified right) margin, meaning that each line in the document varies in length to avoid hyphenated words. But you can select regular justification or space justification so that your text fills the entire line, from the left to the right margins.

```
              Wrong                            Right

        Bill Bailey                     Bill Bailey
        2345 Red Mountain Dr.           2345 Red Mountain Dr.
        Nemo, AR 45667                    Nemo, AR 45667

        July 4, 1990              July 4, 1990

        Jim Smith                Jim Smith
        Smith's Nursery          Smith's Nursery
        2280 Fairfield Ave.      2280 Fairfield Ave.
        Little Rock, AR 45678    Little Rock, AR 45678

        Dear Mr. Smith:          Dear Mr. Smith:
```

Figure 2-8: Typing Your Letter so that Write Can Capture the Address and Print It on an Envelope. The example on the left won't work because the return address is first and is flush against the left margin. The example on the right will work because the addressee information block starts on the first nondate line flush with the left margin.

Regular or microjustification is the capability of the print head to move in horizontal steps slight enough to insert small slivers of space between words, and between letters within words.

When you select space justification, Q&A adds spaces between words in a certain manner to justify the lines. These spaces may vary in size, however, in order to accomplish this, and as a result word spacing may appear greatly uneven.

If you set Justify on by selecting "Yes," and your printer supports micro--justification, Q&A will add spaces *of equal sizes* between words on the lines. If you select microjustification, but your printer does not support it, Q&A will space-justify the document. However, Q&A will not justify any lines ending in a carriage return. If you have a document on your hands with a carriage return at the end of each line, you can use Search/Replace to delete the carriage return. See the section in this chapter covering Search and Search/Replace.

The process of microjustification forces some printers to switch modes in order to calculate and place tiny bits of space where needed between words. This can slow down the printing process considerably. Simple space justifica-tion, on the other hand, doesn't require any special printer modes because only ordinary character column spaces are inserted where necessary. So if you want justified text and fast printing where microspacing isn't important, select "Space Justify" at the Print Options screen.

Either justification option will justify the entire document at print time (don't expect to see justified text on the display screen). If you want to justify only part of a document, see the discussion of the *Justify Y* command in the section on advanced printing techniques further in this chapter.

Print To

Write's Print Options screen is preset to print to PtrA (Printer A). To change the printer selection, simply navigate to the "Print to" line and use the space bar or cursor keys to highlight the desired printer. The printer model and mode corresponding to your selection will display at the bottom of the screen.

If your printer supports several modes, such as draft and letter quality (LQ), you can install the draft mode as PtrA, and the LQ mode as PtrB (see printer installation in Chapter 1). Then, when you want to proofread a document prior to final printing, you can run it out in faster draft mode.

You can install any number of printers or printer modes up to a total of five, but the Print Options screen is *not* the place to install them, only to select from the printers or printer modes *already* installed.

Printing to disk will save the fully formatted version of your document to the filename you specify in ASCII file format, either in IBM ASCII format or Macintosh ASCII format. Any headers, footers, margin settings, and pagination will be saved with the document, but not fonts, text enhancements (such as bold or italic), or embedded printer codes.

To save the document as straight text *without* headers, pagination, and margins, use the "Export to ASCII" option explained in Chapter 9.

When prompted for the filename under which to save the document, Write presumes the current document directory and offers you the complete pathname. Figure 2-9 shows a current directory of C:\QA\DOCS\. If you want to save the document to this directory, all you need to do is type in the document name you've chosen.

If you want to save the document to a floppy disk in drive A:, for example (perhaps to transfer it to another machine, or to keep it off your already overcrowded hard disk), you'd simply type your desired path over the default one and, after having inserted the disk in the target drive, press **<Enter>**.

Page Preview

New: You can see what your printed document will look like before sending it to the printer by selecting "Yes" on the Page Preview line at the Print Options screen, and pressing **<F10>**.

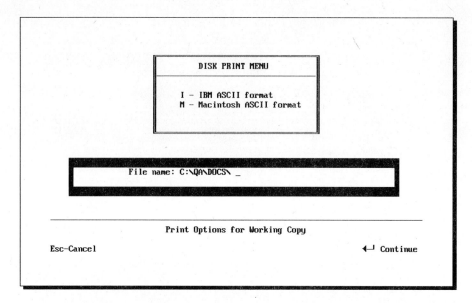

Figure 2-9: Q&A's Disk Print Menu. When you select "Print to Disk" from the Print Options screen, select the format you want to use, and then type the name of the file (with the full pathname) to which to save the document.

Page Preview then looks at your document and its enhancements, your Define Page and Print Options screen settings, and displays a proportional representation of the document on the Preview screen. With the document in preview mode you can zoom in for a close look at a portion of a page, zoom back out again, see facing pages, view previous or subsequent pages, and more. You can then put the finishing touches on that document before you use even a single sheet of paper.

The Preview screen will represent different font sizes, but not different typefaces. For example, a change from 20-point Times to 20-point Helvetica in your document will not be reflected on the Preview screen, but a change from one point size to another will.

Your computer requires a graphics adapter in order for Q&A to show you a preview of your documents. Documents are not editable on the Preview screen. You can change them only by returning to Type/Edit, or to the Define Page or Print Options screen, as the case may be.

The best way to get familiar with the preview mode is to experiment with it, using a document of at least a couple of pages in length.

Table 2-7
Preview Modes Available at the Preview Screen

Key	Action on the Preview screen
<Esc>	Returns you to the Type/Edit screen with the document displayed.
<N>	Normal mode — 25 lines per screen.
<F>	Full-page mode — full view of the current page.
<H>	Half-page mode — half the current page.
<F2>	Returns you to the Print Options screen.
<2>	Displays facing pages — the current page and the next page before or after depending on which is the facing page. In this mode odd-numbered pages are displayed on the right, and even-numbered pages on the left, like books and magazines.
<+> (plus)	Zoom-in key — magnifies an area of the page.
<-> (minus)	Zoom-out key — the opposite effect of zoom-in.
<PgDn>	Scrolls the page down by one screen while in Normal mode.
<PgUp>	Scrolls the page up by one screen while in Normal mode.
<Ctrl><PgDn>	Displays the next document page. Returns you to theType/Edit screen if you're already on the last-page.
<Ctrl><PgUp>	Shows the previous page if there is one.
<→><←><↑><↓>	Moves the entire screen in the direction of the arrow — useful during zoom-in to see more of the page.

When you select "Page preview" from the Print Options screen and press **<F10>**, you'll see the first page of the document in "full page" mode — a representation of the entire page. Then you can use the keys in Table 2-7 to view the document from different aspects.

When you've got the document on the Preview screen and are ready to print it out, press **<F2>**, change the Page preview line at the Print Options screen to "No," and press **<F10>** to print.

Once Q&A has sent your document to the printer, you'll be returned to the Type/Edit screen with the same document displayed. You can now save it using **<Shift><F8>**, or do some more work on it.

Type of Paper Feed

The Print Options screen is set by default for continuous paper feed. This setting is appropriate when you are using the kind of paper where each sheet is attached to the next. Continuous paper is usually pulled or pushed through the printer by a tractor (sprocket) mechanism with pins that line up with holes along the edge of the paper. Printers with only a single-paper feed bin will usually work fine at this setting.

If you're feeding single sheets of paper into the printer and want Q&A to pause after printing each page and prompt you to feed the next sheet, select *Manual* as paper feed type. If your printer has the capability, the manual mode can be used when you've backed out your continuous paper long enough to print a few individual sheets.

If your printer has bins or trays attached to it, you can select from Bin1, Bin2, Bin3, or Lhd (letterhead). Be sure you know which bins contain the type of paper on which you wish to print.

Selecting the Lhd setting will print the first page from Bin1, and all subsequent pages from Bin2 (Q&A presumes you keep your letterhead and second sheets in these two bins). If you're having trouble with proper bin selection, see Appendix B.

Number of Columns

The Print Options screen is preset for single column (normal) printing, but you can print up to eight columns per page. When you select multiple columns, the text in your document is reformatted to fit in the appropriate number of columns as it is sent to the printer (you won't see the multiple columns on the display screen).

The default spacing between columns (the gutter) is .25" (¼-inch). To change it using the Editing Options screen:

1. Select Write Utilities.

2. Select "Set global options" from the Utilities menu.

3. Select "Set editing options" from the Global Options menu.

4. Move to the last item on the screen (Spacing between columns).

5. Type the spacing value desired in whole number, decimal, or centimeter format, being sure to add the inch symbol after a number expressed in inches, or "cm" after a number expressed in centimeters. You can also enter a whole number that represents Ruler Line columns (displayed at the bottom of the Type/Edit screen).

6. Press **<F10>** when finished, and **<Esc>** to return to the Write menu.

If you've opted to have your document printed out in multiple columns, the bottom of the first column will flow to the top of the second column, and so forth, while the bottom of the last column on a page will flow to the top of the first column on the following page. In order to accommodate column printing, Q&A will try to break the text lines between words. But if you've specified many columns, it becomes more difficult to do so. Thus the first part of a word may print on one column line, and the rest of the word on the following line.

Printer Control Codes

Printers contain a built-in language that consists of commands or codes they understand. Activating these codes causes the printer to turn on or off special line spacings, text enhancements, character sets and sizes, and other attributes. Your printer manual tells you what affects your printer is capable of producing along with the special codes needed to control them from within a software package.

There are a number of ways to control from inside Q&A what effects, in addition to normal text output, your printer will produce:

- Set your page characteristics at the Define Page screen, and place text enhancements in the document from the Type/Edit screen. Define Page settings affect the whole document. Enhancing text on the Type/Edit screen affects only the text so enhanced.

- Embed printer control codes in the text of the document during Type/Edit. You type the "on" code at the beginning of the text you want affected, and the "off" code at the end of that section of text. (See "Advanced Printing Techniques" in this chapter.)

- Select the printer mode (if you've installed more than one mode) at the Print Options screen to print draft or letter quality, for example, or portrait or landscape. This selection will affect all the printed text.

- Enter codes in decimal format on the "Printer control codes" line of the Print Options screen. These codes affect the entire printed document.

For example, if you want your document to print with 1½-line spacing, you could use a printer control code to activate it, regardless of the fact that Q&A itself doesn't offer a selection for 1½-line spacing at the Print Options screen.

Or if you want your document to print in letter quality (LQ) mode when only your printer's draft mode has been installed in Q&A, you can override the installed setting by using the control code that turns on your printer's LQ capability.

These control codes can be used to set line lengths, enhancements, vertical line spacing (often in 1/180ths or even 1/360ths of an inch), margins, page length, pitch, and almost anything else you'd like.

Just remember that if you enter these as on codes at the Print Options screen, you don't then have the option of turning them off within the same print job.

Also, your printer may be capable of emulating (imitating) more than one other printer model (Epson, or IBM, or Hewlett Packard, for example), and the codes for printer effects within these emulations may vary. Be sure you select the printer control codes that correspond both to the effect you want *and* the printer emulation (if any) you're using.

Your printer manual contains a section on the codes that can be used to turn on and off the effects the printer is capable of producing. These codes will often be expressed in both *decimal* and *hexadecimal* equivalents. Use the decimal form of the code in Q&A, and separate multiple codes with commas when you type them on the "Printer control codes" line at the Print Options screen. These topics are covered in more detail later in this chapter.

Merge Files

If you're creating a merge document that will bring in information from a Q&A database, type the filename of that database here. The line should be left empty for printing nonmerge documents. (See Chapter 5 for information on how to merge database information with your documents.) However, you can print a quantity of nonmerge documents equal to a certain number of forms in a database by typing in the database filename and, when Q&A presents you with the Retrieve Spec for that database, selecting the forms for which you want a document printed.

Perhaps you have a database of customers, and you want to send a nonmerge form letter only to those within a range of zip codes. You can specify that range at the Retrieve Spec and Write will print out a document for each of the forms that meet your criteria. No database information will be merged with the documents, but the *number* of copies you want will be printed.

Unless you know that the number of forms called by your retrieve criteria will be small, it's wise to first find out how many forms will be involved by querying the database (see the following chapter). Why have your printer working all afternoon when you can print a single copy of the document and then make duplicates on the copy machine?

Appendix B includes a section called "Troubleshooting Common Printer Problems." Check there if you can't get the output you need, or if something unexplained is happening during printing.

Beyond the Basics

Now that you've studied the basic features and functions of Q&A's word processor and know how to format your documents and send them to the printer, let's have a look at some of the more advanced features you can use to manipulate, enhance, and otherwise assist you with your text on the Type/Edit screen.

Following this discussion I'll turn our attention to advanced printing techniques and show you all about how to embed printer control codes in your documents, as well as install and use the fonts you have that your printer supports.

I'll devote the last section of this chapter to Write's global options, where you'll learn how to specify any preset standards you want applied to all new documents you create in Write.

Although the mail-merge and mailing-label options are part of the Write module, these can be more profitably explored after you've created a database or two in Q&A's File module. So I'll hold off discussing these features until Chapter 5.

In addition to the basic typing and editing of text, you may need to call upon Q&A Write's more advanced word processing features. These are simply additional tools that can save you a great deal of time creating, structuring, and fine-tuning your documents. Again, you should take the time to experiment and become familiar with these features on test documents. Then, should you need to make use of them during an actual word processing job, you'll already know how they work and can proceed with confidence.

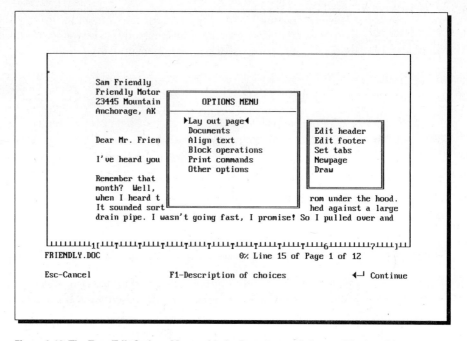

Figure 2-10: The Type/Edit Options Menu with the Page Layout Submenu Displayed.

Advanced Type/Edit Operations

Most of the advanced document operations in the Write word processor are available from the Type/Edit screen by pressing **<F8>** for the Write Options menu. Selecting the operations you want to perform from this convenient menu system saves you from having to remember function key assignments, and is especially handy if you use a mouse. It's entirely up to you whether to use the Options menu or your function keys. You can even use a combination of both.

Figure 2-10 shows the Options menu that displays when you press **<F8>** from the Type/Edit screen.

There are six selections available from the main Options menu:

- Lay out page
- Align text
- Documents
- Block operations

- Print commands

- Other options

Each of these selections leads in turn to a submenu of choices. For example, in Figure 2-10 you can see the "Lay out page" submenu displayed. These submenu selections invoke specific document operations that will be discussed in detail in the pages that follow.

Some of the submenu choices include the function key combinations you can use to invoke the procedure directly from the Type/Edit screen. Where you see ⇧**<F5>**, for example, it means press **<Shift><F5>** to invoke the operation either from the Type/Edit screen, or when the submenu is displayed. **@F5** means **<Alt><F5>**, and **^F5** means **<Ctrl><F5>**. Here's how the Options menu choices stack up should you be anxious at this point to experiment with some of them on a test document:

Lay out page:

- Create or revise document headers and footers
- Set document tabs
- Start a new page
- Use Q&A's Draw feature for lines and boxes

Documents:

- Get a document
- Insert a document into the current one
- View and select from a list of the 12 most recently saved documents

Align text:

- Align text left or right, (also known as flush left or right) or center a line
- Set temporary margins
- Change to single, double, or triple spacing

Block operations:

- Copy or move text within same document
- Delete text
- Copy or move text to another document
- Select text enhancements such as bold, italics, etc.
- Print a block of text
- Capitalize a block of text
- Change a block of text to all lowercase
- Title a block of text (capitalize the first letters of all the main words in a block of text)

Print commands: Insert any of the following special codes in the document at the cursor position:

- Date
- Filename
- Graph
- Join
- Justify
- Line spacing
- Postfile
- PostScript
- Printer
- Program
- Queue
- QueueP
- Spreadsheet
- Stop
- Time

Note that these codes take effect when you send the document to the printer. The codes themselves won't appear in the printed output.

Other options:

- Spelling check
- Thesaurus
- Document statistics
- Hyphenation
- Search and replace
- Restore text
- Go to page/line
- List database fields (for merge documents)
- Save document
- Save document to an ASCII file
- Assign fonts
- Perform a calculation on a column of numbers

If your Q&A menus are set to Automatic Execution at the Global Options screen (available from the Utilities menu), you can select procedures from the Options menu and its six submenus simply by pressing the first letter of the item. The only exception is when two items with the same first letter are on the same submenu. In such cases, pressing the letter invokes the first item on that submenu with that same initial letter. If your menus are *not* set to Automatic Execution, you can still choose from the Options menu by pressing the letter of the option, but you'll need to press **<Enter>** to choose procedures from the submenus.

Block Copy and Move Operations

As you become more familiar with your word processor and begin working with longer, more complex documents and a variety of document types, you may find that you need to move, copy, and otherwise manipulate entire blocks of text.

Below is a summary of what you can do with sentences, whole paragraphs, and even entire document pages. Keep in mind that when you *copy* a block of text you're simply making a duplicate of it without disturbing the original text. When you *move* a text block, however, you're removing it from its location and transferring it to another location.

- Write's Clipboard feature enables you to take a "snapshot" of a block of text in one document and insert it in another document.

- You can copy a block of text in a document and place it elsewhere in the same document.

- You can copy a block of text in a document and create a new document with the copied block.

- You can move a block of text from one location in a document to another location in the same document.

- You can move a block of text from one document and create a new document with the moved block.

- You can insert another document into the one that's on the Type/Edit screen.

Using Write's Clipboard Feature

You can copy a block of text from one document into another — a feature that might come in handy if you need to save and frequently retrieve boilerplate paragraphs for contracts, sales, or customer service letters. When you use the Clipboard to move text from one document into another, the text is not removed from the first document, it is copied. Write takes a "snapshot" of the text you want copied and holds it while you get the target document onto the Type/Edit screen. Here's how you do it:

1. Use the Get command to retrieve the document that contains the text you want to copy to the second document.

2. With that first document on the screen, move the cursor to the beginning of the text to be copied to the Clipboard. Be sure you're in overtype mode.

3. Press **<Shift><F5>** to select the block move function. Alternately, you can press **<F8>** for the Options menu, select "Block operations," and then select "Move" from the submenu.

4. Use the cursor keys to highlight the text you want to add to the Clipboard. Moving the cursor to the right will highlight the line character by character. Moving the cursor down the page will highlight entire lines. Pressing **<Enter>** will highlight the paragraph from the cursor position on down (see Table 2-8).

5. Press **<F10>** when you've highlighted all the text you want picked up by the Clipboard.

6. Now move the cursor *back* to the first letter of the text you just highlighted and press **<F10>** again.

Warning: If you press **<F10>** at any other position the block of text will be copied to *that* location.

7. Press **<Esc>** to exit this first document to the Write menu.

8. Select Get and type in the name of the document you want to copy the Clipboard text *to*.

9. Write will display a warning screen telling you that your last changes to the first document haven't been saved. Select "Yes" to continue. (You can also select "No" to return to the Write menu and save any changes. This won't affect the Clipboard's contents.)

10. With the second document on screen, move, the cursor to the location where you want to insert the Clipboard's contents. Press **<Shift><F7>**. The block copied from the first document will be inserted at the cursor position.

The Clipboard will retain the block until you delete, move, or copy text, or exit from the Write module. So you can continue to copy the block to the same document or to other documents by following steps 7 through 10 above.

Tip: If, when attempting to insert the contents of the Clipboard into the target document with **<Shift><F7>** you get the message "No text to restore" at the bottom of the screen, it means you've selected a block too large for the Clipboard to manage. In such cases you'll either need to repeat the procedure choosing smaller blocks, or use another copying method, such as copying the block to a new document name, and then, from the target document, using the Insert a Document command available from the Options menu.

Text-Blocking Fundamentals

In addition to the Clipboard feature, Write lets you move, copy, delete, enhance, and print text blocks with surprising ease. You simply specify the type of block operation you want to perform, and then highlight the text on which to perform it. You use the same process for selecting text no matter which type of block operation you want.

Table 2-8 lists the operations you can perform on text blocks along with the function key combinations associated with them. Keep in mind that these procedures are also available through the block operations command at the **<F8>** Options menu.

The Pivot Character

In any block operation, text is always selected around what is called a "pivot character." This is the character under which you place the cursor before starting a blocking action. Once you've begun to block your text, moving the cursor in any direction selects all the text between that pivot character and the cursor's new location. On a monochrome monitor blocked text will be highlighted in reverse video; on a color monitor it will show up in a different color from the surrounding text.

You can start your blocking at the beginning of the selected text and work to the right and downward, or start at the end of the selected text and work to the left and upward.

Table 2-8
Block Actions and their Key Combinations

Operation	Key Combination
Copy a block to same document	**<F5>**
Copy a block to a new document	**<Ctrl><F5>**
Delete a block	**<F3>**
Move a block within same document	**<Shift><F5>**
Move a block to a new document	**<Alt><F5>**
Enhance a block	**<Shift><F6>**
Print a block	**<Ctrl><F2>**
Restore a block	**<Shift><F7>**

Capitalize, Lowercase, and Title a block are available only through the Options menu

Blocking the Text

After selecting the block operation to be performed, you'll need to highlight the relevant text. You can use all the standard navigation keys on the numeric keypad (with NumLock off), or use the bank of separate cursor navigation keys found on enhanced keyboards.

You can see how this works by bringing any document onto the Type/Edit screen, pressing **<F5>** to start the copy-block operation, moving the cursor to the right and then down, left, up, and right again, and pressing **<Esc>** when finished to cancel the operation.

While doing this you'll notice that moving the cursor back toward the pivot character *unselects* the text just previously highlighted.

There are a number of key combinations you can use to quickly perform specific block operations (see Table 2-9). For example, pressing the down arrow key during a block operation highlights the rest of the line to the right of the cursor position, and the next line across to the new cursor position. Pressing an Aa-Zz character key when a block operation is on will highlight all of the text from the cursor position though the next occurrence of that character. Pressing the space bar during a block operation selects from the cursor position through the next word.

Pressing **<End>** selects from the cursor position to the end of the line. Pressing **<Home>** selects from the cursor position to the beginning of the line. Pressing **<Tab>** selects the text on the line from the cursor position to the next tab stop. Pressing **<Enter>** highlights to the end of the paragraph from the cursor position on down.

As you can see, some of these block selection moves work very much like the regular document cursor navigation techniques you learned at the beginning of this chapter.

Selecting Progressively Larger Blocks

Multiple presses of the same key you used to begin the blocking operation will highlight increasingly larger blocks of text. The first keypress will highlight the character over the cursor. Pressing the same key a second time will highlight the word; the third time, the sentence; the fourth, the whole paragraph; the fifth, the page; and the sixth, the entire document.

As you do this, Write keeps you informed about what has been blocked so far by flashing a message line at the bottom of the display.

The **<Esc>** key cancels a block operation altogether.

Table 2-9
Summary of Keys Used to Select Text
During Block Operations

More navigation methods are available when the Pivot character is at the beginning of the text to be selected.

Key highlighting action when selecting text from a beginning-of-block pivot character

`<→>`	The next character or space to the right of the cursor position
`Space bar`	From the cursor position through the next word
`<End>`	From the cursor position through the end of the line
`<↓>`	From the cursor position through the end of that line, and the subsequent line up to the new cursor position
`<Enter>`	From the cursor position through the end of the paragraph
`<Tab>`	From the cursor position to the next tab stop
`Aa-Zz`	From the cursor position through the next occurrence of the same letter

Multiple presses of the function key combination that turned on the blocking operation will progressively select the word, the sentence, the paragraph, the page, and then the entire document

Highlighting action when selecting text from an end-of-block pivot character

`<←>`	The next character or space to the left of the cursor position
`<Home>`	From the cursor position to the beginning of the line
`<↑>`	From the cursor position to the beginning of that line, and the previous line from its end to the new cursor position

Copying Text in the Same Document

You can copy blocks of text from one section of a document to another part of the same document. Also, you have the option of creating a brand-new document out of a copied block — this is useful for collecting a library of canned or boilerplate paragraphs you use to compose other documents.

Remember: *Copying* a text block does not delete it from its original location, but *moving* a block does.

To copy a block of text from one part of your document to another part of that same document:

1. With the document in the editor, move the cursor to the beginning or end of the text you want to copy.

2. Press **<F5>**. You can optionally select "Block operations" from the **<F8>** Options menu, and then choose "Copy."

3. Highlight the text you want to copy using one of the methods in Table 2-9.

4. Press **<F10>** to end and confirm the text selection process.

5. Now position the cursor at the exact location where you want the copied text to be inserted.

6. Press **<F10>** and *voila!*

When the block copy operation is done, you'll find the cursor at the beginning of the copied block, not at the originally selected block.

Write remembers the text you block-copy until you delete, move, or copy another block of text, or leave the word processing module. Pressing **<Shift><F7>** following the restore places another copy of the selected text at the cursor location. Press **<Shift><F7>** 20 times and you'll get 20 copies of the same block of text placed in your document.

Copying Text to a New Document

1. With your document in the editor, position the cursor at the very beginning or end of the block you want to copy.

2. Press **<Ctrl><F5>**. Optionally, press **<F8>** for the Options menu, select "Block operations," and then "Copy to file" from the submenu.

3. Highlight the text to be copied using one of the methods in Table 2-9.

4. Press **<F10>** to end and confirm the selection.

5. When prompted, type in the name of the document to have the block copied to. This must be a document that does not already exist (two documents can't have the same name). If you're not sure whether a

document with the new name you want to use exists, press **<Enter>** with the prompt filename blank, and Q&A will show you a list of existing documents in the current directory.

6. Press **<Enter>** and the new document will be created consisting of the block of selected text. The cursor will appear in the *original* document at the point where you began the blocking.

Moving Text within a Document

To move (not copy) text from one location in a document to a new location, follow these steps:

1. With your document in the editor, move the cursor to the beginning or end of the block you want to move.

2. Press **<Shift><F5>**. Optionally, you can select "Block operations," and then "Move" from the **<F8>** Options menu.

3. Highlight the text you want to move using the methods described in Table 2-9.

4. Press **<F10>** to end and confirm the block selection.

5. Move the cursor to where you want the block to appear.

6. Press **<F10>** to execute the move.

The cursor will land at the beginning of the block's new location.

You can press **<Shift><F7>** for additional copies of the moved block. The block can be copied this way until you delete, move, or copy another block, or exit the Write module.

Moving Text to a New Document

1. With your document in the editor, place the cursor at the beginning or end of the block you want to move.

2. Press **<Alt><F5>** to turn on the operation. Or press **<F8>** for the Options menu, select "Block operations," and then choose "Move to file."

3. Highlight the text you want to move to the new document using a method described in Table 2-9.

4. Press **<F10>** to end and confirm the selection.

5. When prompted, type in the name of the document you want the block moved to. It must be a document that does not already exist (unless you want to overwrite an existing document). Leave the name prompt blank and press **<Enter>** to see a list of existing documents.

6. Press **<Enter>** after selecting the filename. When the move operation has been completed, the cursor will appear in the original (source) document at the moved block location.

Inserting an External Document into the Current One

Any Q&A-compatible documents — such as Old WordStar (prior to version 3.3), pfs:Write, IBM Writing Assistant, Lotus 1-2-3 or Symphony spreadsheets, or ASCII text files — can be inserted directly into the document on which you're working. To do so:

1. With your document in the editor, move the cursor to the place where you want the external document inserted.

2. Bring up the Options menu with **<F8>**.

3. Select "Documents," and choose "Insert a document" from the submenu.

4. Type in the name of the document you want to insert and press **<Enter>**. If you've forgotten the name, press **<Enter>** at this point to see a list of available documents in the current directory. Highlight the document you want and press **<Enter>**.

If the document you've selected is in Q&A, pfs:Write, or IBM Writing Assistant format, it will automatically be inserted into the document on your screen.

For other kinds of documents, Q&A will display the Import Document menu. Make your selection from this menu if the document is ASCII, Special ASCII, Old WordStar, or in Lotus 1-2-3 or Symphony format, and Q&A will format the document for Write and bring it onto the screen in the position you indicated in step 1.

If the document is in some other format that can be converted by Q&A, you'll need to import it before you can use it. See Chapter 9 for the word processing programs supported by Q&A, and how to import documents, graphs, and other items from these programs.

If you'd prefer to insert one or more external documents into the current document *only at printing time*, you can use the ***JOIN*** command (see the section on integrating documents at printing time later in this chapter). The ***JOIN*** command is particularly useful when you don't need to see the inserted documents on the Type/Edit screen, or don't want to save the current document with the inserted documents as part of the file. Integrating documents at printing time also conserves memory — a potentially important consideration with long documents.

Deleting a Text Block

It is easy to delete text that you no longer want in a document. Just complete the following steps.

1. Move the cursor to the beginning or end of the text you want to delete.

2. Press **<F3>**. Optionally, you can select "Block operations" from the **<F8>** Options menu, and then choose "Delete."

3. Highlight the text you want to delete using a method shown in Table 2-9.

4. Press **<F10>** to delete the block. The remaining text in the document will be reformatted.

Restoring a Block of Deleted Text

You can restore only the most recently copied, moved, or deleted text. You can make additional copies of such text by pressing **<Shift><F7>** any number of times. To restore the block:

1. Place the cursor at the location where you want the text block restored.

2. Press **<Shift><F7>** to restore the text.

Printing a Block of Text

Any block of text can be printed, whether it's a letter, word, line, paragraph, or several paragraphs. Whatever you can block you can send to the printer. However, only straight, unadorned text can be printed in this manner — no fonts or enhancements allowed. If you prefer to print the block with its enhancements intact, copy the block to a new document using **<Ctrl><F5>**, and then send that new document to the printer with **<F2>** and **<F10>**. To print a block:

1. Make sure your printer is ready for action.

2. With your document in the editor, move the cursor to the beginning or end of the text you want to print.

3. Press **<Ctrl><F2>** to turn on blocking for print. Optionally, you can press **<F8>** for the Options menu, select "Block operations," and then choose "Print."

4. Highlight the text you want to print using one of the methods in Table 2-9.

5. Press **<F10>** to send that block to the printer.

Headers and Footers

You can place headers and footers in your documents to identify running chapter titles, section headings, pages, versions, or dates. Look at books and magazines today and you'll see that most of them, including this one, contain running heads or headers.

A footer is not the same thing as a footnote. Although Write does not support automatic footnote generation, you can still add footnotes to your documents (see the section entitled "Footnotes" in this chapter).

Headers are placed within the top margin of the page, footers in the bottom margin. Thus your top and/or bottom page margins must be wide enough to accommodate the number of lines in your header or footer and leave a little extra space. In a Write document you can have either a header, a footer, or both, but you can't have just a header on some pages and just a footer on other pages in the same document. And because headers and footers are placed in the margins, your top and bottom margin settings determine the vertical space you have available for them. Margins are set at the Define Page screen. Create and edit a header or footer this way:

1. While working on a document, press **<Ctrl><Home>** to move to the top of page 1.

2. Press **<F8>** for the Options menu. Select "Lay out page."

3. Choose "Edit header" or "Edit footer" from the submenu.

   The header window will appear at the top of the screen, the footer window at the bottom. Figure 2-11 shows a document page with the header window open and the header already typed in. Notice the double line separating the header from the main document. The "**#**" tells Q&A to place the consecutive page number here when the document is printed.

4. Type your header or footer text, using the editing features you'd normally use when working on a document.

5. Press **<F10>** when you're done editing and the header or footer window will disappear along with the double line. But Write will keep the header or footer visible on screen.

You can modify a header or footer at any time simply by following steps 1 through 5 again.

Place a pound sign (**#**) in your header or footer to tell Write where you want the page number to appear. If your page numbers will vary in length, you can use extra **#**s as place holders. Write will convert them to spaces if necessary. To print the **#** symbol before the page number in a header or footer, type a

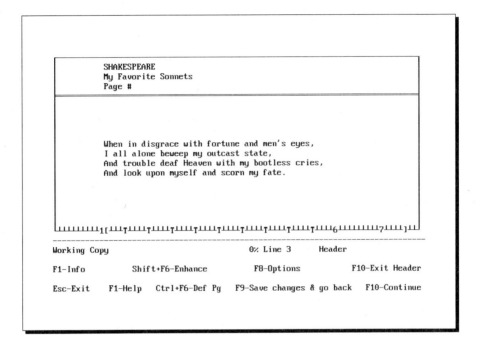

Figure 2-11: A Header Window.

backslash symbol immediately in front of it. For example, "**Page \\#**" typed into a header will produce "Page #15" in the header on the 15th page of the document. Tell Q&A where you want your headers or footers to start at the Define Page screen. You may not want them on the first page, especially if it's a title page.

If your computer's internal clock is running with the correct date and time, you can add these to headers or footers, or anywhere in your document. Type the characters ***@Date(n)*** for the current date, and ***@Time(n)*** for the current time, where *n* is the number that selects the date or time format you want. When Q&A prints the document, these codes are replaced with the actual date and time. You can select from a variety of date and time formats. Table 2-10 shows you a list of those available.

Setting Tab Stops

The **<Tab>** key can be used to indent the first line of a paragraph or to lay out tables and columns that need to be lined up vertically down the page. Once you've got your tab stops set, pressing the **<Tab>** key will move the cursor to the next stop.

Table 2-10
Date and Time Formats Available in Q&A

Time formats:	1 – 4:55 pm	2 – 16:55	3 – 16.55

Date formats:

1 – Aug 31, 1990	8 – 31/08/90	15 – 08-31-90
2 – 31 Aug 1990	9 – 08/31/90	16 – 08-31-1990
3 – 8/31/90	10 – 31/08/1990	17 – 31.08.90
4 – 31/8/90	11 – August 31, 1990	18 – 31.08.1990
5 – 8/31/1990	12 – 31 August 1990	19 – 1990-08-31
6 – 31/8/1990	13 – 8-31-90	20 – 1990/08/31
7 – 08/31/1990	14 – 8-31-1990	

Write has two kinds of tab stops: Regular and Decimal, both of which appear on the ruler line at the bottom of the Type/Edit screen. Regular tabs appear as capital T's, while decimal tabs appear as capital D's.

Text behaves differently around the two types of tab stops. At a regular tab stop any text you type behaves as it normally would — the cursor and your text move from left to right across the page.

At a decimal tab stop, however, the characters you type will be forced to the left until you enter a decimal point (a period). Any characters you enter *after* the decimal point will continue to the right as usual. Using the decimal tab in this manner allows you to right justify your tabular information, such as columns of numbers. To set tabs for the document you're working on:

1. Press **<F8>** for the Options menu.

2. Select "Set Tabs" from the "Lay out page" submenu.

3. Use your left and right cursor keys to move along the ruler line. Type a **T** where you want to place a standard tab stop, type a **D** to place a decimal tab stop. Use the space bar and **<Backspace>** key to erase any unwanted tab stops.

You can set standard tab stops to be applied to all future documents, overriding Q&A's default tab settings.

1. Select Utilities from the Write menu.

2. Select "Set global options" from the Utilities menu.

3. Select "Set editing options."

4. At the Editing Options screen, move to the Default Tab Settings line and type in the tab stops you want, separating each stop with a comma and space.

If you're using proportional fonts in your documents and plan to set up tabbed columns, you must answer "Yes" to the "Set Real Tab Characters" option at the Global Editing Options screen.

You can override default regular tab settings in any document on which you're working by using the **<F8>** Options menu procedure above. When you save a document in Write, your tab settings (whether unique to this document or default) are saved with it. Thus setting new default tab stops will not retroactively affect existing document files.

Temporary Margins

While writing letters and other documents, you may need to indent whole paragraphs. Q&A lets you set up temporary left/right margins in a document for hanging indents, bulleted lists, sequential instructions, and so forth. The following procedure on how to do this is also a demonstration of the concept of temporary margins. The sequence of steps is formatted as you see it on this page by the use of a temporary indented left margin.

To turn on temporary margins:

1. With your document in the editor, move the cursor to the column (horizontal) position on the line where you want the temporary left or right margin.

2. Press **<F6>** — or press **<F8>** and select "Temp margins" from the "Align text" submenu — and type **L** for Left margin, or **R** for Right margin. A temporary left margin will begin on the line *immediately below* the current cursor position. A temporary right margin will begin on the current line. Right and/or left angle brackets (**<>**) will display on the ruler line, marking the temporary margin locations.

3. Repeat steps 1 and 2 if you'd like to set the other temporary margin.

4. Type the paragraph.

5. When done, clear the temporary margins by pressing **<F6>** and then typing the letter **C** while the cursor is still within the indented paragraph. This will clear both left and right temporary margins for the entire paragraph.

6. Change your temporary margins by repeating steps 1 through 3.

When you adopt temporary margins in a paragraph, only that paragraph uses them; other existing paragraphs are not changed. But once you turn on temporary margins in one paragraph, subsequent *new* paragraphs will also adopt those same temporary margins.

To change margins back to normal for your new paragraphs while keeping the temporary margins in your current paragraph intact, type to the end of the paragraph, then type the sequence **<Enter><F6><C>**. This returns the document to normal margin settings for all new paragraphs.

To indent only the first line of a paragraph in the traditional manner, use the **<Tab>** key.

Aligning Text Left, Right, and Center

Centered lines on a page can add a nice effect. Titles, subheadings, and return addresses, for example, are ideal candidates for centering. You center lines one at a time in a Q&A document, either before you are about to type the line, or afterward. Write centers lines between the document's left and right margins. To center a line that has already been typed:

1. With your document on screen, move the cursor to the line you want to center. Anywhere on the line will do.

2. Press **<F8>** for the Options menu.

3. Select "Align text," and choose "Center" from the submenu.

4. Repeat the above steps for each additional line you want centered.

To uncenter a line, choose "Left" in step 3 instead of "Center."

To type a line that self-centers as you type it, follow steps 1, 2, and 3, and then type the line. The cursor will move a space to the right with every *second* character you type. Press **<Enter>** when you've finished typing the line. If your centered line is so long that it wraps to the next line, you'll have to center that next line as well.

If you delete or add characters to centered lines, or change the document's margins, the lines will remain centered, although larger margins may cause a centered line to wrap, in which case you'll need to center the wrapped lines.

Forcing a Page Break

There may be times when you'll want to keep a table or chart from being broken up by a page break, or start a new section of a document on a fresh page.

If you're working on a table, for example, and realize that it's going to extend onto the following page, you can move the cursor to the beginning of the table and force the page to break right there; the table will then start on a new page.

If the table is longer than an entire single page, you're going to have to either redesign the thing, break it somewhere, or insert printer control codes at the beginning and end of the table to temporarily compress the line spacing and perhaps even the character pitch (see the section on "Printer Codes" later in this chapter). You can't decrease the top/bottom margins (or increase the left/right margins) for a single page. If you choose this third alternative, Write will still break the table as it appears on the display, but when it's sent to the printer the proper control codes will cause the table to be vertically compressed due to the decreased line spacing.

If the table or other figure is *still* too long to fit on a single page after being vertically compressed in this manner (verify this using Page Preview), then you'll either have to redesign it or break it at some appropriate point with another Newpage command. To force a page break:

1. With your document on screen, place the cursor anywhere on the line that you want to be *the first line* on a new page.

2. Press **<F8>** for the Options menu.

3. Select "Lay out page," and then "Newpage" from the submenu. The page break symbol (⏎) will appear on the line preceding the break, and the cursor will be moved to the top of the new page.

To remove a forced page break, place the cursor at the page break symbol and press **<Del>**.

Hyphenation

Normally, when a word won't fit on a line, Write wraps it to the next line. You can allow the word to wrap, hyphenate it manually, or insert a soft hyphen. A soft hyphen simply tells Write to hyphenate the word here if it won't fit on the line. To add a soft hyphen to a word:

1. Place the cursor immediately to the right of the character where you want the hyphen should the word need to be hyphenated. You can do this as you're typing the line, or after as you go back through the document.

2. Press **<Alt><F6>** to insert the soft hyphen to the left of the cursor.

To remove a soft hyphen, place the cursor at the character preceding the hyphen (the highlighted character), press **<Del>** twice, and retype the deleted character in insert mode.

Line Spacing

When it comes to setting your document's line spacing, you have five alternatives:

- You can press **\<F8\>** from the Type/Edit screen for the Options menu, and then select the spacing you want from the "Align text" submenu. This sets the line spacing from the cursor position (where you changed the spacing) forward, until you change it again, and makes that selected line spacing visible on screen.

- You can select single or double line spacing at the Print Options screen. This only takes effect when you print the document, and affects the entire document. However, if your screen line spacing is double or triple, a setting of single line spacing at the Print Options screen will not override it, and the document will print with double or triple line spacing as the case may be.

- You can insert the ***Linespace n*** command in your document where you want the line spacing to change during printing. This will affect only the printed document. See the discussion on embedded codes in the "Advanced Printing Techniques Section" in this chapter for more details.

- You can type decimal codes on the "Printer control codes" line of the Print Options screen. These codes are printer-specific, apply to the entire document, and enable you to fine-tune your printed document line spacing practically to any value. Adjustments of up to 1/180ths or 1/360ths of an inch are available on some printers. This methods lets you turn a printer feature (such as a line feed designation) on or off, but not both. See the discussion on printer codes in the "Advanced Printing Techniques" section for more information.

- You can insert the printer control codes in step 4 directly into your document. This allows you to turn a printer feature (such as a line spacing change) on in one place in your document, and turn it off or change it to something else at another point in the document. The advantage is that minute line spacing adjustments are possible where needed.

Most people prefer to work on their documents in single spacing, and then initially print them out double-spaced for proofreading. If you want your document to print triple-spaced, use the Options menu to select triple spacing at the beginning of the document when you're ready to print. You can always change back to single spacing for further editing.

The method you use to set your line spacing depends entirely on your own document editing and printing preferences. The least complicated route is simply to use the preset single line spacing when composing and editing, and then use your Print Options screen to print the document double-spaced if need be.

Goto Command

If you're working on a long document and need to move to different pages and lines, you can use Write's Goto command to accelerate the process. Say you're editing something on page 3 which is referenced again in the middle of page 12. You can tell Write to take you directly to page 12 and set you down on, or very near, the text you want. This saves you from having to scroll down or use the **<PgDn>** key to move through many pages.

1. With your document in the editor, press **<Ctrl><F7>** to display the Goto box (see Figure 2-12). Or, you can press **<F8>** for the Options menu, and select "Go to page/line" from the Other Options submenu.

2. Enter a page number and, optionally, the line number on the page you want to go to.

3. Press **<F10>**. The cursor will move to the specified page and/or line.

If you enter a page *and* a line number, the cursor will move to the beginning of the line on the specified page. If you don't specify a line number, the cursor will move to the top of the specified page. If you enter a line number only, the cursor will move to that line, counting from the first line of page 1.

You can also use the Goto box as a kind of document place marker. Suppose you're on line 15 of page 7 when you need to check something near the end of the document. Bring up the Goto box and press **<F5>** to copy the current page and line number into the box. You can now move around your document, and press **<Ctrl><F7>** and then **<F10>** to return to line 15 of page 7.

Word Count

Write can tell you how many words, lines, and paragraphs are in your document — a handy tool if you must meet a specific word count. With your document on screen, press **<Ctrl><F3>** — or select "Doc Statistics" from the Other Options submenu — and a chart of document statistics will be displayed. The line that reads "Up to cursor" counts from the cursor position to the beginning of the document. The "After cursor" line counts from the cursor position to the end of the document. The "Total" line is a count of the words, lines and paragraph in the entire document.

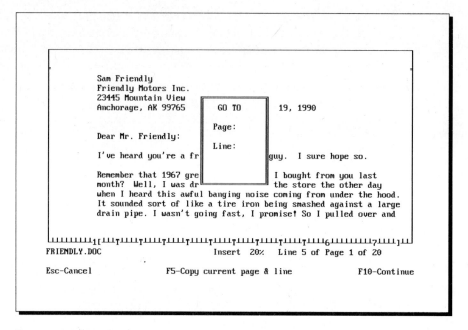

Figure 2-12: A Write Document with the Goto Box Displayed.

Text Enhancements

Text enhancements improve the appearance and readability of your documents. The ability to use boldface, italics, underline, superscript, subscript, strikeout, and different fonts where appropriate gives you the power to create anything from fancy memos and letters to complex contracts, term papers, and books chapters.

You might want to use text enhancements in the following situations:

- Boldface can be used for subheadings, chart titles, table titles, column headings, or general emphasis.

- Italics (letters slanted to the right) are used for titles of books, magazines, movies, as well as for general emphasis. You can also use them for captions and headings.

- Underlining is done for emphasis or to indicate italics.

- Superscript prints the characters slightly above the line. Such characters are used for footnote references and in mathematical formulas.

- Subscript prints the characters slightly below the line. You'll see subscript characters in chemical formulas.

- Strikeout is useful for showing editing changes in a document without deleting any existing text. Areas of the document that have been enhanced with strikeout are printed with a broken line through the selected text.

- Fonts are typefaces in different sizes and styles. Courier, Line Printer, and Helvetica are examples of typefaces. Courier 12-point italics is an example of a font.

Of course, whether you can use some or all of the above enhancements in your printed documents depends on your printer's capability to produce them, and correct installation of your printer and font description files in Q&A. If your printer can't produce a particular enhancement, it will appear in the printed output as plain text.

Fonts must be installed separately before you can assign them to any text in your document (more on this in the "Installing and Using Fonts" section later on in this chapter). To enhance text in your document:

1. After typing the text, move the cursor to the first or last character of the text you want to enhance.

2. Press **<Shift><F6>** for the new Enhancement menu (see Figure 2-13). Optionally, you can bring up the Options menu with **<F8>**, and select "Enhance" from the "Block operations" submenu.

3. Type the code letter or number for the type of enhancement you want.

4. Move the cursor to highlight the text you want to enhance (see the section on Text Block Operations earlier in this chapter).

5. When you've finished highlighting the text, press **<F10>**.

6. To combine text enhancements (bold *and* italics, for instance), repeat steps 1 through 5. However, if you're using a printer that has specific regular, bold, italic, and bold italic fonts (such as the scalable fonts built into the HP LaserJet III), you cannot put one font (bold, for example) on top of another (italic). You have to enhance the regular text with the single bold italic font. (See "Support for HP Printers" later in this section.)

7. To remove enhancements, follow steps 1 through 5, but select **R** (for Regular) at step 3.

In addition to enhancing text *after* you've typed it, you can also turn an enhancement on and continue typing — the next text will take on the enhancement as you type. When you want to apply an enhancement to the word, sentence, or paragraph *you are about to type:*

1. Press **<Shift><F6>** for the Enhancement menu, select the enhancement you want, and press **<F10>**.

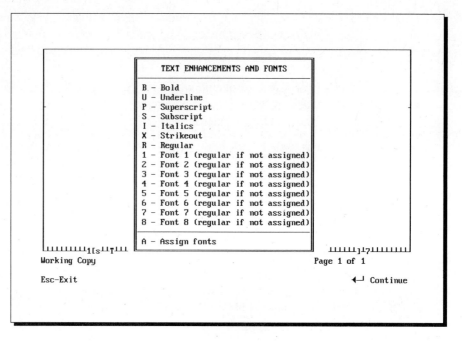

Figure 2-13: The Type/Edit Screen with the Text Enhancements and Fonts Menu Displayed. You assign fonts to your documents at the Font Assignments screen — a procedure covered in the "Advanced Printing Techniques" section later in this chapter.

2. Type your new text in the selected enhancement.

3. To revert to normal text, press **<Shift><F6>**, select Regular from the Enhancement menu, and press **<F10>**, or, press the ←key.

On a color monitor your enhanced text will show up in different colors or shades from the surrounding text (each enhancement will have its own color or shade). A monochrome monitor may show only some enhancements, depending on whether you have a graphics adapter card installed in your computer. But most monochrome monitors will make enhanced text look at least noticeably different than the rest of the text.

The status line at the bottom of your screen will also reflect any enhanced text by displaying the name of the enhancement. Whenever the cursor passes through a section of such text, you'll see "bold," "italics," and others down there on the status line.

Enhanced text is edited the same way you edit any text in Write. When you add characters to an enhanced area, they will take on the enhancement. If you delete an entire section of enhanced text, the enhancement is deleted along with it.

You can speed up text enhancement operations with macros. For example, you could create a macro that would italicize the word just typed. Pressing the macro key combination (such as **<Alt><I>**) would automatically italicize the previous word, and return you to regular text entry mode. See Chapter 8 for information on how to use macros to boost your productivity with Q&A.

All Capitals, All Lowercase, and Titles

You can select a block of text and change it to all capital letters, all lowercase letters, or initial capital letters for titles or subtitles. Changing a block of text to title capitalizes the first letter of every word that is not a preposition or an article such as "the," "a," or "an." Title works on acronyms, too. For example, "ph.d" will be changed to "Ph.D," and u.c.l.a will be changed to "U.C.L.A." However, "ucla" without the periods will be changed to "Ucla," and if the acronym begins with the letter "a," the "a" won't be capitalized.

Q&A's title feature even knows that "mccarthy" capitalizes properly as "McCarthy," and "o'keefe" as "O'Keefe." To change text to all caps, all lowercase, or title:

1. Press **<F8>** for the Options menu.

2. Select "Block operations," and then the mode you want from the submenu.

3. Back on the Type/Edit screen, highlight the text you want affected, and press **<F10>**.

The Draw Feature

If your printer supports graphics characters (the IBM Graphics Character Set, for example), you can enhance your documents with lines, boxes, and other eye-pleasing graphics, and have these printed as they appear on the display (see Figure 2-14).

Not all printers can print the lines you can draw with Q&A. The lines may show on the display, but if your printer lacks the capability to actually print them, or you haven't installed your printer, printer mode, or fonts properly, they may print as dashes, vertical bars, letters, or other characters. Consult your printer manual to find out if your printer has graphics (drawing) capabilities and, if so, how to access them. Many laser printers, including the HP LaserJet, support line-draw characters through a control panel selectable symbol set (a type of built-in font).

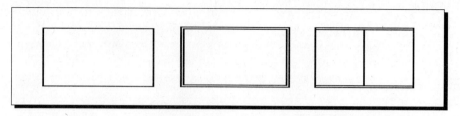

Figure 2-14: A Single Line, Double Line, and Mixed Line Box Created with Write's Draw Feature.

Q&A supports two methods of drawing:

- Using the built-in Draw feature to make single and double lines and boxes.

- Using the **<Alt>** key in conjunction with the numeric keypad to make individual graphics characters which you can string together to form lines, boxes, and other graphic shapes.

To use Write's draw feature:

1. Place the cursor where you want to begin line or box drawing.

2. Press **<F8>** for the Options menu.

3. Select "Lay out page," and then "Draw" from the submenu.

4. If your keyboard has a separate bank of cursor keys, use them to draw single lines and boxes. Otherwise, use the cursor keys on the numeric keypad.

 Note: To draw *double* lines and boxes use the numeric keypad while holding down the **<Shift>** key.

- Press the <→> key to draw a horizontal line from left to right.

- Press the <↓> key to draw a vertical line down the page.

- Press the <←> key to draw a horizontal line from right to left.

- Press the <↑> key to draw a vertical line up the page.

You can alternate between shifted and unshifted modes to produce a mixture of double and single lines and boxes. To draw double lines and boxes only, you can press the **<NumLock>** key to keep from having to hold down the **<Shift>** key.

5. To erase lines, press **<F8>** for the Eraser, and then use the cursor keys to go back over the lines you want to delete.

6. To resume drawing, press **<F8>** again.

7. To move the cursor around *without* drawing or erasing, press **<F6>**. This picks up the "pen" or the "eraser" while you move the cursor around.

8. To resume drawing or erasing, press **<F6>** again.

9. Press **<F10>** when finished.

While you're using the Draw feature, the two lines at the bottom of the screen will tell you whether the pen or eraser is "up" or "down," and which key to press to change modes.

You're in the Draw mode when the cursor is thin. A large flashing cursor indicates you're in Erase mode.

Each time you press a line-drawing key you're creating one segment of a line (a character). These characters or segments are affected by keyboard actions that affect all types of characters.

For example, if you're drawing lines in Insert mode and the cursor is to the left of the line, that line will be moved to the right as you type in that direction.

When you're in overtype mode, whatever is on the line will be replaced by any newly typed characters. Similarly, if you draw a line over text, that text will be deleted and cannot be restored with the **<F8>** erase key. You'll have to retype the text outside of the Draw mode. When typing characters *inside* a box, be sure you're in overtype mode or the vertical line segment to the right of where you're typing will be pushed farther to the right.

Using the IBM Extended Graphics Character Set

This method of drawing is more time consuming because you can only type a single character at a time while holding down the **<Alt>** key and pressing the number combination on the numeric keypad that corresponds to the character's decimal equivalent.

The reward, however, is that you have access to a much wider range of graphics characters, including thick lines, accented foreign letters, and mathematical and other symbols.

The procedure is not as complex as it sounds. Q&A supports the IBM extended graphics character set, and will display these special characters on the screen. If your printer also supports these characters, the printer manual will include a chart showing the characters and their corresponding decimal (dec) codes. The decimal codes are the numbers you type on the numeric keypad while holding down the **<Alt>** key. Figure 2-15 shows a few graphic shapes and symbols you can generate with this method.

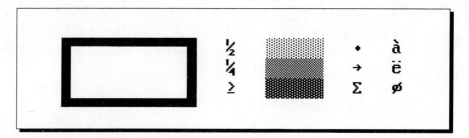

Figure 2-15: Examples of Graphics Shapes and Other Symbols Available from Printers Supporting the IBM Graphics Character Set.

To generate a character from the IBM graphics set:

1. Move the cursor to where you want the character to appear on the screen.

2. While holding down the **<Alt>** key, type the decimal number of the graphics character on the numeric keypad (NumLock must be on, and you must use the numbers on the keypad, not the numbers across the top row of your keyboard). See Appendix C for a summary of the characters and their decimal equivalents.

3. Release the **<Alt>** key and the character will appear.

4. Repeat steps 1 through 3 for any additional characters you want.

The **<Alt>** *decimal number* combination displays IBM ASCII characters from decimal number 33 on up. To access the characters in the lower range, press and hold the **<Alt>** and **<F10>** keys while typing the decimal number. For example, to get a smiling face character, hold down both the **<Alt>** and **<F10>** keys while typing the numeral 1 on the keypad.

Characters from the IBM graphics set behave on screen like any other character. If you type over them, they're gone. And during Insert mode typing they'll be pushed to the right as you type to the left of them on the same line. Appendix C contains a summary of the IBM graphics characters you can access from almost anywhere in Q&A. Decimal numbers 176 through 223 are your best bets for drawing lines, borders, and boxes.

Keep in mind that entire boxes made up of these IBM or Q&A Draw characters (and you can produce some pretty fancy stuff with them) are still just a collection of individual characters on lines, and they can be unwittingly moved or deleted depending on the typing mode you're in and the manner in which you're moving the cursor around with the space bar, backspace, or other keys.

Automatic Spell Checking

Write's built-in spelling checker scans your current document on command and flags the following for you:

- Possible misspellings of words.
- Typographical errors (typos).
- Repeated words (for example, "that that").

You can also check the spelling of single words as you're typing your documents or reviewing them.

Using the spelling checker involves the use of two separate dictionaries: Write's built-in dictionary, and your personal dictionary. When you spell-check a word or document, Write consults both dictionaries, and if it finds a word that's not in either one, the word is highlighted and a menu is displayed (see Figure 2-16) from which you can:

- Tell Write to provide a list of the possible spellings for the word from which you can select the correct spelling.
- Ignore the word and continue.
- Add the word to your personal dictionary.
- Edit the word and then have Write recheck its spelling.

Write begins its spell check from the *cursor position* and continues through to the end of the document. Thus, if you want the entire document checked you must position the cursor at the top of the first page. Here's the procedure:

1. With your document in the editor, place the cursor at the point where you want to begin the spelling check. (Press **<Ctrl><Home>** to move the cursor to the beginning of the document, or place the cursor on or just to the right of the word you want checked.)

2. Press **<Shift><F1>** to spell-check the document. (Press **<Ctrl><F1>** to check only the word at the cursor.) Optionally, you can press **<F8>** for the Options menu, and then select "Spellcheck" from the Other Options submenu. Write will display a "Checking..." message at the bottom of the screen.

   If a double word is located, Write will highlight the second word and give you the message: "Repeated word. Press **<F3>** to delete, or **<Enter>** to continue." Press **<F3>** to delete the second occurrence and continue the spell check. Press **<Enter>** to leave the double word as is and continue the spelling check. If Write locates a word that is not in its main dictionary or in your personal dictionary, the Spelling menu shown in Figure 2-16 displays.

```
                    TERMS AND CONDITIONS

     1) The standard trade discount will be 40%.

     2) The short discoont will be 20% on all other catalog titles.

     3) Any combina  ┌─────────────────────────────┐  books can be
     purchased at t  │                             │
                     │  L - List possible spellings│
     4) Any order w  │  I - Ignore word & continue │  for the
     standard trade  │  A - Add to dictionary & continue │ order filled
                     │  S - Add to dictionary & stop│
     5) You must be  │  E - Edit word & recheck    │   for either the
     standard trade  │                             │  status may be
     required in ad  └─────────────────────────────┘

     6) Orders may be phoned in or mailed in. Purchase order numbers are
     required on all orders.

  [⊥⊥⊥T⊥⊥⊥⊥T⊥⊥⊥⊥T⊥⊥⊥⊥T⊥⊥⊥⊥T⊥⊥⊥⊥T⊥⊥⊥⊥T⊥⊥⊥⊥T⊥⊥⊥6⊥⊥⊥⊥⊥⊥⊥⊥⊥7⊥⊥⊥⊥⊥⊥⊥⊥8⊥⊥⊥]⊥⊥⊥
  CONTRACT.DOC                          0% Line 6 of Page 1 of 6

  Esc-Cancel                                        ←┘ Continue
```

Figure 2-16: Write's Spelling Menu. It pops up when it finds a word not in its main dictionary or your personal dictionary. In this example, the misspelled word "discoont" has been flagged.

3. Press the letter of your choice or **<Esc>** to cancel the spelling check and return to the document.

4. Repeat Step 3 for any additional words flagged by the spelling check.

L — **List possible spellings** displays a list of up to seven alternate spellings. To replace the flagged word with a word from the list, type the number in front of the word, or highlight it and press **<Enter>**. If the list doesn't contain the correctly spelled word, press **<Esc>** to return to the Spelling menu.

I — **Ignore word** tells Write to skip the word and all subsequent occurrences of this exact spelling for the current spelling check session only. Use this if the word is correctly spelled and you don't want to add it to your personal dictionary.

A — **Add to dictionary & continue** adds the word to your personal dictionary and continues the spelling check. Use this option if you want Write to recognize this word from here on.

S — **Add to dictionary & stop** adds the word to your personal dictionary and then cancels the spelling check.

E — **Edit word & recheck** allows you to edit the flagged word without leaving the current spell-check operation. If you've corrected the word's spelling, but Write still flags it as misspelled, you can then add it to your personal dictionary so Write will recognize it in the future.

Adding Words Wholesale to the Personal Dictionary

You don't have to wait until Write flags your special words to add them to your personal dictionary. You can prepare a list of the proper names you're likely to use, along with specialized words, foreign spellings — whatever you like — and enter them directly into your personal dictionary in a separate session. To edit the personal dictionary:

1. At the Write menu, select **G** for Get, type in the filename of the personal dictionary (QAPERS.DCT), and press **<Enter>**. Write will display the Import Document menu.

    If you get the message "QAPERS.DCT does not exist," be sure you're requesting it from the correct directory.

2. Select ASCII from the Import Document menu, and Write will display the contents of the personal dictionary.

3. You can edit the personal dictionary as you would any ordinary document. When adding words to the dictionary, be sure to:

    • Type in your new entries so that the finished list of words is in alphabetical order.

    • Capitalize the words you would normally capitalize in your documents.

    • Use all caps for acronyms like ASCII, ASPCA, and UNESCO.

4. When you've finished editing the dictionary, do not save the dictionary as you would a normal Q&A Write document. The dictionary is an ASCII file and must be saved as such. With the dictionary on screen, press **<Ctrl><F8>** to save it to disk in ASCII format, and under the name QAPERS.DCT.

You can create a Write document containing all the words you want to add to your personal dictionary, and then spell-check on it. As each word is flagged, simply tell Write (using the spelling menu) to add it to the dictionary and continue. This method eliminates the need to alphabetize the words in QAPERS.DCT — Write will do it for you automatically.

Using the Thesaurus

New: Write's built-in thesaurus enables you to find synonyms (words with similar meanings) when the word you've used in the document isn't quite right for the idea you want to express. The words in the thesaurus are cross-linked so you can select a term from a list of synonyms, and get the synonyms for that word, too. To use the Thesaurus:

1. Place the cursor at the word for which you want see available synonyms.

2. Press **<Alt><F1>**. Optionally, you can press **<F8>** for the Options menu, select "Other Options," and then choose "Thesaurus."

3. The word at the cursor is highlighted, and you'll see a list of synonyms. The synonyms will be organized by noun, verb, and adjective, depending on the word you're checking.

4. Move the cursor to the desired replacement word in the Thesaurus screen and press **<F10>** to make the replacement, or press **<Esc>** to return to the Type/Edit screen without making any changes.

You can also look up a word from the list of displayed synonyms. Simply highlight the one you want to check and press **<Alt><F1>** again. Another screen will appear with the available synonyms for *that* word. You can now highlight an appropriate replacement word and press **<F10>** to effect the change in the document, highlight yet another word on the new list to check and press **<Alt><F1>**, or press **<Esc>** to return to the Type/Edit screen without making any changes.

As you search through several levels of synonyms, Write keeps track of each word you've looked up, starting with the word in your document that you initially checked. Press **<F9>** to move back through the looked up words one level at a time, or **<Shift><F9>** to move forward. This feature enables you to easily review the words in several synonym lists, and decide on a comparative basis which replacement word, if any, has the right stuff.

Column and Row Math in Documents

Write knows how to add, subtract, multiply, divide, figure an average, or return a count based on a rows or columns of numbers in a document.

To do column/row math:

1. Type in the numbers either in column (vertical) or row (horizontal) format. The numbers should be right-justified or aligned at their decimal points and single spaced.

2. For column math, place the cursor on the last number in the column. For row math, place the cursor just to the right of the last number in the row.

3. Press **\<Alt>\<F9>** for the Calc menu, or select it from the Other Options submenu. Write will highlight the numbers involved in the calculation and display a menu containing these options: Total, Average, Count, Multiply, Divide.

4. Press the letter for the type of math you want performed.

5. When Write prompts you, move the cursor to where you want the result placed (anywhere in the document) and press **\<F10>**.

Certain rules must be followed when performing math operations in Write:

- Numbers enclosed in parentheses or preceded by a minus sign are treated as negative numbers. To subtract a second number from the first, place a "-" sign in front of the second number (or enclose it in parentheses) and tell Q&A to calculate the total.

- The number of decimal places in the result will equal the largest number of decimal places in any number involved in the calculation.

- When performing an average or division calculation, Write will add two additional decimal places.

- Write looks at columns of numbers from the last one up (where you've positioned the cursor). Your numbers must be placed in a continuous column with no intervening text or lines.

- In row math, Write includes all numbers on the line to the left of the cursor.

- *Total* adds the numbers in the column or row; *Average* produces an average of the numbers in the column or row; *Count* tells you how many numbers are in the column or row; *Multiply* returns the product of all the numbers in the column or row (the first number is multiplied by the second, and that product is multiplied by the third, and so forth); *Divide* divides the second last number in the column or row by the last number in the column or row. Other numbers in the column or row are ignored.

Search and Search/Replace

Write includes a powerful feature that enables you to search your documents for words, phrases, patterns (like phone numbers), sequences of characters, text enhancements, fonts, embedded codes, and so forth. You can optionally tell Write to automatically replace occurrences of these items with other words, phrases, and fonts. This can come in handy if you find out you've spelled a name incorrectly throughout a document, used italics for emphasis when the boss says he now wants boldface, or accidentally used last year's prices.

Up to three elements can be involved in a Search/Replace operation:

- You can simply search without specifying any replacement and make the edit manually.

- You can have Write automatically search *and* replace by specifying both criteria.

- You can limit or expand (customize) your search or search/replace selections to accommodate specific preferences or requirements.

Searching for Text in a Document

Write gives you both Simple and Advanced search options. You select the option that best suits the kind of search or search/replace you're after.

When you issue the command for a Simple search, Write begins from the cursor position and works down through the document, looking for any occurrences of the word, phrase, or enhancement that you've specified as the search criterion. When it reaches the end of the document, the search is continued from the beginning of the document on down to the cursor position. If Write doesn't find a match for your search criteria, it informs you. This Simple search technique can be changed (see the discussion of Advanced search).

To put Write into Simple search mode with your document on screen:

1. Press **<F7>**. Alternately, press **<F8>** for the Options menu, select "Other Options," and then choose "Search & Replace." The Search/Replace box as shown in Figure 2-17 will appear (ignore the "Replace with" and "Method" for the time being).

2. When prompted, type in the word, phrase, or other character string you want to locate in the document.

3. Press **<F7>** to begin the search.

4. If a match is found, Write will highlight it. You can then:

   - Leave the text as is and press **<F7>** to search for the next occurrence.

   - Edit the text (this cancels the search).

   - Press **<Esc>** to cancel the search.

5. If no match is found, Write will advise you and cancel the search.

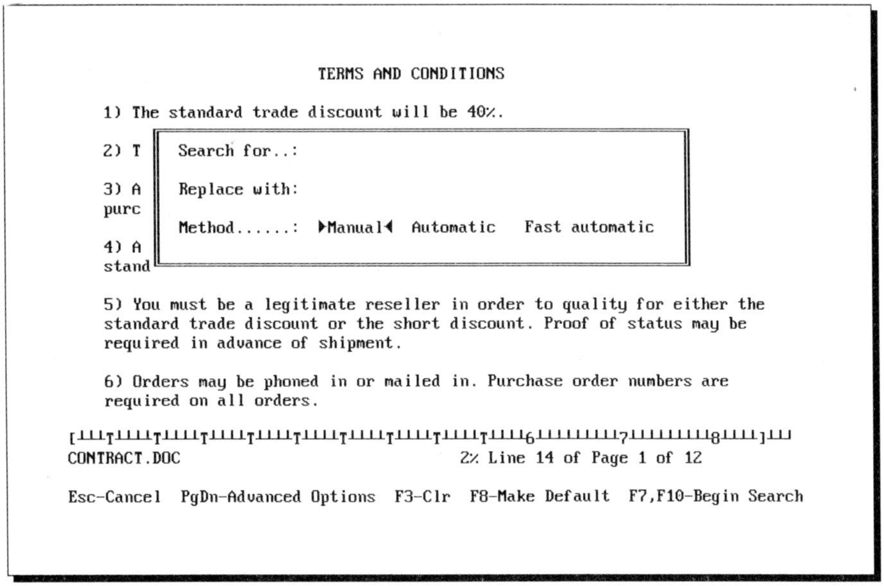

```
                    TERMS AND CONDITIONS

      1) The standard trade discount will be 40%.

      2) T ┌─────────────────────────────────────────────────┐
           │ Search for..:                                   │
      3) A │ Replace with:                                   │
      purc │                                                 │
           │ Method......:  ▶Manual◀  Automatic   Fast automatic │
      4) A │                                                 │
      stand└─────────────────────────────────────────────────┘

      5) You must be a legitimate reseller in order to quality for either the
      standard trade discount or the short discount. Proof of status may be
      required in advance of shipment.

      6) Orders may be phoned in or mailed in. Purchase order numbers are
      required on all orders.
   [⊥⊥⊥τ⊥⊥⊥⊥τ⊥⊥⊥⊥τ⊥⊥⊥⊥τ⊥⊥⊥⊥τ⊥⊥⊥⊥τ⊥⊥⊥⊥τ⊥⊥⊥6⊥⊥⊥⊥⊥⊥⊥⊥7⊥⊥⊥⊥⊥⊥⊥⊥8⊥⊥⊥⊥]⊥⊥⊥
   CONTRACT.DOC                          2% Line 14 of Page 1 of 12

   Esc-Cancel  PgDn-Advanced Options  F3-Clr  F8-Make Default  F7,F10-Begin Search
```

Figure 2-17: Write's Simple Search/Replace Box.

Editing the highlighted text as in step 4 above cancels the search. To continue the search, press **<F7>** again twice. When you press **<F7>** after making a change, the search/replace box will appear with the last "Search for" criterion still in place. Pressing **<F7>** a second time tells Write to look for the next occurrence of that same text. The logic behind this is that you may only want to search for and locate *a single* occurrence of a word or phrase, and then change your search criteria.

If you want to change your search criteria after editing, press **<F7>** to bring up the search/replace box, and then type your new search criterion over the old one and press **<F7>** to have Write search for the word or phrase.

Simple Search and Replace

1. Press **<F7>** while in the document, as above.

2. Type in the word, phrase, or character you want Write to search for.

3. Type in the replacement word, phrase, or character.

4. Tell Q&A which search method to use.

The Manual search/replace method stops at each occurrence and gives you the opportunity to continue or make changes. You can:

- Press **<F10>** to effect the replacement (or make other edits) and then press **<F7>** to resume the search.

- Press **<F7>** to resume the search without making any changes.

- Press **<Esc>** at any time to cancel the search.

The Automatic search/replace method replaces all matches found, pausing briefly to show you each replacement as it occurs. Fast Automatic zooms through the document searching and replacing each and every match without displaying each occurrence.

5. Press **<F7>** to begin the search/replacement routine.

Tip: The following pointers, many not mentioned in Q&A's documentation, may help you decide how best to establish your simple search or search/replacement parameters.

- If you simply want to have Q&A find a particular word, phrase, or other occurrence in your document, use the Manual method with no replacement criteria. If Write finds a match, you can make your edits and/or continue the search, or easily modify your search criteria.

- If you want to search and probably replace (but would like to retain the option of replacing or *not* replacing) type in your "Replace with" criterion and use the Manual method.

- If you want to search *and* replace, and you're sure of what you're doing (changing all occurrences of a text enhancement, or mis-spelled word or name, for example), use the Automatic mode to view each replacement, or the Fast Automatic mode if you want the job done automatically and swiftly without the screen being updated.

- If you want to search and replace in Fast Automatic mode, but wish to verify a few replacements first, start your search in Automatic mode and, if all is going okay, press **<Alt><F7>** to shift into Fast Automatic mode. **<Alt><F7>** acts as a toggle switch between Automatic and Fast Automatic.

- If you want to remove a word or phrase and not replace it, type two periods (..) into the "Replace with" field. Write will then make the deletion and close up the space where the word or phrase was.

Advanced Search

Figure 2-18 shows Write's Advanced search/replace box. You use the same **<F7>** keystroke from inside your document to display the Simple search box, but you then press **<PgDn>** to display the Advanced search box. The optional **<PgDn>** enlarges the box to accommodate additional search or search/replace options. You can press **<PgUp>** again to return to the Simple search box.

The first three lines of the Advanced Search box (as you can see in Figure 2-18) remain the same, and you fill in your "Search for," "Replace with," and "Method" parameters as discussed above.

But you now have the expanded ability to search for parts of words or phrases and upper- and lower-case letters, in addition to specifying what portion of the document Write will search. Keep in mind that Write will preserve both your Simple and Advanced search/replacement settings (if any) until you change them, leave the document, or clear the settings with **<F3>**.

Type: Select "Whole words" if you wish to search for entire words separated from other words. Select "Text" if you're looking for a string of characters, such as a part of a word (for example, when you don't know the exact spelling of a whole word, but know how *part* of the word is spelled). Select "Pattern" if you want Write to look for telephone numbers, account numbers, or other formatted patterns.

Case: This has to do with upper- and lowercase letters. Select "Sensitive" if you want Write to conduct its search based on the exact capitalization entered on the "Search for" line. Select "Insensitive" if you don't want Write to pay any attention to capitalization in its search. Table 2-11 shows some examples of how Write handles case sensitivity.

Range: Select "All" if you want the entire document searched. Select "To end" if you want the search confined to the text from the cursor position to the end of the document. Select "To beginning" to have Write search from the cursor position backward to the beginning of the document.

New: Search Joins: Setting this to Yes tells Write to additionally search documents that are connected to the current document by the ***JOIN***, ***QUEUE***, or ***QUEUEP*** commands, such as chapters in a manuscript. See Advanced Printing Techniques in this chapter for a discussion of these special printing commands.

Changing Search Defaults

The default Advanced search settings are:

- Type = Whole word
- Case = Insensitive

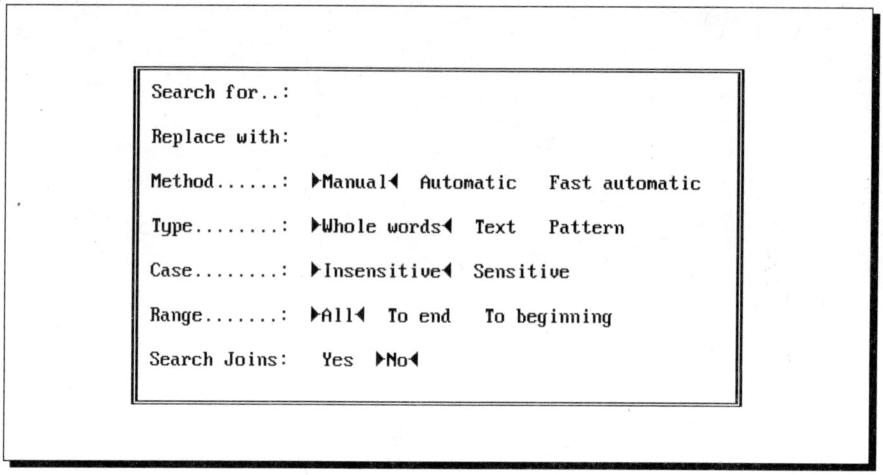

```
Search for..:

Replace with:

Method......:  ▶Manual◀  Automatic    Fast automatic

Type........:  ▶Whole words◀  Text    Pattern

Case........:  ▶Insensitive◀  Sensitive

Range.......:  ▶All◀  To end    To beginning

Search Joins:   Yes  ▶No◀
```

Figure 2-18: Write's Advanced Search/Replace Box. It displays when you press <F7> and then <PgDn>.

Table 2-11
How Write Handles Case Sensitivity

Search Word	Sensitive Finds	Insensitive Finds
case	case	case, Case, CASE, CaSe, cASE
Case	Case	case, Case, CASE, CaSe, cASE
CASE	CASE	case, Case, CASE, CaSe, cASE

- Range = All
- Search Joins = No

You can easily change these. Press <F7> from the Type/Edit screen, and then press <PgDn> for the Advanced box. Change the settings and then press <F8> to establish your settings as the new defaults. These will remain in effect until you change them again, or until you press <F3> when the Advanced box is displayed to restore the original defaults.

Searching for Parts of Words and Character Strings

Write can find any combination of characters (letters, numbers, and symbols). The combination may be meaningful on its own, or it may not. Many words end in "ing," for example. This "ing" all by itself doesn't mean much — it's not a word — but you may need to search for all words that end with it and replace that ending with another text pattern ("ed," for instance).

In such a case you can't search for a whole word, but Write will let you search for any word in the document that contains the text pattern "ing."

If you're going to ask Write to conduct a search/replace operation on a character string such as "ing," you'd be wise to select the Manual mode, otherwise Write would not only change the word "looking" to "looked" (if you specified "ed" in the "Replace with" field) but also "ring" to "red." You can see the mess that could be made of a document by allowing the search/replace operation to go off willy-nilly on Automatic or Fast Automatic.

 Tip: When conducting a search and replace operation on a character string or portion of a word, set the Type field in the Advanced box to "Text." This way Write will know you're looking not for a whole word, but for a specific string or piece of text. Then, when a match is found and the "Search for" pattern is highlighted, you can select from these options:

- Press **<F10>** to make the replacement, and then press **<F7>** to continue the search.

- Press **<F7>** to prevent the replacement at that particular occurrence and search for the *next* occurrence of the pattern.

- Press **<Esc>** to cancel the operator altogether.

Reserved Characters, Wildcards, and Advanced Searches

In addition to its straightforward search features, Write has certain built-in functions, and what are called "wildcard" characters, that you can use when searching and replacing.

Characters that are part of these built-in functions are *reserved*, meaning that you must use them in a special manner when they're part of any search operation.

The character @ is reserved, for example, as are the characters **?** and **..** and **** (backslash). So what do you do if you need to search for any of these characters (called "literal" characters when they're typed in as normal text) in your document?

The **** character, in Q&A, means, "take the following character literally." If you search for a **?** in your document, you need to type **\?** in the "Search for" field of the Search/Replace box.

If you search for the literal **** in a document, your "Search for" criterion would be **** Get the idea?

The \ character has yet another function. You use it to display or replace leading and trailing spaces.

To demonstrate how this works, suppose you had a list of double-dashed items in a document with a single space between the double dashes (——) and the item, and you wanted to replace the single spaces with two spaces. Here's how to do it:

1. With your document in the editor, place the cursor where you want to begin the search and replace operation, and press **<F7>**.

2. In the "Search for" field, type – \ (with *one* space between the – and the \). Press **<Enter>**.

3. In the "Replace with" field, type – \ (with *two* spaces between the – and the \). Press **<Enter>**.

4. Select your search method and press **<F7>** to continue. Write will change all occurrences of a double dash followed by a single space, to a double dash followed by a double space, and let you know when the job is done.

You can also use the \ character to delete the search-for item and replace it with nothing. Other Write reserved characters and their meanings are:

@ Refers to one of Q&A's built-in search functions (see "Searching with Write Functions" in this chapter).

? Is a wildcard character that stands for any single alphabetical or numeric character.

.. Is another wildcard character that stands in place of *several* alphanumeric characters.

Use the \ character when searching for either the @ or ? characters in your documents. To search for a double period, type \.\. in the "Search for" field. If you simply typed in .. to tell Write to locate any occurrences of .. in your document, Write would interpret these as a wildcard and search for *every occurrence of everything in your document!* Table 2-12 shows some examples of how these wildcard characters can be used in searches.

Of course you can't specify wildcards in the "Replace with" field, but you *can* type two dots (..) in the "Replace with" field to tell Write to delete all occurrences of what you've specified in the "Search for" field and close up those vacated spaces in your document.

Searching with Write Functions

Write places invisible codes in your documents as you type. Although the codes themselves aren't displayed, the *effects* of these codes are.

Table 2-12
How to Specify a Wildcard Search in Write

Search for	Write Finds
x?	Any two-letter word beginning with x
?x	Any two-letter word ending with x
???x	Any four-letter word ending with x
x..	Any word beginning with x
..x	Any word ending with x
..x?	Any word with x as its second to last character
x..y	Any word beginning with x and ending with y
x.. y..	Two consecutive words; the first beginning with x and the second beginning with y

For example, you can't see centered line or bold text codes in a Write document, but you *can* see by looking at the displayed document where carriage returns and boldfacing occur.

Using Write's built-in functions, you can search for, and optionally delete or replace, carriage returns, forced new pages, text enhancements, fonts, and centered lines. These functions consist of an @ symbol followed by two letters. Table 2-13 shows a summary of Write's built-in functions.

When searching for a text enhancement or font only, Write looks for the precise point in the document where the enhancement was turned on.

For example, if you italicized a line including ten spaces to the left of it, Write would search for (using @IT) and find the far-left starting point of the enhancement. In this case, the starting point would be the first of the ten spaces in front of the actual text.

On the other hand, if you're looking for an enhanced *word*, the search would stop as soon as the first enhanced letter of that word was found.

You can't search for a text enhancement and replace it with characters. Nor can you search for text, and replace it with an enhancement. Attempting to do so will result in the Write error message: "Enhancement-only searches may not be replaced with data replaces and vice versa."

Here are a few examples of searching and replacing in Write using its built-in functions. When typing the function, the characters following the **@** sign may be typed in either upper- or lowercase letters.

To change all bold text enhancements in the document to italic:

Search for: **@BD**
Replace with: **@IT**

To change all occurrences of regular text "immediately" to boldface "immediately".

Search for: **@RGimmediately**
Replace with: **@BDimmediately**

To change all occurrences of Font 1 to Font 5:

Search for: **@F1**
Replace with: **@F5**

To make all carriage returns visible:

Search for: **@CR**
Replace with: **%%@CR**

The **%** sign is arbitrary. All carriage returns found are identified by **%%** (to make them highly visible) with the actual (but invisible) carriage returns left intact.

After viewing and editing as desired:

Search for: **%%**
Replace with: ****

returns the document to its normal display status, leaving intact any carriage returns that weren't deleted.

If you want to delete all carriage returns and prevent the words just before and after the carriage returns from concatenating (being strung together without a space in between):

Search for: **@CR**
Replace with: **\ ** (backslash, space, backslash)

Pattern Searching

Patterns differ from whole words and text fragments — they're a string of characters connected or formatted in a particular consistent manner. They can consist of any combination of numbers, letters, and symbols. A Social Security number typed as 329-34-8995 represents a pattern with numbers and symbols

Table 2-13
Built-in Functions for Search/Replace Operations

Function	Description
@CR	Carriage return
@NP	New page
@CT	Centered line
@RG	Regular text enhancement
@BD	Boldface enhancement
@UL	Underline enhancement
@IT	Italic enhancement
@SP	Superscript enhancement
@SB	Subscript enhancement
@XO	Strikeout enhancement
@F1	Font 1
@F2	Font 2
@F3	Font 3
@F4	Font 4
@F5	Font 5
@F6	Font 6
@F7	Font 7
@F8	Font 8

(three digits, a dash, two digits, another dash, and then four digits). Likewise, phone numbers typed in the format (415) 344-5619 are patterned. Write can search for such patterns, and when they're found, you can change or delete them, and proceed to the next occurrence of the same pattern.

To find patterns, set the Type line in the Advanced search/replace box to "Pattern".

To locate patterns in the document matching your "Search for" criteria, the following wildcard characters can be used.

9	Matches any one number.
a,A	Matches any one alphabetic character.
?	Matches any one number or alphabetic character.
~	Matches any one non-alphanumeric character.

 Note: These are interpreted by Write as wildcards *only when the search Type is "Pattern."* Using them when the search Type is "Whole words" or "Text" will result in Write looking for their literal counterparts.

You can use the \ character in front of any of these wildcards to designate that a literal character follows, and type a space where a space is part of the pattern.

Here are a few examples of what could be typed in the "Search for" field with the corresponding search action:

99999	Searches for a number with five consecutive digits.
9\9936	Searches for a number with five consecutive digits where the second digit is a 9 and the last two digits are 36.
987/9/9	Searches for a five-digit number where the last two digits are 99.
aa..9\9	Searches for any phrase where the first two characters are letters, followed by any number of alphanumeric characters, and where the last two characters are any digit followed by a 9.
999~..	Searches for a string where the first three characters are digits, followed by a nonalphanumeric character (this would find a social security number typed, for example, as 344-45-4456).
~~~	Searches for an occurrence of three consecutive nonalphanumeric characters. The ~ search criteria can be used to locate the following ASCII characters:

ASCII 1	to	ASCII 47
ASCII 58	to	ASCII 64
ASCII 91	to	ASCII 96
ASCII 123	to	ASCII 127
ASCII 155	to	ASCII 159
ASCII 168	and	above

Q&A Power Feature: The Search/Replace feature brings unexpected power to advanced users who print reports and forms to file or disk and then bring them into the Write for custom "body work." You can have Q&A search for and then replace practically any formatting and enhancement code. For example, you can search for multiple carriage returns and replace them with just one, or have Q&A search and replace consistent strings of spaces.

Imported documents (particularly README files that often accompany shareware and other software programs) are especially prone to having a carriage return at the end of every line, making the document difficult to edit and reformat, and impossible to print justified. Once you've got the document in the editor, however, you can search for all carriage returns, replacing each occurrence with the \ \ code. This adds a space at the deleted carriage return, thus preventing the words just before and after the carriage return from concatenating.

Routine search and replace operations can be automated with macros (See Chapter 8). This can be a real time-saver when editing a variety of documents where your search and replace parameters are exactly the same.

Footnotes

Q&A does not support automatic footnote placement or numbering. But you can still add footnotes to your Write documents with relative ease. The least complicated and best method is to use a superscript number where you want to reference a footnote, and place all your notes at the end of the section, chapter, article, or book.

If someone asks you to put footnotes on the same page as the reference number, refuse. Explain to them that if the document is later revised or reformatted, the footnotes will have to be manually repositioned in an enormous cut-and-paste job.

However, if you really need to have your footnotes appear on the same page as the reference number, here's one unrecommended method:

1. As you compose your document, add your footnote reference numbers where appropriate. Use the Enhancement menu to change these reference numbers to superscript.

2. Compose and save your footnotes in a separate document with the same page characteristics as the master document.

3. When you're ready to print the final version of your masterpiece, use the Clipboard feature to copy your footnotes one by one from the separate footnote document to the master document. You can use Write's Search feature to locate the footnote reference numbers in the master document.

a. Check how many lines the first footnote occupies.

b. Use the Clipboard to copy the footnote to the master document.

c. At the master document page where you want to insert the footnote, place the cursor the number of lines up from the bottom of the page that the footnote will occupy, plus one additional line. For example, if the footnote is four lines, place the cursor five lines up from the end of the page at the beginning of the line.

d. In Insert mode, press **<Enter>** enough times to force the text following the cursor onto the next page.

e. Place the cursor where you want the footnote to start, and press **<Shift><F7>** to restore it from the Clipboard.

f. Create a blank line immediately above the footnote, and type in about 30 or so underscore characters. This provides a pleasing break between the body of the document and the footnote, and should result in the last line of the footnote being the last line on the page.

g. If you miscalculated, and the last line of the footnote is not the last line of the page, you can block and move as many lines of text as are necessary to make it so.

h. Repeat steps **A** through **G** to copy your next footnote into the master document.

If you later revise the document, or change your page characteristics, your footnotes may be thrown out of position. '

Document Templates (Style Sheets)

You can create reusable templates for newsletters, bulletins, letterhead, standard memo layouts, forms, and the like. Often referred to as "style sheets," you design these templates typically with a unique layout, distinctive fixed text, font enhancements, and exclusive Define Page and Print Options settings, and then save them to disk. When you create and save a merge letter (see Chapter 5), you are creating a kind of document template that can be used over and over again.

Suppose you regularly issue company policy or product bulletins that are circulated to employees, and you want to standardize the layout so that each one will be immediately recognized as a policy or product bulletin. All you have to do is design the template in the Write module, incorporating the fixed text, fonts, enhancements, line draw, page characteristics, and print options — everything that won't change from bulletin to bulletin.

When the design is finished, and without adding any variable text, you save the template under a name such as BULLETIN.DOC. Then, when it comes time to produce a bulletin, you retrieve the template, type in the variable text, and then either save the finished production to a different name, or print it out and then clear it from memory. The original template design will still be safely stored on disk for future use.

Document templates also offer a convenient approach to having a variety of different fonts available for documents — this can be a real time-saver if you use more than one printer, or use different styles of fonts for different kinds of documents.

The technique is to create a variety of blank documents, each with its own set of fonts installed at the Font Assignments screen. Then, when you compose the document, the fonts you want will already be there. You simply save the finished document to a different filename so as not to destroy the original template. See the section in this chapter on fonts for more details.

You can also use keyboard macros to create special document effects and page layouts. For example, you can create a series of macros to produce your fixed text, enhancements, page characteristics, and print options for such things as press releases, company memos, and correspondence. These macros are designed to take care of all the details so that all you have to do is type in the variable text and then press **<F2>** and **<F10>** to print. See Chapter 8 to find out how macros can save you time, effort, and frustration.

Program Editing in Write

Write is an ideal editor for creating and debugging programming code. To set up a Write document for program editing, follow these steps:

1. Clear the editor of any document by selecting Clear from the Write menu.

2. From the Type/Edit screen press **<Ctrl><F6>** to bring up the Define Page screen.

3. Move the cursor to the Page Length field, set the Page Length to 0, and press **<F10>**. This gives you a document without page breaks, the length of which is limited only by available memory.

4. Type your program.

5. When you've finished, press **<Ctrl><F8>** to export the document to ASCII format. See Chapter 9 for information on how to set the Default Export Type. You can suppress document margin display at the Set Editing Options screen covered later in this chapter.

Note: The document *must* be exported to "ASCII with CR" (ASCII with carriage returns) in order for a compiler to work with it.

6. Type in a DOS filename for your document and press **<Enter>**.

7. Exit Q&A and compile your program.

To revise a program created in Write, simply bring the ASCII document into the editor, make your edits, and save it again to ASCII format. Most compilers will tell you the line number of any errors found at compile time. With the program in the editor, you can use Write's **<Ctrl><F7>** Goto command to take you directly to the offending line.

Optional Q&A database programming is done in the File module, not in the Write module as above. In Q&A you enter your programming statements at the Programming Spec. See Chapter 4 for the details.

Advanced Printing Techniques

Recall that in Chapter 1 the first thing we did after installing the Q&A program in your computer was to customize Q&A for your printer. This printer installation established a common interface with which Q&A could "talk" (send commands) to your printer, and understand any signals coming back from it. It wasn't appropriate at that stage of your orientation to go into any more detail about the specific aspects of printing in Q&A.

Then, earlier in this chapter, we walked through all the steps required to set up Q&A's Print Options and Define Page screens so you'd understand the basic document formatting and printing-related tools at your disposal. We then explored a variety of text-enhancement features you can use to spruce up your documents.

In this section, you'll learn what embedded printer control codes are and how to place them in your documents. You'll also learn how to install and use fonts, giving you even greater power and flexibility in customizing the appearance of your documents.

Embedded Printer Codes

Printer control codes (sometimes called control codes, printer commands, or command strings) are software-based instructions that you send to your printer. If the instructions are correct, your printer will understand and then act upon them, producing the desired results in your printed output.

Background and Theory

Computer software can be instructed to command a printer's functions or modes by opening up a communication line and then sending codes to turn the functions on and off. The printer accepts this mostly one-way communication as long as the software sends intelligible signals and doesn't attempt to overwhelm the printer with too much too fast. In this sense, the printer is a slave to the computer software. The software calls the shots and the printer complies. It's only when the printer acknowledges receipt of information, doesn't understand the signals, or can't immediately handle the volume of incoming traffic that the flow is reversed, and the printer tells the software, "I'm ready for more" or "back off" for a few minutes and "wait until further notice."

Q&A knows what language your printer understands because you installed your printer and that printer's font description file in Q&A. Q&A is thus able to determine the codes it needs to properly command your printer's operations. These font description files — or printer drivers — are on the Q&A program disks which you copied to your computer's hard disk during the installation procedure in Chapter 1.

When you enhance a portion of text in a document by adding boldface or italics, Q&A looks to the printer file to find which codes your printer requires to print these enhancements. Q&A sends a "Bold-On" code to tell your printer where to start printing boldface, for example, and then a "Bold-Off" code to tell it when to return to normal text printing.

In contrast to this On/Off business, the "Printer control codes" field of the Print Options screen is used to enter printer commands that affect *the entire document*. In other words, this field allows you to enter commands to turn on or turn off particular printer capabilities, but cannot be used to turn printer capabilities both on and off.

In order to tell Q&A where you want particular printer features to start in a document, and also where to stop, use either the Text Enhancement menu available from the Type/Edit screen and highlight the text you want affected (see Text Enhancements earlier in this chapter), or enter the printer control codes right inside your document along with the text.

Which Language Does Your Printer Understand?

Most printers can produce a variety of special modes and effects which can be accessed through software commands. Line-spacing commands, margin commands, expanded, condensed, or shadow printing, and fonts are just a few examples of the kinds of capabilities your printer may possess.

The manual that came with your printer describes these capabilities, and probably provides some sort of chart or table that indicates which codes turn them on and off.

These codes have what are called ASCII decimal equivalents, and it's these decimal equivalents that you can type into your documents to get the special effects you want at printout time.

How to Embed ASCII Decimal Codes into Your Documents

With your document on screen:

1. Position the cursor just *before* the text you want to be affected by the enhancement. (Switch to insert mode if there's already text to the right of where you'll be typing the code.)

2. Type an * (asterisk) and then the letter **P** (for Printer), followed by a space. Alternately, you can press **<F8>** for the Options menu, and select "Printer" from the Print Commands submenu.

3. Type the *ASCII decimal equivalent* for the enhancement On control code, just as it's listed in your printer manual. If there's more than a single code, separate each code from the others with a comma.

4. End by typing another asterisk. For example:

   ```
   *P code1, code2, code3*
   ```

5. Immediately *after* the text you're enhancing, type an asterisk, followed by a **P**, a space, the ASCII decimal code that turns off the special effect, and another asterisk. Should you skip this step, the special effect will be turned on, but Q&A won't know when to turn it off, so the balance of the document from the on code forward will contain the enhancement when printed.

   - If you later decide to change your printer control codes, it's easy to search for them in your documents using ***P** as the search criterion.

   - The control code string you type into your document will not print if it's been typed correctly. Only the enhancement that the code turns on will be visible in the printed document.

   - Many printers have built-in emulation modes to accept the printer control codes of other printers. For example, the Panasonic KXP-1124 emulates both an Epson LQ-2500 and an IBM Proprinter X24. With such printers you use whatever set of commands the printer understands. Consult your printer manual on how to set it up to emulate another printer's commands, and what those commands are.

   - Some printers allow you to use control codes to change character sets (a character set comprises all the numbers, letters, and symbols associated with a given device or coding system. The IBM graphics set is a character set). For example, the Epson LQ-2500 decimal command 27,55 selects the IBM Proprinter Character Set I, and the code 27,54 selects Character Set II.

Examples of Embedding Printer Codes

The Epson LQ-2500 has the capability of printing double-high characters. The command to turn on double-high printing is **ESC+w+1**, but that's not a *decimal* code. The decimal equivalent is **27,119,1** and that's what you'd type to turn on double-high printing in your document if you were using the LQ-2500 or another printer that emulates it.

The decimal code that turns off double-high printing is **27,119,0**. Below is an example of a line of text in a document with these codes strategically placed to turn on, and then turn off again, the enhancement. The control code strings are shown in boldface.

When I was a young boy I lived in ***P 27,119,1*** a very big house***P 27,119,0*** in Brooklyn.

In this example, the words "a very big house" — and only these — would receive the double-high printing enhancement.

Using the same printer in the example above, suppose you wanted to tighten (reduce) the spacing between a set number of lines in your document. Ordinarily, a printer will print six lines to the vertical inch when single spacing, which is equivalent to 10/60ths of an inch per line. The Epson LQ-2500 decimal code to set the line spacing at 8/60ths of an inch (which will squeeze the lines slightly closer together at printing time) is **27,65,8** while the code to set the line spacing at the normal one-sixth inch is **27,50**.

If you wanted the entire document line spaced at 8/60ths of an inch, you could type in **27,65,8** (without the **P** or asterisks) in the "Printer control codes" field of the Print Options screen. But if you wanted only *part* of the document affected, you'd need to embed the on code before the selected text, and the off code just afterward.

Embedded Codes that Aren't Printer Specific

Q&A provides certain standard embedded commands that work no matter what type of printer you have. In other words, you don't need to type ASCII decimal values to invoke them. It converts these standard codes into commands that your printer understands.

For example, you can change the line spacing from single to double anywhere in your document by typing in the code

Linespacing 2 (abbreviated ***Ls 2***)

The "2" in the above example can be any integer from one through nine. So if you wanted to change to triple line spacing, the command would be ***Ls 3*** to turn on triple spacing, and ***Ls 1*** to tell Q&A to revert to single spacing.

You can optionally use the Print Commands submenu to insert a line-spacing command in your document. This embeds the *type* of command, along with the starting and ending asterisks. All you have to do is type in the variable part of the command, which is the number that corresponds to the amount of line spacing you want.

It's wise to place line-spacing commands at the end of the paragraph preceding the one where you want the line-spacing change to go into effect. It's all right to place a line-spacing command on a line by itself (such as on a blank line between paragraphs). Write will ignore the line when printing the document, and won't count it for pagination purposes.

You can also use printer-specific control codes to vary the line spacing in your documents. Some printers allow you control line spacing to within 1/360ths of an inch!

Telling Your Printer to Stop

If you need your printer to stop while you change a print wheel or font cartridge, you can embed a ***STOP*** command in your document. Here's how you do it:

1. On the line *just before* the line of text where you want the printer to stop, type the ***STOP*** command, or select Stop from the Print Commands submenu.

2. Place additional ***STOP*** commands before any other lines where you want a pause in the printing.

During document printing, the printer will pause at a ***STOP*** command, and resume only when you press **<Enter>**. A ***STOP*** command in the middle of a line will cause the printing to pause *before* any part of that line is printed.

Turning Justification On and Off

The ***JUSTIFY Yes*** command (abbreviated ***JY Y***) turns on justification so that your text lines will reach both the left and right margins. Write does this by adding spaces between the words. ***JUSTIFY No*** (or ***JY N***) turns off justification.

To justify the *entire* document, select the type of justification you want at the Print Options screen.

If you're working with tables, charts, or columns and want to preserve the formatting, be sure to turn justification off (***JY N***) just before they begin, and then turn it back on again (***JY Y***) immediately afterward. Of course, if justification is already set to No at the Print Options screen, and you plan to leave it that way, there's no need to use the embedded commands.

Integrating Documents at Printing Time

You can merge text from other Write documents into the current document using the ***JOIN*** command (abbreviated ***J***). This differs from moving or copying text from one document to another in that the merge takes place not on the Type/Edit screen, but during printing.

JOIN makes it easy to merge boilerplate paragraphs (which are themselves document files) into your otherwise original documents automatically, without having to go through the copy or move process. It also conserves memory and disk space since the current or "host" document isn't increased in size by the volume of the external document.

JOIN is especially useful for chain-printing sections of a long contract, for example, where the individual sections or clauses have been saved to different files. In this case you'd place the command to join subsequent documents at the very end of the previous document.

You can merge any number of documents into the host document. At printing time, the documents are merged at the precise locations where you've placed your ***JOIN*** commands. Headers and footers in the external documents are ignored. Only the headers and footers in the host document will be printed out. Here's the procedure for joining documents, using C:\QA\DOCS\CLAUSE-2.DOC as the external Write document for purposes of illustration:

1. Bring the host document into the editor.

2. Navigate the cursor to the location where you want CLAUSE-2.DOC to be merged into the host document at printing time.

3. With the cursor at the beginning of a blank line, type:

    J   C:\QA\DOCS\CLAUSE-2.DOC

    If the external Write document is on disk in the preset drive and directory (for example, if all your documents are located in C:\QA\DOCS\ and Q&A knows this), then there's no need to type the path, only the document name.

4. Repeat steps 2 and 3 for any other documents you want to merge into the host document.

Queuing Documents for Printing

Using the ***QUEUE*** command you can tell Q&A to print a series of documents, one right after the other, in the order you specify. The command to do this is:

*QUEUE *documentname******

Be sure to specify the full pathname of the document if it's not in the default document directory recognized by Q&A.

QUEUE differs from ***JOIN*** — it doesn't merge documents, each is printed with its own headers, footers, and pagination (if any). It works the same way as using the Get and Print commands from the Write menu, so each queued document may have its own Define Page and Print Options specifications.

To ***QUEUE*** sections of a manuscript, for example, you can create a Write document for the purpose, typing each ***QUEUE*** command on successive lines of the document like the one shown in Figure 2-19.

Paginating Across Queued Documents

If you want your queued documents to be continuously paginated, use the ***QUEUEP*** (abbreviated ***QP***) command. Suppose you need to print chapters or sections (each an individual document), paginated as if they were a single document. Instead of using the ***QUEUE** *filename****** command as in Figure 2-19, use the ***QUEUEP** *filename****** command.

Q&A supports a variety of print commands you can use to control document printing, some of which we've covered in detail above. Table 2-15 summarizes these commands.

Support for PostScript Printers

If you're familiar with the PostScript language, you can access advanced PostScript features available in Q&A by using one of the following three methods to send a PostScript command or program to your printer.

1. The ***POSTSCRIPT*** command (abbreviated ***PS***) enables you to insert lines of PostScript code into your document, and send the codes directly to the printer along with the document. PostScript code is included in the command in the following format: ***PS (code)***. The command cannot exceed one line.

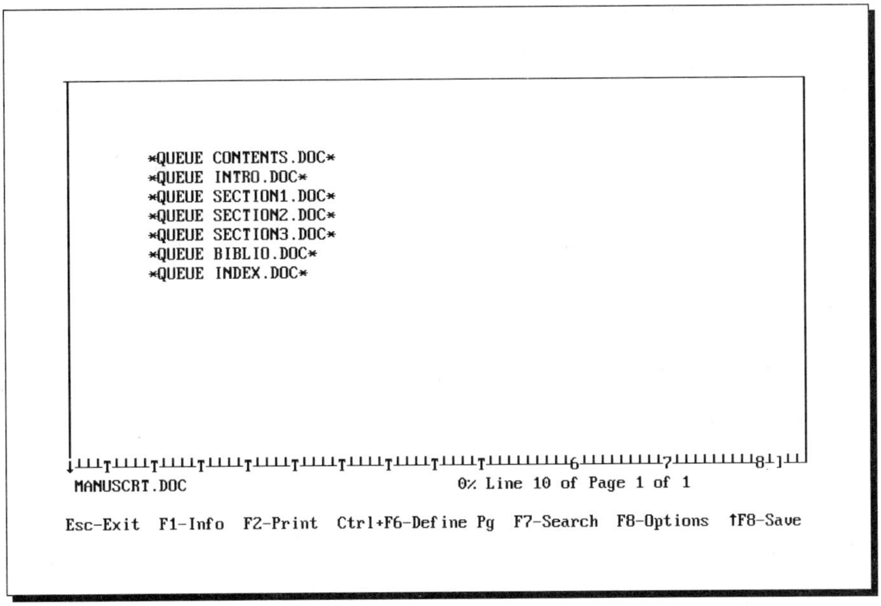

```
*QUEUE CONTENTS.DOC*
*QUEUE INTRO.DOC*
*QUEUE SECTION1.DOC*
*QUEUE SECTION2.DOC*
*QUEUE SECTION3.DOC*
*QUEUE BIBLIO.DOC*
*QUEUE INDEX.DOC*




MANUSCRT.DOC                          0% Line 10 of Page 1 of 1

Esc-Exit  F1-Info  F2-Print  Ctrl+F6-Define Pg  F7-Search  F8-Options  ↑F8-Save
```

Figure 2-19: A Print Queue Document Created in Write.

2. You can use the ***POSTFILE *filename**** command (abbreviated ***PF***) to embed a PostScript program into your document. *Filename* is the complete path, directory, and name of the file that contains the program. Moreover, a string can be passed as an argument to this file by enclosing the string — only the string portion of the command — in quotation marks.

3. If you want to download a PostScript file prior to printing, you can use the "Printer control codes" field at the Print Options screen. Enter the complete path and file specifications, and leave a space between each path/file for multiple files. This method can also be used to download fonts to your printer, or to define functions referenced by the ***POSTSCRIPT*** commands embedded in your document.

Support for HP Printers

Many Q&A users rely on printers from Hewlett-Packard to produce their output. Following is a summary of the special Q&A features that support HP printers. (These comments can also be found in the sections where support of other printers is discussed.) Troubleshooting tips for HP printers (and others) can be found in Appendix B.

Table 2-15
Summary of Printing Commands You Can Embed in Your Write Documents to Control Printing

Insert the commands, along with any arguments they take, at the precise point in the document where you want them to take effect during printing. You can type these commands, or pop them in by selecting them from the <F8> Print Commands submenu.

Command	Abbr.	Application
@DATE(n)	none	Inserts the current date into the document, where *n* is the date format number 1 through 20 (see Table 2-10).
@FILENAME	*@FN*	Inserts the name of the document.
GRAPH	*G*	Inserts a graph imported from another program. More on this in Chapter 9.
JOIN	*J*	Joins two or more Write documents into a single document. Specify the filename(s) of the joined document(s).
LINESPACING n	*Ls n*	Changes the line spacing, where *n* is the spacing from one to nine.
POSTFILE	*PF*	Inserts a PostScript program file in your document. See the section on "Support for PostScript Printers" later in this chapter.
POSTSCRIPT	*PS*	Embeds a PostScript code in a document. See the section on "Support for PostScript Printers" later in this chapter.
PRINTER	*P*	You add the ASCII decimal equivalent of the printer control code to this command.
PROGRAM	*PG*	You can embed valid Q&A programming statements in a document, especially useful for mail-merge applications. See Chapter 5.
QUEUE	*Q*	For use in a printing-queue document. Include in the command the names of the documents to be queued for printing.
QUEUEP	*QP*	Same as the *QUEUE* command except that *QUEUEP* paginates the queued documents as if they were a single document.
SPREADSHEET	*SS*	Inserts a Lotus spreadsheet or portion of one. See Chapter 9.
STOP	none	Instructs printing to pause while you change a print wheel or font cartridge.
TIME(n)	none	Inserts the current time in your document, where *n* is the time format 1 through 3 (see Table 2-10).

Modes Supported

If you're installing an HP LaserJet II, IIP, IID or III, you can install the following five modes: Portrait, Landscape, Legal Portrait, Legal Landscape, and Envelope.

Setting Characters-per-Inch

Q&A gives you a choice of four of the most commonly supported pitches: pica (10 cpi), elite (12 cpi), and compressed (15 and 17 cpi). The Hewlett-Packard Laserjet Line Printer pitch of 16.67 cpi corresponds roughly to Q&A's 17 cpi.

Text Enhancements

If the HP printer you're using has specific regular, bold, italic, and bold italic fonts (such as the scalable fonts built into the HP LaserJet III), you cannot put one font (bold, for example) on top of another (italic) in Q&A. You have to enhance the regular text with the single bold italic font.

Line Draw

Not all printers can print the lines you can draw with Q&A. Others, including many laser printers and the HP LaserJet, support line draw characters through a control panel selectable symbol set (a type of built-in font). Check your owner's manual to see how what type of line draw features your printer supports.

Font Support

Some printers, especially laser printers, support all three types of fonts: built-in, cartridge, and downloadable soft fonts. And several of the new laser printers, such as the HP LaserJet III, have built-in *scalable* fonts that enable you to specify extremely small to very large type sizes.

Hewlett-Packard LaserJets have built-in fonts, and they also support font cartridges as well as downloadable soft fonts. These fonts are shown alphabetically in Q&A's font description file for the LaserJet. Cartridges are listed by the letter of the cartridge (such A, B, or C). Some fonts may be included in more than one cartridge, in which case the cartridges will be listed together followed by the names of the fonts included in them.

LaserJet soft fonts are shown in the Font List with the font name preceded by the words "Soft Font."

Font Description Files

If you're assigning *scalable* fonts for PostScript, Hewlett-Packard, and other laser printers that support these fonts, you can select a point size with each such font you assign. You can accept Q&A's suggested point size, enter any number from 1 to 999, or press **<Esc>** to return to the Font Assignments screen.

QAFONT.EXE enables you to create a Q&A font description file from a selected soft-font file. All the popular HP LaserJet-compatible soft fonts are supported. You can create new font description files for these fonts, or append new descriptions to existing font description files. More on this in Chapter 9.

On Codes

Your printer or font manual will contain a list of the on and off codes you'll need. (This is discussed in more detail in Chapter 9.)

LaserJet Series II on codes, for example, consist of seven elements: font symbol set, spacing (proportional or fixed), pitch, point size, style (Roman or italic), stroke weight (light, medium, or bold), and typeface (the type style, such as Times Roman, Helvetica, etc.).

The **Esc** (or **Ec**) code shown in the printer manual must be converted to its ASCII decimal equivalent before typing it in the On Code field of the Modify Font Description screen. This decimal equivalent is \027. A small left arrow may appear at the beginning of some of the On Code strings. This is equivalent to \027.

HP LaserJet III scalable font on codes are different in only one respect. Instead of the on code containing a point size, you enter an ***** preceding the **v** to indicate a scalable font.

Installing and Using Fonts

A font is a complete set of characters of a consistent and unique typeface. Dot-matrix printers, for example, can usually produce 12-pitch and also 10-pitch printing at the very least, and each can be considered a font. Most printers today have the capability of producing a variety of fonts in addition to the standard 10/12 pitch variety.

It would be impossible to list all the font combinations available for the hundreds of printers people use today — the list would run into the thousands! Look through the manual that came with your printer to find out what fonts it supports. These fonts may be built right into the printer; they may be accessible through special font cartridges that you plug into the printer (which you can purchase from the printer manufacturer or a third-party vendor), or they may be "soft fonts" that either download into your printer's memory before the program loads, or capture the program's output as it is sent to the printer from your application program.

"Soft" Versus "Hard" Fonts

Soft fonts are sometime referred to as downloadable fonts. These are fonts supplied on floppy disks that you copy to your computer's hard disk, and then typically download to your printer prior to loading your application software. Some programs let you download the fonts from inside the program when you're ready to use them, or keep part of the font program in memory to intercept your text on its way to the printer, sending the specified fonts to the printer along with it.

Hard fonts are those that reside not in RAM, but in ROM. These are fonts built right into your printer or supplied in a cartridge that plugs into it.

Hard fonts are immediately available for printing because they're permanently resident in the printer's or cartridge's ROM and don't have to be loaded into RAM. Downloading soft fonts can be a slow process, but soft fonts typically offer a far greater variety of typefaces and can usually be scaled to a wide range of point sizes.

If printing speed is what you're after, hard fonts are the way to go. But if you're more interested in having a large variety of typefaces and sizes from which to pick and choose, soft fonts may be preferable, although there are font cartridges available for laser printers now that answer both needs.

Some printers, especially laser printers, support all three types of fonts: built-in, cartridge, and downloadable soft fonts. And several of the new laser printers, such as the HP LaserJet III, have built-in *scalable* fonts that enable you to specify extremely small to very large type sizes.

The point is, if you already have these fonts, the chances are very good that Q&A will support them for use in your documents and elsewhere in Q&A. The fonts themselves are *not* supplied with Q&A, but the *font description files* are. Font description files enable Q&A to have access to your fonts, and contain the information Q&A needs to apply the fonts you've selected to your document.

Q&A has facilities for creating or modifying font description files. The procedure is for advanced users only, and is covered in Chapter 9.

Installing Fonts

The material in this section presumes you've installed the Font Description file for your printer during the Q&A installation procedure covered in Chapter 1. The Font Description file needs to be available to Q&A in order to assign fonts to your documents.

Also, Q&A must know your printer make and model. If you haven't yet customized Q&A to work with your printer, see the section in Chapter 1 that deals with printer installation. When both your printer make and model — and the correct font description file for it — are properly installed, you can then assign fonts to your documents and print them. If you don't assign fonts to a document, or the font you assign isn't available to Q&A, the default font will print.

There's a difference between *assigning* fonts to your documents, and *using* assigned fonts to enhance your documents. You can assign fonts and not use them, but you can't use fonts unless they've first been assigned at the Font Assignments screen. Here's the procedure for filling out the Font Assignments screen in the Write module.

1. Press **<Ctrl><F9>** from the Type/Edit screen to access the Font Assignments screen shown in Figure 2-20. (You can optionally press **<F8>** for the Options menu and select Assign Fonts from the Other Options submenu or select Assign Fonts from the **<Shift><F6>** Enhancement menu.) Here's where you tell Q&A the name of the font description file you want to use and which particular fonts in that file you wish to make available for use in your document. A document can contain up to nine different fonts — the "Regular" or default font, plus eight others.

2. Place the cursor in the "Font file name" field at the top of the screen and press **<F6>** to see a list of the font files available for use in your document. These are the font files you tagged from the list of the dozens of printer files on the Q&A Master Disk when you installed the program in Chapter 1. Use your cursor keys to highlight the correct font description file for your printer, and press **<Enter>** to make your selection. If the font description file you need isn't there, see "Getting Font Support" in Appendix B.

3. Now that the font description file has been entered in the Font File Name field at the top of the screen, you can select the default (regular) font for your document. This is the font you'll use most often in your document. Press **<Enter>** to move to the Regular field, and then press **<F6>** again for a list of font descriptions. Highlight the font you wish to make the default for your document, and press **<Enter>** to install it on the screen. If you don't select a default font, Q&A will use your printer's internal default font for the regular font.

   If you're assigning *scalable* fonts for PostScript, Hewlett-Packard, and other laser printers that support these fonts, you'll be asked to select a point size with each such font you assign. You can accept Q&A's suggested point size, enter any number from 1 to 999, or press **<Esc>** to

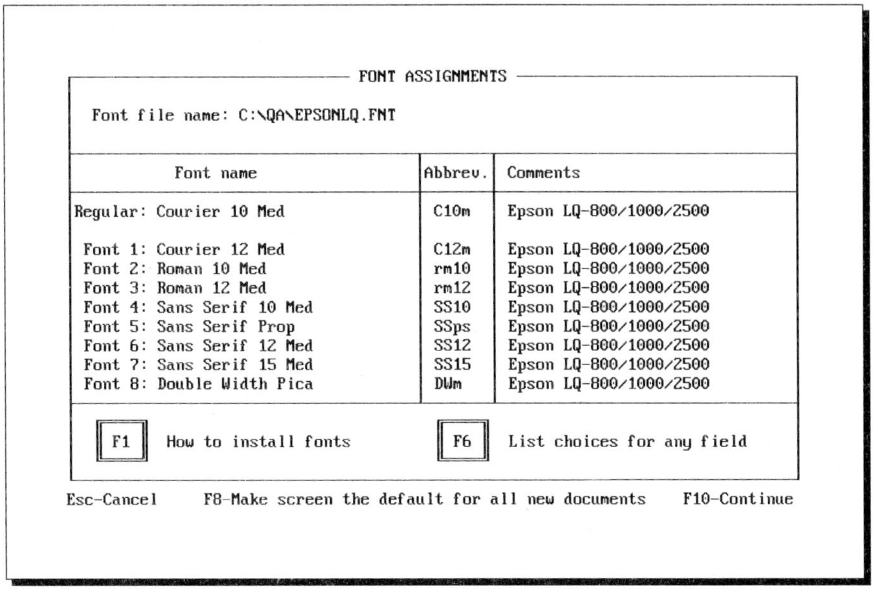

```
┌─────────────────────── FONT ASSIGNMENTS ───────────────────────┐
│                                                                 │
│   Font file name: C:\QA\EPSONLQ.FNT                             │
│                                                                 │
│  ┌────────────────────────────┬────────┬─────────────────────┐ │
│  │        Font name           │ Abbrev.│ Comments            │ │
│  │                            │        │                     │ │
│  │ Regular: Courier 10 Med    │  C10m  │ Epson LQ-800/1000/2500│ │
│  │                            │        │                     │ │
│  │ Font 1: Courier 12 Med     │  C12m  │ Epson LQ-800/1000/2500│ │
│  │ Font 2: Roman 10 Med       │  rm10  │ Epson LQ-800/1000/2500│ │
│  │ Font 3: Roman 12 Med       │  rm12  │ Epson LQ-800/1000/2500│ │
│  │ Font 4: Sans Serif 10 Med  │  SS10  │ Epson LQ-800/1000/2500│ │
│  │ Font 5: Sans Serif Prop    │  SSps  │ Epson LQ-800/1000/2500│ │
│  │ Font 6: Sans Serif 12 Med  │  SS12  │ Epson LQ-800/1000/2500│ │
│  │ Font 7: Sans Serif 15 Med  │  SS15  │ Epson LQ-800/1000/2500│ │
│  │ Font 8: Double Width Pica  │  DWm   │ Epson LQ-800/1000/2500│ │
│  └────────────────────────────┴────────┴─────────────────────┘ │
│                                                                 │
│   ┌────┐                         ┌────┐                        │
│   │ F1 │ How to install fonts    │ F6 │ List choices for any field│
│   └────┘                         └────┘                        │
│                                                                 │
│  Esc-Cancel   F8-Make screen the default for all new documents   F10-Continue│
│                                                                 │
└─────────────────────────────────────────────────────────────┘
```

Figure 2-20: Write's Font Assignment Screen. This is where you tell Q&A which fonts to have available for use in your document.

return to the Font Assignments screen. Ten to 12 points is a typical font size for normal text. A point size of 72 will give you printed characters an inch high.

4. You can now install an additional eight fonts. Simply press **<Enter>** to move the cursor to the Font 1 field, and press **<F6>** again to view the font list. Highlight your selection and press **<Enter>**. Then move to the Font 2 field, and follow the same procedure.

5. If you wish to make this particular Font Assignments screen the default screen *for all your new documents*, press **<F8>**. This ensures that these same font selections will be available (and in the same order you've placed them on the current Font Assignments screen) for use in any documents you create from here on out. In other words, by pressing **<F8>**, this Font 3 will also be Font 3 for your future documents, and so on for all the fonts. But for any document you can always override this default assignment simply by following the above procedure to install the fonts you want for *that* document.

6. When you've installed all the fonts you want to use (you don't have to install all nine fonts, of course), press **<F10>** to return to the Type/Edit screen.

Now that you've assigned your fonts you can proceed to use them in the document on screen or in the one you're about to compose.

If you use several printers, or want to assign a variety of fonts to different types of documents, you can create document template files that contain nothing except filled out Font Assignment screens.

For example, you might want to use a particular variety of fonts for correspondence, another selection for fliers, and yet another collection of fonts for the company policy manual. Just fill out the Font Assignments screens for each of these types of documents and save them with no text (this will also save the Define Page and Print Options settings). You can then go back and use these templates to create your documents, saving the finished documents to a different filename to preserve the original template designs on disk.

Using Fonts in Your Documents

Now that you have the fonts installed and assigned, you can use them anywhere in your document by doing the following:

1. Move the cursor to the beginning of the text you want enhanced in an assigned font.

2. Press **<Shift><F6>** for the Text Enhancement menu (see Figure 2-13). You can optionally press **<F8>**, and select "Enhance" from the Block Operations submenu. Choose the font or enhancement you want; you'll be returned to the Type/Edit screen.

3. Using your cursor keys, highlight the block of text you want changed to the font or enhancement you selected. See Table 2-9 for a summary of keys you can use to block text.

4. Press **<F10>** to apply the font or enhancement to the text just high-lighted. The font or enhancement abbreviation will display on the status line as you scroll through the text.

You can also turn a font "on" and type *new* text — the text will take on the font enhancement until you revert to regular text.

You can unselect an enhanced portion of text by moving the cursor to the beginning of the text, pressing **<Shift><F6>** for the Text Enhancement menu, pressing **R** for Regular (default) text, highlighting the text, and pressing **<F10>** to return that text to the Regular font.

Normally, you can apply more than one enhancement to a block of text. For example, you can boldface a block, and then underline it. But if you're using fonts that include separate bold, italic, and bold-italic fonts in the set, you should use these instead of trying to apply one enhancement on top of another.

If your printer requires a cartridge or soft fonts to be installed in it (or downloaded to it) prior to printing, and you've forgotten to do that, selecting those fonts for your document won't do any good. Q&A does not supply the fonts, only the font description files. So if this happens, save your document, install the fonts according the instructions supplied with the fonts (you may have to exit Q&A to do it), and then retrieve and print your document.

Hewlett-Packard LaserJets and compatibles have built-in fonts, and they also support font cartridges as well as downloadable soft fonts. These fonts are shown alphabetically in Q&A's font description file for the LaserJet. Cartridges are listed by the letter of the cartridge (such A, B, or C). Some fonts may be included in more than one cartridge, in which case the cartridges will be listed together followed by the names of the fonts included in them.

LaserJet soft fonts are shown in the Font List with the font name preceded by the words "Soft Font."

Line and Box Drawing

Q&A Power Feature: Some printers include fonts that contain the IBM graphics character set. Some don't. Q&A version 4.0 beefed-up support for graphics characters for a number of popular printer models, but not all printers.

The best way to find out if your printer supports the graphics characters available on the PC is to consult the manual that came with it. Your printer may have its own set of graphics characters that you can use by typing in the decimal equivalents on your keyboard's numeric keypad while holding down the **<Alt>** key. And while these may show up on your display as different characters altogether, if the decimal codes are correct for your printer, then they should actually print out on paper as expected.

Write Utilities

Write Utilities provide a variety of special tools for carrying out document-related tasks. Don't confuse these word processing utilities with the utilities available from the Q&A Main menu. Figure 2-21 shows the Write Utilities menu.

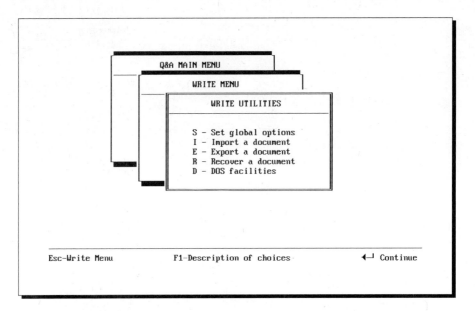

Figure 2-21: Write's Utilities Menu.

Setting Your Global Options

When you select "Set global options" from the Write Utilities menu, the menu in Figure 2-22 will be displayed. From the Global Options menu you can establish preset editing preferences from a variety of document editing options, as well as modify printing and page definition specifications that will affect any future documents you create in the Write module.

In this usage, the word "global" means "everything." When you change a global option you're telling Q&A that from now on you want these new options you're specifying to apply to all the documents you create in Write. In Q&A a change in global options will be reflected in any new documents, but existing documents on disk will not be affected unless you retrieve them from disk and deliberately modify them.

Set Editing Options

Any editing options you set here (see Figure 2-23) will be applied to all new Write documents. Existing documents won't be affected unless you retrieve and change those documents individually. For all but the last two items, use your arrow keys to navigate to the item you wish to change, highlight the desired choice, and then move down to the next item you wish to change. If you wish

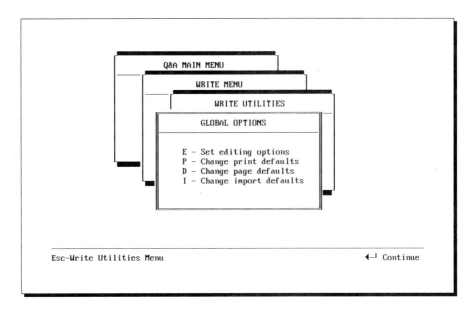

Figure 2-22: The Global Options Menu.

to change the default settings of the last two items, type in the new values. Press **<F10>** when done to save your changes and return to the Global Options menu.

Default Editing Mode: Choose Overtype if you want the cursor to type over (and erase) characters to the right as it moves across the document line on the Type/Edit screen. If you want the text to the right of the cursor to be pushed farther to the right and wrapped onto the next line as you type, select Insert mode. From the Type/Edit screen you can toggle between overtype and Insert mode by using the **<Insert>** or **<Ins>** key, but the selection you make here will be the first mode displayed on the screen when you start on a new document.

Default Export Type: ASCII (American Standard Code for Information Exchange) is a stripped-down text format that's compatible with a wide variety of application programs. "ASCII with CR" places a carriage return at the end of each line of text. Use this if you're sending your documents directly to a printer or communications device, or exporting to another word processor or a program compiler that expects carriage returns to indicate line endings. "ASCII without CR" should be used when you're exporting a document from Q&A to be imported into another word processor.

```
                          EDITING OPTIONS

       Default editing mode...:  ▶Overtype◀    Insert
       Default export type....:  ▶ASCII with CR◀   ASCII without CR
       Automatic backups......:   Yes  ▶No◀
       Use real tab characters:   Yes  ▶No◀
       Show tabs on screen....:   Yes  ▶No◀
       Show returns on screen.:   Yes  ▶No◀
       Decimal convention.....:  ▶American◀    European
       Show margins on screen.:  ▶Yes◀  No
       Show ghost cursor......:  ▶Yes◀  No

       Default import type....:  ▶None◀ ASCII  Special ASCII  Old WordStar  Lotus

       Default tab settings...:   5, 15, 25, 35

       Spacing between columns:   .25"


                    Editing options for all documents

        Esc-Exit                                          F10-Continue
```

Figure 2-23: The Editing Options Screen with Default Settings Shown.

Automatic Backups: Answer Yes if you want Q&A to create a backup copy of your document each time you retrieve it into the editor, and update the backup when you save the document. Q&A-created backup copies use the document name, but with a .BAK extension, and they double the number of document files stored on your disk.

Use Real Tab Characters: Change the setting to Yes if you're using proportional fonts and want any columns in your documents to line up properly.

Show Tabs on Screen: Select Yes if you want an → arrow character to display wherever you've placed a tab in your document. Without the tab character showing, a series of spaces will be indistinguishable from an actual tab.

Show Returns on Screen: A Yes selection displays a ¶ paragraph character wherever you've pressed **<Enter>** in the document. The character won't display at the end of regular wrapped lines. The visible carriage return character could help you when editing documents, but adds clutter to the screen.

Decimal Convention: Select "American" if you want a period for the decimal point. The "European" setting yields a comma.

Show Margins on Screen: Write's default setting shows page margins on the screen as solid lines. Select No for a clear screen.

Show Ghost Cursor: Select Yes if you want a rectangular block on the Type/ Edit ruler line to follow the horizontal motion of the cursor on the screen above. It's useful when you're aligning columns or if you need to count character spaces.

Default Import Type: None is the default. But if you're regularly importing documents in only one of the formats offered, highlight that one as the default type. Write will then recognize the document format automatically and won't have to bother asking you what it is.

Default Tab Settings: Write is preset with tab stops along the ruler line at columns 5, 15, 25, and 35, counting from the left margin. Enter new numbers, each separated by a comma, if you want different or additional tab stops, and tack the letter **D** or **d** onto the beginning of the number to designate a decimal tab stop for aligning columns of numbers.

Spacing Between Columns: .25" (¼-inch) is the default. Enter any new value in inches (with a " sign after the number), in centimeters (with a cm after the number), or in ruler line columns (whole number only). Fractions must be expressed as decimal numbers. Your setting will determine the space Q&A will place between columns should you select column printing from the Print Options menu.

Change Print Defaults

Make this selection from the Global Options menu if you want to change printing default settings for any documents you'll create in Write from here on out (see Figure 2-24). Then, when you send your new documents to the printer, any new global settings will be reflected in the Print Options screens for those documents. Documents saved to disk *prior* to any new default settings will retain the Print Options assigned to them when they were last saved.

The Print Options Defaults screen contains the same choices as the Print Options screen that's displayed when you press **<F2>** to print any document in Write, and these global settings can always be changed for any individual document. See the section earlier in this chapter on printing in Write for a complete description of all the elements of the Print Options screen and tips on how to decide which options to use when printing out your documents.

Change Define Page Defaults

Use this selection from the Write Global Options menu if you want to standardize page format settings for any future documents (see Figure 2-25). Enter those margin, page width, page length, and characters-per-inch values that are most likely to be the values you'll use in your new documents.

```
                            PRINT OPTIONS
                            ============

        From page.............:  1              To page.............:  END

        Number of copies......:  1           Print offset........:  0

        Line spacing..........:  ▶Single◀    Double      Envelope

        Justify...............:  Yes  ▶No◀  Space justify

        Print to..............:  ▶PtrA◀  PtrB    PtrC    PtrD    PtrE   DISK

        Page preview..........:  Yes  ▶No◀

        Type of paper feed....:  Manual  ▶Continuous◀  Bin1   Bin2   Bin3   Lhd

        Number of columns.....:  ▶1◀   2     3     4     5     6     7     8

        Printer control codes.:

        Name of merge file....:


        ─────────────────────────────────────────────────────────────────

        Esc-Exit                      F1-Info                   F10-Continue
```

Figure 2-24: The Print Options Defaults Screen Shown with Default Settings. Changes made here apply only to new documents, not existing ones.

Existing documents won't be affected by changes you make here — they'll retain the page formatting they had when last saved to disk.

Whatever default values you set at this screen can be changed for any document on which you're working. This screen's only purpose is to permit you to establish your own preferred presets. For a comprehensive discussion of the elements of the Define Page screen, see "Defining Your Page Characteristics" earlier in this chapter.

Change Import Defaults

New: You can establish default page formatting for imported ASCII, WordStar, and Lotus files. Notice in Figure 2-26 that the left, top, and bottom margins and page length default to 0, and the page width is extremely wide. These are likely to be the optimum specifications for a document that you plan to do some further work on once imported into Q&A Write. When you have the imported document on the Type/Edit screen, you can then work it over like any Write document, applying enhancements and choosing appropriate Define Page and Print Options.

```
                        DEFINE PAGE



      Left margin: 10              Right margin : 68

      Top margin : 6               Bottom margin: 6

      Page width : 78              Page length  : 66

      Characters per inch............:  ▶10◀   12    15    17

      Begin header/footer on page #...:   1

      Begin page numbering with page #:   1



                   Page Options for New Documents
    Esc-Exit            F1-Help                        F10-Continue
```

Figure 2-25: The Define Page Options Screen Shown with Default Settings. Note that the status line at the bottom of the screen indicates that settings on this screen apply only to new documents.

Import, Export, and Recover a Document

These features are covered in detail, along with importing, exporting, and recovering database files, in Chapter 9.

DOS Facilities

Q&A Power Feature: The DOS file facilities enable you to carry out general housekeeping chores on your document files without having to leave Q&A. Q&A's List Manager, a powerful feature that helps you find, organize, move, and assign 70-character descriptive names to your Q&A document and database files, is covered in detail in Chapter 9. Selecting DOS Facilities from the Write Utilities menu displays another menu from which you can perform the following operations.

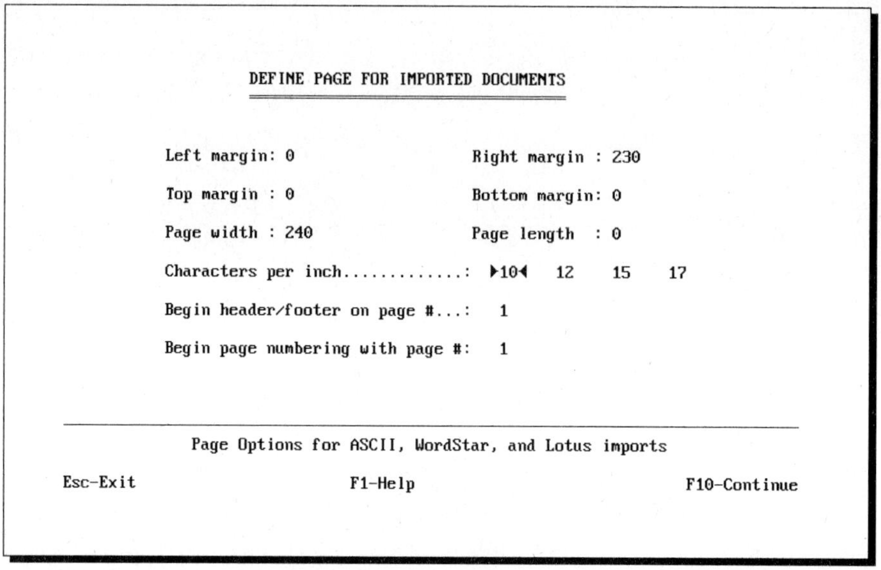

```
              DEFINE PAGE FOR IMPORTED DOCUMENTS


      Left margin: 0                Right margin : 230

      Top margin : 0                Bottom margin: 0

      Page width : 240              Page length  : 0

      Characters per inch............:  ▶10◀   12    15    17

      Begin header/footer on page #...:   1

      Begin page numbering with page #:   1



              Page Options for ASCII, WordStar, and Lotus imports

   Esc-Exit                     F1-Help                    F10-Continue
```

Figure 2-26: The Define Page for Imported Documents Screen. Shown here with default settings.

Rename, Delete and Copy a Document

Use the Rename feature to change your document names if you like. When you select this option, Q&A prompts you for the current name of the file. Type it and press **<Enter>**. Then type in the document's new name and press **<Enter>**, and Q&A will rename the document and confirm the change with a "Rename Operation Completed" message.

Use the Delete option to remove a document from disk permanently. When Q&A prompts you, type in the name of the document you want to delete and press **<Enter>**. Q&A will confirm the deletion with you by giving you the opportunity to give a final "Yes" or "No."

Use the Copy option to make a copy of the document to the same disk (under a different filename), or to a different disk (a floppy, perhaps). When you select Copy, Q&A will prompt for the name of the document to copy, which you type in and then press **<Enter>**. You'll then be asked for the name of the file to copy it to (type it in and press **<Enter>**).

You won't want to copy a document to itself. Doing so will simply overwrite the file with the copy and serve no purpose. So be sure to enter either a different document name, or a different path or directory, so Q&A can put the copy somewhere else.

List Files

When you select this option from the Write Utilities menu, Q&A prompts you for the drive and path. If you press **<Enter>** without changing the drive/path you'll see a list of all the files in the current directory in alphabetical order. If the screen is full, there may be more files on the next screen which you can display by pressing **<PgDn>**.

If you want to view a file list on a different drive or in a different directory, type in the correct drive/path over the current drive/path at the prompt, and press **<Enter>**.

Chapter 9, which covers utilities, contains a more detailed discussion on how to use Q&A's List Manager to search for and manipulate disk files.

Summary

In this chapter you learned to use Q&A's word processor, Write, to create, revise, and store documents. This unexpectedly powerful word processor also lets you format, spell-check, search and replace, enhance your text with special fonts, and print the documents the way you want them to look.

In the next chapter, "File — The Workhorse Database Manager," you will use many of the basics you learned here as you design and enter, update, and print database records.

Chapter 3
File — The Workhorse Database Manager

In this chapter you'll learn how to:

▶ Identify which aspects of your record-keeping and business activities are ideally suited for Q&A File applications.

▶ Recognize the elements of good database form design in Q&A.

▶ Design new database forms to manage customer, employee, and inventory information.

▶ Redesign your forms to accommodate new record-keeping requirements.

▶ Enter new records into your databases.

▶ Retrieve forms already in the files.

▶ View and update the information in your database files.

▶ Print your forms.

This chapter covers the basics of using the Q&A database manager. Here you'll learn the elements of a database, how to design (and redesign) databases, and how to add new records, update, and print.

More advanced features, such as customizing and programming your databases, removing records, mass updating records, and posting values to external databases will be covered in Chapter 4, "Advanced Database Design and Procedures."

You must understand the principles in this chapter before you try to customize or program your database.

Overview

If you've ever worked with forms, records, or file cards, you know how important it is that they be accurately prepared and properly filed for future use. Good record-keeping — the ability to quickly locate recorded information — is essential to any smoothly running work area, department, or business enterprise.

In a business, typical forms or records often include employee records, customer records, supplier records, invoices, purchase orders, and so forth. Q&A is a powerful and reliable record keeper, and offers tremendous flexibility in designing your input forms, as well as in storing, retrieving, and updating the important information contained in them.

In the previous chapter you learned how to prepare, edit, and manipulate documents. Some of what you learned there will be applied to designing basic database forms in this chapter and more advanced database forms in the following chapter.

Documents and database records are entirely different, however, and should not be confused. Word processing documents generally consist of correspondence, memos, and articles written in sentences and paragraphs and intended to communicate thoughts and ideas. Database records are more specialized in that they contain *details* about a subject that were entered into information blanks on a record. Organizing the details in this manner makes it very easy to later retrieve and update the information.

For example, an index card containing a customer's name, address, and phone number would be equivalent to a database record for that customer. The only difference is that instead of using a typewriter or pen to enter the information on the card and then manually filing it along with other index cards, you use the computer's keyboard and display to fill out a blank form, and Q&A and the computer file the information by storing it on disk.

One of Q&A's specialties is merging selected information from your database records with documents you've created in the Write module, giving you the ability to send personalized form letters to all or selected customers in your database simply by typing a single letter and then telling Q&A to place the names and addresses of your customers at the tops of the letters as they are printed.

Merging information in database records with Write documents and mailing labels will be covered in Chapter 5.

What You Can Do with Databases

With Q&A you design database forms that can be made to look very much like the paper forms you may now be using. If you've been typing out invoices in a particular manner, you can design that same invoice form on the computer screen so it can be filled out in the old familiar way and then printed out on paper.

A typical invoice form contains blank areas in which you type the customer's name and address, a description of the items involved in the transaction, prices, shipping charges, sales tax, and a total amount. Filling out a database invoice record is similar, except that you can automate a great deal of the task. Instead of having to type in the name and address, you can have Q&A look up this information for you and place it in the form automatically. Descriptions and prices of invoice items can be similarly looked up and typed in by entering a part number or stock number code. What's more, Q&A can be made to do all the calculations, including multiplying the quantity ordered by the price, and totalling up the invoice.

The beauty of automating your transactions in this manner is not only the speed and ease with which you can create and maintain your records, but in the ability to sort and retrieve them. You can also easily generate reports that tell you about entire classes of records or transactions.

Elements of a Database

Of course, you can't ask the computer for a list of outstanding invoices if there's no database of invoices to begin with. You have to design the input form in Q&A and then begin entering your individual invoices. The more invoice records you add to the file, the more Q&A's powerful features can be tapped to find out about those invoices, either individually or by category or group.

This is true of any aspect of your business. Once your customers' names and addresses have been added to a database, you can manipulate and query that database to find out all sorts of interesting and useful facts and relationships about what's in the file.

Before you get to this point, you must first design the database form.

Database Fields

The basic element of a database form in Q&A is called a *field*. A field is equivalent to a blank space on a form where you would enter a Social Security number, a last name, a part number, a zip code — anything that's logically broken down into its smallest meaningful component.

Some forms you've seen may have called for the entry of a whole name (first name, initial, last name) in a single space. But in designing your database forms it's usually wise to break the name down by providing *four* fields: one for the prefix (Mr., Mrs., Miss, or Ms.), one for the first name, one for the middle initial, and a fourth field for the last name. This gives you the ability to more accurately sort, retrieve, merge, and otherwise manipulate your records and the information in them.

Similarly, if you entered your customers' company names and complete addresses all in one field, it would be difficult to retrieve a list of them by state, by zip code, or alphabetically by company name.

The point is that the more specific the information contained in *each field* in the database, the more versatility you'll have when searching and retrieving your records.

Q&A allows you to have up to 2,045 fields per database form and as many databases as can fit on your hard disk. And in Q&A a field is defined as the information blank *and any descriptive label associated with it*. So if you had the following information blank on a database form:

```
Part Number: X34005-HB
```

the fixed *field label*, "Part Number," along with the variable *field value*, "X34005-HB," would constitute the field. Even If the field were empty (meaning there is no value typed in), the field would still consist of the label *plus* the information blank.

A Database Record

The second element of a database is the individual *record* or *form*. A database may contain a few dozen or hundreds of thousands of records — each record containing information about one particular customer, employee, invoice, supplier, or inventory item. For most purposes, the terms record and form mean the same thing in Q&A. You design the form on screen, after deciding what the database will contain, by placing the information blanks, or fields, on the form.

Figure 3-1 shows an example of an inventory database form with several fields in place. In this example, the form is presented with the field labels (or field names) that will appear on all the records in the database, as well as the specific information about one particular record — in this case, Part Number 211-3X.

The Database File

The third element of a database is the file *taken as a whole* — the collection of all the individual records in the database.

```
PART NUMBER: 211-3X    DESCRIPTION: Black 2-drawer file

SUPPLIER NO: 14    COST: $22.00    RETAIL: $49.95

WEIGHT: 35.5    SHELF LOCATION: B9

PREVIOUS QTY: 15  SOLD TODAY: 3   QTY ON HAND: 12

SOLD YTD: 80    COMMENTS: Legal, 30" high, no lock
```

Figure 3-1: A Sample Database Form for Inventory Items.

Figure 3-1 shows a single database record. If you had 1,000 part numbers, you'd likely have 1,000 records in the inventory file, each containing the specifics about one particular part number. This collection of records is referred to as either *the file* or *the database*, and is stored on disk and identified by you and Q&A by a unique filename.

So a database file contains the records, the records contain the fields, and the fields contain the information. If you search a database for some particular items of information contained in a record, you simply:

1. Tell Q&A which database file to open.

2. Indicate which records in that file you wish to retrieve.

3. View the fields in those records for the information you want. Additional factors have to be considered when designing your databases. For example, you'll need to tell Q&A about the *kind* of information that will be contained in your database's fields. Some fields may contain numbers, while others may contain money values, dates, or normal text.

But ahead of that you'll want to plan your design on paper by determining the *subject* of the database (what will the database keep track of for you — customers? suppliers? employees? invoices?), and how you'll want the form to look on screen.

In this chapter we'll design and work with three simple databases.

 Note: A copy of these databases, slightly modified, is located on the applications disk located in the back of the book. (See Chapter 11 for more information about the applications disk.) Don't use the provided copies yet, however. Creating a database from scratch will help you learn the program.

With a little practice, you'll soon get the hang of creating the forms, adding new records to the databases, and searching for the records you want to see and perhaps update. With no more complexity than this, you'll be able to create entire database applications, and be well on your way to automating as much of your office record-keeping as you want.

In the next chapter I'll move on to Q&A's more advanced database features — powerful tools to help you automate and control data entry, customize your databases for optimum performance, and perform mass operations on entire groups of selected database records.

Designing Your First Database Form

Before designing any database form (often called a *template*), first sketch out your requirements on paper. Doing so stimulates ideas about the information you need to include and how to organize it in the form. Q&A makes it easy to *re*design your database form at any time — add new fields, delete unnecessary ones, and reposition fields on the screen — but it makes sense to get as much of the form design as possible right the first time.

Don't be in a rush when creating a new database form. Consider the elements that will make up the database. Talk to others familiar with the way the records involved with this new database have been filled out and filed up to this point. Find out what items of information should be included in the database, and the order in which they should appear on the display. You want to include in your database all the particular items of information that will be useful to you and your coworkers, and make data entry flow smoothly and logically.

You don't want to pack the database with fields that no one will ever use, or omit fields that will be valuable to the business. Economy should influence your database design. Include too many unnecessary fields and you'll be wasting input time and disk space. Include too few and you won't take full advantage of the benefits offered by automation. Figure 3-2 offers a few suggestions on the information fields a customer file might include.

To start, we'll create a database to include most of the fields shown in Figure 3-2. Later on, to demonstrate how any database form can be redesigned we'll return to it to add a field or two, relocate existing fields, and enhance the form's appearance with a few aesthetic touches.

Speaking of aesthetics, try to make the form as pleasant to the eye as possible. When a database template is thrown together with little regard for the

Customer Database Elements to Consider

Individual's first, middle, and last name
Company name
 — Street address
 — City, State, Zip code (3 fields)
Phone number plus extension (2 fields)
Fax number
Customer number
~~Social Security number~~
Date customer was entered into the computer
Product class (what the customer buys from us)
Account type (retail or wholesale)
Credit limit
Total amount of purchases to date
Comments/notes about customer peculiarities

Figure 3-2: Making a List of the Information Fields to Include in a Customer Database. The Social Security number is crossed off the list because it will probably not be useful in a customer file. If it turns out to be important, you can always add it later.

organization and placement of fields, it can confuse the operator, make data entry more frustrating and difficult, and thus result in more errors.

Also, take care to make your field labels meaningful and as descriptive as possible. *You* may know that "PN" means "Phone Number," but someone else who uses your form later on may have no idea what it means, or may think it means "Part Number." And part numbers in phone number fields make the whole database just that much less useful.

Familiarize Yourself with Q&A'S Database Design Screen

Designing your database form is as simple as typing it on the computer screen while keeping in mind a few fundamental rules on which Q&A will always insist (see Figure 3-3). I'll refer to these rules as our first database creation progresses.

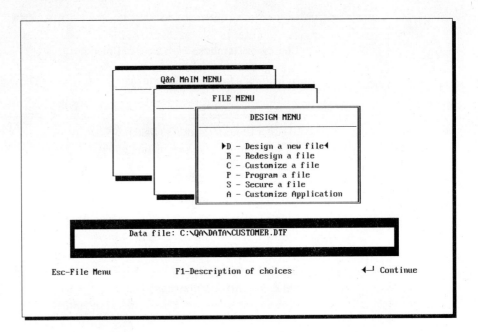

Figure 3-3: The Design Menu.

To get to the database Design menu:

1. At the Q&A Main menu select "File."

2. At the File menu choose "Design file."

3. At the Design menu select "Design a new file."

4. Q&A will prompt you for the name of this new database, and you'll probably want to use a name that describes the contents of the file. In our case it's "Customer." Type in **CUSTOMER** (upper or lowercase is okay). Q&A automatically adds a ".DTF" extension to all filenames in the File module.

Q&A will display a blank design screen (shown in Figure 3-4), ready for you to unleash your creative power.

The design screen includes four special lines at the bottom of the display, similar to those on the Type/Edit screen in the Write module:

The **Ruler** line has built-in tab stops (where the T's appear along the line) and helps you track the vertical distance of the cursor from the extreme left side of the form. Each tick mark is a single character column. Each number on the ruler line represents 10 character columns. A total of 80 horizontal character columns is available. As you move the cursor across the screen, a "ghost

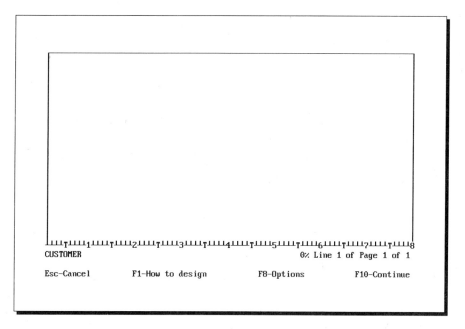

Figure 3-4: Q&A's Database Design Screen.

cursor" on the ruler line follows along to help you track your position on the display.

The **Status** line displays the database name, the percentage of available memory used by the design, the line number of the current screen page, the current screen page, and the total number of screen pages used so far in the form design — it shows 0 percent now because no fields have as yet been placed on the form. Q&A database forms can extend to 10 pages total. With 21 lines to a page, this give you a maximum of 210 lines on which to place your fields. The upper limit on fields per database is 2,045.

The **Message** line is used by Q&A to pass any necessary messages to you during the course of designing your database form.

The **Key Assignment line** offers you four alternatives:

- You can press **<Esc>** to exit from form design. If you try to **<Esc>** after typing anything on the form, Q&A will warn you that the design has not been saved and ask you to confirm. Should you decide at any time that you no longer want the form you've been designing, simply press **<Esc>** and answer Yes to confirm your desire to dump it.

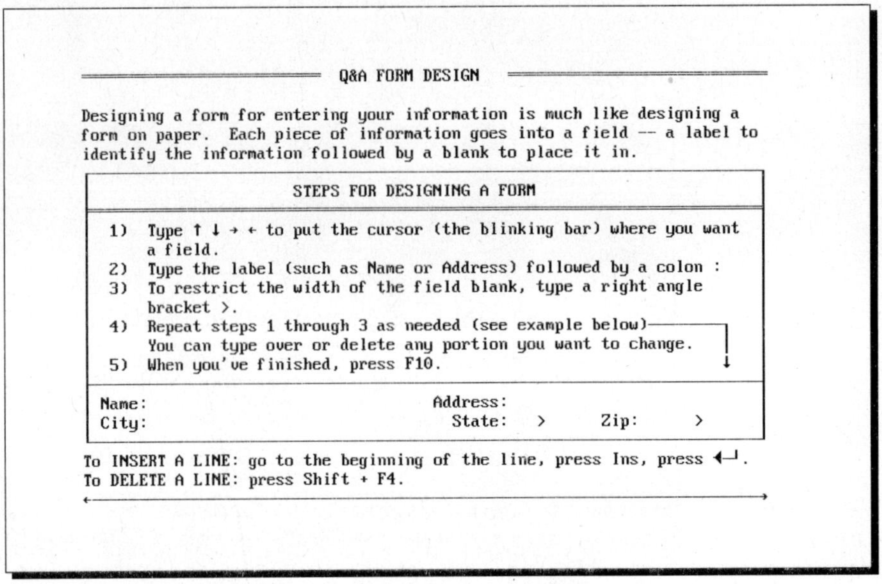

```
============================ Q&A FORM DESIGN ============================

Designing a form for entering your information is much like designing a
form on paper.  Each piece of information goes into a field -- a label to
identify the information followed by a blank to place it in.

  ┌─────────────────────────────────────────────────────────────────┐
  │              STEPS FOR DESIGNING A FORM                           │
  ├─────────────────────────────────────────────────────────────────┤
  │  1)  Type ↑ ↓ → ← to put the cursor (the blinking bar) where you want│
  │      a field.                                                     │
  │  2)  Type the label (such as Name or Address) followed by a colon :│
  │  3)  To restrict the width of the field blank, type a right angle │
  │      bracket >.                                                   │
  │  4)  Repeat steps 1 through 3 as needed (see example below)─────┐ │
  │      You can type over or delete any portion you want to change.│ │
  │  5)  When you've finished, press F10.                           ↓ │
  ├─────────────────────────────────────────────────────────────────┤
  │  Name:                          Address:                          │
  │  City:                             State:  >      Zip:      >      │
  └─────────────────────────────────────────────────────────────────┘

To INSERT A LINE: go to the beginning of the line, press Ins, press ↵ .
To DELETE A LINE: press Shift + F4.
```

Figure 3-5: Q&A's Help Screen Available During Database Design.

- You can press **<F1>** for help with designing your database form (see Figure 3-5).

- You can select design options (set tabs, center a line, uncenter a line, spell-check, draw lines and boxes) by pressing **<F8>**.

- When you finish designing the form, or want to save a partial design so you can take a break and come back to it later, press **<F10>**.

Placing the Information Fields on the Form

In a moment we'll lay out the fields on our Customer database form, typing in identifying labels and telling Q&A how much space to assign to each field. Before doing this, however, you should decide on the number of character spaces to allocate to each field.

A common problem people face after completing a database template is not having made the fields wide enough to accommodate the longest values that will need to be typed into them later during data entry. Everything seems to be going merrily along when up comes a last name like "Forthringstreicher," and suddenly that 15-character-long last name field just isn't long enough.

It's not a serious problem because you can always widen the field. But if you've got your form designed just like you want it, widening a field can upset the placement of other fields and result in a design compromise.

 Remember: Do what you can to predict the longest values your fields will have to accommodate — especially name and address fields — and define your field lengths during the initial design phase with these requirements in mind. It's better to have a little extra room for your data than not enough.

The following steps apply to laying out any database form. Look these over, and then proceed to the design of the Customer template.

1. With the blank design screen on the display, move the cursor to where you want to place your first field. You can place fields anywhere on the screen (you don't have to start at the upper-left corner), and you can place more than one field on a line. Keep in mind that Q&A recognizes the field that is closest to the upper-left corner of the screen as the first field of the form.

2. Type the descriptive field label — a word or two that reminds the user of the kind of information the field contains — followed by a **:** (colon) or a **<** (left angle bracket — Q&A's field delimiter symbol). The colon or **<** instructs Q&A to start the information blank connected to the label here, and continue the field to the right edge of the screen, to the next field, or to the end-field delimiter symbol, whichever comes first.

   Unlike the colon, the left angle bracket will not show on the data entry screen and makes for a less-cluttered form design, especially if the form contains a great many fields.

   Another use for the **<** is to define the beginning of a rectangular information blank (a multiline field) that can extend down the form for many lines, until it is interrupted by another field, ended by a **>** (right angle bracket — also a end-field delimiter), or reaches the bottom of the screen page.

 New: A field label is not mandatory. For example, you can design fields into your form with nothing more than a **<** or **:** to begin the information blank, and optionally a **>** to end it. These types of fields, often called *no-name* or *label-less* fields, are useful for invoice line items composed of groups of fields for part numbers, descriptions, quantities, prices, and amounts.

   A field defined with **<** and **>** during form design will not appear at all on the data entry screen until the cursor enters it, although it will behave like a field in every other respect. Q&A assigns an internal label to such fields so that you can still refer to them in programming statements, reports, and mail-merge applications. See the section on field names in the following chapter for more details.

(In the next chapter, we'll design a sophisticated invoice form that will incorporate a great many of these no-name fields.)

3. End your information blank in one of three ways — with a **>** (right angle bracket), by starting another field label, or at the right edge of the screen. Field labels followed by a **:** and with no end-field delimiter cannot extend onto the next line, whereas a field with a **<** following the field label *can*, as long as no text or other obstruction is encountered (see the discussion of multiline fields later in this chapter).

4. Repeat steps 1 through 3 until you've placed all your fields and the design is complete.

5. Press **<F10>** when finished to save the design. Saving the design does not cast it in stone, however. You can always go back later and redesign the form.

Here's further illustration of the various ways you can set the length of a Customer Name field.

Customer Name: (No end-field delimiter has been specified. The field extends to the right until it meets another field, any character, or the right edge of the screen.)

Customer Name< (The field extends to the right until it encounters another field, any character, or the **>** end-field delimiter. It may extend down several screen lines, but no farther than the bottom of the current screen page. Also, the **<** will not appear on the data entry form.)

Customer Name:	**>** (The field extends to the **>**.)
Customer Name<	**>** (The field extends to the **>**.)
Customer Name:	**Address:** (The Customer Name field ends two character spaces before the Address label.)

Remember: The **>** end-field delimiter will display on the design screen, but will not appear on the data entry screen.

Multiline Fields

When you need to create multiline memo or comments fields for lengthy text, you have two choices: you can design a large information blank into the form, or make the information blank any size and then use the Field Editor when adding or updating records to expand the size of the field in order to enter up to about 16 pages of text. The Field Editor feature is covered in detail later in this chapter.

The multiline field enables you to display all the text in the field without having to move the cursor to the field during data entry and pressing **<F6>** to open the Field Editor. The *dis*advantage of the multiline field is that it takes up a greater amount of space on your form, and you can't surround it with line draw or other ASCII graphics characters.

If you opt for a multiline field, you can design it in one of two different ways. Say, for example, you have a field labeled Product Notes, and you've positioned the label along the left edge of the screen with several blank lines below it. If you follow the label with a colon, and then place the end-field delimiter two lines down at the right side of the screen, the text entry area will look like this:

Product Notes: _____

_____

_____>

If you use the **<** (beginning of field) symbol in place of the colon, however, the same multiline field will give you this rectangular text entry area:

Product Notes< _____

_____

_____>

Note that in either type of multiline field you cannot place any other characters or fields on any of the same lines, and a field cannot extend onto the next screen page.

Adding Nonfield Text to the Form

You can add plain text to the form wherever you like. You might find it useful to add a few lines of instructions at the top or bottom, or down the right side of the screen, to assist the operator during data entry.

Tip: Don't try to squeeze too much text into the form — you can always create custom help screens and display special messages to guide your operator through data entry (see Chapter 4 for more details on this topic).

There's another trick to use if you want to build text instructions into the form design. You can place your instructive text on the next available screen page or pages so that the operator can simply press **<PgDn>** from the data entry portion of the form to access one or more screens of helpful information. Versions of Q&A that preceded 4.0 required you to place at least one legitimate field on every screen page you used; with Q&A 4.0, that's no longer necessary.

Another technique involves placing a series of fields on the screen in the form of a help directory, along these lines:

```
──────────────── HELP  DIRECTORY ────────────────

Place the cursor in the appropriate field and press <F1> for more info.

Shipping methods: > Terms: > Discounts: > Credits: > Backorders: >
```

During data entry, the operator can press **<Tab>** to move to any of these fields, press **<F1>**, and the custom help screen you created for that field will pop up with special instructions on how to handle situations that may arise during input. You can place a custom help screen behind any field on the form — it will be only as far away as the **<F1>** key. This topic is covered in greater detail in Chapter 4.

Cursor Navigation on the Design Screen

The cursor can be moved around the design in the same way you navigate a Write document. Table 3-1 shows what various keyboard actions will do.

Keep in mind that the **<F8>** Options menu, discussed in detail in Chapter 1, is available during database design and redesign, although your menu selections here are limited to the types of operations appropriate to database design.

While you're designing your database, remember that Q&A has design limitations that you can't exceed. Keeping them in mind now will save you a lot of time later (see Table 3-2).

Laying Out the Customer Database

If you plan to embellish your form design with nonfield text, lines, or boxes, this should be taken into account when placing your fields on the form. Don't place a field on the first line of the form if that line is going to be taken up by some descriptive nonfield text. Nor should you begin or end your fields against the left or right edges of the design screen if you plan to draw a box around them. If the first character of a field label is at the extreme left edge of the screen, for example, drawing a vertical line down the first character column will erase it.

During form design you can press **<F8>** for the Options menu and select from a variety of helpful procedures. From the Options menu you can set tabs,

Table 3-1
Cursor Navigation Keys You Can Use to Lay Out
Your Database Form

Key	Function
`<←>`	One character to the left
`<→>`	One character to the right
`<↑>`	One line up
`<↓>`	One line down
`<Ctrl→>`	Next word on the line
`<Ctrl←>`	Previous word on the line

To move up through the form:

Key	Function
`<Home>`	First character of the line
`<Home><Home>`	First character on the current screen
`<Home><Home><Home>`	First character of the form
`<Ctrl><Home>`	First character of the form
`<PgUp>`	To the top of the previous screen

To move down through the form:

Key	Function
`<End>`	Last character of the line
`<End><End>`	Last character on the current screen
`<End><End><End>`	Last character of the form
`<Ctrl-End>`	Last character of the form
`<PgDn>`	To the top of the next screen

Table 3-2
Q&A Database Design Limits (Maximums)

Lines per screen page	21
Lines per record	210
Pages per record	10
Fields per record	2,182
Fields per screen page	248

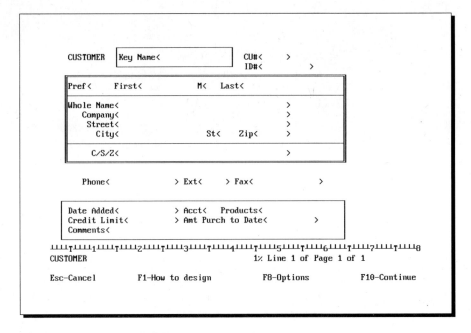

CUSTOMER   Key Name<   CU#<   >
                                   ID#<   >

Pref<   First<   M<   Last<

Whole Name<   >
    Company<   >
     Street<   >
       City<   St<   Zip< >

    C/S/Z<   >

      Phone<   > Ext< > Fax<   >

    Date Added<   > Acct< Products<
    Credit Limit<   > Amt Purch to Date<   >
    Comments<

CUSTOMER   1% Line 1 of Page 1 of 1

Esc-Cancel   F1-How to design   F8-Options   F10-Continue

Figure 3-6: Sample CUSTOMER.DTF Form Layout.

turn on the Draw feature, perform block copy-and-move operations, run a spelling check on field labels and text, and use the thesaurus to check for synonyms.

Also, when designing your initial form, work in overtype mode so that you don't inadvertently displace existing fields and lines. Figure 3-6, a sample CUSTOMER.DTF form design based on the fields suggested in Figure 3-2, shows the raw Customer form layout as it would look on the design screen *before* being saved.

Design Rationale

The following considerations were applied to this particular form design from my own experience with database forms and Q&A. Chances are your own design for a customer file would not look like this at all because your information needs (and thus your field requirements) are unique to your own business. The sample database presented here is only for purposes of illustration and to give you a few ideas you can take advantage of when designing your own forms.

- The form is confined to a single screen page so the operator sees the entire record during data entry, search, and update. Don't crowd your form by squeezing too many fields into a small area, but don't use multiple screen pages if all the fields fit comfortably onto a single page.

- The word "CUSTOMER" has been typed in the upper-left corner of the form. You can add supporting nonfield text anywhere on the form. Just don't place a : or a < after your text, or Q&A will think it's a field.

- Field labels identify the information the blanks will contain, abbreviated where possible to conserve space on the form. No two fields should have the same field label.

- The first characters of the field labels along the left side of the form were typed several character columns in from the left edge of the screen to leave room for line and box drawing; these graphic options were discussed in detail in the previous chapter. You can use them when designing your database forms.

- All the information blanks start with a < instead of a : to give the form a cleaner appearance on the data entry screen.

- A text field, Key Name, is included to make searches for customer records faster. The length of the field is set to 12 character spaces. This is intended to be a special field that will be used to look up the customer's record based on the most meaningful portion of the company name. That's why it was positioned as the first field on the form.

For example, if the company's full name is "Griswold Sporting Goods, Inc." only the word "Griswold" will be typed into the Key Name field during data entry. Then, if the operator should need to retrieve the record from the database, only the key name "Griswold" will need to be entered.

Note: Don't confuse this Key Name field *label* with *keyword*, a special Q&A information type.

- The CU# field was added for customer account numbers, along with a field (ID#) intended mainly for invoice use. The ID# field will contain the first five letters of the Key Name plus the five-digit zip code, so the record can be looked up by an invoice programming statement if the CU# is unknown. Both of these fields, along with the C/S/Z (for combined City, State, and Zip) will be filled in automatically by simple programming statements we'll incorporate into the form in Chapter 5.

- Assuming your company wants mail-merge capabilities and does business with both individuals and companies, the name and address area is designed to accommodate easy mail-merge and invoicing objectives (this topic is discussed in detail in Chapters 4 and 5).

Creating separate fields for the city, state, and zip code in the addresses makes it possible to search and sort customers by any of these criteria. Suppose you need a report of all the customers in Illinois (or Chicago, for that matter), sorted by zip code. If these items weren't in fields by themselves, you'd have a difficult task ahead of you.

As for the individual's name being broken down into several fields, consider what would happen if you wanted to run a mail-merge (see Chapter 5) of personalized form letters addressed to the buyers at your client companies.

If the name "Mr. John Smith" was all in one field, you'd have a heck of a time trying to work out a salutation like "Dear John:" or "Dear Mr. Smith:" because neither "Mr." nor "John" nor "Smith" is in its own field. You *could* address such letters "Dear Mr. John Smith:" but that would make them sound like a canned promotional mailing.

Having both whole names and whole addresses as well as the names and addresses broken down into their constituent parts is a tremendous advantage, as you'll see. We'll add a couple of programming statements here, too, so you won't have to input any of the name or address information twice on the same form.

- All the field lengths have been set to accommodate the data that will later be typed into them. The **St** (State) field will accommodate a three-letter Canadian province abbreviation, and the **Zip** field is just large enough for a 6-character Canadian postal code.

Field Information Types and Format Options

Once you've finished your field layout work and want to save the form design, pressing **<F10>** will take you to the next step in the process — the Format Spec — where you assign the information types the fields will contain, and the way you'd like the *contents* of your fields displayed on your forms.

The procedure involves three steps:

1. Specify **Information Type**. Tell Q&A the *type of value* you plan to enter in each database field (such as money, date, or number).

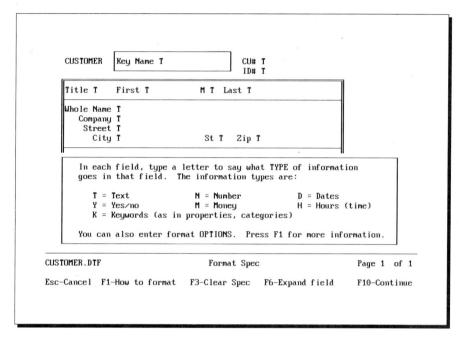

```
        CUSTOMER   Key Name T                        CU# T
                                                     ID# T

        Title T     First T          M T  Last T

        Whole Name T
          Company T
           Street T
             City T                 St T   Zip T

            In each field, type a letter to say what TYPE of information
            goes in that field.  The information types are:

               T = Text            N = Number          D = Dates
               Y = Yes/no          M = Money            H = Hours (time)
               K = Keywords (as in properties, categories)

            You can also enter format OPTIONS.  Press F1 for more information.


        CUSTOMER.DTF                    Format Spec               Page 1  of 1

        Esc-Cancel  F1-How to format   F3-Clear Spec   F6-Expand field   F10-Continue
```

Figure 3-7: Using the Format Spec with the Customer Database Form. When you press <F10> to save your database design, Q&A wants to know what information type each field will contain, and presumes text values for all fields until you specify otherwise.

2. Specify **Format Options**. Tell Q&A how you want the values to be displayed or positioned in the fields on the form (all uppercase, justified right, or numbers with two decimal places, for example).

3. Specify **Global Format Options**. Establish global conventions for how money values, decimal places, dates, and times will be displayed in your database fields.

Figure 3-7 shows the Customer database form at Q&A's Format Spec.

Assigning Field Information Types

The information type of a field may be different from what the field label indicates should be typed into it during data entry.

When you create a field label on your database form, the label serves as a guide to the operator to enter the appropriate information.

For example, you label a field "Phone Number" so that the input operator knows to type the phone number in that field. But to Q&A a phone number

Table 3-3
Database Information Types

Use these codes to tell Q&A the kind of information the field will contain.

Code	Field type	When to specify
T	Text	Name, address, phone number, zip code, mixed text and numbers, descriptive and conceptual information
N	Number	Numerical digits only: quantities, units, measures, numbers for computations.
M	Money	Dollars and cents, currency values
D	Date	Whole dates
H	Hours	Times of day only (not numbers of hours or minutes)
Y	Yes/No	Logical yes/no or true/false
K	Keyword	For categories where there may be more than one entry in the field

isn't a true number because it contains *nonnumerical characters* (parentheses, spaces, or dashes, for example). So the *information type* of the field must be specified as text, even though we tend to think of these as numbers.

Q&A won't use the field label to determine the type of value the field will contain. You have to specifically tell Q&A that a field will contain a number, a date, or a money value.

Careful attention to indicating proper field information types will help ensure a bright future for your database. You want to make sure that dates are understood by Q&A and stored as dates, money as money, and numbers as numbers. And if you don't enter the proper codes now, you may run into difficulty later when you try to perform operations such as searching, sorting, field programming, or arithmetic on these values.

When the Format Spec is displayed, Q&A assumes that all the fields on the form will be formatted as text fields. Table 3-3 shows a list of field information types and the letter codes representing them.

Text: If the field doesn't fit one of the other information types in Table 3-3, leave it as a text (**T**) field. Phone numbers, Social Security numbers, and zip codes with four-digit suffixes ("zip + 4") are text, not numbers. Any mixture of text and digits (sometimes referred to as "alphanumeric") is a text field.

Numbers: If you can (and will) do normal arithmetic on the value, you can code it as a number. Number field values can contain decimal places, but not fractions (such as "$^1/_2$").

If you don't plan to use the number — a zip code, for example — for counting, measuring, adding, subtracting, multiplying, or dividing, make it a text field. Q&A will allow you to enter only numerical digits, commas, and decimal points (periods) in a number field. The Global Format Options screen offers you display options for numbers.

Money: When you type a number into a field formatted for money values, Q&A converts it to dollars and cents. Global Format Options provides you with a selection of display alternatives for money values.

Dates: Any date field must be at least 10 characters in length and contain a whole date that consists of the month, day, and year (but not necessarily in that order). Dates can be entered in a variety of ways, but Q&A will automatically display them according to your preselected format (see Global Format Options discussion).

Hours: The time of day is entered into a field coded to contain hours, and it will be displayed in the format you select at the Global Format Options screen.

The reason Q&A insists on global defaults for numbers, money, dates, and hours is to allow arithmetic operations to be performed on them if required (you'll learn more about this in Chapter 4). For example, if a date format is displayed in a form as 6/23/90 (month/day/year), you'll want all your forms in that database to display any date entered in the same format. This enables you to add and subtract dates, or search on date fields, and get consistent answers from Q&A.

Yes/No: Also called a *logical* or *Boolean* field. Use this information type for fields that will contain values equivalent to yes or no, true or false. A Yes/No field will accept the following values: Y, YES, T, TRUE, 1, and N, NO, F, FALSE, and 0 (zero).

Keywords: An extremely versatile information type, keyword fields can add considerable power to your database applications. You format a field as a keyword field when you want it to contain multiple values, each of which has something in common with the others in the same field. A keyword can be a word, a character, or a phrase. What makes this type of field so unique is that it can contain several entries, and you can still search on a *single* entry.

For example, in our sample Customer database, we labeled one of the fields "Product Class," intending this to be a keyword field. To illustrate what you can do with a keyword field, suppose that you ran a mail-order distributing business selling computers, software, peripherals, add-ons, books, and so forth. You may stock and advertise 1,000 items or more, but each inventory item is classified by what *type* of item it is (such as computer, monitor, printer, keyboard, or book). In other words, you've assigned a product code (in addition to a stock number) to each item. For example, all monitors are product code 512, and all books are coded 650.

Perhaps you track your customers' purchases by product code so that you can periodically mail targeted promotional announcements to them. Here's where the keyword field comes into play.

If a customer has purchased product codes 512, 650, 200, and 340, you can enter all of these values, each separated by a ; (semicolon) in the keyword field, and then later ask Q&A for all the customer records that contain one, several, or any combination of the keywords. You could ferret out only those customers who've purchased a monitor, those who've purchased *both* a monitor and a printer, or those who've purchased *either* one.

In a video store customer database, you could have a keyword field for the general video subject the customer has rented from you (such as adventure, horror, comedy, or how-to), enabling you to sort out and mail a flier announcing a new comedy video to those customers who've rented comedy videos in the past.

People usually have hobbies. In an employee database, you could use a keyword field for hobbies, and separate out those employees who've indicated woodworking or skiing — or sports in general if that was a valid keyword category — when organizing a company athletic team.

Keyword entries must be consistent, however. You couldn't enter "ski trips" for one employee and "skiing" for another, and expect Q&A to recognize the two as the same hobby. You'd have to figure out a standard list of keywords and stick with them.

This discussion only touches on Q&A's powerful search capabilities when it comes to keyword fields. More on this later in the chapter when we look at defining database search criteria.

Entering Information Type and Option Codes

All the fields in our sample Customer database are formatted as text fields except Date Added (a date field), Product Class (a keyword field), Credit Limit, and $Purch to Date (both money fields). So far we have no number, hours, or yes/no fields.

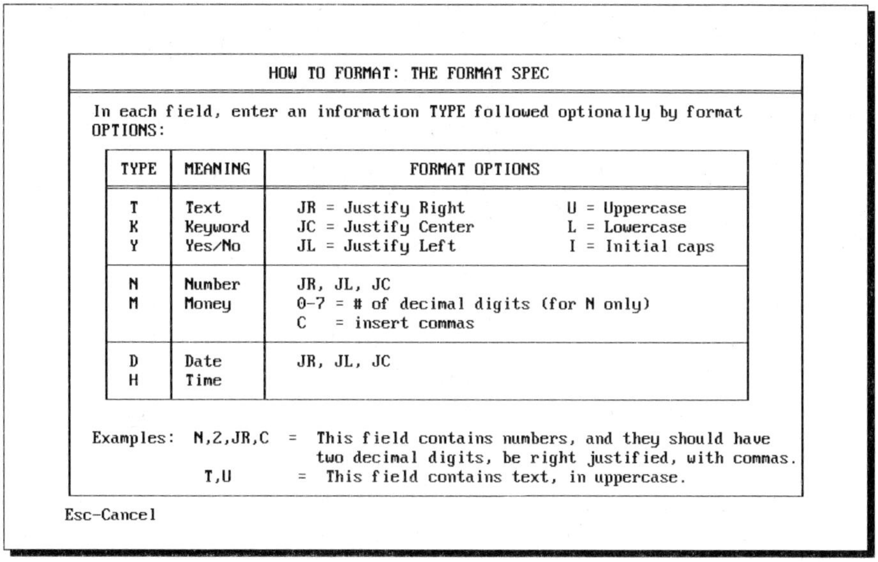

```
┌─────────────────────────────────────────────────────────────┐
│                                                               │
│          ┌─────────────────────────────────────────────┐     │
│          │          HOW TO FORMAT: THE FORMAT SPEC        │     │
│          ├─────────────────────────────────────────────┤     │
│          │ In each field, enter an information TYPE followed optionally by format │
│          │ OPTIONS:                                      │     │
│          │  ┌──────┬─────────┬──────────────────────────┐ │     │
│          │  │ TYPE │ MEANING │       FORMAT OPTIONS       │ │     │
│          │  ├──────┼─────────┼──────────────────────────┤ │     │
│          │  │  T   │ Text    │ JR = Justify Right   U = Uppercase │ │
│          │  │  K   │ Keyword │ JC = Justify Center  L = Lowercase │ │
│          │  │  Y   │ Yes/No  │ JL = Justify Left    I = Initial caps │ │
│          │  │      │         │                          │ │     │
│          │  │  N   │ Number  │ JR, JL, JC               │ │     │
│          │  │  M   │ Money   │ 0-7 = # of decimal digits (for N only) │ │
│          │  │      │         │ C   = insert commas      │ │     │
│          │  │      │         │                          │ │     │
│          │  │  D   │ Date    │ JR, JL, JC               │ │     │
│          │  │  H   │ Time    │                          │ │     │
│          │  └──────┴─────────┴──────────────────────────┘ │     │
│          │ Examples:  N,2,JR,C  =  This field contains numbers, and they should have │
│          │                         two decimal digits, be right justified, with commas. │
│          │            T,U       =  This field contains text, in uppercase. │     │
│          └─────────────────────────────────────────────┘     │
│   Esc-Cancel                                                  │
│                                                               │
└─────────────────────────────────────────────────────────────┘
```

Figure 3-8: File's Format Options Screen. It is displayed by pressing **<F1>** from the Format Spec.

To enter the proper information type for a field:

1. **<Tab>** to move forward, or **<Shift><Tab>** to move back to a field into which you want to change the **T** information type code to another type.

2. Type the code you want over the default **T** (for Text). Either an upper-case or lowercase letter is okay. If the field *is* a text field, just leave the **T** there.

3. Repeat these two steps to enter appropriate information type codes in the other fields.

4. Press **<F10>** when done, or optionally press **<F1>** to see the list of format options.

Field Formatting

At the same time you're entering your information type codes, you can also enter codes to tell Q&A how to present or display your entries in the fields on your form. You may want some of your database text field values to be displayed in all uppercase letters, or justified right, left, or center. To see the list of possibilities, press **<F1>** while at the Format Spec (see Figure 3-8).

If the field isn't wide enough to accept the code, press **<F6>** to expand the field, type in the code (separating each code with a comma), and press **<F10>**

to return to the form. You'll notice a small arrow (→)at the end of the field, indicating that there is more to the code for that field than is visible.

You can see from Figure 3-8 that you have a variety of options when it comes to how Q&A will display the values entered in your database fields. Specifying a text field as **U** for uppercase, for example, results in lowercase letters being converted to uppercase as they're typed into the field during data entry.

If a field is formatted with the **JR** code, the contents of the field, once entered, will be placed at the far right end of the information blank. A **JL** code will place the value at the far left of the field (all fields in Q&A will be displayed left-justified unless you specify right (JR) or center (JC) justification).

For number fields, you can specify how many decimal places the field will accept, and also whether commas should be placed in numbers of 1,000 or more. Commas for money values can also be specified.

Whenever you enter a format-option code, type a comma after the information-type code and then type in the option code. If you're entering several option codes, place a comma between each one.

Field Information Types and Valid Formatting Options

The ability to format a field with the following commands allows text already entered to be changed to the new format.

T (Text), **K** (Keyword), **Y** (Yes/No): These fields can be formatted with the following options: **JR** (Justify Right), **JL** (Justify Left), **JC** (Justify Center), **U** (all Uppercase), **L** (all Lowercase), **I** (Initial capitals, or "caps"). You can select justification *and* all uppercase, all lowercase, or initial capitals. **I** (Initial caps) capitalizes the first letter in the field, and each letter following a space. For example, **T, JC, I** means the text in the field is center-justified and displayed in initial capitals; **K, U** indicates a keyword field displayed in uppercase.

If you format a field for all capital text, lowercase letters will be converted to uppercase as they are typed. An all lowercase field will similarly convert uppercase letters to lowercase.

N (Number): The following option codes can be used for number fields: **JR**, **JL**, **JC**, **C**, **Nn** — where n is the number of digits to the right of the decimal point. For example, **N0, JR** means this is a right-justified number field with no decimal digits and no commas; **N2, C, JC** specifies a center-justified number field with two decimal places and commas.

M (Money): You can use the same format-option codes for money as you can for numbers, with the exception of the decimal digits option. (See Global Format Options discussion.) For example, **M, JR** means format this as right-justified money field.

D (Date), **H** (Hours). You can use **JR, JL, JC,** and Global Format Options.

For our Customer database, we'll let Q&A's justify-left default apply to all fields. The Key Name, CU#, and ID# fields should be set to **U** for all uppercase, and the other text fields, except for zip and C/S/Z can be set to **I** for initial caps. The zip code field should be set to **T** (text) as it's not a number one would use in arithmetic operations — sorting, yes, but arithmetic, no.

Information-type and format-option codes do not have to be permanent. You can always go back and change them later (even after you've added records to your database) should you discover that a different code for a field would be more suitable (you'll find out how to do this in the next chapter). To enter optional formatting codes at the Format Spec:

1. Use **<Tab>** or **<Shift><Tab>** to move to the field for which you want to specify a format option.

2. Type a comma after the information type in that field, and then type the format code. To enter an additional format code in that same field, type another comma, and then enter the second format code. If the field isn't wide enough to display the codes, press **<F6>** to expand the field, type in the code or codes (with a comma between each), and press **<F10>** to return to the form.

3. Repeat steps 1 and 2 to add format codes to other fields on the form.

Initial Caps Format Option

Instructing Q&A in advance to automatically capitalize the first letter of each word in a field can be important if you plan to use the mail-merge feature later on. Suppose your name were (Mrs.) Katherine Jones, and you received a cover letter and catalog from a company you'd purchased from in the past. Which of the below cover letter formats would strike you as more professional?

```
MRS. KATHERINE JONES      SEPTEMBER 6, 1990
1234 HAWTHORNE BL.
SHAWNEE PLAINS, ND 50044


DEAR MRS. JONES:
```

or

```
Mrs. Katherine Jones      September 6, 1990
1234 Hawthorne Bl
Shawnee Plains, ND 50044


Dear Mrs. Jones:
```

People normally don't use all uppercase letters in correspondence; they use an appropriate combination of uppercase and lowercase. Two-letter state abbreviations, however, are typically typed in capital letters.

If you tell Q&A to use the initial capitals (**I**) option for name, address, city, and other text fields, the first letter in the field will be capitalized, along with the first letter following a space. Just remember that if you select the initial caps format option, the "del" in a name like "Maria del Rio" will be capitalized.

Initial caps in name/address fields may *not* be your best alternative if, for example, these fields will only be merged with mailing labels or used to address envelopes. The post office publishes a standardized name/address format for mailing pieces (what the automatic scanners used by the postal service can easily read to determine the delivery destination), and this format includes all capital letters with no punctuation. So the format of your database name/address fields should be determined by what purpose that format is intended to serve.

Consider formatting these fields in initial caps for data entry and merge correspondence, and then changing the format to all caps when you're ready to run mailing labels or address envelopes. Q&A can do it. Formatting options only control how information is *displayed*, not how it's stored in disk.

When you've finished with your information type and format option coding, press **<F10>** to display the Global Format Options screen, the final step in this beginning database design lesson.

Global Format Options

If any of your database fields were formatted as **N** (Number), **M** (Money), **D** (Date), or **H** (Hours), you'll get the Global Format Options screen in Figure 3-9 when you press **<F10>** from the Format Spec. Here you can choose how your date, hour, money, and number values will be displayed when you type these values into your database fields.

To change any of the preset selections, use your cursor keys to navigate to the field, and select the option you want. Press **<F10>** when done to save your new selections.

Currency symbol: This is preset to the good old dollar sign. You can make the currency symbol any characters you'd like. ASCII 156, for example, will give you the British pounds symbol (£). If you're selling to a country that uses another kind of dollar (Australia, Canada), you can type in US$ (United States dollars) as your currency symbol (so you'll get paid in *your* dollars, not theirs), and it will be placed in front of all money values. This, however, may require you to lengthen your money fields by a few spaces to accommodate the additional characters.

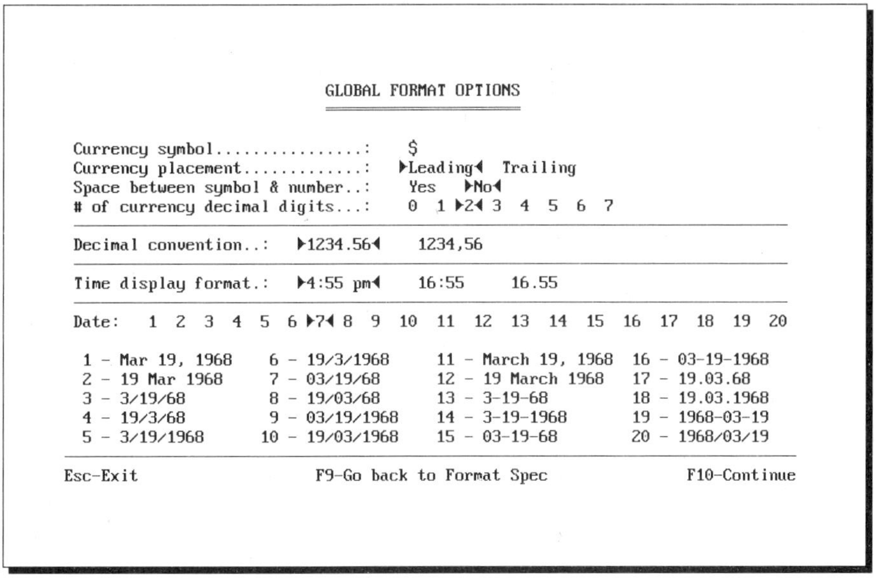

```
                          GLOBAL FORMAT OPTIONS


    Currency symbol...............:     $
    Currency placement............:    ▶Leading◀  Trailing
    Space between symbol & number..:    Yes   ▶No◀
    # of currency decimal digits...:    0  1 ▶2◀ 3  4  5  6  7

    Decimal convention..:  ▶1234.56◀    1234,56

    Time display format.:  ▶4:55 pm◀    16:55     16.55

    Date:   1  2  3  4  5  6 ▶7◀ 8  9  10  11  12  13  14  15  16  17  18  19  20

     1 - Mar 19, 1968      6 - 19/3/1968     11 - March 19, 1968   16 - 03-19-1968
     2 - 19 Mar 1968       7 - 03/19/68      12 - 19 March 1968    17 - 19.03.68
     3 - 3/19/68           8 - 19/03/68      13 - 3-19-68          18 - 19.03.1968
     4 - 19/3/68           9 - 03/19/1968    14 - 3-19-1968        19 - 1968-03-19
     5 - 3/19/1968        10 - 19/03/1968    15 - 03-19-68         20 - 1968/03/19

    Esc-Exit                    F9-Go back to Format Spec             F10-Continue
```

Figure 3-9: The Global Format Options Screen.

Currency placement: Tell Q&A whether you want the currency symbol placed in front of (leading) or behind (trailing) the actual money value.

Space between symbol and number: Change the preset "No" to "Yes" if you want Q&A to add a space between the currency symbol and the money value, for the sake of appearance.

Number of currency decimal digits: The preset is two. You can select from zero to seven.

Decimal convention: The North American custom is to use a period as the decimal between dollars and cents. Other countries use commas to indicate the separation between larger and smaller units of currency. If you select the "," decimal option, you must then use a semicolon (;) wherever you would otherwise use a comma (in programming statements, for example), or Q&A won't be able to interpret your instructions correctly.

Time display format: Let Q&A know here how you want your hours and minutes displayed.

Date format: You have a whopping 20 choices here! Select the one that best suits your fancy. But don't select a format that could result in a date too long to fit in your date fields! If the field is only 10 characters (the minimum for any date field), you can't very well hope to squeeze "January 23, 1990" into it.

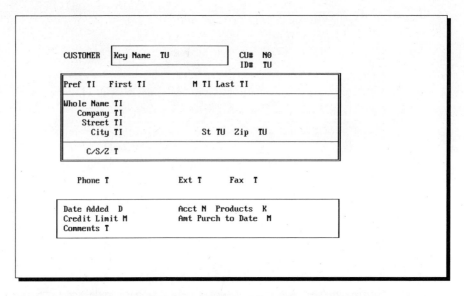

Figure 3-10: Sample Customer Database. It contains information type and formatting option codes in the fields.

You can always go back to the Format Spec from the Global Options screen by pressing **<F9>** (**<F9>** in Q&A usually means "go back"). When you've finished setting your Global Options, or you have no changes to make, press **<F10>**. Figure 3-10 shows our Customer Database form with the format options specified. There are no justification codes here because we're taking advantage of Q&A's left-justify default.

Redesigning Your Database Form

No matter how thoroughly you plan and sketch out your database form before and during the initial on-screen design phase, chances are you'll need to go back several times to rework the form to get it exactly like you want it.

Designing a database form is usually a repetitive process: aesthetics are involved, functionality plays an important role, and the ease with which an operator can move through the form to fill the proper fields has to be a high priority. Such considerations don't always occur to one during the initial design.

Q&A is a forms-based file manager; virtually all the operations you will do with the database — from entering new records, searching, sorting, and updating, to mail merging with documents and creating reports — will involve your database form design. You're going to have to look at it day in and day out.

After you use your form for a while you may realize that you left out a field that should have been included at the start. Or you'll see that a field you've placed over here really belongs over there. Your input operator may bring to your attention a deficiency in the logical flow of fields across and down the screen.

A common situation occurs when too little thought was given to the document or list that the operator would be using to enter the initial batch of forms in the new database.

For example, you may have paper forms with the values running 1, 2, 3, 4, and so on, from left to right across the page, but a database form with the fields running 3, 2, 1, and 4 starting somewhere in the middle of the display. Getting the information out of those documents and into the database would be a tedious chore.

Because you can't easily change the lists or paper forms to input, the database form itself is prime for a redesign. Better yet, the format of the input documents should have been taken into account *before* the database form was laid out, but that's not always practical.

If you're embarking on a form redesign before any records have been added to the database, Q&A won't need to do any reorganizing of the data because there's none to reorganize. But if you've already entered a number of forms, it's a different story.

Depending on how much information has been entered into the database, Q&A will need time to reorganize it in accord with your design changes. This may take only a moment or two. If your database is large with a number of speedy (indexes that are frequently searched) fields, it may take considerably longer. Q&A will let you know it's working and when the reorganizing process has been completed.

Always Back Up Your Database Before Redesigning!

Before you make any modifications to a database, be sure you have a backup copy of it. Q&A will always warn you if you're about to do something that will result in the loss of data, but the ways in which data can be inadvertently dumped or scrambled during a redesign are too numerous to mention. *Always make a backup copy of your database file before making even the smallest change to the form.*

Here's one of the fastest ways to do it:

1. Choose File from the Q&A Main menu.

2. Select Backup from the File menu.

3. At the "Filename" prompt type in the name of the database you plan to redesign.

4. When the "Backup to" prompt appears, type in the other disk or drive you want to back up the file to, and then type in the same database name again. You can't have two identical filenames in the same directory.

If the database is small enough to fit on a floppy disk, back it up to one and tuck that disk away for safekeeping. If your hard drive is partitioned (into drives C: and D:, for example), you can back up the database to another hard disk partition, and use the same filename. If you only have the one hard drive partition, you can back up the file to a different directory.

Getting the Forms on Screen for a Redesign

1. Select File from the Q&A Main menu.

2. Choose Design File from the File menu.

3. Select Redesign from the Design File menu.

4. At the "File name" prompt, type in the name of the database you want to redesign, and press **<Enter>**.

Now, you can:

- Edit a field label.

- Shorten or lengthen an information blank (field).

- Move a field.

- Add a new field.

- Delete a field.

- Add, delete, or change nonfield text.

- Add, delete, or change graphic lines and boxes.

Warning: Unless you're deleting a field altogether, do not change or delete any of Q&A's internal codes. These are the codes AA, AB, AC, and so forth, displayed after each field label on the form. If you change these codes and your database contains data, that data will be in serious trouble! *Leave these codes alone unless you want to permanently get rid of the field and any data it may contain!*

- If you move a field, move the internal Q&A code along with it.

- If you accidentally change or erase a code, type it back in *exactly* as it was, including capital or lowercase letters with no spaces between them.

- If you inadvertently change or delete a code and don't know what to do, press **<Esc>** to back out of the redesign, answer "Yes" to Q&A's warning, and then start at step 1 above again.

During the redesign, your changes to the form are not saved to disk until you press **<F10>**. This means that you're working on a "copy" of your last saved design. When you **<Esc>** from a redesign before saving, your last saved design will remain intact.

5. When you've finished your redesign, press **<F10>** for the Format Spec. If you've shortened or deleted any fields that *may* result in the loss of data, Q&A will warn you and give you the opportunity either to return to the form (with your changes during the current session lost), or confirm that the potential data loss is okay. (If you've shortened the length of a field, any values in that field in the database extending beyond the new field end point will be truncated at that point.)

6. Change the information types and format options for as many fields as necessary. Don't forget to enter new types and format options for any new fields (see the Field Information Types and Format Options sections in this chapter).

7. Press **<F10>** when you finish. If your database contains any money, number, date, or time field, the Global Format Options screen will be displayed for you to make any needed changes.

8. Press **<F10>** to return to the File Design menu.

Changing the Form Design

The same techniques you used during the initial form design can be used for any redesign. Use the cursor keys to move up and down, left and right. In typeover mode you can use the space bar to delete fields. Pressing the space bar in insert mode while to the left of a field will move the field farther to the right, while pressing the **<Del>** key from the same position will pull the field toward the left side of the display. Most all the word processing features you would use to move text around in a document will work when designing or redesigning a database form. (See the section in this chapter on placing information fields in forms.)

Again, be very careful not to change or delete any of Q&A's internal codes unless you want to delete a field, and any data in it, *permanently*.

To change a field label: Because a label is only text, just type over it to change it, or press **<Insert>** to insert characters within it. Be sure not to erase any **<** or **:** symbols — these marks tell Q&A where to begin the information blank.

To shorten or lengthen a field: Simply delete or add spaces between the start of the information blank and its end.

If you shorten the field with the **<Del>** key, any other fields to the right on the same line will be pulled leftward toward the cursor position.

If you use the space bar in insert mode to lengthen the field, any fields to the right of the cursor on the same line will be pushed farther to the right.

If data has been entered into the database, be sure you've backed up this database before shortening any fields.

To move a field: One method of changing the location of a field on the form is to leave the original field where it is and move the cursor to the new location; then type out the field name and demarcation symbols (**:**, **<**, and **>**), being certain to allow the same number of information blank spaces in the duplicate field as in the original field. Type in the Q&A internal field code (field tag) *exactly* as it appears in the original field and then delete the original field.

You can also press **<Shift><F5>** (the Move command), highlight the entire field (from the first letter of the label to the last space or **>** in the information blank), press **<F10>**, move the cursor to the new location, and press **<F10>** again to place the field there. This and other similar procedures can be selected from the **<F8>** "Block operations" submenu.

To add a new field: Use insert mode to avoid accidentally overtyping an existing field.

Move the cursor to where you want the field to begin, and simply type in the field label, along with the **:** or **<** to define the beginning of the information blank. Don't assign an internal field code to a new field — Q&A figures this out on its own.

If you need to add a new blank line to the form, place the cursor at the left edge of the screen on the line below where you want the new line, and, in insert mode, press **<Enter>**. Everything below that line will be pushed down one line to make room for the new one.

Be sure to move the multiline **>** delimiter if you're adding a new line for the purpose of making an existing multiline field longer.

To delete a field: When deleting a field, delete everything connected with it: the label, the field tag, and the colon or angle brackets. Deleting a field means the loss of any data connected to it.

To change a field's information type or format option: When you've finished your redesign, press **<F10>** for the Format Spec. Press **<Tab>** to move to the appropriate fields and enter your new information types and/or format option codes as previously discussed. Press **<F10>** when you've made your changes.

If your database contains any money, number, date, or time fields, the Global Format Options screen will be displayed. Change any settings as necessary, and press **<F10>** to complete the database redesign and return to the File Design menu.

Designing Inventory & Employee Databases

Now that you're familiar with the steps involved in basic database form design in Q&A, and just before we look at how to enter records into the file and search and update existing database records, let's put together a couple simple databases — one to keep track of inventory items and another to record company employee information. In the next chapter we'll design a far more complex database form for invoicing.

Again, please keep in mind that these are only *sample* databases designs suggesting fields that *may* be appropriate. Your own needs are likely to be quite different, and so your fields and form designs will be different.

The form layouts will be shown first, followed by a listing of the fields that were included in the form and a brief explanation as to *why* they were included, along with the widths of the fields, their information types, and suggested format options.

For the inventory database (which I'll name STOCK.DTF), we'll design the form around a hypothetical publisher/distributor who sells books, audiotapes, and videotapes at both wholesale and retail. A specific application such as this calls for an array of different field types and lengths, and will add realism to our queries, reports, and other Q&A activities as we move through the book. In Chapter 10, when we're prepared to integrate our databases into a complete business system, we'll redesign this form to accommodate a wider variety of products and applications.

An Inventory Database Application

The STOCK.DTF form is designed to provide:

- A record of each item in the inventory.

- Up-to-date status of each stock item.

- Basic item activity (bought, sold, received, open purchase orders).

- Particulars about items to answer customer queries.

- Fields to accommodate invoicing and purchase order lookup functions.

```
        Stk#<     >
                                              Date Added<           >
    ┌══════════════════ INVENTORY ITEM ═══════════════════════════┐
    │ Full Title<                                                  │
    │ Short Title<                      >                          │
    │ Author First<              > Author Last<                    │
    └──────────────────────────────────────────────────────────────┘

    HB/PB/AT/VT<   ISBN<           Subject Codes<
    Description<
                                                                    >
    Vendor<                Vendor#<   Case Qty<   Case Wght<   Item Wght<
    Cost<         List<        Discount<   20%<       40%<       50%<    >

    ┌───────────────┬────────────────┬────────────────┬─────────────────┐
    │ Sold Today<   │ Rec'd Today<   │ Qty On Hand<   │ Reorder Level<  │
    └───────────────┴────────────────┴────────────────┴─────────────────┘

    Sold YTD<    Bought YTD<    PO Date<         PO#<     Qty<     Cl?< >
    ┌─────────────────────────────┐          ┌─────────────────────────┐
    │ Physical Count<             │          │ Shelf Location<         │
    └─────────────────────────────┘          └─────────────────────────┘
    ⊥⊥⊥⊤⊥⊥⊥⊥₁⊥⊥⊥⊤⊥⊥⊥⊥₂⊥⊥⊥⊤⊥⊥⊥⊥₃⊥⊥⊥⊤⊥⊥⊥⊥₄⊥⊥⊥⊤⊥⊥⊥⊥₅⊥⊥⊥⊤⊥⊥₆⊥⊥⊥⊤⊥⊥⊥⊥₇⊥⊥⊥⊤⊥⊥⊥₈
    STOCK                                   2% Line 21 of Page 1 of 1

    Esc-Cancel       F1-How to design        F8-Options       F10-Continue
```

Figure 3-11: Sample STOCK.DTF Form Design for Keeping Track of Inventory Items.

- Fields for management decision-making (from the records themselves, or from reports compiled from the records).

- Enough data to assist in the compilation of published catalogs or price listings of available items.

Looking over the form in Figure 3-11, notice how certain associated fields have been grouped by the boxes drawn around them. This breaks the form up into areas and makes it easier to spot the fields you may be looking for during search and update operations. Too many boxes, however, can crowd a form — you want to leave "breathing space" wherever possible.

Figure 3-12 shows the form filled in with sample data. Because of the quantity of fields in this STOCK.DTF form (33 of them so far), an argument could be made for allocating the fields over *two* screen pages instead of the one screen page used here, thus increasing the form's field-to-empty-space ratio and perhaps, for some, adding a measure of visual attractiveness.

Table 3-4 gives a brief rundown of the fields in the STOCK.DTF database form shown in Figure 3-11, along with the purposes they serve (or will serve in the coming chapters) and formatting considerations.

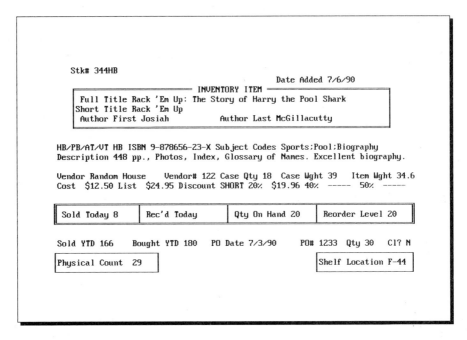

```
     Stk# 344HB
                                      Date Added 7/6/90
                      ═══════════ INVENTORY ITEM ═══════════
                    │ Full Title Rack 'Em Up: The Story of Harry the Pool Shark │
                    │ Short Title Rack 'Em Up                                   │
                    │ Author First Josiah            Author Last McGillacutty   │

     HB/PB/AT/VT HB ISBN 9-878656-23-X Subject Codes Sports;Pool;Biography
     Description 448 pp., Photos, Index, Glossary of Names. Excellent biography.

     Vendor Random House    Vendor# 122 Case Qty 18  Case Wght 39   Item Wght 34.6
     Cost  $12.50 List  $24.95 Discount SHORT 20%  $19.96 40%  ─────  50%  ─────

     ┌───────────────────┬────────────────┬────────────────────┬──────────────────┐
     │ Sold Today 8      │ Rec'd Today    │ Qty On Hand 20     │ Reorder Level 20 │
     └───────────────────┴────────────────┴────────────────────┴──────────────────┘

     Sold YTD 166    Bought YTD 180   PO Date 7/3/90    PO# 1233  Qty 30   Cl? N
     ┌───────────────────────────┐                    ┌──────────────────────────┐
     │ Physical Count   29       │                    │ Shelf Location F-44      │
     └───────────────────────────┘                    └──────────────────────────┘
```

Figure 3-12: The STOCK.DTF Sample Form with Values Entered.

Don't worry if at this point you find yourself wondering why a particular field is there, or how you go about filling it in. We'll customize some of these fields to fill in themselves in the next chapter.

In Chapter 6, many of these fields will play an important role in creating useful management reports.

As you look over these field types, labels, and explanations, do it with an eye toward an inventory database of your own that will meet *your* company's unique requirements.

An Employee Database Application

Now let's create a sample employee database with the filename EMPLOYEE.DTF. We'll make this one a *two-page* form, and add a little artistic flourish to the first of the two screen pages.

This is not a payroll application, and we're not going to attempt to create a database to include the employee's entire employment application, history, or resume. What we want is information about the employee that's likely to be

Table 3-4
Fields in the STOCK.DTF Form

Field Label	Format*	Purpose of the Field
Stk#	5, T, U	First field on the form to aid form retrieval; alphanumeric (text) to handle stock numbers with descriptive letter suffixes. Your stock numbers, of course, may be much longer than the five characters allotted here.
Date Added	13, D	A 13-character date field to record the date a new stock number was added to the file. Later, we'll tell Q&A to auto-type the current date in this field anytime a new stock number is added to the file.
Full Title	54, T	Titles of books and tapes can be long. This field will contain the full title of the item. You could format it as uppercase (U), initial caps (I), or simply rely on the input operator to capitalize as appropriate.
Short Title	30, T	You'll need to contain the length of the title if you plan to use it in an invoice application. This one is limited to 30 characters so it will fit on a single invoice line along with the stock number, list price, net price, and amount.
Author First	15, T	The author's first name.
Author Last	23, T	The author's last name. The author's first and last name are placed in different fields to aid in searching and catalog indexing by author name should that be desired.
HB/PB/AT/VT	2, T, U	This field will contain a code that identifies the item as either a hardbound or paperback book, or an audiotape or videotape. Later we'll restrict the field so the operator will only be able to enter one of these four values.

(continued)

---

* Number of characters, T=text, K=keyword, Y=yes/no, M=money, N=number, D=date, U=uppercase, JR=justify right, N (numeral)=number+decimal digits

Table 3-4 *(continued)*

Field Label	Format*	Purpose of the Field
ISBN	13, T, U	Books have 13-character International Standard Book Numbers (ISBNs) that are important for customer ordering and publisher/distributor cataloging.
Subject Code	31, K	A Keyword field. A title could involve more than one subject (for example, Sports; Biography). The field will contain predefined keywords, so if you or a customer want to know how many titles you have on "sports" or "biography," you'll be able to pull a quick report to answer the question.
Vendor	15, T	This field will contain the abbreviated name of the distributor from which you purchased the item.
Vendor#	3, N	The supplier's preassigned vendor code number. It's been formatted as a number because we may later want to ask Q&A for a list of vendors sorted by vendor number.
Case Qty	4, N	The quantity of this stock number packaged per case, box, or carton. This may be useful if you want to offer customers additional discounts for purchasing by the case (it saves packaging time and materials).
Case Wght	4, N0	The weight of a case or carton of this stock number rounded off to the nearest pound (N0 = Number with no decimal digits). This is useful for calculating shipping charges without having to reweigh the carton.
Item Wght	4, N1	The weight of a single stock number item in ounces, rounded off to the nearest 1/10th of an ounce. This field could be used to tell a customer what the shipping charge on the item will be, or to calculate the total shipping weight of all items on an invoice for billing purposes. *(continued)*

* Number of characters, T=text, K=keyword, Y=yes/no, M=money, N=number, D=date, U=uppercase, JR=justify right, N (numeral)=number+decimal digits

Table 3-4 (continued)

Field Label	Format*	Purpose of the Field
Cost	7, M, JR	What the item cost you. A 7-character field will permit a money value of up to $999.99. The field is formatted for money and justified right.
List	7, M, JR	Your list or retail price for the title.
Discount	T, U	Books are often sold to resellers at what are called "Trade" and "Short" discounts. A short discount is typically 20 percent off list, and a trade discount can be 40 percent off list or more. In this field the operator will be able to enter SHORT or TRADE, but no other value.
20% 40% 50%	7, M, JR	These three fields are all seven-character fields formatted to justify right. Depending on whether Short or Trade was entered in the previous field, we'll have Q&A calculate the net prices for these three fields automatically, based on the list price above.
Sold Today	4, N0	This field will contain the number of units of the stock number sold once the day's invoices have been totaled up and the figures are available. Several quick methods of obtaining the value and posting it to this field will be discussed in subsequent chapters.
Rec'd Today	4, N0	Incoming quantities (from purchase orders) of the stock numbers will be posted to this field.
Qty On Hand	4, N0	This field will show how many of the particular stock number are available to fill orders, and will receive its value based on a calculation between the previous on hand quantity, the quantity sold, and the quantity received.
Reorder Level	4, N0	The minimum quantity permitted before more of the stock number is ordered from the supplier.

(continued)

* Number of characters, T=text, K=keyword, Y=yes/no, M=money, N=number, D=date, U=uppercase, JR=justify right, N (numeral)=number+decimal digits

Table 3-4 *(continued)*

Field Label	Format*	Purpose of the Field
Sold YTD	6, N0	Sold Year-to-Date. the quantity of this stock number sold so far this year. The value in this field could represent sales over any period of time; for example, quantity sold since the stock number was added to the file, or sold month to date. The field will be automatically updated by its current value added to the quantity sold today.
Bought YTD	6, N0	Bought (or purchased) Year-to-Date. The field contains the quantity of this stock number ordered from outside suppliers during the period. It is another automatically updated field.
PO Date	10, D	You may want your stock number records to show if and when a purchase order was placed for more of the item — this is handy if you're low on stock and need quick reassurance that more is on the way.
PO#	5, N0	The number of the open purchase order in case you need to look up that PO.
Qty	4, N0	The quantity of this stock number on order with the above PO#.
Cl?	1, Y, U	A Yes/No field that closes the purchase order and updates the inventory record when the items on the PO have been received and entered into the stock number record.
Physical Count	5, N0	When doing a physical inventory, this field will come in handy. You would enter the count of the item here, and use it as the basis for inventory reconciliation, or preparing inventory discrepancy and valuation reports (more on this in Chapter 6).

(continued)

* Number of characters, T=text, K=keyword, Y=yes/no, M=money, N=number, D=date, U=uppercase, JR=justify right, N (numeral)=number+decimal digits

Table 3-4 *(continued)*

Field Label	Format*	Purpose of the Field
Shelf Location	4, T, U	This field will tell the operator where the item is located in the warehouse. Can be printed on invoices, sales orders, or pick slips to tell warehouse personnel where to find the item. "D4," for example, could be used to denote Unit D, Shelf Number 4.

* Number of characters, T=text, K=keyword, Y=yes/no, M=money, N=number, D=date, U=uppercase, JR=justify right, N (numeral)=number+decimal digits

needed during the course of employment. Figure 3-13 shows the two screen pages, followed by a brief description of the fields.

Notice that in the design of this employee database form, unlike STOCK.DTF, the field labels have been typed in all capital letters, and colons have been used to indicate the beginning of the information blanks that do not extend beyond the line they're on. This is simply a matter of preference.

If your field labels are in caps, you might want to use normal upper- and lowercase (or initial caps) for your field values, in order to provide a better visual contrast between the field labels and their related values.

The fancy border around the form's first screen page was created using ASCII graphics character 177 for the outer portion of the border (one each of these characters along the top and bottom of the screen, and three in a row along the left and right edges), and Q&A's own double-line draw for the inner portion of the border. Borders like this provide a pleasant on-screen visual effect to the form.

To access the IBM ASCII graphic character set, hold down the **<Alt>** key while pressing the decimal number of the character you want (see Appendix C). That character will appear at the cursor position.

To draw lines and boxes, press **<F8>** from the form design screen, and choose Draw from the "Lay out page" submenu. Use your cursor keys for single lines and boxes, and your numeric keypad cursor keys, in conjunction with the **<Shift>** key, for double lines and boxes. Press **<F10>** to end drawing and return to normal text character mode.

```
                              EMPLOYEES

  ┌──────────────────────────────────────────────────────────────┐
  │ LAST:                    FIRST:              MIDDLE:           │
  │ ADDRESS:                            HOME PHONE:                │
  │ CITY:                      STATE:    ZIPCODE:       >          │
  └──────────────────────────────────────────────────────────────┘

     SEX:   BIRTHDATE:            SOCIAL SECURITY NO:        >
     TAX STATUS CODE:   FULLTIME?:  WORK PHONE:        EXT:
     HOBBIES:                                                >
  ┌──────────────────────────────────────────────────────────────┐
  │ HIRE DATE:          POSITION:              DEPT:              │
  │ JOB TITLE:                 SUPERVISOR:                        │
  └──────────────────────────────────────────────────────────────┘

     ┌─Notify in Case of Emergency──────────────┐    ┌──────┐
     │ NAME:                 PHONE:              │    │ PgDn │
                                                      │ More │
                                                      └──────┘
```

```
  HOURLY RATE:       O/T AUTHORIZED?:   O/T RATE:       TOTAL HOURS:     >

  SALARY:         PER:        COMMISSION CODE:   REVIEW DATE:

  REVIEW COMMENTS<
                                                                    >
  BONUS PAID:          BONUS DATE:            >

  ┌──────────────────────────────────────────────────────────────┐
  │ EDUCATION LEVEL:                         DEGREE:              │
  │ SPECIAL COURSES:                                              │
  └──────────────────────────────────────────────────────────────┘

  ┌──────────────────────────────────────────────────────────────┐
  │ SICK DAYS ENTITLED:    SICK DAYS TAKEN:    SICK DAYS REMAINING:  > │
  │ VACATION DAYS ENTITLED:   VACATION DAYS TAKEN:   VACATION DAYS LEFT: │
  └──────────────────────────────────────────────────────────────┘

  NOTES:

                                                                    >
  ⌊⌊⌊⌊T⌊⌊⌊⌊1⌊⌊⌊⌊T⌊⌊⌊⌊2⌊⌊⌊⌊T⌊⌊⌊⌊3⌊⌊⌊⌊T⌊⌊⌊⌊4⌊⌊⌊⌊T⌊⌊⌊⌊5⌊⌊⌊⌊T⌊⌊⌊⌊6⌊⌊⌊⌊T⌊⌊⌊⌊7⌊⌊⌊⌊T⌊⌊⌊⌊8
  EMPLOYEE                  Num                    4% Line 17 of Page 2 of 2

  Esc-Cancel       F1-How to design        F8-Options       F10-Continue
```

Figure 3-13: Sample EMPLOYEE.DTF Two-Page Form Design.

See the section on the Line Draw feature in the previous chapter for more information on how to use these special characters to enhance your screen.

Table 3-5 shows the fields included in the EMPLOYEE.DTF form in Figure 3-13, their lengths in characters, and the information types assigned to them.

Table 3-5
Fields in the EMPLOYEE.DTF Form

Field Label	Format*	Purpose of Field
	SCREEN PAGE 1	
Last	20, T	Last name field. First field of form.
First	15, T	First name field.
Middle	10, T	Middle name field (could be just middle initial).
Address	30, T	Street address.
Home Phone	12, T	Employee's home phone number.
City	25, T	City.
State	2, T, U	State, formatted in all caps.
Zip code	5, N	Zip code, formatted as a number to prevent accidental entry of a letter.
Sex	1, T	Male or female. You'll want to restrict this field so that only an M or F can be entered. Restricting values will be discussed in the next chapter.
Birthdate	13, D	Employee's date of birth.
Social Sec No	11, T	Employee's Social Security #
Tax Status Code	2, T	For a code that will identify deductions for payroll purposes.
Full-time?	1, Y	A Yes/No field — Y indicating a full-time employee.
Work Phone	12, T	Employee may work in another building at a different number.
Ext	5, T	Work phone extension.

(continued)

---

*Number of characters, T=text, U=uppercase, N=number, D=date,
Y=yes/no, K=keyword, M=money

Table 3-5 *(continued)*

Field Label	Format*	Purpose of Field
Hobbies	K	A Keyword field containing one or more employee hobbies.
Hire Date	11, D	The date the employee joined the company.
Position	15, T	What the employee will be doing for the company.
Dept	10, T	The department in which he or she will be working.
Job Title	17, T	Production Manager, Secretary, Salesperson, etc.
Supervisor	24, T	The employee's supervisor's name.
Notify in Case of Emergency:		This is not a field, but only descriptive text.
Name	17, T	The name of the person to call in case of emergency.
Phone	13, T	The emergency phone number.

SCREEN PAGE 2

Field Label	Format*	Purpose of Field
Hourly Rate	6, M	A money field for hourly employees' pay rates.
O/T Authorized?	1, Y	A Yes/No field indicating if the employee may work overtime.
O/T Rate	6, M	Shows the time-and-a-half hourly rate, or hourly overtime rate if salaried.
Total Hours	4, N	The number of overtime hours the employee may work in a given pay period.
Salary	9, M	The employee's salary weekly, semi-monthly, etc.

(continued)

*Number of characters, T=text, U=uppercase, N=number, D=date, Y=yes/no, K=keyword, M=money

Table 3-5 *(continued)*

Field Label	Format*	Purpose of Field
Per	6, T	The time period (weekly, biweekly) covered by the salary figure.
Commission Code	2, T	For certain employees, a code that indicates the level or type of commission (or benefits) plan in effect.
Review Date	13, D	The date of the employee's last evaluation. Another similar field could be added to indicate the next review date.
Review Comments	T	A two-line field to contain significant points raised during the review.
Bonus Paid	9, M	The dollar amount of the bonus.
Bonus Date	13, D	The date the bonus was paid.
Education Level	30, T	Quick reference for employee's educational level.
Degree	17, T	Any college degrees.
Special Courses	56, T	Job-related training or special courses the employee has had.
Notes	T	A large five-line text field to record, perhaps, the actual dates when the employee was absent from work due to illness or vacation, or simply to enter notes or comments about the employee.

Sick Days Entitled, Sick Days Taken, Sick Days Remaining, Vacation Days Entitled, Vacation Days Taken, Vacation Days Left.

These are all two-character number fields to keep track of days off taken by employee.

---

*Number of characters, T=text, U=uppercase, N=number, D=date, Y=yes/no, K=keyword, M=money

Notice how the 44 fields in this form fit comfortably on the two screen pages and that, when possible, associated fields are grouped together to make the form progress in an apparently sensible fashion (I say "apparently" because your own application requirements may make this layout appear crude.)

Notice also how the descriptive field labels will assist the operator during data entry, and that no two fields have the same label.

Note: Try not to use the same exact label for two or more fields — this may create confusion later when designing reports, merging database fields with Write documents, or querying your database via Q&A's Intelligent Assistant or Query Guide.

Assigning labels such as "Phone1" and "Phone2," or "Home Phone" and "Work Phone" beats having two fields labelled "Phone," where they might become confused during certain database operations.

Q & A Power Feature: Q&A offers a wealth of features you can use to further customize and add versatility to your database applications. You can:

- Set up stringent field restrictions to control data entry.

- Make fields you often search speedy (indexed) for fast retrieval.

- Add custom pop-up help screens to your forms to guide your operator along.

- Program your forms for automatic data entry, data validation, and calculations.

- Change the background colors or style of your forms as they appear on screen.

- Hide fields on your forms or make them read-only.

- Construct lookup tables to automatically fill in specified fields during data entry.

The details are covered in the following chapter, along with the procedures for manipulating selected groups of database records, including copying, removing, mass updating, backing up, and posting information from the fields in one database to another.

But since you now know how to complete the form design of a database, modify that design, and assign your field information types and format options, let's cover the procedures for entering, searching, updating, and printing database forms before moving on to the more advanced stuff.

Add Data: Creating New Database Records

Filling in a new record in a Q&A database is referred to as *adding data* — to distinguish it from updating existing records.

Suppose you've added 20 new customers to your customer database. You've filled in the company names, addresses, and so forth — filling in one new record for each of the 20 customers. You now have 20 forms or records in that database.

Suppose you didn't have the all the buyers' names as you were creating those 20 new customer records, but the next day you were handed the 12 buyers' names you were missing. You'd have to call up those 12 records, one by one, and type in the missing buyer's name.

This procedure is called *Search/Update.*

Adding a form is the correct procedure for starting with a fresh blank form on the screen — you're creating the record for the very first time. After you've just finished designing a database form, you use Q&A's "Add data" function to display blank forms to fill in the fields with the data you've designed the database to help you manage.

This is sometimes referred to as *initial loading* because the data is loaded for the first time into the database. This process can sometimes involve hundreds or thousands of new records being added to the database in a single marathon-like stretch of time.

If you've got 250 customer records on typewritten index cards, then your initial load will involve creating 250 new database records, one for each index card in the file. Databases designed to manage transactions like invoices or purchase orders, however, may require no initial loading at all. (Do you really want to enter all those earlier invoices?)

Search/Update is the procedure to use when you need to enter additional data or change existing data on a form that has already been added to the database.

After the initial load is complete, you'll then periodically need to add new forms to the database. You'll get new customers or have new products to sell, and these will need to be added to their respective databases as well.

On a typical day you might get three new customers, hire a new employee, bring a brand-new item into your inventory, enter 30 invoices, and cut three purchase orders. This potentially adds up to modifying five different databases during the course of that day.

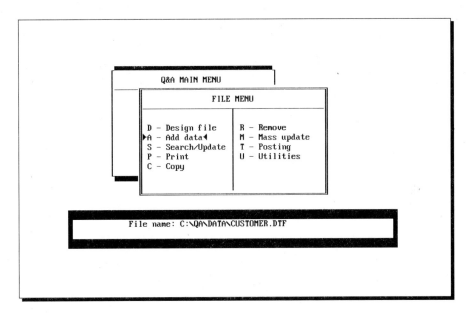

Figure 3-14: The File Menu. Select "Add Data" to enter new records into your database.

If a customer changes his address, for example, or there's a change in the price of a stock item, you'd then, of course, merely update the appropriate records to reflect the new information; you wouldn't create new records and type in the unchanged data along with the changed data all over again. That wouldn't make sense.

How to Enter New Database Forms — Add Data

Following is the procedure for adding new records to your databases. If you have many records to enter, you might consider reading ahead to the next chapter in order to learn how to customize your database forms to help automate data entry and have Q&A check for correct values being entered. Taking advantage of these advanced features where appropriate can cut down on data entry time — and errors — considerably.

To enter a new record into the database:

1. Select File from the Q&A Main menu.

2. Choose "Add data" from the File menu. (See Figure 3-14 above.)

3. Type in the name of the database you want to use and press **<Enter>**. A blank form for that database will be displayed.

4. Type the value in the first field, and then press **<Enter>** or **<Tab>** to move to the next field. Press **<Shift><Tab>** to move back to the previous field. If you need more room to enter text into a field that isn't long enough to accommodate it, press **<F6>** to open the Field Editor and continue entering your information. Press **<F6>** again to close the Field Editor and move to the next field.

5. Repeat step 4 until you've filled out all the fields on the form.

If you're missing a small item of information, and you don't want to interrupt your flow to go and find it, you can always use Search/Update later to call up the record and enter the missing value.

If the record has been messed up and you'd feel better just dumping it and starting over, press **<F3>** and confirm your action by typing **Y** at the warning screen. Q&A will get rid of the bungled record and display a fresh one.

You can also press **<Esc>** while adding a form, and then answer Yes to confirm deletion. This action will place you back at the File menu.

6. When you've finished the form, press **<F10>**. Q&A will add it to the database by saving it to disk, and display another blank form.

If this is your last form of the session, press **<Shift><F10>** to add the form and return to the File menu. If you press **<Esc>** from a blank form, you'll also end up back at the File menu. Pressing **<F9>** will display the *previous* form added during that session.

 Tip: Q&A won't let you add a blank form to the database — you'll get an error message. A form must have something (anything) in it before you can save it with **<F10>**.

If you're filling out a Keyword field with multiple values, you must separate the values with semicolons. If you don't, Q&A will see the entry as one long value. For example, "Tennis;bowling; golf," is correct, whereas "Tennis, Bowling, Golf" — separated by commas — is incorrect for a Keyword field. It makes no difference if you leave a space after each semicolon.

If your database design includes more than one screen page, the second page will be displayed when you press **<Enter>** or **<Tab>** from the last field on the first page.

You can move to the second page from anywhere on the first page by pressing **<PgDn>**. Likewise, you can move from the second to the first page by pressing **<PgUp>**. Pressing **<PgDn>** three times will display page 4 of the form, for example, if your form includes a fourth screen page.

Editing the Contents of a Field

At any time during data entry you can change the information already typed into a field:

- Use **<Enter>**, **<Tab>**, or **<Shift><Tab>** to move to another field on the same line, or your cursor keys to move up and down the form to get to the field you want to edit.

- Use your left/right cursor keys to move inside of a field.

- Use the **<Delete>** key or space bar to erase individual letters or the entire contents of the field, and then type in the new value.

- Pressing **<F4>** deletes the value from the cursor position to the end of the word. **<Shift><F4>** deletes the contents of the field. In a multiline field, **<Shift><F4>** deletes the first line only.

- All of the keystrokes used in the word processor to erase words and characters will work in a database field.

- You can use both overwrite and insert mode when editing field values. Toggle between the two modes by pressing the **<Ins>** key.

You can move back to previous records entered during the current session by pressing **<F9>**, and you are free to edit them. Move forward to subsequent records by pressing **<F10>**.

The status line at the bottom of the display will tell you how many records you've added during the session, the number of the record displayed, and the total number of records in the database.

When you edit a record that has already been saved, and press **<F9>** or **<F10>**, Q&A will save the modified record before moving on to the previous or next one. When you press **<F9>** or **<F10>** to move backward or forward in the stack of records, Q&A may tell you that you're already at the first or last form added during the session and that there are no records behind, or ahead, of the current one.

Table 3-6 summarizes the cursor moves available to you when working with forms.

Data Validation

In Q&A, your first line of defense against the entry of inappropriate values into a database field is the *information type* you assigned to the field at the Format Spec.

Table 3-6
Keys You Can Use to Navigate Between and Within Database Forms

Key	Meaning
<←>	One character to the left
<→>	One character to the right
<↑>	One line up (to nearest field)
<↓>	One line down (to nearest field)
<Ctrl><→>	Next word in the field
<Ctrl><←>	Previous word in the field
<Home>	First character of field
<Home><Home>	First character of the first field on the page
<Home><Home><Home>	First character of the first field of the form
<PgUp>	Previous screen page
<Ctrl><Home>	First form in the stack
<F9>	Previous form
<F10>	Next form
<End>	Last character of the field
<End><End>	First character of last field on page
<End><End><End>	First character of last field on form
<Ctrl><End>	Last form in the stack
<PgDn>	To the top of the next screen page
<Tab>	Beginning of next field
<Shift><Tab>	Beginning of last field
<Enter>	Beginning of next field (beginning of next line in multiline fields)

A number field will only permit digits, commas, periods, plus signs, and minus signs to be typed in. Try typing any other character into a number field and you'll get nowhere.

A money field will react differently. It will allow you to type in the currency symbol (although it's unnecessary) you specified for the database at the Global Format Options screen, and will warn you as you leave the field if the value entered doesn't look like a money value.

For all other information types, Q&A checks for the appropriateness of the value when you move the cursor *out* of the field.

Anything typed into a date field, for example, that Q&A cannot format as a date will earn an error message. Q&A will give you the opportunity to change the value to the assigned information type.

Without using any of Q&A's more advanced field restriction features, the entry of an inappropriate value type will be flagged by Q&A — but you can than overrule the objection simply by pressing **<Tab>** or **<Enter>** to continue on to the next field; the value you entered will be accepted.

There are techniques, however, you can use to make it impossible for invalid data, data types, and ranges of data to be entered into database fields. One of these is Q&A's Restriction Spec, which enables you to place conditions on what can and cannot be entered into any field on the form. Another is to add programming to the field, and perhaps a custom help screen, so that when an out-of-range value is entered, the cursor will be returned to the offending field, the value will be deleted, and the help screen will pop up with specific instructions for entering data in that particular field.

We'll look at these advanced field restriction features in the next chapter.

Q&A'S Ditto Feature

Suppose you're adding a series of forms to a database where all but a few of the fields will contain the exact same values as all the other forms in the series. It would be nice to just "ditto" all the fields in the previous form into the current form, and then edit the few fields that need it.

You can do this in Q&A by pressing **<Shift><F5>**, and Q&A will copy the entire contents of that most recently viewed form into the same fields on the current form.

This feature works on the basis of *the last form displayed*, which means that it will also work if you're looking at a form in Search/Update, go to Add Data in the same database, get a blank form, and press **<Shift><F5>**.

You can also ditto information from the previous form into the current form on a field-by-field basis. Simply move to the field you want to receive the copied value, and press **<F5>**. Q&A will copy to the current form the contents of the same field in the immediately preceding form. However, the ditto feature won't work if you've been moving back and forth between forms with **<F9>** and **<F10>**.

To review:

- Copy a field's value in the previous form to the same field on the current form by pressing **<F5>** with the cursor in the field you want to receive the same value.

- Copy the last viewed form's entire contents to the current blank form in Add Data by pressing **<Shift><F5>**.

Other Q&A Features Available When Entering Data

The following features will be useful to you as you enter data into your databases.

Auto-type the current date into a date field by pressing **<Ctrl><F5>**. You can also tell Q&A to enter the current date on all your blank forms as they come up in Add Data. Or you can add a programming statement to auto-type the date when a specified condition is met (more on this in the following chapter).

Auto-type the current time into an hours field by pressing **<Alt><F5>**. You can also preset Q&A to add the current time to all blank forms as they are displayed for data entry. Or, again, add a programming statement to auto-type the time when a specific condition is met.

Bypass the File menu and go directly from Add Data to the Retrieve Spec (to search for a form or forms) by pressing **<F7>**. Pressing **<Shift><F9>** while in Add Data displays a bypass menu from which you can go directly to the customize facilities for that database (more on this in the next chapter).

When you're in Search/Update, you can press **<Ctrl><F6>** to go directly to Add Data, where a blank form will be displayed for input. These menu bypass keys save you from having to "check in" at the File menu to change between the two different procedures.

Customize your forms. (While this topic is covered in detail in the following chapter, here are the pertinent points.)

- You can change the information types of any of your fields at any time to control the kinds of values entered.

- You can tell Q&A to make one or more fields *unique* to guard against duplicate entries (two or more forms with the same value in a field). This feature works in conjunction with an indexed field.

- Data entry mistakes can be avoided by restricting the range of values a field may contain.

- Fields can be made invisible or placed off limits so the values in them can't be easily changed.

- Fields can be preset to contain commonly entered values, saving time during data entry.

- A lookup table can be constructed to assist data entry by providing frequently entered values that can be auto-typed into the form.

- Fields can be programmed to carry out calculations, display custom help screens and messages, return values based on the contents of other fields, look up information contained in external databases, and move the cursor around the form.

- Q&A's keyboard macro feature (see Chapter 8) can be used to record a series of keystrokes which can then be "played back" to fill out portions of your forms automatically.

- You can create custom help screens for any fields on the form to assist the operator during data entry.

When you press **<F1>** (Q&A's Help key) from Add Data, you get general information on how to proceed — but no information that relates specifically to the application or the particular field in which the operator might be wondering what to enter.

In the next chapter you'll learn how to create custom help so that when the operator presses **<F1>** from a field on the form, a tailored help screen will pop up with the exact information needed.

The Field Editor

New: Q&A File's Field Editor allows you to enter text values that exceed the field's length.

During data entry you can press **<F6>** with the cursor in the field in which you want to enter extended text, and an editing box (78 columns by eight lines) will pop up. Once the Field Editor is open, you can press **<F8>** for the Options menu and virtually all of Write's word processing features are at your disposal (see Chapter 1 for a discussion of these features). You can delete, copy, move, search and replace, scroll up and down, export, import, insert

```
-------------------------------------------------------------------
  HOURLY RATE: $15.50 O/T AUTHORIZED?: Y O/T RATE: $23.25 TOTAL HOURS: 42

  SALARY:            PER:          COMMISSION CODE:    REVIEW DATE: 3/15/90

  REVIEW COMMENTS Good knack for setting up the production line. Makes 110%→

  BONUS PAID: $500.00   BONUS DATE: 3/18/90

    EDUCATION LEVEL: High School              DEGREE: Vocational
    SPECIAL COURSES:
  _____
  Good knack for setting up the production line. Makes 110% of quota 20 days
  out of the month. Always helpful and willing to show others how to do their
  work. Never late for work and doesn't get sick. (Also, he's the only pitcher
  we have on the company baseball team that knows how to throw a curve ball,
  and he can win at least ten games a year for us.)



  _____

  EMPLOYEE                                 0% Line 1 of 5

  Esc-Exit  F1-Info  F2-Print  Ctrl+F6-Define Pg  F7-Search  F8-Options  ↑F8-Save
```

Figure 3-15: The Field Editor. This feature is used to enter lots of information into text fields. Here, the Review Comments field is expanded to enter commentary too long to fit in the field on the form.

documents, use macros, the spelling checker, thesaurus, and so forth. When using the Field Editor, all your actions take place in the editor and not on the form itself.

Figure 3-15 shows the second screen page from the sample employee database we designed earlier. The Review Comments field is the type of field most benefitted by the Field Editor feature.

In this example the Field Editor is being used to hold more information concerning the employee's last review than can fit in the field designed into the form. The display status line indicates what line the cursor is on in the Editor, the total number of lines, and how much of the Editor's memory has been used up. Notice the →at the end of the Review Comments field, indicating that the field contains an expanded value.

Expanded fields can be used wherever you need to enter lengthy descriptions, comments, notes, and so forth. They make it unnecessary to use up valuable template real estate for long multiline entries. The Field Editor can only be opened at fields formatted for text or keyword information types. However, you can press **<F6>** to expand fields formatted for other information types even though you won't be able to take advantage of the Field Editor's word processing-like options. But why would you need such features for date, hours, money, or number fields, anyway?

You also have a special abbreviated Print Options screen available for printing directly from the Field Editor.

When you press **<F2>** from inside the Editor, you can make your usual printer selection (or print to screen or disk), and also enter an offset value, printer control codes, and number of copies. Pressing **<F10>** will then print only the contents of the Editor, not the entire form.

You can enter as much text into the Field Editor as you want, up to the 32K field limit (64K for the entire form). When you're finished with the editor, press **<F6>** or **<F10>** to close the Field Editor and return to the form; there you'll see a right arrow at the end of the field, indicating there's more data in the field than can be displayed.

To edit the contents of any expanded field, you simply place the cursor in it and press **<F6>**. You can then work inside the Editor just like you'd work with a document in the Write module.

The Field Editor can be a powerful data entry and information tool in other ways as well. You can use it to call up entire reports, lists, documents, and other reference information stored on disk. For example, you can view a list of customers showing up-to-date credit status or find out what's currently in inventory without leaving the invoice you're working on. You can answer telephone order queries without having to exit and open another database. Or you can pull up a list of all open purchase orders in the middle of updating a customer record. See Chapter 12 for more ways to get the most out of this versatile Q&A feature.

Retrieving and Updating Database Records _____

There'll be times when you'll need to search your database for particular records to view and perhaps update.

This is an essential database activity, and Q&A makes it as easy as typing in the name of the database, entering your search criteria, and pressing **<F10>** to bring up the record or group of records you want to view and optionally modify.

Add Data is used when adding brand-new records to your database file.

Search/Update will find those stored records for you and display them so you can look at and change them.

You'll use Search/Update to:

- View a specific form or group of related forms.
- Modify information contained in one or more forms, or add new information to empty fields.
- Print a form or group of forms.
- Find and Delete a form from the database.

Search/Update Procedure

When you use Search/Update to find records in a database, Q&A will put you at the Retrieve Spec for that database. *The Retrieve Spec form will look exactly like the form you designed and have been using to add records to your database.* At the Retrieve Spec you can press **<F1>** for help in entering your search parameters. To search for a record or records:

1. Choose File from the Q&A Main menu.

2. Select Search/Update from the File menu.

3. Type in the name of the database to search, and press **<Enter>**.

4. When the Retrieve Spec is displayed, use your navigation keys to move the cursor to the field on which you want to establish your search criteria. (Pressing **<F10>** at the Retrieve Spec will retrieve all the forms in the database and display the first record in the stack.)

5. Type in your search restrictions (see Table 3-7) to define which form or forms you want Q&A to locate. Press **<F6>** to expand the field if necessary to enter your specifications, and **<F6>** again to return to the form (see the section on saving search parameters in this chapter if you want to store your Retrieve Spec parameters for later use).

6. Repeat steps 4 and 5 for other fields you want involved in the search.

7. If you want the retrieved forms sorted in a particular manner, press **<F8>** for the Sort Spec. (There will be more on this later in the chapter.)

8. When you've finished entering your retrieve restrictions and sort criteria, press **<F10>** and the first of the forms (if any) that meet your parameters will be displayed. If more than one form is retrieved, the group of them is called the *stack* or the *answer set.*

9. Change the information on the form as necessary using the usual cursor navigation and editing keys. Press **<F6>** to edit information contained in expanded fields.

10. Press **<F10>** to view the next form in the stack, and **<F9>** to view the previous form in the stack.

Here's a summary of what you can do with retrieved forms:

- You can make changes to the information fields on the form, or add information to empty fields.

- You can press **<Alt><F6>** to view and even edit the forms in a table format. This displays the individual records as rows, and the fields in those records as columns — like a spreadsheet.

- Pressing **<F9>** displays the previous form in the stack; **<F10>** displays the next one. **<F9>** or **<F10>** will save any changes you've made to the current record before displaying the next one.

- **<F7>** redisplays the Retrieve Spec so you can change your search or sort parameters, and search again.

- **<Ctrl><F6>** takes you directly to Add Data after saving the form, bypassing the File menu.

- **<Shift><F9>** produces a bypass menu from which you can go directly to any of the Customize Menu specs.

- You can press **<F3>** to delete the form on the screen, and answer Yes to confirm the deletion when Q&A's warning message pops up.

- You can press **<Shift><F10>** to save any changes made to the current form and return to the File menu.

- Pressing **<Esc>** will take you back to the File menu if no changes were made to the displayed record. If you try to **<Esc>** without first saving a modified record, Q&A will warn you that the changes to it will not be saved.

- You can press another one of the function keys on the key assignments line at the bottom of the screen.

Q&A's record retrieval capabilities can be reduced to three general *types* of search. Within these broad types there are a variety of single- and multifield, and compound search parameters you can specify at a Retrieve Spec. Also, certain information types may require you to enter your criteria in a certain

Table 3-7
Symbols and Codes You Can Use for
Retrieving Database Records in Q&A File

For All Search Restrictions

For use with any information type

.. (two periods)	AND. **X..Y** means X and Y (or from X to Y)
; (semicolon)	OR. **X;Y** means X or Y
/ (slash)	NOT. **/X** means not X
.. (two periods)	wildcard characters (text and keyword)

Exact Match Search Restrictions

All information types including Yes/No fields and Date

X or **=X**	Equal to X
/X	Not X
=	Field must be empty
/=	Field must not be empty
X;Y;Z	X or Y or Z within a single field

Range Search Restrictions

All information types except Yes/No fields

>**X**	Greater than X
<**X**	Less than X
>=**X**	Greater than or equal to X
<=**X**	Less than or equal to X
>**X**..<**Y**	Greater than X and less than Y
>**X**..<=**Y**	Greater than X and less than or equal to Y
>**X**;<=**Y**	Greater than X or less than or equal to Y
MAXn	Highest n (whole number) values
MINn	Lowest n (whole number) values

(continued)

Table 3-7 *(continued)*

Text and Character Search Restrictions

Text and Keyword

?	Any single character
..	Any group of characters
X..	Begins with X.
..X	Ends with X
X..Y	Begins with X and ends with Y
..X..	Includes X
..X..Y..Y	Includes X, Y, and Z in that order
****	Finds literal character following symbol (\? finds question mark)

Special Keyword Searches

X;Y;Z	Finds X or Y or Z in a keyword field
&X;Y;Z	Finds X and Y and Z in a keyword field

Special Usage Searches

..	Finds correctly formatted values (values which are appropriate to the information type the field is supposed to contain)
/..	Incorrectly formatted values (for example, a nonmoney value entered into a money field)
]	For wildcard Date field searches only
~	The tilde symbol means "sounds like." For example, if you were looking for a last name that sounds like "Seegal," but might be spelled "Seigel," "Seegall," "Siegel" or "Seegal" (but you don't know which), you could type in ~Seegal in the last name field and Q&A would find the sound-alikes.

way. But it's less confusing to start off by thinking in terms of the types of searches you can do:

Exact match: Type **BOB** into a field and Q&A will retrieve the forms with **BOB** in that same field. Enter **12345** and you'll get the forms with **12345** in the matching field.

Partial match: Enter a *portion* of the value, and tell Q&A to search for any form where that portion of the corresponding field's value matches what you've specified. Typing **BO..** as your search parameter would give you the forms with **BOB**, **BOZO**, **BOTANY**, and so forth in the matching field. Entering **456..** into a Zip code field would give you all the forms with the **456** zip code prefix.

Range match: Similar to a partial match, but here you're telling Q&A you want all the forms where the matching field contents fall *between* a lower value and a higher one. You might want to retrieve the stack of forms for employees who are between the ages of 55 and 60, the purchase orders that were cut between January and March of 1990, or inventory items that cost you more than $15.00 but less than $50.00.

Simple Searches

A simple search consists of typing at the Retrieve Spec the precise value you want to search for — you're telling Q&A to go and find all the records with an exact match.

For example, if you wanted the employee record for **Tim Smith**, you'd simply type in **Smith** in the Last Name field, then type in **Tim** in the First Name field of your employee database Retrieve Spec, and press **<F10>**. If the record for **Tim Smith** is in the file, Q&A will find and display it for you, so long as "Tim" and "Smith" are *exact* matches for the corresponding database fields.

Suppose you wanted to retrieve all the records of your customers located in California. At the Customer database Retrieve Spec you'd type in **CA** in the State field and press **<F10>**. The stack of California customer records would be retrieved, ready for you to browse through them and edit as necessary.

When your Retrieve Spec search parameters include restrictions in more than one field, Q&A assumes that you want the forms that meet *both* criteria. In other words, when **Tim** was entered into one field, and **Smith** was entered into another field in the above example, Q&A assumed you wanted to see only the records matching both restrictions. If you had merely typed **Smith** into the Last Name field (omitting the **Tim**), Q&A would have retrieved all forms in the database with **Smith** in the Last Name field, including Joe Smith, Fred Smith, and Angelica Smith.

Range Searches

You can restrict your searches to *ranges* of values. Q&A, for example, can retrieve all the forms in a customer database that fall between a specified Zip code range. At the Retrieve Spec you'd simply tell Q&A that you want all the forms from Zip codes 10000 to 19999.

At an inventory database Retrieve Spec you can retrieve all the stock number records with a list price of $30.00 or more, but less than or equal to $40.00. Less than $40.01 would be the same as less than or equal to $40.00 if you're using two currency decimal places.

At an employee database Retrieve Spec you could have Q&A hand you the forms for those employees born after December 31, 1950, or those whose Social Security number fields are blank, but this latter would better qualify as an *exact match* because you're not dealing with a range.

Such range searches involve the use of symbols and simple codes. Table 3-7 summarizes them. The letters *X, Y* and *Z* in the Table represent arbitrary values — substitute your own values for them.

The symbols and codes you use to fill out the Retrieve Spec may depend on the information types contained in the fields involved in the search. The following sections explain what the symbols mean, and when and how to use them to find the forms you want.

Exact Retrieval

Exact Retrieval means that only a form exactly meeting the conditions will be retrieved. Conditions used in Exact Retrieval include the following:

X or **=X** means the value must precisely match the X in this field at the Retrieve Spec. If X is "90505" then only the forms with "90505" in that field will be retrieved.

/X means NOT equal to X, and tells Q&A to find all the forms that do *not* have X in this field. For example, **/CA** in the State field will find all the forms *except* California. **/B..T** in a text field means find all the forms where the value in this field does *not* begin with "B" and end with a "T." The forms containing the words BAT and BULLET in this field would be excluded.

= all by itself means "find all the forms where this field is empty" (nothing in it). A **/=** (*not* empty) code means find all the forms where there is something (anything) in this field.

X;Y;Z means find the forms that contain the value X, or the value Y, or the value Z in this field. For example, **Smith;Jones** would retrieve all the forms where the field matched either "Smith" or "Jones." If the field contained "Smith Jones," it wouldn't work. It has to be one or the other individually.

However, a **Smith..;Jones..** retrieve parameter would locate the forms for "Smith," "Jones," "Smith Jones," "Jonesby" and "Smithers Jonesby."

Range Retrieval

Range Retrieval, unlike Exact Retrieval, retrieves forms whose values fall within certain parameters — greater than, less, more than this but less than that. Conditions used in Range Retrieval include the following:

>X means that whatever is in this field must be greater than X. If X is a number or money value, then the number or money value must be greater than X; if X is a text value, then the word must come later in the dictionary; if X is a date, then the date must be later in time than X. **<X** means the value must be less than or lower than X.

>=X looks for values in that field which are equal to or greater than X. If X is 90000, then Q&A will find the forms with a value in the field of 90000 or higher. **<=X** means find the forms where the value is equal to or less than X.

>X..<Y means find the forms where the corresponding field value is greater than X *and* less than Y. **>X;<=Y** will retrieve all forms where the matching field contains a value greater than X *or* less than or equal to Y.

MAXn finds the *n* number of forms in the database with the highest value in the matching field. If *n* is 20, then Q&A will retrieve the 20 forms with the highest value in this field. In a text field Q&A would retrieve the 20 forms closest to the end of the dictionary. Similarly, **MINn** will retrieve the *n* number of forms with the lowest values in the field.

You can use **MAXn** or **MINn** in only one field per Retrieve Spec, and they're not available for Keyword searches. If you use MAX or MIN without the *n*, Q&A will assume the *n* to be 1 and will retrieve the single form with the highest or lowest value in the matching field.

Special Date Retrieval

You can search on date fields that contain nondate values. For example, when the text "open" was entered into a date field during Add or Update, Q&A warned the operator that the value wasn't correct for a date, but the operator forced the value into the field, anyway. To retrieve all the forms with "open" in the date field, use the **]** (right bracket) followed by the value you want Q&A to look for:

```
Next Appointment:  ]open
```

You can also use the **]** character to retrieve all the records where the date could be any year, month, or day. Here's where the **?** wildcard character comes into play.

Q&A stores dates internally in the following format: YYYY/MM/DD, where the year is four digits, followed by a two-digit month and a two-digit day. So to retrieve all the forms where the month of June was part of the date, you'd use:

```
]????/06/??
```

Use **/..** for incorrectly formatted values other than dates. **/..** finds the forms that contain values that didn't conform to the field's information type but were entered anyway. Use it to locate values in money, Yes/No, and hours fields that are not really money, Yes/No, or hours values.

Incorrect information types can be entered into fields while importing data from another program, and while running a Mass Update that wasn't properly structured. Programming a field incorrectly can also result in incorrect information type values being placed into fields.

Keyword Only Searches

A Keyword field differs from a regular text field in that it may contain multiple entries.

When you search for a value in a text field, Q&A evaluates your search parameters based on what's in the entire field. Keywords, however, are separated by colons and must be searched for as individual values because they *are* individual values.

Tennis;bowling;golf in a Keyword field means this field contains *three* separate values. In a text field these would not be treated by Q&A as three entries, but as one — a single text string consisting of the letters "Tennis;bowling;golf."

When you ask Q&A to search for **X;Y;Z** in a Keyword field, you're asking for all the forms that contain X or Y or Z in the matching field. You'll get the forms that contain X, the forms that contain Y, those that contain Z, and those that contain any combination of the three values.

Asking for **&X;Y;Z** means that you want only those forms that contain all three values in the matching field. For example, **&Sharkhunting;skydiving** will give you only those forms where the matching field contains *both* entries (although they don't have to be in the same order).

Using Multiple Restrictions in a Single Field

Q&A will search your database for forms that meet multiple restrictions. Separate each of your restrictions with a semicolon. For example:

X..Y;Z tells Q&A to search for the forms that contain X through Y, or Z in the matching field. Q&A reads the restriction from left to right.

<X;/>Y finds the forms containing values less than X or NOT greater than Y.

X..;Y..;Z.. in a text or keyword field finds the forms where the matching field value begins with X or Y or Z.

/>Z..<X;= in a number, money, date, or hour field would retrieve all the forms with values NOT greater than Z and less than X or contain no value at all.

Changing the Way Q&A Searches

Unless you modify Q&A's search logic, it will assume you mean AND when selecting search parameters *in two or more fields*.

For example, telling Q&A you want:

Product Code: ..HB

Price: >$15.00

will produce the forms on which the stock code ends in HB and the price is greater than $15.00.

But what if you want the forms where the stock code ends in HB *or* the price is greater than $15.00? To do this you need to press **<Ctrl><F7>** from the Retrieve Spec for the Search Options box and change Q&A's search logic. Figure 3-16 shows what this box looks like when displayed over the Retrieve Spec screen.

On the first line of the box, select the setting that will determine whether Q&A will retrieve the forms that do or do not meet your Retrieve Spec restrictions.

On the second line choose the option that determines whether Q&A will select the forms that must meet all or any of your restrictions.

The **Do** and **Any** selections are useful for searching invoices for a particular stock number, for instance.

Suppose you need to know on which invoices Stk# P93-4 was sold, but you've got 10 invoice line items with as many Stk# fields. What you do is type the P93-4 in all the Stk# fields, then tell Q&A, through the Search Options box, to retrieve all the forms that meet *any* of these restrictions. This way Q&A will find all the invoices where Stk# P93-4 was entered in any of the Stk# fields.

To use the Search Options box:

1. Enter your restrictions at the Retrieve Spec.

2. Press **<Ctrl><F7>** to display the Search Options box.

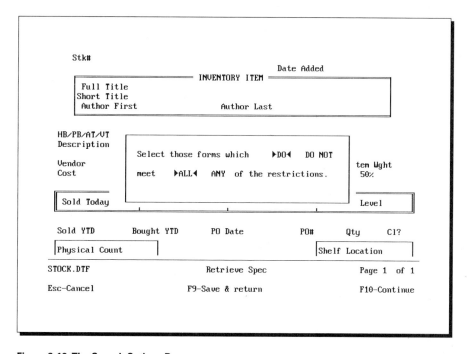

Figure 3-16: The Search Options Box.

3. Use your cursor keys to change the settings.

4. When the settings are the way you want them, press **<F9>** to save your choices without starting the search. You'll be returned to the Retrieve Spec. Or, press **<Esc>** when the box is displayed to cancel any changes and return to the Retrieve Spec.

5. Press **<F10>** to start the retrieve operation.

Table 3-8 shows the relationship between the Search Options box settings and how Q&A conducts its search.

Saving Your Search Parameters

New: Version 4.0 brought with it the ability to save your Retrieve Specs. As you may have gathered, the key to retrieving the exact group of forms you want to view is the restriction or combination of restrictions you enter in selected fields at the Retrieve Spec. Working out a detailed Retrieve Spec can take considerable time and deliberation.

If you'll be using the same Retrieve Spec again, save it to disk so the next time you can ask for it by name and have Q&A fill in all the fields for you.

Table 3-8
Results of Search Options Box Settings

Settings	DO	DO NOT
ALL	Forms that meet all of your restrictions	Forms that don't meet at least one of your restrictions
ANY	Forms that meet at least one of your restrictions	Forms on which all restrictions fail

When you create the specification for the first time:

1. Fill out the Retrieve Spec as you normally would.

2. When all your restrictions have been typed into the selected fields, press **<Shift><F8>**. Q&A will pop up a box prompting you to enter the name of this particular Retrieve Spec.

3. Decide on a descriptive name for the Retrieve Spec ("Active Subscribers," "Invoices with Balances Due," "Employees Past Review Date," "Hardbound Adventure Books," or "Open Purchase Orders," for example), type in the name (up to 31 characters), and press **<Enter>**. Q&A will save your spec with the name you've assigned to it (see Figure 3-17).

4. Press **<F10>** to proceed with the search or **<F8>** for the Sort Spec.

Now when you need to call up this same Retrieve Spec in the future, you simply press **<Alt><F8>** from the Retrieve Spec to see the list of saved Retrieve specs for the database. Highlight the one you want (or type in its name), press **<Enter>**, and Q&A will enter your restrictions in the appropriate fields. At this point you have the following options:

- Press **<F10>** to continue.

- Make a temporary modification to the spec and press **<F10>** to continue.

- Modify the spec and save it with a new name (adding it to the list of saved Retrieve Specs for that database).

- Modify the spec and save it under its existing name. This will overwrite the old spec with the new one.

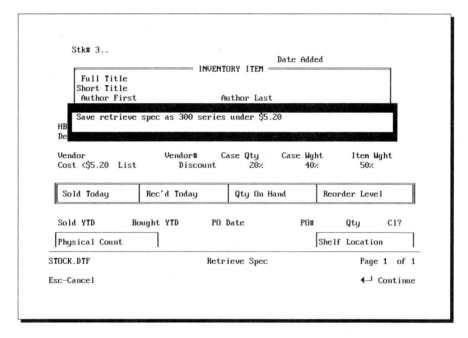

```
    Stk# 3..
                                          Date Added
                           ═══ INVENTORY ITEM ═══
      Full Title
     Short Title
      Author First                  Author Last

     ┌──────────────────────────────────────────────────────┐
     │ Save retrieve spec as 300 series under $5.20           │
 HB  │                                                        │
 De  └──────────────────────────────────────────────────────┘

    Vendor                Vendor#    Case Qty    Case Wght    Item Wght
    Cost <$5.20  List        Discount    20%         40%         50%

    ┌─────────────┬─────────────┬─────────────┬──────────────┐
    │ Sold Today  │ Rec'd Today │ Qty On Hand │ Reorder Level│
    └─────────────┴─────────────┴─────────────┴──────────────┘

     Sold YTD      Bought YTD      PO Date         PO#     Qty      Cl?
    │Physical Count      │            │            │Shelf Location      │
    ─────────────────────────────────────────────────────────────────
    STOCK.DTF                    Retrieve Spec              Page 1  of 1

    Esc-Cancel                                         ◄┘ Continue
```

Figure 3-17: Saving a Retrieve Spec Named "300 Series Under $5.20." The search restrictions here are: the Stock Number begins with a 3 and the cost is less than $5.20.

Using Formulas in Retrieve Specs

You can use programming formulas to retrieve the forms you want to view, update, or print, adding substantial power and flexibility to your retrieve parameters. For example, you can use a formula to retrieve only those forms containing a field with information that matches a field in another database; you can tell Q&A to find any forms that match the result of an arithmetic calculation; and you can use formulas containing the **@Date** function to retrieve records whose dates fall before, or after, a certain number of days from the current date.

I'll reserve our discussion of this feature, however, until the next chapter, where you'll be introduced to Q&A's programming language and built-in functions — options that you can use to tailor your databases for super-high performance.

Sorting Retrieved Forms

Without specifying a sort criteria, Q&A will hand retrieved forms to you roughly in the same order in which they were originally entered.

220 PC World Q&A Bible

But if you want your forms retrieved in some orderly fashion (by date, control number, alphabetically by last name, etc.), enter your parameters at the Sort Spec.

1. Fill out your Retrieve Spec and press **<F8>** before leaving it. The Sort Spec screen will be displayed.

2. Move the cursor to the field on which you want to sort.

3. Type **1** in the primary sort field, followed by an **AS** (for an ascending sort) or a **DS** (for a descending sort). An ascending sort will retrieve the forms with the lowest value first and the highest value last. A descending sort will hand you the form with the highest value first.

   If the field is too small to enter your codes, press **<F6>** to expand it, type in your code, and press **<F10>** again to return to the form.

4. If you want a second level of sort, move the cursor to the appropriate field and enter **2**, followed by an **AS** or **DS**.

5. Repeat step 4 using a sequence of higher numbers for any additional fields on which you want to sort.

6. When you're done with the Sort Spec press **<F10>** to begin the search/ sort operation.

The field with the number 1 in it is the *primary* sort field, meaning that any other sorted fields are sorted relative to it.

If you ask for an ascending sort on zip codes with a 1AS in the zip code field, and also a descending sort on last names with a 2DS in the last name field, Q&A will first sort the forms in zip code order, and then sort the forms by descending last name order within zip code.

In an employee database you might want your primary sort (1AS) on the Department field with a secondary sort (2AS) on the Last Name field. That way you'd get the forms for employees in Accounting in last name order first, and so forth through all the departments beginning with the letters B, C, D, on to the end of the alphabet.

You might want to sort invoices by date (1AS in the Date field), with a secondary descending sort on invoice number (2DS in the Invoice Number field). Doing so would retrieve all the invoices from the earliest date, sorting the invoice numbers within the dates in descending order.

Q&A allows up to 512 sorting levels (depending on field widths), but it's unlikely you'll ever need to sort deeper than a few levels at most.

Keep in mind that number sorts and text sorts behave differently. In a text field, numbers are sorted alphabetically, not numerically. So if you plan to use numbers in a text field, and sort them, make them all the same length by adding leading zeros.

Saving Your Sort Parameters

Saving a Sort Spec for future use works just like saving a Retrieve Spec (see section on saving Retrieve Spec parameters earlier in this chapter). You fill out your Sort Spec as usual, and then press **<Shift><F8>**. Q&A displays the "Save as" box, and you enter the name you want to assign to the spec ("Ascending Subscriber Last Name," "Descending Zip Code Field," "PO Numbers by Date," and so on). The name can be up to 31 characters long.

When you want that same Sort Spec later, you press **<Alt><F8>** from the Sort Spec screen for a list of the Sort Specs in the database, highlight or type in the name of the one you want, and press **<Enter>**. Q&A will fill in your Sort Spec for you, and you can then make a temporary modification if you like, and press **<F10>** to continue. At any time, you can also bring a saved Sort Spec onto the screen, change it, and save it back to disk under the same or a different name.

Viewing and Editing Forms in Table View

New: You can view your database records in a columnar format by pressing **<Alt><F6>** after any retrieved record is displayed.

Q&A version 4.0 added the capability to *edit* your records while in Table View — an extremely powerful feature.

Table View provides you with a different method of looking through your records and updating the information in them. Often referred to as "browse" mode, instead of looking at one record at a time, you can display up to 17 records on the screen at once, making it easier to compare the contents of fields from record to record, see relationships between the same fields in different records, and spot data entry errors.

Table View presents your records in row and column format. Each record in the stack of retrieved forms is represented by a horizontal row, and each field by a column (see Figure 3-18). Scroll vertically to display additional records, and horizontally to display more fields.

You can call up Table View anytime you want to view a group of records together, or when you need to make changes to the records — changes that are more easily done in a table, rather than in a form, environment. You can also create, save, and later recall Table View Specs.

Full Title	Stk#	Date Added	Author Last	Cost
Rack 'Em Up: Th	344HB	7/6/90	Magillacutty	$13.50
The Man Who Inv	348PB	5/25/90	Leecher	$6.90
Looking Through	388PB	4/27/89	Van Buren	$4.45
Exploring the A	245VT	3/29/88	Halerin	$10.00
Bird Songs of t	680AT	7/8/90	Whimple	$3.90
Boating on the	205HB	2/18/88	Somerset	$8.35
The Hollow Glen	299HB	2/2/89	Parsoner	$9.20
Building Your F	410VT	1/20/90	Fletcher	$9.22
How to Avoid Ju	533PB	4/18/90	Retting	$5.10
Help for the Co	314PB	5/3/89	Brooks, M.D.	$5.90
Growing Fruit T	309PB	4/20/90	Donlevy	$6.00
Modernize Your	403VT	9/15/89	Donovan	$8.66
Love Songs of t	199AT	6/18/88	Clark	$3.90
Cruisin' Blues	444HB	3/18/90	Rattle	$8.18
The Omaha Facto	501HB	8/7/90	Patterson	$12.08
Terror on the M	188HB	6/19/88	Falcon	$6.90
Bach's Greatest	218AT	3/14/88	Bach	$4.10

STOCK.DTF   Retrieved form 1   of --   Total forms: 18

Figure 3-18: Table View of 17 Records in an Inventory Database.

When you invoke a Table View of your database records, the first five columns of the table will correspond to the first five fields in the database form — but you can change this. The rows will be displayed in the same sequence in which the forms were retrieved so that they'll be consistent with your Sort Spec. Also, the record you were looking at when you pressed **<Alt><F6>** for the Table View will be highlighted when the table is displayed.

Table 3-9 provides a summary of the keys you can use to navigate around the table in browse mode. You can also use your mouse.

Editing While in Table View

Editing your forms while in Table View is straightforward, and Q&A will still warn you if you attempt to enter an incorrect information type in a field.

Simply move to the field of the record you want to change, and type in the new value. As soon as you press any character key or press **<F5>**, an ordinary cursor replaces the browse mode highlight bar, and you can now edit the field in the usual fashion. Press **<F1>** to see a list of available options and commands.

Once you're in the edit mode, however, your left and right cursor keys won't move you from column to column as they will in browse mode. You'll need to use **<Tab><Shift><Tab>** to move a column at a time.

Table 3-9
Table View Navigation Keys in Browse Mode

Key	Movement
<Home>	Top line of current screen page
<End>	Bottom line of current screen page
<Ctrl><Home>	First row in the table
<Ctrl><End>	Last row in the table
<Ctrl><→>	Five columns to the right
<Ctrl><←>	Five columns to the left
<PgUp>	Previous 17 rows
<PgDn>	Next 17 rows
<↑> or <F9>	Previous row
<↓> or <space bar>	Next row
<→> or <Tab>	Next column
<←> or <Shift><Tab>	Previous column

You can press **<F6>** to expand the field should you need to edit any field whose contents are longer than the displayed column.

When you're done editing Table View, press **<F10>** and you'll be returned to the form. Any changes you made will be saved and the record the cursor was on when you pressed **<F10>** will be displayed.

Note: On a network, Q&A does not lock a record in Table View until you begin to edit it.

Selecting the Order of Fields for the Table View

You can change the order in which the fields appear in the table — this is helpful when you find yourself routinely viewing or editing some fields more than others.

1. Press **<Shift><F6>** from either a displayed record or the Table View of records to get to the Table Spec.

2. Move to the field you want to have displayed in column 1 of Table View, and type **1**.

3. Repeat step 2 typing a **2,3**, and so forth in the fields you want to correspond to those columns in Table View.

4. Press **\<Esc\>** to cancel the operation, or **\<F10\>** to see your newly defined Table View.

Table View is for use during Search/Update only. Use the form itself to add new records to your database.

Any field restrictions, initial values, programming, field templates, or custom help you've designed into the database will work the same way in the Table View as in the standard form view. These features are covered in the next chapter.

Additionally, You can save and recall a variety of Table Views by saving your specs to disk. The procedure is similar to saving a Retrieve or Sort Spec:

1. Press **\<Shift\>\<F6\>** from Table View for the Table View Spec.

2. Number the fields in the order you want them to appear in Table View columns, starting with a 1 in the field you want to be column 1.

3. Press **\<Shift\>\<F8\>** and type in a descriptive name to attach to this particular Table View Spec.

4. Press **\<Enter\>** to save your parameters.

The next time you want a Table View of your retrieved forms, you can then press **\<Shift\>\<F8\>** and select from the specs you've saved, choosing the view that's optimum for your purposes.

Table Views in Action

With a number of Table Views available you can make the process of updating your records proceed much faster because you can control the field/column relationships and scroll between records rather than having to display each one individually.

If you were updating invoice Balance Due fields with payments received, for example, you could create and then select from your menu a Table View that placed the invoice number in column 1, the amount received in column 2, and the balance due in column 3. Then, if your invoice form was programmed to update the balance due with the amount received, entering the payment and pressing **\<Tab\>** or **\<Enter\>** would work the same way without having to navigate the cursor to the end of the invoice as you'd have to do in form view.

You can save and recall a *different* Table View Spec for entering ship dates on your invoices, and yet another spec for simply viewing the forms. So when Mr. Haggerty calls to find out what happened to his parts order, you can tell him, "Oh, let's see — yes, those were shipped two days ago by UPS surface. You should have them by tomorrow."

 Q&A Power Feature: Saved Retrieve, Sort, and Table View Specs support quick and consistent access to your record groups, and can add tremendous versatility to your applications. And when you combine them with programming (see Chapter 4), and keyboard macros (see Chapter 8), the time spent doing routine database chores can be reduced dramatically.

Printing in File

With practically no effort at all you can print entire forms, selected fields from your forms, all forms in the database, and ranges of forms. And with Q&A 4.0 you can assign a variety of fonts to your individual fields to dramatically enhance your printed output.

There may be times when you'll need to print out individual forms as they appear on screen, and with or without the field labels, lines, and boxes that adorn your design.

You may need to print only certain fields to specific locations on the page, to a preprinted invoice form, for example. (A preprinted form in this sense refers to forms — either generic or custom designed — that you've purchased from outside.)

Mailing labels are another common type of printing job. Here you'll place your name and address fields on individual pressure-sensitive labels, or in a format that calls for two, three, or four more labels to be printed across the page.

Q&A takes into account just about every possible database printing requirement, and offers you a tremendous amount of flexibility in the appearance of your output.

But don't mistake form printing for *reports.* Although you can generate report-like output from the File module, if you're looking for a column-style format with calculations, totals, and subtotals, use the Report module discussed in Chapter 6.

Printing Individual Forms

The simplest way to print from File is to print the individual form you have on screen during Add or Update.

When you've finished filling out the form in Add, or when you've retrieved it from Search/Update, you simply press **<F2>** for the Print Options screen, and then **<F10>** to send it to your printer.

This method won't allow for printing with more than a single font, and you won't be able to control where your fields are placed on the printed page — they'll print in the same relative position as they are on the database form — but some flexibility in output is still possible.

At the Print Options screen you can select any installed printer, add printer control codes to enhance your output, select the number of copies to be printed and the number of forms per *paper* page.

If you're printing to custom-made preprinted forms (like invoices), you can tell Q&A to print the field contents without the labels, or you can make your printed output the form itself by printing the labels along with the field contents — a method typically used for invoices, purchase orders, insurance forms, and other types of forms where the printed page serves as a document.

When you print a form from the screen, and opt to print the field labels along with the data, your output will also contain any lines or boxes that are part of the form design, as long as your printer supports these graphics characters. Figure 3-19 shows the File Print Options screen.

Printing a form directly from the screen during Add Data or Search/Update is best when you want to print out each invoice, sales order, purchase order, and so forth, as you go along.

Print to: Select the printer you want, or send your output to disk or screen. As you highlight the various choices, the output medium is displayed along the bottom of the monitor, reminding you of the installed printer or printer mode that corresponds with PtrA, PtrB, and so forth. Print to screen (with "Print field labels" and "Page preview" set to No) to see how the form looks without field labels. Print to disk when you want to save the output in ASCII format, perhaps to port it to the Write module for a little custom body work.

New: Page preview: This 4.0 feature lets you to see what your output will look like when positioned on a whole page. If you're printing more than one form per page and want to see what the output will look like without field labels, or want a preview of multiple labels printed across the page, the Page preview option gives you a look-see beforehand. It can be especially helpful when you're designing a special print spec and want a realistic view of your efforts without having to print out a test run on paper.

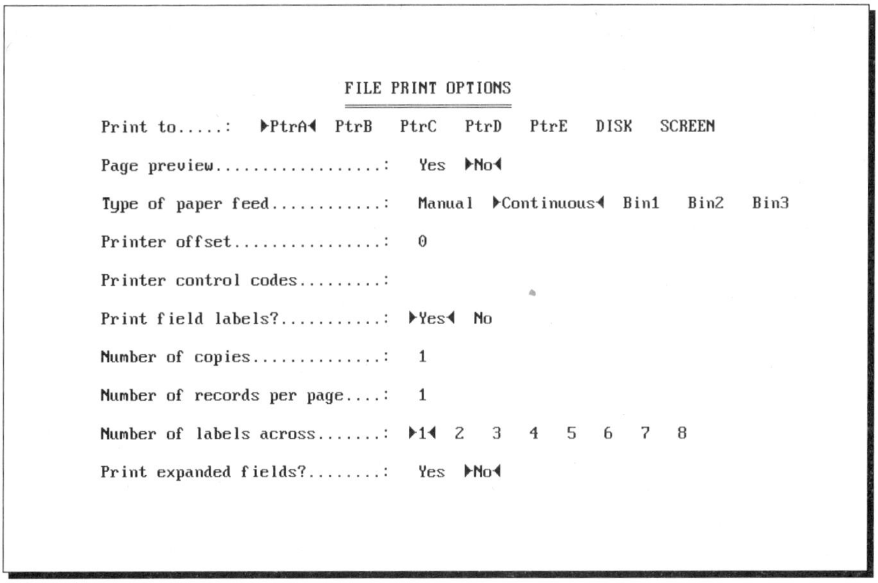

```
                         FILE PRINT OPTIONS

       Print to.....:  ▶PtrA◀ PtrB   PtrC   PtrD   PtrE   DISK   SCREEN

       Page preview.................:   Yes  ▶No◀

       Type of paper feed...........:   Manual ▶Continuous◀ Bin1   Bin2   Bin3

       Printer offset...............:   0

       Printer control codes........:

       Print field labels?..........:  ▶Yes◀  No

       Number of copies.............:   1

       Number of records per page...:   1

       Number of labels across......:  ▶1◀  2   3   4   5   6   7   8

       Print expanded fields?.......:   Yes  ▶No◀
```

Figure 3-19: File's Print Options Screen.

A previewed page displays a *printed* page mock-up based on your font selection, page format, and Print Options settings. If your form is three screen pages long and your Define Page is set for a standard page size, the preview option will display the entire form.

Type of paper feed: Select manual feed to load individual sheets and have Q&A pause after printing a page so you can load the next one. Continuous feed is for printers that handle fanfold paper or feed from a single tray (such as many laser printers). If your printer has more than one paper tray attached, select the appropriate bin.

Printer offset: Allows you to control where the first character will be printed on the page. A value of 2 causes the printer to start printing two characters further to the right on the page than your normal left margin setting. The opposite occurs with a negative offset. Whole numbers only, please — no decimals or fractions.

When printing a variety of forms during the day on a printer with adjustable paper guides, an appropriate offset entered at the Print Options screen for each of your forms saves you having to constantly readjust them.

Printer control codes: These can be entered here to enhance the entire printed form. See "Printing in Write" in the previous chapter for information on using these codes.

Print field labels: Choose Yes if you want your field labels printed along with the field values, or No to print just the values. If you're using a Print Spec, an **L** typed into the field at the Fields Spec will override a No setting at this screen and print that field's label along with the value.

Number of copies: Type the number of copies of the form you want printed.

Number of forms per page: This is per *printed* page, not screen page. If your forms are small, you may want to print several of them on a single sheet of paper. You can type in a number and use the Page Preview option to see what the multiform printed page will look like before sending it to the printer.

Number of labels across: Use this only when printing mailing labels, or printing to a page in a label-like format (multiple forms across the page) — otherwise leave it set at its default of 1. You can print up to eight labels (forms) across a page, depending on the field widths involved, the width of the paper, and the horizontal distance the printhead is able to span.

Print expanded fields: If your form contains expanded fields and you wish to print the long values, select Yes. These will then print in a vertical column the same width as the *un*expanded field on the form. Leaving this option set to the default No will print only up to the end of any expanded fields as they appear on the form, with a small right arrow to indicate that the field contains more data.

Using a Print Spec, as you'll see in a moment, gives you the option of printing any expanded fields on a field-by-field basis.

Define Page Settings

Pressing **<F8>** from the Print Options screen takes you to the Define Page screen shown in Figure 3-20. Here you can change your page width, page length, margins, and printing pitch, as well as add a header and/or footer.

Using the Define Page screen to format the page characteristics of your database forms in File is very similar to formatting your documents in the Write module (see "Defining Your Page Characteristics" in the previous chapter and Chapter 6 for details on Define Page screen choices).

 Tip: When you change any of your page characteristics, including pitch, the entire printed form will be affected — but only the *printed* form. Nothing you do to the Define Page screen in File will change the way your form is displayed on screen; that was fixed with your database form design.

A form can be printed much smaller than screen size by increasing the characters-per-inch, enabling you to fit more forms on the printed page.

```
                          DEFINE PAGE
                          ──────────

          Page width : 80          Page length..: 66

          Left margin: 5           Right margin : 80

          Top margin : 3           Bottom margin: 3

          Characters per inch:    ▶10◀  12   15   17
─────────────────────────────── HEADER ───────────────────────────
    1:
    2:
    3:
─────────────────────────────── FOOTER ───────────────────────────
    1:
    2:
    3:
────────────────────────────────────────────────────────────────
    STOCK.DTF              Define page for current form

    Esc-Cancel            F9-Go Back to Print Options        F10-Continue
```

Figure 3-20: File's Define Page Screen.

When printing individual records to preprinted forms without the benefit of a formal print specification (see below), and you want to use 12 or 15 pitch instead of the default 10, you'll need to fine-tune your left and right margin settings so that the contents of the fields are printed in their correct positions on the form. Remember, changing your pitch will affect the printed page's actual left/right margins if those margins are specified in character columns rather than inches.

Q&A Power Feature: In addition to printing single forms directly from Add and Search/Update, you can design special print specs for printing groups of forms in almost any imaginable format. You can retrieve only those forms you wish to print, select fields to include in lists or mailing labels, and tell Q&A exactly where to print them on the page. Figure 3-21 shows the File module's Print menu. We'll look at each of these selections in the following pages.

Print Menu Choices

Selecting "Design/Redesign a Spec" gives you the tools you need to create and save a custom printing specification.

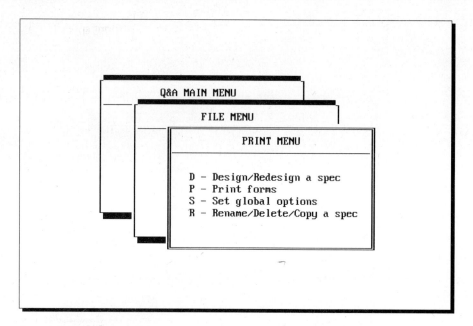

```
                    Q&A MAIN MENU

                         FILE MENU

                              PRINT MENU

                         D - Design/Redesign a spec
                         P - Print forms
                         S - Set global options
                         R - Rename/Delete/Copy a spec
```

Figure 3-21: The File Print Menu.

The Print Forms option is used when you've already set up your spec and want to start printing a batch of forms or parts of forms. Here Q&A always gives you the option of modifying your printing spec for a one-time-only printing job.

If you want to change Q&A's default settings for printing and page options, "Set global options" enables you to do it swiftly. And the "Rename/Delete/ Copy/a Spec" selection helps you carry out a variety of utility-like tasks with your existing print specs.

Designing a Print Spec

A *Print Spec* prints each form in a group of forms the same way. If you print the day's invoices at the end of each day, for example, designing a Print Spec for the job will make it go faster because Q&A will know how you want them printed.

Your spec remembers which forms in the database are to be retrieved (Retrieve Spec), which fields on these forms are to be printed, and where the selected fields are to be positioned on the printed page (Fields Spec). It also contains your Define Page and Print Options settings. As a result, Print Specs give you total *control* over your forms printing.

You can save and later recall up to 40 different print specs for any database. Q&A keeps them stored on disk.

A Print Spec isn't necessary for forms you print one at a time from the screen during Add or Search/Update. In that case you're simply pressing **<F2>** and **<F10>** to send the current record to the printer.

But with single-form printing you must either print all the field labels or none — you have no control over which field values will be printed or where they'll appear on the printed page, and you can't enhance selected fields only. Single-form printing simply duplicates your screen form.

The steps involved in setting up a print spec are as follows:

1. Select "Design/Redesign a Spec" from the Print menu and press **<Enter>**. You'll see a list of print specs already in the database (if you've designed any previously).

2. Type a name for the spec that will identify it for you, and press **<Enter>**. Names can be up to 30 character long. You could call a spec "Four-up Subscription Labels," "Marketing Contact Phone List," or "Today's Purchase Orders."

3. Fill out the Retrieve Spec to tell Q&A what forms to include in the printing job (the **<F1>** Help screen can come in handy here with its list of the various Retrieve Spec codes). Press **<F8>** for the Sort Spec if you want the forms printed in a particular order.

   Filling out the Retrieve and Sort Specs here is done exactly as described earlier in this chapter under "Retrieving and Updating Your Forms" and "Sorting Retrieved Forms." If, when designing your Print Spec, you press **<F10>** with the Retrieve Spec left blank, Q&A will assume you want to print all the forms in the database.

   Also, you can use programming formulas in your Retrieve Spec; for example, with **{@Date}** in the date field of an invoice database, Retrieve Spec selects only those invoices for printing with the current date on them. More about using programming functions and formulas in the following chapter.

   Press **<F10>** when you've finished filling out your Retrieve and Sort Specs.

4. At the Fields Spec you tell Q&A which fields you want printed and where they should appear on the printed page. Either the *Coordinate* or *Free-form* method can be used, but not both in the same spec (more on this in a moment). If you leave the Fields Spec blank and press **<F10>**, Q&A will assume that you want to print all the fields in the same position on

the printed page as they are on the form. Press **<F10>** when your Fields Spec is finished.

You can also select which field labels to print, and assign enhancements and up to nine fonts per form. The steps needed to do this are shown later in this chapter.

5. Make your selections at the Print Options screen, and optionally press **<F8>** to check or change your Define Page settings. Press **<F10>**, Q&A will let you know that your specification has been saved, and ask if you're now ready to print.

6. Press **Y** to run the printing job, or **N** to hold off on it. Either way your spec has been saved to disk.

You can see that a Print Spec is really nothing more than a Retrieve Spec, a Fields Spec, a Define Page screen, and a Print Options screen all saved as a single specification.

Printing Selected Fields Only — The Fields Spec

New: You can take best advantage of a Print Spec by using it to tell Q&A which fields in your selected forms to print, and where these fields should appear on the printed page. This is done at the Fields Spec. Q&A 4.0 users have additional printing options available through the Fields Spec:

- *On a field-by-field basis* you can choose to print just the field label, just the field contents, or both.

- You can enhance just a field label, just the field contents, or both. This means that you can choose to print any of your selected fields in bold or italics, in different pitches, or in proportional fonts, so long as your printer supports them and they've been installed in Q&A (see "Installing and Using Fonts" in the Write chapter). Figure 3-22 shows the Enhancement menu that displays when you press **<Shift><F6>** from the Fields Spec.

- On a field-by-field basis you can decide whether to print expanded values or only the portions of expanded fields visible on the form.

- In coordinate printing, you can specify your page coordinates in inches as well as in columns and rows — this is sensible if you're using proportional fonts for your forms (characters-per-inch aren't very useful for calculating positions of fonts where the characters are all different widths).

Remember: You can press **<F1>** at the Fields Spec for on-line information on how to proceed.

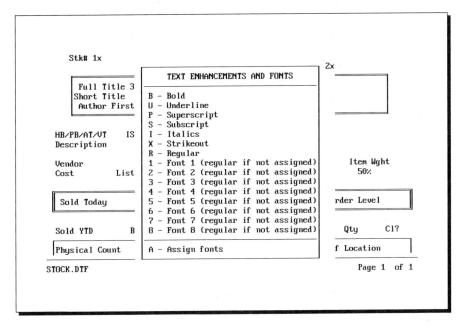

Stk# 1x

```
                         ┌──────────────────────────────────┐                    2x
                         │   TEXT ENHANCEMENTS AND FONTS      │
    ┌──────────────┐     ├──────────────────────────────────┤
    │Full Title 3  │     │ B - Bold                           │
    │Short Title   │     │ U - Underline                      │
    │Author First  │     │ P - Superscript                    │
    └──────────────┘     │ S - Subscript                      │
                         │ I - Italics                        │
  HB/PB/AT/UT    IS      │ X - Strikeout                      │
  Description            │ R - Regular                        │
                         │ 1 - Font 1 (regular if not assigned)│     Item Wght
  Vendor                 │ 2 - Font 2 (regular if not assigned)│        50%
  Cost        List       │ 3 - Font 3 (regular if not assigned)│
                         │ 4 - Font 4 (regular if not assigned)│
    ┌──────────────┐     │ 5 - Font 5 (regular if not assigned)│   rder Level
    │ Sold Today   │     │ 6 - Font 6 (regular if not assigned)│
    └──────────────┘     │ 7 - Font 7 (regular if not assigned)│
                         │ 8 - Font 8 (regular if not assigned)│   Qty      C1?
  Sold YTD       B       │                                    │
    ┌──────────────┐     │ A - Assign fonts                   │   f Location
    │Physical Count│     └──────────────────────────────────┘
    └──────────────┘
  STOCK.DTF                                                        Page 1  of 1
```

Figure 3-22: The Field Enhancement Menu Available at the Fields Spec.

Free-Form Printing

This style is the one to use for printing mailing labels (that are actual forms or parts of forms), or to print portions of forms onto blank paper for lists. If you have an employee database, and want a list of employees with their names printed on the first line, their address on the second line, and phone numbers on the third, Free-form is the way to go. It's usually faster and easier than the coordinate method because you just type the characters **X** or **+** into each of the fields you want to print.

X in Free-form printing means "print this field then move down to the next line (carriage return)."

+ means "print this field and skip a space before printing the next field."

When using the Free-form style, Q&A will print only those fields containing an **X** or a **+** character, and it will print them in the same order as they appear on the form, from left to right, top to bottom. The exception to this is if you leave *all* the fields blank, in which case the entire form will print.

To illustrate a Free-form printing spec, suppose your database fields were positioned like this on the form:

```
First Name: +        Last Name: X>

Street: X                      >

City: +        State: +  Zip: X   >

Phone:         Fax:               >
```

The codes typed into them as above at the Fields Spec would result in the fields being printed like this:

```
James Baldwin
4855 Pacific Hwy
San Diego CA 90124
```

You've told Q&A to print the first name, skip a space, print the last name, go to the next line, print the street, move to the next line, and print the city, state, and zip.

You can see how handy this style would be for printing out mailing labels either on one-up continuous pressure-sensitive labels, or two, three, four, or more across on wider sheets (selected at the Print Options screen).

Other Free-Form Options

Continuing with the above example, if you wanted a blank line between the last line of the first label, and the first line of the next one, you'd simply type a comma and then **2** in the Zip field to tell Q&A to add an extra carriage return (line feed) between the labels. So instead of the zip field containing just the X, it would look like this: **Zip: X,2**.

You can also add extra spaces between multiple fields printed on the same line by typing a comma and then a number after the **+** character. In the example, typing **+,2** into the State field would leave *two* spaces between the state and zip when printed.

Another feature available with the Free-form style allows you to change the order in which the fields will be printed. Suppose you wanted the Last Name field to print first, and the First Name field to follow it on the same line (just the opposite of their locations on the form), all you need to do is type **2X** in the First Name field and a **1+** in the Last Name field. This would tell Q&A to print the Last Name first, followed by a space, and then print the First Name field, followed by a carriage return.

You can specify the maximum number of characters in the field to be printed by adding an *additional* whole number to your code after a comma. Then, if the field contents *exceed* the number specified, Q&A will truncate the value.

The following examples illustrate how you can code your fields to get them to print where you want them on the page or label.

A number directly following an **X** indicates the number of *carriage returns,* whereas a number after a **+** indicates the number of *character spaces* to be left blank.

1+	Print this field first, followed by a space.
3+,5	Print this field third, followed by 5 spaces.
2X,2,10	Print this field second, followed by 2 carriage returns, and print only the first 10 characters of the field.
X,2,15	No order is specified (no number preceding the X). If no order is specified for any of the other selected fields, the first 15 characters of this field will print relative to the other selected fields' positions on the form, followed by 2 carriage returns.
5+,2,5	Print this field fifth, followed by two spaces, and print only the first 5 characters of the field value.

If you want to print an expanded field in Free-form, follow the **X** or **+** with the letter **E**. This tells Q&A to print the contents of the expanded field even though the Print Options screen may say not to.

If you want the field label printed, include the letter **L** as part of the selected field code. If you want to specify a label different than the actual field label, follow the **L** with the label you want to print in parentheses. For example:

3+2,10,L (Surname) means print this field third, stay on the same line, leave 2 spaces, print only the first 10 characters of the field, and print the label "Surname."

When designing mailing labels in Free-form, you don't have to be concerned about controlling how many labels to print *across* a page until you get to the Print Options screen. But the *vertical* space between the labels (the number of lines you want skipped between the last line of one label and the first line of the next one) *does* have to be entered here at the Fields Spec.

An alternative to Free-form designed mailing labels is to use Q&A's built-in mailing label generator available from the Write menu (see Chapter 5). There Q&A provides you with a shopping list of commercial label sizes, and may make the task of label printing easier on you.

If you want to print custom messages on your labels, merge selected database fields into your label format, select a standard label size, or simply don't want to hassle with a Free-form spec, The Mailing Label menu is the way to go. But since that method requires a merge operation, it can take Q&A noticeably longer to prepare for printing when a large number of forms is involved.

Coordinate Printing

The Coordinate printing style is best used when you're printing to preprinted forms (such as invoices, checks, or purchase orders) because it allows you to control exactly where fields and columns will appear on the page.

It works like coordinates on a grid. You select a field and say, "Now start printing the contents of this field on the 12th line of the page and in the 35th column position," and Q&A will print that field right there. There's a Write document file included with the Q&A program called LINE-DOC.DOC. It's a grid numbered in 10-cpi character columns across the top, and six lines to an inch down the left edge. You can print this document out and use it to establish your line and column coordinates for coordinate printing.

To use the coordinate method at the Fields Spec, navigate to a field you want to print and type in the page coordinates: first the line number (row), followed by a comma, and then the character position (column). If you wanted an Invoice Number field to start printing on line 3 in the fifth character position, you'd enter **3,5** in the Invoice Number field.

The coordinates you specify will print based on the margins you've set up for your form at the Define Page screen. If you've set a top page margin of 1 inch, line 1 will be the first line below the top margin. Similarly, if you've set a left margin of an inch, column position 1 will be the first character column immediately to the right of the margin.

If the space available to print a field on a form is limited to a certain number of characters, type the page coordinates in the corresponding field at the Fields Spec, add a comma, and then type a number after the comma to indicate the *maximum* length for a printed value for that field. Q&A will then truncate values that are too long for that page coordinate.

For example, coordinates of 20, 12, 10 mean "start printing this field on the 20th line down and at the 12th character column, and only print the first 10 characters of the field."

New: Q&A 4.0 users can optionally specify page coordinates in inches by telling Q&A, for example, to start printing a field 3 inches down from the top of the page, and 2.5 inches over from the left margin. If you're using proportional fonts and need to have your columns line up, it's the thing to do. When you enter your coordinates in inches, be sure to follow them with a " symbol. For example: 3,2" or 3.5", 2.75.

You can use row and column coordinates for some fields, and inches for others, but you can't specify a row in inches and a column in character spaces within the same field.

Other Field-Specific Options Available at the Fields Spec

New: Using either printing style, Q&A 4.0 users can specify field value *and* field label printing on a field-by-field basis, and add text enhancements to either the label or the value, or both.

To have Q&A print the field label in addition to the field value, type **L** into the field, separated from any other code by a comma. Even if you tell Q&A *not* to print field labels at the Print Options screen, this code will still print that field's label. If you want *all* the labels printed in addition to the field contents, typing **L** into all the fields at the Fields Spec would be a waste of time — just tell Q&A to print the field labels at the Print Options screen.

You can also direct Q&A to print alternate field labels by typing the new label in parentheses directly after the **L** command.

On a field-by-field basis you can also choose to print fields containing expanded values. But you'll need to watch out for these in Coordinate printing since the text could interfere with page coordinates set for other fields. To print an expanded value, type **E** into the field, separated from any other code by a comma.

Q&A Power Feature: Text and font enhancements are also available when creating a version 4.0 Print Spec. The section on installing and using fonts in the Write chapter identifies the steps required to use fonts with Q&A, and the procedure is similar for using enhancements and fonts at the Fields Spec in the File module.

At the Fields Spec, press **<Ctrl><F9>** for the Font Assignments screen. Here you can select your font description file and enter the fonts you want to have available for use in printing your forms.

To assign a font or enhancement (such as bold, underline, or italics) to a field:

1. Move to the field and press **<Shift><F6>**. The Text Enhancements and Fonts menu shown in Figure 3-22 will be displayed.

2. Move the highlight bar to the enhancement or font you want and press **<Enter>**, or select the enhancement by first letter or number.

3. Now use the **<>** key to highlight the field, and then press **<F10>**. If any portion of the field is highlighted, the entire field value will be printed in the enhancement you've selected. If there's an **L** in the field, and you've highlighted that also, the label will be printed in the same enhancement. To enhance the field value but *not* the label, don't highlight the **L**.

If later you want to *remove* the enhancement from the field, follow step 3, select the regular font from the Enhancements menu, highlight the field, and press **<F10>**.

As usual, if you need to expand a field in order to have enough room to type your codes into it, simply press **<F6>**.

Redesigning a Print Spec

Changing your saved print specs is as simple as selecting Design/Redesign a Spec from File's Print menu, and editing any or all of the screens that comprise the spec.

To redesign the spec from start to finish, enter the database filename, type the name of the spec or select it from the list of saved specs, and move back and forth through the screens using **<F10>** and **<F9>**, making the desired changes. When you press **<F10>** from the Define Page or Print Options screen, the modified spec is saved to disk and Q&A will ask if you wish to begin printing.

There is also a special redesign menu available to make changes to a spec during the actual printing process. Pressing **<Shift><F9>** during printing brings up a menu with selections for the Retrieve Spec, the Sort Spec, the Fields Spec, the Print Options screen, and the Define Page screen. You press the letter corresponding to the screen you want, make your changes, and then press **<F10>** to restart printing.

You can repeat this process for each part of the spec you want to edit, but you can't navigate between the screens. To edit several screens you should use the "Design/Redesign a Spec" option from the Print menu and move through the screens in sequence.

You can also press **<F2>** during printing to bring up the Print Options screen. This interrupts the printing until you press **<F10>** again. But if you make any changes to the Print Options screen and press **<F10>**, printing will start over again with the first form in the stack.

Print Forms

Choose Print Forms from the Print menu when you want to print with an existing spec. Q&A shows you the list of print specs for the database you specify, and you can type in the name of the one you want, or highlight it, and then press **<Enter>**.

Q&A Power Feature: When you choose an existing spec, Q&A asks you if you'd like to make any *temporary* changes to the spec for this particular print run (temporary specs aren't saved). Making temporary changes are often a useful alternative to designing an entirely new spec, and can save you time on those ad hoc print runs. You just go in and edit only the necessary screens, pressing **<F10>** at the ones that already meet your parameters. And when you press **<F10>** at the Print Options screen Q&A will print the job with your temporary settings.

Unless the Retrieve Spec last saved with the Print Spec will select the forms you want to print in the *current* job, you'll have to answer Yes to the "Do you wish to make any temporary changes?" question and enter your new retrieve parameters.

For example, if you're preparing to print *today's* invoices, you'll need to ensure that your Retrieve Spec is set to select *only* today's invoices. You could do this by typing today's date in the invoice date field at the Retrieve Spec, or by specifying the new range of invoice numbers to be printed.

On the other hand, if you simply run the customer list the same way every week, and your Retrieve and other specs don't need updating, you'd simply answer No to "Temporary Changes?" and run the job.

Global Options

You can also set printing and page defaults to apply to all new print specs you create. When you change your global options, existing specs won't be affected, only new ones — and these only to the extent that you leave them with the default settings intact at the time you design the spec.

Q&A Power Feature: Appropriate Global Options settings for your database forms printing can prove to be a real time-saver if your Define Page and Print Options are going to be consistent for all the print specs you may design for this database. You can set defaults just for single-form printing (when you print a displayed form while in Add or Search/Update), or for any printing for which you've designed a print spec.

Select "Set global options" from the Print menu, and the Global Options menu (see Figure 3-23) will be displayed.

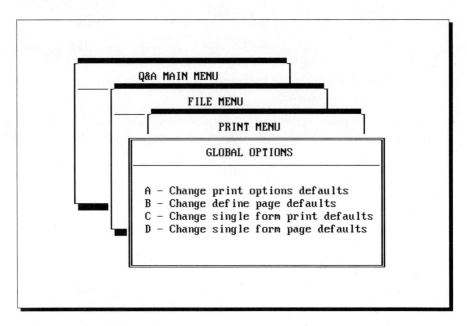

Figure 3-23: The Global Options Menu.

Print Spec Print and Page Defaults

The screen displayed when you select "Change print options defaults" is no different from the usual File Print Options screen, except that any settings you make here will be reflected on the Print Options screens you'll see when you design new print specs.

The same holds true when you select "Change define page defaults" from the Global Options menu. You're presented with a Define Page screen that looks exactly like the usual one with the exception of the status line, indicating that changes made here apply only to new print specs.

If all the forms you'll be printing from designed specs are likely to have the same page characteristics, set your defaults here. Then they'll automatically be reflected in any future Print Spec designs you do.

Single-Form Print and Page Defaults

If you want to establish new defaults for single-form printing during Add or Search/Update (when you print the form that's on screen by pressing **<F2>** and then **<F10>**), select "Change single form print defaults" or "Change single form page defaults" and enter your new settings. Changes made to either of these screens will show up the very next time you print a single form from this database.

If your single forms unexpectedly begin to print with inappropriate page or print characteristics, check your single-form global defaults. People often don't realize that changes here take effect with the very next single form that goes to the printer.

Of course any global default settings remain in effect only until you change them again.

Your Print Specs and Good Housekeeping

The fourth and final selection on your Print menu is "Rename/Delete/Copy a spec."

You might want to give a print spec a new, more descriptive name, especially if you've redesigned it.

If a print spec is no longer of any use, or if you need to get rid of an old one to make room for a new one, you can delete an existing spec. But once you delete it, it's gone forever.

Copying a spec can be a handy tool, especially when you need to design a new one that will contain most, if not all, of the characteristics of one you've already created.

After you've selected "Rename/Delete/Copy a spec" from the Print menu, a Rename Delete Copy menu will be displayed from which you can choose your action. When you do, Q&A will prompt you for the name of the specification. Type in the spec name or press **<Enter>** to see a list of print specs in the database.

If you're renaming or copying a spec, you'll be prompted for the new name. Type it in and press **<Enter>**. If you've chosen to delete a spec, Q&A will ask you to confirm the request before it proceeds with the deletion.

Summary

In this chapter you've learned all the basics of designing a database form, adding, searching, and updating records, and printing your forms in a variety of ways.

In Chapter 4 I'll introduce you to Q&A's more advanced File features. These enable you to fully customize your databases and database procedures to make data entry, retrieval, and wholesale data manipulation easy and efficient, adding considerable power and versatility to your applications where needed.

Chapter 4
Advanced Database Design and Procedures

In this chapter you'll learn how to:

▶ Design sophisticated work-saving data entry forms.

▶ Set up defaults and restrictions on data entry.

▶ Perform speed search and retrieval operations.

▶ Change the way Q&A displays your forms.

▶ Design custom help screens.

▶ Program your forms for fast data entry.

▶ Construct lookup tables to store frequently used data.

▶ Retrieve information into your forms from other databases.

▶ Post values from one database to another.

▶ Place fields and files "off limits" to others.

▶ Update, copy, and remove entire groups of records.

This chapter will show you how to build on the information, tips, and tricks you learned in the last chapter to customize and program your databases. I will also show you how to create an advanced invoice form and then program it, copy, remove, and update records, and post values to external databases.

You must understand the principles in Chapter 3 before you try to tackle the precepts in this chapter.

Overview

Once you've got your basic form designs in shape you can customize them to make them really sing. Customizing a database increases its versatility, performance, and value. You can make the process of adding and updating records easier, faster, and less error prone, and restrict access to selected fields on your forms. You may be looking at an application where you need to link several databases together to form an integrated system. Or your requirements might call for operations to be done on all the records in a database.

Q&A offers a wealth of options to add the degree of sophistication and performance you need, whether your database contains 100 records or half a million. But you should be familiar with basic Q&A form design, and adding, searching, and updating forms, as presented in the previous chapter, before moving into these more advanced procedures.

In this chapter I'll explain each of these custom features in detail, and show you how a number of them work in a sophisticated invoice database that we'll design together from the ground up.

 Note: A copy of this database is located on the free applications disk in the back of this book. (See Chapter 11 for more information about the applications disk.) Don't use the applications disk invoice form yet, however. You'll get a lot more knowledge if you create the form from scratch.

In Chapter 10, which covers how to make your databases work together in a multi-module business system, some of these advanced features will be stretched even further.

What These Custom Features Can Do for You

When it comes to working with the advanced features in Q&A's File module, you're really looking at three distinct types of activities:

- **Adding options to enhance data entry.** Under this heading you have tools to restrict values, construct custom help screens, and increase the speed at which Q&A will retrieve information for you. Simple programming routines can look up values from tables and other databases, move the cursor around the form, perform calculations, and automate other routines to suit your particular data entry needs and preferences.

- **Manipulating groups of records within a database.** Here you have options available to mass update, remove, copy, and merge groups of records, and back up and recover your files.

- **Setting up databases to communicate with each other.** Q&A has features that allow you to look up values from other databases and bring them into the current form, as well as a version 4.0 feature that enables you to post values from one Q&A database to another. Relational-like in performance, these powerful capabilities help you

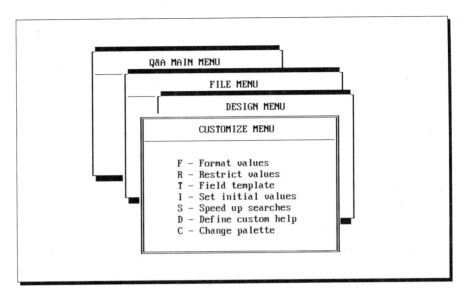

Figure 4-1: File's Customize Menu.

design extensive, fully integrated applications, and get lots of work done with minimal time and effort.

In addition to these, you can select from a variety of import/export formats that let you bring in database files from other programs and freely transfer Q&A data to them. Together we'll explore this aspect of file management in Chapter 9.

Most of the advanced features you'll learn about in this chapter can be protected from unauthorized changes by placing locks on the database that can only be unlocked with a password you assign. Keep this in mind as you read on. There's a special Database Lock screen that you can reach from the Customize Application menu in the File module. This feature is discussed in detail in Chapter 9.

Customizing a Database

You're already familiar with Q&A's Design menu. In the last chapter we used the "Design a New File" selection to create our sample Customer, Stock, and Employee databases.

Figure 4-1 shows Q&A's Customize menu, which branches off from the Design menu. Reach the Customize menu by selecting File from the Main menu, Design a File from the File menu, Customize a File from the Design menu, typing in the name of the database you want to work on, and pressing **<Enter>**.

Because you'll be working with your database forms on a frequent basis now, the way they are displayed on screen can make a big difference. So let's look at the last Customize menu selection first.

Changing Your Screen Attributes

Q&A's Change Palette feature allows you to set foreground and background screen attributes for any database form. The form's actual layout isn't affected, only the way it looks when displayed. Your own personal preferences are the guiding light in choosing a screen palette for your form. If you prefer purple background, for example, but your coworker Susan hates it, well, you and Susan will just have to work out a compromise.

With a monochrome monitor you can highlight the field label or the information blank, have an underline appear in the field where the next value is to be entered, or various combinations of both.

On a color monitor you can set the foreground and background colors, and also highlight the field label or the information blank. The area at the bottom of the screen that Q&A reserves for itself, however, cannot be assigned a different color.

When you select Change Palette from the Customize menu, Q&A displays the default palette for the database. You can see all the palettes by pressing **<F8>** for the next one and **<F6>** to go back to the previous one. You can choose from eight different styles, and have a different palette for each database in your system — this is a good idea if two of your form designs might otherwise look similar.

While you're browsing through the palettes, feel free to type sample entries into the fields to see what they look like with the different screen colors or attributes.

When you've decided which palette looks best to you, press **<F10>** and Q&A will return you to the Customize menu. The palette you've selected will stay in effect for the database form until you change it.

Format Values

In the previous chapter, you learned how to assign information types to your fields (number, money, text, and keyword, for example), formatting your fields for the way you want them displayed on the form (all uppercase, initial caps, justify right, justify left), and setting your global format options for dates, hours, decimal digits, and your favorite currency symbol. The Format Values selection at the Customize menu lets you change any of these at any time.

After your database is up and running, you might decide that all uppercase letters in certain fields is preferable to initial caps, that a different date format has more appeal, or that your left-justified money fields ought to be right-justified so they'll line up in a columnar format on the form.

It's no sweat. To assign a new information type or field format code, simply go into the Format Spec, use **<Tab>** to move to the field you want to change, type the new code, and press **<F10>**. If your database contains any money, number, date, or hour information types, Q&A will bring you to the Global Format Options screen where you can alter these settings, too.

Format changes you have made will be implemented in Add Data and Search/Update from that point forward. For example, a left-justified money field without commas, changed to right-justified *with* commas, will be displayed in the new format when you retrieve any form from that database.

Tip: You can have your name and address fields in a customer database in all uppercase for data entry and mailing labels, and quickly reformat them to display in initial caps for merge-letter addressing and salutations.

Restricting Data Input

Assigning proper information types to your fields at the Format Spec is your *first* line of defense against garbage in the database. Restricting values is the *second.*

When an improper *type* of value is entered into a field, Q&A suspends data entry and displays an error message, prompting the operator to enter a correct type of value.

A *range* restriction on the field serves the same purpose. An out-of-range value entered will result in an error message and the opportunity to correct it.

Your *third* line of defense against invalid entries (which you'll learn about later in this chapter) are field-programming statements that prevent the operator from continuing to the next field if your programmed restrictions are not met.

A typist may not fully appreciate the fact that important business decisions can be based on reports that in turn depend on individual fields in individual database records. You want truth in your database, not error.

Even a single field containing an invalid entry in a single record can throw off an entire report. Thus data entry conventions and restrictions play a crucial role in any automated data management and information system.

Table 4-1: Restrictions for Data Entry

For All Restrictions
(For use with any information type)

.. (two periods)   AND. **X..Y** means X and Y (or *from* X to Y).
; (semicolon)   OR. **X;Y** means X or Y.
/ (slash)   NOT. **/X** means not X.
.. (two periods)   wildcard characters (text and keyword).

Exact Match Restrictions
(All information types including Yes/No fields and Date)

X or **=X**   Equal to X.
/X   Not X.
=   Field should be empty.
/=   Field should not be empty.
!=   Field *cannot* be empty.
!X;Y   Field *must* contain either X or Y.
X;Y;Z   X or Y or Z within a single field.

Range Restrictions
(All information types except Yes/No fields)

>X   Greater than X.
<X   Less than X.
>=X   Greater than or equal to X.
<=X   Less than or equal to X.
>X..<Y   Greater than X and less than Y.
>X..<=Y   Greater than X and less than or equal to Y.
>X;<=Y   Greater than X or less than or equal to Y.

Text and Character Search Restrictions
(Text and Keyword)

?   Any single character.
..   Any group of characters.
X..   Begins with X.
..X   Ends with X.
X..Y   Begins with X and ends with Y.
..X..   Includes X.
..X..Y..Y   Includes X, Y, and Z, in that order.

The Restrict Values option provides you with powerful tools for controlling data entry. The method you use to set up your restrictions here is very similar to how you enter your search parameters at the Retrieve Spec when searching for particular forms — in fact, the codes you use are exactly the same, except *you* have fewer of them.

At any Retrieve Spec you're placing restrictions on the information Q&A will retrieve for you. At the Restrict Values Spec, you're placing restrictions on what you can hand Q&A.

In contrast to the information types you assigned at the Format Spec — which flag the entry of dates that aren't dates and prevent letters from being typed in number fields, for example — the Restrict Values Spec can be used to control *the range* of values permitted, and restrict data entry in other ways as well.

At the Restrict Spec you can set minimum or maximum (or minimum *and* maximum) values that can be entered into your form's fields, and you can prevent the operator from leaving empty a field where a value is required — this is considered by many to be the most valuable restriction of all.

You can also place a ceiling on the dollar amount a purchase order can be worth, or set a minimum invoice order quantity for wholesale accounts. Table 4-1 provides a summary of the restrictions you can use to control the values entered into the fields on your form. Notice that in some cases the restriction depends on the field's information type assigned at the Format Spec. Substitute your own values for the X's, Y's, and Z's.

When you access the Restrict Spec from the Customize menu Q&A will display your form. You enter your restrictions simply by navigating the cursor to the fields you want to restrict, typing in the restriction values, and pressing **<F10>** when finished.

Here are a few examples to get you moving in the right direction:

/= means a value is *recommended* in this field. If the operator tries to bypass the field, leaving it empty, the error message will be, "This field requires a value. Please enter a value before continuing." The operator can then press **<Tab>** or **<Enter>** and proceed to the next field, leaving the recommended field blank.

! placed in front of a restriction makes it a *hard* restriction — meaning that the field *must* contain the correct value or be within the required range before the operator will be permitted to continue or save the form.

! by itself means the field *must* contain a value before the operator will be permitted to leave the field.

HB;PB	in a text field means that values other than **HB** or **PB** will earn the error message, "Warning! Value not in specified range. Please verify before continuing."
>10	means the value should be greater than 10 (or $10.00 in a money field). **!>10** *enforces* a value greater than 10.
!<500	means the value *has to be* less than 500 (or $500.00 in a money field) before the operator can continue or save the form.
>5..<7	means the value needs to be greater than 5 and less than 7.
B..	in a text or keyword field means that the value should begin with the letter B. **!B** makes it a hard restriction.
..B..	in a text or keyword field means that the value *should* include the letter B. **!..B..** means it *must*.

When placing restrictions on your fields it's a good idea to complement them with custom help screens. Then, by pressing **<F1>** your operator can see an explanation or brief summary table indicating what range or type of values *are* permitted.

Q&A Power Feature: You can use the Restrict Spec to maintain an entire list of acceptable values for any field. For example, if 10 different shipping methods are permitted in the Shipping Method field of an invoice, simply type these into that field at the Restrict Spec. Then, during data entry, the operator can press **<Alt><F7>** to pop up the list of restricted values, highlight the one that's wanted, and press **<Enter>** to retrieve it into the field without having to type a single character. When entering lists of acceptable values at the Restrict Spec, be sure each value is separated by a semicolon.

You can also program your custom help screen (or a one-line message) to pop up automatically when an incorrect value is entered. More on all of this later in the chapter.

Field Templates

New: If your forms will contain telephone numbers, Social Security numbers, department prefixes, Zip+4 zip codes, or the like, you can create "templates" or "masks" for these fields that will make entering data into them both faster and less error prone.

At a phone number field, for example, one data entry clerk might type **415-833-3455**, while another might enter **(415) 833-3455**; another might omit the area code altogether and type **833-3455**. So far, that's *three* different formats in a field on which you may later need to search.

Creating a control template for such a field would permit the phone number to be entered only one way: **4158333455**.

The template can't be beaten. If the number is typed with the parentheses around the area code, or a dash between the prefix and suffix, these nondigits will simply be ignored and only the numerical digits will be displayed — the template *fixes* the parentheses and dashes in the field.

Field templates can be created for text fields only. Use the **#** symbol to designate a single number, an **@** symbol to designate an alphabetic character, a **$** symbol to designate any single character that can be typed (including punctuation), and the **** symbol before any character you want Q&A to take literally.

One format for a phone number would be:

Phone Number: (###) ###-#### Extension:

This tells Q&A to display the field as follows when the cursor arrives at it during data entry:

Phone Number: (　　)　　–　　　　Extension:

During data entry the field template is displayed just before and as the value is typed in it. You can use any characters as part of the mask design. But if you use **#**, **@**, or **$**, precede it with **** so that Q&A knows the character is to be taken literally. You can use no more than two characters to separate the parts of any template value.

Here's another example of a field template. A template design like this:

\#PROD-X##/@@-$

limits the user to entering two digits, two alphabetic characters, and finally any character that can be entered from the keyboard. Such a product or account number might wind up looking like this:

#PROD-X45/AC-H

Search/Update on a masked field is handled by Q&A a little differently. If the phone number 4158333455 were masked to display as (415) 833-3455, you would search for all phone numbers with a 415 area code by entering **415..** in the phone number field at the Retrieve Spec. If your search parameter were **(415)..** you'd come up with no forms because only the phone number *digits* — not " **(**" and " **)**" — are part of the field's value. However, when you print a templated field in a form or report, the template will print along with the value.

To create a field template:

1. Select Field template from the Customize menu.

2. Move the cursor to the field you want to mask.

3. Create your template as described above.

4. Repeat steps 2 and 3 for other fields you want to mask.

5. Press **<F10>** when finished.

You can use a template in a field when you want the information blank always to contain specified numbers or letters. For example, you could mask a "Department" field:

Department: F16-###

if you wanted the field always to include the F16 prefix and the dash. The mask could be part of a suffix as well.

 Tip: The following points should be kept in mind where field templates are concerned:

• If you set an initial value for a template, such as a telephone area code (see the next section), enter the initial value without the mask.

• Mass update and programming operations can change the character types you've assigned to a template, permitting a number to be placed into an alphabetic character position, for example. These operations work with stored rather than displayed data — a field template is a display format. Be careful when writing programming statements that change masked field values.

• If you shorten a template after data has been entered, the template will display the truncated value, but the rest of the value will still be stored. To truncate the data to fit the new template, run a Mass update, entering **#1=#1** in the masked field at the Update Spec. Mass update procedures are covered later in this chapter.

Setting Default Field Values

You can preset values for any fields on the form. When adding new forms to the database, the values you enter at the Initial Values Spec will already be entered on the otherwise blank form when it displays.

Set Initial Values can place the date (@Date) and time (@Time) on your forms automatically. Q&A also has a feature called @Number which allows you to increment your forms by 1, or by any other number.

When you type the expression **@Date** into a date field at the Initial Values Spec, Q&A will include the current date on all new forms. Similarly, **@Time** entered into an hours field here will time stamp your forms.

The built-in @Number function entered into a number field at the Initial Values Spec will generate a unique number for your invoices, purchase orders, or other documents that need to be incrementally numbered.

@Number(*n*), where *n* is a digit, will increment your forms by a count of *n*. For example, if you typed the expression **@Number(10)** in a number field at the Initial Values Spec, each form you entered would be automatically numbered 10 higher than the previous one.

Q&A remembers the last number it assigned to a form, even if it was last week or last year. And you can reset the @Number to any new starting number by pressing **<Ctrl><F8>** from any form while in Add Data mode. If you ever need to reset the @Number, reset it to the number that's one less then the next number you want Q&A to return.

To enter initial values on your form:

1. Select Set Initial Values from the Customize menu.

2. Move to the relevant field or fields and type the value you want filled in on all new forms.

3. Press **<F10>** when finished.

When Initial Values Come in Handy

If you're running a sales organization and most of your employees are in the Sales Department, you can set your initial value for the Department field of your employee database to "Sales."

If you're entering a batch of invoices during a promotion for a particular item, you can set your Item# field to whatever the item number is, so you won't have to enter it time and again.

If most of your items are shipping via parcel post, you can set the initial value of your Shipped Via field to "parcel post" and avoid having to type it repeatedly.

When entering a list of addresses into database records that all contain the same city, state, and zip code, you could set these up as initial values and save yourself a lot of keystrokes.

You can also use Q&A's @Ditto feature so long as you were doing nothing but adding forms one after another without leaving the database.

Initial values are like any operator-entered value in that you can edit them on the form at any time. If the Shipped Via field says "parcel post," but this customer wants UPS Ground, you simply type "UPS Ground" right over the initial value and that's how it will stay until you change it.

Initial values are entered by Q&A on the form only during Add Data. If you delete them during Add Data or Search/Update, Q&A doesn't put them back.

Speeding Up Searches

As your database swells with records, and searches and updates become a part of the daily routine, you'll probably find that you frequently search for existing records on relatively few of the fields, and as you keep adding more records to the file, Q&A may take longer to find the forms already entered.

The Speed-up Searches option lets you create indexes for fields on which you frequently search so that your record retrieval commands can be carried out more swiftly. The .IDX file that always accompanies a Q&A .DTF database file contains the index. The index itself doesn't contain any data you can work with, but it tells Q&A where to find it.

A database index works like a book index. You can turn 500 pages of a history book looking for each occurrence of the word "Jefferson," or you can check the index to find out on which pages "Jefferson" is mentioned. If it's a good index, the second method will save you considerable time.

At the Speed-up Spec you enter codes in the fields you want Q&A to index for you. These will likely be the fields normally included in your Retrieve Spec search activities (last names, zip codes, invoice numbers, dates, part numbers, or contract numbers, for example). Then, instead of Q&A having to search through every record in the file to locate the ones you specify at the Retrieve Spec (*any* Retrieve Spec) it will use the index you created to quickly locate and retrieve those records.

Note: Some database operations, such as Posting and using XLOOKUP programming commands, require that the Key field in the external file be indexed. You'll receive a warning message if you attempt an operation requiring a Speedy field where Q&A notices that such a field is not indexed, and you'll then need to exit from the operation, open the appropriate database, index the Key field at the Speed-up Spec, and then return to the operation you were working on.

To index a field, select Speed-up Searches from the Customize menu, move the cursor to the field you want Q&A to index, and type the letter **S**. If you want Q&A to know that this is also a unique field, type **U** after the **S**.

Unique Fields

Invoice numbers, Social Security numbers, company names, and many other types of values are unique, and you can have Q&A warn you whenever a value typed in a field on one record has been entered in the same field in another record. You may even wish to make a last name field unique, so at least the operator will be aware that someone with that last name is already in the file. A duplicate entry would then result in the message:

```
"This field should be unique.
Please verify before continuing.''
```

If you make the field Unique (**U**), you must also make it Speedy (**S**) because Q&A will need to check for duplicate entries each time you enter a value in it. A Speedy field, however, does not have to be Unique.

You can't *prevent* the entry of a duplicate value in a field set up to be Unique (without programming) — Q&A just warns you and then allows you to proceed if you wish.

On the other side of the coin, you can have Q&A check your entries and hand you a warning message if the entry *does not* already exist in the same field of at least one other record in the field. You might want to use this feature to ensure that names or words that are entered frequently are spelled correctly. To have Q&A warn you when the value entered is unique, type **SE** into the appropriate field at the Speed-up Spec.

You can disable Speedy searches and related codes by returning to this spec and deleting the **S** and **U** or **E** in those fields you no longer want Speedy.

If your database is large when you decide to index a field or two, be prepared to give Q&A a little time to complete the task. It will have to look at each record in the database as it creates the index.

You'll notice a performance increase primarily in large databases, although your search parameters would have to include the Speedy field for the performance increase to be noticed. For example, you won't hasten the process by creating an index on only an invoice number field, for example, and then asking Q&A to search *by date* among 10,000 invoices.

By indexing your most important database fields, you'll see a speed improvement in most every Q&A operation involving them, from printing mailing labels

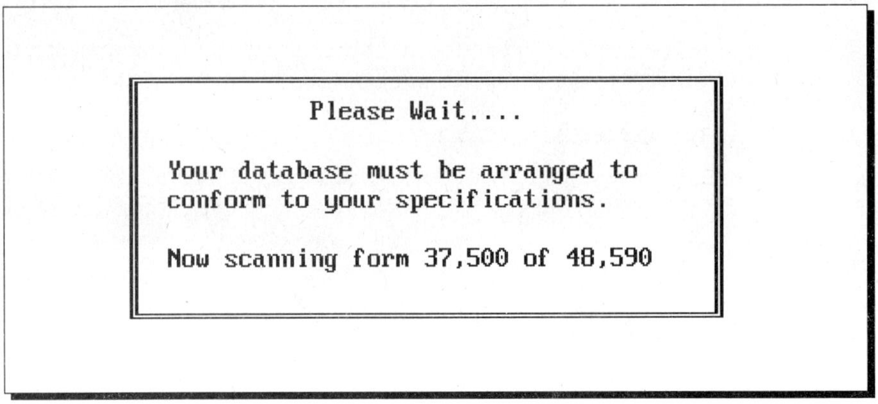

```
                Please Wait....

   Your database must be arranged to
   conform to your specifications.

   Now scanning form 37,500 of 48,590
```

Figure 4-2: Q&A's Status Message. It keeps you posted on Q&A's progress as it indexes your records.

and selected forms, to generating reports, sorting, and running mass updates. The actual printing won't go faster, but Q&A will be able to find the forms more quickly and thus prepare for the job at a faster rate.

Another advantage is that when you retrieve a group of forms by searching on one or more Speedy fields, you can press **<Ctrl><End>** when the first form in the stack is displayed, and Q&A will give you a fast count of the total number of forms in the stack — a useful clue for determining how big the update job is going to be, or about how long the printing will take. Pressing **<Ctrl><Home>** returns you to the first form in the stack.

In databases where there is no control number or date to search on (customer or supplier files set up by name), it can help to design a special Speedy field into the form to contain a value that will help during Search/Update activities.

For example, if "Griswold Sporting Goods" in zip code 40532 was one of your customers, you could enter "Griswold" or "GRIS40532" in your special field, making it easier to specify that record when you wanted to look it up. And if this field was indexed, Q&A would locate it for you considerably faster.

Later, when you learn how to do a little programming, you'll find that you can have Q&A automatically fill in special fields like the above from the other data that you enter. In other words, you won't have to type "GRIS40532" when adding the form, it will be done for you by a programming statement. This is another example of customizing your database forms and automating data entry.

Speed vs. Memory

You can have up to 115 Speedy fields per database, but each one adds a little overhead.

In a large database there may be a perceptible delay while Q&A checks the index for Unique field duplicates, and then indexes the Speedy fields after you press **<F10>** to add the new form. The more fields that are indexed, the longer it will take.

Indexes are extra, additional files that also consume hard disk space. The more fields you make Speedy, the bigger the file grows. But this may not amount to much unless you're critically short of hard disk space.

You can see how much additional hard disk space indexing another field requires. Check the file size (it's in bytes) of the database and write down the number. Add the Speedy field at the Speed-up Spec and let Q&A create the new index. Now go back and check the file size again. The difference will be the additional bytes needed to store the new index.

Indexing an additional field in a database of 20,000 records may add only another few thousand bytes to the file.

Creating Custom Help Screens

Behind any data entry operation waits Q&A's own context-sensitive help system. When you press **<F1>** during input the general help screen for adding/ updating displays, explaining how to add and update.

But your application may require more help than this. In addition to Q&A's built-in help, you may need *field-sensitive* or other custom help to guide the operator through the form.

Once you've designed a custom help screen for a field, pressing **<F1>** while the cursor is in that field will pop it up on screen. Unlike Q&A's full-page help screens, your custom screens are limited to eight lines of text at 60 characters per line — but you can work around this limitation.

You won't have to write a single character of programming code to place help screens behind your fields, that is, unless you want to have them pop up automatically without the **<F1>** key being pressed.

Figure 4-3 shows what a custom help screen looks like when displayed in our sample STOCK database.

Here, during data entry, the operator could press **<F1>** to bring up this screen for instructions on what codes are permissible *for this field*.

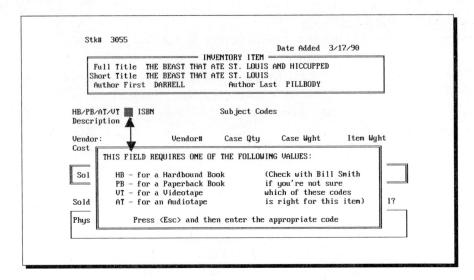

Figure 4-3: A Custom Help Screen. It will guide the operator during data entry.

At the Restrict Values Spec you may have told Q&A that this field could only contain the values HB, PB, VT, or AT, which would cause a "Value out of range" error message to be displayed if the operator attempted to enter, for example, "HT" in this field.

But the error message would not indicate *what* values are permissible. And that's where your custom help screens can eliminate operator frustration and speed data entry. With Q&A's error message displayed, the operator would only need to press **<F1>** to pop up the help screen shown in Figure 4-3.

Tip: Help screens can be made even more valuable by programming them to pop up immediately when an incorrect value is entered.

For instance, in the above example had the operator typed "HT" in the field and then tried to exit the field, your custom screen could be programmed to pop up automatically.

Restrict Values settings take priority over programmed help screens. In other words, an out-of-range value would earn Q&A's own error message first, followed by your custom help screen at the next **<Tab>** or **<Enter>**. So if you plan to program a help screen to pop up at the entry of an incorrect value, consider removing the restriction, and add programming to make the cursor stay put and redisplay the help screen until the value is correct.

If you've given the field a *hard* restriction using the **!** character at the Restrict Spec (available in version 4.0), you may not be able to program an automatic pop-up help screen at all since Q&A's own error message would take precedence. In such a case the operator would have to press the **<F1>** key to see your screen.

I'll get to the how-to on this programming business later in the chapter. For now, follow the procedure below and design a standard custom help screen for a field in a database you already have.

How to Create a Custom Help Screen

1. Select Define Custom Help from the Customize menu after telling Q&A which database you want to work with. Your form will be displayed.

2. Press **<F8>** to move to the field for which you want to design custom help. Press **<F6>** to go back to a previous field. You'll notice that each field will be highlighted as you move around the form, indicating that whatever you type the displayed box will be the help screen for that field.

3. Enter your text for the relevant field's help screen using the usual Write module editing keys. You can use all uppercase letters or a column-like format for emphasis. Make your help screen easily readable by not cramming it with wall-to-wall text.

You can't use text enhancements here such as bold or underline, and Q&A's Draw feature won't work, but you *can* add borders and boxes using ASCII Graphics characters. Figure 4-4 shows a help screen using a variety of ASCII characters.

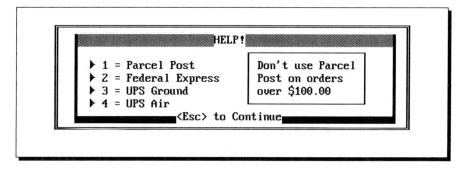

Figure 4-4: Dress Up Your Help Screens for Impact with ASCII Graphics Characters.

4. Repeat steps 2 and 3 to create help screens for other fields on the form. When you're finished, press **<F10>** to save your work and return to the Customize menu.

Now add a dummy form to your database (or retrieve an existing form), and when the cursor is in a field for which you designed a help screen, press **<F1>** and *voila!* Press **<F1>** again and Q&A's own help screen will be displayed.

By default, custom help screens do not stay displayed while typing during data entry — as soon as you begin typing, the help screen disappears. You have the option, however, of keeping your help screens displayed while typing information into a field. To change custom help to *concurrent*, press **<F5>** at the Help Spec, and choose **C**; to change help screen display back to the default *nonconcurrent* mode, choose **N**.

Although these custom screens are limited to one per field, you can use the screens of several fields to chain-link multiple screens and tie them to a single field. You'd write a short programming statement to make the first screen pop up automatically on the entry of an incorrect value, and have the operator press **<Enter>** to display the second and even third help screens while the cursor remained in the offending field. You'll find out how to program such options later in the chapter.

Whenever a field requires a particular kind or range of value, a custom help screen only the **<F1>** key away can make data entry orderly and efficient, and help cut down on the boo-boos.

The Programming Menu

Figure 4-5 shows Q&A's Programming menu. Reach this menu by choosing Program a File from the Design menu after entering the name of the database you're planning to further customize.

Q&A's programmable form capabilities give you ultimate control over what happens when information is entered on a database form.

You can program a form to automate data entry such as retrieve values from tables and other databases and enter them into the current form, calculate field values, determine overdue dates, control cursor movement on the form, and much more.

With programming you can also pass messages to the typist, make help screens pop up, and take field values apart or string them together in order to make use of the results in other fields.

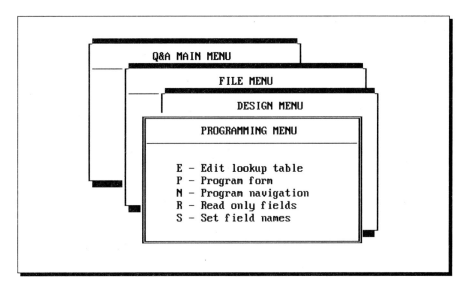

Figure 4-5: The Programming Menu.

There is an infinite number of ways in which you can use programming to get the job of data entry done faster and with fewer errors, as you'll see.

But before discussing Q&A's programming features and many built-in functions, and before beginning to program the sample invoice form, let's look at the three selections on the Programming menu in Figure 4-5 that won't require any programming knowledge to set up.

The Edit Lookup Table option lets you construct tax tables, shipping weight tables, part number, and even name and address tables with information that you can bring into your forms automatically during data entry. Designing a lookup table for your database requires no programming; retrieving values from it to place into your records, however, requires some programming.

The Read Only Fields selection enables you to protect fields so they cannot be changed from the keyboard during data entry. However, Read-only Fields *can* be changed by programming statements, copy operations, mass update, and posting.

And the Set Field Names option provides a way to assign descriptive names to any fields on your form that do not have field labels, so that during mail-merge, programming execution, and other operations, Q&A (and you) will know which fields are involved.

Edit Lookup Table

Selecting Edit Lookup Table from the Programming menu lets you create or edit a table of values tied to your database. The values in this table can be retrieved into your form during data entry using Q&A's LOOKUP command — a simple programming statement discussed in detail a bit later in this chapter.

The role of a lookup table is to hold the values that you will use in your forms frequently. Where appropriate, it's faster to have Q&A find a value in the table and bring it into your form than it is for you to type the value into your form from the keyboard.

A database lookup table shouldn't be confused with Table View. Table View is for browsing through or editing forms that have already been added to the file; a lookup table contains values you normally use to complete your forms *before* they become part of the database.

Author's Tip: The following ideas for using a lookup table are my own, not mentioned in Q&A's documentation:

- Place suppliers names and addresses in the lookup table, and then simply enter a key value (a one- or two-character code) on your purchase orders to "pull" the information into your form from the table.

- Descriptions of your inventory items, along with their prices, can be keyed to stock numbers in the lookup table. You enter the stock number on your form, and the item's description and price are "typed" in your form for you.

- Your table can contain shipping charges keyed to weights. When your invoice calculates the weight of the order, the lookup table can place the shipping charges in the invoice.

- United Parcel Service zones can be placed into the lookup table keyed to the customer's three-digit zip code prefix. You have Q&A look at the first three digits of the zip code, look up the zone in the table, and place it on your manifest record or invoice.

- If your company does business under several commercial names, you can use the lookup table to enter the appropriate company name and return address on your invoices, purchase orders, and other business documents.

- A business whose customers are mostly local can place the cities and state in the table keyed to the zip code, eliminating the need to type the city and state on customer database forms.

KEY	1	2	3	4
A	Barnes & Gobel→	P.O. Box 1755	Detroit, MI	48157
B	Barnes Videos	P.O. Box 1940	Detroit, MI	48157
C	Barnes Distrib→	1645 Commerce→	Flint, MI	48435
5	$12.50	$15.50	$17.00	$19.00
6	$13.70	$15.90	$17.20	$19.80
7	$14.20	$16.60	$17.90	$21.00
8	$15.00	$17.35	$18.40	$21.90
9	$15.90	$18.20	$18.90	$22.30
10	$16.80	$19.00	$19.40	$23.85
11	$18.00	$21.30	$22.00	$24.90
004	8	12	22	
006	NO	15	25	
010	8	12	22	
100	8	12	22	
200	8	12	22	
300	8	12	22	
324	8	12	22	

INVOICE.DTF	Lookup Table	Page 1 of 8

Figure 4-6: A Lookup Table Showing Page 1 of 8.

- You can place state abbreviations and starting and ending zip code ranges in the table, and use programming statements to check data entered by the operator against the values in the table. If an incorrect state abbreviation, or an out-of-range zip code for the state is entered, you can have a help screen pop up to notify the operator. See Chapter 12 for a sample application.

- Tax tables for different states can be stored for automatic retrieval.

- Bonus factors, rates, charts — any group of related values that can be structured in a table format of four columns or less — is a candidate for a lookup table.

With these ideas in mind, review Figure 4-6, which shows a lookup table with three different categories of values entered. Reading down the table in Figure 4-6 you'll notice the three categories of values:

- The first three rows contain company names and addresses keyed to one-letter codes (A, B, and C) in the Key column. These could be primary suppliers for which you frequently cut purchase orders, or names under which your company does business.

- The next seven rows contain rate information tied to weight values in the Key column.

- The rest of the table contains shipping zones tied to zip code prefixes in the Key column.

Now you can't tell from looking at the table that these are necessarily weight values, shipping rates, service zones, and zip code prefixes, but this sample table illustrates that you can have any number of different categories of values in a single lookup table — which is just as well, since you get only one of these tables per database.

The first column of the table is called the *Key column* and contains the values you want Q&A to look up in order to locate other information in the table.

The *Numbered columns* (1 through 4) contain the information you want retrieved into your forms.

The arrows you see at the ends of some of the values in the numbered columns indicate those values are longer than can be displayed in the column.

Q&A allows you one key column and four numbered columns. If you need more columns than that you should consider creating and then storing the values in another database, and then using Q&A's XLOOKUP command to retrieve the values you need from there — this topic will be covered later in this chapter.

You don't have to use all the columns in the lookup table, but an entry in any of the numbered columns requires an entry in the corresponding Key column. An entry in any column can be up to 240 characters long, and you expand the field for a long entry by pressing **<F6>**.

To create a lookup table:

1. Select Edit Lookup Table from the Programming menu after telling Q&A which database you want to work with.

2. In the Key column, type the values you'll be entering on your form that Q&A will use to find a match in the table. Use the **<Enter>** key to move down to the next line.

3. In the numbered columns type the information you'll want retrieved and placed into the fields on your form. Use the **<Tab>** key to move from column to column. Don't enter values on a subsequent page until the last line of the current page has a value in it.

4. Press **<F10>** when finished to save the table and return to the Programming menu.

When typing your information in the table, make your columns consistent for each lookup category. For example, if you're using the table to store frequently needed names and addresses, put all your names in column 1, all your street addresses in column 2, and your cities, states, and zips in column 3. This will help avoid confusion when writing your lookup commands to retrieve the values.

You can also use a lookup table to validate information entered in a form — not necessarily to retrieve information into it. For example, you can validate correct state abbreviations entered into an address database by typing the correct abbreviations in the table. You would need a programming statement in the State field in the database to check the values in the lookup table against the abbreviation entered, and display a message or help screen if a match can't be found.

You can beef up the restriction even further by using two lookup table columns for the starting and ending zip codes that correspond to the states listed in the Key column. This way you can trap both invalid state abbreviations *and* out-of-range zip codes. You'll need a little programming to accomplish it, but you'll see how it's done when you get to that section and Chapter 12.

Editing the Lookup Table

To delete a row in the table, put the cursor on it and press **<Shift><F4>**. Q&A will close up the empty row and add a blank row at the very end of the table.

To insert a new row, place the cursor in the first character position of the Key column, go into insert mode, and press **<Enter>**. Q&A will open up a row for you across all five columns, and force all the other rows down a line.

If you're not in insert mode, pressing **<Enter>** moves the cursor to the beginning of the next line.

Open more space for typing longer values by pressing **<F6>**.

Here are some additional points to keep in mind when working with lookup tables:

- Q&A treats all lookup table values as *text* values — including digits. It sees 1001 as a text string having no numerical significance other than knowing that 1002 comes after it. But if you retrieved 1001 into a number field on your form, it would now be formatted as a true number.

- The field in the database that you're using to find a match in the lookup table must be formatted as a text information type. You can retrieve a text value from the lookup table into a number field, but the match field in the database cannot be a number field.

- When Q&A looks for a key value in the table it starts at the top of the table and takes the first exact match it finds. So if your table includes two identical key values, Q&A will take the first occurrence.

- If you have two categories of identical key values, but with different column values associated with each one, you can place a character in front of all the key values in one category, and have Q&A do the same with the value in the form before the value is looked up. That way you'll get the value from the category you want.

- A special programming formula is available to tell Q&A to retrieve the *next lowest* value in the key column if an exact match isn't found. You can use this feature when the key value you want to match falls within a range.

For example, shipping zone 7 might cover zip code prefixes 480 through 550. Your key column would have 480 on one row, and 551 on the next row down. Any value from 480 through 550 looking for a match would connect with the 480 row because that's the exact or the next lowest value. This feature frees you from having to type in the table every single value in the entire range.

- Lookup table size is limited by the amount of memory in your system, up to a maximum of 64,000 characters. In a 512K RAM system you'll have enough memory for about 600 lines with an average line of around 100 characters. Q&A warns you when you're approaching the limit. You'll then have room for about 1,000 more characters. If you go over the limit, you'll have to delete some characters before you can exit.

- You can't do sorts or automatic search and replace on lookup table values. These tables aren't for values that constantly change and require frequent updating. If you've got a 900-line lookup table with 50 values that have to be changed, you'll have to page through the table until you find those values, and edit them one at a time.

If the information you want to have Q&A look up and retrieve into your forms tends to change often, or if the volume of lookup table items is extremely large, consider constructing another database to hold the values. While lookup table values are retrieved more rapidly into your forms because Q&A doesn't have to open another file to get them, external databases may offer you more flexibility since you can update records more easily, and sort and retrieve them on any field.

You'll learn how to write short programming statements to retrieve lookup table values into your forms when you read the section on lookup commands later in the chapter.

Read-only Fields

Version 4.0

New: With Q&A 4.0 you have the option of designating fields on your form to be viewed, but not changed from the keyboard. Additional levels of security are available for your databases from Q&A's Security menu. These are discussed in Chapter 12. You can also place locks on your database so that unauthorized procedures can't be accessed without a password. Chapter 9 includes a section on how to protect your data files from unauthorized tampering.

When you specify a field as Read-only, only programming statements, posting procedures, and mass updates can change its value. The typist cannot get the cursor into the field — even if it's empty — until the restriction is removed; and you can protect *that* with a password.

If a Read-only field is the first field on the form, the cursor will bypass it during Add and Update and prompt for a value in the next unrestricted field. If the Read-only field contains Main Program programming statements (programming options are discussed further ahead in this chapter), these will be executed as if the field were a normal read/write field.

Set a field to Read-only to protect it from inadvertent or deliberate changes during normal data entry, or when you want its value changed only by programming statements and/or mass update or posting routines.

The following types of fields are candidates for Read-only status:

- Fields containing customer numbers, part numbers, dates, and other values that won't change, where the value is generated as the result of a programming statement, or an @Date or @Number function predefined at the Initial Values Spec.

- Key fields containing values involved in XLOOKUP routines — to avoid XLOOKUP failures when a command in another database may depend on this field's matching value to complete the look up.

- Salary, bonus, and review information that the operator is permitted to see but not change (note: such fields can be hidden from view altogether using 4.0's extended security features — see Chapter 12).

- Any fields containing values that should only be edited by a supervisor or manager.

To make a field Read-only, select Read-only Fields from the Programming menu, move to the fields you want to protect and type **R** in each one. Then press **<F10>** to save your changes and return to the Programming menu.

Read-only status can be disabled simply by deleting the **R** in the fields you want returned to normal read/write status.

 Note: You can also *hide* fields on forms so they can't even be viewed during data entry. Fields can be hidden, for example, in an employee field where you want to allow all users access to employee names, addresses, phone numbers, extensions, hobbies, and so forth, but wish to control who can view salary, bonus, and review comments information. See Chapter 12 for details on creating Field Restriction Groups.

Set Field Names

Later in this chapter we're going to design and program a sophisticated invoice form. In order to have enough space to design in Stock Number, Description, Quantity, Price, and Amount fields all on a single line, you'll be making these labelless or "no-name" fields. In other words, the information blanks will not be preceded by the usual descriptive labels.

When programming a form it's often necessary to *reference* other fields on the form in your formulas. And mail-merge operations can be a problem when you need to merge a database field into your document, but that field has no identifying label. Version 4.0 solved the problem with Field Names.

Fields are referred to in a number of ways depending on what operation you're doing in Q&A:

- When you redesign a form, you'll see Q&A's internal *Field Tags* such as AA, AB, and so forth. These tags should never be changed or deleted unless you're deleting the entire field and any data associated with it. Q&A uses these tags internally. You never refer to them when using the product.

- A field can include the normal descriptive *Field Label* that precedes the information blank.

- During programming you'll assign *Logical Field Numbers* to your fields so you can easily reference them in programming formulas.

- And with version 4.0 you can assign *Field Names* to your fields. These can then be used to identify labelless fields during mail-merge, and also in place of Logical Field Numbers in programming expressions.

To use this feature, select Set Field Names from the Programming menu. Q&A will display the Field Name Spec for the database. Notice that all the field names contained inside the information blanks are the same as the Field Labels. These are Q&A's default field names for your fields.

However, if any of your field labels are not unique, the field name of the first field will be followed by the number 1, the second with a 2, and so forth, as follows:

Label	Name	Label	Name
Date:	Date1	Amount:	Amount1
Date:	Date2	Amount:	Amount2
Date:	Date3	Amount:	Amount3

If you have any information blanks on your form that are *not* preceded by a field label, the first one will be assigned F0001, the second, F0002, and so on.

Tip: At this point it would be wise to give your labelless fields more descriptive names. Instead of:

Stk No.	Description		Price
<F0001>	<F0002>	>	<F0003>
<F0004>	<F0005>	>	<F0006>

which you'll see at the Field Names Spec, a more useful approach would be:

Stk No.	Description		Price
<Stk#1 >	<Desc1>	>	<Price1>
<Stk#2 >	<Desc2>	>	<Price2>

and so forth. This way if you should ever need to use these fields in a mail-merge, need to reference them by name in a programming formula, or use them with the Query Guide or Intelligent Assistant (Chapter 7) they'll be readily identifiable to you and others who will use your form.

If your field labels are already descriptive, there's no point in changing their default field names. Doing so, in fact, could later cause confusion. To change a Q&A assigned field name:

1. Select Set Field Names from the Programming menu. You'll be placed at the Field Name Spec for the database.

2. Move to the field whose name you want to change, and type the new name over the old one. Press **<F6>** to expand the field should you need more room.

3. Press **<F10>** when finished to save your changes and return to the Programming menu.

When you edit a field name at the Field Name Spec, that field name will not change, even if you later redesign your form.

For example, suppose the field label and default field name are "Phone No.," and you change the field name to "Phone1." Subsequently changing the label to "Home Phone" while redesigning the form will *not* change the Field Name. If you want the field name changed to "Home Phone," you'll have to go to the Field Name Spec and change it.

On the other hand, if you haven't changed the field name, then giving the field a new label during redesign *will* result in the field name being updated to match the new label.

Tip: When assigning field names, don't use symbols or words that Q&A reserves in its programming language, such as **<**, **>**, GOTO, IF, THEN, ELSE, CNEXT. You'll find out what these mean in the section on programming just ahead in this chapter.

If you have a field label that contains an operator such as **List Price * .25**, this might be harmless as a field *label*, but it may be confusing to Q&A as a field *name* because it means *List Price multiplied by .25*. Such field names should be enclosed in quote marks and preceded by the **#** sign.

When designing your database, be sure all your labeled fields have unique field labels and don't contain mathematical operators like **+**, **-**, **/** and *****, and you won't have to be concerned about the Field Name Spec, except perhaps to assign names to your labelless fields.

Programming a Database

Q&A Power Feature: Programming your database can catapult it to a new level of performance. Why spend 60 keystrokes typing the supplier's name and address into that purchase order when you can have Q&A type them for you? Why have to stop in the middle of data entry to add up the amount column and figure the sales tax on invoices when Q&A can do it for you automatically? And why be forced to press **<Enter>** 15 times to bypass those empty fields and get the cursor over to where you need it?

These are just a few of the rather modest benefits you can reap with some very basic programming. With a little effort, you can turn that tedious database into a roaring tiger of an application that practically enters data into itself.

You're now at that point where programming becomes essential in order to add to your Q&A applications the power you are likely to need. You've learned how to design, redesign, and customize a database file. You've seen how to add, search, retrieve, and update records. You've been exposed to a variety of different types of databases and the tools you can use to enhance their utility and performance. In the pages that follow you'll explore the Q&A programming language in some detail, showing you how and when to use it to bring increased productivity, flexibility, and amazing power to your applications.

The databases you routinely use may require no programming at all — programming in Q&A is entirely optional. But often even modest databases, such as customer name and address records, can benefit from the addition of a little programming here and there to make data entry proceed faster and more reliably.

Programming in Q&A is a good place to start if you've never before been exposed to programming. Its syntax is not difficult to learn, and after a little exposure and practice you'll discover that the door to enhancing your databases with programming is wide open.

How Programming Works in Q&A

In Q&A you type programming parameters into the fields of your database form at the Program Spec. These parameters, called *programming statements, commands,* or *formulas,* you then set to execute according to specific instructions. Programming in Q&A thus involves two elements, both of which are entirely under your control. For each field in each database you're programming, you specify:

- What you want your programming formulas to do. This involves typing out one or more valid programming statements.

- When you want the programming statements executed.

A programming command is nothing more than a series of instructions that you embed into the database to have Q&A do something for you automatically at a particular point during the data entry process. When Q&A executes your programming only the current form in the current database is affected. For example, you cannot embed a programming statement in database A which, when executed, changes something in database B, although you can program database A to *retrieve* information from other databases.

To *update* database B from the values in database A you use the Posting feature (covered later in this chapter) which does *not* involve programming.

The Q&A programming language and built-in functions offer you infinite options when it comes to specifying *what* your programming statements do when executed. As to *when* you want them to execute, you can choose among the following alternatives:

- When the cursor leaves any field on the form whose contents have just been altered. This is referred to as automatic execution of the *Main Program.*

- When you direct Q&A to execute the Main Program by pressing the **<F8>** "calc" key. This is known as manual execution. For programming purposes, the term *calc (calculation)* means the same thing as *execution.*

- When the cursor enters a field containing a statement that is only to be executed *on-field-entry.* This type of statement will not execute if the cursor is *backed* into the field.

- When the cursor exits a field to the right containing a statement that is only to be executed *on-field-exit. On-field-exit* statements will not execute when the cursor is backed into the field (you have to exit the field to the right again to execute them).

- When a new form is first displayed during Add Data, or an existing form is first displayed during Search/Update. This is referred to as *on-record-entry* execution. You can specify only *one* field's programming to execute in this fashion. The *on-record-entry* and *on-record-exit* fields can be the same or different fields.

- When the form is saved to the database file during Add Data or Search/Update (when you press **<F10>** or **<Shift><F10>**). This is called *on-record-exit* execution. You can specify only *one* field's programming to execute in this fashion.

Note that on-record-entry, on-record-exit, and Main Program statements will not trigger on-field-entry or on-field-exit statement execution. These latter two types of statements execute only when the cursor either enters or leaves the fields that contain them.

You can use a combination of the above execution options when programming your form. Depending on your requirements, you may wish some programming statements to be executed on a field-by-field basis as you're moving through the form, while holding off on others until you've reached a certain point on the form and press **<F8>** (the manual calc key), or until the record is saved to disk with **<F10>** or **<Shift><F10>.**

Q&A gives you complete control over what your programming formulas do, and *when* they do it. You don't have to write a lengthy program to cover the whole operation of filling out a form. You write statements only for the fields where you want something to happen other than having the cursor simply move across the form to the right and down.

You don't have to add any programming at all to your database, however. It's entirely optional.

If you're using only one simple database to keep track of your customers' names and addresses, there may not be much in the way of help that programming can offer. It's where your applications begin to expand and grow more sophisticated that you'll recognize the need to build more automation into them.

Field Navigation vs. Form Programming

Q&A version 4.0 has two layers of programming: *Field Navigation Programming* and *Form Programming*. You add programming statements to your database to control two different broad types of action.

- You tell Q&A to perform a calculation, add two field values together, look up a value from the lookup table or another database, and so forth. This is referred to as *Form* or *Calculation* programming, and is done at the Program Spec.

- Using symbols and abbreviations such as GOTO, you control the movement of the cursor on the form during data entry. This is *Navigational* programming, and is done at the Navigation Spec.

A simple navigational programming statement might include the Q&A programming language equivalent of: "When the cursor leaves this field, move the cursor to field X" — where "X" is another field somewhere on the form.

To illustrate, suppose you have an invoice form with enough lines to enter 10 items, their descriptions, prices, quantities, and amounts, but the customer is ordering only two items.

Without programming the form for cursor navigation, the order entry operator, after entering the two items, would have to press a number of keystrokes to get the cursor past all the unused line-item fields and down to the bottom of the invoice where the total, sales tax, and so forth would be calculated and entered.

In Q&A you can add programming which says: "If the cursor leaves this field without a value having been entered (the assumption is that there are no more items to enter on the invoice), then skip the subsequent line-item fields and move the cursor directly to the subtotal field at the bottom of the form."

This statement is essentially navigational because you're not asking Q&A to calculate or look up any values, or really do anything else except to move the cursor to a specified field if a certain condition is met (exiting from an empty field in this example). However, the statement *does* require Q&A to check to see if the field has been left blank, so *this* part of the statement is not navigational, but involves an evaluation.

Why Two Programming Levels?

With version 4.0, Symantec is making Q&A databases *interoperable* with other kinds of computers and operating systems so that Q&A can work with non-DOS computers in multiuser environments.

Other environments (and versions of Q&A designed to be used on non-DOS computers) may require that navigational and calculation programming be separated from one another, and so 4.0 users are being encouraged to program their databases accordingly.

In Q&A 3.0, both types of programming were included in a single statement at the Program Spec. You're discouraged from doing this in version 4.0 without placing the navigational portion of the statement in the corresponding field at the Navigation Spec, *especially if you plan to share your databases with other types of computers (such as the Apple Macintosh) on a multiuser network.*

Q&A 4.0 won't prevent you from including calculation and nagivational programming statements together, but it's something to keep in mind if your databases will be shared on a network.

Tip: If you include your navigational programming along with your calculation programming at the Program Spec, you should *not* use the following cursor commands in your programming statements:

- **CNEXT** (to move the cursor to the next field).
- **CPREV** (to move the cursor to the previous field).
- **CHOME** (to move the cursor to the first field on the form).
- **CEND** (to move the cursor to the last field on the form).
- **PgDn** (to move the cursor to the first field on the next screen page).
- **PgUp** (to move the cursor to the first field on the previous screen page).

Instead, use GOTO(*field identifier*) commands to move your cursor, for the following reason: If, after you've programmed the form, you redesign the database and change the positions of your fields, cursor navigation commands other than GOTO(*field identifier*) may move the cursor unexpectedly to the wrong field. For example, the **CNEXT** cursor navigation command moves the cursor from the field in position A to the next field (in position B) in the original form design. But if field B is moved to another position on the form during redesign, it may not now be *next* to field A, and so the CNEXT command may not now give you the cursor move you need.

Q&A Field Programming Essentials

To tell Q&A to execute the field's formula when the cursor enters the field, you type a **<** in front of the Field ID number.

To execute the formula as the cursor is leaving the field, you indicate so by typing a **>** in front of the Field ID number. For example:

<#40: (formula) means execute the formula when the cursor *enters* field #40

>#50: (formula) means execute the formula when the cursor *leaves* field #50

You can override the execution of an on-field-entry or on-field-exit statement by typing a GOTONP(*field reference*) in the corresponding field at the Navigation Spec. This tells Q&A to move the cursor to the specified field without executing the programming. If you need to turn off a field's programming, but don't wish to erase the statement, this is the way to go. Later, if you want to revert to having the field's programming execute during data entry, you simply edit the GOTONP statement in the Navigation Spec.

Here's the procedure for adding programming formulas to your database. Following this, I'll devote a considerable number of pages to exploring all the Q&A programming options available to you. Although the procedure below pertains to the Program Spec, filling out the Navigation Spec is very similar. The difference is that the Navigation Spec is concerned with cursor navigation rather than calculations and formulas.

To add programming to a Q&A database:

1. Select File from the Main menu, and then select Design a File from the File menu.

2. Select Program a File from the Design menu, and enter the name of the database you wish to program.

3. At the Programming menu, choose Program form. This will take you to the Program Spec for the database.

4. Move the cursor to the first field for which you want to write a programming statement, and type the number sign in it (**#**) followed by a number — for example: **#5**. This is the field ID number, also referred to as the logical field number.

5. Follow the field ID number with a colon, and then type your programming statement. For example:

`#5: If #5 < #3 then #4 = "Yes"`

You can press **<F1>** from the Program Spec to get a summary of Q&A's programming options. If your statement is simply setting the field equal to something, you can omit the colon and use an equal sign, as follows:

`#5 = #3`

If you need more space to type your statement, press **<F6>** to expand the field, type the statement, and then press **<F10>** to return to the form.

6. Move the cursor to any fields *referenced* by the programming statement you just typed, and type the appropriate field ID numbers into them. (When you tell Q&A to set field #5 equal to field #3, for example, you need to identify field #3 with its own field ID number.)

 Remember: In a programming statement, if you refer to another field by *field name* rather than by field ID#, that referenced field need not have a field ID# unless it, too, contains a programming statement. You can refer to a field either by field ID# or by field name.

You can clear the entire programming specification by pressing **<F3>.**

7. Repeat steps 4 through 6 for any additional fields you wish to program.

8. When you've finished writing your programming statements, press **<F10>** to save your work and return to the File menu. You should now add a dummy form to test out your programming, returning to the Program Spec to make revisions where necessary.

Later on I'll give you some tips to keep in mind while programming. But you'll need to be a bit more familiar with the basics of programming before you'll be able to take advantage of them.

Writing Programming Statements

Programming in Q&A can be as easy as typing in the following expressions into the appropriate fields at the Program Spec.

Simple Statements

Simple statements are unconditional: A times B equals C, as indicated in the examples below.

`#6=#10*2`

Meaning: multiply the value in field #10 by 2 and place the result in field #6.

```
#12=@Date+30
```

Meaning: add 30 days to the current date and place the new date in field #12.

```
>#6=#3-1
```

Meaning: subtract 1 from field #3 and place the result in field #6 *when the cursor exits field #6.*

```
>#6: #7 = #6 + 10
```

Meaning: as the cursor *leaves* field #6, add 10 to the value in field #6 and put the result in field #7. Notice the colon after the field ID number.

Warning: Always use the colon immediately after the field ID number when you're not making a simple assignment to the field that contains the programming statement.

```
<#3 = #1; goto #9
```

Meaning: when the cursor *enters* field #3: Copy the contents of field #1 to field #3, and then move the cursor to field #9. *Programming statements in Q&A are always executed from left to right.*

If you'll be entering cursor moves at the Field Navigation Spec (which you're encouraged to do in Q&A 4.0), the above field should be identified as field #3 in the Navigation Spec also to avoid confusion. But you wouldn't type the same command as above at the Navigation Spec. You'd only enter the portion of the statement that indicates the cursor move, such as: **<#3: goto #9**. You could then reduce the above statement at the Program Spec to: **<#3 = #1** (without the **goto #9**).

If/Then Statements

If/Then statements are conditional. *If* the comparison is true, *then* carry out the statement that follows. The formula is:

```
>#10: If #10 = #5 then goto #12
```

Meaning: when the cursor leaves field #10, *If* the value in field #10 equals the value in field #5, *then* move the cursor to field #12. Otherwise, the cursor would be moved to the very next field on the form. Since the execution of the "goto" portion of this statement depends upon a comparison of values, your navigation statement at the Navigation Spec would have to include the entire expression.

```
<#10: If #10 <> #5 then goto #12
```

Meaning: when the cursor enters field #10, *If* the value in field #10 is *not* equal to (<>) the value in field #5, *then* move the cursor to field #12. Otherwise, the cursor remains in field #10 until you move it out with a keyboard command.

```
#100: If #200 > #198 and #15=#10 then #100=200
```

Meaning: when the statement is executed, if #200 is greater than #198 *and* #15 is equal to #10, *then* set field #100 to 200 ("200" in this case is a value, not a field ID#).

If/Then/Else Statements

If/Then/Else statements provide a third option. *If* a comparison is true, *Then* carry out action A, *otherwise* (*or else*) carry out action B.

```
>#20: If #30 = #50 then goto #32 else goto #34
```

Meaning: when the cursor leaves field #20, *If* fields #30 and #50 contain the same value, *then* move the cursor to field #32; *otherwise* move it to field #34.

```
<#100: If #20 > #100 then goto #105 else #100 = #20; goto
#110
```

Meaning: when the cursor enters field #100, *If* field #20 *is greater than* field #100, *then* move the cursor to #105; *otherwise*, make field #100 equal to field #20 and move the cursor to field #110.

You'll notice that the final portion of the expression, **goto #110**, is preceded by a semicolon. The ";" separates each of two or more statements typed in the same field.

In Q&A programming you can use braces to set off a group of statements that you want executed when some preceding condition is met. For example:

```
#250: If #200 < #150 then {#255=5;#260="Have a nice
day!";goto #261}
```

Notice the **{}** (braces). Use these when you have a number of commands you want executed only when the preceding If/Then condition is true.

In the above statement, if the value in field #200 is less than field #150's value, then the three commands following the opening brace are executed; whereas if the condition proves *not* to be true (i.e., field #200 is *not* less than field #150) then the commands inside the braces are *not* executed.

You can use the word **BEGIN** in place of the **{** symbol, and the word **END** in place if the **}** if you like. But wherever you start a phrase with **{** or **BEGIN**, you must also end it with **}** or **END**.

And and *Or* in a Statement

And and *or* can be used to make something happen when *both* things are true, or *either* is true.

```
#50: If #50="Y" and #12 > 10 then #14=#12*.065
```

```
#50: If #50="Y" or #12 > 10 then #14=#12*.065
```

In the first of the two statements above, both conditions must be true before the value in field #12 is multiplied by .065 and placed in field #14.

In the second statement, only *one* of the two conditions need be true for the final part of the programming to execute.

```
#55: If #33=30 and not #30<5 then #40=@Date-30
```

In this statement: *not* carries out some action if the condition is *not* true.

Use ◇ to indicate *not equal to*. For example:

```
<#10: If #3 <> #2 then {#12 = 5; goto #15} else goto #20
```

Multiple statements are those that include a number of statements strung together. Using colons and braces, you can separate the statements and have Q&A execute them in groups.

For example:

```
#80: If #80>#15 then #85=3; If #90>#4 then #91="Time for
Lunch"
```

Another example, using braces:

```
>#80: If #40>#15 then {#20=15; goto #25} else {#20=25;
goto #30}
```

In place of the { } you can use the terms **BEGIN** and **END**.

Q&A executes cursor moves as soon it sees them. In the statement: **<#2: #3=#8;goto #15;#4=#3*#7**, the **#4=#3*#7** part of the statement will not be executed because the cursor is moved out of the field before Q&A has had a chance to read it. Remember that statements are read from left to right.

Q&A also offers a long list of programming *functions* that you can incorporate into your formulas to calculate averages and totals, round off numbers, pop up your help screens, turn numbers into text values for creating strings, turn text values into numbers, and retrieve information from a lookup table or another database. See the section on Q&A's built-in functions later in this chapter.

Programming Execution Options

You've seen that Q&A executes programming commands on-field-entry with the **<** preceding the field ID#, and on-field-exit with the **>** symbol preceding the field ID#. You have other execution options as well.

Context Functions and Programming Execution

You can place an @Add or @Update context function in your statements, so they'll execute only when adding or updating your forms. **If @Add** in a statement tells Q&A to execute what follows only if the form is being added. **If @Update** limits the execution of what follows to when the form is being updated. Use these context functions in conjunction with If/Then statements.

For example:

```
#40: If @Update then #30 = #45/10
```

instructs Q&A to divide the value of field #45 by 10 and place the result in field #30 *when, and only when the form is being updated.* If this is a new form in Add Data, the statement will not execute.

Manual vs. Automatic Calculation

In Q&A's preset manual mode, programming statements are recalculated (executed) by pressing the **<F8>** calc key with the record on screen. In automatic mode, which you can set by pressing **<Shift><F8>** and typing **A**, all programming statements are recalculated every time the cursor leaves a field that has just been altered. On-field-entry-and-on-field-exit programming statements (those preceded by **<** or **>**) are not affected by either manual or automatic calculation; neither are on-record-entry or on-record-exit statements.

Automatic calculation can slow down data entry if a great many fields need to be recalculated as you move around the form, or if the calculations are complex.

Once you've selected automatic calculation mode, it remains in effect until you change it by pressing **<Shift><F8>** and typing **M**. You'll then need to press **<F8>** when you want Q&A to perform the calculations.

When Q&A is calculating your statements in this manner (when you're not using **>** or **<** to control execution), they'll be executed in Field ID number order, from lowest to highest — keep this in mind when calculations in one field depend on the results of another or others.

Also keep in mind that when you move the cursor out of a field that contains an on-field-exit statement, any Main Program statements are executed first if "calc" is set to automatic. Q&A executes the Main Program, and *then* the on-field-exit statement. You can change this default, however, and have your on-field-exit statements executed first.

To change the default:

1. Use Add Data to display a blank form for the database whose Main Program calculation mode you want to change from Manual to Automatic, or to set the on-field-exit execution to before or after Main Program execution.

2. Press **<Shift><F8>** to display a box with the calculation options.

3. Type **A** for Automatic or **M** for Manual calculation of the Main Program (the Manual setting requires the **<F8>** key to be pressed to execute the Main Program during data entry).

4. Select Yes or No for Main Program before field exit, and then press **<F10>** to save your changes. These settings will stay in effect until you change them again.

On-Record-Entry vs. On-Record-Exit Calculations

You also have the option of telling Q&A to perform the calculations in any single field when the form is first displayed, and to perform the calculations in the same field or a different one as the last thing it does just before saving the form (when you press **<F10>** or **<Shift><F10>**). To specify fields that contain on-form-entry and on-form-exit calculations, press **<F8>** at the Program Spec for the Entry/Exit box and enter the field ID numbers.

On-form-exit calculations can be used to validate data that have been entered or to time-stamp the form. On-form-entry statements are useful for calculations based on time spans such as a comparison between the date already on the form and the current date. For example, you could use an on-form-entry statement to calculate the number of days that have elapsed since the invoice date, or to flag an appointment date that's only two days away.

You can also use an on-form-entry statement to place the cursor in a particular field depending on the identity of the user, or to copy information into the form from the previous form. (See the @USERID and @DITTO programming functions discussed later in this chapter.)

Although you can specify only one field for an on-record-entry calculation, and only one field for an on-record-exit calculation, you can use these to recalculate a whole series of dependent fields, so long as each such Field ID number, and the calculations to be performed in those fields, are specified in the single field whose programming is set to execute on-record-entry or on-record-exit.

Table 4-2
Operators That Can Be Used in
Programming Statements

Op	What it does	Example
+	Addition	#10=#5+#8+#9
–	Subtraction	#10=#4-#3
*	Multiplication	#10=#5*#2
/	Division	#10=#5/#3
+	Equal to	#10=#5
<	Less than	If #10<#3 then #10=#3
>	Greater than	If #2>#10 then #3=#5
<=	Less than or equal to	If #10<=#5 then #6=#3
>=	Greater than or equal to	If #10>=#5 then #6=#4
<>	Not equal to	If #4<>#5 then goto #15
AND	Both comparisons true	If #4>#3 and #5=#3 then goto #10
OR	Either comparison true	If #4>#3 or #5=#3 then goto #10
NOT	Reverses comparisons	If not #5=3 then #5=#10/#4

Mathematical and Other Operators

Operators are used to perform calculations on numbers and numeric field values. You may need to program Q&A to add the values in two or more fields and place the result in another field, or multiply two values and then divide the result and either place *that* in a field, or use it in yet another calculation. Table 4-2 summarizes the operators available to you in Q&A, including their use in a variety of statements. Where the number is *not* preceded by the # sign, Q&A will assume it to be a number, not a field ID#, and will operate with it accordingly.

Table 4-3
Operator Precedence

Precedence	Operator
Calculated first	( )
	* /
	+ −
	<> <= >=
	NOT
Calculated last	AND OR

Precedence of Calculation

Q&A evaluates all programming formulas from left to right, but certain operators take precedence over others, and values enclosed in parentheses take precedence over all other calculations. For example: 3+6/2=6, but (3+6)/2=4.5. So be sure to use parentheses whenever in doubt about what part of the formula will be calculated first.

Table 4-3 shows the order in which Q&A sees operators in a programming formula. Operators on the same line in the table have the same precedence.

Using the Program Editor

New: For your programming statements that are longer than the field, press **<F6>** for the Program Editor and enter them there. Working inside the editor at the Program Spec is virtually the same as working on a document in the Write module — you have most of the word processing features at your disposal. While in the editor you can press **<F8>** for the Options menu, and select the procedure you want from the submenus. The chapter on Write contains the details on using these features.

When you've finished writing the statement, press **<F10>** to close the editor and return to the form. If Q&A finds an error in your syntax, it will let you know and position the cursor near where it found the error. You'll then need to review that part of the statement and correct it where necessary.

Printing Programming Statements

You can get a printout of your programming in the current field by pressing **<F2>** from *inside* the editor. You then select your options from the Field Print Options screen, and press **<F10>** to print out the field's contents.

```
                         SPEC PRINT OPTIONS


    Print to.....:  ▶PtrA◀ PtrB   PtrC   PtrD   PtrE   DISK   SCREEN

    Page preview.................:   Yes  ▶No◀

    Type of paper feed...........:  Manual  ▶Continuous◀  Bin1   Bin2   Bin3

    Print offset.................:   0

    Printer control codes........:

    Print field labels?..........:  ▶Yes◀  No

    Number of copies.............:   1

    Number of forms per page.....:   1

    Print expanded fields?.......:  ▶Yes◀  No


    STOCK.DTF             Print Options for current form
    Hewlett Packard LaserJet II/D/P/III (Port) »» LPT1
```

Figure 4-7: The Spec Print Options Screen. Reviewing your programming statements on paper saves you from having to use **<Tab>** to move between fields and constantly open and close the Program Editor.

If you want a print-out of the entire programming specification — a very useful tool that lets you review and compare all your programming statements in field ID number order (with or without field labels) — press **<F2>** from the Program Spec while *outside* the editor.

Figure 4-7 shows the Spec Print Options screen. Be sure to set the "Print Expanded Fields?" line to Yes so the printout will include any programming statements longer than their corresponding field widths.

Programming Tips

Author's Tip: These programming tips have been compiled by me through my knowledge of Q&A and programming. Most of these tips are not mentioned in Q&A's documentation.

- Before entering the Program Spec, sketch out your statements on a field-by-field basis; make notes on what you want the statements to do during data entry, and when you want them executed.

- Work out in advance which fields you'll be programming, and assign field ID numbers to them before typing in your programming statements.

- When assigning field ID numbers, increment them by 5 or 10. This way, if you design in new fields later on and wish to program them, you can maintain a logical sequence of field ID numbers.

- If you plan to use field names (rather than field ID numbers) as references in your programming statements, be sure you've assigned any labelless fields appropriate field names at the Field Names Spec. This makes it easier to identify such fields throughout Q&A.

- Once you've typed all your field ID numbers, and before typing your statements, save the design so that Q&A can check for any duplicate field ID numbers before you type a lot of statements containing field references.

- After entering a statement, check to see how it works during data entry before programming the form further. From the Program Spec you can press **<Ctrl><F6>** to display a blank form in Add Data mode, bypassing the menu system. But first be sure the programming statement you've just written is acceptable to Q&A by closing the editor or moving out of the field. After you've entered some "live" data to test your programming, you can press **<Shift><F9>** and then press **P** to return directly to the Program Spec. These bypass features allow you to move back and forth quickly to test and debug your programming.

- Design extra fields into the database and use them to store intermediate results. This helps you pinpoint where your programming goes wrong. You can delete the extra fields once the programming is working to your satisfaction.

- As you proceed with your programming, occasionally run a print-out of your spec. It's easier to view your statements on paper than it is to constantly move around the form to review the statements already typed.

- For long, complex statements, test small portions of the statement wherever possible, before stringing the whole statement together. If the results are undesirable, this makes it easier to spot and debug the flaws.

- Incorrectly formatted fields can hinder programming execution. Q&A sees text in a number field as 0 (zero); fields formatted for dates which contain nondate values are seen as blank. If your programming statement isn't returning what it should, check the field's information type and be sure the value is appropriate. All lookup commands treat data in key fields and columns as text, and return only text values. If your programming expects values from these commands to be numbers, for example, the programming won't work unless you use a Q&A built-in function to convert the value.

- If you're using any of Q&A's built-in functions in your programming (see the section on Q&A's built-in functions later in this chapter), be sure you know the kind of value the function expects (number, text, date, etc.), as well as the kind of value it returns.

- "Calc" or Main Program statements are executed in field ID number order. Where calculations in one field are dependent on the calculations in other fields, be sure you've got the field ID numbers in the proper sequence.

- From inside the Program Editor you can define a macro and record a lengthy programming statement, and then play back the macro to enter the same statement in another field. This is useful where you need to type a number of lengthy statements that are almost identical except, perhaps, for field references. You can use the Search/Replace feature to locate all occurrences of a certain field reference, and replace them with a different field reference, saving hundreds of keystrokes.

- You can copy a programming statement to an ASCII document file from inside the Program Editor, import the file from inside another field's Program Editor, and then edit the statement. This beats retyping several long statements that are practically identical.

The Lookup Commands

The ability to look up and retrieve information from tables and other databases is a powerful relational-like feature and an essential one if your database applications are to expand and be used interactively.

 Q&A Power Feature: If you're using only one database, then Q&A's *external* lookup commands won't be of any value to you. External lookups retrieve values from databases other than the current one. *Internal* lookup commands, on the other hand, return information from a lookup table tied to the current database. And by *current* is meant the database in which the lookup command was programmed. You can also do an *internal* lookup to the current database

Table 4-4 Q&A's Lookup Commands		
Used for	**Statements**	**Functions**
Internal	LOOKUP	@LOOKUP
lookups	LOOKUPR	@LOOKUPR
External	XLOOKUP	@XLOOKUP
lookups	XLOOKUPR	@XLOOKUPR

(@*filename*) perhaps to find and retrieve a value for the current form, or simply to have Q&A check out something that's elsewhere in the same file on which you're working.

Table 4-4 summarizes the various lookup commands available in Q&A, and a description of each one follows.

A Note on Statements vs. Functions

Statements and functions are both programming terms, and they have different meanings.

Generally, a programming *function* is a process or instruction that produces or returns a value. Instructions that return the time, date, and incremental numbers (@Time, @Date, @Number), for example, are functions — they hand you a value, a piece of information about something.

Functions, however, don't say what to do with the value once it's been retrieved or calculated. You have to specify, additionally, where you want the value to be placed. The delivery man arrives with your new 24-inch TV; now you have to show him where to put it.

Statements, on the other hand, are commands a programmer uses to get something done — a value copied from one field to another, the cursor moved. A programming statement can *include* a function; the function returns the value, and the statement says what's to be done with it (such as place it in a field). The LOOKUP statement is a good example. It both finds a value in a table *and* places it in the field you've specified.

In Q&A, all functions are preceded by the @. And when you use any function like @LOOKUP or @DATE to have Q&A return a value for you, remember to also specify what you want done with the value, or *where* you want the value to appear. You might want the value returned to a field, or compared with another value (as in an If/Then expression) with some other action dependent on the result of the comparison. Sometimes, the only way to have Q&A find or calculate what you want is to embed one function inside another. This is perfectly permissible when using functions.

Internal Lookups

LOOKUP is used to find exact matching values in the lookup table attached to the database. It's a complete programming statement that retrieves a value from the table and places it in the designated field on your form. If you need to refamiliarize yourself with how to create and edit a database lookup table, see the section on it earlier in this chapter.

The formula for a LOOKUP statement is:

LOOKUP (*key, column, field ID#*)

- **key** is the ID# of the field containing the value that has a matching value in the table.

- **column** is the column number in the table that holds the information you want to retrieve into your form.

- **field ID#** is the destination field where you want the retrieved information placed.

The @LOOKUP command is not a complete statement but a *function*. It returns a value from the lookup table but doesn't tell Q&A where to put it — you have to additionally assign a field ID# to say where the value should go.

With the LOOKUP statement you say: **LOOKUP (#40,1,#42)**, and Q&A retrieves the value from the first column of the lookup table that corresponds to the key field matching the value in field #40, and places that value in field #42 in your form.

To get this done with the @LOOKUP command, you'd have to say: **#42=@LOOKUP (#40,1)**. You see, in the @LOOKUP command you're telling Q&A where to put the value independently of the function because the function itself doesn't specify it.

The formula for the @LOOKUP function is:

@LOOKUP (*key, column*)

where *key* is the ID# of the field containing the value that has a corresponding value in the table, and *column* is the column number in the table that holds the information you want to retrieve.

When should you use one and not the other? The advantage of @LOOKUP is that it can be included in derived report columns, and used in formulas for other Q&A operations as well (for example, when you want values compared). LOOKUP statements, on the other hand, specify a field where the value should be placed and thus can't be used except in instances where a field is available (such as on a form).

LOOKUPR and @LOOKUPR work like the above two commands except that they retrieve the *next lowest value* from the table if an exact match cannot be found. They allow you to retrieve values from lookup tables when those values fall within a ranges.

Suppose you needed to look up a particular delivery zone based on a zip code, where each zone covered a range of zip codes. You could enter into the Key column of your table the zip code that corresponds to the bottom of each range, and place the corresponding zones in column 1 of the table. Then, when you use the zip code to find the zone, Q&A hands you the zone corresponding to the next lower zip code if an exact match were not available in the Key column.

The formulas for these two range value LOOKUP commands are:

LOOKUPR(*key, column, field ID#*)

@LOOKUPR(*key, column*)

where the *key* is the ID# of the field that contains a matching value in the Key column of the table; *column* is the column number (1, 2, 3, or 4) in the table that contains the value you're after; and *field ID#* is the number of the field on the form where you want the value placed (the destination field).

With @LOOKUP, as you can see, you must additionally specify the field that is to receive the value.

External Lookups

When you need to have Q&A "look outside" to another database for information to retrieve into your forms, you use the *external* lookup commands. There are four different external database LOOKUP commands, just as there are four different commands you can use to find information in an internal lookup table.

The XLOOKUP statement returns a value from an external database and places it in the designated field. Later, when programming the invoice database, you'll see how valuable this capability can prove to be. Without it you wouldn't be able to look up customer names and addresses from the Customer database, or item descriptions and prices from the Stock file, and place these into the invoice during data entry.

The formula for the XLOOKUP statement is:

XLOOKUP(fn,pkf,xkf,lf,field ID#)

- **fn** is the external database *filename* — in quotes — from which the statement retrieves its information.

- **pkf** is the *primary key field*, the ID# of the field in the current database that has a matching field in the external database.

- **xkf** is the *external key field*, the name — in quotes — of the field in the external database that matches the primary key field of the current database.

- **lf** is the *lookup field*, the field label — in quotes — of the field in the external file whose value you want brought into the current database.

- **field ID#** is the number of the field in the current database where you want the retrieved value to appear (the destination field).

New: Q&A version 4.0 added an exciting new feature to the XLOOKUP command — the capability to handle up to 17 lookup and destination field ID#'s in a single expression. Before this, you could only return a single external value per statement.

You specify the filename, the primary key field, and the external key field as usual, and then specify your *first* lookup field and field ID#, your *second* lookup field and field ID#, your *third*, etc., as follows:

#3:XLOOKUP("Stock",#10,"Stk#","Description",#12,"Price", #13,"Discount",#14,"Qty in stock",#15........)

You can also use the @XLOOKUP function to retrieve a value from an external database, so long as you specify where the value is to be placed. The @XLOOKUP formula is the same as the XLOOKUP's except for the *field ID#* inside the formula. Here's a comparison of the two commands. In a database programming expression either would accomplish the same thing:

XLOOKUP("Stock",#10,"Part Number","Price",#20)

#20=@XLOOKUP("Stock",#10,"Part Number","Price")

Notice that the XLOOKUP statement contains the field where the value is to be placed, whereas the @XLOOKUP function is *preceded* by the target field.

@XLOOKUP functions are expressed as follows:

@XLOOKUP(fn,pkf,xkf,lf)

and the definitions for the four items contained in the function are the same as those defined for the XLOOKUP statement above.

Unlike the XLOOKUP command, you can use the @XLOOKUP function in report-derived columns, mass updates, at Retrieve Specs in merge documents, and inside other functions or statements. When @XLOOKUP returns a blank value, though (the lookup field in the external file is blank), and a target field has been specified, the blank will replace the value in the target field. The XLOOKUP command, in contrast, will *not* change the target field if the lookup field is empty.

XLOOKUPR and @XLOOKUPR are also available for you to use when programming external database lookups. Like their LOOKUPR and @LOOKUPR *internal* counterparts discussed above, they return the next lowest value if an exact match isn't found.

Points to Remember When Working with External Lookup Commands

When you're working with external lookup commands, keep in mind the following points:

- There must be matching fields in both the primary and external databases (the *pkf* and the *xkf* must be the same). For example, if you want to look up the Customer Number from an invoice form, both the customer file *and* the invoice file must contain fields whose values will match. Moreover, they must be of the same information type (the *pkf* and the *xkf* must *both* be numbers, text, etc.)

- The external key field *must* be indexed (a Speedy field).

- The external key field has to be unique. In other words, you can't expect to get a proper match on the "Phone number" field in the external file if that database has two "Phone number" field labels.

- When you specify the external filename, you may need to include the complete drive, path, and filename. When you don't, Q&A uses the default drive and path you've set for your data files. If all your data files are in the same directory, and you've told Q&A so at the Set Default Directories screen, then you won't need to specify the pathname in your XLOOKUPs.

- You don't need to include the .DTF extension when you specify the external filename.

- You can perform an "external" lookup within the same database by replacing the name of the external database with **@filename**. This tells Q&A to retrieve the information from the current file, and can be used to bring balances forward or maintain running totals.

Version 4.0

- You can lookup directly to a dBASE II, III, or IV file by specifying the external file with its .DBF filename extension and, if it's a dBASE II or III file, the filename and path of the index file ending with an .NDX extension. If you don't specify an index file path as the *external key field* parameter, Q&A assumes it is searching for a dBASE IV file with an .MDX filename extension. In addition, since dBASE has case-sensitive indexing, be sure to use the appropriate upper- or lowercase lookup field in your lookup command. If the dBASE field label is in uppercase, specify the lookup command in uppercase characters also.

  dBASE stores memo field data in a file with a .DBT filename extension. So when Q&A is looking up a dBASE memo field, it assumes the same name and path as the .DBF file, and automatically searches for a file with the .DBT extension.

- You can use field ID numbers instead of field labels to specify the external key field and external lookup field, for example, **XLOOKUP ("Customer", #4, "X#3", "X#4", #5)**. You just put an "X" in front of the external field ID numbers and enclose them in quote marks. The advantage to this method is that it can reduce keystrokes where your field names are longish.

- To use the @XLOOKUP function, your configuration system file (CONFIG.SYS) must be set to allow more than eight files open at the same time, or Q&A will give you an error message.

- An external lookup can fail in a number of ways: the external key field can't be found by Q&A, it isn't indexed, the value you want retrieved can't be found, etc. Q&A is pretty good about letting you know *why* the lookup failed, and you should be able to quickly track down and correct any problem.

Q&A'S Built in Functions

Q&A Power Feature: To add even more power to database applications, Q&A provides an array of built-in programming functions in addition to the lookup commands. Because these are functions, you sometimes have to specify the fields where the values returned by them are to be placed on your forms.

You can embed functions within other functions, and the value returned by one function can be used by another function within the greater programming expression.

For example:

#10=@TEXT(@WIDTH(#10),"!")

means fill the width of field #10 with exclamation marks. Here, the @WIDTH function returns the value (the width of field #10, in characters), which is then used by the @TEXT function. If field #10 were five characters long, the function would place five **!** characters in it.

You can also use functions in If/Then and If/Then/Else statements.

The following is a list of all Q&A's built-in functions along with their abbreviations. You have the option of using either the entire function name in your programming expressions, or the abbreviation. Abbreviated function names help reduce your overall character count, saving memory, and make for less typing.

Note: The term *return*, when used in describing the action of a function, means that the function calculates, gets, or creates a piece of information when executed.

Date and Time Functions

Date and time functions return various forms of the date and time.

@D(date) Enables you to use a date constant in a function. For example, in the expression: **#10=#8 - @D(January 1, 1992)**, #10 will get the value 30 (days) if #8 is January 31, 1992.

@DATE, @DA Returns the current date, including day, month and year, in the format specified at the Global Format Options screen for the database. Q&A's internal date format is YYYY/MM/DD.

@DOM(n), @DM(n) Returns the integer of the day of the month of date *n*. If the date is 3/15/92, @DOM returns 15. *N* can be a field ID number, a field name, or expression that evaluates to a date.

@DOW$(n), @DW$ Returns the name of the day (Monday, Tuesday, etc.) of date *n*. *N* can be a field ID number, a field name, or an expression that evaluates to a date.

@MONTH(n), @MT(n) Returns the integer of the month of date *n* (1 through 12). *N* can be a field ID number, a field name, or an expression that evaluates to a date.

@MONTH$(n), @MT$(n) Returns the name of the month (June, July, etc.) of date *n*. *N* can be a field ID number, a field name, or an expression that evaluates to a date.

@T(time) Allows you to use a time constant in a function, similar to the way @D(date) works.

@TIME, **@TME**   Returns the current time of day. **#1 = @Time** places the time (including a.m. or p.m.) in field #1.

@YEAR(*n*)   Returns the year (1991, 1992, etc.) of date *n*. *N* can be a field ID number, a field name, or an expression that evaluates to a date.

Numbering Functions

Numbering functions return incremented numbers to the form.

@NUMBER, **@NMB**   Returns a number always 1 greater than the last one. Use it on invoices, purchase orders — any documents you need to number incrementally. Entered at the Initial Values Spec, it automatically assigns the next number (in Add Data only) when the next form is displayed, and the number won't change when updating.

@NUMBER in a programming expression will produce a new number each time it is executed, but you can control this with "If @Add then..." or other If/Then statements.

Press **<Ctrl><F8>** during Add Data to reset @NUMBER to a new starting number. You get only one @NUMBER per database.

@NUMBER(*n*), **@NMB(*n*)**, where *n* is an integer, returns a number always *n* greater than the last one. Works like @NUMBER except that it allows you to control the increment. A positive *n* increases the number, a negative *n* decreases it.

See Chapter 12 for a special note on using @NUMBER with shared databases.

Context Functions

Context functions work only with If/Then statements in Add Data and Update Modes.

@ADD, **@AD**   Executes the statement only when in Add Data mode. Use only in If/Then statements. For example: **#12: If @Add then**....

@UPDATE, **@UD**   Executes the statement only when in Search/Update mode. Use only in If/Then statements. For example: **#20: If @Update then**....

Financial Functions

Financial functions calculate values on financial forms: interest payments, investments, repayments, annuities, and the like.

Divide interest rate percent by 100 to get the decimal equivalent. Multiply the decimal interest rate by 100 to get percent equivalent. Convert monthly interest to annual interest with the formula:

```
Annual Interest = @EXP(1 + Monthly Interest,12) - 1.
```

Convert annual interest to monthly interest with this formula:

Monthly Interest = @EXP(1 + Annual Interest, 1/12) - 1.

See "Mathematical Functions" below for an explanation of the @EXP function.

@CGR(*pv*, *fv*, *np*), **@CR(*pv*, *fv*, *np*)** Calculates the rate of return of an investment, where *pv* represents the present value, *fv* the future value, and *np* the number of periods. Returns the rate of return in decimal form.

@FV(*pa*, *i*, *np*) Calculates the future value of a stream of payments where *pa* is the payment, *i* is the periodic interest rate (in decimal form), and *np* is the number of payments.

@PMT(*pv*, *i*, *np*), **@PT(*pv*, *i*, *np*)** Calculates the payments on a loan where *pv* is the present value, *i* is the periodic interest rate (in decimal form), and *np* is the number of payments.

@PV(*pa*, *i*, *np*) Calculates the present value of an annuity where *pa* is the payment, *i* is the periodic interest rate (in decimal form), and *np* is the number of payments.

@IR(*pv*, *pa*, *np*) Calculates the interest rate of a loan where *pv* is the present value, *pa* is the amount of the payment, and *np* is the number of payments. Returns the interest rate in decimal form.

Mathematical Functions

Mathematical functions return values on various math problems; absolute value, average, highest, lowest, square root, and the like.

@ABS(*n*), **@AB(*n*)** Returns the absolute value of *n* where *n* is a number entered as a constant, a field ID#, a field name, or an expression that evaluates to a number.

@AVG(*list*), **@AV(*list*)** Returns the average of the values of all the field ID#'s or field names in the list. The list can be individual field ID#'s or field names separated by commas, as in this example: **(#40, #42, #48)**, or consecutive, as in this example: **(#40..#45)**. When using this latter method, Q&A calculates the average of the values in fields #40 through #45 inclusive.

@EXP(*n*, *m*), **@EX(*n*, *m*)** Raises *n* to the *mth* power. *N* can be a field ID number, a field name, or an expression that evaluates to a number.

@INT(*n*), **@IT(*n*)** Returns the integer portion of *n* where *n* is a number entered as a constant, a field ID#, or an expression. **#10=@INT(2.344)** places 2 in field #10. **#10=@INT(#5)** returns the integer portion of the value in field #5 and places it in field #10.

@MAX(list), **@MX(list)** Returns the highest number on the list of field ID#'s or field names that hold the values. The list can be individual field ID#'s or field names, separated by commas, or consecutive fields like **(#55..#65)**.

@MIN(list), **@MN(list)** Returns the lowest value number from the list of field ID#'s or field names. See @MAX.

@MOD(x,y), **@MD(x,y)** Returns the smallest nonnegative number that results when y is repeatedly added to or subtracted from x. Where x and y are both positive numbers, the function returns the remainder that results when x is divided by y. If y is zero, then zero is returned.

@ROUND(n,m), **@RND(n,m)** Rounds off the value of n to m decimal places, where both n and m are numbers entered as constants, field ID#'s, field names, or expressions that evaluate to numbers. M must be in the range -15 to +15.

@SGN(x) Returns the sign of x where x is a text value entered as a constant, a field ID#, field name, or an expression that evaluates to a number. @SGN returns 0 if x equals 0; returns 1 if x is greater than 0; and returns a -1 if x is less than 0.

@SQRT(n), **@SQ(n)** Returns the square root of the value in field n. The absolute value of the number is used if the number in the function is negative. N can be a constant, a field ID, a field name, or an expression that evaluates to a number.

@STD(list) Calculates the standard deviation of the values in the list. The list can be field ID numbers or field names. Separate each field with a comma, or use consecutive fields, such as **(#60..#70)**. Blank fields are ignored. Standard deviation is the square root of the variance. See @VAR.

@SUM(list) Returns the sum of the values of all the field ID#'s or field names in the list. The field ID#'s or field names can be separated by commas, or expressed as a consecutive series as in **(#701..#710)**.

@VAR(list) Calculates the variance of the values in a list of field ID#'s or field names. Blank fields are ignored. The list can be individual field names separated by commas, or expressed as a consecutive series as in **(#10..#16)**.

Text and String Functions

Text and string functions give you a variety of commands.

Note: You can join words and other text strings together simply by using the plus (**+**) sign. For example:

> where field #10 contains "Christine" and field #11 contains "Anderson", the expression: **#12 = #10 + " " + #11** results in field #12 getting the value: "Christine Anderson"

@ASC(*x*), **@AS(*x*)** Returns the ASCII decimal equivalent of the first character of *x* where *x* is a text value entered as a constant, a field ID#, a field name, or an expression. The *x* must be placed within quote marks if it's a text/string value.

@CHR(*n*), **@CH(*n*)** Returns the ASCII character equivalent of *n*, where *n* is an ASCII decimal value.

@CLEAR(*list*) Clears a list of fields of their values; doesn't return a value.

@DEL(*x*,*n*,*m*), **@DE(*x*,*n*,*m*)** Returns *x* with *m* characters deleted starting at position *n*, where *x* is a text value (or the field ID# or field name that contains a text value), and *n* and *m* are numbers entered as constants, as field ID#'s, field names, or expressions. For example: **#10 = @DEL (#5,6,5)**, where field #5 is SMITH90456, would place SMITH in field #10, since "9" is the character in the 6th position, and "90456" are the five characters to be deleted.

@DITTO(*list*), **@DI(*list*)** Returns the values from the listed fields of the previous form and places them in the same fields of the current form. This function works in Add Data only, and is useful, for example, for copying field values like cities, states, and zip codes where these are consistent from one form to the next during a data entry marathon. The list can be field ID numbers or field names.

For example:

```
#15:  @Ditto(#5,#7,#10..#15,#19).
```

You can't make @DITTO *equal* to a field reference.

@FILENAME, **@FN** Returns the name of the current file. Sometimes used in XLOOKUP statements or @XLOOKUP functions (without quote marks). It is also used in document headers or footers to return the document name.

@HELP(*n*), **@HP(*n*)** Displays a user-defined help screen for field *n*. Typically used in If/Then statements to pop-up help screens where appropriate.

For example:

```
<#30: If #10 = "UPS" then @help(#30)
```

pops up the help screen for field #30 if field #10 contains the text "UPS." *N* can be a field ID number or a field name. A help screen must be defined for field *n*. You can't set a field equal to @HELP.

@INSTR(*x*,*y*), **@IN(*x*,*y*)** Returns the position (an integer) of the first occurrence of the string *y* in the text.

For example:

```
#20 = @INSTR(#5,"song")
```

where field #5 contained the value: "I wrote a song," would set field #20 equal to 8 because the "s" in "song" is the 8th character in the field. @INSTR is often used within other functions, where @INSTR finds the first occurrence of a character in a field, and another expression then does something based on the position of that character. For example, @INSTR could be used to locate the position of an unwanted comma in an address field which could then be deleted, or the text after the comma moved somewhere else. Note the double quote marks around the string portion of the argument.

@LEFT(x, n), **@LT(x, n)** Returns *n* characters from field *x* starting at the leftmost position (and working right) in *x*, where *x* is a text value, a field ID number or a field name, and *n* is a number. **#10=@LT(#4,2)** places HB in field #10 where field #4 is HBO12X. See @RIGHT and @MID.

@LEN(x), **@LN(x)** Returns the length in characters of the contents of field *x*. @WIDTH returns the *length of the field* in characters, whereas @LEN returns the value's character count. *X* can be a field ID number or a field name.

@MID(x, n, m), **@MD(x, n, m)** Returns *m* characters from text *x* starting at position *n*, where *n* and *m* are numbers. *X* can be a field ID number or a field name.

For example:

```
#20 = @Mid(#10,4,5)
```

where field #10 contains **XT245-B3HBB**, places "45-B3" in field #20 because "4" is the fourth character of the text and "45-B3" contains five characters.

@MSG(x) Displays a user-defined message *x* on the Message Line at the bottom of the screen. *X* can be a string, field name, field ID number, or expression — usually an expression. The message can be a maximum of 80 characters.

An example would be:

```
>#10: If #10 < 5 then @MSG("This person looks too young
to be hired");goto #10.
```

Place quote marks around the actual message. On monochrome monitors, @MSG messages may be difficult to see.

@NUM(x) Returns the number represented by field *x*. If text characters are mixed in, @NUM removes them and brings together the digits.

For example:

```
#10 = @NUM(#5)
```

where field #5 contained the value **255BH**, would place the number 255 in field #10. Note that @NUM returns a *text* value.

@REPLACE(expression, x, y) Replaces every occurrence of *x* in an expression with *y*, and returns the modified expression.

For example:

where **#1=@replace(#2,"JJ","John Jones"')** and **#2="JJ,JJ"**

field #2 will get "John Jones, John Jones."

@REPLIFER(expression, x, y) Replaces the first occurrence of *x* in an expression with *y*, and returns the modified expression. Given the same arguments as in the @REPLACE example above, @REPLIFER would return "John Jones, JJ" to field #2.

@REPLLAS(expression, x, y) Replaces the last occurrence of *x* in an expression with *y*, and returns the modified expression. Given the same arguments as in the @REPLACE example above, @REPLLAS would return "JJ, John Jones" to field #2.

@RIGHT(x, n), **@RT(x, n)** Returns *n* characters from *x* starting at the rightmost position (and working left) in *x*, where *x* is a text value and *n* is a number. **#10=@RT(#5,3)** places HBO in field #10 where field #5 is A2133HBO. *X* can be a field ID number or field name.

@TEXT(n, x) Returns a text value consisting of *n* characters of *x*, where *n* is the total number of characters you want, and *x* is a text value (letter, symbol, digit, or other character).

For example

#30=@Text(20,"-")

places twenty dashes in field #30. Use quotes around the text value.

@WIDTH(n), **@WTH(n)** Returns the integer which is the width of the field n in characters. *N* can be a field ID number or field name. @LEN counts the number of characters *in the value*, whereas @WIDTH counts the total number of character spaces in the field.

Miscellaneous Functions

The next few commands, while important, don't fit into any particular category.

@ERROR Returns True (or 1) if the most recent XLOOKUP command failed, or False (0) if the most recent XLOOKUP succeeded. False (0) is returned if there was no XLOOKUP at all.

For example:

```
#20: If @error = 1 then @Help(#20)
```

pops up the custom help screen for field #20 if the most recent XLOOKUP failed.

@REST(*field,expression*) Returns a value based on a comparison between two or more arguments. If the expression matches the value in the field, a "Yes" is returned. Otherwise, a "No" is returned. The field argument can be a field ID number or a field name.

For example:

```
#5=@Rest(Size,"Small")
```

returns a "Yes" to field #5 if the value in field #3 is equal to the word *small*, and returns a "No" if it isn't.

```
#5=@Rest(#10,@Month$(@Date))
```

returns a "Yes" to field #5 if the current month is the same as the month in field #10, and a NO if it isn't.

@SELECT(*n,x;y;*...) Returns the *n*th item (always text) from the list *x;y*... Three arguments are required: The first must be the ID number or the name of the field containing a number or expression with a whole number value, followed by a comma. The second, third, etc. arguments are expressions, usually text strings, each separated by a semicolon or comma. You can use numbers during data entry to select from @SELECT's items.

For example:

```
@select(#20,"UPS";"FED-X";"PARCEL POST")
```

if #20 is 1 then "UPS" (the first item) is returned. If #20 is less than one or, in this case, greater than 3, the last item from the list is selected. @SELECT can be used instead of multiple If/Then statements.

Typecasting Functions

Typecasting functions convert values between different information types. For example, you may need to convert a money value to a number, or vice versa, or a number value to text.

@STR(n) Returns the text equivalent of *n* where *n* is a number entered as a constant, a field ID#, a field name, or an expression. Use @STR to concatenate a number with a text value to create a new string value.

@TONUMBER(x), **@TN(x)** Converts *x* to a number. *X* can be a text value, field ID number, field name, or expression.

@TOMONEY(x), **@TM(x)** Converts *x* to a money value. *X* may be a text value, a field ID number, field name, or expression.

@TODATE(x), **@TD(x)** Converts *x* to a date value. *X* can be a text value, a field ID number, field name, or expression.

@TOTIME(x), **@TT(x)** Converts *x* to a time value. *X* can be a text value, a field ID number, field name, or expression.

@TOYESNO(x), **@TY(x)** Converts *x* to a Yes/No value. *X* can be a text value, a field ID number, field name, or expression.

Lookup Functions

Lookup functions are meant to be used in conjunction with the lookup table.

@LOOKUP(key,column), **@LU(key,column)** Returns a value from the lookup table where *key* is the name of the Key column item you're looking up in the table (or any expression that evaluates to the name of the item), and *column* is the numbered column in the table that contains the information you want retrieved.

@LOOKUPR(key,column), **@LUR(key,column)** Returns the next lowest value from the lookup table if an exact match isn't found, where *key* is the name of the Key column item you're looking up (or any expression that evaluates to the name of the item), and *column* is the numbered column in the table that contains the information you want retrieved.

@XLOOKUP(fn,pkf,xkf,lf), **@XLU(fn,pkf,xkf,lf)** Returns a value from an external database, where *fn* is the external *filename* — in quotes — that contains the information, *pkf* is the *primary key field* (the ID# of the field in the primary file that has a matching field in the external file), *xkf* is the *external key field* — in quotes — that matches the value in the primary key field, and *lf* is the *lookup field* that contains the value you're retrieving.

@XLOOKUPR(fn,pkf,xkf,lf), **XLR(fn,pkf,xkf,lf)** Returns the next lowest value from the external database if an exact match isn't found. Takes the same arguments as @XLOOKUP.

There are lookup *statements* that correspond to the above functions. See the section on lookup commands earlier in this chapter.

Network Functions

Network functions are to be used only if Q&A is running on a network.

@GROUP Returns the name of the field protection group assigned to the user. Useful in an If/Then statement, perhaps on record entry, to control the cursor.

@USERID Returns the User ID to the specified field — useful if you want to be able to determine who added the record or updated it last. Combining **@USERID** with the date and time (as a string expression), and making the field Read-only, stamps the form with a secure "who and when."

Subroutine Programming

A subroutine is a portion of a larger program that's set aside to perform a specialized recurring function. It's designed to be called on again and again. In a Q&A database any commands or programming expressions can be used in a subroutine and executed from any other part of the form. Subroutines are particularly useful when you need to have the same programming command repeated a number of times during data entry.

New: Subroutine programming in Q&A involves the use of three commands: GOSUB, RETURN and, optionally, STOP. GOSUB starts the subroutine, telling Q&A to transfer programming control to another field on the database form. Once that programming is executed, the RETURN command — required in the field containing the subroutine — transfers control back to the field that called the GOSUB. Before the matching RETURN is executed, however, you can program other statements, including cursor navigation statements, as well as other GOSUBs with their own RETURNs.

Subroutines can only be executed when the cursor enters the field containing the GOSUB — so fields containing a GOSUB command need to be preceded by < in the Program Spec.

Here's an example of a GOSUB/RETURN:

```
<#31: If #14 = "Y" then GOSUB #60; #32 = #32 + 1; goto #33
```

```
<#60: #80 = @Sum(#15..#30);RETURN
```

The statement in #31 means: *If #14 is "Y" then transfer control to field #60.* Field #60 (containing the subroutine) says: *Add up the values in fields #15 through #30, place the result in field #80, and then return control to field #31.* When control is passed back to field #31, the statements following the GOSUB, `#32 = #32 + 1; goto #33`, are executed.

The field referenced by a GOSUB can be either a field ID number or a field name.

You can program a STOP command to end subroutine execution, even where one or more RETURNs may still be pending. Since STOPs produce no system messages, you may want to program an @Msg message or custom help screen to display to instruct the operator on the next action. STOP commands can also be used in If/Then statements, so that if some condition is (or isn't) present, the subroutine can be halted and control passed back to the user.

Indirection

New: Indirect field references are possible in Q&A with the @FIELD statement. @FIELD(x), abbreviated @(x), is an indirect field reference that returns the value of field *x*.

For example:

```
#2 = @(#1)
```

gets the value from field #1 and looks for a field name or field ID number that matches that value. If it finds one, the contents of that matching field are copied to field #2. You can use one or more indirect field references in almost any programming statement. Field names and field ID numbers are permitted, and you can include arithmetic operators, text, and other built-in functions as parameters within an @FIELD expression.

Special rules pertaining to the expression supplying the indirect reference are as follows:

- If the value in the expression is text, Q&A looks for a field with that name. If none is found, the value is converted to an integer and Q&A then searches for a matching field ID number. But if the value in the expression is anything other than text, Q&A will only look for a matching field ID number.

- If the above search doesn't find a field then, of course, Q&A considers the reference undefined, and makes no assignment. But if the value in the referenced field was going to be used in a calculation within an expression, the indirection returns an ERR.

Retrieve Spec Programming _____

Calculations, along with most all of Q&A's built-in functions, can be used at any Retrieve Spec in the product; the only exceptions are @DITTO, @HELP, @MSG, @NUMBER, @TOTAL, @AVERAGE, @COUNT, @MAXIMUM, and @MINIMUM. As you become familiar with these particular functions you'll see why. Some of them don't return values, others require a list of fields for their argument, and others return values which would be useless at a Retrieve Spec. @ADD and @UPDATE context functions are permitted, but of what use would they be in retrieving database records?

Programming functions can be used along with calculations and the regular Retrieve Spec restrictions covered in some detail in the last chapter. Functions add power and a great deal of flexibility in establishing your exact retrieval parameters. For example, one of the most basic of all the functions, @DATE, can make things just plain easier.

In Q&A version 3.0 you had to tab to the date field and type today's date or press **<Ctrl><F5>** every time you wanted to retrieve the forms with the current date on them. With 4.0 you can simply save the @DATE spec, call it up with a couple of keystrokes, and you've got the current date on your Retrieve Spec no matter what day of the century it is (see "Naming and Saving Specs" further ahead).

Alas, however, programming functions are not the same as programming statements — and you *cannot* use statements, such as If/Then constructions, at a Retrieve Spec.

When you enter an expression into a field at a Retrieve Spec, type braces around the expression, like this:

Invoice Date: ={@DATE}

Notice the = (equal) sign in front of the opening brace. In this case we're setting the **Invoice Date** field *equal to* the function which returns the current date. So the equal sign falls *outside* the braces.

Now you can add other nonprogramming-related restrictions as well. If these are invoices we're retrieving, for instance, you might add to the same Retrieve Spec:

Shipping Method: UPS

Invoice Amount: >$499

These two additional Retrieve Spec parameters, in conjunction with the @DATE function, tell Q&A to find today's invoices that are to be shipped via UPS and are worth $500.00 or more.

If you wanted to retrieve all the inventory records where the list price is the same as the discount price (ie., no discount has been established for some items, and you want to find which ones), your Retrieve Spec parameter would be:

List: ={Discount Price}

Here's another example of using a formula at a Retrieve Spec. Suppose you wished to retrieve all the invoices where the shipping charge is greater than ten percent of the order value (assuming these are both fields on the form) you would enter:

Shipping: >{Order Value * .10)

Use field names, not Program Spec field ID numbers, when referring to fields in Retrieve Spec expressions.

There's practically no limit to the retrieve criteria you can establish using formulas and Q&A's built-in functions. Suppose you wanted to include in a report all the purchase orders where the PO amount exceeded the credit limits in the corresponding Vendor file records. You could this @XLOOKUP function at the PO database Retrieve Spec:

PO Amount: >{@Xlookup("Vendor.dtf", "Vendor No", "Vendor No", "Limit")}

Assuming "Vendor No" (Vendor number) is a field in both PO.DTF and VENDOR.DTF, this expression would include the forms you want in the report. When using a lookup function in a Retrieve Spec, you have to obey all the standard rules that apply to lookup commands.

These are just a few examples of how you can use calculations, field references, and programming functions at any Retrieve Spec. If you should try to use an expression that Q&A doesn't allow, it lets you know with a warning message and places the cursor near where the error is. You can return to the spec with **<Esc>**, or press **<F1>** for help.

Naming and Saving Specifications

The more you use Q&A, the more likely you'll benefit by saving certain specifications as you create them. Q&A retrieves, sorts, prints, generates reports, and carries out a number of other operations based on your specifications, or *specs*. The spec always looks like a duplicate of the design of your database form.

If you get into the habit of naming and saving your specs, you'll have them for future use. Why retype a complex Retrieve Spec you routinely use when you can just press a couple of keys and call it up?

Keep in mind as you read the following sections that you can save almost any spec in Q&A. Of course, there's no point to saving a spec you'll probably never use again. But a named and saved spec may help you out of a mess. If the spec was inappropriate and you wound up with an unwanted result, you can always go back to the spec to find out why. If you didn't save the spec, how are you going to retrace the steps that led to the unwanted result?

You can name and save the following specs:

- Retrieve Specs
- Sort Specs
- Report Specs
- Mass Update Specs
- Merge Specs
- Post Specs
- Duplicate Records Specs
- Table View Specs

Q&A always reminds you to save a Report Spec. With the other specs you have to take the initiative. To save any type of spec other than a Report Spec, follow these steps:

1. Fill in the spec.

2. Press **<Shift><F8>**. A box displays prompting you to type the name of the spec. The name can be up to 31 characters long (it's not a DOS filename, but is stored on disk along with the database). Type a name that describes what the spec is for or what it does, perhaps even adding a date abbreviation to time-stamp it for future reference.

3. Press **<Enter>** or **<F10>** to save the spec to disk under the name you just gave it.

When you want to reuse a spec:

1. Get the blank spec on screen.

2. Press **<Alt><F8>** for the list of names specs.

3. Highlight the one you want and press **<Enter>**. The blank form is filled out with the selected spec.

4. Press **<F10>** to use the spec.

Using Restricted Values to Create "Pick Lists"

 Q&A Power Feature: At any database Restrict Spec you can press **<F6>** at any field to open up the Field Editor, allowing you to enter hundreds of permissible values for the field, each separated by a semicolon as required by Q&A. Then, during data entry, you can move the cursor to that field, press **<Alt><F7>** to display the list of those restricted values, highlight the one you want, and press **<Enter>** to retrieve it into the form. You can do tricks with this feature to produce what is known as a "pick list" — a list of values *from an external database*. It's an understated feature in Q&A, but a powerful and versatile one. I'll show you one way you can use it.

Although this section covers an advanced use of Restrict Spec capabilities, I'll be referring to report design and macros here. So you'll need to study the material in Chapters 6 and 8 before attempting this procedure. Chapter 12 contains a similar advanced application tool, but one that does not bring the Restrict Spec into play.

Suppose you have a used vehicle business and maintain an inventory of several hundred vehicles in a Q&A database, VEHICLES.DTF, and you want a pick list of these inventory items that you can pop up from inside *another* database, OUTFIX.DTF, during data entry. OUTFIX.DTF is a work order form that you fill out each time you send a vehicle to an outside service for mechanical work, painting, reupholstering, and so forth. Each vehicle may be sent out to several different shops before it's ready to go out onto the lot and be offered for sale.

Your VEHICLES.DTF form contains, among others, the following fields, shown here with sample values entered:

MAKE: Ford   **YEAR:** 87   **MODEL:** LTD   **COLOR:** Red   **STK#:** 477

When you fill out an OUTFIX.DTF work order form to send a vehicle out for service, you enter a code into the Vehicle field that describes the vehicle, such as **Ford 87 LTD Red 477**, but you'd prefer to have a pop-up list available from within the OUTFIX database that shows all your inventory items, so you can press **<Alt><F7>**, highlight the subject vehicle, and press **<Enter>** to retrieve it into the form. In essence, what you need is a series of acceptable (Restrict Spec) values for the field that is as up-to-date as your inventory.

Of course, when a new vehicle is brought into inventory, a new VEHICLES.DTF form is filled out immediately, so the vehicles database is always current. But you want to avoid also having to add new vehicles to the Vehicle field at the OUTFIX.DTF Restrict Spec, yet you want that field's restrict values to be current. Using the Report module, the Write module, the Restrict Spec, the word processor-like capabilities of the Field Editor, and a macro, you can have Q&A update your Respect Spec in OUTFIX.DTF automatically with a keystroke or two, and have the pick-list you need.

Your first step is to design a report that shows all your current vehicle codes in alphabetic order by make (Ford, Chevy, Nissan, etc.). Keeping in mind that you can automate this entire procedure with a macro, here are the steps.

Report Design

Design your report in the Vehicles database by completing the following specs:

1. At the report Retrieve Spec select all items in your current inventory.

2. At the Column/Sort Spec, type **1AS,I** into the Make field, and subsequent column numbers into the other four fields, Year, Model, Color, and Stk# respectively, making all the columns invisible.

3. Create a Derived column, using the following formula (note the semicolon at the end of the formula, which will be used to separate each restricted value):

   #1+" " +#2+" "+#3+" "+#4+" "+#5+";"

   The window that displays the list of restricted field values when **<Alt><F7>** is pressed during data entry is only 19 characters wide; values longer than this are perfectly acceptable, but you can only *see* the first 19 characters (spaces included) until the value is actually retrieved into the record. Bear this in mind, because if you need to see the entire value in the pop-up window, it has to be 19 characters or less.

4. At the Print Options screen choose Disk on the "Print to" line.

5. At the Define Page screen, set your page width at 80, your page length to a number greater than the number of records you would ever likely have in the inventory file, your right margin to 80, and your left, top, and bottom margins to 0.

6. Print the report to disk, and save it to the filename RESTRICT.DOC.

Editing in the Write Module

Edit the report in the Write module by completing the following steps:

1. Bring the ASCII-formatted RESTRICT.DOC onto the Type/Edit screen. Your page length should be set to 0 so there are no page breaks.

2. Using **<Shift><F4>**, delete the column heading along with the dashed line underneath it so all you have left is the row of raw inventory codes, each ending with a semicolon.

3. Now do a fast/automatic search and replace on carriage returns: Search for **@CR** and replace each occurrence with **** (nothing). When the operation is done you should have a continuous stream of alphabetically

sorted vehicle codes with each code followed by a semicolon. Some codes may wrap — don't worry about that.

4. Save the report to Q&A Write format with **\<Shift\>\<F8\>**, overwriting the ASCII document with the same name.

At the OUTFIX.DTF Restrict Spec

The final step in creating the restricted values list (the document you just saved to disk) is to retrieve it into the Restrict Spec by completing these steps:

1. At the Restrict Spec for OUTFIX.DTF, move the cursor to the Vehicle field and press **\<F6\>** to open the Field Editor.

2. Press **\<F8\>** for the Options menu, and select Documents, then "Insert a Document." When Q&A prompts for the filename, type RESTRICT.DOC and press **\<Enter\>**.

The document will flow into the editor formatted for the editor's maximum line length, and with the required semicolon separating each vehicle code. This text, which was originally a report, and then a Write document, has now become a list of restricted values.

Now when cutting your outside work orders in OUTFIX.DTF, you can move to the Vehicle field and press **\<Alt\>\<F7\>** to display the alphabetical list of all the vehicle codes in inventory. If the list is long, you can press the first letter of the vehicle make and the first code with that letter will display. When you've got the one you want, simply press **\<Enter\>** to retrieve it into the form.

This entire procedure (from generating and printing the predesigned report to disk and working it over in the Write module, to updating the Restrict Spec with it) can be macro driven so that you can always have the current list of available vehicles for display during data entry. Figure 4-x is a sample report created with the Restrict Spec.

A few points to keep in mind, however. You'll want the macro to include the command to overwrite the out-of-date RESTRICT.DOC on disk each time with the new RESTRICT.DOC, and also to block-delete the existing "document" in the Restrict Spec before inserting the new one.

A technique similar to this one can be used in any situation where you could benefit from pick lists available during data entry. In this case, if you ran the macro right after selling a vehicle or bringing one into stock your restricted values list would always be current. It's a no-programming technique for viewing and grabbing external database information during data entry that will save you a great deal of time and keystrokes while reducing input errors.

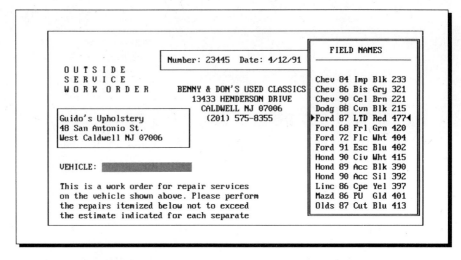

Figure 4-8: Sample Restrict Spec Report. With the cursor in the highlighted Vehicle field, the operator presses <Alt><F7> for the list of values, highlights the right one, and presses <Enter> to retrieve the value into the field.

Designing the Sample Invoice Form

Now let's take some of the things we've learned in this chapter, as well as the previous one, and apply them to the development of a rather advanced invoice application.

First, you'll lay out the template, positioning and labeling the fields. After that, you'll assign information types to the fields and add other custom features where appropriate. Once the design is complete you'll add programming statements where needed to enhance the form's efficiency during data entry.

An invoice form design is a good example to use because it involves interaction with a lookup table and other databases, requires programming for calculations and cursor moves, uses a variety of information types, and is particularly well suited to the addition of custom help, field restrictions, initial value presets, and other features we've looked at up to this point.

The invoice form, as it will be designed in the following section, is included on the Applications disk that came with this book. Don't worry if it's not the exact invoice you want — you'll be able to modify its design and programming to suit your needs.

Sample Invoice Design

Keep the following ideas in mind when you set out to create an invoice form:

- Keep your own information needs foremost in mind.
- Look at your invoice from your customer's eyes.
- Lay out your invoice from an order entry point of view.

Automated invoicing applications have tremendous advantages over their ancient typewritten counterparts. Not only are they faster, mathematically inclined, and more mistake-proof, but they're a treasure trove of management information.

They tell you who ordered what, when, what's selling, dollar volume, sales tax, freight charges, terms, balances due, who needs dunning, payments received, back orders, preferred shipping methods, weights, who entered the invoice, *and just about anything else you want to design into them.* Daily, weekly, or monthly reports compiled from invoices reveal the costs, margins, activity levels, and relationships that are the keys to keeping on top of your business. Thus they can be a primary source of management information.

Assumptions for the Invoice Application

Your particular invoice design requirements will depend on what your business does, what it sells, to whom it sells, and what you and your customers need to see on the invoice.

Our sample invoice will be designed so that it can be printed either to your custom preprinted forms, or to an 8½-by-11-inch blank page (multipart continuous, or single sheet). In the former instance, you'll print only the field contents; in the latter instance you'll print the entire form just as it appears on screen — field labels, values, lines, boxes, and all.

The form itself will include enough fields for ten invoice line items, although you can design the form to handle many more than that. By *line item* is meant one invoice line containing one stock number and its corresponding description, quantity, price, and amount. You'll make use of Q&A's lookup commands to retrieve information into the invoice from a lookup table, and from the customer, stock, and shipping rates databases.

Creating the Invoice Screen

Since the invoice form will take three screen pages to lay out, Figures 4-9 through 4-11 show you each screen page as it appears when completed on the design screen, and Figure 4-12 then shows the entire form with the *Field ID Numbers* in place.

A brief discussion of the fields will follow each screen page so you'll understand why they're there, and how they fit into the overall design and purpose of the form.

Once the invoice layout has been completed, you'll learn about the suggested field widths, information types, formatting, and the other Q&A features you can tap to enhance the form.

After you've got the design of the form down pat, you can proceed to a discussion of the programming statements needed to control data entry and perform calculations, as you explore the form and function of each the many programming features available in Q&A.

Creating Invoice Screen 1

The layout starts on line 3 of Q&A's database design screen with the first field label (**#** for "Company Number") at the very left edge. Two blank lines are left at the bottom of the form, also, making the form a total of 62 lines on a 66 line 8½-by-11-inch page. This should accommodate most any printer.

The black lines to the left and right of **INVOICE** are ASCII graphics characters. **INVOICE**, **Ship to**, and **Sold to** are not field labels, just added text. The boxes underneath these, and also the segmented box at the bottom of the page, are drawn using Q&A's Draw feature, available by pressing **<F8>** from the design screen.

All information blanks start with **<** rather than **:** because these do not show up during data entry, making for a less-cluttered form.

A number of labelless fields are included in the design. The three fields below the **CU#** ("Customer Number") field are for your company's name and address. They're 35 characters wide and will be filled in automatically from the lookup table, based on the one-character value entered in the **#** field.

The field immediately to the right of the **CU#** field is date field where the actual order shipping date will be entered.

The **Invoice No** field contains the invoice number filled in automatically with the next number using Q&A's @Number feature at the Initial Values Spec. The **Date** field is also preset at the Initial Values Spec using the built-in the @Date function.

The four labelless fields each under **Ship to** and **Sold to** are for the customer's address which Q&A will retrieve from the Customer file. They're 35 characters each in length.

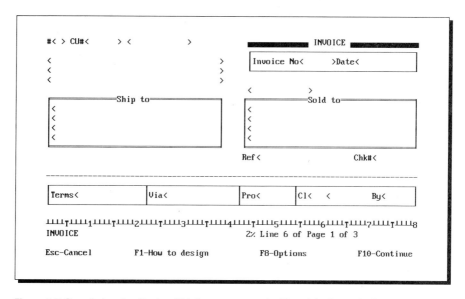

Figure 4-9: Sample Invoice Design. This is screen page 1 of 3, as it looks on the form design screen. Remember that Figure 4-9 shows the form on the design screen before it has been saved.

The **Ship to** address was placed beneath the shipper's name and address so the invoice can to be folded and used as a shipping label.

The 10-character field just above **Sold to** is where the operator will enter the abbreviated name-plus-zip code lookup value to pull in the **CU#** (Customer Number) if it's unknown.

The **Ref** field is for the customer's P.O. number, buyer's name, or the date the order was received. The **Chk#** field contains the customer's check or money order number if he has remitted.

The **Terms** field will return the terms of the order (such as Paid, Net 30 Days, and Pro-forma) based on the entry of a one-digit code. The **Via** field will likewise return the shipping method (UPS Ground, Federal Express, Parcel Post, etc.) with a one-character value entered.

The **Pro** field can contain a code that corresponds to a special promotion you've done, enabling you to pull reports to see the results of your advertising.

The **CL** field to the right of that is for the customer class or account type (wholesale, retail) and will be looked up by Q&A from the customer file and placed here automatically.

```
Figure 4-9: Sample Invoice Design, Screen Page 2 of 3.

    Stk#            Description       Ord  Shpd  List    Net    Amount

     1<      <                         <    <    <       <      <
     2<      <                         <    <    <       <      <
     3<      <                         <    <    <       <      <
     4<      <                         <    <    <       <      <
     5<      <                         <    <    <       <      <
     6<      <                         <    <    <       <      <
     7<      <                         <    <    <       <      <
     8<      <                         <    <    <       <      <
     9<      <                         <    <    <       <      <
    10<      <                         <    <    <       <      <

     <
                                                                      >

          ┌─In Stock─┐  ┌─Status─┐   ┌─On Order─┐      ┌─Discount─┐
          │ <        │  │ <      │   │ <        │      │ <        │
          └──────────┘  └────────┘   └──────────┘      └──────────┘
    └┴┴┴┴┬┴┴┴┴┴1┴┴┴┴┬┴┴┴┴2┴┴┴┴┬┴┴┴┴3┴┴┴┴┬┴┴┴┴4┴┴┴┬┴┴┴┴5┴┴┴┴┬┴┴┴┴6┴┴┴┴┬┴┴┴┴7┴┴┴┴┬┴┴┴┴8
    INVOICE                              4% Line 1 of Page 2 of 3

    Esc-Cancel        F1-How to design        F8-Options        F10-Continue
```

Figure 4-10: Sample Invoice Design, Screen Page 2 of 3.

The second field in that last box will contain the invoice cost-of-goods-sold figure, calculated by a programming statement to be composed later on.

The last field on the screen, **By**, is for the name or initials of the person entering the invoice.

Creating Invoice Screen 2

Figure 4-10 shows screen page 2 of the invoice layout. Notice at the very top of the page the nonfield text that indicates the information to be entered into each of the seven columns.

The columns will work as follows once the form is programmed:

1. Type the **Stk#** (stock or item number) and then press **<Tab>** or **<En-ter>**.

2. Q&A looks up the **Description** and **List Price** from the *external* STOCK database and enters these in values columns 2 and 5 respectively.

   At the same time, the **In Stock, Status, On Order**, and **Discount** windows at the bottom of the screen are filled in with information retrieved from the same **Stk#** record in the external STOCK database. These tell you how many of the item are **In Stock**, any special **Status** with respect to the stock item, whether any more are **On Order**, and the

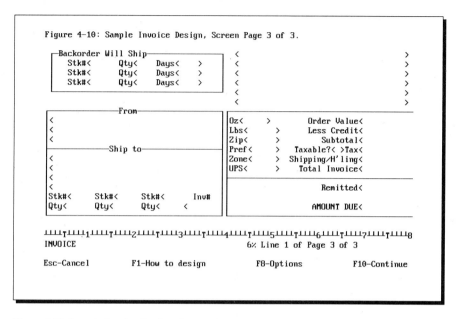

Figure 4-11: Sample Invoice Design, Screen Page 3 of 3.

type of discount that can be extended — helpful information during order entry.

3. The quantity ordered (**Ord**) and quantity to be shipped (**Shpd**) are next entered in columns 3 and 4. And since the **List** field has already been looked up and entered by Q&A, the cursor will jump to the **Net** field where you can enter any applicable discount, or leave the field blank where the net price is the same as the list price.

4. After entering a value in the **Net** field, the amount column is calculated automatically and the cursor moves to the next line.

5. If you now enter a *second* item number, the process beginning at step 2 above starts all over again, and so forth down through the 10 invoice lines. But if you exit to the right from a *blank* stock number field, our programming will assume there are no more items to enter and will move the cursor to the large multiline field below line item 10 where you can enter comments, a thank-you, a pitch to buy something else, or announce a coming event.

Creating Invoice Screen 3

Figure 4-11 shows the final screen page of the invoice form. The six wide labelless fields at the top right will later be used to contain special text and programming statements to look up and calculate values. Don't be concerned with them at this point.

The **Backorder Will Ship** box contains fields for ordered items and quantities that are out of stock and to be shipped later. The **Days** fields let the customer know about how long before these back-ordered items will ship. The area can handle up to three back-ordered items. If more fields than that are needed, better have a heart-to-heart talk with your purchasing agent.

The large box in the lower left of the form is an extra shipping label for large orders or back orders. The back-ordered items and quantities (if any) are copied from the corresponding fields in the **Backorder Will Ship** box, and the invoice number is entered in the field below **Inv#** along with both the shipper's and customer's names and addresses.

This area can be detached from the invoice, held until the back-ordered items arrive, and then used as a shipping label. The **Inv#** connects it with the proper invoice. The two blank lines below the box could contain a text field advising the customer: "These are back-ordered items not shipped on our original invoice No. 2334."

If you're having custom-designed invoice forms printed, tell the printer to run a perforation around the box so you can remove it easily from the invoice. If you're having three-part forms printed, you'll have three extra labels for each invoice.

The lower-right area of the form contains fields for calculating the weight and shipping cost of the invoice, and totaling up the invoice. This will be discussed in greater detail when the form is programmed.

Once the invoice is finished you can print it out or save it to disk, and run your daily totals and shipping manifest, and update the stock records with the invoice quantities that should be deducted from inventory (because they've been sold). The best way to map out and manage these activities is discussed later in this chapter, and in Chapters 10 and 11.

Logical Field Numbers at the Program Spec

The first thing you want to do when preparing to add programming to your Q&A form is to assign Field ID numbers to the fields that will be involved in any programming formulas or cursor moves. These are variously known as field numbers, field ID's, or logical field numbers. If you'll be entering cursor moves into fields at the Field Navigation Spec, and formulas into the same fields at the Program Spec, you'll probably want these numbers to correspond, although they don't have to.

Tip: If the field is *not* going to include a programming formula or cursor move, and won't be referenced in any other field's formula, then you don't have to assign it a number. Note that you can use field names — rather than field ID numbers — as references in Q&A programming. But if you're programming a form containing fields without labels it's easy to lose track of your references. Moreover, field ID numbers generally require fewer keystrokes compared to field names.

We still need to assign information types to invoice fields, format them for display, establish initial values, field restrictions, and so forth — and normally you'd want to do all of these things *before* you added field ID's and started programming the database.

But here you'll add field ID numbers *first*, so you can then refer to these fields by their numbers as we discuss the form field by field.

In Figure 4-12 you can see the whole form with all the field ID numbers entered at the Program Spec. A few of the fields are too small to display their ID numbers, and in these you'll see the usual →symbol indicating there's more.

Notice that in Figure 4-12 the field numbers aren't numbered from left to right with #1, #2, and #3. There's a reason for this.

You may find after you've programmed your form that you need to add more fields. Had you numbered all the fields in increments of 1, your *new* field's ID numbers would be out of sequence with the other field ID numbers around them.

Field ID numbers are for reference; they don't have to be in consecutive order. But if you assign them in a logical sequence it will help you when writing your programming formulas.

The sequence applied in this example starts with #2 in the first field of the form (the **#** field is only one-character wide, so you see the →instead of the ID number), and generally incremented the field ID numbers by twos.

In the line items area of the invoice, you assigned #101 to the first **Stk#**, #201 to the first **Description**, #301 to the first **Order Quantity**, and so forth, allowing associated fields to be referenced in programming statements.

To enter field ID numbers into the fields on your form:

1. Tell Q&A the name of your database when prompted, and select Program Form from the Programming menu. The Program Spec will be displayed.

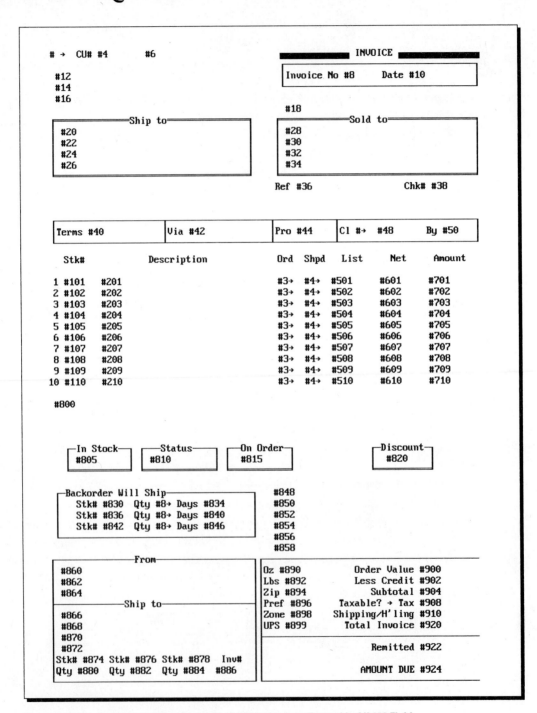

Figure 4-12: The Complete Invoice Form with Field ID Numbers Entered in All 168 Fields.

2. Move to the fields in which you plan to use a formula or that will be referenced in another field's formula, and type the **#** sign followed by an integer. Working left to right down the form, I strongly recommend that you increment your numbers by 2's, 5's or even 10's, in case you need to add fields at a later date and want your ID numbers to stay in numerical sequence.

Press **<F6>** if you need to open the Program Editor for more space in a field Press **<F10>** or **<F6>** to close the Editor and return to the form.

3. After your fields are numbered, it's a good idea to save the Program Spec *before* entering any formulas. This way Q&A can check to make sure you haven't entered any duplicate field ID's.

See Table 4-5 for a summary of suggested field widths and formatting. These are already built into the invoice form on the Applications disk that came with this book, but you can certainly change them to suit your own needs.

Before diving into the next section you should familiarize yourself with Q&A's built-in functions and the basics of formulating a programming statement; otherwise you may find the material too difficult. If you don't understand something, take a moment to go back and read the section again. All the tools you'll be drawing on to program our invoice form were discussed at some point earlier in this chapter.

Programming the Invoice Form

We'll add programming to our invoice one field at a time, referring to the fields by their field ID numbers. Many of the fields on the invoice form don't have labels (although they've been assigned field names at the Field Names Spec) so field ID numbers will give us a more consistent reference.

Each programming statement will be explained, and you should refer to Figure 4-12 and also Table 4-5 to find out exactly to which point on the form the statement applies and how the programming relates to data entry. A number of fields don't appear in the programming summary that follows, which simply means these fields don't require any programming.

To ease the process, you can display the INVOICE.DTF Program Spec on your computer's monitor while reading this section, and follow along that way.

Incidentally, all of the GOTO statements in the Program Spec are alongside our programming commands so you can readily observe how cursor control works in relation to the form's layout, in relation to the programming formulas, and how data entry is to proceed.

Table 4-5
Sample Invoice Form Field Particulars
(Field widths are approximate)

ID#	Width/Format*	Additional Parameters and Comments
#2	1, TU	For a one-character code that will retrieve the shipper's name and address from the lookup table.
#4	5, N0	The customer number will be entered here to retrieve the name and address information from the customer record. Your help screen should explain how to enter the ID and what to do if it's unknown.
#6	10, D	The ship date of the order, updated by a Posting Spec.
#85	5, N0	Set field to @Number at Initial Values Spec, and make it a Read-only field so it can't be changed.
#10	10, D	Invoice Date. Set field to @Date at Initial Values Spec, and make it a Read-only field.
#12	35, T	Name of shipper, retrieved from lookup table. Fields #14 and #16 for the shipper address, also from lookup table.
#18	10, T	If Customer ID# unknown, operator will type first five characters of name plus zip code to check if customer has an ID# in customer file. If so, it will be retrieved into the CU# field. Place a help screen here to guide operator.
#20	35, T	Fields #20-#26 contain Ship-to name and address retrieved from customer file.

(continued)

* T = text, U = uppercase, N(n) = number + decimal places,
  D = date, M = memory, JR = justify right, Y = yes/no

Table 4-5 *(continued)*

ID#	Width/Format	Additional Parameters and Comments
#28	35, T	Fields #28-#34 contain Bill-to name and address.
#36	15, T	Customer reference (P.O. number). Help screen here.
#38	10, T	Check or money order reference.
#40	15, T	Invoice terms auto-typed from code entered. Add a help screen to tell operator the codes that correspond to different invoice terms.
#42	15, T	Shipping method auto-typed from code entered. Add a help screen to show permitted codes and corresponding shipping methods.
#44	6, T	A code that ties customer order with your promotion.
#46	2, T	Customer type or class is retrieved from customer file and entered here.
#48	7, N	Cost of items sold on invoice, formatted as a number field to mask its purpose.
#50	6, T	Order entry clerk's initials.
#101	5, T	Fields #101-#110 are for stock numbers. Format them as numbers if your stock numbers are pure integers. If you need more than a 5-character width, steal space from the Description column. Be sure to format all of these the same way, and place help screens behind at least the first one.

(continued)

Table 4-5 (continued)

ID#	Width/Format	Additional Parameters and Comments
#201	30, T	Fields #201-210 are for item descriptions, filled in automatically by programming.
#301	3, N0	Fields #301-#310 contain the order quantities which the operator types in.
#401	3, N0	Fields #401-410 contain the quantities that will ship on the invoice.
#501	7, M, JR	Fields #501-#510 contain list prices retrieved from the stock item file.
#601	7, M, JR	Fields #601-#610 contain the net prices.
#701	9, M, JR	Fields #701-#710 contain the extended amount.
#805	5, N	Shows quantity in stock of item number being entered.
#810	10, T	Shows any special condition attached to item.
#815	5, N	Tells operator how many of the item, if any, are on order from *your* source.
#820	5, T	Allowable discount retrieved from stock number record.
#830-#846		Format the **Stk#** and **Qty** fields the same as the others above. The **Days** fields should be three-character number fields.
#848-858		These will be used to contain programming statements. Leave them formatted for text.

(continued)

Table 4-5 *(continued)*

ID#	Width/Format	Additional Parameters and Comments
#860-#864		Same as Fields #12, #14, and #16 above. Automatically filled in.
#866-#872		Same as #20, #22, #24, and #26 above. Automatically filled in.
#874-#884		Same as #830-#846 above. Automatically filled in.
#886	5, N	Invoice number automatically entered.
#890	4, N0	Weight of order in ounces.
#892	3, N0	Weight of order converted to pounds.
#894	3, N0	Zip code returned from Customer file.
#896	5, N2	Zip code prefix for UPS shipping rate calculation.
#898	5, N2	UPS service zone.
#899	7, N2	UPS shipping charge, formatted as a number field.
#900-#904		All nine-character, right-justified money fields.
#906	1, YU	Taxable? Yes/No.
#908-#924		All nine-character, right-justified money fields.

Field #2

```
>#2: If @update then goto #38; If #2="A" or #2="B" then
{lookup(#2,1,#12); lookup(#2,2,#14); lookup(#2,3,#16)}
else {@msg("Enter A or B to retrieve shipper's name and
address into form"); goto #2}
```

If the form is being retrieved for update, the @update function at the beginning of the command moves the cursor *immediately* to the **Chk#** (Check Number) field (#38) and the rest of the statement is ignored (because the cursor was moved as soon as the "goto" command was encountered). We're moving the cursor to field #38 when updating on the assumption that the fields above that point aren't likely to be changed, whereas one or more fields below #38 are. If this is a brand-new invoice being entered, the @update command is ignored and the rest of the statement is executed.

If it's a new invoice, the lookup table is searched for a value that matches the one you entered in field #2. If **A** was entered in field #2 then Company A's name and address (the shipper) is retrieved into fields #12-#16. If you enter **B** in field #2, then the values in the **B** row of the lookup table are brought into the form in fields #12-#16. You must enter an **A** or a **B** in field #2 or a message will be displayed and the cursor won't move.

You have a choice of using either of the two companies, each with its own name and/or address.

The next field on the sample invoice form requires information from the Customer database to be looked up and brought in to the invoice. Here's the statement that will fill out the **Sold to** area, and the customer's account type.

Field #4

```
>#4: If @Add then {xlookup("customer",#4,"CU#","whole
name",#28,"company," #30, "street",#32,"c/s/z",#34,"acct
type",#46); If #34=""then goto #20 else goto #18}
```

The statement above retrieves the name and address information from the Customer database, along with the account type, when in Add Data mode. It then checks to see if field #34 contains a value. If it does, then the lookup was successful and the cursor does not need to go to field #18 (see #18 below), so it is sent to field #20, the first line of the **Ship To** address.

Once you specify the external filename, the primary key field, and the external key field in an XLOOKUP statement, you can name up to 17 lookup fields and destination fields in the same statement.

You may need to take another look at the Customer database form designed in the last chapter to understand the relationships between the fields there, and those in the XLOOKUP statement above. Figure 4-13 shows the Customer form.

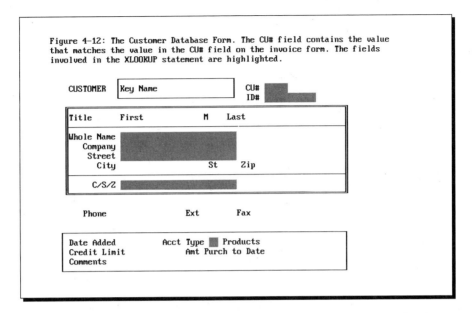

Figure 4-12: The Customer Database Form. The CU# field contains the value
that matches the value in the CU# field on the invoice form. The fields
involved in the XLOOKUP statement are highlighted.

Figure 4-13: The Customer Database Form. The CU# field contains the value that matches the value in the CU# field on the invoice form. The fields involved in the XLOOKUP statement are highlighted.

Field #18

```
>#18: If #34=" " then (xlookup("customer",#16,
"ID#","CU#",#4);goto #4} else goto #20
```

This statement tells Q&A to use the **ID#** typed in this field to retrieve the **CU#** from the Customer file, place it in field #4, and move the cursor there; but that part of the statement executes only if field #34 is blank. Otherwise, the cursor is moved to field #20 (the **Ship to** area) on the assumption that the customer's name and address were retrieved into fields #28-#34.

To illustrate, suppose an order came in from Atlantic Book Co. in zip 80345, but you don't have the customer number. The **Key Name** field in the Customer database should contain "Atlantic," and the **ID#** field should contain ATLAN80354. You know that this will probably find the record *and* the needed **CU#** if the company is in the file, so ATLAN80354 is entered.

If the lookup fails (no matching record with ATLAN80354 is found), the cursor will be in field #4 and it may be assumed that the customer is not on file. At this point, you should ditch the form with **<Esc>** and **Yes**, and add the new customer to the Customer file before cutting the invoice.

Remember: You can create a macro to take you directly to a new customer form in Add Data and another macro to return you from there to invoice input, making these transitions between files swift and smooth. See Chapters 8 and 10.

Field #20

```
>#20: If #20="" then {#20=#28;#22=#30;#24=#32;#26=#36;
goto #36} else goto #22
```

If you exit from an empty field #20 then the information in the **Sold to** fields will be copied into the **Ship to** fields and the cursor will be moved to field #36. Should this customer have a different shipping address, type it in fields #20-26.

Field #22

`>#22: goto #24` Moves the cursor to the next **Ship to** address line.

Field #24

`>#24: goto #26` Moves the cursor to the last **Ship to** address line.

Field #26

`>#26; goto #36` Moves the cursor to the **Ref** field.

Field #40

```
>#40: If #40= 1 then #40="Net 30 Days"; If #40=2 then #40=
"Net 10 Days"; If #40=3 then #40= "Net 10th Prox"; If
#40=4 then #40= "Net Due"; If #40=5 then #40= "COD"; If
#40=6 then #40= "Paid"; If #40=7 then #40= "Pro-forma" If
#40="" then {@msg("Enter a number 1 through 7 to specify
terms, or press <F1> for help"');goto#40}
```

Here you enter a one-digit number (1-7), and the If/Then statement returns the matching terms. If the field is left blank an @Msg displays telling you to press **<F1>** for the help screen (showing the acceptable codes) and the cursor will be returned to the field.

Field #42

```
>#42: If #42 = 1 then #42="First Class"; If #42=2 then
#42= "Parcel Post"; If #42=3 then #42= "Book Post"; If
#42=4 then #42= "UPS Ground"; If #42=5 then #42= "UPS
Second Day"; If #42=6 then #42= "UPS Next Day"; If #42=7
then #42= "Fed Express"; If #42=8 then #42= "Truck
Freight"; if #42=9 then #42= "Will Call"); If #42="" then
{@msg("Enter a number 1 through 9 to specify shipping
method, or press <F1>"); goto #42}
```

The programming for this field is structured along the lines of field #40. Your help screen shows the acceptable codes and what they mean.

Field #44

```
>#44: goto #50
```

You enter a code in this field that identifies the advertisement or promotional program that brought in the order. You can require a value be entered by setting the field to **/=** or **!** at the Restrict Spec. You could also provide a custom help screen that summarizes the codes and the ads or campaign they identify.

Field #48

This field will contain the calculated cost of goods sold on the invoice once the ordered items and quantities have been entered. Field #848 below contains the programming statement.

We're now into the line items area of the invoice. It's here that the item numbers in the order are entered, along with the quantities and any discounts. Sample programming statements for the first line are shown below. With only two exceptions these statements will apply to all ten lines.

Figure 4-14 shows the Stock database form designed in the previous chapter with a few minor changes (see Chapter 11 for the Stock database on the Applications disk supplied with this book). The following programming statements retrieve a number of values from this database in order to help automate the entry of invoice line items, and provide you with useful information about each item as it is entered.

Field #101

```
>#101:xlookup("stock",#101,"stk#","description",#201,"list",
#501,"on  hand",#805,"status",#810,"on  order",#815,
"disc",#820);  goto #301
```

The statement retrieves the **Description** and **List** (list price) values from the Stock database, and also returns the values for the **In Stock**, **Status**, **On Order**, and **Discount** boxes below the line item area. Notice that all the lookups are dependent on the stock number in field #101. Upon exiting field #101, the cursor is moved to field #301 for entry of the quantity ordered.

 Note: Fields #102-#110 contain the same programming statements as #101 except for the field references. On the *second* invoice line, for example, the references to #101, #201, and #501 become #102, #202, and #502 respectively.

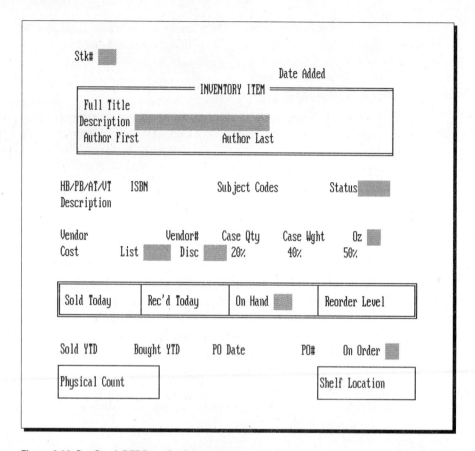

Figure 4-14: Our Stock.DTF Form Revisited. The key field (Stk#) and lookup fields are highlighted.

Fields from fields #102 to #110 should contain an added conditional statement, so that when **<Tab>** or **<Enter>** is pressed from an empty field, the cursor will be moved to field #800 on the assumption that there are no more line items to enter. You can precede the statements in these fields with:

```
>x If x = "" then goto #800;
```

where *x* is the field ID# of the **Stock Number** field.

Field #401

```
>#401: goto #601
```

The quantity shipped is entered in this field, and the cursor jumps to field #601 when you exit the field as field #501 already contains the list price.

Note: Here's where the **In Stock**, **Status**, and **On Order** windows can come in handy. You can see how many of the item you have, and if more are on the way. The information bears on the quantity entered into this shipped field.

Fields #402 to #410 contain the same statement except for the field reference. On the next invoice line, for example, **>#401: goto #601** becomes **>#402: goto #602**, and so forth on through the remaining lines.

Field #601

>#601: If #601=0 then #601=#501

If you move the cursor out of the blank **Net** field, the **List Price** from the previous field is copied into it. You can use an alternative programming statement as follows:

>#601: if @add then {if #601=0 then #601=#501 else #601 = #501- (#501*#601*.01)}

This statement executes only when entering a new invoice. If the operator leaves field #601 without a value (no discount is involved), the value from field #501 will be copied into it. The "else" portion of the statement multiplies field #601's value by the list price, the result is multiplied by .01, and the new result is subtracted from the list price to get the net price. So if the list price is $10.00, a value of 20 entered into field #601 results in a net price of $8.00. The **Discount** window below the **Net** field reflects the maximum allowable discount, in our case, in terms of "trade" or "short" discount.

Note that the programming statements for fields #602 to #610 are the same as #601 except for the field references. On the second invoice line, for example, #601 becomes #602, and #501 becomes #502, and so forth through the remaining invoice lines.

Field #701

<#701: #805=""; #810=""; #815="";#820=""; #701=#301*#601; goto #102

When the cursor *enters* the **Amount** field for this item, the **In Stock**, **Status**, **On Order**, and **Discount** fields are blanked out for this line item, the net price is multiplied by the order quantity in field #301 with the result placed in field #701, and the cursor is moved to the next invoice line.

The programming for fields #702-#710 are the same as that just shown for #701 except for the references to fields #701, #301, #601, and #102. On the second invoice line, for example, these references change to #702, #302, #602, and #103 respectively. When you get to field #710, however, you'll want the cursor to go to #800 when it exits field #710, the last field of the line item area.

Field #800

```
>#800:If @sum(#301..#310) > @sum(#401..#410) then goto #830
else goto #848
```

This is the large, multiline remarks field just below the line items area of the invoice. The programming totals up the **Quantity Ordered** and **Quantity Shipped** fields, and if the latter is less than the former, the cursor is moved to the **Backorder Will Ship** box to enter back order information. Otherwise the cursor is moved to field #848.

Fields #830 through #846

Program your cursor moves from these fields so that if the cursor exits any blank **Stk#** fields, it will move to field #848; and when the cursor exits any **Days** field (except for the last one) it will move to the next **Stk#** field. When the cursor leaves field #846, it should move to #848.

Now add programming statements to field #848 and #850 to calculate both the cost of goods sold on the invoice and the total weight of the order, by looking up the data in the Stock file item by item and performing arithmetic on the returned values.

Field #848

```
<#848:  #48  =(@xlookup("stock",#101,"stk#","cost")*#301)
+(@xlookup("stock",#102,"stk#","cost")*#302)
+(@xlookup("stock",#103,"stk#","cost")*#303)
+(@xlookup("stock",#104,"stk#","cost")*#304)
+(@xlookup("stock",#105,"stk#","cost")*#305)
+(@xlookup("stock",#106,"stk#","cost")*#306)
+(@xlookup("stock",#107,"stk#","cost")*#307)
+(@xlookup("stock",#108,"stk#","cost")*#308)
+(@xlookup("stock",#109,"stk#","cost")*#309)
+(@xlookup("stock",#110,"stk#","cost")*#310);  goto    #850
```

The @XLOOKUP *function* is used here because we want to tell Q&A just once where to put the values it's looking up, multiplying, and adding together. Had XLOOKUP *statements* been used, the field where the value was to be placed would have to have been included *with each lookup expression.*

The invoice can handle up to ten ordered items. The statement returns the cost of each stock number, multiplies it by the quantity ordered, and adds it to the next one on down through the ten line items. Blank invoice line item fields return 0 (zero) and don't distort the calculation. The total cost of goods is returned to field #48, and the cursor is moved to field #850.

Field #850

```
<#850:   #890=(@xlookup("stock",#101,"stk#","weight")*#401)
+(@xlookup("stock",#102,"stk#","weight")*#402)
+(@xlookup("stock",#103,"stk#","weight")*#403)
+(@xlookup("stock",#104,"stk#","weight")*#404)
+(@xlookup("stock",#105,"stk#","weight")*#405)
+(@xlookup("stock",#106,"stk#","weight")*#406)
+(@xlookup("stock",#107,"stk#","weight")*#407)
+(@xlookup("stock",#108,"stk#","weight")*#408)
+(@xlookup("stock",#109,"stk#","weight")*#409)
+(@xlookup("stock",#110,"stk#","weight")*#410);
#892=#890/16*1.05; goto #852
```

This statement calculates the total weight of the order based on the weights in the Stock file and the quantity of each item on the invoice. The result, placed in field #890, is then divided by 16 (to convert it to pounds) and multiplied by 1.05 (to account for packaging), and field #892 gets the new result.

Field #852

```
<#852:   #894=@Xlookup("Customer",#4,"CU#","Zip");#896=
@left(#894,3);If #42="UPS Ground" then {lur(#896,1,#898);
#899=@xlu("Upsrates",#892,  "Weight",#898)};  If  #42="UPS
Second Day" then {lur(#896,2,#898);#899=@xlu
("Upsrates",#892,  "Weight",#898)}  ;  If  #42="UPS Next Day"
then  {lur(#896,3,  #898);#899=@xlu("Upsrates",#892,
"Weight",#898)};  goto  #900
```

This complex multiple statement finds the UPS rate that corresponds to the type of UPS service specified on the invoice, the destination zip code prefix (the first three digits of the customer's zip code), and the total weight of the order.

Field #894 gets the zip code retrieved from the Customer file, and the @left function returns the three-digit prefix to field #896. The series of If/Then statements — using the type of UPS service indicated in field #42 and the *range* lookup function — then find the UPS zone in the lookup table and place it in field #898. The final lookup function retrieves the UPS rate from the external UPS rates database (based on the weight and zone), and returns it to field #899.

 Warning: The INVOICE.DTF lookup table containing the zip code prefixes and corresponding zones, along with the UPS rates database — both included on the Applications disk — contain out-of-date values for a specific pickup area. These zones and rates are not valid for your location. If you plan to use this feature of the Invoice application, you'll have to consult the UPS prefix and rate charts for your own area to update both the lookup table and the UPS rates database. Until you do this, you should have Q&A bypass field #852 by replacing the "goto #852" at the end of field #850's programming with "goto #900."

Field #900

```
<#900: #805=""; #810=""; #815=""; #820="";
#900=@sum(#701..#710); #860=#12; #862=#14; #864=#16;
#866=#20; #868=#22; #870=#24; #872=#26; #874=#830;
#876=#836; #878=#842; #880=#832; #882=#838; #884=#844;
#886=#8; goto #902
```

This statement first ensures that all the fields below the line item area of the invoice are blanked. It then uses the @Sum function to total up the **Amount** column for field #900. The remaining portion of the expression fills in all the fields in the extra shipping label with values already entered elsewhere on the form.

Field #902

```
>#902: #904=#900-#902; goto #906
```

The **Subtotal** field receives the difference between the **Order Value** and any credit entered here, and the cursor is moved to the **Taxable?** field.

Field #906

```
>#906; if #906="Y" then #908=#904*.065; goto #910
```

Calculates and enters the sales tax amount in field #908 if there's a "Y" in field #906, and the cursor is moved to field #910. The tax rate used here is 6.5 percent. You'll need to substitute your own local sales tax rate.

Field #910

```
>#910: #920=#904+#908+#910; goto #922
```

The operator enters the shipping/handling charge in field #910, and when the field is exited the **Total Invoice** is calculated and the cursor is moved to the **Remitted** field.

Field #922

```
>#922: #924=#920-#922; goto #924
```

The amount remitted is entered in field #922 and the balance due on the invoice is calculated when you press **<Tab>** to move out of the field.

Field #924

```
<#924:@msg("Press F2 then F10 to print invoice -- F10 to
add it to file")
```

This is the last field on the form. You can now print the invoice or save it to disk to print later with other invoices. If you need to make any changes to an invoice before saving it, or when updating it in Search/Update mode, use your cursor navigation keys to get to where you want to go. After making your corrections, you should then move the cursor back through to the bottom of the form so that any dependent fields have a chance to recalculate.

For example, if you change a quantity and don't give the programming that comes after that point on the form a chance to reexecute, your total cost of goods sold, weight, and probably your money fields near the bottom of the form, will be off.

Really, you should not print or save the invoice until the cursor has reached the **Amount Due** field — the last one on the form.

Now that we've finished with our sample invoice form, let's look at the remaining Q&A features you can use to help you manipulate and better manage your data files. In Chapter 10 you'll find out how to update your inventory records from your invoices using Q&A's Post feature, and in Chapter 11 I'll give you some tips on customizing the databases on the Applications diskette to your needs.

Copying Forms, Form Designs, and Databases

Q&A's Copy feature lets you copy your records (or portions of them) from one database to another, copy your form's design, or copy the entire database file.

Remember: You don't use Copy to back up your databases — Q&A has separate features for that which you'll learn about in Chapter 9 and Appendix G.

Use the Copy command when you want to move records elsewhere. Copy doesn't remove them — it just duplicates them. As your database grows and adding new forms to it becomes slower, you may want to create a "temporary" database by copying the design of your original database, and then entering your new forms in the temporary database. At the end of the day or week you can copy these records into the "mother" database and then remove the originals from the temporary file.

Another advantage to temporary databases is that you can do operations on a day's worth of invoices, for example, without having to work with the entire file. Searching, sorting, running reports, posting the days sales, and so forth, will proceed much faster when you're working with 200 invoices instead of 10,000.

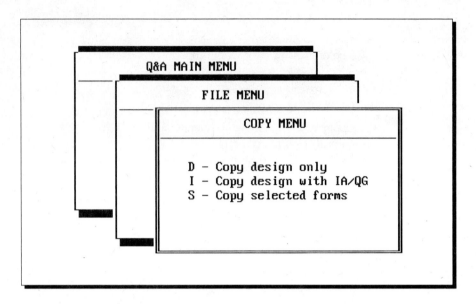

Figure 4-15: The Copy Menu.

You can also copy selected fields from one database to another by creating a target database and telling Q&A which records and fields from the *source* database to copy into the *target* file. This would be useful for copying only invoice numbers, item numbers, and quantities from a selected group of invoices into a different database that contained fields for these values only. You could then run transaction and summary reports to tell you about which items are selling.

Making a copy of the database *design* — which includes all of your saved file, report, mass update, programming, and other specifications — is necessary for creating the temporary database mentioned above, but can also be useful when modifying an existing form design, especially before any records have been added to the file. You can redesign the *copy* with the original file design safely tucked away.

Finally, you can copy the entire database — design, forms and all. Again, this doesn't destroy the original database, it copies it to another location — another directory or drive — on your hard disk.

When you select Copy from the File menu, you'll see the Copy menu as pictured in Figure 4-15.

Copy Design Only

When you copy the design of a database you're copying the form design along with its saved specifications — but no records. What you'll have is an empty file to which you can add records. The copied database will behave just like the original.

Use the following procedure to make a copy of your database design:

1. From the File menu select Copy.

2. Type the name of the database that uses the design you want to copy, and press **<Enter>**. Or press **<Enter>** with the filename empty to see a list of the databases in the directory, highlight the one you want, and press **<Enter>**.

3. From the Copy menu choose Copy Design Only.

4. Type the drive, path, and filename of the new database, and press **<Enter>**. Q&A will get right to work making the copy, placing it in the drive and directory you've specified. If it's a large form with lots of fields, it'll take a few moments.

Should Q&A encounter any problems, such as deficient disk space, the copy process will be aborted and Q&A will display a message explaining why.

Copy Design with IA/QG

If you've been using Q&A's Intelligent Assistant or Query Guide with your database, you'll probably want to copy that, too, along with your form design. If so, choose the appropriate option from the Copy menu.

On the other hand, if you want to remove the IA and Query Guide (see Chapter 7) from your database, along with everything you've taught it, you can choose Copy Design Only, and then copy all your records into the new file. If you need to, you can then rename your database with its original name.

The procedure for copying with the IA and QG information intact is similar to the method for copying database designs. The only difference is that you choose Copy Design with IA/QG.

Copy Selected Forms

Use this option to copy individual records, or portions of records, into another database. There has to be another database design already *there*, of course, to accept the records. You can't copy database records to nowhere.

The procedure for copying records is unique because you have to select the records you want copied, and also tell Q&A where the field values in the source database are to be placed in the target database. You'll need to fill out both a Retrieve Spec and a Merge Spec. Here's how you do it:

1. From the File menu select Copy and type the name of the database that holds the records you want to copy.

2. From the Copy menu choose Copy Selected Forms, and type the name of the destination (target) database when prompted. If you can't recall the name, delete any database name on the filename line, press **<Enter>** to see the list of databases in the directory, highlight the one you want, and press **<Enter>**.

3. At the Retrieve Spec for the source database, enter your parameters to tell Q&A which forms you want copied to the target file. If you press **<F10>** without selecting specific records, *all* the records in the source database will be copied to the target file. If you want your records copied in sorted order, press **<F8>** for the Sort Spec. Press **<F10>** when your Retrieve and (optionally) Sort Specs are as you want them.

4. Fill out the Merge Spec by telling Q&A which *fields* in the source file you want copied to the target database (more on this below). If the form designs of your source and destination databases are identical, and you want all the fields copied just as they are, press **<F10>** without entering anything in the Merge Spec. Q&A will begin copying.

When Q&A copies forms it appends them to the end of the destination database. While it's busy copying, you'll see the first page of each record displayed.

Again, if you don't fill out the Merge Spec, the value in the first field of the source database will be copied into the first field of the destination file, the value of the second field of the source database will go to the second destination database field, and so on. The Merge Spec enables you to specify both the source and destination fields.

When you look at the Merge Spec, you're looking at the *source* database form, *not* the destination file's form. In Figure 4-16 you'll see that the CU# field has the number 4 in it, the Wholename field has the number 1 in it, the Phone field has the number 2 in it, and the "Amt Purch to Date" has the number 3 in it. These numbers tell Q&A what fields in the destination file are to receive the copied values.

In this example, the first field of the destination database gets the Wholename values from the selected records, the second field of the destination database gets the Phone values from the selected records, and so forth. In the destination database, Q&A counts the fields from the top left of the form to bottom right.

```
CUSTOMER   Key Name                          CU#   4
                                             ID#

Title       First          M     Last

Whole Name  1
    Company
    Street
       City                      St    Zip

     C/S/Z


     Phone  2                Ext        Fax


 Date Added              Acct     Products
 Credit Limit            Amt Purch to Date  3
 Comments


 CUSTOMER.DTF               Merge Spec          Page 1  of 1
```

Figure 4-16: The Merge Spec. The numbers entered in the spec tell Q&A which fields to copy and where they go in the destination database.

Tip: Whenever you're copying selected fields, have a printed copy of the destination database to hand with the fields numbered from top left to bottom right. That way you can be sure the numbers you enter at the Merge Spec correspond to the appropriate fields in the target file's form.

If you're routinely copying from and to the same databases, and your Retrieve and Merge Specs are always the same, name and save your specifications. It'll help speed up the process and make it less error-prone. To save Retrieve and Merge Specs simply press **<Shift><F8>** after filling in the spec, give the spec a descriptive name, and then press **<Enter>** to save it to disk.

Tip: Don't confuse Copy Selected Records with either Mass Update or Posting:

- When you copy selected records — either entire records or only certain fields within those records — *you're creating new database records in the destination file.* Mass Update and Posting do not create new records but simply update *existing* records.

- Use Mass Update, not Copy or Posting, when you have a set of update specifications to execute on a group of (or all) records in a file. You can make use of Q&A's built-in functions and programming statements (including XLOOKUP and If/Then commands) when mass updating. Records can be mass updated in the Intelligent Assistant module, but they cannot be copied or posted from there.

- Use Posting to update field values in field "B" from related field values in file "A" — for example, to reduce the On-Hand quantities of items in an inventory file from quantities sold on invoices or to update master payroll summary records from pay period detail records. Posting allows you to specify — on a field-by-field basis and without the need for programming statements — that a posted value is to replace, be added to, subtracted from, or multiplied or divided by, the value in the target field in the destination file. This type of update procedure cannot be accomplished through Mass Update without a more complex set of parameters requiring programming.

- In Mass Update and Posting procedures you can optionally specify that existing programming statements in the target file are to be executed on the target records as those records are updated. This feature is not available when using Copy Selected Forms.

See the sections ahead on Mass Update and Posting for more on the ways these procedures differ from one another and how to use them to accomplish the kind of task you have in mind.

Copying a Whole Database

You can choose any of three methods to copy your entire database, form design, records, and all.

1. You can copy the design and, when that's finished, copy all the records to it.

2. Use Q&A's DOS File Facilities (available from the Utilities menu) to copy the whole database.

3. Back up the Database file.

The first of these three methods takes the longest, but is also the "healthiest" for your database. When you copy a design and then the forms, the empty spaces in the file which develop from heavy database usage are taken out as the file is renewed during the copy process. But this can also be accomplished — and faster — by *recovering* your database (more on this in the chapter on Utilities).

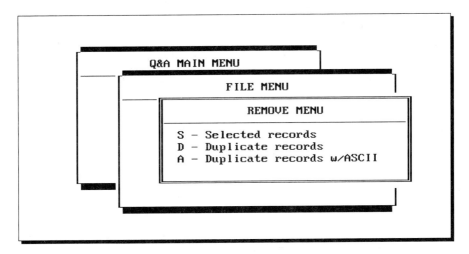

Figure 4-17: Files's Remove Menu.

Using Q&A's Backup feature, or DOS File Facilities, copies the database "holes" and all — but does it much faster. The Backup feature copies both .DTF (database) and .IDX (index) automatically. When using DOS you have to copy each file separately (don't ever copy a .DTF file without its .IDX companion).

Using the Backup command from the File Utilities menu is covered, along with the other File Utilities, in Chapter 9.

Removing Records

The Remove command lets you delete a selected group of records all at once; for example, customers who haven't bought anything from you in a couple of years. When you choose Remove from the File menu, and enter the name of the database from which you want to remove records, the Remove menu appears, offering three choices (see Figure 4-17).

When you simply want to remove a group of records from the database, choose Selected Records from the Remove menu and (carefully!) fill out the Retrieve Spec to tell Q&A which forms you want deleted. When you do this and press **<F10>**, Q&A displays a warning box telling you how many forms are about to be sent to the Great Beyond. Answer Yes if you're sure, No if you're not. A Yes answer will delete the selected records permanently.

You can, of course, delete individual records with the **<F3>** key during Search/Update. Your Retrieve Spec would be the same, but you'd then have the opportunity to view each record before deleting it from the file.

To delete an *entire* database — forms, form design, report specs, and all — use Q&A's DOS File Facilities, available from the Utilities menu. More on this in Chapter 9.

Removing Duplicate Records

New: Choosing Duplicate Records from the Remove menu lets you locate and delete records that have matching field values and are likely to be duplicates. When you select this option, Q&A takes you to the Duplicate Spec where you type **D** or **DEL** into the fields you want checked for duplication. In those fields where you want Q&A to match case (upper/lowercase letters) identically, use the code **DS** instead. The more fields you include in your specification, the less likely you'll be to lose forms that aren't really duplicates.

For example, if you typed **D** into the last name field, and let it go at that, all the Smith records save the first one would be gone forever. Typing **D** in the last name *and* the zip code fields would delete all but one of the Smith records with the same zip code.

If the fields selected for the duplication check and removal are Speedy, the process will run faster. Even a single Speedy field among those selected helps improve performance. And if one of the Speedy fields is also Unique, that's even better.

When you've finished filling out the Duplicate Spec and press **<F10>**, Q&A will find the duplicate records and ask you to confirm deletion. The removal operation retains the first record in a group of duplicates, and removes any duplicate records that follow it. From the Retrieve Spec you can press **<F8>** and fill in a Sort Spec to control which record comes up first in the group.

An ASCII Backup File for Removed Duplicates

You can also have Q&A save any duplicates to an ASCII file using the "Duplicate Records with ASCII" selection from the Remove menu. This works the same way as Remove Selected Records, except that a file is created in which you can later review the removed records using Q&A's word processor. Having a log of all removed records is cheap insurance. Use this option at least until you're a seasoned pro at removing those duplicates.

Mass-Updating Records

Q&A Power Feature: When you need to change the information in a group of records all at once, mass update is the way to do it.

Suppose the bonus factor increases by two percent for all 60 salesmen in the company, the boss wants a five percent across the board increase in the prices of your inventory items, you decide you'd like you give all your customers customer numbers, or you need to create a new field on your form, multiply the values in two existing fields, and put the result in the new field.

All of this — and much more — can be done with Q&A's Mass Update feature.

Here's the step by step procedure, followed by a few examples:

1. From the File menu select Mass Update and then enter the name of the database from which you'll select your forms.

2. Fill out the Retrieve Spec carefully so that only the forms to be mass updated are selected. You can use a previously saved Retrieve Spec — **<Shift><F8>** displays the list. You can also use the **<F8>** Sort Spec to control the order in which Q&A retrieves the records.

3. At the Update Spec, move the cursor to the fields you want to update, including those that will be referenced or involved in the update, type a pound (**#**) sign and a unique number after each, and type the change, either directly or as a calculation (more on this below). Statements entered at the Program Spec for the database will *not* be executed during mass update unless you specifically indicate so — only your Update Specs will be executed (see the section on calculation options later in this chapter). However, you can copy your Program Spec to the Update Spec with **<Shift><F5>**. This might save you some time if your Update Specs are similar or identical to your statements at the Program Spec.

4. Press **<F10>** to start the update. The forms will be counted and you'll be asked to confirm.

5. Select No to update all the forms automatically without any further involvement on your part. Select Yes if you want to see each form before it's updated. Yes tells Q&A to display each form that meets your Retrieve Spec, and you can then press:

   - **<Shift><F10>** to update the displayed form.

   - **<F10>** to *not* update that one, and get the next one.

   - **<Ctrl><F10>** to update the rest in the stack automatically.

   - **<Esc>** to abort the procedure at any time.

Entering the correct values at the Retrieve Spec is extremely important and merits thorough consideration before embarking on an update that may affect dozens or hundreds of records. Further, you should save your Retrieve Spec by pressing **<Shift><F8>** after the spec has been filled out.

Tip: Mass Update Specs should likewise be named and stored on disk, at least until you're sure that no forms have been adversely affected. Saved Mass Update and Retrieve Specs enable you to review exactly what you did, and more easily undo any damage that may have been done.

For example, a five percent increase in the price fields of the wrong group of inventory records can be mass updated *back* to the earlier values so long as you know exactly which records were involved in the update to begin with.

Save your Retrieve and Update Specs by pressing **<Shift><F8>** from either spec, and entering a name that describes the nature of the mass update.

When you fill out your Update Spec, place a **#** and a number in each field that will be updated or involved in the update (#1 in the first field, #2 in the next field, etc.), then enter the update value or the calculation. If you were changing all **Position** fields from "Salesman" to "Salesperson," for example, you'd type in the **Position** field: **#1= "Salesperson"** (hopefully you will have specified "Salesman" in the **Position** field at your Retrieve Spec!).

At the Update Spec you can enter a direct change, as is the above example, a change as a calculation, or a change as an If/Then statement.

Here are a few examples.

- To add 10 percent to the prices in a **Price** field: **Price: #1 = #1 * 1.1**.

- To reduce salaries by two percent: **Salary: #1 = #1 * .98**.

- To incrementally number all forms after a field was created (in redesign) to hold the numbers: **Customer Number: #1 = @Number**

- To mark every 25th record with an **X** in a database, where the records are not incrementally numbered, you'd first have to add two new fields to the database, say, **Customer Number** and **Test Mail**, and then enter your update spec as follows:

    ```
    Customer Number #1 = @Number

    Test Mail #2: If @Int(#1/25) = #1/25 then #2 =
    "Y" else #2 = ""
    ```

    And you'll have a **Y** in every field of the 25th record.

From the Retrieve Spec you can optionally press **<F8>** for the Sort Spec if you want to specify the sequence in which the records will be updated.

Calculation Options

New: You can also press **<F8>** from the Update Spec to select calculation options. It's optional. If your database contains on-record-entry statements, on-record-exit statements, or calc statements, you can select Yes or No for each of these *types* of formulas (not field by field) and have them executed or not executed during the mass update. The on-record-entry statements will be executed first, followed by the mass update statements, the calculation statements and, finally, the on-record-exit statements. *On-field-entry* and *on-field-exit* statements cannot be executed during a mass update. There is no navigation programming available in an Update Spec — GOTOs and GOSUBs are not permitted. See Figure 4-18.

In any mass update, it's always prudent to select Yes to confirm that you want to update the records individually. Then, if all seems to be going okay, you can press **<Ctrl><F10>** to have Q&A update the remaining records in the stack automatically.

Posting Values to External Databases

With Q&A's Posting feature, you can copy a value from one or more fields in a *source* database to selected fields in the *target* database — and you can choose either to replace the values in the target file with the source file values, or use arithmetic operators to do addition, subtraction, multiplication, and division with them.

This powerful counterpart to XLOOKUP rounds out Q&A, enabling it to provide what, to many users, are the two essentials of a multidatabase application: the ability to *retrieve* values from external databases, and the ability to *place* values in external database fields.

New: Until Q&A 4.0 was released you could post in a rudimentary fashion with the Copy command, but you had no way to select a group of source *key* and *post* fields and update the corresponding target *post* field in the external records without copying the source fields over one at a time to a different database, and then use mass update with external lookup commands to update the target file. It was complicated, tedious, and for advanced users only — in short, a workaround for a Q&A limitation. But 4.0's posting facility now makes updating records in external files a snap.

To illustrate, suppose you have an Invoice database and a Stock database like the ones featured in this chapter. Using the Posting feature, you can have Q&A look at the stock numbers sold on each invoice entered during the day, find the

Stock database records that match them, and deduct the quantities from the Stock database **Qty On Hand** fields. This can help you maintain a running inventory with the speed and convenience of a mass update.

With the Posting feature you can select one field in your source database and one field in your destination database. You can also select a *group* of fields in your source database to post to a corresponding field in the target file.

Posting is the perfect solution for updating fields in summary records from their related detail record fields in other files. Master payroll summary records can be updated from detailed pay period records, for example; an outstanding balance field in your customer records can be updated from invoices as a defense against customers exceeding their credit ceilings; order shipment dates can be posted to invoices; purchase order numbers, dates, and item quantities can be posted to related records in an inventory field; call reports can be posted to their corresponding master customer/prospect records; payments on account can be posted to individual invoices or accounts receivable records; and other types of bookkeeping procedures — such as posting to ledgers — are possible.

Designing a Posting Spec

1. Select T - Post from the File menu to design or execute your Posting Specification. You'll be prompted to type the name of the database whose values you want to post (the *source* database), and the name of the database you want to receive the posted values (the *destination* or *target* database). Enter the two filenames.

2. The Retrieve Spec for the *source* database will then display, and you can enter the parameters that will select the forms that contain the fields you want posted to the *target* database (for example, invoices with today's date). You can use an existing Retrieve Spec by pressing **<Alt><F8>** and choosing the spec from the list of saved specs. Press **<F10>** from the completed Retrieve Spec, and Q&A will display the Posting Spec — the form layout for the *source* database, the one you're posting *from*. Figure 4-18 shows the Posting Spec for INVOICE.DTF, the database designed earlier in this chapter, with the Posting box open at the first **Ord** field.

3. If you've already designed a Posting Spec, press **<Alt><F8>** for the list of saved Posting Specs, highlight the one you want, and press **<Enter>**. If you're designing a new Posting Spec, press **<Tab>** or **<Enter>** to move to the first *source post field* on the form. In Figure 4-18 this is the **Ord1** field — we've named it that at the Set Field Names Spec since it

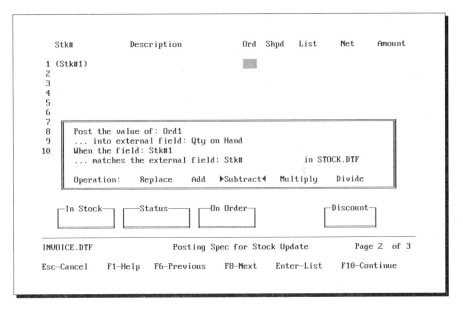

```
       Stk#              Description           Ord  Shpd   List     Net     Amount
   1 (Stk#1)                                    ▓
   2
   3
   4
   5
   6
   7
   8     Post the value of: Ord1
   9     ... into external field: Qty on Hand
  10     When the field: Stk#1
         ... matches the external field: Stk#              in STOCK.DTF

         Operation:    Replace    Add   ▶Subtract◀   Multiply    Divide


   ┌─In Stock─┐   ┌──Status──┐   ┌─On Order─┐         ┌─Discount─┐
   │          │   │          │   │          │         │          │
   │          │   │          │   │          │         │          │
   └──────────┘   └──────────┘   └──────────┘         └──────────┘

   INVOICE.DTF             Posting Spec for Stock Update        Page 2  of 3

   Esc-Cancel   F1-Help   F6-Previous   F8-Next   Enter-List   F10-Continue
```

Figure 4-18: At the Posting Spec with the Posting Box Displayed. This is page 2 of the Invoice form (source database), where stock numbers and quantities were entered as invoice line items during data entry. The highlight is on the first **Ord** field.

has no field label. The *source post field* name automatically appears in the posting box as you move from field to field.

4. Type the field label of the field in the destination file to which you want to post the value from the *source post field*. Optionally, you can press **<Alt><F7>** for a list of fields in the destination file, highlight the one you want, and press **<Enter>**.

5. Move down a line in the posting box, and type the name of the *source key field* whose value has a matching value in the destination file. In Figure 4-17 this is the **Stk#1** field. Optionally, you can press **<Alt><F7>** for a list, highlight the field you want, and press **<Enter>**.

6. On the next line in the posting box, type the name of the *destination file key field* that matches the *source key field* (or you can press **<Alt><F7>** for a list).

Warning: The destination file key field must be indexed. If it's not, it won't be on the list, and Q&A will prevent you from proceeding until you've indexed the field at the Speed-up Spec. The *source key field* does not have to be indexed.

7. Now highlight the operation you want done between the *source post field* and *target post field* values: Replace, Add, Subtract, Multiply, or Divide (see Table 4-6).

8. Press **<F7>** to close the Posting box and **<Tab>** to move to the next *source post field*, or **<Shift><Tab>** to move to a previous one. Q&A remembers the posting box you just filled out.

9. Repeat steps 4 through 7 for all the fields whose values you wish to post to the corresponding target file fields.

10. Press **<F10>** when you're finished filling out the Posting Spec, or option-ally press **<F8>** for the Calc Options screen (see the Calculation Options section in this chapter) if you want programming statements in the destination file executed during the post. You may wish to save and name a new Posting Spec at this point. To do so, press **<Shift><F8>**, type a descriptive name of the spec (such as "Daily Invoice Post to Stock") and press **<Enter>**.

When you've completed your posting spec, Q&A will tell you how many forms will be posted, and ask if you'd like to confirm each post individually. Choose No to have Q&A proceed with the batch posting, or Yes to confirm each post individually. Pressing **<Esc>** returns you to the Posting Spec.

If you choose to confirm each post, you can then press:

- **<Shift><F10>** to update the form.
- **<F10>** *not* to update the form and get the next one.
- **<Ctrl><F10>** to have the rest of the forms in the stack updated automatically.
- **<Esc>** to abort the operation.

Table 4-6 shows the operations you can have Q&A perform on the *target post* field during the posting. By default, Q&A *replaces* the value in the target file post field with the value from the source file post field.

Posting Failures

As you're designing a posting specification, Q&A keeps tabs to make sure your external key fields are indexed, and the source and target fields exist.

You can still run into problems, however, should someone redesign one or both of the forms, change a field name, disable a Speedy field, or move, delete, or rename a file after the Posting Spec has been designed.

To help identify any posting errors that occur *during* a batch post, Q&A automatically creates a *Posting Transaction Log* each time you post.

Table 4-6
Summary of Posting Operations

Operation	Result of the Operation
Replace	Replaces the value in the destination field with the value in the source field.
Add	Adds the value in the source field to the value in the target field, and places the sum in the target field.
Subtract	Subtracts the value in the source field from the value in the destination field, and places the difference in the destination field.
Multiply	Multiplies the value in the destination field by the value in the source field, and places the result in the destination field.
Divide	Divides the value in the destination field by the value in the source field, and places the quotient in the destination field. For example, if the destination field is 12, and the source field is 4, the destination field will get the value 3.

The log is an ASCII file that records the name of the source database, the name of the destination database, and the contents of any source key fields which didn't have matching destination database fields. Q&A stores this file under the name *sourcedatabasename*.PST (for example, INVOICE.PST if you posted from the invoice file). After posting, you can view this ASCII file in the Write module and ascertain where, if at all, the post may have gone wrong.

 Tip: Be aware, however, that Q&A logs as "posting failure" instances where one or more *post-from* fields in the source file were empty during the post, resulting in no actual posting from such fields having taken place. This would occur, for example, where post-from line item fields in invoices or purchase orders were blank. Such posting "failures" aren't really failures because, after all, finished invoices and POs typically have empty line item fields (that is, the invoice can accommodate ten items ordered, but customers usually order only one or two item).

A batch post — like a mass update — can, when designed or executed improperly, wreak havoc on your data. You'd be wise to restrict access to these operations, and Q&A has tools that help you to do it. See Chapters 9 and 12.

```
                        Auto Program Recalc
                        ═══════════════════

        Choose the programming statements you would like executed
        during the batch post [or Mass Update].


             On record entry statements:       Yes   ▶No◀

             Calculation statements....:       Yes   ▶No◀

             On record exit statements.:       Yes   ▶No◀


        Note:  On field entry statements and on field exit statements
               will not be executed.
        ───────────────────────────────────────────────────────────
        INVOICE.DTF            Batch Post Calculation Options
                                  [Mass Update Calculation Options]

        Esc-Exit      F1-Help            F9-Batch Post Spec        F10-Continue
                                                                   [Update Spec]
```

Figure 4-19: The Auto Program Recalc Screen. Use it to tell Q&A which types of programming statements in the destination file you want executed during a posting or mass update operation.

Posting and Mass Update Calculation Options

If the target database contains on-record-entry, on-record-exit, or calculation (Main Program) statements, you can choose which of these three *types* of statements to have Q&A execute during a posting or Mass Update operation. By default, Q&A will not execute any programming statements during a post or Mass Update.

As you'll see in Chapter 10, this recalc feature is handy for posting quantities of items sold on invoices to the corresponding stock records. Not only will we post the quantities sold, we'll also have Q&A automatically update several additional fields in the target stock file during the posting operation.

When you're finished with your Posting or Mass Update Spec and want to specify programming execution in the target file, press **<F8>** for the Auto Program Recalc screen shown in Figure 4-19, choose Yes or No for each *type* of programming statement, and press **<F10>** to save the spec and begin the posting or Mass Update. Pressing **<F9>** from the Auto Program Recalc screen returns you to the spec where you can change your parameters if you like.

New: When posting, Q&A's actions on the target file take place in the following order:

1. The first record is retrieved.

2. The on-record-entry programming is executed in the record if specified on the Auto Program Recalc screen.

3. The value is posted in accord with any specified arithmetic operator or updated in accord with the Mass Update Spec, depending on which type of operation is being carried out.

4. Main Program statements are executed in the record if specified on the Auto Program Recalc screen.

5. The on-record-exit programming is executed in the record if specified on the Auto Program Recalc screen.

6. The record is put away, and next record is retrieved.

7. The process starts over with step 2 above.

Summary

In Chapter 1 you learned how to use the Write word processor, including the wealth of tools Q&A provides to help you create, enhance, format, and other-wise manipulate your documents.

In the last two chapters we've covered all the essentials of database design and customization. You've been exposed to several types of databases, as well as all the features Q&A makes available to help make your data entry and data file management more productive.

Mail-merge applications involve both the Write and File modules, and require familiarity with both. So now that you have the prerequisites you can safely move on to this new ground.

You may have noticed that three submenus weren't covered during our exploration of Q&A's File module. We've reserved our File Utilities menu discussion for Chapter 9, The File Security menu for Chapter 12, and the Customize Application menu for Chapter 8, although you're certainly at liberty to skip ahead to these other chapters depending on your interests and needs.

Chapter 5
Mail Merge and
Mailing Labels

In this chapter you'll learn how to:

▶ Recognize when Q&A's mail-merge feature is the right choice for the task you want to perform.

▶ Fine-tune your customer database to make the most of mail-merge applications.

▶ Create and print personalized form letters.

▶ Exploit the information in your databases to produce a variety of powerful business documents.

▶ Design and print mailing labels in all sizes, formats, and quantities.

▶ Program your merge documents to include calculated values and information from multiple databases.

This chapter will help you fine-tune your customer database (you originally created it in Chapter 3) to allow you to maximize mail-merge applications. From there, you will be able to create personalized form letters with the information in your databases. Finally, you will learn how to prepare and print customized mailing labels.

The first part of this chapter deals with mail-merge applications; ways to create and print mailing labels are found at the end of the chapter.

Overview

One of today's fastest rising stars in the world of business/consumer relations is the computer mail-merge application.

Companies are looking for better ways to integrate form letters and other business documents with information from their databases — merging the two into a personalized format that will not only be well received by the customer, but that can be mass-produced with minimal effort.

With mail merge you can let your customers know, in a more personal way, that you're thinking of them.

The three elements needed to create any kind of mail-merge application are: an able word processor to compose and edit your merge documents, one or more databases containing the information to be merged with these documents, and software capable of automating the merge process.

Q&A provides all three. You add the creative touch and the printer.

In this chapter you'll learn how to use Q&A to design several mail-merge applications, and then how to use Q&A's exceptional mailing label generator to select or design the exact size and format of mailing label you need — labels that you can print out one at a time, or by the tens of thousands.

Mail Merge Applications

If small to medium-size businesses possessing a mail-merge capability tend to make a common mistake, it's that they *under-utilize* this powerful capability.

The perception is that mail merge is only good for personalizing form letters to customers. Maybe the software package being used doesn't support merge printing much beyond the everyday "Thank you for inquiring..." or "We'd like to introduce to you to..." form letter. On the other hand, it could be that it didn't occur to anyone to think beyond this to the *additional* ways the capability can be exploited to harvest a far greater variety of benefits to the company.

In addition to easily creating personalized form letters in Q&A, you can also design virtually push-button applications for:

- Sending out reminders on invoice balances now due, or purchase-order items that haven't been received from suppliers.

- Producing monthly statements. (Chapter 12 features a comprehensive billing statement application.)

- Printing payroll and accounts payable checks with informative stubs.

- Generating magazine subscription or service renewal cards with creative ad hoc messages.

- Merging a great deal more into personalized form letters than just customer names and addresses, such as announcing new products available in which only *particular* types of customers are likely to be interested.

And much, much more.

Q&A Power Feature: The greater the variety of databases you maintain (customer, inventory, invoice, purchase order, to name a few), and the more information these files contain, the more you can take advantage of Q&A's tremendous document-merge capabilities to communicate to the people and organizations crucial to your own business success.

Still, for most companies, the primary focus of mail-merge activity is customer relations and the customer database. And indeed, the *way* information from this file is merged into documents can make the difference between a successful promotional campaign and one that produces only ho-hum results. So we're going to spend some time fine-tuning our customer file.

The Customer Database Revisited

Recall that in Chapter 3 we designed a sample customer database form. Then, in Chapter 4, we built a complete order entry invoice application from the ground up, and you learned how to add programming to your forms to control and automate data entry.

In this chapter, before we go into the information you'll need to integrate database information with documents in the Write module, we'll first reexamine and improve on our customer form *especially* for use in mail-merge applications. The ease with which a typist can enter and search for specific records, and the useful information they reveal about your customers, is one thing. How that information looks when printed in a personalized merge letter that will be *received* by the customer, is quite another.

Figure 5-1 shows the sample customer form as we've designed it so far. Field ID numbers have been entered in those fields that will be referred to in programming statements. If you need a refresher course on programming a database form, refer to the previous chapter.

In Chapter 3 a number of reasons were given as to why the form was designed as you see it in Figure 5-1. We've made a couple of additional modifications to enhance the form's capabilities as a mail-merge tool. In a moment you'll perhaps better understand the rationale behind the form design as we view it from the dual perspective of data entry and mail merge.

You'll notice, for example, that the name and address area of the form includes fields to contain essentially the same information twice. We have a field for the customer's title (Mr., Mrs., Dr., etc.), as well as fields for the first name, middle initial, and last name. Then, right below that we have a "Whole Name" field.

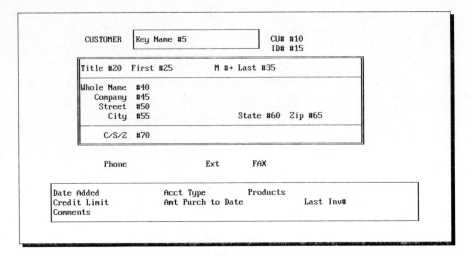

Figure 5-1: The Sample CUSTOMER.DTF Form with Field ID Numbers Entered at the Program Spec. This is the Customer database form on the Applications disk that came with this book.

These are followed by fields for the company name (if any), the street address, city, state, and zip code, and then another field (C/S/Z) which *combines* the city, state, and zip into a single line.

The question is, are we going to have to type the customer's name and address once, and then have to type these values again for the Whole Name and C/Z/S fields? No, I wouldn't make you do that. What we will do is *customize* the form so that Q&A will fill in the Whole Name and C/S/Z fields, as well as the CU#, the ID#, and the Date Added fields for us.

By design, we're incorporating into this form the following capabilities:

- Automatic generation of both a sequential customer number and a special identification number that will speed order (invoice) entry considerably.

- Fast *individual* record search and retrieve on a key name field.

- Merge-*ability* with personalized form letters. We need the name parsed (divided into parts) so that we can address the customer or buyer ("Dear Dr. Smith:" or "Dear Francine:").

- The Whole Name field will generate a name line in the address block of the merge letter that won't contain unsightly blank spaces should some of the forms be missing a middle initial.

- The single city, state, and zip field (C/Z/S), coupled with the Whole Name field will save time and effort in the following ways: when selecting the fields for the name, address, city, state, and zip in the address portion of a merge letter or mailing label, we'll only need to deal with *half* the number of fields. In our invoice/order entry application, only *four* lookup fields will be required instead of eight, which simplifies invoice design and programming.

While your application needs may be entirely different than these, your customer database is your most valuable asset, and the information in it will be used in a variety of ways. Thus it's worthwhile to carefully consider *how* it will be used. This will give you an end product that's not only efficient from a data-entry perspective, but highly versatile.

Customizing the Customer Form

To refresh your memory on how the sample invoice application was programmed to look up information from the customer database, you may want to review that section in the last chapter. The discussion which follows here will pertain to it.

Two of the fields on the customer form can be assigned preset values at the Initial Values Spec. The CU# field should be an @Number field, so as each new form is filled out, Q&A will assign the next number in sequence; and the Date Added field should be preset with the @Date function to return the current date. It tells you *when* the customer came on board.

You'll want both the CU# and ID# fields to be Speedy fields, as they're *external key fields* in the invoice lookup commands. If the database will be large, you can also make the Key Name field Speedy if you'll be using it to search for individual forms. An indexed zip field will retrieve your forms faster when sorting by zip code for mailing labels. You need zip code sorting to take advantage of presorted bulk mailing rates.

The CU#, ID#, and Date Added fields should be read-only so they can be changed *only* by programming formulas.

The Phone Number and Fax fields should be field *templated* (see Field Templates in Chapter 4) to speed operator entry and cut down on data entry errors.

Programming the Customer Form

Only some of the fields on the customer form in Figure 5-1 have been assigned field ID numbers. These will either contain programming statements or be referenced by statements in other fields. What follows are the statements to be entered into the fields at the Program Spec, along with a brief explanation of what they accomplish during data entry.

Note: If this database will be shared on a network, you should enter the cursor navigation portions of your programming statements at the Field Navigation Spec rather than at the Program Spec. See Chapter 4.

Field #5: Enter the key name for the individual (last name) or company during data entry. The cursor moves to #20 on field exit because fields #10 and #15 are Read-only.

You *could* have Q&A create the Key Name field for you by returning the company name or, if no company name, the individual's last name. Making key names out of company names, however, may require some thought on the part of the input operator if the value is to be limited and meaningful. But on the other hand, if you're dealing *only* with surnames, you probably won't need a Key Name field to begin with. The purpose of the field, after all, is to contain something *meaningful* that can be remembered or quickly inferred from a longer name to aid in the retrieval of *individual* records. (Of course if the zip code is known during Search/Update, the record can be retrieved on the ID# field.)

Fields #20, #25, and #30: No programming required. You fill in the title, first name, and middle initial of the individual customer or commercial buyer during data entry.

Field #35: >#35: If #30=" "then {#40=#20+" "+#25+" "+#35} else {#40=#20+" "+#25+" "+#30+" "+#35}; goto #45

Here's where the parts of the name are strung together to create a full name for the Whole Name field. The If/Then/Else logic is needed to account for the possibility of a missing middle initial. Tell Q&A to add a space in a computed string value by typing a double quote mark, adding a space, and then typing another double quote mark. When you want Q&A to check for a blank field, the space between the quote marks isn't used.

Fields #40, #45, #50, #55, and #60: No programming required. You enter the company name (if any) and the customer address information during data entry.

Field #65: >#65: #70=#55+" "+#60+" "+#65; #15=@left(#5,5)+@str(#65);goto#75

A lot of action takes place after the zip code has been entered and you exit the field. First, a string value is created from the city, state, and zip fields, similar to the way in which the Whole Name field was produced.

Next, the customer's ID# is created by pulling together the first five letters of the Key Name field and the five digits of the zip code. So customer Farnwick Book Company in zip 20546, with the Key Name FARNWICK, will get

FARNW20546 for an ID#. This will enable Q&A to return the CU# when the CU# isn't known during invoice order entry.

Finally, the cursor is moved to #75 and the rest of the customer's particulars are entered.

We haven't included any @Add or @Update context functions in our programming for the simple reason that a customer's name could have been misspelled during data entry and will have to be corrected, or an address may change. If the form has to be updated along either of these lines, the CU# will remain constant, but the ID# will be updated if either the Key Name or the zip field is updated, so long as the cursor passes through the zip field.

An alternate way of executing the programming in the form is to eliminate the *on-field-exit* stipulation in the two programmed fields, and have Q&A calculate the derived field values when the cursor leaves *any* field (automatic "calc" mode). Given our programming, this would be clumsy because only a portion of the derived fields would be filled in until the cursor passed through the fields containing the *final* portions of the string values.

A second alternative is to use the **<F8>** "calc" key (manual mode) once the form is filled out or updated.

A third alternative is to have Q&A execute the programming statements when the form is saved. You can specify fields that hold on-form-entry calculations (when the form is displayed), and on-form-exit calculations (when you press **<F10>** or **<Shift><F10>** to save the form) by pressing **<F8>** from within the Program Spec (see the previous chapter to review these topics).

Now that we've got the customer form ready to go (assuming we've added some new records to the file), let's use it in a standard merge letter. Here you'll see the steps involved in creating a merge document. Then, later in this chapter, I'll show you how to add more power to your mail merges by drawing on Q&A 4.0's merge programming feature and other features as well.

Creating Your Merge Document

Here are the steps involved in creating personalized form letters or any merge document. Following this we'll look at each of the key steps in greater detail. Refer to the chapter on Write if you need help with any of the word processor features.

1. Compose your merge document (pitch letter, thank you letter, new product announcement, etc.) as usual in Write, or use one that's already been written.

2. Move the cursor to the location in the document where you want to insert the first database merge field. Press **\<Alt\>\<F7\>** and enter the name of the database whose field values you want to use in your letter (or press **\<Enter\>** to see a list of available files in the current directory, highlight the one you want, and press **\<Enter\>**).

3. Q&A will display a window showing you the list of fields available in the selected file (see Figure 5-2). Use the cursor keys to move to the field you want to insert at the cursor position and press **\<Enter\>**.

   The field names are displayed in the window in alphabetical order. Pressing a letter will take you to the first name that begins with that letter. You can also use the **\<PgUp\>**, **\<PgDn\>**, **\<Home\>**, and **\<End\>** keys to move up and down the list.

   You can bypass the window and type your database merge fields directly into the document, as long as you type the field name exactly as it appears in the Field Name list, and enclose it in asterisks.

   Field names appearing on the list may not match the labels on your database form if you've changed them at the Field Names Spec. When Q&A displays the list of fields in the merge file, it uses the database's field *names* as opposed to its field *labels*.

4. Repeat steps 2 and 3 to place additional merge fields in the document. Once a merge field is in place, you can relocate it as you would any text block, but it's faster simply to place the field in the right location the first time. You can place the same merge field in the document more than once.

5. When you're finished, press **\<Shift\>\<F8\>** to save the document in the usual manner. Or print it, and save the merge document later. It's wise, however, to save the document before you proceed.

If you're merging database fields that have no field labels, Q&A will have assigned *field names* to them (F0001, F0002, etc.), and it is *these* names you'll see when the window containing the list of fields is displayed for you to select your merge fields. You can view and change these field names at the Field Names Spec in the File module (covered in the last chapter), and you should do so to avoid any confusion when creating your merge documents.

If your database contains duplicate field labels (such as two fields labeled "Phone"), Q&A will have numbered them "Phone1," "Phone2," and so forth, and this is how they'll appear in the select merge fields window. You can give these fields more descriptive names at the Field Names Spec if you wish.

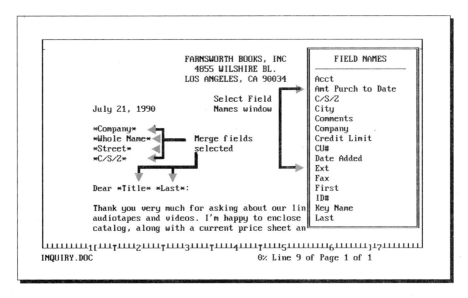

Figure 5-2: The Select Field Names Window. Highlight the field you want inserted at the cursor position and press <Enter>.

New: The Field Names option became available with Q&A version 4.0. And it's an important feature since it allows you to use labelless fields in your database forms and still have readily identifiable field names to work with in your merge documents.

A Few Tips on Creating Merge Letters

Author's Tip: The following suggestions come from my own experience with Q&A mail merge. Many of these tips are not mentioned in Q&A's documentation.

- In the Figure 5-2 merge letter a date has been typed. If this same letter is to be used routinely, you can type ***@Date(n)*** where you want Q&A to place the current date in the document. Substitute the number of the date format you want for the *n*. Chapter 3 contains a table showing the 20 different date formats available in Q&A.

- The letterhead in Figure 5-2 has been typed. Of course, you can use your own custom letterhead.

- You can type your merge fields manually, rather than choosing them from the list. If you do, be sure that the field names are enclosed in asterisks. If you miss an asterisk, Q&A will print the merge field data as literal text.

- When placing your merge fields, leave a space where you want a space in the printed document. In Figure 5-2 a space has been left between *Title* and *Last* so the two field values won't run together.

- A printed merge field will start at the location of the left asterisk and continue to the right, using as many spaces as needed to print the contents of the field. When field values vary, Q&A closes up any unused spaces during printing.

- Note the colon placed after the *Last* field. You have to type this in the merge document because it's not a field value.

- We can mail the merge letter in Figure 5-2 to companies *and* individuals. Note that *Company* is the first field in the name/address block. This line will simply be blank in printed merge letters with no Company value in the database. And it won't upset the look of the letter at all.

- You can locate your merge fields strategically so the letter can be folded and placed into a standard business window envelope, eliminating the need for a label or typed envelope.

- When you add an enhancement (bold or italics, for example) to a merge field, be sure to *enhance the entire field*, including the beginning and ending asterisks.

- You can create reports or modified database layouts in the Write module that are actually merge documents, giving you tremendous flexibility over the final look of your forms or reports when printed. You can place the database fields anywhere on the page (enclosing them in asterisks), and use programming expressions to calculate column totals and even include information from other database files. You'll get one form or report per page at printing time, and you can use the Retrieve Spec to tell Q&A which forms to include in the printing. This is not the same as printing a report or form to file or to disk at a Print Options screen and then bringing it into the Write module for modification. But you can do this, too, and turn that database form or a report itself into a merge document!

- Use macros to run your routine mail merge and mailing label jobs, having the macro pause, if necessary, to enter any variable Retrieve Spec parameters. Creating and using macros to automate recurring chores is covered in Chapter 8.

• Create a special Mail Merge menu that includes the merge letter and mailing label applications you most frequently run. Then record a macro and install it as an alternate program selection on the Q&A Main menu, so that a single keystroke from the Main menu takes you directly to your custom Mail Merge menu. Custom application menus are covered in Chapter 8; installing alternate programs and macros on the Q&A Main menu is covered in Chapter 9.

Option Codes to Control Text Positioning

You may have fields in your merge database that are justified center or right, leaving spaces between the start of the information blank and the first character of the value. For example:

Customer Name: Bob Jones

If, in your merge letter, you typed the following:

...Thank you again for writing, *Customer Name*, and please feel free to contact us...

It would print in your merge letter as:

...Thank you again for writing,   Bob Jones, and please feel free to contact us...

To correct the problem, enter **(T)** between the field label and the right asterisk, like this:

...Thank you again for writing, *Customer Name (T)*, and please feel free to contact us...

This trims out the space left by special database field formatting.

Tabular Positioning

Two codes are available for positioning merged information that you want to appear in columnar form: the **(L)** left justify and **(R)** right justify commands. You place these commands inside the asterisks to control where the database merge information begins and ends.

When you want a column to be left justified, type **(L)** before the ending asterisk. Type **(R)** before the ending asterisk if you want the column right justified. The example below shows how this works:

`*Descrip1  (L)`	`*`		`*Price1  (R)*`
`*Descrip2  (L)`	`*`		`*Price2  (R)*`
`*Descrip3  (L)`	`*`		`*Price2  (R)*`
19 characters		4 spaces	

This arrangement tells Q&A to start printing Descrip1, left justified, and continue for 19 characters. If the Descrip1 value is shorter than 19 characters, Q&A will pad the space, and then insert the four spaces between the two columns. The prices in the corresponding column will be right justified, and the result will print like this:

```
Harry's War              $15.95
See Spain in a Day        $7.95
Navy Encyclopedia       $119.95
```

Spacing Problems

When some of your merge fields are blank, depending on where those fields are in the merge document, you may need to do two things. For example, suppose your merge fields are set up like this in the document:

First Name *Middle* *Last Name*:

But some of the forms in the merge database are missing a middle initial. The result will show up in the printed letter as:

```
Robert    Clark:
```

with *two* spaces between the first and last names for those forms without a middle initial. This, of course, is bad form.

The first way to correct the problem is to add a field to your database form, along with a programming statement in it, that *combines* the elements of the name into a single field. This is exactly what we've done with our customer database, and you won't have this kind of problem when merging names in our documents.

The second method is to create *two* documents, each with different merge fields:

Document #1 *First Name* *Middle* *Last Name*
Document #2 *First Name* *Last Name*

and then use one Retrieve Spec for those forms where there *is* a middle initial (the middle initial field is not blank), and another Retrieve Spec for those forms where there is *not* a middle initial (the field is empty).

At the *first* Retrieve Spec, in addition to whatever other retrieve parameters you're specifying, you'd type **/=** (this means "not blank") in the middle initial field. This would retrieve the forms containing the middle initial.

Then, to run the *second* part of the job, you'd type **=** ("empty field") in the middle initial field (with any other retrieve specifications the same as the first job), which would merge print the forms with the missing middle initial.

So if you're merge printing with this database often, your best solution is to have a field that combines the separate parts of the name into a whole name, as we've done with our customer file.

But Q&A gives you a *third* solution to this common mail-merge dilemma — you can use an arithmetic operator along with the merge field.

Suppose your database contains fields like this:

First Name: Last Name:

and one of the fields in the merge database is empty. When that merge letter is printed, it will look like this:

```
Dear Freddy :
```

There's an unwanted space between the "y" in Fredd, and the colon because the last name field was empty in the database. You can remove the space caused by blank database fields by adding this expression to your merge document:

Dear *program{First Name+" "+Last Name}*:

You can also substitute the field ID numbers in the Program Spec of the merge file for the field names shown in the example. You'll learn more about using calculations and programming expressions in merge documents a little later on in this chapter.

Printing Your Merge Letters

The database fields you've inserted into your document are merged with it at printing time. When your merge document is finished and you're ready to print, here are the steps you follow:

1. If the merge document is already on the Type/Edit screen, press **<F2>** for the Print Options screen; otherwise choose Get from the Write menu, type the name of your document, and bring it into the editor.

2. Change your print options as necessary. If the "Name of Merge File" line at the bottom of the screen is empty, type the name of the database that contains the merge information. Press **<F10>** when you're ready to roll.

3. Should any of the merge fields in your document not match those in the selected database, you'll get a warning message to that effect, along with a list of the field names Q&A can't identify. At this point you can press **<Esc>** to return to the editor to make your changes. You can also have Q&A ignore these unidentified merge fields by pressing **<F10>** to

continue. Or, you can press **<F8>** for the Identifier Spec. (More on that later.)

4. At the Retrieve Spec, tell Q&A which forms you want to include in the printing. Press **<F8>** to fill out the Sort Spec if you want the documents printed in a particular order.

 Note: It's always a good idea to have Q&A retrieve and print your merge documents in some sorted order. This way if something goes wrong in the middle of the job you can go back to the Retrieve Spec and enter the parameters that will resume the printing where it stopped.

Also, if your Retrieve Spec is at all complex and you'll be using the same retrieval parameters again, fill out the spec and press **<Shift><F8>** to save it for future use. See Chapter 3 for details on how to use the Retrieve and Sort Specs, and Chapter 4 for how to use calculations and programming expressions at any Retrieve Spec.

5. Press **<F10>** to print. Q&A will prepare an internal merge file and then begin printing. Q&A creates a temporary file on your hard disk during merge printing. If it can't find enough room to do this, you'll get an error message.

The Identifier Spec

If Q&A can't match one or more of your document merge fields with the fields in the database, the reason will usually be that you typed in the merge field names incorrectly (they don't match the field names exactly). You can correct this without editing your document by using the Identifier Spec to enter substitute field names (see Figure 5-3).

At the Identifier Spec you type only those field names in the merge document that don't match the field names in the database (Q&A lets you know which ones these are before you get to the Identifier Spec). This saves you having to edit the document itself.

Simply move to the first field that *is* the field you want merged and type the field name that Q&A has flagged as unidentified. For example, the database field label might be "Last," but you typed "Last Name" as the merge field name in the document. To correct this situation without editing the document, you'd type "Last Name" in the "Last" field at the Identifier Spec.

Repeat this procedure for any other unidentified field names in your document, and press **<F10>** when done for the Retrieve Spec.

The Identifier Spec can come in handy when you've got several merge fields you want to print on one line of the merge document, but the field names are too long to all fit on the one line. One solution is to use Program Spec field ID

```
        CUSTOMER   Key Name                      CU#
                                                 ID#

        Title      First          M    Last

       Whole Name
          Company
           Street
             City                   St    Zip

        ┌─────────────────────────────────────────────────────────┐
        │ If all the field names in your document match field labels in your │
        │ database, press F10 to continue. If not, type the names as they appear │
        │ in the document in the corresponding fields here, and press F10. │
        │                                                          │
        │ If you are NOT SURE whether everything matches, press F10 anyway. Q&A │
        │ will tell you which ones don't match and give you another opportunity │
        │ to match them up.  If everything matches, Q&A will take you to the │
        │ Retrieve Spec.  (Esc will cancel this message). │
        └─────────────────────────────────────────────────────────┘

        CUSTOMER.DTF              Identifier Spec           Page 1  of 1

        Esc-Cancel      F3-Clear Spec      F6-Expand field      F10-Continue
```

Figure 5-3: The Identifier Spec. If any of your document merge fields don't match those in the database, you can enter the substitute field names you used in the merge document.

numbers instead of field names, but then you'll likely have to *go* to the Program Spec of the merge file to find out what the field ID numbers are.

The easier way is to use arbitrary short field names — abbreviations of the longer field names — in the merge document, and then enter them in the appropriate fields in the Identifier Spec so that Q&A will know the field references for which they're being substituted.

Unfortunately, you can't name and save an Identifier Spec, as you can most other specs throughout Q&A. So if you'll be using the same merge letter frequently, you should create a macro that fills out the Identifier Spec for you (see Chapter 8).

Speaking of macros, you can use them to run all your routine mail-merge and mailing label tasks, recording them so they pause at points where you're likely to need to enter variable information (such as at the Retrieve Spec, where you select the records whose information is to be included in the merge letter).

For example, suppose you have a personalized merge letter that thanks new customers for their first order. Your customer file contains the date new customers were added to the file, and you routinely print these letters every Friday afternoon. It would be a time-saver to simply press a couple of keys to print out the letters. You could even fill out, name, save, and then reuse a

Retrieve Spec that selects only those forms on which the dates are less than a week old:

```
Date Added: >{@Date-7}
```

The Retrieve Spec is filled out like any File module Retrieve Spec — you tell Q&A which forms from the database to use in the merge operation, and optionally, the order in which you want them retrieved and printed. Remember, you can save your Retrieve and Sort Specs for future use, and you can also use valid Retrieve Spec calculations and functions to have Q&A fetch the precise group of forms you need (using programming expressions at the Retrieve Spec was covered in the last chapter).

After you've typed your retrieval parameters you can press **<F8>** for the Sort Spec if you want the documents printed out in order by zip code, last name, the date the form was added, or whatever you need.

Mail-merge Programming for Advanced Users

Version 4.0

New: Q&A version 4.0 brought an exciting new feature to advanced mail-merge applications that enables you to use programming expressions in your merge letters, and even bring information into your documents from multiple databases. Couple this with a programmable Retrieve Spec and you've got a powerful application tool in your hands.

You can have Q&A do arithmetic on field values in the merge file (or on external database fields), with the result placed where you want it in the document; Q&A can parse a field value, or join together two or more values in the database and merge the new value into the document. The possibilities are endless.

You do this by embedding the programming expressions where you want the values to appear in the document when it's printed. You'll need to know either the Program Spec field ID numbers or the names of the fields that will be included in the expression.

The formula for an embedded programming expression is:

```
*program {expression}*
```

where the expression is the formula or function that will return the value. "Program" can be abbreviation to just "pg." Be sure to leave space to the left of the opposing brace.

```
             *pg{@xlookup("customer",#4,"CU#","company")}*
             *pg{@xlookup("customer",#4,"CU#","whole name")}*
             *pg{@xlookup("customer",#4,"CU#","street")}*
             *pg{@xlookup("customer",#4,"CU#","C/S/Z")}*

             Dear *pg{@xlookup("customer",#4,"CU#","first")}*:

             Thank you for your order of *Date* which was shipped to
             you on *Shipdate* by *via*.

             This is your first order with us and we appreciate your
             business. How did you hear of us, by the way?

             Enclosed with the shipment was our invoice No. *Invoice
             No.* for *Total Invoice*. Our terms are *Terms*.

             Please call me at (701) 656-6678 if you have any
             questions. Again, we appreciate your business, and look

NEWCUST.DOC                              0% Line 12 of Page 1 of 1

 Esc-Exit  F1-Info  F2-Print  Ctrl+F6-Define Pg  F7-Search  F8-Options  ↑F8-Save
```

Figure 5-4: Sample Merge Letter With Xlookup Programming Expressions Embedded to Look Up Items From the Customer Database.

For example, suppose your database records contained both a customer credit limit and a current balance, and you wanted to encourage those customers with a large limits and low current balances to borrow some more money. You could do something along this line in a merge letter:

...Our records indicate that you have a credit limit with us of *Credit Limit* and a current balance of only *Current Balance*. This means that we're prepared to loan you an additional $*pg{Credit Limit - Current Balance}* to help you buy that new car or fix up the house...

At your Retrieve Spec, you would tell Q&A to select the forms where the credit limit was a specified amount greater than the current balance, and you'd get all the customers who are preapproved to borrow from you.

You can use the @XLOOKUP function in your merge programming expressions to merge information from external files. Suppose you wanted to send personalized follow-up letters to all your customers whose invoices contained a code identifying them as first-time buyers. Since the invoice is linked to the customer file by the customer number (CU# as we've been using it in our sample databases), you can use the invoice database as the *primary merge file*, and the customer database as the *secondary merge file*. This allows you to select at the Retrieve Spec only new customer invoices entered, say, during the last month. Figure 5-4 shows a sample letter with both primary (invoice) and secondary (customer) merge fields inserted in the document.

Atlantic Booksellers
Mrs. Julie Howitzer
14866 Naples Ave.

Dear **Julie:**

Thank you for your order of **9/12/90** which was shipped to you on **9/23/90** via **UPS Ground.**

This is your first order with us and we appreciate your business. How did you hear of us, by the way?

Enclosed with the shipment was our Invoice No. **12334** for **$323.40.** Our terms are **Net 30 Days.**

Please call me at (701) 656-6678 if you have any questions. Again, we appreciate your business and look

Figure 5-5: A Sample of the Printed Merge Letter. The merged information is shown in boldface.

In Figure 5-4, we're pulling up the company name, the buyer's name, the address, and the buyer's first name from the external customer file (CUSTOMER.DTF), using the CU# as the link between the invoice and customer databases.

We're merging the other particulars such as invoice date, ship date, shipping method, invoice number, invoice amount, and terms, from the primary merge file (INVOICE.DTF).

You'd have to be careful with your Retrieve Spec here, because in this case you'd want to include in the merge printing only new customer invoices entered within a well-defined time period. Figure 5-5 shows what the output of the sample merge letter would look like.

You can use the @DOW$ function to return the day of the week from a date in a client contact database. @Month$ can be used to return the month of a date in a file. You can get the total of a list of database fields in your merge letter using @Sum. And using @XLOOKUP to external or secondary merge files, you can conjure up a practically limitless number of ways you can use mail merge to create extremely useful documents.

Q&A places a few limitations on the mail-merge programming option:

- The programming expression cannot exceed 80 characters (it can wrap onto the next line, however).

- No single expression can return more than a single value.

- Programming functions that will not work are @Number, @Number(*n*), @Help, @Msg, @Add, @Update, and @Ditto (these cannot be used at Retrieve Specs either).

- You cannot use programming statements such as If/Then, If/Then/Else, XLOOKUP, and so forth.

When you're creating your merge document, you can get a list of the fields in any database by pressing **<Alt><F7>** and entering the name of the file. You can then highlight the desired field and press **<Enter>** to place it at the cursor position.

If you want to see a list of fields from a database *other* than the one you selected earlier, press **<F2>** from the Type/Edit screen to get to the Print Options screen, move to the "Merge File Name," and delete the filename. Then press **<F9>** to return to the Type/Edit screen, and press **<Alt><F7>**. Q&A will prompt you for the name of the file whose list of fields you wish to see. Type the name of the database and press **<Enter>**.

Remember: Use the "program" or "pg" command for any programming expressions; place the expressions themselves inside braces and the entire merge component inside asterisks. Also, make sure that your *primary* merge file is entered at the Print Options screen when you send the job to the printer.

You'll want to be extra careful when creating merge documents that contain programming expressions. Before you get the hang of it, unexpected results could occur in the printed output. Your best bet is to create the document and merge print it with a single database record (selected at the Retrieve Spec) to see how it looks. If the output is as you want it, then fill out your Retrieve Spec to include all the records to be merged and print away!

Status Messages During Merge Printing

When you press the final **<F10>** to begin the merge operation and printing, Q&A will count up the forms that meet your retrieve parameters and let you know how many documents are about to be printed. You can press **<Enter>** to continue or **<Esc>** to cancel. Before continuing you should check to make sure your printer has enough paper and that it's properly aligned.

If you're merging addresses onto envelopes, and you've specified envelope printing at the Print Options screen, Q&A will pause when necessary for you to put the next envelope in the printer.

Mailing Labels

Q&A's powerful mailing label generator lets you select from more than 50 predefined label formats (including audio cassette and videotape formats) from companies such as Avery — or you can design your own at Q&A's Define Label screen.

You can also produce mailing labels directly from File without using the Mailing Label option on the Write menu.

Printing labels from File involves setting up a *free form* Print Spec to tell Q&A where to place the selected field contents on the label (see Chapter 3). Then, at the File Print Options screen, you tell Q&A how many you want printed across the page. Printing labels from file is faster where a great many records are involved, since there is no merge aspect to it. So if you simply need to pump out 5,000 four-across address labels, or even a quantity of continuous pressure-sensitive labels, the File module may be your best option.

But you have more room for creativity when using the mailing label generator in the Write module. For example, you can add a special ad hoc message to the label that will print right along with the name and address. If you're mailing to several different lists, and the address label will be affixed to an order form or reply envelope with the address showing through the outer envelope's window, you can add different key codes to the labels so you can evaluate response rates.

Since the Write module mailing label feature generates labels in a merge operation, you have other options as well. You can, for instance, create large "mailing labels" that are actually survey cards, subscription renewal, or payment overdue notices, and run these off on preprinted forms or three-up on a page. You can merge names, addresses, and other information from a database with such "documents," and add "teasers" and other messages to the printed output.

You'll see an example of how this can be done after we've looked at the mechanics involved in designing mailing label applications.

How to Create a Mailing Label Spec

Figure 5-6 shows one page from the list of predefined labels that Q&A displays when you select the Mailing Labels option from the Write menu. Here's the procedure for selecting a predefined label format:

1. Select Mailing Labels from the Write menu and the list of Q&A supported labels will be displayed (see Figure 5-6).

```
                        LIST OF MAILING LABELS

 Avery 5160 1" x 2 5/8" HP          Avery 5198 Audio Cass. HP II
 Avery 5160 1" x 2 5/8" HP II       Avery 5199-1 2/3" x 5 7/8" HPII
 Avery 5161 1" x 4" HP              Avery 5199-2 1 5/6" x 3" HPII
 Avery 5161 1" x 4" HP II           Avery 5260 1" x 2 5/8" HP
 Avery 5162 1 1/3" x 4 1/4" HPII    Avery 5260 1" x 2 5/8" HP II
 Avery 5162 1 1/3" x 4" HP          Avery 5261 1" x 4" HP
 Avery 5162 1 1/3" x 4" HP II       Avery 5261 1" x 4" HP II
 Avery 5163 2" x 4" HP              Avery 5262 1 1/3" x 4 1/4" HPII
 Avery 5163 2" x 4" HP II           Avery 5262 1 1/3" x 4" HP II
 Avery 5164 3 1/3" x 4" HP          Avery 5262 4" x 1 1/2" HP
 Avery 5164 3 1/3" x 4" HP II       Avery 5262 4" x 1 1/2" HP II
 Avery 5197 1 1/2" x 4" HP          Avery 5266 3 1/2" x 5/8" HP
 Avery 5197 1 1/2" x 4" HP II       Avery 5266 5/8" x 3 1/2" HP II
 Avery 5198 Audio Cass. HP          Avery 5267 1/2" x 1 3/4" HP

                                    Press PgDn for more

          Enter name:
 _____

 Esc-Exit    F1-Help  F3-Delete  F5-Copy  F7-Search  F8-Rename  F10-Continue
```

Figure 5-6: Page 1 of 2 of the Custom Label Formats Available from Q&A. These are all pre-defined, and there's over 50 standard label formats from which to choose, including predesigned labels for audio cassettes and videotapes. You can select the label format you want or create your own.

2. Using your cursor navigation keys, place the highlight bar over the label format you want. Notice that as you move the highlight the label description will appear on the "Enter Name" line at the bottom of the screen. Highlight the size of label you want and press **<F5>**. You'll be prompted to enter a name for the label. Type a name that will help you later identify the label or project. You can use up to 32 characters.

Remember: Don't use the original label. Make and work with a copy of it so you can use the original label template in the future.

3. Now select the new label you just copied from the list (Q&A lists label names in alphabetical order) and press **<F10>**; the Mailing Label screen shown in Figure 5-7 will be displayed with Q&A's default merge fields already entered.

Some labels come on sheets and are designed for laser and other sheet-fed printers; others are designed to be tractor- or pin-fed and come in long, continuous forms perforated after so many labels. "1-UP" means one label across.

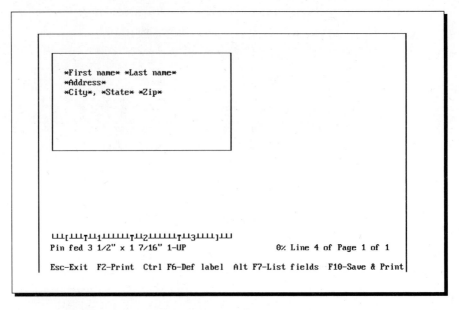

```
    *First name* *Last name*
    *Address*
    *City*, *State* *Zip*




    └└┌┴┴┴┬┴┴1┴┴┴┴┴┴┬┴┴2┴┴┴┴┴┬┴┴3┴┴┴┘┴┴┘
    Pin fed 3 1/2" x 1 7/16" 1-UP              0% Line 4 of Page 1 of 1

    Esc-Exit  F2-Print  Ctrl F6-Def label  Alt F7-List fields  F10-Save & Print
```

Figure 5-7: The Mailing Label Editing Screen. Here you edit your label, placing your merge fields where you want them to print in relation to the label edges and other merge fields. This step of the process is just like placing merge fields in documents.

4. If Q&A's default merge field names are the same as those you want to merge from your database (which is unlikely), you can press **<F10>** to continue. Otherwise, you'll need to delete the merge fields in the label, and either type your own or have Q&A place them on the label for you.

5. To have Q&A place your fields, position the cursor where you want the beginning asterisk defining the merge field to appear, and press **<Alt><F7>**.

6. At the prompt, type the name of the appropriate database, and press **<Enter>**.

7. Select from the list the field you want to merge with the label and press **<Enter>**. The procedure for placing merge fields on labels is identical to placing them in merge documents. In fact, your label *is* a merge document that will be printed in label format.

8. When you've finished editing your label, press **<Shift><F8>** to save it. (See the section later on printing when you're ready to print.)

With the mailing label on screen, you can add enhancements and fonts, just as you would any Write document.

You can also add text to the label wherever you want. Working inside the label box is just like working inside the Write editor except that here your page is defined by the label size. If you're adding text, be sure not to enclose it in asterisks, or Q&A will think you mean a merge field and you'll receive an error message at printing time. Also, be sure the length of any merged database value won't exceed the space alloted for it in the label. Otherwise, the value will wrap onto the next label line during printing and may disort any labels after that point.

You can use the usual merge document **L** and **R** commands to justify your field values left and right, as well as the **T** command to remove space from irregularly justified database fields.

Now, before we discuss label printing, let's look at what it takes to create your own custom label format.

Creating a Custom Label

You can design your own mailing label if the size you want doesn't appear on the list. You can also design a "mailing label" as big as a screen page for frequently needed forms like reply cards, announcements, overdue payment reminders, subscription renewal notices, and the like.

These can be preprinted with your company logo and address on attractively colored index stock (heavier than paper) and ordered as pin-fed, perforated, continuous forms that you can load into your dot-matrix printer and run off by the thousands. Perforated index cards and even post cards are available for laser printers. Any commercial forms printer can handle the job and they're normally quite inexpensive.

A typical size is $8\frac{1}{2}$-by-$3\frac{2}{3}$-inches, giving you the equivalent of three forms to a standard size page. You simply print them, separate them, and insert them in standard window envelopes so the address block is visible.

Such forms are easy to work out when you use Q&A's Define Label screen (see Figure 5-8), because here you simply specify the form's physical dimensions right on screen.

Designing Your Custom Label

Here's the procedure for designing your own custom label.

1. Select Mailing Labels from the Write menu.

2. When the list of available sizes is displayed, assign a name to your custom label by typing it in on the "Enter Name" line. Make your name descriptive so you can later connect it with the project. The name can be up to 32 characters long. Press **<F10>**.

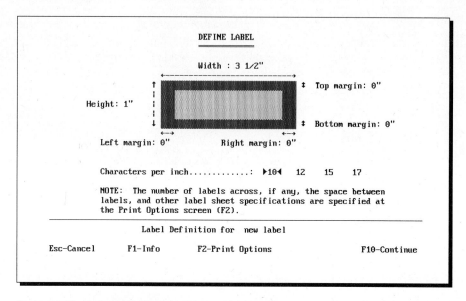

Figure 5-8: The Define Label Screen. Use it to specify the label size you want Q&A to generate. Here you also select the number of characters-per-inch you want printed. Proportional fonts, when specified, override the cpi setting.

3. A default label size of 3½-by-¹⁵/₁₆-inches will appear on your screen with no default merge fields in place. To specify new dimensions, press **<Ctrl><F6>** for the Define Label screen shown in Figure 5-8.

4. Enter the label or form dimensions by using your cursor keys to navigate to the dimension you want to change, and typing in a new value. Type your dimensions in inches and include the inch symbol (") after the number. You can use decimal places but not fractions.

Use the following as a guide when entering your dimensions:

Width: Measure from the extreme left edge of the label to the right edge. You're measuring the label surface only, not the backing or out to the tractor holes (if your labels or forms include these).

Height: Measure from the extreme top of the label *to the top edge of the label below it.* Many labels have ¹/₁₆-inch gaps between them, and this must be included in your height measurement or the labels will not print correctly.

Left margin: This is the distance from the left edge of the label to where you want the first character of text to be printed.

Right margin: This is the distance from where the last character of the text will end to the right edge of the label.

Top margin: Measure this distance in *lines*. It's the number of lines from the top edge of the label to where you want the first line of text.

Bottom margin: The distance *in lines* from the bottom edge of the label to the last line of text above.

When you print labels two or more across (two-up, four-up, etc.), Q&A will add a default of ¼-inch space between them. If the spacing for your labels is different, you can change it at the Set Editing Options screen. You get to this screen by selecting Write Utilities, and then Global Options. At the Editing Options screen change the "Spacing Between Columns" setting to the correct distance.

Characters-per-Inch

When entering your label dimensions, be sure you have enough room for the text you'll be inserting. You can choose from 10, 12, 15, or 17 characters-per-inch (or you can "font" the text on your labels to get smaller or larger characters). If you choose 10 cpi when your label is only 3 inches wide, and you're inserting merge fields whose values may exceed 30 characters, some of those lines will wrap during printing.

With a 3-inch wide label, and left and right margins set to 0, you've got room for 30 characters at 10 cpi and 36 characters at 12 cpi. But to take a text line to the maximum width of the label means that there's no margin for error when the printhead meets the paper.

When you've got your dimensions typed the way you want them, press **<F10>** and you'll see the label sized for you on the screen with the right margin left open. Type your text and place your merge fields in the usual way. You can use calculations and programming expressions just as you can when creating a merge document. You can add enhancements, too. **<Shift><F6>** brings up the enhancement menu; **<F8>** displays the Options menu; and **<Ctrl><F9>** displays the Font Assignments screen.

When you've got your label just how you want it, press **<F10>**.

Printing Labels

Figure 5-9 shows the Mailing Label Print Option screen. With your label dimensions now specified, and your text and merge fields in place, you can now prepare for printing.

```
                       MAILING LABEL PRINT OPTIONS


    Number of copies.......:   1          Print offset...........:   0

    Print to...............:  ▶PtrA◀  PtrB   PtrC   PtrD   PtrE   Disk

    Page preview...........:   Yes  ▶No◀

    Type of paper feed.....:   Manual ▶Continuous◀  Bin1   Bin2   Bin3   Lhd

    Number of labels across:  ▶1◀  2    3    4    5    6    7    8
    Space between labels...:   0"
    Lines per label sheet..:   66
    Blank lines at top.....:   0
    Blank lines at bottom..:   0

    Printer control codes..:

    Name of Q&A merge file.:   E:\QA4BETA\DATA\CUSTOMER.DTF


    _____

                     Print Options for MYLABELS

    Esc-Exit      F1-Help           F9-Save changes & go back      F10-Continue
```

Figure 5-9: The Mailing Label Print Options Screen.

Note, however, that you can always go back. You can return to the Define Label screen by pressing **<Ctrl><F6>**, or to the label display with **<F9>**.

The menu items are briefly explained here:

Number of copies: Select the number of copies you want. This is handy if you're printing one-up, pressure-sensitive labels with no merge fields, such as labels for your return address. However, don't type 1,000 unless you want that many copies. This line is for *copies*, not labels with merge fields. If you want to print out two *sets* of merge labels, type **2**.

Print offset: Enter any print offset value. A positive value prints the first character farther to the right; a negative character starts the printing farther to the left. Unless you know you'll need an offset, leave it blank.

Print to: Select your printer or printer mode, type of paper feed, and the number of labels to be printed across the page.

Page preview: You can preview a page of labels by setting page preview to yes, and pressing **<F10>**.

Number of labels across: Your "Lines per label sheet" value should be set to however many lines your printer is capable of printing on a page. For a standard page, this will be 66. For 1-inch-high pressure-sensitive labels, the value will be 6 (6 lines to an inch — the page is 6 lines in height). Be careful when using laser printers. Many of these can print only 60 lines at 6 lines to an inch.

Blank lines at top: You can increase this value if the text is not printing on the first line of the first label or row.

Blank lines at bottom: Decrease this value if the last row of labels on a sheet isn't printing.

Printer control codes: Enter any printer control codes you want.

Name of Q&A merge file: Type the name of the primary merge file if it's not already entered, and press **<F10>**.

When you press **<F10>** from the Print Options screen, Q&A saves your settings along with the label design, and takes you to the Retrieve Spec. Here, you select the forms you want to include, and optionally press **<F8>** to enter your sorting parameters.

Q&A's on-line help is excellent throughout the label-making process, and is only the **<F1>** key away. The help facility also includes a trouble-shooting guide with some excellent suggestions on how to correct for spacing and other label-related problems.

Summary

In this chapter you have used both the Write and File modules as you learned how to use Q&A's powerful mail-merge capabilities and the mailing label generator.

In Chapter 6, you will learn about a new module: Report — The Information Generator, which allows you to create and print columnar reports from your databases. The information can be sorted, arranged, enhanced, and displayed on screen or printed according to your specifications.

Chapter 6
Report — The Information Generator

In this chapter you'll learn how to:

▶ Recognize when a Q&A report will answer your database query needs.

▶ Design simple reports with subtotals and totals.

▶ Create sophisticated reports with custom formatting, calculated columns, and information from external databases.

▶ Dress up your reports with fonts and other enhancements.

▶ Preview and print your reports.

▶ Establish default settings for all your reports.

Although you can print lists and other report-like output from your database records in the File module, Report gives you more power and flexibility when you need a tabular format with calculations and special formatting.

In this chapter you will learn to design, enhance, and redesign reports. Along the way, you will also learn about such specialized types of reports as keyword and crosstab reports.

At the end of the chapter are "More Ideas on Working with Reports," which will provide you with tips I have picked up through my own experience.

Overview

Your database files contain records, and these records contain fields with variable information typed into them during the data entry process.

When you design a report, you fill out a Retrieve Spec to tell Q&A which records are to be included in the report. For example, if you want a report to show the totals of last month's invoices, you specify at the Retrieve Spec that only those particular invoices are to be included.

To specify which *fields* in those selected invoices are to be included in the report, you fill out a Column/Sort Spec. When the invoice form displays on screen, move to the fields you want included and type a number that corresponds to the column number (from left to right) where you want the information to appear in the printed report.

At the Column/Sort Spec you can also enter codes that tell Q&A how you want the rows in the report sorted, along with codes that specify any special column headings, formatting, enhancements, and calculations you want in the report.

Your reports can include headers and footers. In addition, you can direct Q&A to automatically date and time-stamp a report each time you run it.

You can select from a variety of print options for your reports as well. You can specify that your report be single- or double-spaced, suppress the splitting of records at page breaks, and print only the report totals, for example.

You can also use Q&A's powerful @XLOOKUP feature to include information from other databases in your reports. Q&A provides you with a wide range of built-in report functions that enable you to add *derived columns* to your reports — columns that use the information contained in other report columns to display revealing information and relationships not contained in the database records themselves.

The Report module is easy to use. Once you know how to use the File module, you already know much of what it takes to design even sophisticated reports. The three basic requirements of a finished report are:

- A database from which information will be extracted and included in the report.

- A report design, that includes instructions on selecting the appropriate records, identifying the fields to be used, and specifying page and printing parameters.

- Printing the report.

You can design and save up to 200 different reports for any database, and produce many more than that on an ad hoc basis. A report can contain up to 50 columns with no limit on length and up to 16 derived columns.

Once you've completed a report design, Q&A stores all the report specifications with the database. When you want to run the report again, you simply choose it from a list. It makes no difference if you've added or removed database records or changed the information in them. When you run the report, Q&A will take all of this into account and generate the output, based on the information that's currently in the database.

If you're using Q&A in a multiuser environment — meaning that you are using a shared database to generate your report — Q&A will use the information in the records that is current at the precise moment you issue the command to output the report. Others on the network can continue adding and updating records in the same database while the report prints out.

A Quick Sample Report

Using the Stock database we designed earlier in the book, you'll produce a simple report that lists the stock numbers, titles, authors, and prices of all the records in STOCK.DTF. Since we're including all the records in the file, our Retrieve Spec will be blank. Figure 6-1A shows the Column/Sort Spec with the columns and sorting criteria specified; Figure 6-1B shows what the printed report looks like.

Q&A automatically sets the column titles and column widths based on the field labels in the database and the longest values entered in those fields. You have complete control over these settings, however, as well as over the spacing between columns. You'll see the wealth of report design tools available to you to customize your output as you read through the chapter.

The Report Menu

Figure 6-2 shows the Report menu displayed when you select Report from the Q&A Main menu.

The selection you make at this menu depends on what you want to do in the Report module:

Design/redesign a report: Choose this when you're creating a report for the first time or modifying an existing report design.

Print a report: Use this option when you want to run a report that's already been designed and saved. Q&A will present a list of reports on file and give you the opportunity to make temporary design changes for this printing only.

Set global options: You can establish page, printing, and formatting defaults for all your future reports. Changes made to global options will not affect existing reports unless you redesign them.

Rename/Delete/Copy: You can change your report names, delete saved reports that are no longer useful, and copy the designs of existing reports to use for new reports.

```
      Stk#  2
                                           Date Added
                       ═════ INVENTORY ITEM ═════
      ┌──────────────────────────────────────────────────────┐
      │ Full Title                                            │
      │ Short Title  1,AS                                     │
      │ Author First                  Author Last   3         │
      └──────────────────────────────────────────────────────┘

      Type    ISBN              Subject Codes
      Description

      Vendor                Vendor#     Case Qty     Case Wght      Item Wght
      Cost  4       List  5    Discount    20%          40%           50%

     ┌────────────────┬──────────────────┬──────────────────┬──────────────────┐
     │ Sold Today     │  Rec'd Today     │  Qty On Hand     │  Reorder Level   │
     └────────────────┴──────────────────┴──────────────────┴──────────────────┘

      Sold YTD       Bought YTD      PO Date         PO#      Qty      C1?
     ┌───────────────────────────────┐         ┌──────────────────────────────┐
     │ Physical Count                │         │ Shelf Location               │
     └───────────────────────────────┘         └──────────────────────────────┘
      STOCK.DTF               Column/Sort Spec for Figure 6-1B Report    Page 1  of 1

      Esc-Cancel  F1-Info  F6-Expand    F8-Derived Columns    F9-Go back   F10-Continue
```

Figure 6-1A: The Column/Sort Spec for STOCK.DTF. Five fields have been selected for inclusion in the report, and one has been coded AS to specify an ascending sort on that field. The numbers typed in the selected fields indicate their column positions in the printed report.

```
              Short Title          Stk#    Author Last     Cost      List
      ----------------------------- -----  -------------   ------    ------
      Bach's Greatest Hits         218AT   Bach            $4.10     $9.95
      Backwater Fishing            533PB   Nelson          $2.35    $16.40
      Bird Songs of New Jersey Shore 680AT Whimple         $3.90     $9.95
      Boating on the Detroit River 205HB   Somerset        $3.35    $19.95
      Building Your First Fence    410VT   Fletcher        $9.22    $29.95
      Cruisin' Blues               444HB   Rattle          $8.18    $19.95
      Exploring African Wilderness 245VT   Halerin        $10.00    $25.00
      Growing Fruit Trees          309PB   Donlevy         $6.00    $14.95
      Help for the Common Cold     314PB   Brooks, M.D.    $5.90    $16.95
      Hollow Glen Mystery          299HB   Parsoner        $4.20    $23.45
      How to Avoid Jury Duty       533PB   Retting         $2.10    $14.95
      Looking Through the Lens     388PB   Van Buren       $4.45    $10.95
      Love Songs of the Sparrow    199AT   Clark           $3.90     $9.95
      Man Who Invented Ball Bearings 348PB Leecher         $6.90    $12.95
      Modernize Your Kitchen       403VT   Donovan         $8.66    $19.44
      Rack 'Em Up                  344HB   Magillacutty    $4.50    $22.50
      Terror on the Nile           188HB   Falcon          $6.90    $18.95
      The Omaha Factor             501HB   Patterson      $12.08    $28.50
```

Figure 6-1B: The Finished Report. Note that the order of the columns matches the numbers typed in the corresponding fields at the Column/Sort Spec in Figure 6-1A, and also that the first column is sorted alphabetically by title.

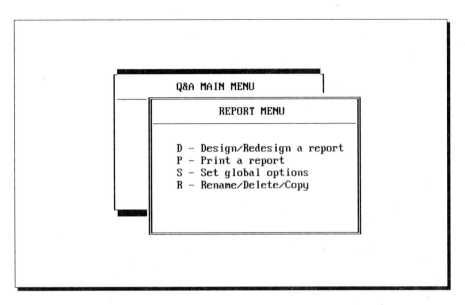

Figure 6-2: The Report Menu.

When you select either Design/Redesign a Report or Print a Report, Q&A shows you the list of reports in the database (see Figure 6-3). If you're creating a report specification for the first time, you'll assign to your report a descriptive name up to 30 characters in length, and then move on to the Retrieve and Column/Sort Specs.

If you selected Print a Report from the Report menu, you can use the cursor keys to highlight the report you want to run. Then, if you have no temporary changes to make, Q&A will generate the report for you.

If you're designing a report for the first time, or redesigning an existing report, Q&A will take you to the Report Type screen shown in Figure 6-4. Here you'll specify if the report is to be a standard columnar-style report, or a crosstab report. Crosstab reports (which will be covered later in the chapter) require special formatting, so Q&A needs to know this in advance.

The steps previously outlined are required once you've selected Design/ Redesign a Report from the Report menu. They're preliminary to actually designing the report in detail. With these handled, you now proceed to the Retrieve and Column/Sort Specs, and then the Print Options and Define Page screens. All of these steps taken as a whole constitute your report specification that Q&A will save for you at the end of the process.

```
                        LIST OF REPORTS IN DATABASE
      Physical Inventory Report
      Titles, Vendors, and Prices
      Titles in Low Stock Condition
      Titles Added in 1990
      Daily Sales Report
      Year-to-Date Sales Report
      Update List for Phone Orders
      Titles on Order from Vendors
      Video/Audiotape Titles
      Titles Less than 5 in Stock
      All Title Run for Sales Book
      YTD Sales vs. YTD Cost of Goods




               Enter name: Stock Titles by Alpha


      STOCK.DTF
```

Figure 6-3: The List of Reports. This uses the Stock database as an example. Here you assign a name to your new report or highlight the existing report you want to run. Both standard columnar and cross-tabulated reports are listed together, so you may want to place a code at the beginning of your crosstab reports to identify them as such.

```
                              REPORT TYPE
                              ══════════


                   Select the type of report you want.


                ▶C - Columnar◀       X - Crosstab


        Press F1 if you need help deciding what kind of report you want.




      STOCK.DTF                Stock Titles by Alpha

      Esc-Main Menu            F1-Description of choices         ↵ Continue
```

Figure 6-4: Q&A's Report Type Screen. Use it to specify a standard columnar report or a crosstab report format.

Designing a Report _____

The following are the steps involved in designing any new report in Q&A. Each of these steps will be explored in detail in this chapter. Remember that you can press **<F1>** for help with any of the steps in this procedure.

1. Select Design/Redesign from the Report menu.

2. Type the name of the database that contains the information for the report, and press **<Enter>**. If the name is already on the prompt line, just press **<Enter>**. To view a list of all the databases in the current directory, press the space bar, press **<Enter>**, highlight the file you want, and press **<Enter>** again. The list of reports for the selected database will be displayed.

3. If you want to redesign an existing report, highlight it and press **<Enter>**. If this is a new report, assign a name to it and type it at the "Enter Name" prompt (report names can be up to 30 characters long). Press **<Enter>**.

4. At the Report Type screen, indicate whether this is to be a standard columnar-style report or a crosstab report. Press **<F10>**.

5. Fill in the Retrieve Spec to tell Q&A which forms from the database to include in this report and press **<F10>**. Note: As is the case throughout Q&A, you can use a saved Retrieve Spec. If you do, you can also use the **<Ctrl><F7>** search option to tell Q&A whether the records you're retrieving meet your Retrieve Spec parameters.

   Although Q&A saves your report Retrieve Spec when it saves the report design, you can add any Retrieve Spec to the list of saved specs by pressing **<Shift><F8>**, and you can use a saved spec by pressing **<Alt><F8>**. See the discussion on naming and saving specs in Chapter 4 for more details.

6. Fill out the Column/Sort Spec to indicate which fields will be included, and their column order in the report. Use this spec also to indicate your sorting criteria (if applicable) and any formatting or enhancement options. Press **<F10>**.

7. At the Print Options screen, tell Q&A where to print the report, and select all the related items. Press **<F8>** for the Define Page screen.

8. Select the Define Page options to set margins, characters-per-inch, and create headers and footers for your report. Press **<F10>**.

Q&A will now advise you that your specifications have been saved. You can go ahead and print the report now, or opt not to print it at this time.

The Retrieve Spec

You select the database forms you want to include in your report the same way you retrieve a group of forms in the File module. Since you already know how to do this, I'll provide a brief review of the procedure here. For more details on filling out any Retrieve Spec, see Chapter 3.

Enter your Retrieve Spec parameters as follows:

1. Move to a field where you want to set up search restrictions. (If you press **<F10>** with a blank Retrieve Spec, all the forms in the database will be included in the report.)

2. Type the search/retrieve restrictions that will find only the forms you want (see Table 6-1). You can edit any retrieve specification typed in a field in the same way you edit text anywhere in the program. Press **<F6>** to expand the field to accommodate longer search restrictions, and press **<F3>** if you want to clear the spec and start over.

3. Repeat steps 1 and 2 for other fields that will contain retrieval restrictions.

4. Press **<F10>** when you're done to bring up the Column/Sort Spec.

You can also use calculations, @XLOOKUP, and other programming functions in your Retrieve Spec to further define your selection criteria. See Chapter 4 for more information on how to do this.

For example, if you want to include in your report only the invoices with today's date, you can type **{@Date}** into the Invoice Date field. Invoices with other than the current date will then be excluded. **{@Date-1}** would get you yesterday's invoices.

Table 6-1
Summary of Search/Retrieve Restrictions for Report

For All Search Restrictions
For use with any information type

.. (two periods)	AND. X..Y means X and Y (or *from* X to Y)
; (semicolon)	OR. X;Y means X or Y
/ (slash)	NOT. /X means not X
.. (two periods)	wildcard characters (text and keyword)

(continued)

Table 6-1 *(continued)*

Exact Match Search Restrictions

All information types including Yes/No fields and Date

X or =X	Equal to X
/X	Not X
=	Field must be empty
/=	Field must not be empty
X;Y;Z	X or Y or Z within a single field

Range Search Restrictions

All information types except Yes/No fields

>X	Greater than X
<X	Less than X
>=X	Greater than or equal to X
<=X	Less than or equal to X
>X..<Y	Greater than X and less than Y
>X..<=Y	Greater than X and less than or equal to Y
>X;<=Y	Greater than X or less than or equal to Y
MAXn	Highest *n* (whole number) values
MINn	Lowest *n* (whole number) values

Text and Character Search Restrictions

Text and Keyword

?	Any single character
..	Any group of characters
X..	Begins with X.
..X	Ends with X
X..Y	Begins with X and ends with Y
..X..	Includes X
..X..Y..Y	Includes X, Y and Z in that order
****	Finds literal character following symbol. (\? finds question mark)

(continued)

Table 6-1 (*continued*)

Special Keyword Searches

X;Y;Z	Finds X or Y or Z in a keyword field
&X;Y;Z	Finds X and Y and Z in a keyword field

Special Usage Searches

..	Finds correctly formatted values (values that are appropriate to the information type the field is supposed to contain)
/..	Incorrectly formatted values (for example, a non-money value entered into a money field)
]	For wildcard Date field searches

The Column/Sort Spec

After you've told Q&A which forms to pull for your report, you'll come to the Column/Sort Spec. This screen is the heart of the report design procedure. There's so much you can do here to customize your report that it will take the better part of this chapter to tell you about it.

It's not that the Column/Sort Spec is complicated. On the contrary — you simply type the codes that tell Q&A what you want your printed report to include, as well as how you want it to look. However, this spec offers such a wealth of options that you can easily be tempted to go further than may really be necessary in customizing your reports.

If your reporting needs are simple, you probably won't need to take advantage of the abundance of sophisticated features offered at this step in the report-making procedure. But if you need power reporting with derived columns, special formatting, enhancements, custom column headings, and so forth, the tools that Q&A provides here can probably get you the exact report you want with minimal fuss, once you're familiar with the options you can specify and the codes that activate them.

I'll start with the specifications *you must enter* at the Column/Sort Spec to get any kind of sensible report. Later, I'll look at each of the more advanced options from which you can pick and choose to fine-tune and fully customize your printed reports.

Selecting Fields and Column Order

A column in a report corresponds to a field in the database from which the report is drawn. This isn't true for *derived columns*, however, which are columns that contain information from other columns or calculations on field values.

We'll look at these derived columns later. For now, think of a report column as representing a field in the database.

When you select the fields you want to include in the report at the Column/Sort Spec, you're also telling Q&A that these are report columns and that you want them in the order specified.

To select your fields and order your columns:

1. Make sure you have the Column/Sort Spec on screen (it will tell you at the bottom of the display, and also give you the report name and the selected database). The blank Column/Sort Spec looks just like the data entry form, and also like the Retrieve Spec form (and Merge Spec form). Check to make sure you're at the correct screen.

2. Move to the field you want to make the *first* column in your report, and type **1** — don't type **#** in front of it as you would at the Program Spec.

3. Move the cursor to the field you want to make the *second* column in your report and type **2** into that one.

4. Repeat this procedure for each field you want to appear in the report, typing **3**, **4**, **5**, **6**, **7**, and so forth, into each successive field. Typing **5** in the field tells Q&A that this is to be the 5th report column, as long as numbers 1 through 4 are typed into other fields.

Tip: You don't have to use consecutive numbers. In fact, there's an advantage to incrementing your column numbers by two's or even five's — it enables you to insert additional columns later should you need to redesign your report to include more information.

Advanced users should keep in mind that a number must be entered in any field that will be used for calculations or will be referenced later in a derived column, even if that field's information won't show up in the final report in a column of its own.

Note: The numbers you're using to order your columns at the Column/Sort Spec have no relation to the field numbers you use when programming your form at the Field Programming Spec — the two specs have nothing in common.

If you simply want a straight, unsorted columnar report with no subtotals, totals, or special formatting, you can now press **<F10>** to proceed to the Print Options screen and print the report out. That's all there is to it. Otherwise, read on.

Sorting Codes

Reports typically include subtotals and totals. A report with subtotals indicates that the items (rows) included in the report have been grouped in some meaningful manner. For example, you might want to sort an employee report by department, with a subtotal of salaries for production, accounting, sales, and so forth. Or you might want a monthly invoice report that shows subtotals by invoice date, by advertising response code, or both, with a grand total at the bottom.

In order perform any calculations other than grand totals or a total count of the items, you must sort your data. Here's how you do it.

1. At the Column/Sort Spec, move to any field you want to sort on. The field must contain a column-ordering number.

2. After the number, type a comma, and then **AS** for ascending order, or **DS** for a descending sort.

3. Repeat these steps for each numbered field you want to sort on, pressing **<F6>** to expand the field if you need more room.

If you need a review, there's more detailed information on specifying sort criteria in Chapter 3. The Help screen at the Column/Sort Spec (see Figure 6-5) gives you a summary of the codes you can enter to specify sorting and other criteria you may need to enter at this spec to get the report you want.

When you specify an ascending sort on a column, all the text in that column will be arranged in order from A to Z. A sorted number field will display the numbers from lowest to highest in the corresponding report column. If no sorting order is specified, the rows in the report will appear in the order in which Q&A retrieved the forms, which may be no logical order at all.

Figure 6-6A shows a simple report of inventory items with no sort criteria specified. Figure 6-6B shows the same report sorted by list price.

Keep in mind that text fields containing numbers sort in a pseudoalphabetic fashion, for example, 1, 11, 199, 2, 2344, 25, and so forth. The only way to overcome this is to make sure that any numbers in your database text fields are all the same length. Leading zeros can be added when entering data. Standard zip codes in text fields will sort properly since they're all five digits (90254, 02345, and so on).

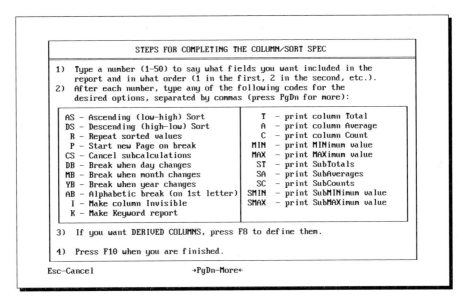

```
╔══════════════════════════════════════════════════════════════════════╗
║              STEPS FOR COMPLETING THE COLUMN/SORT SPEC                  ║
╠══════════════════════════════════════════════════════════════════════╣
║  1)  Type a number (1-50) to say what fields you want included in the   ║
║      report and in what order (1 in the first, 2 in the second, etc.).  ║
║  2)  After each number, type any of the following codes for the         ║
║      desired options, separated by commas (press PgDn for more):        ║
║  ┌──────────────────────────────────┬─────────────────────────────┐   ║
║  │ AS - Ascending (low-high) Sort   │  T   - print column Total   │   ║
║  │ DS - Descending (high-low) Sort  │  A   - print column Average │   ║
║  │  R - Repeat sorted values        │  C   - print column Count   │   ║
║  │  P - Start new Page on break     │ MIN  - print MINimum value  │   ║
║  │ CS - Cancel subcalculations      │ MAX  - print MAXimum value  │   ║
║  │ DB - Break when day changes      │ ST   - print SubTotals      │   ║
║  │ MB - Break when month changes    │ SA   - print SubAverages    │   ║
║  │ YB - Break when year changes     │ SC   - print SubCounts      │   ║
║  │ AB - Alphabetic break (on 1st letter) │ SMIN - print SubMINimum value │║
║  │  I - Make column Invisible       │ SMAX - print SubMAXimum value │   ║
║  │  K - Make Keyword report         │                             │   ║
║  └──────────────────────────────────┴─────────────────────────────┘   ║
║  3)  If you want DERIVED COLUMNS, press F8 to define them.              ║
║                                                                        ║
║  4)  Press F10 when you are finished.                                   ║
╠══════════════════════════════════════════════════════════════════════╣
║  Esc-Cancel                        →PgDn-More←                          ║
╚══════════════════════════════════════════════════════════════════════╝
```

Figure 6-5: Page 1 of the Column/Sort Spec Help Screen.

You can use Q&A's @NUMBER feature to create five-digit stock numbers prefixed by a code like "PN" for "Part Number." Such special numbers are text values to Q&A, but will respond properly to sorting.

Here's an example of how you could do it at the Field Programming Spec:

```
<#2: #2="PN-" + @Right("00000" + @Str(@Number),5)
```

This function gives you sequential part numbers, the first of which would look like this: PN-00001. Or you could reset your @NUMBER to 5000, for example. As a result, the first number returned would be PN-05001. The leading zeros enable you to sort on these text fields, so long as all the part numbers contain the same prefix. Sorting on fields formatted as numbers or money doesn't present this problem.

New Pages for Sorted Columns

If you want your report to start on new page when there's a break in the sorted column, you can enter **P** in that field at the Column/Sort Spec.

For example, you may need to sort a sales lead report by state so you can hand your salesmen the report pages for the states in their respective territories. Normally, Q&A would start the next state right below the last one, but you can remedy this with the **P** code.

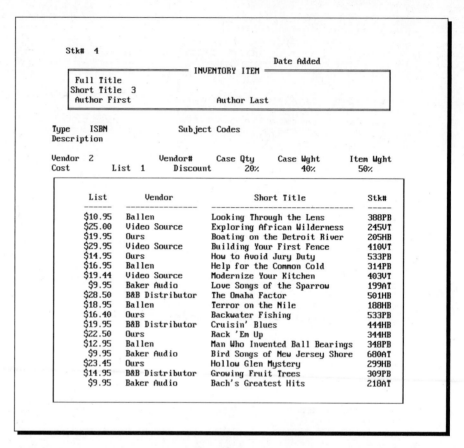

Figure 6-6a: Part of the STOCK.DTF Form at the Column/Sort Spec. No sorting is specified, resulting in the report rows appearing in random order.

In a 1,AS state field you simply type a comma after **AS** and type **P**. the field now contains 1,AS,P and Q&A knows to start a new page whenever the state value changes.

Repeating Values in Sorted Columns

Ordinarily, when you sort a report column and there are duplicate values in that column, Q&A will print each duplicate value only once.

For instance, if column 1 contains sorted employee last names and column 2 contains their first names, the last names will appear only once, even though you may have three Smiths and a family of Joneses working for the company. In such a report you'd want Q&A to *repeat* those sorted last names. You do this by typing a comma and then **R** after the code that's already in the sorted field — for example: 1,AS,R.

```
      Stk#   4
                                              Date Added
                      ═══════════ INVENTORY ITEM ═══════════
         ┌──────────────────────────────────────────────────────┐
         │ Full Title                                            │
         │ Short Title  3                                        │
         │ Author First               Author Last               │
         └──────────────────────────────────────────────────────┘

      Type    ISBN             Subject Codes
      Description

      Vendor  2            Vendor#     Case Qty      Case Wght      Item Wght
      Cost         List ▶1,AS◀  Discount      20%           40%           50%
         ┌──────────────────────────────────────────────────────────────┐
         │   List         Vendor              Short Title         Stk#   │
         │   ──────    ─────────────    ──────────────────────   ─────  │
         │   $9.95     Baker Audio      Love Songs of the Sparrow  199AT │
         │   $9.95     Baker Audio      Bach's Greatest Hits       218AT │
         │   $9.95     Baker Audio      Bird Songs of New Jersey Shore 680AT │
         │   $10.95    Ballen           Looking Through the Lens   388PB │
         │   $12.95    Ballen           Man Who Invented Ball Bearings 348PB │
         │   $14.95    Ours             How to Avoid Jury Duty     533PB │
         │   $14.95    B&B Distributor  Growing Fruit Trees        309PB │
         │   $16.40    Ours             Backwater Fishing          533PB │
         │   $16.95    Ballen           Help for the Common Cold   314PB │
         │   $18.95    Ballen           Terror on the Nile         188HB │
         │   $19.44    Video Source     Modernize Your Kitchen     403VT │
         │   $19.95    Ours             Boating on the Detroit River 205HB │
         │   $19.95    B&B Distributor  Cruisin' Blues             444HB │
         │   $22.50    Ours             Rack 'Em Up                344HB │
         │   $23.45    Ours             Hollow Glen Mystery        299HB │
         │   $25.00    Video Source     Exploring African Wilderness 245VT │
         │   $28.50    B&B Distributor  The Omaha Factor           501HB │
         │   $29.95    Video Source     Building Your First Fence  410VT │
         └──────────────────────────────────────────────────────────────┘
```

Figure 6-6b: The Report with AS Ascending Sort Code Entered in the List Field. The report is now sorted from lowest price to highest.

If the column is *not* sorted, **R** will accomplish nothing because Q&A always repeats values in nonsorted columns.

You can change Q&A's default setting so that it will *always* repeat values in a sorted column by using Report's Global Format Options. Here's what you do:

1. Choose Set Global Options from the Report menu.

2. Choose Columnar Global Options.

3. Select Set Format Options.

4. Change "Default to Repeating Values" from No to Yes and press **<F10>** to save the change.

Global Options settings affect all new reports you create — not existing report designs. However, if you print an existing report using Design/Redesign, any global options settings that have changed since that report was designed will be reflected in it. You'll find out how to change these global defaults to suit your reporting preferences later in the chapter.

Breaking Columns by Date

You may need your sorted date columns to break on days, months, or years so you can get daily, monthly, or yearly subtotals. You can do this using **DB** (Daily Break), **MB** (Monthly Break), and **YB** (Yearly Break) codes entered at the Column/Sort Spec.

Suppose you use a purchase order database and want to see purchase order expenditures by month, with another subtotal by year, and then a grand total. Such a report would give you a clear picture of *when* the company's money is being spent, and how much is being committed in some months compared to others. Figure 6-7 shows a comparison between a report with no date breaks, and the same report with a month date break code (1,AS,MB) entered in the date field at the Column/Sort Spec.

The date-breaking codes you enter (**DB**, **MB**, or **YB**) apply only to the sorted date column, not to the column that includes the actual subcalculation. In other words, in the purchase order form at the Column/Sort Spec, you'd enter your date-breaking codes in the purchase order *date* field, not the money field, and then you'd enter your subtotal and total codes in the money field. Q&A would then break the report when the month and year changed, and give you the dollar subtotals and a grand total (more on specifying totals and subtotals later in this chapter).

DB Daily Break: Q&A breaks the column and does subcalculations (if any) when the *day* changes.

MB Monthly Break: Q&A breaks the column and does subcalculations (if any) when there's a change in the *month*.

YB Yearly Break: Q&A breaks the column and does subcalculations (if any) when the *year* changes.

P.O. Date: 1,AS,MB,YB

gives you a report that breaks at the sorted date column 1 whenever the month or the year changes.

P.O. Date: 1,AS,MB
Supplier: 2
P.O. Amount: 3,ST,T

gives you a report that breaks at the sorted date column 1 when the month changes, and also provides monthly dollar subtotals and a grand total.

```
P.O. Date        Supplier              P.O. Amount
-----------      ----------------      -----------
5 Jun 1990       Video Source              $244.15
9 Jun 1990       Ballen Books              $122.88
12 Jun 1990      Ballen Books              $432.88
7 Jul 1990       Baker Audio                $88.00
19 Jul 1990      Video Source              $335.00
28 Jul 1990      B&B Distributor           $590.00
7 Aug 1990       B&B distributor           $238.00
22 Aug 1990      Baker Audio               $420.50
29 Aug 1990      Ballen Books              $230.55
```

```
P.O. Date        Supplier              P.O. Amount
-----------      ----------------      -----------
5 Jun 1990       Video Source              $244.15
9 Jun 1990       Ballen Books              $122.88
12 Jun 1990      Ballen Books              $432.88
                                       -----------
Month Total:                              $799.91

7 Jul 1990       Baker Audio                $88.00
19 Jul 1990      Video Source              $335.00
28 Jul 1990      B&B Distributor           $590.00
                                       -----------
Month Total:                             $1013.00

7 Aug 1990       B&B Distributor           $238.00
22 Aug 1990      Baker Audio               $420.50
29 Aug 1990      Ballen Books              $230.55
                                       -----------
Month Total:                              $889.05

==================================================
Total:                                   $2501.96
```

Figure 6-7: Two Reports. The top report includes no date-break codes — it is simply sorted by date. The bottom version is the same report, but with a month-break code in the date field, and with monthly subtotals and a grand total.

You can use these codes in any combination within a single date field, but if you use more than one code, the code that breaks at the smallest interval of time should be typed first, with each such code separated from any others by a comma.

The procedure for entering date-breaking codes at the Column/Sort Spec is the same as entering all the codes we've discussed so far: go to the field, type a comma after the last code already there, and then type the date-breaking code or codes. Repeat the step for other sorted date fields you want to show up in the report with date breaks.

Table 6-2 shows a summary of the sorting codes you can use in a report.

Column Calculations

Reports typically include calculations on columns, such as subtotals, totals, counts, and averages. Table 6-3 shows a summary of the column calculation codes you can specify in your fields at the Column/Sort Spec.

You can also create *derived* report columns to show calculations made between field values, or based on totals, subtotals, or other column calculations. You'll see how to create these special columns later in the chapter.

The procedure for entering calculation codes is the same as the other codes discussed so far. Move to the field in which you want to enter a calculation code, type a comma after any code already there, and type the calculation code. The codes listed in Table 6-3 are ordinarily used for columns containing number or money values, although you can enter a count or subcount in a text field because this code simply tells you how many entries the report contains. If you need more space to enter the code, **<F6>** will expand the field.

Codes that perform calculations based on *all* the values in the column (**T**, **A**, **C**, **MIN**, **MAX**, **STD**, **VAR**) can be used even when the report contains no sorted values. But the codes that call for *sub*calculations depend on column breaks and thus require that you specify a sorted column.

Moreover, columns with subcalculations cannot be the first column of the report. Typically, a primary sorted column is the first report column, with any calculated columns appearing somewhere to the right of it.

Here's an example of a Column/Sort Spec with codes entered for various calculations:

P.O. Date: 1,AS,MB,YB
Supplier: 2
P.O. Amount: 3,SC,C,ST,T,SA,A

These Column/Sort Specs produce a three-column report:

- The first column contains the dates in ascending order, with breaks where the month or year changes.

- The second column lists the suppliers.

Table 6-2
Sorting Codes Available in Q&A Reports

Code	What it does
AS	Ascending sort
DS	Descending sort
YS	Ascending sort by year (can't be used with other sorting codes)
MS	Ascending sort by month (can't be used with other sorting codes)
CS	Cancels subcalculations (see next section)
P	New page when the sorted value changes
R	Repeat sorted values
AB	Break and do subcalculations when the first letter in the field changes.
DB	Break and do subcalculations when day changes
MB	Break and do subcalculations when month changes
YB	Break and do subcalculations when year changes

- The third column shows a subcount, a dollar subtotal, and a dollar subaverage when the month or year changes, and shows a grand count, grand dollar total, and grand dollar average at the bottom of the report.

Canceling Subcalculations

Subcalculations (**ST**, **SC**, **SA**, etc.) are triggered every time there's a break in a preceding sorted column. For example, if the first column is sorted and the second column contains a sort code also, Q&A will trigger subcalculations when there's a break in *either* column — which may make for a messy report.

If you want to suppress subcalculations when the values in specific sorted columns change, type **CS** (Cancel Subcalculations) into those fields at the Column/Sort Spec.

Table 6-3
A Summary of Column Calculation Codes You Can Enter at the Column/Sort Spec

Code	What it does	Where it appears
Calculation codes		
T	Prints column total	Bottom of column
A	Prints average value	Bottom of column
C	Prints count of entries	Bottom of column
MIN	Prints column's minimum value	Bottom of column
MAX	Prints column's maximum value	Bottom of column
STD	Prints column's standard deviation	Bottom of column
VAR	Prints column's variance	Bottom of column
Subcalculation codes		
ST	Prints subtotals	At column breaks
SA	Prints subaverages	At column breaks
SC	Prints subcounts	At column breaks
SMIN	Prints minimum values	At column breaks
SMAX	Prints maximum values	At column breaks
SSTD	Prints substandard deviation	At column breaks
SVAR	Prints subvariance	At column breaks

To illustrate the procedure, suppose you want an invoice report sorted by ascending date in column 1, additionally sorted by ascending customer name in column 2, and with subcalculations on the total invoice amounts in column 3.

You don't want subtotals and so forth in column 3 when the customer name changes in column 2, yet that's what you'll get if you don't suppress those subcalculations by entering **CS** in the customer name field.

Here's an example of how the spec might look:

Invoice Date: 1,AS,MB
Customer Name: 2,AS,CS
Invoice Amount: 3,ST,T

- Column 1 is sorted by ascending date with a break when the month changes. This is the *primary* sort field.

- Column 2 is sorted by ascending alphabetical customer name, but only where there are duplicate dates in column 1. This is the *secondary* sort field. **CS** typed in this column suppresses column 3 subcalculations when the value in column 2 changes.

- Column 3 shows a subtotal figure only when there's a break in the month in column 1. No subtotals are triggered on a break in column 2. Column 3 also shows a grand total of the dollar amounts of all the invoices in the report.

Formatting Columns

The columns in your reports can be formatted to display their values according to your needs and preferences. This is the Report module counterpart to the Format Spec you use in File when assigning information types and formatting options. In Report, however, you enter your formatting codes at the Column/Sort Spec.

Why would you want to format your report columns?

You may want to center a column, justify it left or right, print its values in all uppercase letters, use a different date or hour format, treat a number value as money, or vice versa.

Q&A automatically formats report column values as they appear in your records in File. If the Date field in the database form is justified center, the corresponding column in the report will also be justified center. The formatting codes you enter at the Column/Sort Spec override these presets and provide an extra degree of flexibility in the design and look of your report output. Table 6-4 shows a summary of the formatting codes available for use in your reports.

When you want to add formatting codes to your report:

1. Move to the field you want to format. It must contain a column number at the very least.

2. Move the cursor to the space after the last code entered.

3. Type a comma, then **F**.

4. Type all your formatting codes inside of a single set of parentheses. For example: **Last Name: 1,AS,F(U,JR)**. When you include more than one formatting code in a field, separate each of them with a comma. In any one field you can use only one justification code; either **C** or **WC**; and only one of the **Dn**, **Hn**, **Nn**, **M** or **T** codes. If you need more space, press **<F6>** to expand the field.

5. Repeat steps 1 through 4 for any other fields you want to format.

Custom Column Headings and Widths

Q&A defaults to using your field labels as report column headings, and is preset to size columns based on the length of the longest value in the corresponding database field that will be included in the column.

Depending on your needs, you can assign more descriptive column headings to your reports. For example, if the field label for the customer's last name is simply **Last**, you can make its corresponding column heading read **Last Name**. Some of your database fields may not have labels at all; in this case, Q&A uses the field name. But where you're including these in your reports, you'll probably want to head the columns with something descriptive.

When you specify a column width, values exceeding it will be truncated. If you make a number or money column so narrow that the values won't fit, Q&A will fill the space with asterisks, and any calculations assigned to that column will go to pot.

To change default column headings and widths:

1. Move to any field that will be included in the report.

2. Move the cursor to the space following the last code entered.

3. Type a comma, and then **H**.

4. Type your column heading and/or width information inside parentheses following the **H**. First type the width (in character spaces or inches — inches must be followed by the **"** symbol) followed by a colon (**:**). Then type the heading, using the capitalization you want. If you want to split your heading onto multiple lines, separate the parts of it with exclamation points (**!**).

5. Repeat steps 1 through 4 for any other field to receive new column heading and/or width specifications. Press **<F6>** to expand those fields that aren't wide enough to accommodate your codes.

You can specify hanging indents for any right-justified multiline or expanded text fields you want to include in your report. The first line of the field value will print normally, and subsequent lines will be indented the number of characters or inches you choose.

Table 6-4
Formatting Codes Entered at the Column/Sort Spec to Override Default Formatting

Code	What it does
JR	Justifies right (automatic with number & money columns)
JL	Justifies left (automatic with text fields)
JC	Justifies center
U	Prints all uppercase letters
I	Prints initial uppercase letters
L	Prints all lowercase letters
C	Prints numbers with commas
WC	Prints number & money values without commas
TR	Truncates values that don't fit in a column
Dn	Prints the date in the n date format (1-20) from Global Format Options
Hn	Prints the time in the n time format (1-3) from Global Format Options
Nn	Prints the number with n decimal digits (1-7)
M	Treats the value as money
T	Treats the value as text

After you type **H**, type the column width, a colon, the indent value, another colon, and then the custom column name, all within parentheses. Here's an example:

Comments: 4,H(15:2:Supervisor!Review!Comments)

This tells Q&A to make this the fourth column of the report, make it 15 characters wide, indent the second and subsequent lines of the text two character spaces, and head the column "Supervisor Review Comments" split onto three lines. The column would then print looking like this:

```
Supervisor
  Review
 Comments
 _ _ _ _ _ _ _

He has always
  been a good
  employee but
  last quarter
  he started
  to....etc.
```

If you want a ! to appear in a column heading, type a \ (backslash symbol) just before it. Q&A will then print the ! but not the \. A ! in a column heading with no preceding \ tells Q&A to split the heading at that point.

Column widths and indent values can be expressed in characters or inches. But when you specify a column width *and* an indent value in the same field, both of them must be expressed the same way (you can't express a column width in inches and an indent value in the same column in characters).

If your report will be printed in a proportional font, you'll want to set your column widths and indent values in inches.

You can assign a column width without an indent value or a custom column heading. Likewise, you can enter a column heading without a column width. But where you specify an indent, you must also enter a column width. The indent, of course, can't exceed the width.

User-defined Report Labels

The Column/Sort Spec is home to a variety of custom report elements. You use it to order report columns, enter sorting parameters, control column formatting and width, and specify custom headings and indent values.

New: Q&A 4.0 users can use the Column/Sort Spec to assign alternate names to report labels, and specify custom report separator lines, as well.

You can change "Total" in your report to read "Subtotal" or "Grand Total." "Month Total" can be changed to "Monthly Subtotal," "Total for the Month," or "New Total." Table 6-5 summarizes the codes you can use to tell Q&A to print different aggregate labels.

You assign your new label by typing the text inside parentheses following the code. For example:

TL(Grand Total)

tells Q&A you want "Grand Total" to print in the report instead of the "Total" label.

STL(Subtotal)

prints the word "Subtotal" at report subtotal breaks rather than the word "Total."

You use these label codes in conjunction with column calculation codes. In other words, if a column was coded for a subtotal (**ST**), you wouldn't want to enter a custom label code for an average, unless the column also included the code calling for the calculation of the average value.

To define special text for your report labels:

1. At the Column/Sort Spec, move to the first field that contains the calculation code you want to redefine.

2. Type a comma after the last code entered in the field.

3. Type the label code as in Table 6-5 and follow that with your label text inside parentheses.

4. Repeat these steps for other calculated columns whose labels you want to redefine.

In addition to adding your custom labels, you can also specify the type of horizontal separator lines you want your report to contain. Q&A defaults to single dashed lines (– – –) beneath column headings and at subaggregate levels (subtotals or subaverages, for example), and prints double-dashed lines (= = = = = = = =) at aggregate (column total, column average, etc.) levels.

You can enter codes in your fields at the Column/Sort Spec to tell Q&A which kind of separator line you want for that column. The codes include **HS** for a header separator line, **SL** for a single-dash line, and **DL** for a double-dash line.

If you want to specify that a different sequence of characters print as separator lines, follow the code with the sequence of characters inside parentheses. For example, the heading separator –+–+–+–+ would be typed in the field as **HS(-+-+)**, telling Q&A to print a dash, a plus sign, a dash, and so forth. Typing **HS(—)** uses the specified line-draw character as the separator line between the heading and the report body, and **DL(=)** prints a solid double line for aggregates.

Table 6-5
Summary of Report Label Codes

Code	Label Text Affected
TL	Total
AL	Average
CL	Count
MINL	Minimum
MAXL	Maximum
STDL	Standard deviation
VARL	Variance
STL	Subtotal
SAL	Subaverage
SCL	Subcount
SMINL	Subminimum
SMAXL	Submaximum
SSTDL	Substandard deviation
YTL	Year total
YAL	Year average
YCL	Year count
YMINL	Year minimum
YMAXL	Year maximum
YSTDL	Yearly standard deviation
MTL	Month total
MAL	Month average
MCL	Month count
MMINL	Month minimum
MMAXL	Month maximum
MSTDL	Monthly standard deviation

You enter these specifications into the Column/Sort Spec fields in the usual manner. Remember to press **<F6>** to expand the field if you need more room.

Invisible Columns

You can make a column invisible even though you may be sorting on it, or though its values are being used for calculating a derived column.

An invisible column can be used like any other column except that it will not print in the report. So you wouldn't want to spend time formatting, enhancing, or creating special labels for it.

Invisible columns are valuable when you have sensitive data in fields that need to be a part of the Column/Sort Spec for sorting or calculation purposes. For example, you might want a report showing bonuses sorted by increasing salaries, but you don't want salaries to appear in the output. You simply make the salary column invisible so it won't print.

In this case the invisible salary column, since the sort is based on it, must have a lower column number than the bonus column.

Invisible columns can also come in handy when the data in them is needed in the first column for primary sorting purposes, but the information itself doesn't add to the value of the report. For example, if you want to sort an inventory report by stock number, but the stock numbers themselves would be of no value to any other part of the report, that column could be made invisible.

Invisible columns are sometimes necessary when you have too many columns and the report is too wide for the page. If the columns are needed for sorting or calculation purposes, but aren't essential in the printed report, just make them invisible and you'll free up the space.

An invisible column requires an ordering number at the Column/Sort Spec, just like any other field used in a report. Move to the field you want to make invisible and type **I**. No matter where the **I** is typed, the field containing it will not print as a report column, and the appearance of the output will look perfectly normal.

Derived Columns

Ordinarily, a report column corresponds to a field in the database — you type a **1** in a field at the Column/Sort Spec to tell Q&A to make it the first column in the report. But there will be times when you'll need to generate report columns that don't correspond to any particular field. You may need to add two fields together, multiply one field by another, or operate on columns containing calculations such as totals or subtotals and place the results of *these* calculations in columns of their own.

These special columns are called *derived columns* because the information in them is *derived* from a source other than the contents of a single field in the database. You can create up to 16 derived columns in a Q&A report.

Figure 6-8 shows the Derived Column screen, which you reach by pressing **<F8>** from the Column/Sort Spec.

You'll notice in Figure 6-8 that four groups of fields are available for derived columns on the screen. If you need more, simply press **<PgDn>**.

Each derived column includes three fields: Heading, Formula, and Column Spec. Use these to tell Q&A what text to print at the top of the column, what formula to use to calculate its information, and where to place the column in the printed report.

Heading: Use this line to type the heading you want to assign to the derived column. Unlike regular columns, you have to create the heading because there's no field label to serve as a default heading. You can head a derived column **Sales x Price**, **Salary plus Bonus**, or **Income less Expenses**. You can split your headings just li ke you can in regular report columns using the **!**. The heading **Percent!of Total!Bonuses** would print on three lines. If you want the column to begin with a number, type a colon and then the number. If the column will be invisible, you won't need a heading at all.

Formula: Here you type the calculation formula that will generate the data for the column. A formula typically includes other report columns and arithmetic operators, but derived columns can do much more than this, as you'll see.

Column Spec: This line functions in a capacity similar to the fields at the Column/Sort Spec. Here you enter your column number, any sorting criteria, calculation codes if you want totals or subtotals, and any special formatting.

Here's the procedure for creating a derived column. More details on this subject follow later, along with descriptions of how you can use these columns for much more than just calculations.

1. With your Column/Sort Spec filled out and displayed, press **<F8>**. You'll see the derived column screen shown in Figure 6-8.

2. Type the heading for the first derived column and press **<Enter>**.

3. Type the formula that will be used to calculate the derived column, then press **<Enter>**.

4. Enter the column's specification as you normally would at the Column/Sort Spec (column number, sorting, formatting, calculation codes, etc.) and press **<Enter>**.

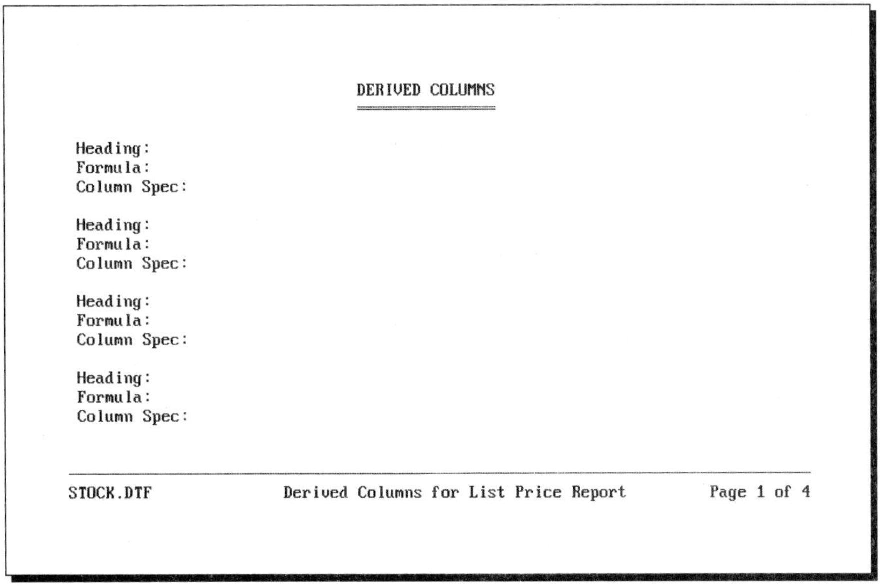

```
                          DERIVED COLUMNS
                          ═══════════════

       Heading:
       Formula:
       Column Spec:

       Heading:
       Formula:
       Column Spec:

       Heading:
       Formula:
       Column Spec:

       Heading:
       Formula:
       Column Spec:


       _____

       STOCK.DTF         Derived Columns for List Price Report      Page 1 of 4
```

Figure 6-8: The Derived Column Screen.

5. Repeat steps 2 through 4 for any other derived columns you need. You can have a total of 16. When your first four derived columns are filled out, press **<PgDn>** if you need more.

6. When you've finished, press **<F10>** to move on to the Print Options screen, or press **<F9>** to go back to the Column/Sort Spec.

Figure 6-9 shows a simple derived column report that multiplies the quantity in stock in an inventory database by the cost of the item, producing a current inventory valuation at cost report.

Deciding on the Correct Derived Column Formula

A typical formula includes adding together or multiplying two or more regular columns, such as **#3*#4**, or **#5+#7+#9**. Use **+** for addition, **–** for subtraction, **/** for division, and ***** for multiplication. Even though ordinary report column numbers don't require **#** in front of them, you must use **#** when referencing another column in a derived column formula.

Parts of formulas enclosed in parentheses are calculated first, followed by multiplication and division, followed next by addition and subtraction. When in doubt about how Report will calculate a formula, enclose the appropriate parts of your calculations in parentheses to avoid ambiguity.

```
        Stock No: 1, AS
        Qty on Hand: 2
        Cost: 3

        Derived Column
        Heading: Value at Cost
        Formula: #2*#3
        Column Spec: 4, T


   Stock No.   Qty on Hand     Cost     Value at Cost
   _____   _____   _____    _____

     122H           344       $1.75          $602.00
     133B           200       $9.20         $1840.00
     212C            99      $15.30         $1514.70
     213D            12       $2.50           $30.00
     288F           922       $4.45         $4102.90
                                          ==============
   Total:                                    $8089.60
```

Figure 6-9: A Simple Derived Column. This column is used to report on the value of an inventory at cost.

For example, in the expression **#4-#3*100**, Q&A first multiplies the value in #3 by 100, then subtracts that product from the value in #4. If you want the difference between #3 and #4 multiplied by 100, then your expression should read **(#4-#3)*100**.

Here are a few more examples of straightforward derived column calculations:

#2+#4-#7   Returns the difference between column 7 and the sum of columns 2 and 4.

#5/#2*5   Divides column 5 by column 2, and multiplies the result by the number 5 (*not column 5*).

#8*(#2-#1)   Subtracts column 1 from column 2, and multiplies the difference by column 8.

Cumulative Derived Columns

A derived column can be set up to print running totals. Suppose you have a sorted Invoice No. (column 2) without breaks for subcalculations, and an Invoice Amount field (column 3) where you're asking for subtotals. You can make a derived column called **Total Sales** (#4) using the formula **#3+#4**.

```
        Date: 1,AS
        Invoice No: 2,AS,CS
        Invoice Amt: 3,ST

        Derived Column
        Heading: Total Sales
        Formula: #3+#4
        Column Spec: 4


  Date      Invoice No   Invoice Amt   Total Sales
--------    ----------   -----------   -----------
9/10/90        1234        $233.44       $233.44
9/10/90        1235        $342.22       $575.66
9/10/90        1236        $215.33       $790.99
                          -----------
Total:                      $790.99

9/12/90        1255        $654.66     $1,445.65
9/12/90        1256        $102.40     $1,548.05
9/12/90        1257         $80.50     $1,628.55
                          -----------
Total:                      $837.56

9/16/90        1258        $800.40     $2,428.95
9/16/90        1259        $320.00     $2,748.95
9/16/90        1260        $205.30     $2,954.25
                          -----------
Total:                     $1325.70
```

Figure 6-10: A Derived Column that Reflects a Cumulative Running Balance.

Report will add the value from the previous row of Total Sales to the current row of Invoice Amount and place the result in the current row of Total Sales.

In this case, your Column/Sort Spec and single derived column would be set up as in Figure 6-10.

Notice that the derived column actually references itself in its own formula. When the date changes you'll get a subtotal in the Invoice Amount column, but none in the derived Total Sales column. Total Sales will simply continue to increase by the values in the Invoice Amount column. Had a *grand total* been requested in the Invoice Amount column, that figure would match the last entry in the cumulative Total Sales column.

Here's another example of a useful cumulative derived column in a simple financial application. The application includes database fields for Client#, a Transaction code, Deposit, and Withdrawal, and you want a report that shows cumulative balances by Client#, and subtotals when the Client# changes.

```
Client#    Trans Code   Deposits    Withdrawals   Cum Balance
--------   ----------   ---------   -----------   -----------
   122         111      $350.00       $250.00       $100.00
               122      $100.00         $0.00       $200.00
               121      $500.00       $200.00       $500.00
                                                   ----------
Total:                                              $800.00

   123         122      $100.00         $0.00       $100.00
               121      $600.00       $300.00       $400.00
               111      $200.00        $50.00       $550.00
                                                   ----------
Total:                                             $1050.00
```

Figure 6-11: An Advanced Derived Column Report with Running Balances by Client Number.

Your Column/Sort Spec, simplified here, would reflect the following:

```
Client#: 1,AS
Trans Code: 2,AS,CS
Deposits: 3
Withdrawals: 4
```

with these two derived columns:

```
Heading: Cum Balance
Formula: ((#1=#20)*#10)+#3-#4
Column Spec: 10,ST
Heading:
Formula: #1
Column Spec: 20,I
```

resulting in a report like that in Figure 6-11.

Formatting Derived Columns

You have to be alert while formatting derived columns when you're operating on both a money and a number value, a date and a number value, and so forth. Usually, Q&A will format the column's information as you want to see it. But your best bet is to type the formatting code you want, such as **Dn**, **Hn**, **M**, **Nn**, or **T**. See Table 6-4 for the codes you can type on the derived Column Spec line to ensure you'll get the results you need.

Derived Column Summary Functions

Using Report's summary functions, you can use the totals, subtotals, and the results of calculations in one column to produce calculations in derived columns.

For example, regular report column totals are not database fields — they are generated by the Report process, and as a result you can't refer to them by field ID# in a derived column formula. What you need to do in such cases is use a Report summary function.

For example, suppose you need a derived column value to reflect a percentage based on the total of another column. Because you can't directly refer to the other column's total, use the @TOTAL summary function. Table 6-6 shows the summary functions available for use in derived columns, and derived columns *only*.

To illustrate the most commonly used summary function, @TOTAL, Figure 6-12 shows a Column Sort Spec and derived columns for a report that generates percentages of total products sold by salesmen within three regions. Calculations in the derived columns are based on totals taken from regular columns, and the derived columns specify their own column totals and subtotals.

Summary functions can also be used to retrieve values calculated in columns with a day, month, or yearly break. You specify this by typing the **DB**, **MB**, or **YB** date-break code after the column information in the summary function. For example, to have Q&A display the totals values produced in column 5 when the day changed, you would type:

```
@Total(#5,#4,DB)
```

Derived Column Lookup Functions

You can use lookup functions, *but not lookup statements*, in derived columns. Why? — because a lookup statement is a programming command that returns a value from a lookup table or an external database and specifies which field in the primary database is to receive the value. In a report you don't have fields, so such statements aren't valid.

On the other hand, a lookup function simply returns a value from an external database, and in a derived column you can specify that *the column* is to contain the value. Thus you can use the @LOOKUP and @XLOOKUP functions in your derived columns.

All of Q&A's lookup commands are discussed in detail in Chapter 4, and you should refer to that material to find out how to specify them and what they do.

Table 6-6
Derived Column Summary Functions

Use these in your derived column formulas to reference the results of calculations in other columns.

Function	What it does
Grand Summary Functions	
@Total(n)	Returns the grand total of values in column *n*
@Average(n)	Returns the grand average of values in column *n*
@Count(n)	Returns the total count of values in column *n*
@Minimum(n)	Returns the minimum of all values in column *n*
@Maximum(n)	Returns the maximum of all values in column *n*
@Std(n)	Returns the standard deviation of all values in column *n*
@Var(n)	Returns the variance of all values in column *n*.
Subsummary Functions	
@Total(n,m)	Returns the subtotal of values in column *n* on a break in column *m*
@Average(n,m)	Returns the average of values in column *n* on a break in column *m*
@Count(n,m)	Returns the count of values in column *n* on a break in column *m*
@Minimum(n,m)	Returns the minimum value in column *n* on a break in column *m*
@Maximum(n,m)	Returns the maximum value in column *n* on a break on column *m*
@Std(n,m)	Returns the standard deviation in column *n* on a break in column *m*
@Var(n,m)	Returns the variance in column *n* on a break on column *m*

```
Column/Sort Spec
Region: 1,AS
Salesman: 2,AS
Item: 3,AS,CS
Qty: 4,T,ST,SC,F(N0)

Derived Columns
Heading: % of Total!Items by!Salesman
Formula: #4/@Total(#4,#2)*100
Column Spec: 5,T,ST,F(N2)

Heading: % of Total!Items by!Region
Formula: #4/@Total(#4,#1)*100
Column Spec: 6,T,ST,F(N2)

Printed Report
```

Region	Salesman	Item	Qty	% of Total Items by Salesman	% of Total Items by Region
North	Falk	Blender	44	48.89	33.33
		Dryer	13	14.44	9.85
		Fan	33	36.67	25.00
	Total: Count:		90 3	100.00	68.18
	Murray	Fan	12	28.57	9.09
		Sink	12	28.57	9.09
		Washer	18	42.86	13.64
	Total: Count:		42 3	100.00	31.82
Total: Count:			132 6	200.00	100.00
South	Edwards	Blender	38	54.29	21.97
		Dryer	3	4.28	1.73
		Fan	12	17.14	6.94
		Washer	17	24.29	9.83
	Total: Count:		70 4	100.00	40.47
	Martin	Blender	9	8.74	5.20
		Fan	80	77.67	46.24
		Sink	5	4.85	2.89
		Washer	9	8.74	5.20
	Total: Count:		103 4	100.00	59.53
Total: Count:			173 8	200.00	100.00
West	Jones	Fan	17	48.57	25.00
		Sink	3	8.57	4.41
		Washer	15	42.86	22.06
	Total: Count:		35 3	100.00	51.47
	Smith	Blender	17	51.52	25.00
		Dryer	9	27.27	13.24
		Fan	7	21.21	10.29
	Total: Count:		33 3	100.00	48.53
Total: Count:			68 6	200.00	100.00
Total:			373	600.00	300.00

Figure 6-12: Sample Column/Sort and Derived Column Specs with Summary Calculations and Resulting Report.

As the @LOOKUP function returns a value from the lookup table associated with the database in which you're working, you can use it in a derived column formula to bring information from the table into the column.

The formula for an @LOOKUP function is:

@Lookup(*key, column*)

Where:

key   is the field ID# in the database of the item you're looking up in the table. In a derived column, the *key* is the Program Spec field ID#, not the numbered column in the Column/Sort Spec.

column   is the column number in the table (not the report column) that holds the value you want to retrieve. The value is always on the same row as the key's value.

When you need to include external database information in a report, use the @XLOOKUP function. Keep in mind as you design your report that it will be a product of the information in the *current* database, and only the current database, unless you create a derived column and use the @XLOOKUP command properly in the column formula.

The formula for an @XLOOKUP function is: **@xlookup(*fn, pkf, xkf, lf*)**

Where:

fn   is the name of the external database (filename) — in quote marks — from which you want to retrieve a particular value for your derived column.

pkf   is the *primary key field*, the field ID# (not the column number) in the primary or current database that has a matching value in the external file. No quotes.

xkf   is the *external key field*, the field label — in quote marks — in the external file whose values match those of the *primary key field*.

lf   is the *lookup field*, the field label — in quote marks — of the field in the external file whose values you want to retrieve into the derived column.

Suppose you have an invoice file containing the following fields (among others, of course):

```
Customer ID#:
Customer Name:
Invoice Date:
Invoice No:
Balance Due:
```

```
            At the Column/Sort Spec for INVOICE.DTF:

      Customer ID#: 3,I
          Customer Name: 1,AS
          Invoice Date: 4,AS
          Invoice No: 5
          Balance Due: 6

          Derived column:

          Heading: Telephone
          Formula: @Xlookup("Customer",#1,"Customer ID#","Telephone")
          Column Spec: 2

          Your report would look like this:

      Customer Name        Telephone   Invoice Date   Invoice No   Balance Due
      --------------       ---------   ------------   ----------   -----------
      Johnson Supply       212-435-5677  3/9/90          1255        $233.45
                           212-435-5677  3/12/90         1344        $104.40
                           212-435-5677  3/27/90         1480        $210.33

      Krager Products      415-899-1233  3/12/90         1346        $490.50
                           415-899-1233  3/30/90         1550         $99.00

      McCallister, Inc.    213-433-5678  4/2/90          1620        $233.45
                           213-433-5678  4/9/90          1730        $400.60
                           213-433-5678  4/12/90         1800        $222.22
```

Figure 6-13: Report Specs and Sample Report for Customer Follow-up on Overdue Invoices.

And a customer database that includes these fields:

Customer ID#:
Telephone:

And you want to pull a report on the 30-days-or-more outstanding (unpaid) invoices that shows the Invoice Date, the Invoice Number, the Balance Due, and the Customer Name and Telephone.

All the data for the report is in the invoice file except for the customer's phone number. But you need that in the report because you want to call the customer to find out if his check is in the mail. So you'll need a derived column with an @XLOOKUP function to pull it in from the external customer database.

After selecting at the Retrieve Spec only those invoices more than 30 days old with balances due, Figure 6-13 shows how you could set up your columns to generate a report that would group overdue invoices by customer name:

You could get fancy with this report by suppressing repetition of the phone number and specifying subtotals for overdue invoices when there's a break in the customer name, but the report used in the example gives you an idea of how the @XLOOKUP function works in a Report derived column, and how useful it can be.

More Ideas on Derived Column Reports

You're not limited to summary and lookup functions in derived columns. You can pick and choose from Q&A's built-in functions to generate a variety of report formats (see the discussion in Chapter 4 of Q&A's built-in functions).

Underlining Blank Fields in a Report

Suppose you want to create a report for the purpose of getting others to fill in missing information in a particular column when you need the data to round out your records.

Printing the report in the usual manner would give you blanks in your columns where no corresponding value in the database exists, making it hard for people to spot and thus write in the requested information.

Tip: With a little derived-column know-how, and two built-in functions, however, you can have Q&A print the report with an underscore emphasis in the "fill-in" column.

Let's assume that your personnel database contains all your employees' names, addresses, and so forth, but you're missing their titles. In the Title field at the Column/Sort Spec you'd type: **Title:8,H(20),I** (making the title the eighth column, 20 characters wide, and invisible. You'd then create your derived column as follows:

```
Heading:  20:Title
Formula:  @left(#8+@text(20,"_"),20-20*(#8<>" ")+@len(#8))
Column Spec:  9
```

The formula, an exotic @LEFT function, prints 20 underscore characters in column #9, but only where the invisible column #8 contains no entry (a blank value in that particular record).

A report like this could be passed around the office for employees to fill in missing information; sales prospectors could fill in their appointment or call-back times.

Numbering the Lines in a Report

You can set up a derived column to number your report lines sequentially:

Heading: `Line!Number`
Formula: `#1+1`
Column Spec: `1`

Resulting in a report that looks like this:

```
Line
Number   Make          Year   Cost
```
1	Chevrolet	1988	$2344.00
2	Ford	1987	$1955.00
3	Dodge	1990	$3995.00
4	Toyota	1985	$1455.00
5	Ford Pickup	1964	$980.00

Multiple Fields in a Single Column

When printing names and addresses in reports, you may want to format the information in a single column — not easy to do when the name, address, city, state, and zip may each have their own field in the corresponding database.

Tip: Figure 6-14 shows a Column/Sort Spec and two derived columns that will print the information as a block in column 1 of a report.

These specs would give you a report as follows:

```
Name/Address              Phone

Barney Morris             (313) 544-7866
Morris Pipe and Supply
21334 14th St.
Freeberg, MI 48965
```

In the first derived column 30 blank spaces are added after each field. The width of the columns is then limited to 30 characters by the second derived column, forcing the text of each field to wrap underneath on consecutive lines. Columns can be made wider or narrower by changing the value of 30 in the two derived columns to any desired column width.

For this example to work properly, the zip code must be a text field.

```
Column/Sort Spec:
First Name: 1,I            Last Name: 2,I,AS        Phone: 10
Company: 3,I
Address: 4,I
City: 5,I                  State: 6,I   Zip: 7,I

Derived Columns:
Heading:
Formula: @Text(30," ")
Column Spec: 8,I

Heading: 30:Name/Address
Formula: #1+" "+#2+#8+#3+#8+#4+#8+#5+," "+#6+" "+#7
Column Spec: 9,AS
```

Figure 6-14: Specs for a Report with Several Fields in a Single Column.

A Derived Column Report that Ages Invoice Balances

Tip: Here's a sample report specification that demonstrates how you can make database information appear in a report column only when certain conditions are present. This example generates a report of aged balances from an invoice database that contains the following fields, shown here with the Column/Sort Spec filled out:

```
Invoice Number: 2,AS,CS,H(:Invoice)
Billing Date: 3,H(:Date)
Account Name: 1,AS,H(:Account)
Balance Due: 4,I
```

The report has three columns with total amounts for invoices that are 0 to 30 days old, 31 to 60 days old, and more than 60 days old. You'll need the following three derived columns:

```
Heading: 0-30 Days
Formula: (@Date-#3<31)*#4
Column Spec: 5,ST,T

Heading: 31-60 Days
Formula: (@Date-#3>30 and @Date-#3<61)*#4
Column Spec: 6,ST,T

Heading: Over 60
```

```
      Account        Invoice   Date     0-30 Days  31-60 Days  Over 60
  ------------------  -------  --------  ---------  ----------  ---------
  The Book Nook        10222  6/15/90      $0.00       $0.00    $102.40
                       10287  7/16/90      $0.00      $65.95      $0.00
                       10344  8/21/90     $44.80       $0.00      $0.00
                       10357  8/24/90     $37.50      $00.00      $0.00
                                         ---------  ----------  ---------
      Total:                             $82.30      $65.95    $102.40

  Midwest Books        10288  7/14/90      $0.00     $234.50      $0.00
                       10319  7/17/90      $0.00     $335.44      $0.00
                       10347  8/22/90    $155.80       $0.00      $0.00
                                         ---------  ----------  ---------
      Total:                            $155.80     $569.94      $0.00
```

Figure 6-15: Using the Built-in Date Function. You can exploit the built-in date function (and other functions as well) to fashion conditional-like statements for use in derived column formulas.

Formula: (@Date-#3>60)*#4
Column Spec: 7,ST,T

The colon at the beginning of the heading in column 6 allows the heading to begin with a number.

The @DATE formulas used in the derived columns are actually statements which can be true or false depending on the difference between the current date and the invoice date. A true statement becomes a 1 when used in a formula; when multiplied by a number from a field (#4 in this case), the result is the number in that field (the invoice amount).

On the other hand, a false statement in a formula returns a zero — and when you multiply any value by zero you get zero. So the invoice amount will be 0 in the two columns (out of the three) where it doesn't belong.

A report generated with these specs will look like the one in Figure 6-15.

The sample report in Figure 6-15 shows only a portion of the output. The actual report would continue listing all the invoices selected at the Retrieve Spec, and provide column totals at the bottom.

When working with the Retrieve Spec, be sure to choose only those invoices showing a balance due. Otherwise you'll have every invoice in the database in on the game, including those paid in full months ago!

A Report that Serves as a Billing Statement

Tip: You can design a report that produces billing statements you can send to customers who haven't paid up. Assume you have the following fields in your invoice database:

CU#: (customer number)
Name: (customer name)
Addr1: (street address)
Addr2: (city, state, zip)
Invoice No: (invoice number)
Date: (invoice date)
Amount Due: (outstanding invoice amount)

At the report Retrieve Spec, tell Q&A to include in the report only those invoices showing an amount due.

Set up your Column/Sort Spec as follows:

```
CU#: 1,AS,H(!Account!Number),F(JC),P
Name: 4,I
Addr1: 5,I
Addr2: 6,I
Invoice No: 8,F(JC),H(7:Invoice!Number)
Date: 9,AS,CS,F(JR),H(10:Invoice!Date)
Amount Due: 10,ST,H(8:Balance!Due)
```

The **P** code in the CU# field tells Q&A to start a new page when the customer number changes, giving you one statement per customer. The name and address columns are invisible — use a derived column to turn them into a single report column. Sort on the Date column so the earliest invoices will appear first on the statements. In the Amount Due column you'll ask for a subtotal, which you'll get each time the CU# changes.

Assuming the widths of the name and address fields in the database are 22 characters, you'll need these two derived report columns:

```
Heading:
Formula: @text(22," ")
Column Spec: 2,I


Heading: 22:Bill to:
Formula: #4+#2+#5+#2+#6
Column Spec: 3,AS,CS
```

```
Ballen  Booksellers            ▬▬▬ STATEMENT ▬▬▬
5454 NE Winona Drive
Freemont, CA 94988                      Statement Date: Oct 9, 1990


      Account                     Invoice  Invoice  Balance
      Number         Bill to:     Number    Date     Due
      ------        -----------   -------  -------  -------
       1211    BILL SOFRIN          3349   8/19/90  $420.55
               3244 E MAIN ST
               LOS ANGELES CA 90344
                                    3444   8/25/90  $102.45
                                    3533   8/30/90  $288.47
                                    3644   9/15/90  $390.00
                                                    -------
      Total:                                        $1201.47


~~~~~~~~~~~~~~~~~~~~~~~~~~~~~~~~~~~~~~~~~~~~~~~~~~~~~~~~~~~~~~
~~~~~~~~~~~~~~~~~~~~~~~~~~~~~~~~~~~~~~~~~~~~~~~~~~~~~~~~~~~~~~

          Please remit the Total Amount Due shown above
              Deduct any invoices already paid
           Include your Account Number on your check
```

Figure 6-16: An Example of a Balance Due Statement.

You'll need a special Define Page setup, too, along the lines of the one shown here. You may need to experiment a bit depending on your printer's capabilities.

Page width: 85   Page length: 66
Left margin: 1   Right margin: 80
Top margin: 10   Bottom margin: 20
Characters per inch: 10

Header Lines: (your company name and address, etc.)

```
1: Ballen Booksellers!  ▬▬▬ STATEMENT ▬▬▬
2: 5454 NE Winona Drive!
3: Freemont, CA 94988! !Statement Date: @Date(1)
```

Footer Lines: (to print below the statement total)

```
1: !Please remit the Total Amount Due shown above
2: !Deduct any invoice amounts already paid
3: !Include your Account Number on your check
```

At the Print Options screen, tell Q&A to center the output on the page. When you print the "report" you'll get a statement for each customer with one or more invoices with a balance due — a page for each account number that will look like Figure 6-16.

Pushing the Envelope on Reports

When working with Report's derived columns keep in mind that you can return the value of a built-in function to a report column as easily as you can return the value from the same function to a database field.

This is difficult for many people to grasp. You'll find them testing and working out various complex formulas in the Field Programming Spec to enhance data entry in the File module, yet they'll shy away from using some of the same functions in derived columns, even though the variety of report formats available to them with functions is practically limitless, and the potential feedback from such reports could be tremendously useful.

For example, consider the @XLOOKUP command and the fact that you can have up to 16 derived columns in a report. Here is a level of reporting power that makes it possible not only to use the information from several databases in a single report, but to operate on that information from column to column.

Q&A Power Feature: Considering that you can embed functions within other functions, you have more tools at your fingertips to create extraordinarily informative and useful reports.

Experimenting in the Report module can be loads of fun, and once you set your mind on obtaining the report you really want, chances are that with a little persistence you'll be able work out the particulars of even the most sophisticated set of report specifications.

After all, if the information you need is in your Q&A database files or can be derived from the information in those files, it's only a matter of working out the proper specs to pull it out and format it exactly as you want to see it.

You don't even need the printer when prototyping a report. Simply print the report to your display from the Print Options screen, look it over, and go back and alter your specs as necessary until you've got it looking right. *Then* print.

Keyword Reports

You'll need to take a somewhat different approach when dealing with keyword fields in a report. Keyword fields, as discussed in Chapter 3, contain a variety of items separated by semicolons.

Remember: The keyword field has to be the first field in a keyword report, and you must also follow the report column number with a comma, and then the letter **K**.

Sports	Last Name	First Name	Ext
Baseball	Buchanan	Fred	344
	Williams	Peter	320
	Gonzales	Ernesto	144
	Jorgensen	Emily	142
Basketball	Chamberlain	Walter	220
	Buchanan	Fred	344
Football	Carswell	William	130
	Buchanan	Fred	344
	Dakota	Joe	115
Golf	Ontiveros	Gary	201
	Sasson	Sandra	402
	Dakota	Joe	115
Tennis	Sasson	Sandra	402
	Buchanan	Fred	344
	Chamberlain	Walter	220

Figure 6-17: A Keyword Report.

The **K** indicates a keyword report type. Q&A then knows that it will be dealing with multiple entries in this field and can search for the particular items you've entered at the Retrieve Spec.

The keyword capability lets you create report sections categorized according to the entries in a keyword field. Fields without keywords can also be sorted and formatted, but you must enter all the specifications in the usual manner.

Suppose you have a "sports interest" keyword field in your employee database, which, for purposes of illustration, I'll limit here to the following possible entries: football, basketball, baseball, tennis, and golf.

Further, perhaps you want to generate a report showing in which sports each employee has an interest, and you want the report sorted by type of sport, with the employee name and extension.

Here's what the included fields in your Column/Sort Spec would look like, with Figure 6-17 showing a portion of the report based on these specifications:

Last Name: 2   **First Name:** 3   **Ext:** 4
Sports: 1,K

You don't have to specify a sort on a keyword field. Q&A will automatically display the entries in ascending order.

You can further restrict which keywords will be the basis of your report. For example, if you were working up a company softball team and you wanted a keyword report that would include only those employees interested in baseball, you would type the word **baseball** at the Retrieve Spec, in the Sports keyword field. Q&A would generate a report with the names and extensions of all the employees who may be inclined to participate.

If you wanted to find everybody whose records indicated an interest in *both* tennis and golf, your Retrieve Spec parameter would be:

Sports:&tennis;golf

The **&** tells Q&A you want to include the employee records where the keyword field contains *at least* tennis *and* golf. Your report will still display keyword entries other than tennis and golf, but only from those records where the Sports field contains both tennis and golf as a minimum.

Semicolons are crucial to accurate keyword field searches. If there are no semicolons between multiple entries, Q&A will treat the entire field as one long keyword, and you won't get a decent report.

You can run an unrestricted keyword report to find which records in the database contain faulty keyword field entries — they'll stick out like sore thumbs in the printed report. You can then use Search/Update in File to edit them as necessary.

Cross-tabulated Reports

 Note: Most of the features available for the reports discussed in this section are the same as those available for standard Q&A reports covered up to this point. Familiarize yourself with these features and procedures before designing the type of report discussed here. In other words, you should know how to design an ordinary Q&A report before proceeding to the advanced material presented here.

Q&A version 4.0 added a cross-tabulate (crosstab) feature to the Report module, enabling you to generate reports that summarize information from your databases.

The term *crosstab* comes from the report's capability to present your data in a different fashion than a standard Q&A report. In an ordinary Q&A report you're working mainly with individual records, or portions of records, which make up

```
                                  Product Sold
                         _____
                                                              Total
   Sales Rep            286           386          486      Sales Amount
   _____                                                ============

   Jones              $3555.33     $6066.88   $10462.32      $20084.53
   Martin             $5068.73     $5133.44   $29928.65      $40130.82
   Scott             $10953.64     $2334.99    $7856.45      $21145.08
   Smith              $3745.09     $5099.99   $13711.87      $22556.95
   ==============     =========    ========   =========      =========

   Total Sales Amount $23322.79   $18635.30   $61959.29     $103917.38
```

Figure 6-18: A Crosstab Report. This shows the total sales for each sales rep for each product.

the *rows* of the report, and the fields in those same records which compose the *column* values. You can specify summary calculations, such as totals, subtotals, averages, and others.

In a crosstab report, the emphasis is on summary information — in fact, the entire report is a summary. The values that go into the report are taken from your database, as they are for any report, but the difference is that Q&A can cross-tabulate information across three database fields, summarize the values in the selected fields, and show you the results of any calculations you've specified.

When you design a crosstab report you specify the *row field,* the *column field,* and the *summary field.* Figure 6-18 shows a sample crosstab report that summarizes the sales of four sales reps and three products.

The sample crosstab report in Figure 6-18 looks somewhat different from a standard Q&A columnar report. It reports on four sales reps and three products: 286, 386, and 486 computer systems. There is a record in the SALES.DTF database for each individual sale. The database could also be a collection of invoices or sales orders, as each such document would reveal the salesperson, the system sold, and the dollar amount of the transaction. The following fields in that SALES.DTF file were used to produce this crosstab report:

Sales Rep: Row
Product Sold: Col
Sales Amount: Summary

The Sales Rep field has been designated as the report *row,* indicating that a listing of all the Sales Reps shown will be included, running down the left side of the report.

```
                                   Product Sold
                          ---------------------------------     Average
          Sales Rep          286       386       486         Sales Amount
          --------------------   ---------  ---------  ---------   ============
          Jones              $1777.67  $3033.44  $5231.16       $3347.42
          Martin             $1689.58  $2566.72  $5985.73       $4013.08
          Scott              $1564.81  $2334.99  $7856.45       $2349.45
          Smith              $1248.36  $2550.00  $4570.62       $2819.62
          ====================  ========  =========  ========   ============
          Average Sales Amount  $1554.85  $2662.19  $5632.66       $3149.01
```

Figure 6-19: The Crosstab Report in Figure 6-18. Here the averages, instead of totals, are specified.

The Product Sold field is designated as the *column* so that each of the different values in this field will be displayed as a report column under the column title, Product Sold.

Q&A has been instructed to generate the report's summary on the Sales Amount field, the field that contains the information that interests you the most.

So the result is a cross-tabulated summary report showing the performance of each salesperson *by product*. If you didn't need to see a summary by product, you could create a standard columnar report to show the total overall sales by salesperson. The crosstab feature makes it possible to summarize information across *three* database fields.

In a crosstab report, Q&A defaults to providing totals. But you can also specify average sales by product, a count of sales by product, the minimum or maximum sales by product, and so forth. If the Sales Amount field is specified as **Sales Amount: Summary, A** where **A** indicates *average*, and we keep our Sales Rep and Product Sold fields as they are, Q&A will produce the report in Figure 6-19.

As you can see in Figure 6-19, the crosstab report now shows us the average dollar sale amount cross-tabulated by salesperson and product. You can easily determine the average amount Jones and the others are getting for each of the three computer systems, what the overall average is per sale, and what the overall average is per sale by product.

If you want to generate a report that would summarize sales by total dollar amount and average dollar amount, and simultaneously show a *count* of the transactions by product and salesperson, your summary field would contain the

```
                            Product Sold
                   -------------------------------
Sales   Rep      286          386          486        Sales Amount
-----   ---   ---------    ---------    ---------      ============
Jones   Avg   $1777.67     $3033.44     $5231.16      $3347.42
        Tot   $3555.33     $6066.88     $10462.32     $20084.53
        Cnt   2            2            2             6

Martin  Avg   $1689.58     $2566.72     $5985.73      $4013.08
        Tot   $5068.73     $5133.44     $29928.65     $40130.82
        Cnt   3            2            5             10

Scott   Avg   $1564.81     $2334.99     $7856.45      $2349.45
        Tot   $10953.64    $2334.99     $7856.45      $21145.08
        Cnt   7            1            1             9

Smith   Avg   $1248.36     $2550.00     $4570.62      $2819.62
        Tot   $3745.09     $5099.99     $13711.87     $22556.95
        Cnt   3            2            3             8
======  ===   =========    =========    =========     ============
Sales   Avg   $1554.85     $2662.19     $5632.66      $3149.01
Amount  Tot   $23322.79    $18635.30    $61959.29     $103917.38
        Cnt   15           7            11            33
```

Figure 6-20: A Combination Crosstab Report that Shows Totals, Averages, and Counts.

codes **Sales Amount: Summary, A, T, C** where **A** tells Q&A to average the transaction amounts, **T** specifies totals in addition to averages, and **C** indicates that you want counts cross-tabulated, too.

Figure 6-20 shows this combination crosstab report.

The report in Figure 6-20 is a treasure trove of information. It provides a number of criteria by which you can evaluate the performance of the sales staff and make decisions on where you need to focus your marketing efforts. For example:

- More 286 systems are being sold than the others, and it looks like Scott is pushing them.

- Martin has sold more 486 systems than the other sales reps, and his dollar volume and average sales amount are the highest.

- Most of the company's revenue is coming from sales of 486 systems, but more individual 286 systems are being sold than either 386 or 486 systems.

- Revenues during the period covered by the report were $103,917.38 on sales of 33 computer systems, with an average sales amount of $3,149.01.

Much more can be gleaned from the crosstab report in Figure 6-20, but you get the idea.

Because crosstab reports derive their information from three database fields, one of each of which you designate as the *row* field, the *column* field, and the *summary* field (although a summary field can also be a row or column field), you can describe what you want in the report along the following lines:

- I want the **total sales** for each **sales rep** for each **product**, where the database includes a sales amount field (summary), a sales rep field (row), and a product field (column).

- I need to compare the **total salaries** for each **department** for each **sex** (male/female), where the database includes a salary field (summary), a department field (row), and a sex field (column).

- Show me the **total value at cost** for each **inventory item** for each **category of product**, where the database contains fields for inventory item (row), product category (column), and the total value at cost (summary) would be *derived* from the quantity in stock and unit cost fields (yes, you can use derived columns in crosstab reports).

Terminology

Using the sample report in Figure 6-20, the following terminology applies to crosstab reports:

- Column and row *titles*: Product Sold is the column title, and Sales Rep is the row title.

- Column and row *headings*: 286, 386, and 486 are the column headings, and Jones, Martin, Scott, and Smith are the row headings.

- The report *results* are the values computed by the report process and displayed at the intersections of row headings and column headings.

- The *summary column* is the last column of the report. In Figure 6-20 the summary column contains three summary values.

- The *summary row* is the last row of the report. In Figure 6-20 the summary row contains three summary values.

Defining a Crosstab Report

Designing a crosstab report is similar to designing a standard columnar report with a few exceptions. Instead of working with a Column/Sort Spec, you enter your specifications at the Crosstab Spec. The two specs look alike on screen (the data entry form for the database is displayed), and you fill them out in a similar fashion (typing in your report specifications, such as formatting, header, and calculation codes in the selected fields).

At the Crosstab Spec, however, you don't number your columns, you specify the *row field,* the *column field,* and the *summary field* — a crosstab report can display a maximum of three fields.

Here's the procedure for designing a simple crosstab report. (A more detailed explanation of the available options follows this outline of the procedure).

1. At the Report menu select Design/Redesign a Report and press **<Enter>**.

2. Enter the name of the database from which the report will draw its information.

3. At the List of Reports, assign a descriptive name to the report (up to 30 characters) and press **<Enter>**.

4. At the Report Type screen, select Crosstab and press **<Enter>**.

5. Fill in the Retrieve Spec to tell Q&A which forms to include in the report, and then press **<F10>**.

6. At the Crosstab Spec, type **R** or **ROW** into one field whose values you want to display as report rows; type **C** or **COL** into one field whose values you want to display as report columns; and type **S** or **SUMMARY** into the one field on which you want the report to be summarized. To suppress the printed display of the summary column or summary row, type **NS** into the COL or ROW field. You can optionally enter the same formatting, alternate heading, and summary calculation codes that are available with standard Q&A reports. You can also press **<F8>** for the Derived Column screen, and include a derived column as a row, column, or summary field. Press **<F10>** when finished. (Because columns are displayed across the page, and report *width* is usually more confining than length, you might want to keep this in mind when specifying which field values will generate the rows and which will produce the columns of the report.)

7. At the Crosstab Grouping Spec tell Q&A how to group the rows and columns. For example, if Salary is specified as a row or column field at the Crosstab Spec, you'll get a row or column in the report for every unique salary value in the database, making the report unreadable. The same thing would occur on date fields or other fields where there are numerous unique values. The Grouping Spec allows you to specify ranges of salaries and other grouping functions (more on these later in this chapter) that serve to contain or control the report output. Press **<F10>** when you've filled out the Grouping Spec.

8. You are now at the Print Options screen, and from here you can optionally press **<F8>** for the Define Page screen. Press **<F10>** from either screen to have Q&A save your report design and ask if you'd like to print the report.

9. Answer Yes to print the report, or No to return to the Report menu.

The Crosstab Spec

Filling out a Crosstab Spec is similar to filling out the Column/Sort Spec, and most of the options available for standard reports are available for crosstab output as well.

The major differences are:

- In a crosstab report you select only three database fields: the row, column, and summary fields. A summary field can also be a row or column field. Derived columns can be included, but you can still have only one row, one column, and one summary field in the printed report.

- Q&A is preset to display your row field and column field values in ascending order. If you want either displayed in *descending* order, you specify this by typing a comma, and then **DS** after the ROW or COL designation.

Making the Row or Column Field also the Summary Field

The summary field can be the same as either the column or row field. You specify this by typing **S** (for Summary) following the ROW or COL in the appropriate field. For example, if you want to determine the count of employees (in an employee database) for each sex (male/female) for each department, and sex was to be the crosstab column title, type **Sex: Col, Summary** (or **C, S**) in that field at the Crosstab Spec.

Table 6-7
Crosstab Report Default Summary Field Calculations

Info Type	Q&A will Calculate
Text	Count
Number	Total
Money	Total
Keyword	Count
Date	Count
Hours	Count
Yes/No	Count

Field Information Types and Calculations in Crosstab Reports

If you don't specify a summary calculation in the summary field at the Crosstab Spec, Q&A will determine the information type of the field's values from the database Format Spec and default to the summary calculations in Table 6-7.

All the calculation codes available for standard reports are available for crosstab reports as well. These are shown in Table 6-8.

You can specify more than one summary calculation code in the summary field. This was done in the report shown in Figure 6-20. Enter your calculation codes, separating each with a comma.

For example, **Sales Amount: Summary,A,T,C** calls for the summary average, total, and count to be computed and displayed in the report.

Formatting Crosstab Reports

You specify your report display formatting codes in exactly the same way as at the Column/Sort Spec for standard Q&A reports: by enclosing any of the codes in Table 6-9 in parentheses following an **F** for format. Where no formatting is specified, Q&A defaults to the formats as specified at the Format Spec and Global Format Options screens.

Table 6-8
Crosstab Report Calculation Codes You
Can Specify in the Summary Field

Code	Calculation Type
T	Total
A	Average
C	Count
MIN	Minimum
MAX	Maximum
STD	Standard Deviation
VAR	Variance

For example, to right-justify the row field (Sales Rep) in Figure 6-19 and display the entries in all capital letters, type **Sales Rep: Row,F(U,JR)**.

When used in the row or column field, formatting codes apply only to the values which appear as headings, not to the row or column titles. When used in the summary field, formatting codes apply to the computed summary values.

Alternate Row and Column Titles and Widths

As with standard Q&A reports, you can use the **H** code to assign alternate headings and column widths. Alternate headings replace the default field label for the row or column title. For example, if you want to change the Sales Rep row in Figure 6-18 to "Rep," and limit it to 8 characters, type **Sales Rep: R,H(8:Rep)** in the field at the Crosstab Spec and Q&A will truncate any salesperson names longer than 8 characters.

Alternate headings can also be split across two or three lines with the **!** command. For example:

```
Sales Rep: R,H(9:Jones Mfg!Marketing!Field Rep)
```

yields a row title split onto three lines, and a row width of 9 character columns.

An alternate heading for the summary field will be used as headings for the summary column and summary row, the last column and row of the report. Where no alternate heading for the summary field is specified, the summary calculation (Total, Average, Count, etc.) will be printed.

Table 6-9
Formatting Codes

Formatting codes are to be typed
between parentheses following the **F** code

Code	Report Display Format
JR	Justify right (automatic for number and money fields)
JL	Justify left (automatic for text fields)
JC	Justify center
U	All uppercase letters
I	Initial capital letters
L	All lowercase letters
C	Print numbers with commas (automatic in money fields)
WC	Print numbers *and* money values with *no* commas
D*n*	Use date format *n* from the Global Format Options screen
H*n*	Use hour format *n* from the Global Format Options screen
N*n*	Prints the number with *n* decimal digits (0-7)
M	Treats the value as money
T	Treats the value as text

Adding a Scale to Your Crosstab Report Values

If your crosstab report will contain extremely large numbers, you may need to scale them down one or more orders of magnitude. You can enter a Scale command in the row, column, or summary field at the Crosstab Spec to bring the report into proportion for the sake of readability.

The formula for the Scale command is: **Scale(n),** where *n* is the number of units or order of magnitude in which the values are to be represented in the report. You can abbreviate the Scale command as **S,** but you must follow it by a positive or negative number in parentheses.

For example, if you wanted to represent 500000 as 500, you'd type **Scale(1000)** in the appropriate field to indicate that the values are to appear in units of a thousand. In this instance you'd probably want to explain the report's scale in a header at the Define Page screen to avoid confusion among those who will read the report.

Keywords in Crosstab Reports

If the row or column field in a crosstab report is a keyword field, Q&A will automatically group according to the individual keywords.

Keywords are treated as they are in a standard report — Q&A sees multiple keyword entries as if they were in separate records in the database.

Suppose you want a crosstab keyword report for an employee database to show a correlation between sports interests and department. The Crosstab Spec:

```
Department:  Col,Summary
Sports:  Row
```

will yield a report that looks like the one in Figure 6-21.

Crosstab Report Derived Fields

You can press **<F8>** from the Crosstab Spec to define any derived fields you want to include in your report. The Derived Spec screen is similar to the Derived Column screen for standard Q&A reports except that you have only three available fields. One of these can be the column field, another the row field, and another the summary field.

If you make a derived field a row, then you can't have another row field elsewhere for the current report. The same holds true for column and summary fields. You can specify only one of each per crosstab report.

The procedure for defining a derived field is discussed in detail in the previous section on standard report derived columns, and you should refer to that before attempting to create any crosstab derived fields.

Briefly, type your text for the column, row, or summary field heading at the Heading line; type the derived field formula (arithmetic, @LOOKUP, @XLOOKUP, or other built-in function) on the Formula line; and then enter the field's specifications on the Crosstab Spec line, which would include specifying whether the field is to be the row, column, or summary field, and any calculations, special formatting, etc. that you want.

In a crosstab derived field, you cannot manipulate the column directly, but you *can* manipulate fields which, although they're not included in the report, *are* in the database.

```
                         Department
                  --------------------------------
Sports            Sales  Acct   Prod   R&D  Admin  Count
-----------       -----  -----  ----   ----  -----  =====
Tennis              1      2      1      3     2      9
Golf                4      1      0      2     1      8
Baseball            3      1      9      0     2     15
Skiing              2      5      0      0     4     11
===========       =====  =====  ====   ====  ====   =====
Count              10      9     10      5     9     43
```

Figure 6-21: A Simple Crosstab Keyword Report. This shows a count of the people in each company department interested in a particular sport.

To do this, move to the fields at the Crosstab Spec whose data you want to use in the report, and type unique numbers (1, 2, 3, etc.) in each of them. You can then use those numbers in your derived field formula (#1+#2, for example). This is identical to defining a column as invisible in a standard columnar report for the purpose of using its data in a derived column.

The numbers you type in the fields whose values you want to use for your derived field, however, have no affect on where the columns or rows are placed in the report, or on any sorting order. They are strictly for use in crosstab derived field formulas.

Viewing Report Results as Percentages

If you've requested a total or count summary calculation for your crosstab report — or if either of these are the default — you need not create a derived field to view report values additionally as percentages. At the crosstab Print Options screen you can tell Q&A to display report results as straight numbers (the default), as a percent of the total, as a percent of the row, as a percent of the column, or normalized (above or below average). This saves you the trouble of redesigning the report when you simply want to view the same data from a different angle.

See the Print Options section later in this chapter for more details on choosing these alternative views of report results.

```
                                Salary
                   ----------------------------------------
Department    <$20000   >=$20000..<$30000   >=$30000   Count
----------    -------   -----------------   --------   =====
Accounting       2              1               1        4
Engineering      1              3               2        6
Marketing        2              3               3        8
Production       8              4               2       14
Purchasing       1              1               1        3
===========   ========   =================   ========   =====
Count           14             12               9       35
```

Figure 6-22: A Summary Report of Salary Ranges by Department.

The Grouping Spec

Unless you group your crosstab data by ranges, months, years, intervals, letters of the alphabet, or some other grouping arrangement, your report will print a row for every unique database value in the row field, and a column for every unique database value in the column field.

If you're looking for summaries by department, and there are only ten departments in the company, you won't run into trouble.

But if you're after summary figures on salaries, for example, and the salary field in your database contains a hundred *different* salary values — well, you can see what you'd be up against. You have a maximum of only 50 columns in a report, and, besides, what point would there be in producing a summary of each unique salary value?

 Q&A Power Feature: The crosstab Grouping Spec (see Figure 6-23), which you see after pressing **<F10>** from either the Crosstab Spec or the Derived Column Spec, allows you to enter your ranges or other grouping criteria so that your report will reflect the data you need to see, and to organize it in a sensible summary style.

Suppose you wanted to see a count of employees by specific salary ranges by department. the Crosstab Spec could be as simple as the following to produce the report in Figure 6-22:

Department: R,S,F(JC)

Salary: C

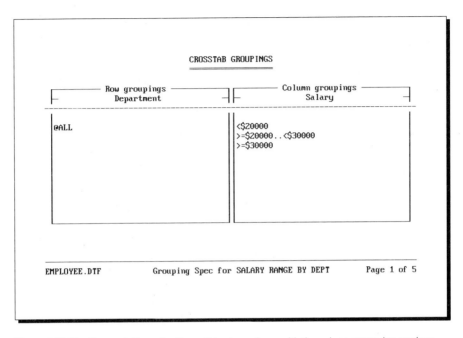

CROSSTAB GROUPINGS

Row groupings ——————— Column groupings ———
Department   Salary

@ALL

<$20000
>=$20000..<$30000
>=$30000

EMPLOYEE.DTF   Grouping Spec for SALARY RANGE BY DEPT   Page 1 of 5

Figure 6-23: The Crosstab Grouping Spec. It is shown here with the values entered to produce the report in Figure 6-22.

If you don't specify the *range* of salaries you want to see in the report columns, Q&A will print a column for every unique salary in the database. But that's not what you want — you want a report that looks like the one in Figure 6-22.

In the Figure 6-22 report, we're asking Q&A for a count of the employees, by department, who make under $20,000 per year, those who make between $20,000 and $29,999.99 per year, and those who make $30,000 or more per year. We've also specified a center-justified format for the report rows so the numbers won't appear at the extreme right edge of the columns, as number and money values will, by default.

The ranges here have been assigned at the Grouping Spec shown in Figure 6-23. Department is the row field, and we've typed **@ALL** to tell Q&A to include all the departments in the company. Salary is the column field as well as the summary field, and we've typed in the ranges desired. These ranges will serve both as the column headings and as the parameters by which Q&A will calculate the column entries. The ranges look like they belong in a Retrieve Spec, but they serve a different purpose here — they *group* the values as you want to see them presented in the report; they *do not* determine what forms will be included in the report.

If you want a count of employees in the same salary ranges for Accounting and Manufacturing only, instead of **@ALL** in the row field (the left side of the screen), type

```
Accounting
Manufacturing
```

in the first two lines under Row Groupings. The Row Groupings correspond to the row field (Department, in this case) of the report, and the Column Groupings correspond to the column field (Salary ranges). Again, you're not filling out a Retrieve Spec here, you're merely telling Q&A to group Accounting and Manufacturing and display only these departments in the report.

The Crosstab Grouping Spec gives you ten lines per page, and five screen pages. Thus you can enter up to 50 separate grouping parameters for both row groupings and column groupings.

If you need more space for an entry, press **<F6>** to expand the field. You'll then have enough room for up to 240 characters.

Built-in Grouping Functions

To make grouping values easier, you can use the predefined grouping functions which are summarized in Table 6-10. These aren't the same as programming functions that return values to columns or database fields; Q&A uses them internally to group data according to your specifications. You're not limited to one of these grouping functions per row or column. You can enter multiple groupings in the fields of the spec.

When you fill out your Grouping Spec and press **<F10>**, Q&A takes you to the Report Print Options screen. From here you can optionally press **<F8>** to set your page parameters and then go ahead and print the report.

Defining your report's page characteristics and selecting the appropriate printing options are similar to printing from both Write and File, but the differences are enough to make a separate discussion of these procedures worthwhile — they'll be covered in more detail in a subsequent discussion.

Before you print your report, however, you may want to take advantage of the Q&A version 4.0 feature that allows you to select among a variety of enhancements to dress up your output. Depending on the capabilities of your printer, you can embellish portions of your reports (or the entire report) with boldface, italics, and even different fonts.

For standard Q&A reports, you add your enhancements at the Column/Sort Spec. For crosstab reports, you do it at the Crosstab Spec.

An appropriately enhanced report can be more eye-catching, more readable, and can help you present your data (and emphasis) more clearly.

Table 6-10
Grouping Functions Available for Use at
the Crosstab Grouping Spec

Function	Purpose
@ALL	Includes each unique value of the row or column field as a row or column heading.
@ALPHA	Groups data by the first letter of the value, A through Z. The letter is automatically capitalized in the report and is followed by two dots.
@RANGE(*x,y,z*)	Groups data into a set of predefined ranges where *x* is the number that starts the range, *y* is the size of the interval, and *z* is the number of intervals. For example, if you wanted to group salaries into 15 intervals of $5000 each, your range grouping specification would be: **@Range(0,5000,15).** This saves you from having to type all 15 ranges at the Grouping Spec. **@RANGE** can be abbreviated as **@R.**
@INTERVAL(*n*)	Groups data into *n* number of intervals or ranges of equal span, where the range is determined automatically by Q&A. Use **@INTERVAL** (abbreviated **@I**) instead of @RANGE when you want range groupings but don't know the minimum and maximum values in the field. If you don't specify the *n* parameter, Q&A will attempt to compute an "ideal" set of 8 to 12 equally sized ranges between the highest and lowest field values in the database.
@DAY	Groups data by day of the year. Since a day is the smallest component of a date, the @ALL function will work just as well.

(continued)

Table 6-10 *(continued)*

Function	Purpose
@DOW	Groups data by days of the week, producing a maximum of seven groupings. For example, all Mondays would be grouped, no matter the month or year. Q&A abbreviates the days of the week as necessary to make the report fit on the page.
@DOM	Groups data by days of the month, producing a maximum of 31 groups. The first days of any month are grouped, the second days of any month are the next group, and so forth, regardless of the month or year.
@MONTH	Groups data by months, producing a different grouping for each month of each year for which there is data in the answer set. Q&A abbreviates the months as necessary to make the report fit on the page.
@MOY	Groups data by months of the year (regardless of the year), producing a maximum of 12 groups. Q&A will abbreviate the months as necessary to make the report fit on the page.
@YEAR	Groups data by years. As many groupings are produced as there are different years in the answer set. Q&A will abbreviate the years to the last two digits as necessary to make the report fit on the page.

Enhancing Your Q&A Reports

Version 4.0

New: Fonts and other enhancements can be assigned to your Q&A reports at any of the following screens:

- Standard Column/Sort and Derived Columns Specs.
- Crosstab and Derived Fields Specs for crosstab reports.
- Print Options screen, Printer Control Codes line.
- Define Page screen header and footer lines.
- Global Set Column/Heading Widths screen.

Making fonts *available* for use in your reports is one thing. The process of actually using them in the report is quite another.

Q&A ordinarily creates enhancements such as bold, italics, underline, superscript, subscript, and strikeout when you select these at any enhancement menu (see Figure 6-24). But in order to use a particular *font* other than the default font in your report, you must first install that font. So the following three steps are involved.

1. If you haven't already done so, install your printer in Q&A as discussed in Chapter 1.

2. In the Report module, at any of the screens except the Retrieve Spec and Print Options screen, press **<Shift><F6>** for the Enhancement menu, and select **A** for Assign Fonts. With the cursor in the Font File Name field, press **<Enter>** to see a list of available font files for your printer, highlight the one you want, and press **<Enter>**. You can now install your default font and up to eight additional fonts. When you've installed all the fonts for use in your reports, you can press **<F8>** to make this Font Assignments screen the default for all new reports, or press **<F10>** to make the fonts available for the current report only.

3. During Report Design/Redesign, at any of the screens except the Retrieve Spec and Print Options screen, press **<Shift><F6>** for the Enhancement menu, and select the font you want to use. Highlight the portion of the report you want enhanced by moving the highlight bar over the appropriate codes, and press **<F10>** to confirm the enhancement.

Installing fonts at the Font Assignments screen in Report (see Figure 6-25) is identical to the procedure discussed in detail in the section on installing and using fonts in the Write module, in Chapter 2. Even though you may have already installed your fonts for Write documents, you'll need to repeat the process if you want to have fonts available for use in reports. Chances are,

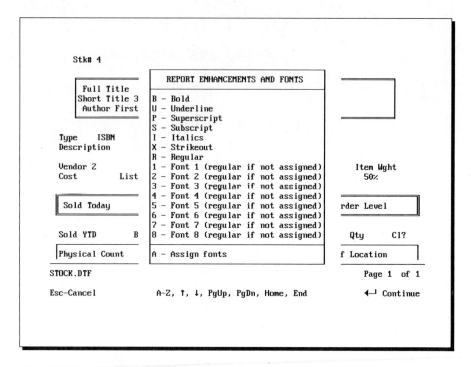

```
        Stk# 4

          ┌─────────────┐ ┌──────────────────────────────────┐ ┌──────────────┐
          │  Full Title │ │    REPORT ENHANCEMENTS AND FONTS  │ │              │
          │ Short Title 3│ │B - Bold                          │ │              │
          │ Author First│ │U - Underline                     │ │              │
          └─────────────┘ │P - Superscript                   │ └──────────────┘
                          │S - Subscript                     │
    Type     ISBN         │I - Italics                       │
    Description           │X - Strikeout                     │
                          │R - Regular                       │
    Vendor 2              │1 - Font 1 (regular if not assigned)│   Item Wght
    Cost         List     │2 - Font 2 (regular if not assigned)│    50%
                          │3 - Font 3 (regular if not assigned)│
                          │4 - Font 4 (regular if not assigned)│
     ┌─────────────┐      │5 - Font 5 (regular if not assigned)│ rder Level
     │ Sold Today  │      │6 - Font 6 (regular if not assigned)│
     └─────────────┘      │7 - Font 7 (regular if not assigned)│
    Sold YTD      B       │8 - Font 8 (regular if not assigned)│    Qty    Cl?
     ┌──────────────┐     │A - Assign fonts                  │ f Location
     │Physical Count│     └──────────────────────────────────┘
     └──────────────┘
    STOCK.DTF                                                     Page 1  of 1

    Esc-Cancel           A-Z, ↑, ↓, PgUp, PgDn, Home, End        ↵ Continue
```

Figure 6-24: Report's Enhancement Menu. You can select Bold, Underline, Superscript, Subscript, Italics, and Strikeout enhancements for your reports without having to install fonts at the Font Assignments screen. If you want to "font" your report, however, the fonts you use must be installed.

however, that you'll want to draw from the same set of fonts for all future reports. If so, then you'll only need to fill out the Font Assignments screen in Report once, and by pressing **<F8>** can make the screen the default for all future reports.

Notice in Figure 6-24 that you can select both enhancements and assigned fonts for your reports from the same menu. Ordinary enhancements (bold, italic, etc.) are built in — Q&A will create the enhancement for you when you select it from this menu. But you can't select a font for your report unless that font has been installed at the Font Assignment screen.

For example, if the default internal font for your printer is Courier 10, you can't select Courier 12 unless your printer supports that font and it's been properly installed at the Font Assignments screen as a font selection. When a selected font isn't available, Q&A will use your printer's default internal font.

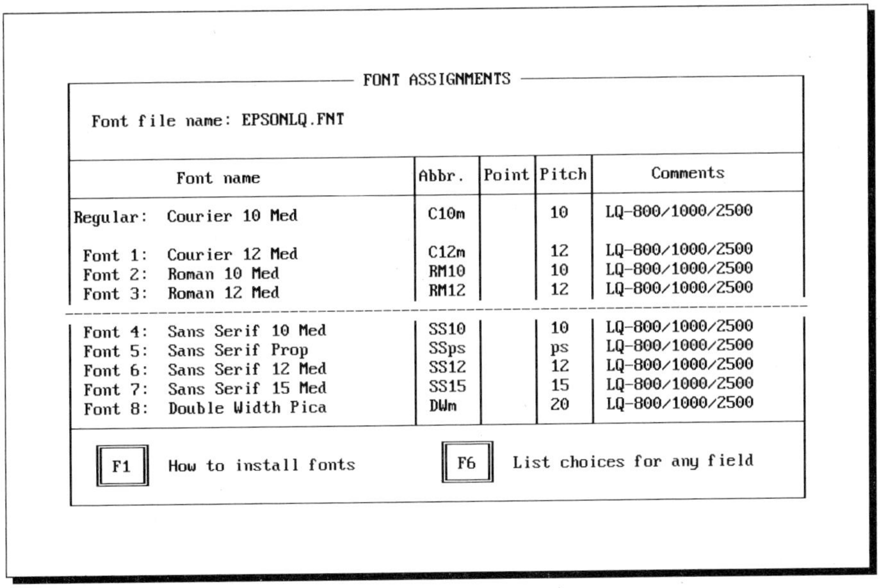

```
┌──────────────────────────────────────────────────────────────────┐
│                                                                    │
│  ┌─────────────────── FONT ASSIGNMENTS ────────────────────────┐  │
│  │                                                              │  │
│  │   Font file name: EPSONLQ.FNT                                │  │
│  │  ┌─────────────────────────────┬─────┬─────┬─────┬────────┐ │  │
│  │  │          Font name           │Abbr.│Point│Pitch│Comments│ │  │
│  │  ├─────────────────────────────┼─────┼─────┼─────┼────────┤ │  │
│  │  │ Regular:  Courier 10 Med     │C10m │     │ 10  │LQ-800/1000/2500│ │  │
│  │  │                              │     │     │     │        │ │  │
│  │  │ Font 1:   Courier 12 Med     │C12m │     │ 12  │LQ-800/1000/2500│ │  │
│  │  │ Font 2:   Roman 10 Med       │RM10 │     │ 10  │LQ-800/1000/2500│ │  │
│  │  │ Font 3:   Roman 12 Med       │RM12 │     │ 12  │LQ-800/1000/2500│ │  │
│  │  ├─ ─ ─ ─ ─ ─ ─ ─ ─ ─ ─ ─ ─ ─ ─ ─ ─ ─ ─ ─ ─ ─ ─ ─ ─ ─ ─ ┤ │  │
│  │  │ Font 4:   Sans Serif 10 Med  │SS10 │     │ 10  │LQ-800/1000/2500│ │  │
│  │  │ Font 5:   Sans Serif Prop    │SSps │     │ ps  │LQ-800/1000/2500│ │  │
│  │  │ Font 6:   Sans Serif 12 Med  │SS12 │     │ 12  │LQ-800/1000/2500│ │  │
│  │  │ Font 7:   Sans Serif 15 Med  │SS15 │     │ 15  │LQ-800/1000/2500│ │  │
│  │  │ Font 8:   Double Width Pica  │DWm  │     │ 20  │LQ-800/1000/2500│ │  │
│  │  └─────────────────────────────┴─────┴─────┴─────┴────────┘ │  │
│  │                                                              │  │
│  │   ┌────┐                        ┌────┐                       │  │
│  │   │ F1 │ How to install fonts   │ F6 │ List choices for any field │  │
│  │   └────┘                        └────┘                       │  │
│  └──────────────────────────────────────────────────────────────┘  │
│                                                                    │
└──────────────────────────────────────────────────────────────────┘
```

Figure 6-25: The Font Assignments Screen. Press **A** from the enhancement menu to install and assign up to nine fonts for use in reports. The "Font File Name" is the printer driver or Font Description File that comes with Q&A, and contains the information that tells Q&A how to use the fonts. Font files can hold dozens, even hundreds, of font descriptions.

This becomes clear once you grasp the difference between a simple *enhancement* and a *font*. As long as your printer supports text enhancements such as bold and italics, you don't need to install these as fonts at the Font Assignments screen — Q&A will create them for you.

Fonts, on the other hand, *must* be installed at the Font Assignments screen if you want to make use of them in your reports. Moreover, Q&A doesn't supply the fonts themselves, only the *Font Description Files* that tell Q&A how to use the fonts.

Most printers contain a variety of internal fonts that you can install as alternate font selections. You can also purchase fonts in the form of font cartridges that plug into your printer — or soft fonts that you download to your printer prior to starting Q&A.

Figure 6-25 shows a sample Font Assignments screen with installed fonts for the Epson LQ series of dot-matrix printers.

Font assignments are saved with each report when you press **<F10>**. Pressing **<F8>** from the Font Assignments screen makes the same set of fonts available for all future reports in addition to the current one.

The steps you follow to select an enhancement or font for your report, and the portion of the report affected, varies depending on where you are in the report design process, as well the type of report you're creating. Let's look at each of the screens in Report from which you can access the enhancement menu and the procedure you use for assigning the available enhancements to portions of your report.

Enhancing at Column/Sort and Crosstab Specs

During the report design process most of the action takes place at the Column/Sort Spec for standard columnar reports, and at the Crosstab Spec for crosstab reports. Also, you designate most of your report enhancements at these screens. Unless otherwise noted, the procedure for enhancing either type of report is the same, and in this context I'll use the Column/Sort Spec to show you the steps involved.

To add enhancements to your report:

1. Be sure the Column/Sort Spec is displayed and filled in for the report you're designing.

2. Move the cursor to the field that contains the code representing the report information you want to enhance.

3. Position the cursor beneath the code whose enhancement will be reflected in the printed report.

4. Press **<Shift><F6>** for the Enhancement menu shown in Figure 6-23, press the letter or number of the enhancement you want, or highlight it and press **<Enter>**. You'll notice that the code corresponding to the cursor position is now highlighted.

5. Use the right arrow key to extend the highlight to include other portions of the report you want in the same enhancement (see the next section for an example of the codes that can be enhanced, and what enhancing them does for the printed report).

6. When you've highlighted all the codes you want enhanced in that particular field, press **<F10>**.

7. Repeat steps 2 through 5 for other fields that contain codes for report information you want to enhance.

An Example of Enhancing Codes at the Column/Sort Spec

Here's an example of a series of codes typed in a field at the Column/Sort Spec:

```
1,AS,C,CL(Grand Count),T,TL,H(15:Cost x Count)
```

These codes specify that this is the first column in the report, the column values are to be sorted in ascending order, the entries in the column are to be counted and totaled, the count and total labels are to be printed as "Grand Count" and "Grand Total," respectively, at the bottom of the report, and the column is to be headed "Cost 3 Count."

- When the **1** is enhanced, Q&A prints the values in the column (and only the values) in the selected enhancement. It does not enhance any calculation codes, headings, or any other portion of the report.

- Highlighting the **AS** does nothing, since there is no text associated with sorting criteria. You can highlight it, but when you press **<F10>** the enhancement will be stripped.

- Highlighting the **C** makes the Count data value (the actual count of the column entries) come out in the enhancement. The label, "Grand Count," will *not* be enhanced.

- Highlighting the **CL** where it is *not* followed by a new label in parentheses enhances the report label "Count." Where the **CL** *is* followed by a new label in parentheses, highlighting the **CL** by itself does nothing, whereas highlighting the text in parentheses (**Grand Count**) enhances this user-defined label in the printed report.

- Highlighting the **T** code enhances the data on the "Total" line at the bottom of the report, but not the "Total" label.

- Because it is not followed by a user-defined label in parentheses, highlighting the **TL** code enhances the label "Total." By highlighting both the **T** and the **TL**, the label *and* the data appear in the printed report in the selected enhancement. Thus if you're not defining a new label, yet you want the default label to appear in the enhancement, you must type **TL** in the field and then enhance it. Without the label code there's no way to tell Q&A you want the label enhanced. See Table 6-5 for a summary of report label codes.

- Highlighting the user-defined column heading inside the parentheses selects it for enhancement. You enhance a user-defined heading letter by letter. If you want the entire heading to appear in the enhancement, highlight all the characters in it. If you want to enhance a Q&A default column heading (the field label), type **H** in the field with no parentheses following it, and then enhance the **H**.

Tip: When enhancing only certain portions of the report forces you to skip the codes in between:

1. Position the cursor at the first code that corresponds to the portion of the report you want highlighted.

2. Press **<Shift><F6>** for the Enhancement menu, and then press the letter or number of the enhancement you want.

3. Use the right arrow key to move the highlight bar over the relevant code or codes.

4. Press **<F10>** to confirm the enhancement.

5. Now move the cursor to the *next* code in the field to be enhanced and return to step 2.

6. Repeat this procedure until only the appropriate codes are enhanced (the others remain unenhanced).

7. To remove an enhancement, start with step 1, and select Regular from the Enhancement menu.

In the following series of report codes typed in a field at the Column/Sort Spec:

```
1,AS,C,CL(Grand Count),T,TL,H(15:Cost x Count)
```

the only items that will be enhanced in the printed report (shown here in boldface) are the Count data, the Grand Count label, and the Cost 3 Count column heading. The column data, the Total data, and the Total label have not been enhanced.

You can select any number of enhancements or fonts within a single field at the Column/Sort Spec. For example, you can italicize the column data, underline the Count label, embolden the Total data *and* label, and print the column heading in a special font.

If you want the entire report printed in the same font or enhancement, use the Printer Control Codes line at the Print Options screen (see the section on Print Options in this chapter) or make the enhancement your "regular" font at the Font Assignments screen. To enhance report headers and/or footers, use the Define Page screen (see the section in this chapter on the Define Page screen).

The procedure for adding enhancements to derived columns is virtually the same as at the Column/Sort Spec. However, enhancing anything in the formula field will accomplish nothing. You can enhance only the Column Heading, as well as any relevant codes in the Column Spec field.

In crosstab reports you can enhance the Row, Column, and/or Summary field codes (**R, C,** and **S**) and thereby enhance the data in these areas of the reports. You can add enhancements to any user-defined headings, labels, titles, headers, and footers.

You can also apply enhancements at the Grouping Spec. When you enhance any of the predefined grouping functions, all rows or columns pertaining to that particular grouping will print with the enhancement. If you want to enhance only *selected* rows or columns within a group, type their values, precede each of them with % and apply the enhancement to them. This tells Q&A to enhance only *those* values in the Grouping Spec.

Enhancements will not display when printing a report to screen. But you can select Page Preview at the Print Options screen to get a WYSIWYG view of the output — a real time-saver when you're not sure if the printed output will be up to your standards. By previewing the report you can see it as it will appear on the printed page with all enhancements intact. You can then return to the Column/Sort or Crosstab Spec, change your specifications, and preview the report once more to make sure everything looks as it should.

Redesigning a Report

Chances are you'll need to redesign certain reports, especially right after you've run them for the first time. The more complex your report specifications, the greater the likelihood that you'll want to modify certain items at the Column/Sort Spec, the Define Page screen, and so forth.

You can get your report specs awfully darn close before you even print to paper by using the Page Preview or Print to Screen selections available at the Print Options screen — and you should take advantage of these features to save yourself time and paper. When you choose Design/Redesign a Report from the Report menu, the procedure is similar to designing a brand-new report, except that the report will already have a name, and the screens involved in the specification will contain the codes and values you entered during the initial design (or last redesign) process. You can move back and forth between your Retrieve and Column/Sort Specs and your Define Page and Print Options screens, and edit any of the specifications as you see fit.

Copying Your Initial Report Design Before Redesigning

Before embarking on a report redesign, however, consider copying the report specification to a new report name. You can do this at the List of Reports screen — the first screen that displays during redesign. Copying the complete report spec is cheap insurance. If you find yourself wondering what the original specs were after having made extensive changes to, for example, a Column/Sort Spec, you'll have the original report design available for reference, and even to restore if necessary.

"On-the-Fly" Redesign

You can redesign a report during the actual output process. Pressing **<Shift><F9>** during printing interrupts printing and displays a special redesign menu from which you can select any of the report specifications (Retrieve Spec, Column/Sort Spec, Derived Columns Spec, Print Options screen, or Define Page screen) for the current report.

This special Redesign menu is typically used for quick changes to a report design that can be made at a single spec — it won't let you move back and forth between the specs. If you need to edit two or more specs, your best bet is to use the Design/Redesign a Report selection at the Report menu and move through the specs sequentially.

You can also interrupt a printing operation with **<F2>.** This cancels the printing and places you back at the Print Options screen, from where you can press **<F8>** to check or change or your Define Page settings, or press **<F9>** to move back to the Column/Sort and Retrieve Specs. When you resume printing, Q&A starts from the beginning with your new settings now in effect.

Pressing **<Esc>** during output cancels printing, too. Your printer will continue to print until its buffer is emptied. Turning it off and then on again empties the buffer and resets it for the next printing job. It also returns the printer to its internal default settings.

Printing a Report

You print your reports from the Print Options screen. The Print Options screen also offers many enhancements for a report.

The Print Options Screen

When you press **<F10>** from the Column/Sort Spec, the Crosstab Grouping Spec, or any Derived Columns screen, the Print Options screen is displayed (see Figure 6-26). Print options for both standard and crosstab reports are the same except for the following:

- At the crosstab Report Print Options screen you can choose how you want your summary results displayed (as numbers, percentages, or normalized — more on these later).

- There is no Print Totals Only option at the crosstab Print Options screen.

```
                        REPORT PRINT OPTIONS
                        ━━━━━━━━━━━━━━━━━━━━━

     Print to.........:   PtrA  ▶PtrB◀ Ptr(.  PtrD   PtrE   DISK   SCREEN

     Page preview............:   Yes  ▶No◀

     Type of paper feed.......:   Manual  ▶Continuous◀  Bin1   Bin2   Bin3

     Printer offset...........:   0

     Printer control codes.....:

     Print totals only........:   Yes  ▶No◀

     Justify report body......:  ▶Left◀  Center   Right

     Line spacing.............:  ▶Single◀  Double

     Allow split records......:  ▶Yes◀  No
    ─────────────────────────────────────────────────────────────────────
     STOCK.DTF              Print Options for List Price Report
     Hewlett Packard LaserJet II/D/P/III (Port) »» LPT1
     Esc-Cancel       F8-Define Page        F9-Go back            F10-Continue
```

Figure 6-26: The Print Options Screen for Standard Q&A Columnar Reports. The crosstab Print Options screen is similar except that it does not allow for the Print Totals Only, and Allow Split Records options. Moreover, the crosstab Print Options screen allows you to choose how you want your report results displayed; as numbers, percentages, or in a normalized fashion.

- There is no Allow Split Records option at the crosstab Print Options screen.

To change your Print Options settings:

1. Move the cursor to the item you want to change.

2. Make the change either by typing a new value where required, or using the cursor keys to highlight the appropriate selection.

3. Repeat these steps for other Print Options you want to change.

4. Press **<F10>** to start printing, or optionally press **<F8>** for the Define Page screen.

You can set global Print Options defaults for all new reports. You can also press **<Shift><F9>** to stop printing output and go to a special redesign menu. This menu lets you go back to any of the report specs, alter them, and return to printing with your new specs in place. Both of these will be covered later on in the chapter.

The first five items on the Print Options screen are the same as the choices you have at the Write and File Print Options screens. Here's a review of how to use them.

Print to: Here you select your output medium. As you highlight each printer (PtrA through PtrE) Q&A displays, at the bottom of the screen, the name of the printer, the printer mode (Portrait or Landscape, for example), and the port to which it's connected.

Select the Disk option to print the report to disk in ASCII format.

Choose the Screen option to preview the raw report on screen without headers, footers, or margins, fonts or other enhancements. You can then use the cursor keys to move up, down, and across the report since it's likely to be both longer and wider than the monitor.

New: **Page preview:** If your computer supports graphics (meaning it has a graphics adapter installed) you can get a WYSIWYG preview of your report as it will look on the printed page with headers, footers, margins, line spacing, and all enhancements intact. The preview option takes into account the printer you've selected and the page characteristics established at the Define Page screen.

With Page Preview set to Yes, the first page of your report will be displayed in the full-page mode, so long as the physical page is no wider than 24 inches. You can then zoom in or out, preview other pages, and so forth (manipulating the Page Preview screen is covered in detail in Chapter 2).

Q&A Power Feature: The Page Preview is a useful report design tool. Use it to view the effect of all your report specifications before ordering a hard copy print-out. You can't edit your report in the preview mode, but by pressing **<Esc>** from the preview screen, and then pressing **<F9>**, you can return to any of the various report design screens, make your changes, and then get an updated preview. It saves paper, as well as the time it can take waiting for a report to print out in order to see what it looks like.

Type of paper feed: Select manual, continuous, or the appropriate bin. Manual feed stops after each page and waits for you to insert the next page and press **<Enter>**. If your printer has only one bin, continuous feed will probably work fine.

Printer offset: A positive number adjusts the printhead to start printing further to the right, whereas a negative number prints the first character of each line farther to the left. A value of 1, for example, results in printing starting one character column further to the right. Offsets come in handy when you're printing a variety of documents on the same printer and want to avoid having to manually adjust the printer's paper feed with each different report, form, or document.

Printer control codes: Enter any special codes, such as font On codes, that you want to apply to the entire report. These codes are typically entered in decimal format, and are normally listed in your printer manual. See the section on Printer Control Codes in Chapter 2 for a more detailed discussion.

Print totals only: Select Yes to suppress printing of report details, and to print subtotals and totals only — giving you a summary report.

Justify report body: Select Left (the default) to print the report on the left side of the page. The Center selection prints the report between the left and right margins, and Right prints the report flush right with the right margin.

Line spacing: Choose single or double report line spacing. You can also control line spacing via a printer control code. For example, if the Page Preview reveals that the last few lines of your report are spilling onto another page, you can reduce the normal 1/6-inch line feed so the entire report will print on one page.

Many printers allow you to control line feed in increments of 180ths of an inch or even 360ths of an inch. Using a printer control code that sets the line feed to 1/8th of an inch, for instance, enables you to print an additional 20 lines on a 10-inch page. The trade-off is less empty space between printed lines, which may reduce readability.

Allow split records: Selecting No amounts to "widow" and "orphan" control for your reports. If a record involves more than a single report line (for example, when the value in a column wraps to the next line), Q&A will print the whole record on the page if it can, or move the whole record to the next page of the report, thereby maintaining the integrity of the column value and making the report easier to read.

If you *don't* want your output controlled by Q&A in this manner (for instance, where your report contains many multiline values and suppressing record-splitting would make the report run to too many pages), set this option to Yes and allow Q&A to split any such records. The switch has no effect when printing output is directed to the screen.

Crosstab Report Print Options

The Print Options screen for crosstab reports offers neither the "Print Totals Only" or the "Allow Split Records" options — these wouldn't be useful in summary reports.

Q&A Power Feature: But a crosstab Print Options feature that could be *very* useful is the "Show Results as" option that allows you to see report calculations in a number of different ways: as numbers, as percent of total, row, or column, or normalized.

If your report is set to print summary calculations of total and/or count, here are your printing alternatives, available at the crosstab Print Options screen. Keep in mind that the terms "results" and "answer set" refer to the relevant summarized values only in those records that have been selected for inclusion in the report at the Retrieve Spec.

Number: The default crosstab summary result display. Report summary values will print just as you've indicated at the Crosstab Spec.

% Total: Displays the results as a percentage of the total value for all summary field values in the answer set.

% Row: Displays the results as a percentage of the grand total or grand count for the row.

% Column: Displays the results as a percentage of the grand total or grand count for that column.

Normalized: Displays report results as an amount above or below an average, giving you a kind of scale. The average would be 100. Indexes over 100 represent data above the crosstab average, while indexes below 100 represent data below the average. Normalization shows whether a value is worse or better than the computed average, and by what relative amount. Q&A computes the index by dividing the result value by the average value and then multiplying the quotient by 100.

Having these display options available at the crosstab Print Options screen means that you don't have to redesign the report to see your report data from a variety of angles. You can run the same report several times, each time selecting a different display result — giving you information that may be more meaningful than simple raw summary totals and counts.

The Define Page Screen

Pressing **<F8>** at the Print Options screen takes to you to Report's Define Page screen where you can set the dimensions of the page, its margins, the character density, and add headers and footers to the report.

The Define Page screen is identical to the File module's Define Page screen and is shown in Figure 6-27.

The section on the Define Page screen in Chapter 2 contains a thorough discussion of the points to keep in mind when setting your page dimensions, margins, and characters-per-inch. Although the discussion there is centered on page definition for Write documents, many of the tips apply equally well to page setup in the Report module. You might want to review that material if you're experiencing any difficulties.

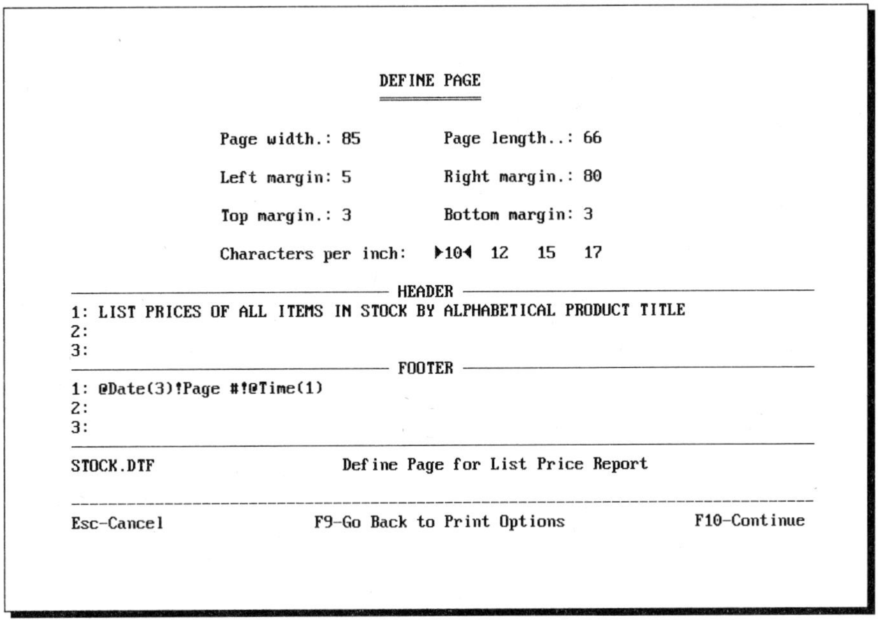

```
                              DEFINE PAGE
                              ==========

              Page width.: 85        Page length..: 66

              Left margin: 5         Right margin.: 80

              Top margin.: 3         Bottom margin: 3

              Characters per inch:   ▶10◀  12   15   17
 ─────────────────────────────── HEADER ───────────────────────────────
 1: LIST PRICES OF ALL ITEMS IN STOCK BY ALPHABETICAL PRODUCT TITLE
 2:
 3:
 ─────────────────────────────── FOOTER ───────────────────────────────
 1: @Date(3)!Page #!@Time(1)
 2:
 3:
 ───────────────────────────────────────────────────────────────────────
 STOCK.DTF                   Define Page for List Price Report
 ───────────────────────────────────────────────────────────────────────
 Esc-Cancel            F9-Go Back to Print Options         F10-Continue
```

Figure 6-27: Report's Define Page Screen. It shows sample page dimensions, margins, character density, and a header and footer for the current report.

Except for the header and footer, Figure 6-27 shows Q&A's default settings. You can, of course, change any of these to suit the particular page characteristics of your report; and when the report design is saved (just before printing), your Define Page settings are saved, too.

To enter new page characteristics:

1. Move to the item you want to change.

2. Type the new value where appropriate, or highlight your choice in the case of characters-per-inch.

3. Repeat these steps for any other values you want to change.

4. Type your report headers or footers in the space provided. You can include @DATE and @TIME notations so that the report will include the system date and time it was printed. A page notation (#) can also be included to facilitate report page numbering.

5. Press **<F9>** to return to the Print Options screen, or **<F10>** to save the design and print the report.

Page Measurements

Margins and page dimensions can be entered at the Define Page screen in either inches or lines and columns.

To indicate inches, follow the number with the inch symbol ("). Specify fractions of an inch with decimal numbers. When using inches, the right margin value is entered as inches from the *right edge* of the page.

When specifying your margins and page dimensions in lines (rows) and columns, only whole number values are acceptable. Page length and top and bottom margins are entered as lines, while page width and left and right margins are entered as character columns (character spaces). When using character columns instead of inches, the right margin must be entered as characters from the *left edge* of the page.

Characters-per-Inch and Margins

When you change the characters-per-inch value at the Define Page screen, you're also changing the basis on which any character column values for left/right margins are computed by Q&A.

In other words, left/right margins and page widths, where entered in character columns, are dependent on the report's current characters-per-inch value.

A cpi setting of 10, for instance, means that a left margin setting of 10 will result in a true one-inch left margin. A cpi setting of 12, however, means that a left margin setting of 10 will result in a printed left margin of ten 12-cpi columns, or something less than an inch.

Table 6-11 shows Q&A's minimum and maximum page measurements at various character per inch settings.

The minimum and maximum page lengths are 1 and 32 inches, respectively. In lines, the minimum and maximum page lengths are 6 and 192, respectively.

Headers and Footers

A header or footer, or both, can add a nice touch to your report.

Use headers and footers to:

- Tell the reader what the report is about.

- Add descriptive or explanatory comments to the report.

- Paginate the report.

- Date-stamp and time-stamp the report, so readers will know exactly when it was printed.

Table 6-11					
Minimum and Maximum Page Dimensions					
		Character Columns			
Width	**Inches**	**10 CPI**	**12 CPI**	**15 CPI**	**17 CPI**
Minimum	1"	10	12	15	17
Maximum	58"	580	696	870	1000

Your report can contain up to three header lines and three footer lines, so long as your top and bottom page margins are wide enough to accommodate them.

Headers and footers, when you type them at the Define Page screen, are printed with each report page. You can paginate your report by typing **#** in a header or footer. Q&A will place the page number where you've typed **#**. If, for example, you want the headers on the first and second pages to include Page #1, Page #2, etc., you'll need to type Page ##. Q&A will then interpret the second pound sign as the page number location.

To date-stamp your report, type the notation **@DATE(n)** in a header or footer, where *n* is the particular date format (1 through 20) that you want printed. See Table 2-9 in Chapter 2, or any Global Format Options screen, for a summary of all the date and time formats. For example, @DATE(1) produces a Sep 15, 1989 format; @DATE(3) produces a 9/15/89 format; and @DATE(11) produces a September 15, 1990 format.

You can similarly time-stamp your report by typing **@TIME(n)** in a header or footer, where *n* is the time format (1, 2, or 3) you want printed in your report.

Header and footer text is normally centered on the page, but you can control this using exclamation points. Text to the left of the first **!** will print flush left. Text to the right of the **!** will print flush right. Text centered *between* exclamation points will be printed centered. For example, if you typed in a header as follows:

```
@Date(11)!List of Available Products!Page #
```

the date would print flush left, the report title would be centered, and the page number would print at the right margin.

Remember, be sure your top and bottom margins are set to allow enough lines for your header and/or footer. If your top margin is set to 2, for instance, Q&A won't be able to print your entire three-line header.

If you want the literal characters **!** or **#** to print in a header or footer, precede them with a backslash (****). Q&A will then know you want the character printed as is.

You can enhance your headers or footers while at the Define Page screen. Move the cursor to the place in the header or footer where you want the enhancement to begin and press **<Shift><F6>** for the Enhancement menu. Select the enhancement you want, highlight the appropriate text, and press **<F10>** when you're finished. Enhance other header or footer lines the same way.

When Your Report Is Sent to the Printer

When you press **<F10>** from either the Print Options screen or the Define Page screen, Q&A will save your entire report specification, and ask if you're ready to begin printing. If you answer Yes, and Q&A can't make the entire report fit on the page, you'll get a warning message as shown in Figure 6-28.

Here are the options you have if your report turns out to be too wide to print:

- You can choose **C** to cancel printing and return to the Report menu.

- You can select **E** to edit your specifications and reprint, which typically involves selecting narrower margins and/or a higher character density at the Define Page screen.

- You can tell Q&A to truncate the right portion of the report that makes it too wide to print on the page.

- You can have Q&A split the report across pages. This can turn out to be cleaner than it may sound. What Q&A does when you split the report is simply divide it so that all the columns that will fit on the page will be printed on the first page, and the remaining columns will be printed on the following page. Headers and footers are repeated on the split pages, and all the lines in the report are properly aligned.

 Tip: If you don't want to truncate or split the report, ask yourself the following questions:

At the Define Page Screen: Can I decrease my left and right margins, increase my page width, and/or increase my character density?

At the Column Sort Spec: Can I safely eliminate one or more columns from the report? If calculations in Column B are dependent on values in Column A, but I don't really need to see Column A in the printed report, should I just make Column A invisible? Should I decrease the width of some of the columns by specifying special column widths and headings with the **H** code?

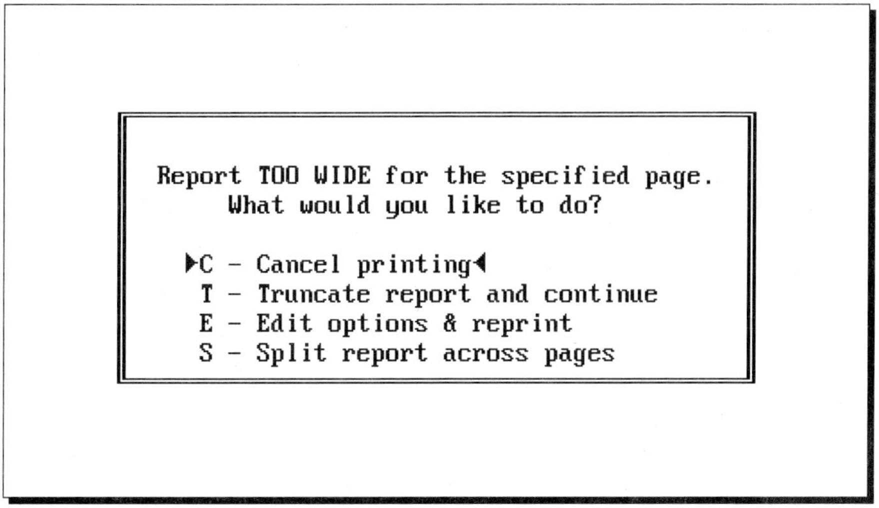

```
    Report TOO WIDE for the specified page.
         What would you like to do?

    ▶C - Cancel printing◀
     T - Truncate report and continue
     E - Edit options & reprint
     S - Split report across pages
```

Figure 6-28: The Report Is Too Wide for the Page.

Set Format Options (Report Global Options): Should I reduce the default spacing between columns? (If you do so you'll need to run through the report redesign process so the global change will take effect. You don't have to change any of your report specs, however.)

General: Do I have wider paper I can load to print this report, or a printer that will accommodate wider page settings? Can I use a printer control code at the Print Options screen to print at compressed 20 characters-per-inch? Can I use landscape mode and legal size paper to run the report on my laser printer?

Use a Utility Program: Funk Software makes a product called Sideways — a utility that imports documents and rotates them 90 degrees to print vertically down multiple sheets of fan-fold paper, instead of in the usual horizontal format. With Sideways installed in your computer, make sure your report Define Page settings are as follows for any report you want to print using the utility:

```
Page Width: 240
Right Margin: 240
Left, Top, and Bottom Margins: 0
```

Set your Page Length to match Sideways' number of lines per page.

At the Print Options screen, select Print to Disk, and don't specify any Printer Control Codes. When you press **<F10>** Q&A will prompt you for a disk file name, and save the report in ASCII format (stripped of all enhancements). You can then use Sideways to print the report.

Q&A allows a maximum report width of 240 characters. If you go over the limit you'll have to trim the report width by deleting as many columns as are necessary.

Printing a Report

Select Print a Report from the Report menu when you want to print a report you've already designed and saved, or when you want to print a temporary report whose design you don't want to save.

When you choose Print a Report and enter the name of the database, Q&A will show you the names of the reports whose specs are already on file. To run a report, highlight it or type its name and press **<Enter>**. To create an ad hoc report whose specs will not be saved, press **<Enter>** without giving Q&A the report name.

When you enter the name of an existing report, Q&A asks if you want to make any temporary changes to any of the report's specifications. Answer No to run the report right away, or Yes if you want to make changes for this printing only.

By answering Yes, you'll go through all the spec and options screens one by one. Don't be afraid to edit the specs — Q&A throws these temporary changes away after printing and hangs on to the specs that were saved when you last designed or redesigned the report.

To print a new temporary report without giving it a name, press **<Enter>** from the List of Reports screen, and move through the specs one by one, filling them out as appropriate. The word "New" will display on the status line to remind you that this is a throw-away report design. Once the report is sent to the printer, Q&A will place you back at the Report menu.

Don't use Print a Report when you want your specifications saved to disk. Use it only when you want to print an existing report, or design and print a temporary report.

Report Global Options

Choose Set Global Options from the Report menu when you want to establish new default settings for all new reports in the database. You can globally set new defaults for column headings and widths, special format options, and page and print options for columnar reports, and set new print and page

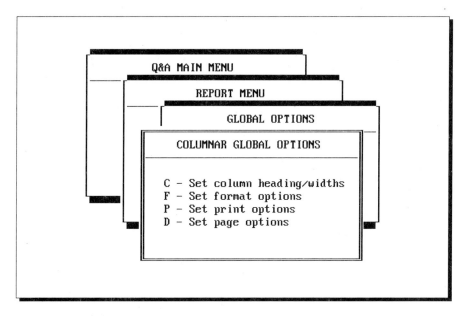

Figure 6-29: Setting New Report Design Defaults at the Global Options Menu.

options for crosstab reports. Existing reports will not be affected by changes to any global options unless you redesign those reports individually.

Figure 6-29 shows the Columnar Global Options menu.

Setting Column Headings and Widths

Q&A automatically uses your database's field labels as report column headings, centers the headings over their columns, spaces the columns evenly, and adjusts columns widths to accommodate the information in the column.

You can change any or all of these defaults, however, and have them apply to all new reports you create in the database.

When you select **C** from the Columnar Global Options menu, Q&A displays the database form. You can then:

1. Position the cursor on any field whose column heading, width, and/or indent value you want to change and type the defaults for all new reports. Press **<F6>** to expand the field if it looks as if you'll need more room.

2. Type the new column width in characters or inches (inches must be followed by the " symbol). Optionally:

- Type a colon and then type the default indent value for this field. If the column width is specified in inches, the indent value must also be specified in inches. You cannot enter an indent value unless you've also specified a width, and the indent must be less than the width.

- Type a colon and type a new column heading. The column width, indent value, and heading must be separated from one another by colons.

- Press **\<Shift\>\<F6\>** to add an enhancement to your column heading if you want.

3. Repeat steps 1 and 2 for any other fields you want to change.

4. Press **\<F10\>** when finished to return to the Columnar Global Options menu.

To use a number as the first character in a column heading, precede it with a colon. To run a heading on two or three lines, type **!** where you want the split to occur.

Set Format Options

Select **F** from the Columnar Global Options menu to set new format options as shown in Figure 6-30.

Number of spaces between columns: Q&A's default "Variable" format option setting places five spaces between columns where space permits, compressing the space to as little as two spaces where necessary. You can specify a fixed number of spaces (from 1 to 9) at this line.

Default to repeating values: The default setting does not repeat values in sorted columns unless you override it with the **R** code at the Column/Sort Spec. If you want sorted column values to repeat in the majority of your reports, set this line to Yes and save yourself the trouble of having to enter **R** at the Column/Sort Spec.

Action on blank value: By default, Q&A prints a zero wherever a money or number field in a report column is blank. You can globally change this by selecting Leave Blank.

Action on column break: Q&A is preset to skip a line at column breaks. Change the default to Don't Skip Line if that's what you want.

When you've finished setting your Global Format Options press **\<F10\>** to save the changes and you'll be returned to the Columnar Global Options menu. Any changes you've made to this spec will not affect existing reports unless you redesign those reports individually.

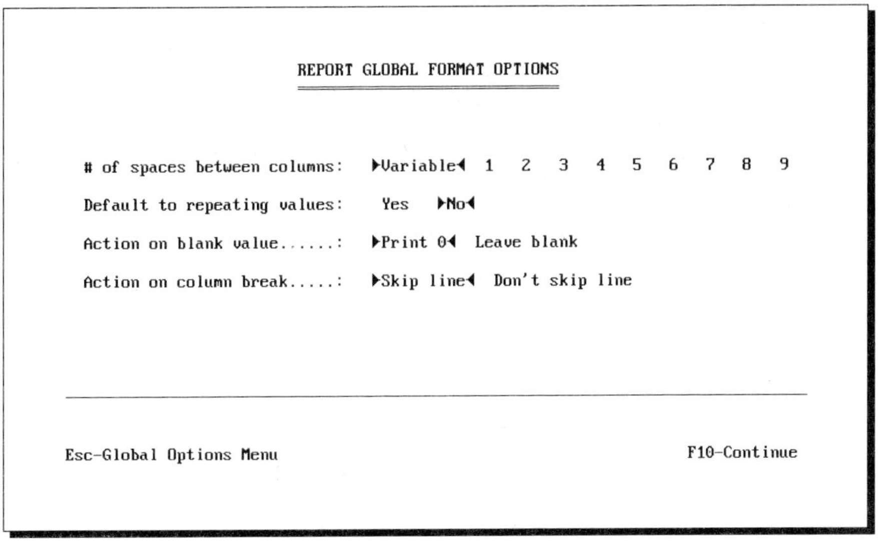

```
                        REPORT GLOBAL FORMAT OPTIONS


    # of spaces between columns:   ▶Variable◀  1   2   3   4   5   6   7   8   9

    Default to repeating values:    Yes    ▶No◀

    Action on blank value......:   ▶Print 0◀  Leave blank

    Action on column break.....:   ▶Skip line◀  Don't skip line




    ────────────────────────────────────────────────────────────

    Esc-Global Options Menu                            F10-Continue
```

Figure 6-30: The Set Format Options Screen.

But a word of warning: Should you take an existing report through the Design/Redesign a Report process and then save the report (even if you haven't made a single change to any of the specs), that report will now contain any new Global Format Option changes that have been made since it was last saved.

This can be a source of confusion when suddenly a report that printed fine the day before, is now "TOO WIDE," even though you haven't changed anything that would cause this to occur.

What can happen is that the default column space at the Global Format Options screen was changed to a higher value, and when you sent your report to the printer via Design/Redesign (and thus resaved it), the *changed* column width value became part of the "new" report spec, making it now "TOO WIDE."

Setting new default Print and Define Page options is the same as selecting these options at the regular Print Options and Define Page screens, except here your settings will be reflected in these screens for all new reports. This applies to crosstab reports as well as to standard columnar reports.

Use the report-specific Print Options and Define Page screens when you want to make changes to individual reports only. Enter your new global printing and page options when you want to change the default settings for all future reports.

Modifications made to any global options are never cast in stone. You can always come back later and change them again. Q&A provides the facility to enter global defaults simply as a convenient way to establish custom presets for your reports, making the job of report design that much easier and faster.

Rename/Delete/Copy

This final selection on the Report menu allows you to change a report's name, delete a report design permanently, and make a copy of a complete report specification.

Copying a report design can save time and effort when designing a new report whose specs will be similar to an existing one. It's also a good policy to copy a complex design to a new report name and work with the copy during redesign rather than the original. If you muck up the redesign, you'll still have the original specification to fall back on.

You can save up to 200 report designs per database. But it's always a good housekeeping practice to remove any reports that are out of date or no longer useful. You can't selectively back up only reports to disk because Q&A stores report designs with the database. So if there's a chance you might need that report again, you're better off saving it. But saved reports — just like anything you save to disk in a computer — take up space.

Tip: You don't have to select Rename, Delete, or Copy from the Report menu. For some, it's easier to carry out these operations from the List of Reports screen in the database in which you're working. Simply highlight the report you want, and press **<F3>** to delete it, **<F8>** to give it a new name, or **<F5>** to make a copy under a new name. Q&A provides the usual prompts and warnings to confirm the actions.

More Ideas on Working with Reports

Tip: Here are a few additional tips to keep in mind when you're working with reports:

- You can build your reports a step at a time using the Query Guide (QG) available in the Intelligent Assistant (IA). You can also run pre-defined reports via the QG. Report *designs* created in the QG, however, are for one-time use only. (See the following chapter.)

- You can also use the IA to design ad hoc reports, or to run an existing report. Report *designs* you create from scratch using the IA are not saved, however (see the next chapter for more on this).

- You can print your reports to disk at the Print Options screen, and then bring them into the Write module for a little custom "body work." Suppose you need to add comments to a report, and there's not enough space on the Define Page header and footer lines. You can print the report to disk, bring it into the word processor, and supplement it with as much text as you like (you can also enhance it there).

  If some of the report columns wrap when you bring the report onto the Type/Edit screen, it means your page isn't wide enough. Just press **<Ctrl><F6>** for the Define Page screen, and adjust your margins and/or page width to accommodate the report's width.

- You can run predesigned reports with macros. In fact, you can create a custom Report menu that lists all your routine reports, and run a report from this menu simply by highlighting it and pressing **<Enter>**. Chapter 8 tells you how to create macros and custom menus.

You can even go a step further by installing a macro on the Q&A Main menu that "calls" your custom report menu. Installing alternate programs and macros on the Q&A Main menu is covered in Chapter 9.

Summary

In this chapter you learned to use the Report module at times when you need a tabular format, with calculations and special formatting.

In the next chapter, you will learn about Q&A's English-language interface, which allows you to request certain actions from Q&A's database using English rather than computer commands.

Chapter 7
Q&A's English-Language Interface

In this chapter you'll learn how to:

▶ Recognize when the Intelligent Assistant can simplify your database managements tasks.

▶ Teach the Assistant about your databases.

▶ Use plain English commands to get information from your forms.

▶ Have the Assistant create reports and update records.

▶ Build complex queries and reports with ease using the Query Guide.

This chapter will show you how to teach and use the Intelligent Assistant and new 4.0 Query Guide, which allow you to communicate with Q&A in plain English. Also included in this chapter are instructions for renaming the Intelligent Assistant.

Overview

For many, Q&A's Intelligent Assistant (IA) is the most fascinating aspect of the entire package. It represents the first attempt to bring to everyday microcomputer users a natural language interface that can be used to query information in databases, retrieve and update forms, generate lists and reports, and answer a host of other questions — all by merely typing in sentences in ordinary conversational English. For example:

```
Show me the Ed Barnes form.
Get the record for part number B6088.
What's the phone number at Murray's Hardware?
What's the total amount of the July 1990 invoices?
Who makes more than $20,000 a year?
```

```
What's Jane Fergusen's department?
List our San Diego customers.
What are their phone numbers?
Show the P.O.'s where the total amount is more than $2,000.
Which employees work full-time?
List them by department with extensions.
Change the Consolidated Supply fax number to 313-565-4566.
Delete part number X22B4.
```

These sample commands and questions, you may have noticed, pertain to specific databases. Some of the requests refer to information that would be contained in a customer file or an employee file, while others obviously involve querying an invoice, purchase order, or inventory database.

This is the first thing you need in order to use the IA — a database with records in it. Once you have that, you can teach the Assistant about your database, and then start using it to manipulate the records in your files and obtain information from them.

Using English phrases, questions, and sentences, you can:

- Have the IA generate one-time reports.

- Run predesigned reports.

- Get a new form to fill in.

- Find and display a single form or group of forms.

- Change information on one or more forms.

- Ask who, what, when, how many, and Yes/No questions about the database.

- Order calculations to be performed.

- Define synonyms such as "client" for "customer."

- Get comparative information, such as "which stock numbers are priced between $10 and $15?"

- Ask follow-up questions, such as "Who are their suppliers?"

The Intelligent Assistant already knows about 600 words, and once you decide to work with a file through the IA, it learns any words associated with your database through a brief initialization process. You can then teach it any special words it will need to know in order to respond to your requests more efficiently.

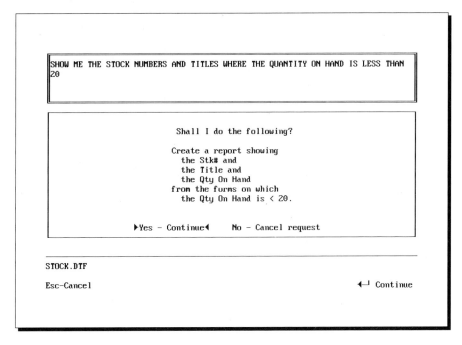

Figure 7-1: Asking the Intelligent Assistant to Produce a Report from the Inventory Database.
The IA evaluates the request and displays its plan of action before proceeding.

Figure 7-1 shows an example of a command entered in the Intelligent Assistant's Request box, and the way in which the IA responds and asks for confirmation. Figure 7-2 shows the requested report.

How the Assistant Learns

Through a series of simple lessons, you teach the Assistant the finer points of the database, such as which fields uniquely identify your forms, which fields contain names, which fields contain locations such as addresses, or warehouse shelves or bins, the units of measure to work with, and any special synonyms, adjectives, or verbs you'll be using to formulate your requests and commands.

As for the content of your database, the IA learns this on its own. When you introduce the IA to your database for the first time, it looks at the field names, each field's information type, and the values in the fields by reviewing the

```
┌─────────────────────────────────────────────────────────────────┐
│ SHOW ME THE STOCK NUMBERS AND TITLES WHERE THE QUANTITY ON HAND IS LESS THAN │
│ 20                                                                │
└─────────────────────────────────────────────────────────────────┘

Stk#          Short Title              Qty On Hand
─────    ─────────────────────────    ───────────
388PB    Looking Through the Lens          15
245VT    Exploring African Wilderness       9
403VT    Modernize Your Kitchen            12
501HB    The Omaha Factor                  18
348PB    Man Who Invented Ball Bearings    15
680AT    Bird Songs of New Jersey Shore     8

218AT    Bach's Greatest Hits              12


─────────────────────────────────────────────────────────
STOCK.DTF
****************************** END OF REPORT *******************************
```

Figure 7-2: The IA Producing the Requested Report.

entire database as a whole. This doesn't mean that you have to teach the IA each time you add, delete, or modify a record. The only time the IA may need a refresher course is when you modify the structure of the file by redesigning it, or when you change the information types of any of the fields.

The IA's ability to handle English requests is a function of the vocabulary it understands and your clear and sensible use of the language. If the IA doesn't know the words, it can't sing the tune. If your request is phrased illogically, it won't understand what you want. The IA draws its vocabulary from three sources:

- Its own extensive built-in vocabulary.

- The words, terms, and values it gleans from your database field names and field contents.

- New words — synonyms, adjectives, and verbs — that you teach it so you can communicate your requests more naturally.

Teaching the Assistant is easy and can be quite fun. The IA is a quick study and never forgets. The first time you teach it about a database, however, expect the process to take some time. After all, you're learning, too. But the more you train the IA to interpret your requests correctly, the more you'll learn about the teaching process itself, and the faster each new lesson will go. You'll better understand the meaning of this as we proceed through this chapter.

There are certain things that the IA *cannot* be taught. For example, you can't ask the IA to bring a document into the word processor, modify a font file, print mailing labels, export a file to Paradox, run a macro, or add a new field to the database. These are all outside the realm of ordinary database operations.

You can, however, have the IA run a mass update, delete a group of forms, tell you the current date or time, or calculate the result of an arithmetic expression, as you'll see.

Building Queries and Reports Step by Step

 New: Q&A version 4.0 added a special *Query Guide* (QG) feature to the Intelligent Assistant module that enables you to select query and report-generating options from structured lists. In other words, instead of typing your request, as you must for the Intelligent Assistant, you build your query step by step simply by choosing from a variety of canned procedures or fragments of statements.

Using the Query Guide, you interact with Q&A through a kind of dialogue whereby your query, or the objective you have in mind, is defined a step at a time until Q&A is able to deliver exactly what you want. This way, you don't have to be concerned about how to properly phrase your request, or whether or not it will be understood, because the Guide leads you along until you've told it what it needs to know to retrieve and display the database information you want.

When you enter the Query Guide you're first asked about the nature of your request. It wants to know, for example, if you'd like it to:

- Look at a form or group of forms.

- Produce a report.

- Count the forms in the file.

- Have the data summarized.

- Run a predefined operation.

Once the QG understands the broader aspect of your query, it then leads you through several more steps as it helps you frame your command more precisely one part at a time.

When you opt to type your entire request in English, the IA must break down the command into its logical components. Once it understands the words you've used, and then the request as a whole, it can proceed to carry out your wishes.

The Query Guide assists you by using a different method. Rather than translating your command, it displays a list of predefined commands and prompts you to select one.

Do You Really Need the Assistant?

For the most part, the IA functions mainly as a sort of Retrieve Spec and ad hoc report generator. When you tell the Assistant, for example:

```
Get me the Bronson record
```

what you're asking the IA to do for you, in effect, is to go to the Retrieve Spec, type **Bronson** into the last name field, and press **<F10>** to bring up the form.

Which is easier and faster — using the IA or using the Retrieve Spec? It depends on your familiarity with the product and your personal preferences. Let's compare the two search/retrieve methods starting from the Q&A Main menu:

Retrieving Bronson's form using the Intelligent Assistant:

1. Select Assistant from the Main menu.

2. Select Ask Me to Do Something from the Assistant menu.

3. Enter the name of the database.

4. Type the request Get me the Bronson record.

5. Press **<Enter>**.

6. Press **Y** or **<Enter>** to confirm the IA's plan of action. The Bronson record is displayed.

Retrieving Bronson's form using the Retrieve Spec:

1. Select File from the Main menu.

2. Select Search/Update from the File menu.

3. Enter the name of the database.

4. Use **<Tab>** to move to the last name field.

5. Type **Bronson**.

6. Press **<F10>**. The Bronson record is displayed.

As you can see, the two methods of retrieving the form involve about the same number of steps. The difference is that when using the Retrieve Spec you don't have to go through the process of teaching the Intelligent Assistant anything about the database.

The IA's facilities may indeed make using Q&A easier for those who feel more comfortable with English dialogue than with entering parameters on-screen in order to control the desired file and print operations.

The question is: what will you be using the IA *for*?

If you want to take the time to teach the Assistant about your database — including the synonyms, verbs, and adjectives you and others may use to formulate queries; *and* if the people using the computer *need* an English-language interface — then by all means set up your databases for use with the IA.

Or, depending on the level of English-language interaction you need, and the types of queries you normally formulate, you may be able to get everything you need from the Query Guide without having to interact with the Assistant at all.

On the other hand, if you and the others in your office who use Q&A find that the Retrieve Spec and report design process are easy enough (especially if you want to *save* your retrieval parameters and report formats — something the IA and QG *can't* do), and if no one is really dependent on English to get the information that's needed, you don't have to use the Intelligent Assistant at all.

Drawbacks of Using the Intelligent Assistant

When you type a request for the IA to carry out, it first analyses each and every word to make sure it understands what you're asking, and then checks with you to make sure you agree it's got it straight. This can take time, especially if there are words in the request it doesn't know, if it doesn't quite understand what you mean, or if it needs you to clear something up before proceeding.

And if several people are using the Assistant — different people pose questions in different ways and use a variety of words — you may find yourself spending more time teaching the IA than it would take to show the others how to fill out a Retrieve Spec or design a report.

There is some overhead connected with the IA as well.

Once you've taught the Assistant about your database, each record you add to the file needs to be looked at by the IA. In a large database, this can result in a noticeable delay when adding forms. This same effect is also true once you've taught the Query Guide. The more you teach either of these assistants and the more records added to the file, the more it can slow down database performance.

The IA and QG create and store indexes so they can search for requested information faster. Index files use disk space — a factor you may need to consider if your hard disk is already near capacity.

Many users, after a little experience with Q&A, find that they no longer depend on the IA at all, and in fact sometimes take steps to remove the Assistant from a database by copying the file design to a new name, copying the existing records to the new file, and then deleting the original file.

If you'd like to try the Intelligent Assistant and Query Guide, the best approach is to teach them about one database, and then use them with that database for a time to see how you are getting along. It may turn out that as you become more familiar with Q&A, you'll find yourself going to the IA and QG less frequently. On the other hand, your Assistant may prove so valuable that you'll want to teach it about all your database files.

Accessing the information in your data files through the Intelligent Assistant module is entirely optional — you may never need or want to use it. But by reading this chapter, you'll gain a better understanding of how the Assistant works and what it can do for you. As a result, you'll be in a better position to determine whether or not the IA is right for you and your particular database management needs.

 Warning: Always back up your database before teaching either the Intelligent Assistant or the Query Guide. Unexpected disasters such as partial or total power failures can occur. Having an up-to-date copy of your file elsewhere can save you hours or even days of work.

The Assistant Menu

When you select Assistant from the Q&A Main menu, the Assistant menu shown in Figure 7-3 displays.

Here's a summary of your choices:

Get acquainted: This selection takes you to a series of informative screens that briefly explain what the IA is and what it can do. You're also encouraged to run the easy IA tutorial that comes with Q&A so you can get a feel for what's required of you in order to take advantage of the Assistant's capabilities.

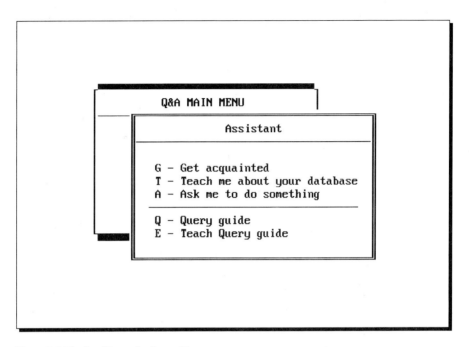

Figure 7-3: The Intelligent Assistant Menu.

Teach me about your database: When you've decided to use the IA to query your database, this selection starts the teaching process. Give the Assistant the name of the database; the IA spends a few moments analyzing the structure and content of the file, and then proceed to several lessons whereby you teach the IA what it needs to know in order to process your requests more efficiently. You *can* use the IA in a limited fashion without first teaching it, but it will still have to examine your file and the records contained in it before you can enter a request. More on how to do this later.

Ask me to do something: Choose this when you're ready to type an English-language request, normally after the IA has been taught about the database. The IA asks for the name of the file and then presents you with the Request box where you enter your command. If the database has not yet been prepared for use with the Assistant, the IA offers to carry out this necessary step now and gives you the option of proceeding or not.

Query Guide: When you want to build your request by means of a point-and-shoot exchange with Q&A, you enter the Query Guide and select alternatives from a series of predefined lists. If you haven't yet initialized the Query Guide, you'll need to give it a few moments to scan your file and compile information from your forms. If the database contains a great many records, this may take a while.

Teach Query Guide: Invoke this menu selection when you want to tell the Assistant which fields in the file to establish as query fields. These are normally the fields in your database that you'll search on or need to include in reports. The Query Guide creates indexes for the selected fields and displays their values in alphabetized scrollable lists during the query-building process. You then select from these lists to specify the information to be included and the actions you want performed.

Having the Assistant review the records in your database prior to using the Request box or Query Guide is best done when the file contains only a few dozen records. If you go to the IA for the first time with a file that contains thousands of forms, be prepared to wait a while as your forms are reviewed and the information in them is compiled. It's a one-time process that doesn't require any interaction on your part, however. And once the IA has collected the information it needs (and saves for future use), it returns control of the program to you.

The Query Guide

Although the Query Guide (QG) is part of the Intelligent Assistant module, teaching it about your database involves far less time and consideration than the more detailed process of preparing the IA to accept English-language requests. For this reason I'll discuss the procedure for setting up the Query Guide first, and later describe how to prepare the IA for accepting and acting on commands typed by hand.

When you select Teach Query Guide from the Assistant menu and enter the name of the file, the IA presents you with the form you designed for the database. Figure 7-4 shows the STOCK.DTF form as it would be displayed during the beginning of the procedure.

Notice in Figure 7-4 that the bottom of the displayed STOCK.DTF form indicates "Query Guide Teach." This is actually a Speed-up Spec. When you teach the QG, you type **Q** in those text and keyword fields:

- That have values you want the Guide to include in scrollable pick-and-choose lists, when the time comes for selecting them.

- That you'll likely want to search on when retrieving forms for your queries and reports.

The first time you enter the QG in this manner, the box shown at the bottom of Figure 7-4 will be superimposed over the lower portion of the form, with the message prompting you to type **Q** in the fields whose values you'll want displayed during the query- or report-building process.

```
      Stk#
                                            Date Added
                              ═══════ INVENTORY ITEM ═══════
         ┌──────────────────────────────────────────────────┐
         │ Full Title                                        │
         │ Short Title                                       │
         │ Author First                    Author Last       │
         └──────────────────────────────────────────────────┘

      Type    ISBN               Subject Codes
      Description

      Vendor                 Vendor#    Case Qty    Case Wght    Item Wght
      Cost         List        Discount    20%         40%          50%
      ┌─────────────────┬─────────────────┬─────────────────┬─────────────────┐
      │ Sold Today      │ Rec'd Today     │ Qty On Hand     │ Reorder Level   │
      └─────────────────┴─────────────────┴─────────────────┴─────────────────┘

      Sold YTD        Bought YTD        PO Date           PO#      Qty      C1?
      ┌──────────────────┐                      ┌──────────────────┐
      │Physical Count    │                      │Shelf Location    │
      └──────────────────┘                      └──────────────────┘
      STOCK.DTF                       Query Guide Teach              Page 1  of 1

      Esc - Cancel    F1 - Help     F3 - Clear Spec    F3 - Mark All     F10-Continue

         ┌──────────────────────────────────────────────────────────────┐
         │ Type a ``Q'' in each text or keyword field that you wish to index│
         │ for use by the Query Guide.  For example, if you wish to have    │
         │ access to a scrollable list of cities in your database while in  │
         │ the Query Guide, type  ``Q'' in the ``City'' field.             │
         │                                                                 │
         │ SUGGESTION: Start by pressing F5 to mark all fields indexable by the│
         │ query guide with Qs.  Then remove the Qs from those fields that │
         │ you do not wish to index. To unteach the database, remove all Q's.│
         └──────────────────────────────────────────────────────────────┘
```

Figure 7-4: The Query Guide. It is displaying the form from the selected database.

If the form contains a lot of text fields you want indexed, you can press **<F5>** to mark *all* the fields and then delete the **Q** from those you do *not* want to teach. You can unteach the database by removing all Q's — the **<F3>** key will do it.

The Guide can still be used even without any indexed fields, but won't be able to present you with a list of values for those fields from which you can pick and choose when the time comes.

After you've typed **Q** in all the fields you want indexed and pressed **<F10>**, you're ready to build your query or report.

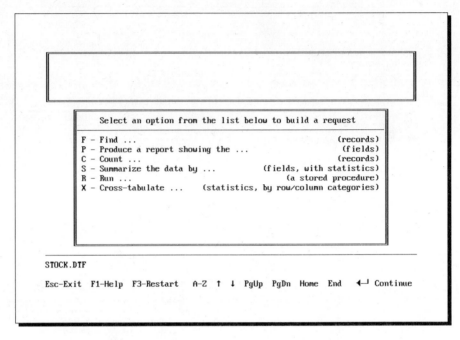

Figure 7-5: The Query Guide Presenting a List of Options. Choose the one you want and press <Enter>.

Using the Query Guide

Once the Guide has been initialized, you can select Query Guide from the Assistant menu to begin the process of building your request. Figure 7-5 shows what the first screen looks like when you enter the Guide to build a request.

The empty area at the top of Figure 7-5 corresponds to the Request box where, if you were using the Intelligent Assistant, you would type your command word by word. When using the Query Guide, however, the English-language command is automatically typed for you as you proceed through the menus making your selections and building your query or report piece by piece.

Notice in Figure 7-5 that the QG offers you a total of *six* possible ways to proceed with your query. If you choose the first option, Find, the QG assumes you want to look at one or more forms. The three dots (...) that follow each selection indicate that at subsequent menus this information (in this case, *which* records) will also have to be selected. You can press the letter that corresponds to the selection, or highlight it with your cursor keys and press **<Enter>**, or point and click your mouse.

Here are the phrases from the opening Query Guide screen and an explanation of what they lead to in the query-building process.

F - Find ... (records) Use this selection when you want to view (or view and update) one or more records in the database. The Query Guide will then help you choose the specific records you want, and the order in which you want to view them.

P - Produce a report showing ... (fields) Select this option to run a one-time report from information in the database. The QG will then take you through the report-building process a step at a time, enabling you to choose the fields and records to be included in the report and how you want the report information sorted and displayed.

C - Count ... (records) Choosing this item results in a count of the forms in the database that meet the parameters you select at subsequent menus.

S - Summarize the data by ... (fields, with statistics) Select this menu item when you want to see a summary of fields by average, total, maximum, minimum, count, variance, or standard deviation. The QG will ask you to specify the fields along with the type of summary information you're after.

R - Run ... (a stored procedure) This selection enables you to run a report or print spec previously designed, named, and saved to disk. You cannot run a Batch Post, Mass Update, or other stored procedure from the Query Guide.

X - Cross-tabulate ... (statistics, by row/column categories) Use this option to create an ad hoc crosstab report. The QG will ask you select your row, column, and summary fields, and specify which records you want included in the report.

Continuing with this example, if you choose Find, this word will be typed in the Request box and the QG will now take you to the second menu in the chain, shown in Figure 7-6.

At this second menu in the query-building process, the QG has entered the first portion of your request in the Request box, shown at the top of Figure 7-6. Suppose that you now want to select only those records from the database that meet certain requirements. Your next step would be to press **R** to tell the QG that this is how you wish to proceed. You are now three steps into the query-building process, as Figure 7-7 shows.

As Figure 7-7 illustrates, your request has been extended to include "Find the records where." It's not a complete query yet, and the QG prompts you to indicate a field in the database that contains the information on which you want to search.

```
┌─────────────────────────────────────────────────────────────┐
│ Find                                                          │
│                                                              │
│                                                              │
└─────────────────────────────────────────────────────────────┘

        ┌───────────────────────────────────────────────────┐
        │      Select an option from the list below to build a request │
        │ ─────────────────────────────────────────────────────── │
        │ R - the records where ...                         │
        │ A - ALL the records ...                           │
        │ C - the current record.            (last record entered) │
        │                                                   │
        │                                                   │
        │                                                   │
        │                                                   │
        └───────────────────────────────────────────────────┘
    ──────────────────────────────────────────────────────────
    STOCK.DTF

    Esc-Backup  F1-Help  F3-Restart  A-Z  ↑  ↓  PgUp  PgDn  Home  End  ↵ Continue
```

Figure 7-6: The Find and Show Option. You've told the QG that you want it to Find and show records. Now it wants to know which records you want to see.

```
┌─────────────────────────────────────────────────────────────┐
│ Find the records where                                       │
│                                                              │
│                                                              │
└─────────────────────────────────────────────────────────────┘

        ┌───────────────────────────────────────────────────┐
        │                  Select a field                   │
        │ ─────────────────────────────────────────────────────── │
        │ Author First                                      │
        │ Author Last                                       │
        │ Bought YTD                                        │
        │ Case Qty                                          │
        │ Case Wght                                         │
        │ Cl?                                               │
        │ Cost                                              │
        │ Date Added                                        │
        │ Description                                       │
        │ Discount                                          │
        │ Full Title                                      ↓ │
        └───────────────────────────────────────────────────┘
    ──────────────────────────────────────────────────────────
    STOCK.DTF      33 FIELDS

    Esc-Backup  F1-Help  F3-Restart  A-Z  ↑  ↓  PgUp  PgDn  Home  End  ↵ Continue
```

Figure 7-7: Getting Specific. You've told the QG that you want to select and show a specific record or group of records. Now the QG wants you to indicate the retrieve parameters.

```
Find the records where Author Last



                         Select a constraint on the text or keyword field

              B - begins with ...                   (a character sequence)
              E - ends with ...                     (a character sequence)
              C - contains ...                       (a character sequence)
              M - matches ...                        (a character sequence)
              S - matches the SOUNDEX pattern ...       (a letter sequence)
              A - appears alphabetically ...      (before/after/first/last)
              N - does not ...                           (one of the above)
              I - is ...                          (blank or correctly formatted)




     STOCK.DTF

     Esc-Backup  F1-Help  F3-Restart  A-Z  ↑  ↓  PgUp  PgDn  Home  End  ←┘ Continue
```

Figure 7-8: Indicating Restrictions. The QG requesting that you place a constraint on the selected field value so it will know exactly what record or records to retrieve.

Notice that the screen displays the number of fields in the database (33 in this case). The QG presents the fields to you in alphabetical order, and if the appropriate field is not displayed, you use your navigation keys to move down the list until the one you want is highlighted. You then press **<Enter>** and the QG adds *that* to the query in the Request box above.

Anytime you want to start the query-building process over from the beginning, press **<F3>**. Press **<Esc>** to back up to the previous menu.

Suppose you selected Author Last — a field label in our STOCK.DTF database that contains the author's last name; the next step in the query-building process would be to choose the actual name contained in the selected field on the record you want the QG to display, as shown in Figure 7-8.

The query in the Request box in Figure 7-8 has now been extended to the still incomplete but now more well-defined command, "Find the records where Author Last." And all that's left for us to do is to specify the value for the Author Last field.

Suppose you're looking for an exact match on the author's last name field. The author's name is Parsoner, and you want the QG to find and display that

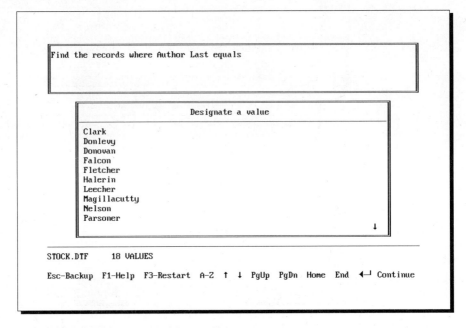

```
Find the records where Author Last equals




                              Designate a value
         Clark
         Donlevy
         Donovan
         Falcon
         Fletcher
         Halerin
         Leecher
         Magillacutty
         Nelson
         Parsoner
                                                                      ↓

   STOCK.DTF      18 VALUES

   Esc-Backup  F1-Help  F3-Restart  A-Z  ↑  ↓  PgUp  PgDn  Home  End  ←┘ Continue
```

Figure 7-9: The QG Displaying the Values for the Selected Field. Move to the value you want and press **<Enter>** to retrieve the matching record.

particular record. In this case you can choose Begins with ... (a character sequence), and type **P**. Or, you can press **M** for "Matches," because "Parsoner" is also a character string.

Select Matches, and you're taken to the next and final menu in the process, shown in Figure 7-9.

You're now at the point in the query-building process where having taught the QG makes a difference. Had you opted not to "teach" the Guide about this Author Last field, it would not now be able to display the list of values from that field, and you'd be forced to type the name "Parsoner" in order to retrieve that record. Selecting Parsoner now from the list of field values completes the query as follows:

Find the records where the Author Last equals Parsoner.

The request is logically complete, and so the action of retrieving the actual record can now take place.

But you may *not* have completed the request just yet. What if you had several books in stock authored by Parsoner, and you wanted to display the record of just one of them? In this case you'd need to further define your

```
┌─────────────────────────────────────────────────────────────────┐
│ Find the records where Author Last equals Parsoner                │
│                                                                   │
└─────────────────────────────────────────────────────────────────┘

     ┌───────────────────────────────────────────────────────┐
     │       Select an option from the list below to build a request │
     │                                                         │
     │   & - and the ...                              (field)  │
     │   . - .                          [to execute the command] │
     │   S - sorted by ...                  (values from the field) │
     │   D - sorted by decreasing ...       (values from the field) │
     │   O - or ...                         (alternate constraint) │
     │                                                         │
     │                                                         │
     │                                                         │
     └───────────────────────────────────────────────────────┘

   STOCK.DTF

   Esc-Backup  F1-Help  F3-Restart  A-Z ↑ ↓  PgUp  PgDn  Home  End  ←┘ Continue
```

Figure 7-10: A Logical Query. If you don't need to further define your search parameters, you can execute the command as is.

request by adding another search restriction or two. So the *sixth*-level menu comes up after "Parsoner" has been selected, and you're given the option of running the command as it is or further defining your search parameters. Figure 7-10 shows where you stand at this point.

At this point you can add one or more *additional* field restrictions (using "and" or "or" criteria), have the QG display the requested forms in sorted order, or execute the request as it stands in the box above the menu.

You can also press **<F3>** to start the query-building process from the beginning, or **<Esc>** to move back through the menus to reformulate your request.

Before you use the Query Guide for anything more than a simple search such as the one we've conducted here, you should be familiar with the elements of specifying search restrictions. There's a detailed discussion of these and a complete table of search restrictions included in Chapter 3.

Generating a Report Through the Query Guide

Building a report using the Query Guide is somewhat more involved because the process requires that you specify a number of fields to include as report columns. But it really isn't any more difficult.

```
┌──────────────────────────────────────────────────────────────────────┐
│ ┌──────────────────────────────────────────────────────────────────┐ │
│ │Produce a report showing the Title and the Stk# and the Cost and the│ │
│ │Qty On Hand from the forms where Type equals HB sorted by Title.    │ │
│ └──────────────────────────────────────────────────────────────────┘ │
│                                                                        │
│          Title              Stk#    Cost   Qty On Hand                  │
│     ─────────────────────   ─────   ──────  ───────────────            │
│                                                                        │
│     ─────────────────────   ─────   ──────  ───────────────            │
│     Boating on the Detroit River  205HB  $3.35      1120               │
│     Cruisin' Blues          444HB   $8.18         22                   │
│     Hollow Glen Mystery     299HB   $4.20        840                   │
│     Rack 'Em Up             344HB   $4.50       1034                   │
│     Terror on the Nile      188HB   $6.90         67                   │
│     The Omaha Factor        501HB   $12.08        18                   │
│                                                                        │
│                                                                        │
│     ──────────────────────────────────────────────────               │
│     STOCK.DTF                                                           │
│     *************************** END OF REPORT ************************** │
└──────────────────────────────────────────────────────────────────────┘
```

Figure 7-11: A Simple Report Produced by the Query Guide.

Suppose you wanted to generate a simple ad hoc report showing the title, stock number, cost, and quantity on hand of all your hardbound books, sorted by title — the report as shown in Figure 7-11.

You can see from the Request box in Figure 7-11 the language it took to create the report. Obviously, a number of menus were involved in the request, with the selection at each menu adding to the request (extending it) until the report was completely defined and the QG was told to execute the command.

Here are the steps that generated the Figure 7-11 report:

1. Query Guide was selected from the Assistant menu.

2. At the first menu Produce a Report... was selected.

3. The Select a Field option was chosen, and "Title" was specified as the first field (column) in the report.

4. Using the "& - and the ... (field)" option, the following additional fields were selected for inclusion in the report:

   • Stk# (stock number)

   • Cost (the price paid for the item)

   • Qty on Hand (the quantity of the item currently in stock)

5. Next, the "F - from ... (records)" option was selected to tell the Guide that it was time to specify the retrieval parameters.

6. "R - the records where ..." was next selected to set up the QG to accept the retrieve specs.

7. The QG then asked us to Select a Field to search and retrieve on, and we chose Type because that's the database field that contains information designating the stock item a hardbound book (HB), a paperback book (PB), an audiotape (AT), or a videotape (VT).

8. We then chose "M - matches ... (a character sequence)" from the next menu, and highlighted the code **HB** to indicate that we wanted to include only hardbound books in the report.

9. The QG then offered sorting options, and we selected "S - sorted by ... (values from the field)," and chose to sort the report on the Title field.

10. Finally, the QG was told to Execute the Command, and the screen report shown in Figure 7-11 displayed.

Once the report was displayed, we could have sent it on to the printer by pressing **<F2>**, selecting our print options and/or page characteristics, and pressing **<F10>** to print.

Now that you know the basics of using the Query Guide to retrieve records and run a report, you should take the time to experiment with it, using your own database or the sample employee database supplied with the program. Once you run a few queries and create a few ad hoc reports, the procedure will become practically second nature.

Using the Query Guide is also a good way to prepare yourself for working with the Intelligent Assistant, because the QG reveals how your requests are formulated in English as you move through the hierarchy of menus building your queries and reports.

In addition, the Query Guide is a powerful database query tool in itself, and its facilities may provide everything you need without ever having to type a single command.

In addition to simple search/retrieve operations, and one-time reports, use the QG to:

- Retrieve a sorted stack of forms to update.

- Get a quick count of the number of forms in the file that meet your search restrictions.

- Get a quick summary report on specified records, with counts, averages, totals, and maximum and minimum values.

- Create a one-time report cross-tabulated on two database fields, with a summary field that includes a variety of revealing statistics.

- Run a predefined report or File print spec. (These selections show you the list of existing report designs or print specs for the selected database.)

If you already know how to design standard and cross-tabulated reports from the discussions in Chapter 6, using the Query Guide will be a snap from the very first time you use it. But even novice users will find the QG easy to use.

Teaching the Intelligent Assistant

Teaching the Intelligent Assistant to proficiently process English-language commands is more involved than teaching the Query Guide to index the fields in your database. Yet the IA, once properly taught, can carry out your commands faster because you type your requests directly without having to proceed through a hierarchy of menus.

When you first introduce your database to the IA, it takes a few moments for the Assistant to scrutinize the structure of the file and then review all the records in it. The fewer records in the database, the less time it will take to prepare the IA for the lessons that follow.

You can use the Assistant to query your database without teaching it. But this requires familiarity with your database's field labels, as well as the IA's own built-in vocabulary.

Figure 7-3 shows the Assistant menu. This section of the chapter is devoted to the second item on that menu, "Teach Me About Your Database" — the selection which takes you to the Basic Lessons menu shown in Figure 7-12 after you've entered the name of the database you want to teach the IA.

Basic Lessons

The Basic Lessons menu enables the IA to learn the text and keyword values in a database, what the database keeps track of, which fields identify your forms, which fields can answer the "where" questions, and the field names that you will substitute for the defaults.

Basic Lesson 1 — Learn Values for Assistant

If you plan to have the IA recognize all the text and keyword values in your file so you can ask for the Bronson record, or the record that contains Part

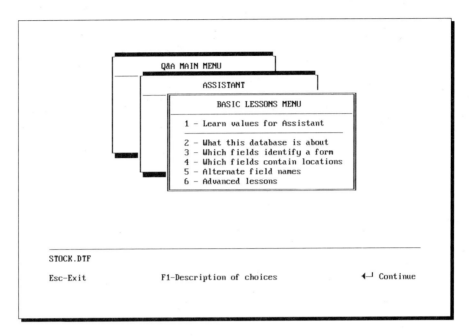

Figure 7-12: The Basic Lessons Menu in the Intelligent Assistant Module.

Number 388PB, select this item from the Basic Lessons menu and give the IA a few moments to scan your forms and compile the information.

If you don't plan to include specific text or keyword values in your requests, such as, "List the Stock Numbers where the Price > $5.00" — where no actual field value is mentioned in the command — you can skip this procedure and move on to Lesson 2.

Tip: Teaching the IA the important text values in your file — those that are likely to be the ones you'll often search on and use in reports — of course adds considerably to the Assistant's capabilities. But consider the cost. If your database has 20 text fields, then the IA will index each of them. If the file also contains several thousand records, those indexes will be fairly extensive and may eat up a little too much hard disk real estate for your liking.

On a large hard disk with a great deal of free space, the extra storage space required seems negligible. But on a 20-megabyte drive that's 90 percent full, you may want to refrain from educating the IA completely. If the number of records in the file is relatively small — say in the hundreds, and they aren't large multipage records loaded with text fields, then you'll probably want your Assistant to be as smart as possible, which would include an active awareness of all the text values in the file.

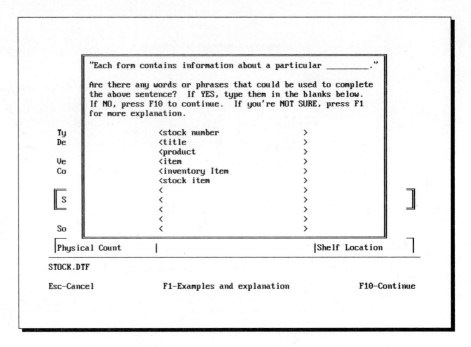

"Each form contains information about a particular _____."

Are there any words or phrases that could be used to complete
the above sentence? If YES, type them in the blanks below.
If NO, press F10 to continue. If you're NOT SURE, press F1
for more explanation.

```
Ty                     <stock number            >
De                     <title                    >
                       <product                  >
Ve                     <item                     >
Co                     <inventory Item           >
                       <stock item               >
                       <                          >
  S                    <                          >
                       <                          >
So                     <                          >
```

|Physical Count | |Shelf Location |

STOCK.DTF

Esc-Cancel   F1-Examples and explanation   F10-Continue

Figure 7-13: Teaching the IA the Subject of the Database.

Basic Lesson 2 — What This Database Is About

Here's where you tell the Assistant what this database keeps track of. In an inventory file this could be stock numbers, part numbers, or, in the case of books and such — titles. In a personnel database, each record would contain information about a particular employee. Records in a vendor file would keep track of vendors or suppliers, and the primary subject of a customer file would be customers or clients.

In the case of a customer file, for example, what would happen if you asked the Assistant for a list of customers? If you don't tell the IA that *customer* is the subject of the database, the IA wouldn't know how to handle the request if the word *customer* isn't in the database.

You see, even though the file is named CUSTOMER.DTF, this tells the IA nothing — it's just a filename. So you need to teach the Assistant about the subject of the database.

Figure 7-13 shows the screen that appears over your database form when you select Lesson 2 from the Basic Lessons menu. Here, we're teaching the IA about the Stock (inventory) database.

As illustrated in Figure 7-13, we've typed a number of terms which we may later use to get information from this file. You may recall that we have text fields on this form labelled Short Title and Full Title, as well as a Stk# field, so we have to be careful here.

In a business that sells books and tapes, these items are often referred to as *titles*. And since we may want to ask the IA, "List all the titles and prices," the IA should know that each record in the database keeps track of a particular title so that it can sensibly respond to such a request.

We also may want to tell the IA, "Show me the stock numbers where the vendor is Random House." So even though Stk# is the label of a field in the database, in this case it's also the *subject* of the database, although spelled differently. To the IA, "Stk#" and "Stock Number" don't mean the same thing unless you tell the IA they *are* the same thing.

For a customer file you'll use terms like *customer, client,* or *patron* to describe the subject of the database.

In a personnel file, terms like *employee, worker, person, staff member, staffer,* and *individual* are appropriate.

Ordinarily, you'll enter the singular form of the word. But where you have irregular plurals like "people," enter both "person" and "people."

When you're finished with this lesson, press **<F10>** to return to the Basic Lessons menu. You can come back later if you think of a new item to add.

Basic Lesson 3 — Which Fields Identify a Form?

In this lesson the IA will ask you to identify any fields in the database that you'll always want to appear as columns in requested reports.

For example, you might want a report that lists the prices of your inventory items. If you typed **What are the prices?** in the Request box, the IA would hand you a list of prices that would have little meaning without another column identifying the particular items to which these prices are connected.

So you'd probably want to tell the IA to always include at least the stock number in any report.

In a personnel file the employee's last name, and perhaps department, would be needed in any report you might request.

To select the fields you want the IA to always include as report columns:

1. Move the cursor to the field you want to make the first column in any requested report, and type **1**.

2. Move to the field you want to make the second column in any report, and type **2**.

3. Repeat the procedure, typing increasingly higher numbers in any other fields you'll always want included in your IA reports.

If you want to suppress the appearance of identification columns specified in this lesson, you can later include in your request the abbreviation WNIC ("With No Identification Columns").

Press **<F10>** when you've finished with this lesson. You'll be returned to the Basic Lessons menu.

Basic Lesson 4 — Which Fields Contain Locations?

When you ask "where" questions, you're generally looking for a location, such as an address, a department, or a warehouse shelf or bin.

At this lesson you tell the Assistant how to answer any "where" questions you may pose by typing numbers into the fields on your form that contain locations.

Street addresses, cities, states, and zip codes are all location fields. You number your location fields in the order you want them displayed by the IA. For example, you'd ordinarily type **1** in a street address field, **2** in the city field, **3** in the state field, and **4** in the zip code field. Then, when you ask the IA:

```
Where is Johnson Pipe Supply?
```

the IA will respond with the whole address.

If you have an inventory database with warehouse locations for your stock items, when you ask the IA:

```
Where is part number X3455?
```

it can give you the shelf or bin number.

Some databases contain multiple addresses, such as a home and business address. Later on you'll learn how to teach the IA to keep the two separate and display only the address you want.

When you've finished entering the numbers for your location fields, press **<F10>** to return to the Basic Lessons menu.

Basic Lesson 5 - Alternate Field Names

This is an important lesson because it provides the Assistant with the synonyms by which you might refer to the fields in your database. Try to resist the temptation to enter field *values* as alternate field names. That's not what you want to do here.

You may want to refer to the Last Name field as *surname;* you might need to request information about the Manager field by using the word *boss* or *supervisor;* there may be times when you'll forget that the field label is Phone, and

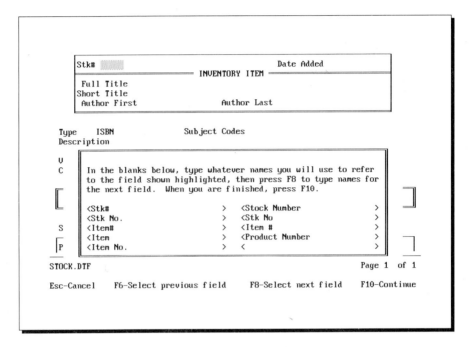

Figure 7-14: Alternate Field Names Defined for the Stk# Field.

request the *phone number, phone#, or phone no;* And if the field label is Stk#, you may want the IA to be able to respond to a request that refers to the field as *stock number, stk no, stock no, stk#,* or *stock #.*

At the Alternate Field Names screen, shown in Figure 7-14, you fill out a separate alternate name list for each field on your form. You can enter alternate names for all your fields or none of them. Press **<F8>** to select the next field, and **<F6>** for the previous field. Use the cursor keys to move between items on the alternate names list for the field you're in.

Tip: When you're teaching the IA, keep in mind the following:

- You don't have to enter the plurals of your alternate field names unless the plural form of the word is irregular (doesn't end with an "s," "es," or "ies."

- Each alternate name must be unique. For example, you can't assign the synonym "name" to both the First Name and Last Name fields.

- The first name on the alternate list is the field name, and this will become the column heading in any reports generated by the IA. You can replace the original field name with another by typing over it,

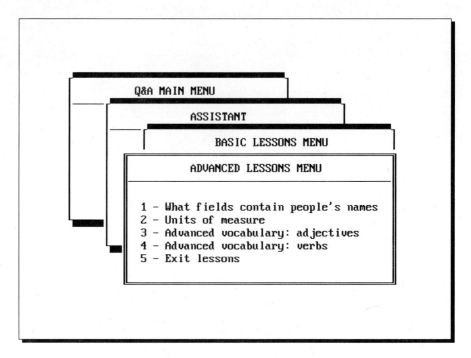

Figure 7-15: The Intelligent Assistant Advanced Lessons Menu.

and this new top name will head your report columns. But if you replace the first field name with another, you'll probably want to retype the original top name somewhere else on the list so the Assistant will know it.

Press **<F10>** when you've finished with this lesson to return to the Basic Lessons menu.

Advanced Lessons

After educating your assistant in the basics, you'll probably want to move on to the more advanced lessons where you'll tell the IA which fields contain people's names, which fields contain units of measure, and which adjectives and verbs you'll use when typing your commands into the Request box.

When you select Advanced Lessons from the Basic Lessons menu, the Advanced Lessons menu displays as shown in Figure 7-15.

Advanced Lesson 1 — Which Fields Contain People's Names

You'll probably need to ask "who" questions of the IA from time to time. If your database contains the names of people, questions like these can be posed:

```
Who is the buyer at Consolidated Metals?
Who is in the accounting department?
Who works part time?
Who was billed on invoice# 2345?
```

This lesson also teaches the IA to treat several fields containing parts of names as a unit, and allows you to retrieve information for "Edward" even if Edward's form shows his name as the longer string "Edward James Smith."

With titles, first names, middle initials, last names, and suffixes like "Jr." or "M.D." in a database, the IA won't know how to respond to requests for such names unless you tell it that these are *partial* name fields.

Figure 7-16a and 7-16b show a Customer database form at the People's Names lesson, and the chart summarizing the codes you use, which you can view by pressing **<F1>**.

If there are more than two names on the form, type **1** in the fields that contain the first person's name, and **2** in the fields that contain the name of the second person. In Figure 7-16a, the Whole Name field is the same person, so that gets a **1** also.

Now you have to tell the Assistant what part of the name the field contains. For the first person's title, type **T** after the **1**; for that same person's first name type an **F** after the **1**; the middle initial field gets a **1M**; the last name field gets a **1L**; and the suffix field, if any, gets a **1S**.

The second person's name fields, if any, get the same **T**, **F**, **M**, **L**, and **S** codes, each preceded by **2**. Should the second person's name field contain the whole name, type **2W** in that field.

So long as you've told the IA that a whole name field is a name field, you can refer to it by using any of the words entered in it. For example, if a whole name field contains "Fred Bingles," you can refer to the person as "Fred" or "Bingles;" however, if there's another person in the file with the first name of Fred, the IA will be forced to ask you for clarification.

When you've entered your name codes and press **<F10>** the box in Figure 7-17 appears. When you're dealing with composite names (several fields contributing to the identity of the person), the IA also needs to know if you'll refer to the person by any special words or phrases. Since our Customer database contains retail customers as well as commercial companies where a

```
         CUSTOMER   Key Name                    CU#
                                                ID#

        Title 1T   First 1F       M 1M Last 1L

        Whole Name 1W
           Company
            Street
              City                 St    Zip


          Are there any fields that contain a person's name?

          If YES, then press F1 so that I can tell you what I need to know.

          If NO, then just press F10 to continue to the next lesson.



        CUSTOMER.DTF                               Page 1  of 1

        Esc-Cancel            F1-Examples and explanation    F10-Continue
```

Figure 7-16a: People's Names Lesson. You teach the IA about people's names by typing special codes in the fields that contain parts of names and whole names. This is the top portion of a customer database form showing the codes entered to denote the component parts of the name, and also the whole name.

```
           =========== FIELDS THAT CONTAIN PEOPLE'S NAMES ===========

         Each form in your database may have fields that contain the names of
         one or more people.  To teach me about them, do the following.

         1. Type 1 in the field or fields that contain the name of the
         first person, 2 in the field(s) for the second person, if any,
         and so on -- one number per person (see example).

         2. Type an abbreviation after the number to indicate whether the
         field contains a whole name or part of a name:

         W = Whole name      F = First name     T = Title (Mr., Mrs.)
         M = Middle name     L = Last name      S = Suffix (Ph.d, Esq.)

             For example:
            ┌─────────────────────────────────────────────────────────┐
            │                    EMPLOYEE FORM                         │
            │                                                          │
            │    Last name: 1L         First name: 1F      Title: 1T   │
            │                                                          │
            │    Manager: 2W                                           │
            └─────────────────────────────────────────────────────────┘

         Esc-Cancel
```

Figure 7-16b: People's Names Lesson. This chart displays when you press <F1> at this lesson.

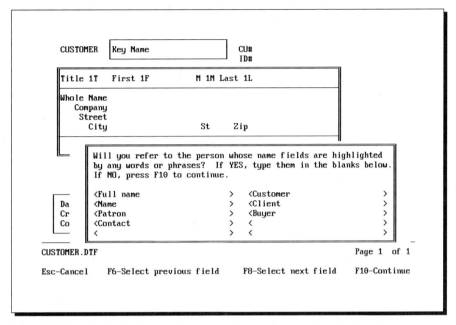

Figure 7-17: Substitution for Names. Your assistant wants to know if you'll refer to the person by any words or phrases.

buyer's name may be entered in the name field, we've typed a variety of words by which we may refer to the contents of the name fields.

We could now ask the Assistant:

Who is the buyer at Allied Distributing?
Who is my contact at Barnes Book Company?
List the customers who...
Which clients are in San Diego?
Show me the names of...

and we'd get the name or names of the individuals.

Notice that we didn't code the Company and Key Name fields as name fields. This lesson is for the names of people only. The Key Name field could contain a company name or a person's last name — or an abbreviation of either (to help the operator retrieve the record faster). But, strictly speaking, it's not a valid person's name field.

If you're teaching the IA about an employee database which includes whole name fields for a supervisor's name and the name of someone to contact in case of emergency, code these **2W** and **3W,** respectively, thus informing the IA that these are indeed name fields, but not *primary* name fields.

When you've coded all the name fields as above, press **<F10>** to save your specifications and return to the Advances Lessons menu.

Advanced Lesson 2 — Units of Measure

If the information type of any fields in the database is numeric, the IA will need to know the *units of measure* that apply to those fields.

For example, a numeric field's value might be expressed in inches, feet, square feet, acres, miles, ounces, pounds, tons, days, hours, months, years, quarts, gallons, or any other unit of measure.

If you intend to ask the Assistant questions such as:

```
Which products weigh less than 12 ounces?
Who is more than 50 years old?
How many hours does Otis Winkler's form show?
List the houses greater than 5000 square feet
Which trucks get at least 5 miles per gallon?
```

the IA will need a reference so it can process your request without stopping for clarification.

When you enter the Units of Measure lesson, numeric fields will be highlighted with a string of pound or number signs (**#**). Use **<F6>** and **<F8>** to move forward or back to each numeric field that has a unit of measure, and type the appropriate measurement term in the box provided. If you're not sure about what to enter, press **<F1>** for examples and explanations.

Money fields aren't highlighted at this lesson. The IA already knows that these contain dollars or whatever currency you specified at the Global Format Options screen.

Not all numeric fields necessarily include units of measure — a field may contain simply a count or a total. Our sample Stock database, for instance, contains several quantity fields (such as On Hand and On Order) which aren't measured in gallons, inches, or any other special units. Furthermore, their field names would ordinarily be specifically referred to in any IA request. So there's no need, at this lesson, to specify units of measure for them.

However, you may need to add synonyms to such fields at the Alternate Field Names lesson. For example, although "cubic feet" may be the specified measurement, you may want to query the field's value by asking about the "volume." If a field is labeled Qty in Stk (meaning "quantity in stock"), synonyms such as Quantity in Stock, Qty in Stock, or even QIS, may come in handy when querying the database through the Intelligent Assistant. You could phrase your question as follows:

```
What is the QIS of PN T344XPB?
```

and the IA would tell you how many of that part number are currently on hand.

If there are no numeric fields on your form when you enter this lesson, the IA tells you so. Should this database contain one or more fields that *are* numeric but haven't been designated as information type **N,** you can exit this lesson, go back to the Format Spec, change the information types to **N,** and then return to this lesson to specify any appropriate measurements.

Proper information types entered at the Format Spec, and appropriate units of measure specified for numeric fields at this lesson, enable the Assistant to interpret and correctly handle these kinds of queries.

Advanced Lesson 3 — Adjectives

Adjectives help describe or add meaning to subjects. When someone says "He's the *tallest* kid on the block," or "That car gets the *best* (or *highest*) gas mileage," an order of comparative magnitude is being expressed to add meaning to the statement.

People often ask questions that contain these kinds of qualifiers. For example, you might ask the Assistant "Whose salary is the *highest?*" Who is the *youngest* employee?" "Which part number is the *most expensive?*" "What is the *cheapest* stock item?" or "Who are the three *top* salespeople?" As long as the information about salaries, ages (or birth dates), part number prices, and salespeople's volume is in the database, you'd expect the IA to know what you mean.

The IA comes with many of the comparative adjectives people ordinarily use already built in. In this lesson you assign opposite pairs of adjectives to any numeric and currency fields where you want to be able to ask questions about their high and low values.

Be particularly careful to tell the IA about adjectives you may use that are irregularly formed, such as *good, better,* and *best,* or *bad, worse,* and *worst.* Normally, the IA can figure out regularly formed adjectives such as *older* and *oldest,* so long as you've defined the adjective *old.* In other words, if the magnitude of the value described by the adjective increases when it ends in "er," and is expressed as the maximum when it ends in "est," you only have to teach the IA the higher or lower value, and it will be able to figure out the others.

Table 7-1 summarizes the adjectives in the Assistant's built-in vocabulary.

All the comparative adjectives in Table 7-1 can apply to any field. In this lesson you need to teach your assistant any other adjectives you'll use which relate to specific fields. In a birthday or age field you might want to teach the

Table 7-1
Adjectives the IA Already Knows

above	below	under
big	bigger	biggest
early	earlier	earliest
few	fewer	fewest
great	greater	greatest
high	higher	highest
large	larger	largest
late	later	latest
little	littler	littlest
long	longer	longest
low	lower	lowest
many	more	most
maximum	——	minimum
much	less	least
small	smaller	smallest
top	——	bottom

IA *old* and *young* (it would then be able to figure out *older, oldest, younger,* and *youngest.* In a numeric field containing a value expressed in some physical dimension, you could enter *tiny* as a low value and *huge* as a high value. *Teenie-weenie* could be a low value and *humongous* a high value.

Remember: The high/low relationships you establish in this lesson should pertain to a particular field and only to that field. This doesn't mean that you can't use the same pair of adjectives in more than one field, only that you should consider whether the adjectives you specify *apply* to the field in question before teaching them to your assistant.

Also, you'll want to avoid defining as adjectives terms that are better suited for the next lesson on verbs. For example, you may want to use the verb *paid* when asking for information in a salary field ("How much is Fred Johnson *paid?*"). In this case, the IA would know what *lowest paid* and *best paid* (or *highest paid*) mean.

When you enter Advanced Lesson 3, the IA displays your database form design with pound or number signs (#) in all the numeric and money fields. Move the cursor between fields using the <F6> and <F8> keys, and at each such field type any high- and low-value adjectives you might use when asking the IA about the information in the field.

When you've finished specifying your high- and low-value adjectives, press <F10> to return to the Advanced Lesson menu.

Advanced Lesson 4 — Verbs

Verbs are a class of words that tell what's being done or express action. When you say "Let's *move* the car" or "*Hand* me the newspaper," you're using the verbs *move* and *hand* to describe the action involved.

The IA's built-in vocabulary contains a number of verbs that you can use to command the Assistant. You may want to tell the IA to *"Run* the New Customers report," *"Show* invoice number 12334," *"List* the POs for June 1990," *"Count* the forms where Ballentine is the supplier," or *"Increase* the retail prices of all videos by .05."

Table 7-2 shows the verbs the IA already knows.

Using just the verbs listed in Table 7-2 you'll be able to obtain the record, report, or other information you need from your assistant. But chances are that you'll want to use additional verbs — verbs you're accustomed to using in your ordinary conversational English.

In an employee database, you might want to ask "When was John Obermeyer *hired?* The verb *hired,* in this case, relates to the field on the form that shows Date Hired. "Who was *brought on board* after April 1, 1990?" also associates the verb phrase *brought on board* with the Date Hired field.

Verbs such as *earn* and *paid* are typically associated with salary fields. For example, "How much is Jim Haggerty *paid?*" or "What does Jim Haggerty *earn?*" These would be entered at this lesson as verbs, not in the employee name field, but in the salary field, because you're asking for salary values.

In an invoice database, you might ask the Assistant, "How much did we *bill* all customers in May, 1990?" or "When did we *prepare* invoice number 35466? Here, the verb *bill* refers to the invoice Total Amount field, and the verb *prepare* is associated with the Invoice Date field. "How many POs have we *prepared* since January 1, 1990 and what is the dollar amount total?" asks the

Table 7-2
The Intelligent Assistant's Built-in Verbs

add	define	find	print	set
blank	delete	get	remove	show
change	display	increase	replace	subtract
count	divide	list	report	sum
create	enter	make	run	total
decrease	erase	multiply	search	

Assistant to return a count of the number of purchase orders entered since January 1, 1990, along with the grand total dollar amount.

The verbs you add to the IA's fund of knowledge must be unique from field to field; the same verbs can't be used to refer to two different fields. Moreover, your verbs can't duplicate field labels or any synonyms you've already defined for other fields. For example, if an inventory database field is labeled Cost, you can't add *cost* as a verb. Or if *pay* is an alternate field name for Salary, you can't add *pay* as a verb. However, since the IA treats verbs and alternate field names in a similar manner, "How much does part number X344B cost?" and "What is the cost of part number X344B?" produce the same answer.

Verbs ending with "s," "es," "en," "ed," and "ing" are recognized by the IA once the root verb is established. For example, when your assistant sees *hired* or *hires* in your request, and the verb *hire* has been taught, it will know how to respond.

If you plan to use any irregular verbs, such as *sell* and *sold*, you must enter both of these terms as verbs. Listing only *sell* enables the IA to understand both *sell* and *selling*, but not the past tense *sold*.

Sometimes verbs are expressed as a combination of words: "When was part number B234 *brought in?*" "Who does Nancy Smith *report to?*" If you're likely to use such verbs you must teach the Assistant the entire combination, as well as any other forms of it you may use in your requests.

To enter verbs at this lesson, use **<F8>** to move forward to the next field and **<F6>** to move back to the previous field. You can list up to ten verbs for any field.

When you've finished adding your special verbs, press **<F10>** to save your work and return to the Advanced Lessons menu. "Exit Lessons" will be high-lighted. Press **<Enter>** to return to the Intelligent Assistant menu.

Using the Intelligent Assistant

Now that you've taught your assistant what it needs to know to understand and process your requests, you can select "Ask Me To Do Something" from the Intelligent Assistant menu, and the Request box shown in Figure 7-18 will appear, ready for you to type your command.

It's not mandatory that you first teach the IA before asking it to do something. Using only the IA's built-in vocabulary and the field labels and field values in your database, you can have the IA retrieve and change forms, perform calculations, and produce reports. If you plan to refer to *field values* in your requests, however, at the very least you'll need to select the Learn Values for Assistant option, and give the IA a few moments to compile the contents of the fields in your database.

I'll discuss querying an untaught Assistant later in this chapter. For now it's assumed that you've gone through the basic and advanced lessons one by one, and that the IA is now prepared to respond to your requests typed in the Request box.

To use the Request box, type your question or command in ordinary English and then press **<Enter>**. The usual editing and cursor keys are at your disposal. If you've left out a word, for example, use the cursor keys to return to that area of the request, press **<Ins>**, and type the missing word.

When you've typed your request and pressed **<Enter>** to have it carried out, the IA first evaluates the request to make sure it understands what you want. If no further clarification is needed, the IA responds by displaying a "plan of action" (a confirmation of your request in its own terms), and asking you if that's what you really want.

If your Assistant has correctly interpreted your command, you then press **<Enter>** or **Y** (for "Yes") to have it carried out. If the IA's interpretation is *not* consistent with what you want, you then press **N** (for "No") and rephrase your request in terms you think it *will* understand.

Your assistant may stop in the middle of evaluating your request to ask for clarification. Perhaps a field label or an adjective or verb used in your request is the same as a word in the IA's built-in vocabulary, you've used a word the IA doesn't know, or you've phrased the command in such a way that a single reference could apply to more than one field in the database. I'll cover such situations in the pages that follow.

```
┌──────────────────────────────────────────────────────────────────┐
│  ┌────────────────────────────────────────────────────────────┐  │
│  │ LIST THE STOCK NUMBERS WHERE QTY IN STK < 10 SORTED BY TITLE │  │
│  │                                                              │  │
│  └────────────────────────────────────────────────────────────┘  │
│  ┌────────────────────────────────────────────────────────────┐  │
│  │      Type your request in English in the box above, then     │  │
│  │      press ↵ .                                               │  │
│  │      Examples:                                               │  │
│  │      ``List the average salary and average bonus from the    │  │
│  │      forms on which the sex is male and the department is    │  │
│  │      sales."                                                 │  │
│  │      ``Get the forms of the Administration employees,        │  │
│  │      sorted by city."                                        │  │
│  │                                                              │  │
│  │              Press │ F1 │  for more information.             │  │
│  └────────────────────────────────────────────────────────────┘  │
│  ──────────────────────────────────────────────────────────────  │
│  STOCK.DTF                                                        │
│                                                                   │
└──────────────────────────────────────────────────────────────────┘
```

Figure 7-18: The Intelligent Assistant's Request Box. This is where you type your question or command.

Questions and Requests

An Assistant that's been properly taught will be prepared to respond to a wide variety of questions phrased in ordinary English. The following are a few examples of the types of questions and requests you can ask:

"What," "Which," and "Who" Questions

- What's the address of John Franklin?

- What's the average cost of our stock items?

- Which invoices show a total amount greater than $500?

- Which employees live in San Diego?

- Which customers are wholesale accounts?

- Who does Carl Martin report to?

- Who lives in San Diego?

- Who was hired before Jan 1, 1988?

- Who supplies PN 122HB?

- What's the fax number and buyer's name at Acme Pool Supply?

"How Many" Questions

- How may stock numbers are in the inventory?
- How many male employees are in the production department?
- Count the invoices for Drexel Lumber Co.
- Give me a count of the purchase orders.
- How many customers do we have?
- How many retail customers do we have?

"Where" Questions

- Where is PN 433BX?
- Where does Jim Fergeson live?
- Where is Jim Fergeson?
- Where is Drexel Lumber Co.?

"When" Questions

- Who was brought on board after June 15, 1990?
- When was Susan Warner hired?
- What's the date?
- What time is it?
- What purchase orders were prepared in the last 60 days?
- Which June 1990 invoices are for Micro Supply?

Complex Questions

- Which customers are wholesale or have a credit limit greater than $5,000?
- Whose salary is higher than Ferguson's and works in Production?
- Which orders have a balance due between $100 and $250?
- Get me the forms where the type is clothbound or video and sort them by title.
- List employees who have no emergency contact, show their departments and extensions, and sort them by last name.
- List the April 1990 purchase orders sorted by company, and show the date and amount.

- Who doesn't work in Sales and makes more than the average salary in Accounting?

Run a New Report Requests

- Show me a list of the employees who live in San Marcos.

- Who works in Accounting?

- Give me a list of the stock numbers supplied by Ballentine sorted by title.

- Show the wholesale customers and phone numbers sorted by company.

- List the invoice numbers, dates, and customers where the balance due is greater than $100.

- Show me a list of the purchase orders for Random House.

- Display the names, salaries with totals, and bonuses with totals, sorted by sex.

Run Predefined Reports Requests

- Run the Bonuses report.

- Show me the Phone Directory.

- Run the Backorder report.

- Get me the Active Titles report.

Add/Search/Sort/Display Forms Requests

- Add form.

- I want to create a new form.

- Add a new inventory form with X344B in the Stk# field and $12.95 in the list price field.

- Get Bob Gruel's form.

- Show me the forms for all the videos.

- Let me see all the forms where the supplier is Ballentine.

- Get the forms for employees in R&D, sorted by Last Name.

- Show me the forms where the resale number is blank, sorted by company.

- I want all the forms where the date is later than May 12, 1990.

Change Values in Forms and Delete Forms Requests

- Add $1,000 to Jim Fergeson's salary.
- Change the supplier on part number BX43 to Random House.
- Increase all prices by 5 percent.
- Increase all prices by $2.50.
- Delete the form for PN X3344.
- Remove Jane Martin's form.
- Erase any forms where the supplier is Martin Press.

Calculations Requests

- What's 15,856 divided by 8?
- 87 + 33 * 7.5
- Multiply the Qty on Hand by the Cost for all stock numbers and show the total.
- Qty on Hand * Cost with total.

Add and Use Synonyms Requests

- Define "clothbound" as "HB."
- Define "videotape" as "VT."
- List the videotapes with titles and prices, sorted by title.
- Define "address" as "street, city, state, and zip code."
- What's Brad Lensky's address?
- List the employees phone numbers and addresses, sorted by department.

Using the Assistant without Teaching It

You can use the Intelligent Assistant to query your database, display and change forms, and generate reports without first teaching it any of the Basic or Advanced Lessons discussed earlier in this chapter.

If you'll be referring to database *field values* in your requests, however, the IA will need to know what those values are. Select "Learn Values for Assistant" at the Advanced Lessons menu, and allow the IA to take a few moments to compile the information from your records.

Even without this step you'll still be able to enter requests, as long as the words you use are either in the Assistant's built-in vocabulary or are database field names.

Before you can query a database through the IA you must first allow the Assistant to become familiar with the file. This requires no more involvement on your part than simply giving the Assistant permission to proceed with initialization. Once familiar with the structure of your database, and without teaching it any further lessons, the IA is prepared to process your requests.

Here are a few examples of requests you could make of an untaught Intelligent Assistant:

- Cromwell form   (to display the form of employee or company named Cromwell)

- Telephones   (to list all the phone numbers)

- Last Names   (returns a list of the last names)

- R&D Secretaries   (shows the names and salaries of the secretaries in the R&D department)

- Salary >=$20,000   (shows names and salaries for employees who make $20,000 or less)

- 345/15   (divides 345 by 15)

Even more complex requests are possible without teaching the Assistant:

- Stk#s, Titles, Prices, sorted by Title.

- Dept, Last Name, First Name where Department = Sales or Production.

- Invoice Number, Date, and Amount where Balance Due > $10.

- Purchase Order No and Amount where Date > July 14, 1990 sorted by Vendor.

- Companies where City = Chicago sorted by Company.

- Last Name, First Name, Salary with total and average by Department.

You can also enter synonyms (alternate field names) directly at the Request box without having to go through the menu system and teaching process. For example:

- Define "Paperback" as Type = "PB"

- Define "Book" as Type = "HB" or Type = "PB"

You can then tell the IA to "List the Paperbacks" or "Show me a list of the Books and Prices sorted by Title."

- Define "Big Cheese" as Position = "President"

- Define "hangs out" as "Street, City, State, Zip Code"

- Define "poor slobs" as Salary "< $10,000"

After all this, you could ask the Assistant: "Tell me where the Big Cheese hangs out" or "List the poor slobs in Production by Last Name" (although the phrase "hangs out" is a verb, it can still be defined as a synonym for expediency).

Formulating your requests to match the IA's built-in words and your database's field names (including any synonyms you've defined) may be a feasible shortcut where there are few fields on the form and you can remember the vocabulary. But where the database will be queried frequently through the Assistant (especially by others as well as yourself), and you want it to be able to respond quickly to a wide range of questions posed in natural conversational English, taking the IA through the lessons one by one is well worth the effort in the long run.

Retrieving and Updating Forms

From the many examples above you already know how to instruct the Intelligent Assistant to retrieve a record. When you want just one record, use the word "form" or "record" in your request; when you want a group of forms, specify "forms" or "records."

Once the record is displayed, you can edit it as though you were in Search/ Update in the File module.

If you've had the IA retrieve a stack of forms, press **<F10>** when you've finished editing the first record, and the next record in the stack will be displayed. Continue the procedure until you've viewed and updated all the records in the group.

You can also change the information on a record or records by typing in the change in the Request box. For example:

```
Change the location of part number X3455 to "F12".
Change The Book Nook's phone number to "212-454-5677".
Add $150 to the bonus of all employees in production.
Make Sarah Johnson's salary $25,000.
```

 Tip: When using the Request box to add new information to a form, put any new text values inside quote marks as in the first two examples above. You don't need quotes around numbers, money, times, or dates. Also, don't include a period inside any quote marks unless you want the IA to interpret the period as part of the field label or value.

Running Reports

When you ask the Assistant for a report, you'll need to specify what fields are to be columns, and which forms are to be included.

The easiest way to specify the fields is simply to include the field labels (or alternate field names) in your request. For example, to see the Stk#, Title, and Price fields from all the forms in the database, just say:

```
Show the stk#, title, and price.
```

You could also say:

```
Create a report showing all the stock numbers, titles,
and prices.
```

The first way of wording the command provides the IA with the precise field names you want included in the report, although the wording in the second command may be more natural for you and will produce the same report.

In either case, the stock number will be the first column in the report, the title will be the second, and the price will be the third, since that's the order in which you requested them.

An exception to this rule comes into play, however, if you've assigned Identification Columns in Basic Lesson 3. If, when you were teaching the IA, you specified that the Title field always be included in any report as the first column, then that's the way the IA will display it: Title, then Stk#, and then Price.

The IA can also handily process a request for a report with an arithmetically derived column. For example, if you wanted a report showing the value of your on-hand inventory at cost with a grand total, you could make the following request:

```
List the titles, stock numbers, and cost * qty on hand
with total.
```

Requesting Totals and Subtotals

When you want the column grand total displayed, follow the field name with the phrase "with total." For example:

```
Show me the names and salaries with total.
```

The phrase "with total" calculates and display the totals of all numeric columns in the report. You can control which columns are totaled by specifying "with total for (field name)." For example:

Show me the Shipping Charges and Amounts with total for Amount Due.

When you want subtotals to appear at sorted column breaks, use the phrase "with total by (field name)" or "with subtotal by (field name):"

Show the Employees, Hire Dates, and Salaries with total by Department.

The Department field will then display as the first column of the report, with breaks for subtotals on salary when the department changes.

To get subtotals *and* a grand total of the salaries in the above example:

Show the Employees, Hire Dates, and Salaries with subtotal by Department and total.

Count, average, minimum, and maximum are specified in the same way.

Selecting and Sorting Forms

Where you want restrictions placed on the forms to be included in the report, the IA needs to know this. For example, if you want only the employee forms on which the department is Sales and the Salary is greater than $25,000, your request can be made along these lines:

Show the salary where the department is sales and the salary > $25,000.

See Table 7-4 at the end of the chapter for a summary of how to specify restrictions.

To have the IA produce a sorted report, tell your assistant which fields to sort on. This is as simple as adding to your request the phrase:

sorted by title.
sorted by department.
sorted by last name.
sorted by zip code.

Sorted fields will display as the first column in any report. You can sort on more than one field, in which case the first sorted field will be the leftmost column, the second sorted field will follow it as column 2, and so on, in the same order in which you requested the sorts.

If you want a *descending* sort, specify "by decreasing (*field name*)" in your request.

```
┌─────────────────────────────────────────────────────────────────┐
│ SHOW ME THE TITLES, STOCK NUMBERS AND PRICES SORTED BY COST       │
│                                                                   │
│                                                                   │
└─────────────────────────────────────────────────────────────────┘

  Cost            Short Title           Stk#    List
  ─────     ───────────────────────     ─────   ──────
  $2.35     Backwater Fishing           533PB   $16.40
  $3.35     Boating on the Detroit River 205HB  $19.95
  $3.90     Love Songs of the Sparrow   199AT   $9.95
  $3.90     Bird Songs of New Jersey Shore 680AT $9.95
  $4.10     Bach's Greatest Hits        218AT   $9.95
  $4.20     Hollow Glen Mystery         299HB   $23.45
  $4.45     Looking Through the Lens    388PB   $10.95
  $4.50     Rack 'Em Up                 344HB   $22.50
  $5.90     Help for the Common Cold    314PB   $16.95
  $6.00     Growing Fruit Trees         309PB   $14.95
  $6.90     Terror on the Nile          188HB   $18.95
  $6.90     Man Who Invented Ball Bearing 348PB $12.95
 ─────────────────────────────────────────────────────────────────
  STOCK.DTF

  Esc-Cancel   F2-Reprint      { → ← ↓ ↑ PgUp PgDn }-Scroll   F10-Continue
```

Figure 7-19: A Sorted Report. A specified sorting order takes precedence over identification fields.

Figure 7-19 shows a sorted report where the identifying fields were Stk# and Title. The sorting parameter ("sorted by cost") takes precedence over these identification fields and appears in the report as the first column. "Title" has already been defined as a synonym for the field label Short Title, "stock number" has been defined as a synonym for Stk#, and "Price" has been defined as a synonym for List (List Price).

Ordinarily, you don't have to say, for example, *"sorted* by department" in your requests. The Assistant will usually know what you mean when you simply say "by department."

```
Display a list of the books by title.
List the invoices by date and by customer.
Show me the POs by date and by vendor.
Create a report showing the employees in Production by
hire date.
```

You *must* use the words "sorted by," however, if the item you're sorting on is also used to describe the subject of the database in addition to being the field name.

The query:

List the titles by title.

produces a report of titles sorted by values in the Title field so long as "title" hasn't been listed as a subject of the database at Basic Lesson 2 (What this database is about).

If "title" *is* a subject of the database, and you want a report sorted on the Title *field*, your request must specify:

List the titles sorted by title.

You can add a special phrase to your request when you need to control what columns appear in the displayed report. The abbreviation **WNIC** (With No Identification Columns) tells the Assistant to suppress the display of the columns specified in Basic Lesson 3.

Where your request places restrictions (such as sorting) on the forms to be selected for the report, you can suppress the display of those columns by adding **WNRC** (With No Restriction Columns) to the end of your command.

And if you want the IA to prevent the display of any columns except those explicitly asked for in the request, use the abbreviation **WNEC** (With No Extra Columns). Using **WNEC** is the same as specifying *both* **WNIC** and **WNRC**.

Working with Your New Assistant

Once you've taken your assistant through the basic and advanced lessons and begin using it, most of the work will be done. The more carefully and comprehensively you've taught the IA, the less it will have to stop to request clarification from you as it evaluates your requests. But the teaching process is likely to continue for a time, especially at the beginning. This is to be expected as you get adjusted to working with the IA.

Tip: Here are some principles and techniques you can employ to get the most from the Assistant.

Forms, fields, and values — The Assistant can "think fast" when your requests include explicit references to these fundamental database building blocks. As you define new synonyms and reteach the Assistant, remember to keep these basic elements in mind.

Use familiar terms — those that the IA already knows from its built-in vocabulary, the database field names, values, and words you've taught it. If it doesn't know a word, it will have to stop and ask for clarification. At this point, you'll need to decide whether you want to teach the word, or just avoid using it

```
Built-in Words Screen Page 1

                          BUILT-IN VOCABULARY


A               ANY         BELOW       COME           DECREASE     ENTRY
ABOUT           ANYONE      BEST        COMMENCING     DEFINE       EQUAL
ABOVE           APPEAR      BETTER      CONCERN        DEFINITION   ERASE
ACCORDING       APRIL       BETWEEN     CONSTRAINT     DELETE       EVERY
ADD             ARE         BIG         CONTAIN        DESCENDING   EVERYBODY
AFTER           AS          BLANK       COULD          DETAIL       EVERYTHING
AGAIN           ASCENDING   BOTH        COUNT          DEVIATION    EXCEED
AGAINST         ASSIGN      BOTTOM      CREATE         DIFFERENCE   EXCLUDE
AGO             AT          BREAK       CROSSTAB       DISPLAY      EXCLUSIVE
ALL             AUGUST      BUT         CROSSTABULATE  DIVIDE       EXIST
ALONG           AVERAGE     BY          CURRENT        DO           F
ALPHABETICAL    AWAY        CALCULATE   CUT            DURING       FALSE
ALSO            B           CAME        DAILY          EACH         FEBRUARY
AM              BE          CAN         DATA           EARLY        FETCH
AMONG           BEEN        CHANGE      DATABASE       EITHER       FEW
AN              BEFORE      CHRISTEN    DATE           EMPTY        FIELD
AND             BEGIN       CHRISTMAS   DAY            END          FILE
ANNUAL          BEING       COLUMN      DECEMBER       ENTER        FILL
```

Figures 7-20a, b, and c: Words in the IA's Built-in Vocabulary. You can display the word list by pressing <F6> from the Request screen and selecting Built-in Words.

```
Built-in Words Screen Page 2

    FIND        HIM            LARGE     MINIMUM    NULL        PRESENT
    FOLLOWING   HIS            LAST      MINUS      NUMBER      PREVIOUS
    FOR         HOUR           LATE      MINUTE     OCTOBER     PRINT
    FORM        HOW            LEAST     MONTH      OF          PRODUCE
    FOUND       I              LESS      MORE       OK          PRODUCT
    FROM        ID             LET       MOST       ON          PROGRESSION
    GET         IDENTIFICATION LIKE      MUCH       ONE         PUT
    GIVE        IF             LIST      MULTIPLY   ONLY        QUOTIENT
    GOOD        IN             LITTLE    MUST       OR          RAISE
    GOT         INCLUDE        LOOK      MY         ORDER       RANK
    GRAND       INCLUSIVELY    LOW       N          OUT         RATIO
    GREAT       INCREASE       M         NAME       OVER        RECENT
    HAD         INFORMATION    MADE      NEGATIVE   OVERALL     RECORD
    HALF        IS             MAKE      NEITHER    PAST        REDUCE
    HALLOWEEN   IT             MANY      NEW        PATTERN     REMOVE
    HAS         JANUARY        MARCH     NEXT       PERCENT     REPLACE
    HAVE        JULY           MATCH     NO         PLUS        REPORT
    HE          JUNE           MAXIMUM   NON        POOR        RESET
    HELP        JUST           MAY       NOT        PORTION     RESPECT
    HER         K              ME        NOVEMBER   POSITIVE    RESTRICTION
    HIGH        KNOW           MEAN      NOW        PRECEDING   RETRIEVE
```

Figure 7-20b

```
Built-in Words Screen Page 3
    REVERSE     STANDARD         TABLE     TO        WHAT      YEAR
    RUN         START            TAKE      TODAY     WHEN      YES
    SAME        STATISTICS       TELL      TOMORROW  WHERE     YESTERDAY
    SEARCH      STILL            THAN      TOP       WHETHER   YOU
    SEE         SUBAVERAGE       THANK     TOTAL     WHICH     YOU'LL
    SELECT      SUBCALCULATION   THAT      TRUE      WHO       YOUR
    SEPTEMBER   SUBCOUNT         THE       TWICE     WHOM      Z
    SEQUENCE    SUBMAXIMA        THEIR     UNDER     WHOSE
    SET         SUBMAXIMUM       THEM      UP        WILL
    SHALL       SUBMINIMA        THEN      US        WITH
    SHE         SUBMINIMUM       THERE     USE       WNEC
    SHOULD      SUBTOTAL         THESE     VALUE     WNIC
    SHOW        SUBTRACT         THEY      VARIANCE  WNRC
    SINCE       SUBVARIANCE      THING     VERSUS    WON'T
    SMALL       SUCCEEDING       THINK     WANT      WORSE
    SOME        SUM              THIS      WAS       WOULD
    SORT        SUMMARY          THOSE     WE        WRITE
    SOUND       SYNONYM          THROUGH   WELL      WRT
    SOUNDEX     T                TIME      WERE      Y

         %  (  )  *  +  ,  -  /  /=  ;  <  <=  <>  =  >  ><  >=
```

Figure 7-20c

in requests. Figures 7-20a, b, and c shows all the words even the untaught IA already recognizes.

At the Request screen, you can press **<F6>** to look at the vocabulary the IA already understands. Press **B** to see the IA's built-in words, **F** to see the field names, or **S** to view all the synonyms you've taught the Assistant. You can then add or delete field names and synonyms in addition to viewing them.

To teach the IA a new word, press **<F8>** from the Request screen, and then choose the *type* of word you want to add to your Assistant's vocabulary:

W - a word for the subject of the database.

F - a field name (alternate field name).

S - a synonym.

O - other.

Special terms — The IA's built-in vocabulary contains certain words with special meanings. Table 7-3 summarizes the ones you're likely to use in your requests.

Table 7-3
Special Built-in Words and Their Meanings

Word	What It Means/Examples
Alpha	Abbreviation for alphabetical.
Between	Indicates lower and upper limits to follow.
Better	Specifies higher numeric/money value.
Best	Specifies highest numeric/money value.
Blank	Contains no value. For example, "Show the forms where the Fax Number is blank," or "Set all Review Comments to blank."
Cut	Decrease. "Cut all prices by 2 percent."
Delete	Eliminate. "Delete the Brower Inc. form." "Delete Bret Turner's Review Comments."
Respect	With respect to. "...sorted respect Last Name."
Set	Change or assign value. "Set the price of part number B33X-1 to $12.95."
Top	Highest value. "Show the top 10 products by decreasing YTD sales."
WNEC	With No Extra Columns. The report will contain only those columns explicitly requested.
WNIC	With No Identification Columns. Suppresses the display of report columns specified at Basic Lesson 3.
WNRC	With No Restriction Columns. Columns with restrictions on them are not displayed in the report.

One request at a time, please. You'll confuse the IA if you ask for two or more unrelated pieces of information in the same report. In the example:

```
Show the prices of the videos by title and the costs of
all paperback books.
```

Two different reports have been requested. You could probably get all the information you want by rephrasing the request as follows:

Show the prices and costs of the videos and paperbacks by title.

This would give you a report with the titles of the videotapes and paperbacks in sorted order in the first column, followed by the stock number (an identification field), list price, and cost.

Follow-up questions — Once the Assistant has answered a request, you can ask a follow-up question based on the original one. If your first question is:

What's Fred Belkor's department?

After you get your answer, you can then immediately follow up that request by asking:

Show me his review comments.

The Assistant then displays his review comments because you've used a pronoun (in this example, his), and the IA assumes you want the comments associated with the same form.

Follow-up questions can also be asked where the IA's answer to the original request is displayed as a report. Your first request might be:

List the hardbound books where the cost > $25 sorted by title.

Once the report is displayed you can then press **<Esc>** and type:

Who are their authors?

This produces a report showing the same books sorted the same way, but this time with a column displaying the authors of the selected books. The follow-up request, "Who are *the* authors," however, wouldn't work because you haven't used a pronoun to connect the second request with the first one.

Restoring a previous request — After the Assistant answers your request to display a form or forms, the request is erased. You can restore it, however, by pressing **<Esc>** to go back to the Request box, and then pressing **<Shift><F7>**.

Where you haven't asked to view entire forms — for example, where a report has been requested and is displayed — you can press **<Esc>** to clear the screen and then press **<Shift><F7>** to restore the last request. You can now modify the command to get a modified report.

Using shorthand — When typing out your requests, shorthand will speed things along. For example, you can use the "greater than" sign (**>**) instead of typing "greater than." Instead of typing "Create a report showing the..." you could get the same information by saying "List the..." You'll get a sense of this the more you work with your assistant.

Specifying restrictions is easy. You can use the "greater than" symbol (**>**), the "less than" symbol (**<**), the equal sign (**=**), and the word "between" to have the IA retrieve only the forms you want.

```
List the Titles where price > $10.
Get the forms where Qty On Hand < 5.
Show me the forms where the YTD Sales is between
50 and 500.
List the invoice numbers where customer = Bill Stafford.
List the invoice numbers where customer is Bill
Stafford.
```

When using the word "between" to retrieve selected forms, always type the lower value first.

You can place more than one condition in your retrieve specification. For example:

```
List the employees whose salaries are > $15,000 AND who
work in Marketing.
```

```
Show me the workers who were hired before July 23, 1989
OR whose social security number is blank.
```

Arithmetic problems — These are normally solved by the IA in left-to-right order as the parts of the problem are expressed in the request. You can change that order by placing the parts of the expression you want evaluated first inside parentheses. This overrides the English rule with the math rule.

If you want math precedence rules to apply to your request, use the operator symbols (*****, **/**, **+**, and **-**) instead of their English word equivalents, along with parentheses to tell the Assistant which parts of the expression to evaluate first.

Punctuation — Avoid using colons and semicolons in your requests — they'll just confuse the Assistant. You can use commas when specifying report columns, or type **and** to separate the fields, as in the following two examples:

```
List the part numbers, descriptions, prices, qty on
order.
```

```
List the part numbers and descriptions and prices and
qty on order.
```

You don't need to end a question with a question mark, or a command with a period. The IA evaluates your request based on the words you use and their order, not the punctuation at the end of the sentence.

If you use quotation marks to specify a new text value for a record or group of records, or when defining a new synonym, make sure the close quote mark comes before any punctuation, otherwise the IA may "think" the period, comma, or question mark is part of the new value or synonym.

The IA uses commas to separate items in a series. So, if you use a comma when specifying a name like "Bill Fredrickson, M.D." (where each component of the name is in its own field), the IA will think you want the form for "Bill Fredrickson" *and* anyone who has "M.D." in his name.

However, you *do* include in your requests the periods in the parts of names (initials, titles, prefixes, and suffixes) where they'd normally be placed in proper English usage. Hopefully, the proper punctuation was included when the titles or suffixes were typed in their respective fields during data entry.

Yes/No fields — When you want to display the contents of a Yes/No field in a report, you have to use the word "field" in your request. For example, if your customer database includes a Yes/No field labeled Subscriber, and you want that field included as a column, ask for it explicitly:

```
List the customers, phones, and subscriber field where
city is Los Angeles.
```

Speeding up the IA — If the Assistant seems to be taking too long to display the answers to your request, go to the Speed-up Spec in the File module and type **S** in those fields on which you most frequently ask the IA to retrieve and sort.

Indexing just any *displayed* field probably won't help. You want to speed up only those fields you're having the IA use to *select* your forms.

Adding Synonyms

A synonym is a word or phrase having a meaning that is the same or nearly the same as another word or phrase. *Sharp* is a synonym of *keen; residence* usually means *home; Where* a person *resides* is where he *lives*. Leaf through any thesaurus, or use an on-line thesaurus such as the one available in the Write and File modules, and you'll usually discover many alternate words or phrases that can be used in place of the subject word.

Synonym definitions can be important when requesting information from the Intelligent Assistant because people normally use them in ordinary conversational English. You have your set field names and the IA's own built-in vocabulary, but when you teach your assistant new words that represent those it already knows, you can then phrase your requests more naturally, and the IA will know what you mean.

Synonyms can be defined in three ways: as alternate field names in Basic Lesson 5 during the teaching process, by typing the synonym definition into the Request box, and by calling up the IA's Synonym box and entering the alternate word along with its definition. If the synonym is *not* an alternate field name, then you'll need to use either the second or third method. A synonym, as defined for the Assistant, can be as rudimentary as a single word defined in terms of another word that the IA already knows, or a word or abbreviation that represents an entire phrase or calculation.

For example, *residence* can be defined as a synonym for the address, city, state, and zip code fields. Then, when you want the IA to return a person's complete address, you can type:

What is Jane Farley's residence?

You could define *particulars* as height, weight, date of birth, salary, position, and phone number if you frequently needed to see these items together. You could then tell the IA:

Show me Gary Jacobsen's particulars.

If you like the word *generate*, you could define it to mean *run*. Since the IA understands *run*, you can then have the IA:

Generate the Hot Prospect report.

Defining a Synonym at the Request Box

When you enter a synonym at the Request box, type it as a command in one of the two following formats:

DEFINE word AS definition

or:

DEFINE word TO BE definition

where *word* is any word or phrase you want to teach the IA, and *definition* is the word or phrase that the IA can recognize. The following example shows a synonym that might be defined for the IA in a purchase order database:

DEFINE open AS Date Closed field is blank

Here, it's assumed that the purchase order form includes a field labeled Date Closed (which contains the date the goods were received). By defining "open" in terms of a blank Date Closed field, you're making it possible for the Assistant to understand what you mean when you say "open." You could then type your request:

```
┌─────────────────────────────────────────────────────────────────┐
│ DEFINE SYNONYM                                                    │
│                                                                  │
│                                                                  │
│                                                                  │
│    Type the synonym you want to teach me in the first column and the word or │
│    phrase it stands for in the second.  (Ex:   New York   -  NY ) │
│    ┌───────────────────────────┐   ┌───────────────────────────┐ │
│    │ OVERDUE                   │   │ AMOUNT DUE > $1.00 AND INVOICE DATE IS │
│    └───────────────────────────┘   │ LESS THAN 30 DAYS BEFORE TODAY │
│    ┌───────────────────────────┐   │                           │ │
│    │                           │   │                           │ │
│    └───────────────────────────┘   │                           │ │
│    ┌───────────────────────────┐   │                           │ │
│    │                           │   │                           │ │
│    └───────────────────────────┘   └───────────────────────────┘ │
│                                                                  │
│    ──────────────────────────────────────────────────────────── │
│    INVOICE.DTF                                                    │
│    Esc-Cancel     F3-Delete synonym                  F10-Continue │
└─────────────────────────────────────────────────────────────────┘
```

Figure 7-21: The Define Synonym Box.

Show me the open POs.

and the IA would produce a report showing your identification fields (perhaps the PO number, date, supplier, item ordered, and quantity) from just those forms where the Date Closed field is empty.

Using the Synonym Box

The Synonym box is handy when you want to define several synonyms at a time. You can reach it by typing "Define Synonym" into the Request box, or by pressing **<F6>** from the Request screen, and then pressing the letter **S** for Synonym. Figure 7-21 shows the Define Synonym box.

In Figure 7-21 we're working with an invoice database and telling the Assistant that when we use the word "overdue" we mean the invoices where the Amount Due is greater than $1.00 and the invoice is more than 30 days old. Once the synonym is defined for the IA, we can then type our request:

Show me the overdue invoices.

and the IA immediately converts the synonym "overdue" into the definition (the language it uses to process requests) and offers its plan of action for what it thinks is the report we want. And in this case the IA's plan corresponds with our own.

Without the synonym "overdue" defined, you could get the same report by typing into the Request box:

```
Show me the invoices where the amount due > $1.00 and
the invoice date < 30 days before today.
```

But because of the IA's understanding of "overdue," the report could likewise be produced simply by typing the word "Overdue" all by itself into the Request box.

The above examples demonstrate how a single word can be used to define a complex procedure. Another alternative would be to design the reports in the Report module, and then tell the Assistant:

```
Run the Open PO report.
```

or:

```
Run the Overdue Invoice report.
```

To add a new definition at the Synonym box, type the synonym you want to define in the left-hand field, move the cursor to the definition field on the right, and type the definition. Remember, the definition you enter must be expressed in terms the IA can understand. If you're not sure whether the IA can "think" with the definition, press **<F10>** to save it, and then try it out at the Request box. You can always come back and edit it.

Viewing the Synonyms

You can get the list of synonyms defined for the IA by typing **List Synonyms** into the Request box, or by pressing **<F6>** from the Request screen, and selecting **S** for "Synonyms."

Once at the Synonym box you can delete or change synonyms by using the cursor and editing keys. Press **<PgDn>** to see any additional synonyms. With the cursor at a particular synonym or definition, you can press **<F3>** to delete it.

More Tips on Defining Synonyms

Tip: Here are some other examples to help you define synonyms for the IA.

- You can create an "empty" synonym (one that has no meaning to the IA) by defining it with double quote marks. For example:

```
DEFINE deadbeat AS ""
```

This word, when used in a request, will then simply be passed over as if it weren't there.

- When defining a synonym that contains "to be" or "as," put both the synonym and its definition in quotes:

   DEFINE "slow as molasses" AS "overdue"

You can define a new synonym in terms of a previously defined synonym.

- The IA recognizes regular plurals — those formed with "s," "es," and "ies," but it can't recognize irregular plurals like feet/foot, man/men, or person/people. These plural forms will have to be defined or entered at the Alternate Field Names Lesson.

- When using a mathematical expression in a synonym definition, enclose the expression in parentheses. For example:

   DEFINE value at cost AS (Cost * Qty On Hand)

- To have the IA show you the definition of a synonym, type in the Request box:

   Show the definition of synonym word

   where *word* is the synonym word or phrase.

- To remove a synonym, type:

   Delete synonyms

   and the Assistant will display the Synonym box so you can place the cursor at the synonym you no longer want, and press **<F3>** to delete it.

   The command:

   Delete the synonym word

   where *word* is the synonym, will remove that particular synonym.

 Warning: Be careful with this one. If you fail to use "synonym" in the command, the IA thinks you want to delete all the database forms that meet the definition.

Sometimes the Assistant Needs a Little Assistance

When you type a question or command in the Request box and press **<Enter>,** the IA first checks it over see if it understands what you've asked (you can watch it "think" as the highlight moves through the request word by word). If no further clarification is needed, the Assistant then formulates and displays a plan of action, as shown in Figure 7-22.

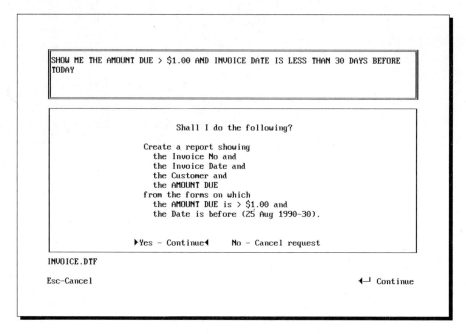

SHOW ME THE AMOUNT DUE > $1.00 AND INVOICE DATE IS LESS THAN 30 DAYS BEFORE
TODAY

                    Shall I do the following?

            Create a report showing
                the Invoice No and
                the Invoice Date and
                the Customer and
                the AMOUNT DUE
            from the forms on which
                the AMOUNT DUE is > $1.00 and
                the Date is before (25 Aug 1990-30).

          ▶Yes - Continue◀   No - Cancel request

INVOICE.DTF

Esc-Cancel   ←⏎ Continue

Figure 7-22: An "Overdue" Request. The synonym "overdue" is converted back into the definition to produce a report of overdue invoices.

If the IA seems prepared to deliver what you want, you can press **Y** (for "Yes") or **<Enter>** to proceed. If something about the IA's plan isn't right, though, you'll want to select No or **<Esc>** and take a good hard look at the way you've worded your request. In such a case the IA evidently "understood" your request as it was phrased (it "knew" the words), but since it proposed to display something other than what you want, chances are you've left out a comma, typed an incorrect field label, or perhaps used a synonym that doesn't have quite the right definition.

When you've confused the Assistant by typing an ambiguous question, impossible request, or illogical command, the IA will let you know by displaying the warning screen in Figure 7-23.

In the Figure 7-23 example, the request asks for a range of invoices, but the range hasn't been fully defined. Furthermore, even if the request included "...between $100 and $200..." the IA would need clarification since the field that these money values relate to hasn't been specified. In other words, there could be 20 fields on the form that contain money values. Which of these money fields is being referred to here?

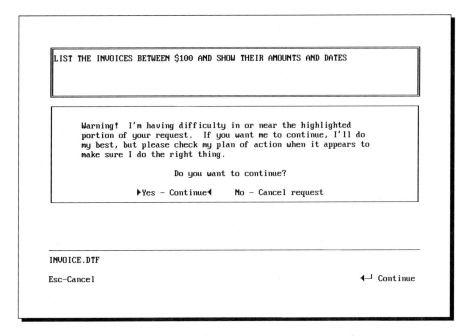

Figure 7-23: An Illogical Request and the IA's Response.

Where the IA doesn't understand a word, it will tell you so and present you with the following list of alternatives:

E - Edit the highlighted word.   **S** - See or change my vocabulary.
T - Teach me a new word.   **G** - Go ahead (the word doesn't matter).

E - Edit the highlighted word: The word may be wrong or misspelled. Select this option to return to the Request box to edit the word. When you're done, press **<Enter>** and the Assistant will reevaluate your request.

T - Teach me a new word: You can teach the Assistant the word without losing your request. When you select this option, the IA takes you to another screen with the following choices:

W - a word for the subject of the database.
F - a field name.
S - a synonym.
V - a verb.
O - other (select this if you are not sure).

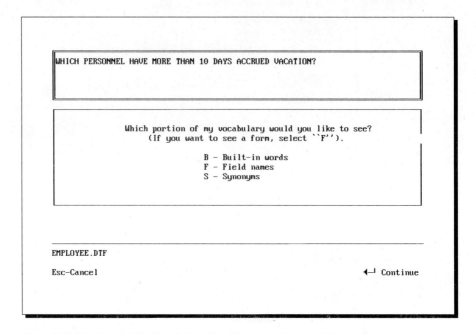

```
┌──────────────────────────────────────────────────────────────────────────┐
│  ┌────────────────────────────────────────────────────────────────────┐  │
│  │WHICH PERSONNEL HAVE MORE THAN 10 DAYS ACCRUED VACATION?              │  │
│  │                                                                     │  │
│  └────────────────────────────────────────────────────────────────────┘  │
│  ┌────────────────────────────────────────────────────────────────────┐  │
│  │          Which portion of my vocabulary would you like to see?       │  │
│  │             (If you want to see a form, select ``F'').              │  │
│  │                                                                     │  │
│  │                       B - Built-in words                            │  │
│  │                       F - Field names                               │  │
│  │                       S - Synonyms                                  │  │
│  │                                                                     │  │
│  └────────────────────────────────────────────────────────────────────┘  │
│  ──────────────────────────────────────────────────────────────────────  │
│  EMPLOYEE.DTF                                                              │
│                                                                           │
│  Esc-Cancel                                                   ↵ Continue  │
│                                                                           │
└──────────────────────────────────────────────────────────────────────────┘
```

Figure 7-24: Viewing the IA's Vocabulary. The IA wants to know which vocabulary you want to view and perhaps change. The Assistant's built-in vocabulary is off limits.

Selecting **W, F,** or **V** takes you to the appropriate lesson (bypassing the Lesson menu) where you can teach the Assistant just as you did during the Basic and Advanced Lessons. When you've entered the new word you can then press **<F10>** to return to the Request box where the IA will now reevaluate your request.

If you select **S,** the IA opens up the Synonym box where you can add the synonym and its definition, and then press **<F10>** to return to the Request box to have the IA reevaluate your request.

The **O** selection displays a help screen suggesting that you either go back to the Lesson menu and teach the word at the appropriate lesson, or rephrase your request in words the IA already understands.

You can't add to the Assistant's built-in vocabulary, but you *can* define a synonym with a built-in word as the definition.

G - Go ahead (the word doesn't matter): The word may be unimportant to the request. This option tells the IA to continue evaluating the request ignoring the highlighted word.

S - See or change my vocabulary: When you choose this the IA will display the screen in Figure 7-24, and you can check the built-in vocabulary, or view and add to the Alternate Field Names or synonym vocabulary. Looking over these vocabularies helps you determine which words the Assistant already knows, and you can then use a substitute word in your request if you prefer not to add the new word at this time.

Retrieval Restrictions in Your Requests

The Assistant can respond to all the usual Retrieve Spec symbols used in the File and Report modules. Table 7-4 includes a summary of the most commonly employed restrictions, including the symbols and optional words or expressions you can use to specify them in your requests.

Specifying Totals and Subtotals for Reports

The following terms allow the IA to complete requests for totals and subtotals in various reports:

With total   Gives you a total for the specified column. For example, "Show the Invoice Numbers and Amounts with total." You can also use *average, maximum, minimum,* and *count* in the same manner.

With total by,   Displays the subtotal of the values in the column at
with subtotal by   each column break. For example, "Show the Last Names and Salaries with total by Department." *Average, maximum, minimum,* and *count* can be specified in the same way.

Printing

The Assistant will not print directly to your printer even if you use the word "Print" in your request. When the IA produces its response, it will always be displayed on screen.

Reports and individual forms — once displayed by the IA — can be sent to your printer by pressing **<F2>** to bring up the Print Options screen. From there you can optionally press **<F8>** to define your page characteristics, select your character density, and add a header or footer, (including pagination) to the report if you like.

Table 7-4
Summary of Restrictions for Use with
the Intelligent Assistant

Word/Phrase	Symbol	What it means
Is, equals	=	Matches, equals. Used to retrieve exact matches.
Matches		Can be used to retrieve partial matches. Company matches "Bre.." finds all companies that begin with the letters B-R-E (items to be matched must be typed inside quote marks like "Bre..").
Is greater than, is after	>	Greater than, later than, or occurs later in the alphabet.
Is less than, is before	<	Less than, earlier than, or occurs earlier in alphabet.
Is greater than or equal to; Is on or later than	>=	Greater than or equal to; appears in alphabet at or later than; comes earlier or at the same time.
Is less than or equal to; Is on later than	<=	Less than or equal to; appears in alphabet at or earlier than; comes earlier or at the same time.
Is not, is not equal to	/=	Doesn't equal, isn't the same as.
Not		Negates next term or condition. For example, "Last Name is not Smith" or "Price is not between $10 and $15."
Begins with, starts with		Initial letter(s) is/are.
Ends with		Final letter(s) is/are.
Contains, Includes		Includes the letter(s).Can be used with Keyword fields. Field entries must match those specified.

(continued)

Table 7-4 (continued)

Between	Follow between with the two items, lowest item first. For example, "between 15 pounds and 20 pounds"or "between Silverstein and Smith" (shows the names that fall alphabetically between the two).
Earliest	Earliest date.
Latest	Date closest to current date.
Top	Maximum value. Can also be used to retrieve a group, such as "Top 5 salaries."
Bottom	Minimum value. Can also be used to specify a group, such as "Bottom 3 hourly rates."
Greatest	Highest single number/money value.
Least	Lowest single number/money value.
And	Both conditions must be met.
Or	Only one of the conditions must be met.

From the Print Options screen you can select Page Preview to see how the report will look on the printed page. You can also print to disk if you want the report saved in ASCII format. This enables you to then import the report into the word processor where you can dress it up with enhancements, preview it again, and even print multiple copies.

IA responses, other than reports and forms, can be printed by using the <Shift><PrtSc> keystroke combination. This bypasses the Print Options screen and sends whatever is displayed directly to the printer.

Renaming Your Assistant

While at the Request box for any database, you can rename your assistant. The new name will appear on the Q&A Main menu, and everywhere in the module where the original name appeared.

The "personalized" name can be any word or phrase up to 12 characters in length, as long as the first letter of the name is not the same as the first letter of any other selection on the Main menu.

The name-change command, typed in the Request box, can be expressed in a number of different ways. To change the IA's name to "Genius," for example, use one of the following commands:

```
I dub you Genius
I dub thee Genius
I christen you Genius
I christen thee Genius
I name you Genius
I name thee Genius
Change your name to Genius
Your name is Genius
```

Summary

In this chapter you have learned about Q&A's Intelligent Assistant — when you should use it and how you should use it. You also have been given enough information to learn IA drawbacks, the main ones being the additional disk space that it takes up, that it can slow database performance, and the fact that you may be able to execute your requests more quickly yourself than the IA can, especially after you become more familiar with Q&A's database manager.

Chapter 8

Q&A Macros and Custom Application Menus

In this chapter you'll learn how to:

▶ Recognize when macros can really boost your productivity.

▶ Use simple macros to automate repetitive tasks.

▶ Create sophisticated macro-driven "mini-programs" to automate complex batch processing routines.

▶ Install macro selections on the Q&A Main menu.

▶ Design your own menus to display and launch macros.

▶ Create a complete custom menu system to replace Q&A's menus.

▶ Protect your macro files.

This chapter will cover macros from basic to more advanced, as well as customizing macros for your needs. The first part of this chapter discusses the macro menu and teaches you to define, run, and save macros.

The second part concerns advanced techniques — editing and embedding macros within other macros, among others.

The last part of this chapter gives you information on tailoring your macros and creating custom menus to suit your specific needs.

Note for users upgrading from version 3.0: Although macros created in Q&A version 3.0 should execute satisfactorily in 4.0 without modification, remember that new selections have been added to some 4.0 menus; there are new submenus, and function key assignments have been added to new operations such as Posting, saving and recalling specs, and invoking the Options menu in File, to name a few. Your safest bet is to not simply take it for granted that your macros will work in 4.0 as they did in 3.0, but to observe them in action when you first run them in 4.0 — being especially watchful of long, complex macros,

macros that cross menus, and macros that use function key combinations that weren't previously defined by Q&A itself.

Macros created in 3.0 can be edited in 4.0 Write to turn the display off during execution, for example, or to call a custom menu upon completion. (These options are discussed later in this chapter.) Before doing so, however, you should first confirm that any such 3.0 macros are working smoothly in 4.0.

Overview _____

A macro is a stored series of keystrokes which can be replayed to accomplish a specific and useful task. It's like having Q&A press the keys or click the mouse so you don't have to.

Macros automate tedious and often repeated tasks, or a series of tasks, that would otherwise require you to press all the keys or manually choose items from menus. They're tremendous productivity boosters, functioning as powerful mini-programs. Q&A macros require absolutely no programming skill to write or master. If you know how to specify a procedure in Q&A by pressing the keys that carry it out, you can record that procedure in a macro and have Q&A carry it out for you automatically the next time.

Q&A provides a macro recording facility that remembers all your keystrokes. When you've finished recording the macro, you save it, and then play it back whenever you want to accomplish the same task ("playing back" a macro is synonymous with "running," "launching," "invoking," or "executing" the macro).

The term "macro" is short for "macro-command" — a command more embracing than other keyboard commands because it can itself invoke a whole series of commands.

For example, you can select a Q&A menu item by pressing the letter of the item. That's one command. But *with one keyboard command* you can accomplish the following six steps:

1. Select File from the Main menu.

2. Choose Backup from the File menu.

3. Type **C:\QA\DATA\CUSTOMER** as the database to back up.

4. Type **CUSTBACK** as the name of the backup file.

5. Answer Yes to overwrite the older backup file.

6. Press **<F10>** to effect the backup.

You've done with *a single keystroke combination* what would otherwise have required 20 or more individual keypresses. And this is only a modest illustration of what macros can do to enhance your Q&A productivity.

In Q&A a macro is normally defined by its *identifier*— the keystroke combination that invokes or triggers the macro. This is typically an **<Alt>** or **<Ctrl><key>** combination, such as **<Alt><C>** or **<Ctrl><L>**. When you've recorded a series of keystrokes that you've identified as **<Alt><C>**, for example, whenever you press **<Alt><C>** that macro plays back the exact same sequence of keystrokes you recorded, and carries out the task for which it was created.

You can also record and save a macro by assigning a descriptive name to it. You can then launch the macro by selecting it by name from a menu or list.

A Q&A macro can have both an *identifier* and a *name*, making it possible to invoke the macro by pressing its identifying key combination and also by selecting it by name from a menu.

Whether you want to automate three or *3,000* keystrokes, macros can be used to handle simple routines like taking you from the Q&A Main menu to Add Data or Search/Update in your Customer file, all the way to fully automating complex batch-processing tasks such as moving selected records to a new file, mass-updating them, and then running a series of reports on the updated file.

Q&A macros can be more than just convenient little short-cuts. The more sophisticated your applications, the more important macros become in your overall mix of data entry and processing tools.

What follows are just a few of the thousand-and-one things you can automate with macros.

Word Processing

- Type your name and address at the top of letters.

- Load a document "template" that contains the font assignments, Define Page specifications, and Print Options settings you need for a particular kind of word processing job.

- Assign fonts and enhance text.

- Type "canned" sentences and paragraphs.

- Type often-used headers and footers.

- Bring any of a series of custom style sheets into the editor and place the cursor right where you want it.

- Change function key assignments and reconfigure your keyboard to suit your preferences.

- Select a predefined mailing label application and print the labels.

- Select a merge letter application and print the letters.

File and Report

- Fill in fields with frequently used information and move the cursor around the form.

- Fill in Retrieve, Sort, Post, and Mass Update Specs, or recall saved specs.

- Get a table view of selected records and place the cursor in the column you want, in edit mode.

- Run routine mass updates.

- Carry out daily, weekly, or monthly batch posting operations.

- Back up selected data files.

- Call up and print out a stored report, or a series of reports.

- Run an entire end-of-day batch-processing routine that prints the day's invoices, runs your reports, and does all your posting.

Intelligent Assistant/Query Guide

- Run frequently needed reports.

- Call up routinely updated forms.

- Carry out the keystrokes to name the database and place the cursor in the Request box, ready for your command.

- Automate the Query Guide to run reports or retrieve selected records for viewing or updating.

Using macros, you can go from anywhere inside Q&A to any other place. You can start out at the Main menu, go into the Report module, call up a saved report and run it; you can move from the Main menu to the Write module, retrieve a file you've been working on, and place the cursor at the end of the last paragraph; or you can get from almost anywhere in the program back to the Main menu.

You can place your most precious macros right on the Q&A Main menu and launch them with a single keystroke, the same way you launch any menu selection. Macros can also be used to display special menus you create. And you can select from these menus the particular macros you want to run.

The way you use Q&A determines the kinds of macros you'll create — they're personal productivity tools that complement your applications and make them sing with efficiency. And recording and using them in Q&A is a snap.

Q&A macros will only work from inside Q&A. However, there are a number of utilities on the market, such as ProKey and SuperKey, that enable you to record and run macros across applications, while you're in DOS, in Q&A — anywhere. In other words, these terminate-and-stay-resident (TSR) macro programs can be tailored to cut-and-paste, type text, enter commands, and so forth, no matter the program in which you're working. They typically require 75K to 150K of RAM. If you need macros you can run from inside *and* outside of Q&A, they're worth checking out.

The Macro Menu

Figure 8-1 shows the main Q&A Macro menu that displays when you press **<Shift><F2>** from anywhere in the program.

Briefly, here's what the selections on Q&A's Macro menu do for you. I'll discuss each of these in more detail in the pages ahead.

Run Macro — When you choose Run Macro, Q&A presents a scrollable menu of macros in the macro file currently in memory. Highlight the macro you want to execute, and press **<Enter>** to launch it.

Define Macro — This selection prepares Q&A to "remember" your key-strokes during the macro recording process. You use Define Macro when you record a new macro, or redefine an existing macro.

Delete Macro — Enables you to erase a macro you no longer use or want.

Get Macros — You can save your macros to different macro files that Q&A stores on disk. When you want to bring another macro file into memory, choose Get Macros and type the name of the macro file you want Q&A to load.

Save Macros — When you've finished using macros created during the current Q&A session and want to save them, Save Macros allows you to type the drive, path, and name of the file where the macros are to be saved for future use.

Clear Macros — You can clear a macro file currently in memory and have all the old macro identifiers available for use.

```
                    MACRO MENU
              ─────────────────────

              R - Run Macro
              D - Define Macro
              X - Delete Macro
              G - Get Macros
              S - Save Macros
              C - Clear Macros
              ─────────────────────

              M - Create Menu
```

Figure 8-1: The Q&A Macro Menu.

Create menu — This selection enables you to create or change a custom application menu that lists the different macros available to be executed from it. Custom menus are called by macros, and you can even replace Q&A's regular menus with menus of your own design. You can also create a custom macro menu by choosing Create Application menu from the Customize Application menu in the File module.

The Run Macro selection is placed in the first position on Q&A's Macro menu for a good reason. Once you've recorded and saved a number of macros, you'll likely use Run Macro more often than any of the others. But for those new to macro recording in Q&A, it's best to start at the beginning, where you first define your macros.

 Note: If your application has been custom designed, the designer may have locked users out of Q&A's Macro menu, in which case you won't be able to define, clear, or delete macros, or create or edit a custom application menu. In order to access these macro features, you'll need to exit Q&A and either autoload another macro file, or rename the file before restarting Q&A. Before attempting this, however, you should consult with the person who designed the application.

The Define Macro Procedure

You can define a macro from anywhere in Q&A. When recording your first few you should keep them simple until you've gotten the hang of it. With the following steps you can record and save a macro. There are variations on these steps, which will be covered in detail later in the chapter.

1. Press **\<Shift>\<F2>**. The main Macro menu in Figure 8-1 displays.

2. Select Define Macro.

3. Q&A will display the message, "Type the macro identifier, or press **\<Enter>** for none." While holding down **\<Alt>**, **\<Ctrl>**, or **\<Shift>**, press any character or function key to identify the macro (for example, **\<Alt>\<C>**). This is called the *macro identifier* or *key identifier*. A flashing square will appear in the lower right area of the screen, letting you know that the macro recorder is on and your keystrokes will now be recorded.

   If you've entered a macro identifier that has been previously defined, Q&A informs you, "That key is already defined (or, That key is already used by Q&A) Do you want to redefine it? (Y/N):" Type **Y** if you want to overwrite the existing definition, or **N** to stop the macro process and begin again with step 1 above.

   You can record a macro *without* first assigning a macro identifier to it. Later, when you've finished recording the macro and save it, you can assign a name to it. A macro can be assigned both an identifier (for example, **\<Alt>\<C>**) and a name. But it must have at least one or the other.

4. Type the sequence of keystrokes you want Q&A to record, save, and automatically type for you when you again press the same macro identifier or select the macro by name from a custom menu. Because Q&A remains active when you're recording the macro, the result of each keystroke is displayed (or the command is carried out) just as if you were pressing the same keys without the recorder on. Should you get into trouble, you can press **\<Shift>\<F2>**, and then press **\<Esc>** to cancel the process, and then start again with step 1.

5. When you've finished typing all the keystrokes in the macro, press **\<Shift>\<F2>** to end macro recording. The flashing square disappears and Q&A displays the Macro Options box shown in Figure 8-8 (see the section "Custom Applications Menus"). Your macro identifier (if you've assigned one) will show on the Macro Name line. I'll go into more detail on using the Macro Options box later. For now, simply press **\<F10>**, and the default macro filename, QAMACRO.ASC will display.

If you haven't assigned a macro identifier, the words "No Name #*n*," where *n* is the number Q&A has temporarily assigned to the macro, will appear on the Macro Name line.

6. Press **<Enter>** to save your macro to this file, or type a new filename over the existing one, and then press **<Enter>** to save the macro to *that* file.

Your macro has now been recorded and saved.

Recording a Simple Macro

Before we discuss the other selections on the Macro menu, let's create a simple macro that will take you from Q&A's Main menu to a blank form for data entry. This macro assumes that you can make Q&A menu selections merely by pressing the first letter that corresponds to the selection. In other words, you have "Auto Execution" at Q&A's Set Global Options screen set to Yes.

Suppose you have a customer filenamed CUSTOMER.DTF, and during the day you frequently need to add new customer records to it. Here's how you create a simple macro to eliminate the keystrokes normally involved with selecting File from the Main menu, choosing Add Data from the File menu, typing in the name of the database, and pressing **<Enter>**.

1. At the Q&A Main menu, hold down the **<Shift>** key and press the **<F2>** key. The Macro menu in Figure 8-1 will appear.

2. Select Define Macro.

3. When prompted for the macro definition, hold down the **<Alt>** key and type **C** (for "Customer"). If a message appears warning you that a keystroke combination is already spoken for and asking if you want to redefine it, answer No, start again with step 1 above, and this time use a letter other than **C**. The square in the lower-right-hand corner of the screen will begin flashing, telling you that Q&A's macro recorder is on, and your keystrokes will now be recorded.

4. Now type **F** for File, **A** for Add Data and, when prompted, type **CUS-TOMER**. Using upper- or lowercase characters is okay, and you don't need to type the .DTF file extension.

 Note: It's a good idea when recording a macro to include the full drive and path of any filename reference, especially if you use different drives (or hard drive partitions) to store your files. Include **<Shift><F4>** in the macro to erase whatever is on the filename line before typing in your drive, path, and filename.

5. Press **<Enter>** and a blank form for customer data entry should display.

6. Now hold down the **<Shift>** key and press **<F2>** again. Press **<F10>** when the Macro Options box displays, and Q&A will ask you if you want to save this macro to QAMACRO.ASC (Q&A's default macro file).

7. Press **<Enter>** and your macro will be saved. That macro will now be available to you whenever you press **<Alt><C>**, as long as QAMACRO.ASC (the file it was saved to) is in current memory.

To test the macro, go back to the Q&A Main menu, press **<Alt><C>** (or the macro identifier you used), and a blank customer database form will be displayed, ready for input. From here on out you'll only need a single key-stroke combination to go from the Main menu to Add Data in the Customer file, whereas before the same procedure may have required 11 or more individual keypresses.

If you found yourself pressing **<Alt><C>** frequently during the course of the day to add new customer forms, you could install this macro right on the Main menu, and launch it by simply typing the letter **C**. This technique is discussed in detail later in this chapter.

Redefining, Undefining, and Deleting a Macro

When you *redefine* a macro you overwrite the existing recorded keystrokes with a series of new ones. Q&A places no limits on your ability to rerecord a macro using the same macro identifier; it simply reminds you if a macro with that identifier already exists. You can optionally edit the macro file directly in the Write module. This saves you the trouble of rerecording lengthy macros that may contain erroneous keystrokes (more on this later in this chapter).

To redefine a macro, follow the steps under "The Define Macro Procedure," listed earlier, using the same macro identifier (for example, **<Alt><C>**). When you attempt to define a macro using an existing identifier, Q&A will warn you that you're about to overwrite the macro previously defined, and asks if you want to do this. Type **Y** for "Yes" and the flashing square will appear in the lower-right corner of the screen. You can now rerecord the macro.

To get rid of an existing macro and replace it with nothing, you can *un-define* it. You do this by Pressing **<Shift><F2>**, selecting Delete a Macro from the main Macro menu, highlighting it on the displayed list, and pressing **<Enter>**.

You can also undefine a macro by pressing **<Shift><F2>**, choosing Define a Macro, typing the existing macro identifier, answering **Y** to overwrite the macro, and then saving the new definition to the macro file with no recorded keystrokes.

Clearing an Individual Macro from Current Memory

If you want to record a new macro with an existing identifier and then save the new macro to a different macro file, you'll need to clear that existing macro from current memory first. Here are the steps:

1. Press **\<Shift\>\<F2\>** for the Macro menu.

2. Select Define Macro, and enter the identifier of the macro you want to clear.

3. Answer Yes when Q&A asks if you want to redefine this existing macro.

4. When the flashing square appears in the lower-right-hand corner of the screen, press **\<Shift\>\<F2\>**, and then press **\<Esc\>**.

This clears that macro so you can now use the same identifier for another macro. When you've finished recording the new macro and save it to disk, the original macro will be overwritten by the new one if you save the new one to the same file that contains the original macro. Unless you want to replace that original macro, save the new one to a new macro file.

Q&A lets you redefine any key on the keyboard — including function keys. If you redefine a key ordinarily reserved by Q&A and then clear it, the original Q&A system definition is restored until the next time you load Q&A.

If you want to restore a Q&A system key completely, use one of the two *undefine* options above. For example, if you've redefined the **\<F10\>** key and later decide that you want **\<F10\>** to work the way it ordinarily does in the program, simply redefine it containing no keystrokes, or delete it with the **X** option from the Main Macro menu.

Clearing an Entire Macro File from Memory

The buffer that holds macro files in RAM is only so large (3K is the default size). If the buffer is nearly full (for example, when a large macro file is in memory), you may run into an out-of-memory problem during the recording of a macro.

Although Q&A provides a way to increase macro buffer size when you load the program (explained later in the chapter) this is of little use when you're in the middle of recording a complex macro and find yourself up against the macro buffer limit.

There is no easy method of determining *exactly* how many keystrokes will fill up the macro buffer, but it's unlikely that you'll run into a full buffer problem unless the macro file currently in memory contains a great many macros, or very lengthy ones. If you're not sure how many bytes a macro file contains, use the DOS File Facilities to find out.

Suppose you're preparing to record a rather lengthy macro. You know that your buffer limit is 3K and that QAMACRO.ASC is currently in memory. When you highlight QAMACRO.ASC at the List Manager (more on this in the following chapter), you see that this file *already* contains 2.8K. Chances are that the buffer may fill up before you can finish recording your new macro, and you should either delete a few unnecessary macros from QAMACRO.ASC or increase your default buffer size (both of these options are discussed later in this chapter).

When you're about to record a particularly long and complex macro, the best thing to do is to clear the current macro file from memory so the buffer will be empty. Then you can record and save even extremely lengthy macros without the risk of running out of buffer. You clear your current macro file by pressing **<Shift><F2>**, and selecting **C** for "Clear Macros."

As soon as you select Clear Macros, Q&A clears the current file from memory without warning, so you'll want to make sure that any unsaved macros up to this point are first saved.

When you clear a macro file, all the macro identifiers used in any macro file become available for reuse. Although any macro files stored on disk are unaffected by the Clear command, you will lose stored macros if you now record a macro and save it to disk *under an existing macro filename.* The file will now contain only the macro just saved. So you need to be especially careful when saving a macro to an existing filename *that is not currently in memory.*

Running Macros

To play back a previously defined and saved macro, choose Run Macros from the Q&A Macro menu. You can also press **<Alt><F2>** to get the same list from almost anywhere in Q&A. With the list displayed (see Figure 8-2) you can scroll through the macro selections, highlight the one you want to run, and press **<Enter>** to run it.

 Note: If you're working with an application that's been custom designed, pressing **<Shift><F2>** may display the List of Macro Names instead of Q&A's standard Macro menu.

The list of Macro Names includes all the macros in the current file in alphabetical order. Macros that haven't been assigned descriptive names (at the Macro Options box that comes up when you've finished recording a macro) will be displayed with their identifiers only (**<Alt><C>** and **<Alt><G>** in the sample list in Figure 8-2).

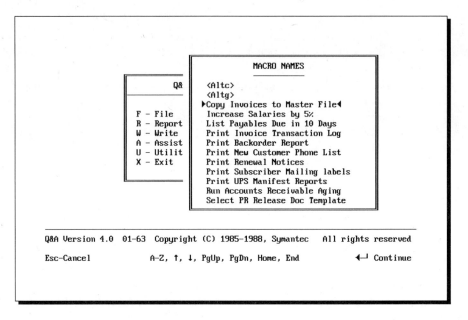

```
                                              MACRO NAMES

                             Q&          <Altc>
                                         <Altg>
                                        ▶Copy Invoices to Master File◀
             F - File                    Increase Salaries by 5%
             R - Report                  List Payables Due in 10 Days
             W - Write                    Print Invoice Transaction Log
             A - Assist                   Print Backorder Report
             U - Utilit                   Print New Customer Phone List
             X - Exit                     Print Renewal Notices
                                          Print Subscriber Mailing labels
                                          Print UPS Manifest Reports
                                          Run Accounts Receivable Aging
                                          Select PR Release Doc Template


  Q&A Version 4.0  01-63  Copyright (C) 1985-1988, Symantec   All rights reserved

  Esc-Cancel                    A-Z, ↑, ↓, PgUp, PgDn, Home, End              ↵ Continue
```

Figure 8-2: Macro File List. It displays the list of macros in the current macro file. Highlight the one you want to run and press **<Enter>**. These are all the macros in the macro file that's in memory. The way they behave when executed depends on from where in the program you began recording them and from where you launch them. The List of Macro Names can be displayed by pressing **<Shift><F2>** for Q&A's Macro menu, and then selecting **Run Macro**. Optionally, you can press **<Alt><F2>** for the same list.

If there are more selections than can be displayed on the first page of the list, use the cursor navigation keys to scroll down, page down, return to the top of the list with the **<Home>** key, or go to the end of it with **<End>**.

You can also type the letter that corresponds to the first letter of a selection, and Q&A will take you to the first macro on the list that begins with that letter.

Once you've highlighted the macro you want, press **<Enter>** to run it.

Any macros that include identifiers such as **<Alt><C>** can still be invoked from anywhere in Q&A without having to access the List of Macro Names. If you want to run an **<Alt><C>** macro, for example, you simply press **<Alt><C>** and Q&A will play it back. But in order to play back a macro with a name (but no key identifier), you have to select it either from the Macro Names list shown in Figure 8-2, or from a custom menu you've designed.

Descriptive macro names are, of course, optional. But they can be a powerful aid to organizing, identifying, and launching your macros. And because you have 31 character spaces to play with when naming a macro, you can choose a name that describes *where* in Q&A you should be when you run a macro.

However, keep in mind that if you have custom menus in addition to many macros, each with a longish descriptive name, you're eating up considerable macro buffer space. After four or five custom menus, with five to nine selections on each, you may well find yourself up against Q&A's default 3K macro file buffer limit and be forced to increase the size of the buffer. That's easily done, though, and another few kilobytes stolen from RAM to accommodate your swelling macro file isn't likely to noticeably affect Q&A's performance.

Assigning names to macros, increasing your macro buffer size, and creating custom macro menus are discussed later in this chapter.

Using Alternative Macro Files

When recording a lengthy macro or a number of macros that you want to store together in the same macro file, you can save them to a file other than QAMACRO.ASC (the startup macro file that loads into memory by default when you load Q&A).

Doing this enables you to keep specific macros and macro files *out* of current memory so they can't accidentally be triggered — you load them only when needed.

For example, you might have a file of macros that assist you with normal daily routines such as adding new forms, searching, typing your name and address on letters, loading specific document templates into the Write editor, and so forth. If these macros are called into action frequently during the course of the day, you'll probably want them in the QAMACRO.ASC file so they'll be auto-loaded with the program.

But suppose at the end of each day you need to run a series of reports, have Q&A post values from the records in one file to those in another file, run a mass update, back up your files, and other similar activities. These are more complex and powerful macro procedures that might be better off in a macro file of their own.

The Get Macros command from the Macro menu retrieves the macro file that you specify and loads it into memory, replacing the current macro file. The current file isn't overwritten or changed in any way, it's merely "swapped out" for the new file.

But if the macro file you're about to "swap out" contains macros that have not yet been saved, be sure to save the file *before* selecting Get Macros to bring the other file into memory. You can have only one macro file in memory at a time, and as soon as you select Get Macros, type the filename, and press **<Enter>**, any unsaved macros will be lost.

Saving Macros

When you've finished recording a macro that you want stored for future use, it's a good practice always to save it right then and there. Then, should you clear the file from memory or exit Q&A, that macro won't be lost.

Q&A doesn't force you to save a macro, however. When you press **<Shift><F2>** to end macro recording, **<F10>** at the Macro Options box, and then press **<Esc>**, that macro will still be available for use during the current Q&A session, as long as you assigned it a key identifier either just before you started recording it, or at the Macro Options box.

The Save Macro command is used in this situation. If you have one or more macros in memory that have *not* been saved but that you want to save, before you Clear Macros or exit Q&A you should:

1. Press **<Shift><F2>**, and select Save Macros.

2. Press **<Enter>** to save the macros to the default filename, or type another name for the new macro file and press **<Enter>**. You can add an extension such as .MAC to remind you later that this is a macro file.

Once you've saved your macros as previously described, they will remain in your computer's memory. You can continue to use them, add new macros, clear them from memory, or load a different macro file. Again, when you load a different macro file using the Get Macros command, it completely replaces the other one (which is now safely stored on disk).

Whenever you save a macro, keep these points in mind:

- When you save a macro to the macro file currently in memory, the macro is *added* to that file.

- When you save a macro to a macro file that is *not* currently in memory, that file will be overwritten, and will then contain *only the macro just saved to it.*

Tips on Recording and Using Macros

Author's Tip: These ideas, most of which are not in Q&A's documentation, will help you avoid problems that commonly crop up with beginning macro users.

- Set your Q&A menus to Automatic Execution so you can select menu items by typing the letter that corresponds to the item. Then, when recording macros that select items from Q&A menus, you won't have to include an **<Enter>** keypress. You can set your menus to Automatic Execution at the Set Global Options screen, available from the Utilities menu.

- Q&A is active during macro recording — the keys you press become part of the macro *and* carry out the command on screen. This interaction can be confusing, especially if you're recording your first macro. Start small; record a few simple macros in the Write module to get a feel for how the process works. You don't necessarily have to save your experimental macros.

- You cannot define a macro that loads a different macro file. Nor can you use a macro to create another macro, although you can have a macro *run* or *call* another macro — this is called *embedding* or *nesting* macros, and is covered later in this chapter.

- If you frequently change drives in Q&A, you should take this into account when recording your macros. If you've been working in a file located on drive D:, for example, and then invoke a macro to call a file on drive C:, the macro may type the filename with a drive D: path. When drive changes are a normal part of your Q&A activities, include the drive name and full path of the file when you record its name in the macro.

- If you need your macro to be in insert mode (rather than the default overtype), press **<Alt><I>** as the first step during macro recording. The **<Ins>** key is just a toggle switch, and doesn't guarantee that insert mode will be on or off.

- When recording a macro that you'll want to use again, it's a good practice to save it as soon as you've typed the last keystroke. It's better to wind up with a macro you don't need (you can always delete or undefine it) than to inadvertently dump a valuable macro that's taken time and considerable concentration to properly record.

- If you clear a macro file, record a new macro, and then attempt to save it to the cleared filename (no longer in memory), the entire file will be overwritten and any macros in it will be lost. Use the Clear Macros command to empty the macro buffer, or to record a new macro with an identifier that already exists in another macro file, and save your new macro to a new filename. You can always use the Write module to copy individual macros from one macro file to another.

- A macro will play back its recorded keystrokes when invoked, regardless of where you are in the program. If a particular macro was recorded starting at the Q&A Main menu and you later invoke it from elsewhere in the program, it's not likely to work properly.

When in doubt about *where* to start recording a macro, you can always start at the Q&A Main menu. You can make the first five keystrokes in your macro **<Esc><Esc><Esc><Esc><Esc>**. As a result, when you invoke the macro from almost anywhere in Q&A, it will first escape to the Main menu, and then begin from there.

- It's important both when recording a particular macro and when launching it to keep these two factors in mind:

  Where was I in Q&A when I *began recording* this macro?

  Where am I in Q&A when I give the command to *run* this macro?

If you recorded the macro starting from the Type/Edit screen in the Write module, for example, and later launch the macro from Q&A Main menu, the macro will produce unwanted results. Why? — because you need a common starting point. When you invoke the macro *it doesn't know that it was recorded starting at the Type/Edit screen in Write. All it can do is replay the keystrokes recorded in it.*

To avoid problems here, record your Q&A macros to start from a common reference point — the Q&A Main menu. If you include five **<Esc>** keystrokes as the first five commands in the macro, the macro will first return to the Main menu before carrying out its task. You can then feel confident that invoking that macro from almost anywhere in Q&A will produce the results you want.

There's an exception to this rule, however, which comes into play whenever an **<Esc>** keystroke forces you to answer "Yes" or "No" in a dialogue box before allowing you to escape from the operation, such as when you've made an unsaved change to a database record or a Write document. But the five **<Esc>** commands at the beginning of a macro will *always* work if the macro is launched from any menu in the Q&A system.

Clearly, there's no point in having a macro first return to the Q&A Main menu and then come all the way back around before it simply boldfaces a line of text or types a message on an invoice. Besides the sheer inconvenience, you'd get into trouble because Q&A wouldn't let you escape from the document or record without confirming that you don't want to first save it.

But the kinds of macros that carry out more complex procedures, such as moving between various menus and opening files, are more reliable when they begin their actions starting from the Q&A Main menu. This becomes especially important when recording macros that you'll launch from your own custom designed menus, as you'll see.

- Pressing **<Esc>** during macro *recording* does not stop the recording process, but simply adds the **<Esc>** keystroke to the macro. If you want to abandon a macro in the middle of recording it (you've made a few too many mistakes), press **<Shift><F2>**, and *then* press **<Esc>**. Now select Clear Macros from the Macro menu, and the abandoned macro's key identifier will be released from memory (along with any other recorded macros that have not yet been saved to disk). You can now use Get Macros to reload the macro file just cleared, and rerecord the macro.

- Pressing **<Esc>** *during macro playback* aborts the macro. It's like a STOP switch that turns off the macro at that point without removing the macro from memory or affecting it in any other way. Pressing **<Esc>** during macro playback, however, doesn't *undo* whatever the macro has already done.

Macros recorded starting at one point in Q&A and then played back from another can seem to go "haywire" during playback and can often wind up doing something quite unexpected. The more complex your macros, the greater care you should take to work them out before you record them and put them into use. Be especially careful with macros that cross Q&A menus. You could wind up renaming a file or report — or worse, *deleting* one — if you don't take into account all the possible screens and selections that could be encountered by the macro during playback.

- Whenever you redesign a form or move, add, or delete a field, take into consideration any existing macros that involve the file. Yesterday, six **<Tab>** presses from the first field in the STOCK.DTF Retrieve Spec may have placed you in the Sold Today field. Today, if that same field is no longer the seventh field on the form and you run the same macro, you're likely to get eye-opening results.

- When recording a macro that selects an item from a list (Report names, saved Retrieve, Sort, Posting Specs, etc.), record the *name* of the item in the macro, rather than using your cursor keys to highlight it. As you add items to these lists, the relative positions of the selections on the lists change. The specific name of something positively identifies it, whereas a position-only indicator in a macro accepts whatever is in that position on the list at the time the macro is run.

- When recording a macro that runs a printing job, it's wise to include (at the very least) the proper printer selection at the Print Options screen. This way, if someone changes the Print Options for that report to print it to a different printer, the macro will still select the correct printer.

Here's an example: Suppose you want to make sure that the report your macro will generate is always printed to Printer B. While recording the macro, you come to the Print Options screen. At the Print-to line, press **<Home>** to move the highlight to PtrA. Now press **<»>** once to select PtrB. Continue recording your macro. The Printer B selection for this report is now built into your macro.

- Extremely complex macros can be recorded in sections. For example, you invoke **<Alt><A>** to run the first part of a procedure and then press **<Alt><B>** to run the second half. This will make it easier to track down what happened if something goes wrong. During playback, macros follow the exact keystrokes you recorded in them. If part of the macro's job is to retrieve selected forms, but one day there are no such forms that meet the recorded parameters, the macro will faithfully try to carry out its mission anyway, and the results could be interesting.

- Any character or function key, optionally entered with **<Ctrl>**, **<Alt>**, or **<Shift>**, can identify a macro, but be prudent when it comes to selecting your identifiers. Use regular **<Alt><key>** and **<Ctrl><key>** combinations until you've become familiar with the procedure. Until you're sure of what you're doing, avoid using single keys as macro identifiers, or redefining any Q&A-reserved function keys.

  You can opt to assign longer names to your macros and invoke them only from macro menus. This topic, as well as how to install macros on your Q&A Main menu, is discussed later in the chapter.

- You can place pause codes in a macro to temporarily suspend macro playback for variable keyboard input. More on this later in the chapter.

- There are certain keys on your keyboard that *cannot* be part of a macro identifier, such as **<NumLock>**, **<Scroll Lock>**, and **<Caps Lock>**. Should you attempt to redefine these keys in a macro, Q&A won't acknowledge that they've been pressed.

- Advanced users who have created or edited a macro file on the Type/Edit screen in Write may see an error message like the following when a macro file is retrieved into memory:

  There's a bad macro definition near macro 5.

  This means there's a typo or some other error in the fifth macro in the file, and the file will need to be brought into the editor so the problem can be corrected. This brings us to our next topic.

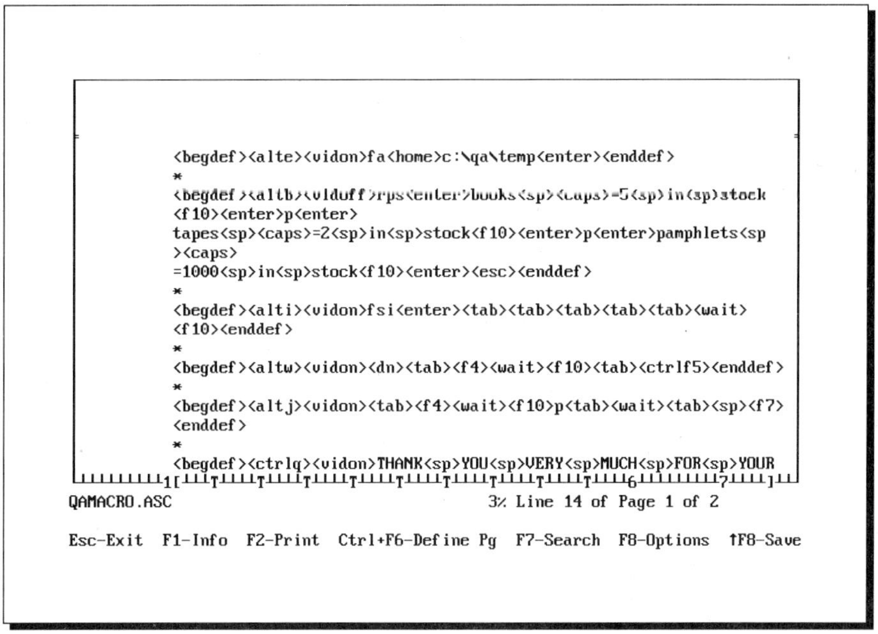

```
        <begdef><alte><vidon>fa<home>c:\qa\temp<enter><enddef>
        *
        <begdef><altb><vidoff>rps<enter>books<sp><caps>=5<sp>in<sp>stock
        <f10><enter>p<enter>
        tapes<sp><caps>=2<sp>in<sp>stock<f10><enter>p<enter>pamphlets<sp
        ><caps>
        =1000<sp>in<sp>stock<f10><enter><esc><enddef>
        *
        <begdef><alti><vidon>fsi<enter><tab><tab><tab><tab><tab><wait>
        <f10><enddef>
        *
        <begdef><altw><vidon><dn><tab><f4><wait><f10><tab><ctrlf5><enddef>
        *
        <begdef><altj><vidon><tab><f4><wait><f10>p<tab><wait><tab><sp><f7>
        <enddef>
        *
        <begdef><ctrlq><vidon>THANK<sp>YOU<sp>VERY<sp>MUCH<sp>FOR<sp>YOUR
```

QAMACRO.ASC   3% Line 14 of Page 1 of 2

Esc-Exit F1-Info F2-Print Ctrl+F6-Define Pg F7-Search F8-Options ↑F8-Save

Figure 8-3: A Sample Macro File in Write.

Advanced Macro Options

Once you understand how to record and play back your macros, and feel comfortable doing so, you can take advantage of several Q&A features to help you fine-tune how macros are selected and how they perform in your applications.

- You can use the Write module to edit your macros much as you would edit a document.

- You can assign descriptive names to your macros and launch them by name from custom menus that you create.

- You can even create custom macro menus to bypass or replace Q&A's regular menus.

Editing Macro Files in Write

Figure 8-3 shows a macro file that has been brought onto the Type/Edit screen in the Write module.

During macro recording you may inadvertently press a wrong key or two, but choose to continue with the recording process anyway; you may have forgotten to have your macro return you to the Main menu or to some other menu where you wanted the macro to end. You could have any number of reasons for modifying a macro.

In such cases it may prove far easier to edit the text of the macro than to rerecord the whole thing all over again.

Because a macro file consists of plain text in ASCII format, you can type your own macro definitions directly into a macro file or combine individual macros from different macro files to create new files. All of Write's regular word processing features such as copy, clipboard copy, search, replace, delete, and so forth, are at your disposal.

To bring a macro file onto the Type/Edit screen:

1. Select Write from the Main menu.

2. Choose Get from the Write menu.

3. Type the name of the macro file (if you only have one macro file, it will likely be QAMACRO.ASC), and press **<Enter>**.

4. Since macro files are in ASCII format, Q&A will display the Import Document screen shown in Figure 8-4.

5. Select **A** for ASCII, or just press **<Enter>**, and the macro file will display on the Type/Edit screen as in Figure 8-2.

Q&A macro files contain regular macros as well as macros that define the structures of custom menus. Although either type of macro can be edited in Write, menu macros involve additional special elements which will be discussed later in this chapter. Below is a sample nonmenu macro, along with a description of its components. There are no hidden codes in a macro file. All macro elements are visible and editable.

```
*
<begdef><altc><vidoff>fa<capsf4>c:\qa\data\customer<enter>
<enddef>
*
```

Q&A uses asterisks to separate individual macros in the file. There are no spaces in a standard macro command, although macros which take up more than one line on the Type/Edit screen may have varying line lengths.

You can use the otherwise empty lines that begin with asterisks to type in comments about your macros. You can even add special comment lines to the

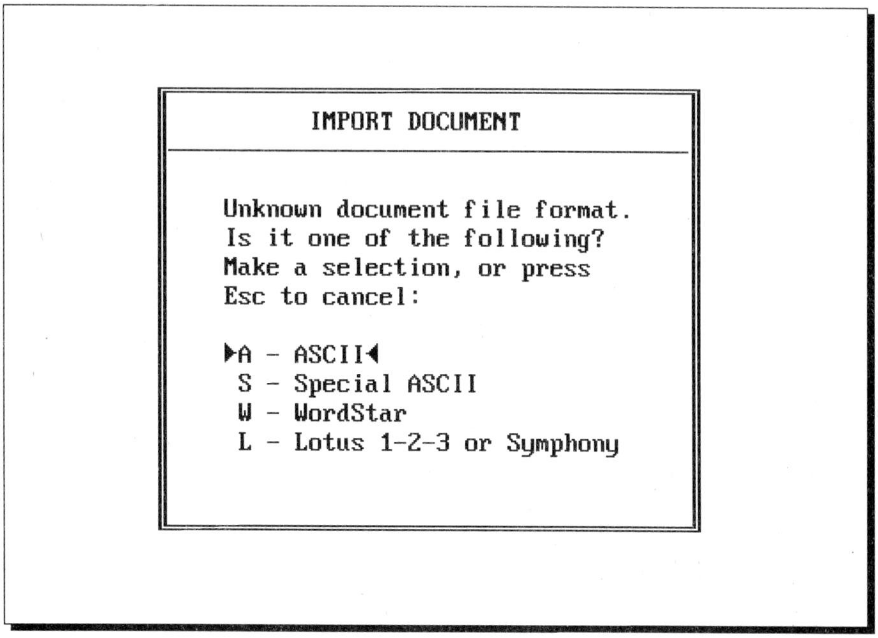

```
┌─────────────────────────────────────────────┐
│              IMPORT DOCUMENT                  │
├─────────────────────────────────────────────┤
│                                              │
│   Unknown document file format.              │
│   Is it one of the following?                │
│   Make a selection, or press                 │
│   Esc to cancel:                             │
│                                              │
│  ▶A - ASCII◀                                 │
│   S - Special ASCII                          │
│   W - WordStar                               │
│   L - Lotus 1-2-3 or Symphony                │
│                                              │
└─────────────────────────────────────────────┘
```

Figure 8-4: Editing a Q&A Macro File. Because macros are stored in ASCII files, Q&A displays the Import Document screen when you bring a macro file into Write.

macro file so long as any such line begins with an asterisk. Macro file comments enable you to more readily identify what your macros do when editing them on the Type/Edit screen.

Every Q&A macro commences with **<begdef>** — short for BEGin DEFinition. Each macro similarly ends with **<enddef>**.

The **<altc>** in the above example is the macro identifier — the keystroke combination that invokes the macro from the keyboard. A macro can be a **<nokey>** macro, meaning that it does not have a key identifier. In such a case the macro name will appear in quote marks following the **<name>** tag.

The **<vidoff>** code indicates that the display is off during macro execution, and the words "Macro working..." flash on the screen. The **<vidon>** code means any screen changes are visible during macro execution.

The **fa** portion of the macro includes the keystrokes that define the Q&A menu selections during macro recording. The **f** stands for File — the first key pressed to select the File module from the Main menu. The **a** stands for Add Data — the selection made from the File menu.

The **\<capsf4\>** is the **\<Shift\>\<F4\>** key combination that clears the drive/path/filename line when Add Data is selected from the File menu.

The **c:\qa\data\customer** string is the correct drive, path, and filename for the data file we want, along with the characters **c u s t o m e r** which open the CUSTOMER.DTF file in Add mode. The **\<enter\>** string corresponds to pressing the **\<Enter\>** key to confirm the filename and bring up a new form for data entry.

If the optional tag **\<wait\>** appears in the macro, it means that Q&A pauses at this point for user input from the keyboard (see the section on macros with pause codes later in this chapter).

The optional **\<keyname\>** tag is used with **\<wait\>** to determine the keystroke that ends the pause. By default, Q&A uses the **\<Enter\>** key to resume macro playback. You can use another key, such as **\<F10\>**, to resume macro playback after the entry of variable data. All you need do is change the **\<enter\>** to **\<F10\>** when editing the macro.

Special "Text" for Noncharacter Keys

Noncharacter keys show up in macros looking a bit odd at first. For example, **\<Shift\>\<F9\>** pressed during macro recording shows up in the macro file as **\<capsf9\>**. Such keys require special attention when editing macro files and must appear between angle brackets (**\<\>**) with their names typed differently from the way you might think of them or be used to seeing them. When you type your own commands directly into a macro file, don't forget to type these key names inside the angle brackets.

Table 8-1 shows you several examples of noncharacter keystrokes and how they must be typed when editing a macro.

There are a number of highly specialized commands and command strings associated with macros that call custom menus. Editing these kinds of macros presents a special case, although the general procedure for editing any macro is the same. You'll find out later in this chapter what to watch for when editing your custom menu macros.

Tips on Editing Macro Files

Author's Tip: These tips, mostly undocumented by Q&A, will make it easier to edit your macro files.

- You can print a copy of your macro file by pressing **\<F2\>** and **\<F10\>** with the file displayed on the Type/Edit screen. Reviewing macros from a printout is often easier than staring into the screen trying to figure out which macro does what — and you can jot down notes on a printout.

Table 8-1
Angle Brackets Define Noncharacter Keys

Key/Combination	Typed as
Alt-C	`<altc>`
Alt-7	`<alt7>`
Backspace	`<bks>`
Home	`<home>`
Ctrl-Home	`<ctrlhom>`
Ctrl-PgUp	`<ctrlpgu>`
Ctrl-Enter	`<ctrlent>`
Ctrl-F5	`<ctrlf5>`
Alt-F2	`<wait>`
→	`<rgt>`
←	`<lft>`
↑	`<up>`
↓	`<dn>`
Escape	`<esc>`
Insert	`<ins>`
Enter	`<enter>`
F2	`<f2>`
Shift-F1	`<capsf1>`
Shift-Tab	`<capstab>`
Tab	`<tab>`

- If, while editing a macro file in Write, you make an accidental deletion or realize you've probably done something you shouldn't have and aren't sure what, you can always press **<Esc>** to back out of the editing session. Since you're working with a copy of the actual file that's stored on disk, any changes you make won't affect the stored version of the file until you save the edited version.

- The page characteristics of a macro document aren't likely to be important. There's no point in trying to change margins, page length, the line lengths of the individual macros, or other elements to enhance the on-screen appearance of an existing macro file. Macros are saved in a page format that corresponds to the default settings at your Define Page for Imported Documents screen.

- The last macro you recorded and saved will be the last one in the displayed file. You can use the Move command to change the relative positions of the macros in the ASCII document, if having them in specific positions within the file make them easier for you to locate and edit.

- When you edit a macro, be sure not to leave any spaces. Pressing the space bar during macro recording is reflected in the macro as the string **<sp>**. Individual macros are continuous strings of definitions whether they're half a line in length, or several pages.

- Use the insert mode to add commands or text to a macro and **<Del>** to erase them.

- You can delete macros that are no longer used by placing the cursor on the line and pressing **<Shift><F4>**. Be sure that the *entire* macro is deleted, and that each remaining macro is separated from the others by an asterisk. There is no asterisk above the first macro in the file or below the last one.

- When macro files are loaded into memory, they're held in a macro buffer — an amount of RAM that Q&A sets aside for the particular macro file. By deleting individual macros that are no longer used, you free up their identifiers for use with new macros and increase the amount of RAM that Q&A now has available for any new macros added to the same file.

- Q&A's default macro Buffer size is 3K but you can increase buffer size with a DOS command-line switch when loading Q&A. At the DOS prompt, type **QA -b***nnnnn* where *nnnnn* is the number of bytes to reserve for the macro buffer. For a 7,000-byte (7K) buffer you'd type **QA -b7000**. The space and dash are important. When specifying buffer size, the minimum is 300 and the maximum is 30,000. A user-defined buffer command is stored in the QA.CFG file along with other user-defined settings.

- During playback, if your macro winds up at the File menu but you'd prefer it to finish at the Main menu, you can insert an **<Esc>** command just before the **<enddef>**. If your macro winds up two menu levels deep but you'd like it to finish at the Main menu, insert *two* **<Esc>** commands before the **<enddef>**.

- When you edit a macro file, you can save the edited version to a new filename, load that file (Get Macros), and run the edited macros to verify that they're working as you want them. If they're not, you still have the original unedited macro file on disk for insurance. If the edited macro file is working okay, simply change its name back to the original filename.

- Using Write's Clipboard feature, you can copy individual macros from one file and insert them into another macro file. See Chapter 2 for details on using the Clipboard.

- After editing a macro you should always test it before turning the application back over to the user. Watch the display carefully with your fastest finger poised over the **<Esc>** key. This way, should the macro start to go haywire, you can simultaneously spot where it happened and type **<Esc>** to kill execution. You should now review the macro in Write and edit it as necessary. Then test it again.

The objective is to have that macro work exactly as it should every time it executes. Sometimes it takes a little trial and error before it dawns on you what's causing it to be unpredictable. Common problems are: missing drive and path parameters (or a typo) when the macro types a filename, failure to take into account a Q&A dialogue screen (for example, when your Retrieve Spec turns up no matching forms), and launching (or having recorded) the macro starting at the wrong location in the program.

See the section "Tips on Recording and Using Macros" earlier in this chapter for more on troubleshooting macro problems.

Saving a Macro File in the Editor

When you've finished editing a macro file on the Type/Edit screen, you'll want to save your changes. The procedure differs from the method you use to save a regular Write document (don't use **<Shift><F8>** or Save from the Write menu).

When you're ready to save your changes, press **<Ctrl><F8>** and confirm the filename by pressing **<Enter>**. This saves the macro file in ASCII format.

After you've made changes to a macro file and then saved it, those changes are not yet available in memory. Before your changes are reflected in the way the edited macro runs, you must first load the modified macro file into RAM. You do this by pressing **<Shift><F2>**, selecting Get Macros, typing in the proper macro filename, and pressing **<Enter>**.

There are a few additional tricks you can do to make your macros work harder for you.

Macros with Pause Codes

You can cause a macro to halt temporarily while you enter a filename or a value, or select an option from a menu or screen. This can be extremely useful in a variety of situations.

Suppose you want a macro to save a document, then pause for you to enter the name of the next document you want to work on. You could record a macro for each document you may want to retrieve, but it would be faster to have a single macro that saves the current document and then prompts you for the name of the next one.

You can do this by entering a *pause* code while you're recording the macro. Here's the procedure:

1. Begin recording the macro in the usual way.

2. While recording the macro, press **<Alt><F2>** at the point where you'll later want the macro to pause for keyboard input. The cursor changes to a large flashing rectangle to let you know the macro is now in *pause* mode.

3. Type whatever you might type during macro playback. This variable information will not be saved as part of the macro.

4. To end the *pause* state and restart the macro definition, press **<Alt><F2>** again and continue recording the macro.

5. Repeat steps 2 through 4 at each point where you want the macro to pause for variable keyboard input.

Now, when you play back the macro, Q&A will temporarily halt it at those places where you entered the pause codes, the cursor will change to the flashing box, and you can enter anything you want. When you've done so and pressed **<Enter>**, playback resumes and the rest of the macro runs until another pause code is encountered.

During playback, if the macro is in pause mode and you need to press **<Enter>** but you don't want playback to resume, type **<Alt><F2>** instead. In this way, **<Alt><F2>** acts like **<Enter>**, but doesn't resume macro playback.

Following a pause code, Q&A resumes playback when the **<Enter>** key is pressed. You can make any key the key that resumes playback, however, by editing the macro in the Write module. The pause in the macro is indicated by the **<Wait>** code immediately followed by the default **<Enter>**. For example, if you want to make **<F10>** the key that resumes macro playback, simply change **<Enter>** to **<f10>** and save the file back to disk with **<Ctrl><F8>**. This doesn't redefine the **<F10>** key, but merely assigns it as the key that resumes playback after *that* pause code in *that* particular macro.

When recording pause codes in macros for the entry of variable record retrieval parameters at Retrieve Specs, keep in mind the possibility that the parameter(s) entered may result in no matching records found. When Q&A can't find any records to match your Retrieve Spec parameter(s), it presents you with a dialogue box where only certain keystrokes are valid: **<Esc>**, **N**, or **2** cancels the retrieve operation and displays the previous menu; **<Enter>**, **<F10>**, **Y**, or **1** redisplays the Retrieve Spec with the same parameter(s).

If you fail to take into account the possibility of no records found to match the Retrieve Spec, and if your macro was designed to execute additional operations on the retrieved data, the macro will continue to attempt to execute, hammering away at the dialogue box until one of the above keystrokes is encountered. Because the result may be totally unwanted, you should always test-run such macros to see what happens when there *are* records to retrieve, as well as when there *aren't*.

Here are a few examples that demonstrate the use of macro pause codes:

- If you frequently search for records in any file on a single field (for example, on an invoice number, customer number, P.O. number, or stock number), you can create a macro that will take you to the Retrieve Spec and pause while you enter the value that will find the records you want.

 Note: You can use the cursor navigation keys to move the large pause indicator to any other field, enter the retrieve parameter, and then press **<Enter>** to resume playback.

For example, where your macro pauses at the Retrieve Spec for entry of the Customer Number, you can move the pause indicator to the Last Name field, type the last name as your retrieve parameter, and then press **<Enter>** to bring up the record.

- If you frequently run routine reports, record a macro that pauses at the List of Reports screen for you to highlight the report you want. When the macro resumes, it prints the report without any further keystrokes.

- Create a macro that pauses for the database filename you want to back up. You enter the name and the macro takes care of the rest.

- When copying an invoice number from an invoice to a customer record, fill out the invoice, and invoke the macro to save it and pause for the customer number (which should already be on the invoice). Enter the customer number, and the macro retrieves the customer's record from the customer file, pausing at the field that contains the latest invoice number. Type the invoice number (or, better yet, program the customer file to look up the number from the invoice) and press **<Enter>**. The macro then resumes and displays another blank invoice for data entry.

- When updating invoices with actual ship dates, create a macro that contains the **<Ctrl><F5>** date stamp and pauses for you to enter the invoice number. As each invoice is retrieved, the macro auto-types the current date (the ship date), and then prompts for the next invoice number.

- When posting quantities of sold or received items to their corresponding stock number records, record a macro that pauses for you to enter the stock number, retrieves the record, pauses again for you to enter the quantity, and then pauses for the next stock number.

Note: In the last three examples, a Posting Spec might prove more efficient than using macros.

Nested Macros

You can embed macros up to five levels deep. This means that you can have the first macro call a second macro, and the second macro call a third, and so forth. The way you do this is by typing *another* macro identifier *while* you're defining a macro.

When Macro A contains the key identifier of Macro B, for example, Macro B will be executed at the point where it's encountered in the macro string. When Macro B has finished executing, control passes back to Macro A, and Macro A will continue to execute starting with the command that immediately follows the call to Macro B.

Several of the sample pause-code macros just mentioned are especially amenable to nesting. Here's how nested macros work.

Suppose you have an **<Alt><N>** macro that types your name, "Robert Evans Parsons." You want to define another macro (**<Alt><P>**) that types your phone number, and a third macro (**<Alt><A>**) that types your name, phone number, and complete address:

```
Robert Evans Parsons
(205) 554-3456
555 N. Elm St.
Birmingham, AL 36787
```

As you're defining **<Alt><A>**, instead of retyping your name and phone number, simply press **<Alt><N>** and then **<Alt><P>**, and Q&A will type your name, phone number, and address. **<Alt><N>** and **<Alt><P>** become part of the macro definition for **<Alt><A>**.

You can still invoke **<Alt><N>** if you want only your name typed, or **<Alt><P>** if you want just your phone number typed, but **<Alt><A>** will call the other macros into action and you'll get the whole nine yards. You should record the **<Alt><N>** and **<Alt><P>** macros *before* you nest them in the **<Alt><A>** macro definition, but it's not mandatory.

Sample Nested Macro Application

Nested macros can help you get more work done than the example above might indicate. You can use nested macros to create looping macros to update a series of records rapidly. A looping macro runs the same procedure repetitively until either the end of the macro is reached or you end it by pressing **<Esc>**.

Let's use the earlier example of updating invoices with their actual shipping dates.

Near the end of each day, Marty from shipping brings you a list of the 50 invoice numbers that were packed and shipped out during the day. You want to record today's date on each of the shipped invoices so when customers call you can retrieve their invoice and advise them that the order was shipped on such and such a date and by whatever means indicated on the invoice.

You need a tool that enables you to rapidly retrieve only the selected invoice forms from Marty's list and enter today's date on them. These original invoices could have been entered days ago, a week ago, or longer, and it's unlikely that the orders were shipped in invoice number order. Here's how you could handle the update with a nested macro; the macro identifiers used here are arbitrary.

1. The macro I'll call **<Alt><A>** takes you from the Q&A Main menu to the INVOICE.DTF Retrieve Spec with the following steps:

    a. Selecting File from the Main menu.

    b. Selecting Search/Update from the File menu.

    c. Typing **INVOICE**, the name of the database or invoice.

    d. Pressing **<Enter>**.

    e. Calling the **<Alt><B>** macro from the first field of the INVOICE.DTF Retrieve Spec.

2. The macro I'll call **<Alt><B>** calls the **<Alt><C>** macro repeatedly, and does nothing else but continue to call the **<Alt><C>** macro.

3. The macro I'll call **<Alt><C>** begins at the first field of the INVOICE.DTF Retrieve Spec, and updates the invoice in the following manner:

    a. Moving the cursor to the invoice number field.

    b. Blanking any value in the field with **<Shift><F4>**.

    c. Pausing for the operator to enter an invoice number.

    d. Retrieving the invoice when the operator presses **<Enter>**.

    e. Moving the cursor to the ship-date field.

    f. Entering the current date with **<Ctrl><F5>**.

    g. Saving the updated form and getting a blank Retrieve Spec with **<F7>**.

Figure 8-5 shows the above three macros on the Type/Edit screen.

Once you invoke **<Alt><A>** from the Q&A Main menu, the only keyboard actions required are to type the invoice number and press **<Enter>**, type the next invoice number and press **<Enter>**, and so on. The above **<Alt><B>** macro calls the **<Alt><C>** macro a total of 25 times, but you could have it call the **<Alt><C>** macro 50 or 100 or more times.

The **<Alt><B>** macro can also be edited to return the operator to the Main menu after the final **<Alt><C>** macro call. If there are still more invoices to update, the **<Alt><A>** macro can be invoked a second time.

Only two of these macros are recorded live — the **<Alt><A>** and **<Alt><C>** macros. Record the **<Alt><C>** macro first, save it, then type the **<Alt><B>** macro in the editor. Now you can record the **<Alt><A>** macro which calls the **<Alt><B>** macro (which in turn calls the **<Alt><C>** macro).

This concept can also be applied to updating purchase orders from a list of purchase orders on which the items have been received from suppliers. It could also be useful in updating inventory records from a report showing items and quantities sold, enabling you to keep running inventory balances.

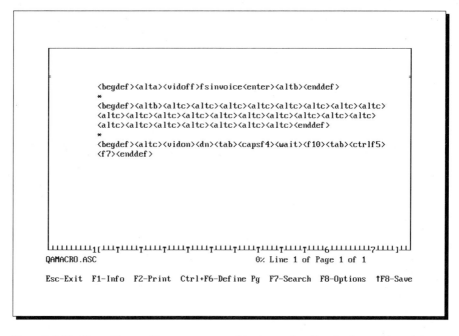

```
       <begdef><alta><vidoff>fsinvoice<enter><altb><enddef>
       *
       <begdef><altb><altc><altc><altc><altc><altc><altc><altc><altc>
       <altc><altc><altc><altc><altc><altc><altc><altc><altc><altc>
       <altc><altc><altc><altc><altc><altc><altc><enddef>
       *
       <begdef><altc><vidon><dn><tab><capsf4><wait><f10><tab><ctrlf5>
       <f7><enddef>
```

```
QAMACRO.ASC                                 0% Line 1 of Page 1 of 1

Esc-Exit  F1-Info  F2-Print  Ctrl+F6-Define Pg  F7-Search  F8-Options  ↑F8-Save
```

Figure 8-5: The Three Macros. These macros combine to create a "looping" macro to update a group of invoices whose items have been shipped. Notice that the last thing the **<Alt><A>** macro does is call the **<Alt><B>** macro, and the only thing the **<Alt><B>** macro does is repeatedly call the **<Alt><C>** macro. It's the **<Alt><C>** macro that updates the invoice and prompts for the next invoice number.

Nested macros can be linked together to perform thousands of repetitive actions in mass update operations as well. For example, you have the first macro call a second macro 20 times, have the second macro call a third macro 20 times, have the third macro call a fourth macro 20 times, and have the fourth macro do the actual update operation. In this example you have 20 multiplied by 20 and again by 20, or a total of 8,000 operations performed.

Installing Macros on the Main Menu

The invoice updating macros described above would make an ideal candidate for inclusion on the Q&A Main menu. This way, the operator can launch the daily routine with a single keystroke.

The Q&A Main menu will accommodate up to six macros or alternate programs. In Chapter 9 you'll see how to install alternate programs on the Main menu and launch them from inside Q&A.

```
                        ALTERNATE PROGRAMS


        You can install up to six alternate programs for the Main Menu.
        You can then execute those programs by selecting them at that menu.
        When you exit from these programs, you will return automatically
        to the Main Menu.

                Alternate program 1: Alt S
                Menu selection.....: Shipdates
                Alternate program 2: Alt O
                Menu selection.....: Open PO's
                Alternate program 3: Alt C
                Menu selection.....: Customer Srch
                Alternate program 4: Alt D
                Menu selection.....: Daily Reports
                Alternate program 5: Alt T
                Menu selection.....: Tbl Vu Items
                Alternate program 6: Alt M
                Menu selection.....: Mthly Summary


        Esc-Exit                                         F10-Continue
```

Figure 8-6: The Alternate Programs Screen. Use the Alternate Programs screen to install your macros or alternate programs on the Q&A Main menu. Notice that the first letters of the menu selections are the same as the letters in their corresponding macro identifiers on the Alternate Program lines.

To install a macro on the Main menu:

1. Select Utilities from the Main menu.

2. Choose Set Alternate Programs from the Utilities menu. The Alternate Programs screen in Figure 8-6 displays.

3. At the first available Alternate Program line, type the identifier of the macro you want to install on the Main menu. The identifier *cannot* include any letter which is already on the Main menu (for example, F, R, W, A, U, and X) if your menus are set to Automatic Execution.

4. On the next line, type a description for the macro that will enable you to identify it. This description will be included on the Main menu. You can use up to 13 characters in your description.

 Note: The first letter of the description must match the character in the corresponding macro identifier.

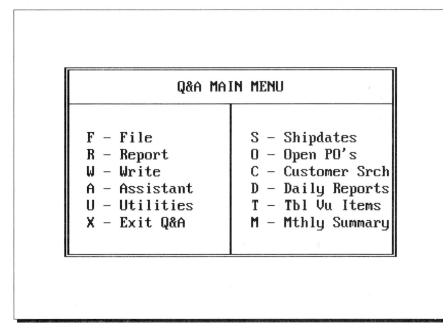

```
┌─────────────────────────────────────────────┐
│                Q&A MAIN MENU                  │
├───────────────────────┬───────────────────────┤
│  F - File             │  S - Shipdates         │
│  R - Report           │  O - Open PO's         │
│  W - Write            │  C - Customer Srch     │
│  A - Assistant        │  D - Daily Reports     │
│  U - Utilities        │  T - Tbl Vu Items      │
│  X - Exit Q&A         │  M - Mthly Summary     │
└───────────────────────┴───────────────────────┘
```

Figure 8-7: Six Macros Installed on the Q&A Main Menu.

5. Repeat steps 4 and 5 for other macros you want to install on the Main menu. When you're finished, press **<F10>** to save the screen and **<Esc>** to move to the Main menu where you'll see your macros installed as in Figure 8-7.

Notice that in Figure 8-7 the macro for entering the invoice ship dates is not **<Alt><A>**, as in the example in the previous section but **<Alt><S>**. This is because **<Alt><A>** would conflict with the **A** selection for the Intelligent Assistant on the opposite side of the menu.

If you want to install an existing macro on the Main menu with an identifier that conflicts with an existing Main menu selection, you'll need to use Write to change its identifier at the Type/Edit screen.

Autostart Macros

You can specify that a macro be launched automatically as soon as Q&A loads. Only macros named **<Alt><0>** through **<Alt><9>** can be autostarted, and their numbers must be typed using the number keys across the top of the keyboard, *not* the numeric keypad.

You indicate which autostart macro to launch by typing the macro number after an **m** on the DOS command line:

QA -m3 <Enter>

tells Q&A to play back the **<Alt><3>** macro as soon as the program is loaded into memory. Be sure to leave a space between the **QA** and the **-m3**.

Autostart macros are otherwise no different from any other Q&A macro. However, they must be in the default macro start-up file, which is normally QAMACRO.ASC.

Q&A has an *autoload* feature that enables you to select a macro file other than QAMACRO.ASC to be loaded with Q&A. More on that in the next section.

How can you use an autostart macro? The possibilities are endless, but here are a few examples:

- To bring up a fresh, blank form for the database in which you most often work.

- To call up your "To-Do" list for the day.

- To automatically retrieve, update, or tag selected records that contain date-sensitive information (such as invoices with balances due, or sales follow-up records). You could use an autostart macro to display a table view (or print a report) of sales leads that need to be contacted today as promised.

- To retrieve the chapter in that book you've been working on.

- To place a custom application menu on screen from which the operator can select the appropriate activity.

- To pop up the password screen for you to enter your user ID and password before starting your Q&A session. For example, following the procedure below you could have Q&A run an **<Alt><9>** macro at start-up:

  1. From the Q&A Main menu define the macro as **<Alt><9>**.

  2. With the recorder running, press **<F6>** to display the password box, type your User ID, and press **<Enter>**.

  3. Now save the macro to QAMACRO.ASC.

  4. Start Q&A with the DOS command **QA -m9**.

As soon as Q&A loads, the macro displays the password box with the user ID already typed and the cursor on the password line. You simply type your password and press **<Enter>** to start your Q&A session.

Autoload Macro Files

Version 4.0

New: With Q&A 4.0 you have the option of stipulating the macro file to be loaded when you start the program. If you don't specify one, Q&A will load it's default macro file, QAMACRO.ASC, at start-up.

To have Q&A load a macro file other than QAMACRO.ASC at start-up, use the following command line option at the DOS prompt:

    QA -al<filename>

where **al** stands for Auto Load, and *filename* is the complete path and name of the macro file you wish to load with Q&A.

If you wish a macro file other than QAMACRO.ASC to *always* load with Q&A, the following switch specifies it as the default macro file:

    QA -ad<filename>

where **ad** stands for Auto Load Default, and *filename* is the complete path of the macro file you wish to make the default macro file.

You can, of course, make any other macro file the default at any time simply by replacing the *filename* parameter.

If you specify a nonexistent filename after either of the switches, or if the QA.CFG (configuration) file cannot be found, Q&A will load the default macro file.

Custom Application Menus

A macro must have some form of identification tag attached to it. This can be a plain old macro identifier such as **<Alt><C>**, or you can assign descriptive names to your macros and launch them from custom-designed menus.

When you press **<Shift><F2>** from anywhere in Q&A you get the Macro menu shown in Figure 8-1. This is Q&A's built-in Macro menu and shouldn't be confused with any special macro menus that you design, which function more like macro lists. With these custom menus, instead of pressing the key combination to play back a macro, you can simply select the macro you want to run, just as if you were selecting an item from a Q&A menu.

Q&A Power Feature: With custom menus and named macros, you can control from *where* in the program your macros are launched. The need to remember specific **<Alt><key>** or **<Ctrl><key>** macro identifiers can be eliminated. It's a breakthrough feature that enables you to better control how your applications are used by others, and in fact allows you to create entire stand-alone applica-

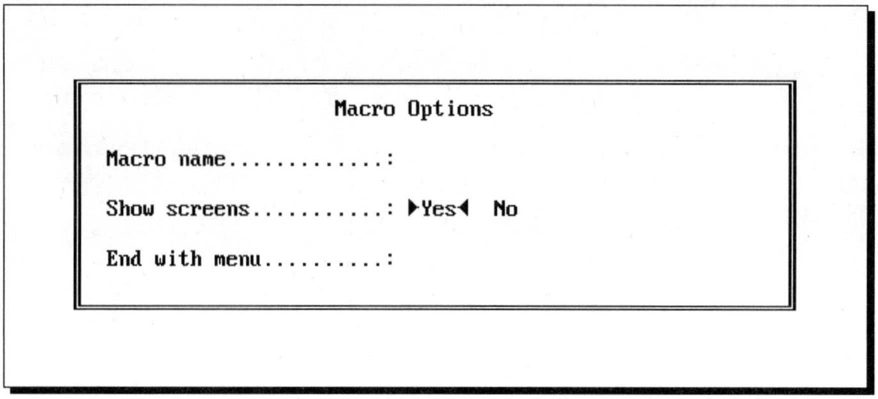

```
                          Macro Options

Macro name.............:

Show screens...........: ▶Yes◀  No

End with menu..........:
```

Figure 8-8: The Macro Options Box. It displays when you press <Shift><F2> to end macro recording.

tions, completely changing Q&A, if you like, from a general purpose database program into a custom menu-driven application program.

The first item on Q&A's built-in Macro menu is "Run Macro." It's first on the menu because it's the selection that is likely to be most often be used. When you press **<Shift><F2>** the "Run Macro" selection will already be highlighted, so you can simply press **<Enter>** to see the list of all the available macros in the current macro file, highlight the one you want to run, and press **<Enter>** again to launch it.

You can also press **<Alt><F2>** from almost anywhere in Q&A to view the list of macros in the file that's currently in memory, and then launch the macro of your choice. Giving your macros descriptive names enables you to more easily remember which macros do what.

Naming Macros

The procedure you use to assign a name to a macro after recording it is essentially the same as the Define Macro Procedure given earlier in this chapter, with the addition of a couple of steps:

1. Press **<Shift><F2>** for the Q&A Macro menu.

2. Select Define Macro.

3. If you want to assign an identifier to the macro now, type the keystroke combination and press **<Enter>**, or optionally press **<Enter>** to proceed without an identifier. The flashing square in the lower-right

corner of the screen lets you know that your keystrokes will now be recorded.

4. Record your macro in the usual manner, with pause codes as appropriate.

5. After the last macro keystroke, press **<Shift><F2>**. The Macro Options box in Figure 8-8 will display.

6. The cursor will be positioned on the Macro Name line in the Macro Options box. If you entered a macro identifier at the beginning of the recording procedure, this line will display that identifier. You can leave the identifier as is, type your descriptive macro name over it, or type the name on the blank line. Typing a name over a key identifier doesn't change or erase the key identifier if one was assigned to the macro. Your descriptive name can be up to 31 characters in length. For example:

Macro name..............: Copy Invoices to Master File

or Find Customer by Last Name
or Run Sales Summary Report
or Table View B of Open POs

And so forth.

Q&A won't let you proceed unless a name or key identifier appears on this line.

7. Show Screens is where you tell Q&A to keep the display on as the macro is executing, or to turn it off during macro playback. If you select Off, the message, "Macro Working..." will display during macro playback. If your macro contains pause codes, those screens that require the user to enter variable data will display each time the macro encounters a pause code.

8. The "End With Menu" selection is optional. If you want to have the macro call a custom menu after playback, enter the menu name, or press **<Alt><F7>** for a list of custom menu names. Even if no custom menus have as yet been designed, you can still enter a menu name and design the menu later. (Details on custom menu design to come.) It's best to design such custom menus in advance, however, because if a menu isn't active or doesn't exist when called by a macro, macro playback will terminate at that point.

9. Press **<F10>** when finished with the Macro Options box, confirm the file where you want the macro saved and press **<Enter>** to save the macro to disk. If you want to use the macro for only the current session (you don't want to save it to disk), press **<Esc>**. The macro will then be available for use until it is cleared or you exit Q&A.

Creating Special Application menus

 Q&A Power Feature: Q&A provides an assortment of powerful tools that enable you to customize virtually the entire look and operation of the program. You can create custom menus that are called at the end of macros. And you can even *replace* the Q&A standard menus with menus of your own.

Having Q&A call a custom menu at the end of a macro puts you in control of what actions are taken next. For example, your first macro may perform a mass update or copy operation on a selected set of database files. When this macro is finished, you may need to limit the operator's next action to a choice of printing a report connected to the previous operation, selecting a table view, running a backup on a file, or returning to the Q&A Main menu.

With a custom menu displayed after the original macro is finished, you can regulate what the operator does next. Macros display your custom menus, and your custom menus launch your macros.

You can gain even more control over what operations are performed by designing custom menus to replace Q&A's own menus.

Here's the procedure for creating a custom application menu:

1. Press **<Shift><F2>** for Q&A's built-in Macro menu (optionally, you can choose File, then Design File, then Customize Application, then Create Application menu, and then proceed to step 3 below).

2. Select **M** for Create menu. Q&A displays the List of Menu Names.

3. To create a new menu, press **<Enter>** to get to the Macro menu Options screen shown in Figure 8-9.

4. Enter the name you want to assign to the new menu. The name can be up to 31 characters including spaces. The name you assign here can be used to "call" this menu from other macros. You can press **<Alt><F7>** from this line to view a list of all the Q&A menu names. If this custom menu will display in place of a standard Q&A menu, ordinarily you'll use the Q&A menu name as your custom menu name. Otherwise, use the list of Q&A menus to *avoid* assigning a Q&A menu name to your custom menu. (See Table 8-2 for special Q&A menu names.)

5. Set Display status to Full Screen if you want only your custom menu to display when called. Select Overlay if you want whatever screen may be behind the menu to partially display along with the custom menu.

6. Set the Status line to Active if you want the menu fully operational. Select Inactive if you want this menu temporarily removed from use.

```
                        MACRO MENU OPTIONS
                        ══════════════════

        Menu name...........: File Search Menu
        Display.............: ▶Full screen◀  Overlay
        Status..............: ▶Active◀          Inactive
        Menu returns........:   Yes    ▶No◀
        On Escape, show menu.:
    ┌─────────────────────────────────────────────────────────┐
    │             Menu Title...: File Search Menu               │
    │─────────────────────────────────────────────────────────│
    │  Item 1: Invoice Search      Macro Name: search invoice   │
    │  Item 2: PO Search           Macro Name: search po        │
    │  Item 3: Customer Search     Macro Name: search customer  │
    │  Item 4: Stock Search        Macro Name: search inventory │
    │  Item 5: Employee Search     Macro Name: search employee  │
    │  Item 6: Vendor Search       Macro Name: search vendor    │
    │  Item 7:                     Macro Name:                  │
    │  Item 8:                     Macro Name:                  │
    │  Item 9:                     Macro Name:                  │
    └─────────────────────────────────────────────────────────┘
```

Figure 8-9: The Macro Menu Options Screen. Here you enter your custom menu name, menu selections, and their corresponding macro names. The sample menu shown includes macros that take you to the Retrieve Specs of the selected files. In this case, the Menu Name is the same as the Menu Title, but this isn't mandatory. Notice that each item starts with a different letter, enabling any item to be selected from the menu simply by pressing the first letter of the selection.

7. Set Menu Returns to Yes if you want to display a custom menu when **<Esc>** is pressed from a Q&A function, provided you got to that function using a macro. Otherwise, set this line to No. If this is a "Menu Returns" menu, it should overlay the Q&A Main menu as all macros on it need to be defined from this point.

8. If you want another menu to display when **<Esc>** is pressed from this menu, type the *name*, not the title, of that menu on the On Escape, Show Menu line. When you have several layers of custom menus, pressing **<Esc>** displays the previous menu in the hierarchy. You can press **<Alt><F7>** here to view a list of menu names already assigned.

9. Enter the Menu Title you want at the top of your custom menu when it's displayed. It doesn't have to be the same as the menu name. The Title can be up to 31 characters including spaces. Press **<Alt><F7>** for a list of Menu Titles already assigned.

10. Type the first item that you want included on the menu. Type the item *exactly* as you want it to appear when the menu is displayed. For example, if you want the item to be displayed as Backup Stock File, type it exactly like that. You can use up to 22 characters including spaces. If you want to be able to select menu items by pressing the first letter of the item, be sure all items in this column of the Macro menu Options screen start with a different letter.

11. In the field opposite the item, type the Macro Name exactly as it's entered in the Macro Options box (see Figure 8-8). You can press **<Alt><F7>** to get a list of macros in the current file, highlight the one you want, and press **<Enter>**. The Macro Name can be the descriptive name for the macro, or the macro identifier, such as **<Alt><G>**. You've got 31 spaces, the same number as in the corresponding field in the Macro Options box.

12. Repeat Steps 5 and 6 for other items you wish to add to your custom macro menu. A custom menu can contain up to nine selections and their corresponding macros.

13. When you're satisfied that the menu is complete, press **<F10>**, confirm the macro file you want your custom menu design saved to (it should be the same file that contains the macros included on the menu), and press **<Enter>** to save the new menu to disk. The entire custom menu design now exists as a highly specialized macro definition.

You can always go back and change any item on any Macro menu Options screen, including the menu name, title, item descriptions and macro names, by following the above procedure. You can also use the word processor to directly edit the macro that creates the custom menu.

Tip: Using the Macro menu Options screen to modify a custom menu is preferable to editing the macro in Write because it's usually easier to work with a form rather than lines of often complex macro code.

Custom menus can be accessed by having the macros that call them installed on the Q&A Main menu. The procedure for installing macros as alternate programs on the Main menu was discussed earlier in this chapter. You can also call a custom menu by pressing the Key Identifier of the macro that calls it. This could be as simple as pressing **<Alt><M>** from the keyboard. Chapter 12 shows a good example of this.

Figure 8-10 shows the Q&A Main menu with four menu-calling macros installed. Each macro is tied to a custom menu, which in turn is tied to a specific Q&A operation.

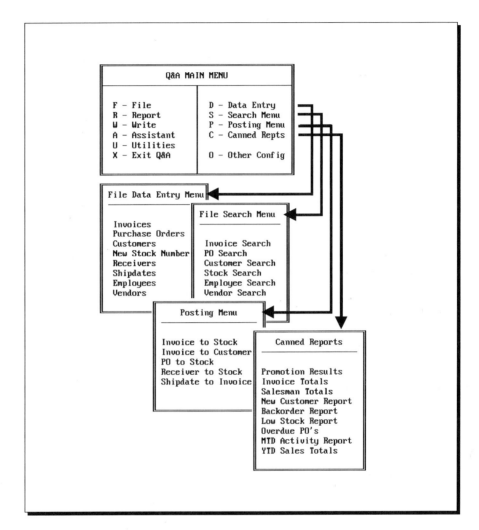

Figure 8-10: Four Menu-Calling Macros Installed on the Q&A Main Menu. The four custom menus correspond to the Main menu macros. The Other Config selection swaps out the current Q&A configuration for an alternate configuration, enabling you to have a second Q&A Main menu with its own set of alternate programs/macros. See Chapter 9 for details on how to create alternate Q&A configurations.

Calling a Menu

The third line of the Macro Options box in Figure 8-8 ("End Macro with Menu") offers you the option of having the macro call a specified menu when the macro has finished. If you want the macro to call a menu upon completion, you enter the menu name when you've finished recording the macro and the Options box is displayed. Press **<Shift><F7>** from this line to view the list of existing custom menus.

You can enter a menu name even if the menu does not yet exist, giving you the option of creating the macro first, and then editing the macro in Write to add the menu name once the menu has been designed.

Menu Management — the Essentials

You can call a custom menu as the last thing a macro does, and that menu can even replace a standard Q&A menu. When you want to replace a Q&A menu, assign that standard Q&A menu's name to the custom menu.

When you replace a Q&A menu with your custom menu, the custom menu displays whenever you call for that Q&A menu. Q&A's standard functions on the replaced menu aren't gone — you can always access them by starting a macro from the replacement menu with the first letter of the Q&A function you want.

Remember that Q&A calls menus and macros the same way — be careful when assigning names to your macros. Should you name a macro after a Q&A menu, you can call that macro from a standard Q&A menu. For example, if you name a macro Report menu, every time you select Report from the Q&A Main menu, Q&A would run the macro instead of displaying the standard Report menu. If you've designed a custom Report menu you want displayed, and that's what the macro calls, fine.

Some Q&A menus present a special case, for example, their names appear more than once in Q&A's own menu system. Table 8-2 shows a summary of these Q&A menus and the custom menu names you must use if you want to replace them.

A Complete Custom Menu Structure

If your objective is a self-contained, stand-alone application in Q&A, you can design it to be completely independent from Q&A's standard menu structure.

In such an application you won't use any Q&A menus at all, and you should define all your macros from the point of the Q&A Main menu.

You can even create a custom menu named "Macro menu" to replace Q&A's built-in Macro menu. With this in place, the user will get *your* macro menu when pressing **<Shift><F2>** and will have no access, unless you permit it, to

---

Table 8-2
Standard Q&A Menu Names, and the Custom
Menu Names that Replace Them

Q&A Menu Name	Custom Menu Name
Rename/Delete/Copy (File)	File Print Rename/Delete/Copy
Rename/Delete/Copy (Report)	Report Rename/Delete/Copy
Print Global Options (File)	File Print Global Options
Report Global Options	Report Global Options
Columnar Global Options	Report Global Options Columnar
Crosstab Global Options	Report Global Options Crosstab
Global Options (Write)	Write Utilities Global Options
Assistant Menu	Assistant Menu (even if you've changed your assistant's name)

---

either the List of Macro Names or the Macro menu Options screen. The only way the user could circumvent such a restriction would be to exit Q&A and rename the macro file in DOS (see the section in this chapter on protecting a macro file).

You can use several features available on the Macro menu Options screen (see Figure 8-9) to add control to your custom menu structure.

The first is On Escape, Show menu. Here you enter the name of the menu you want the user to see when escaping from a menu. In other words, when designing menu C, you enter menu B if you want menu B to display when escaping from menu C. This way, if your menu structure goes several layers deep, pressing **<Esc>** from a menu displays the previous menu in hierarchy.

The second menu control feature at the Macro menu Options screen is Menu Returns. In a hierarchy of custom menus, each menu should be considered a "Menu Returns" menu so long as the custom menu from which they were invoked is also a "Menu Returns" menu.

"Menu Returns" always returns the user to the position of the Q&A Main menu, so any macros on such menus must be defined as though they were starting from the Q&A Main menu. If you use "Menu Returns" with a menu structure that overlays the Q&A Main menu, the user will be brought back to the point of the Q&A Main menu regardless of where the custom menu was executed. So specify "Menu Returns" only in a custom menu structure that overlays the Q&A Main menu.

If you replace the Q&A Main menu, you'll need a macro on that custom menu to exit the program. You can do this by offering an **X** selection as the last item on your custom menu, where the key identifier for the macro is **<Alt><X>**. But because the macro definition ends after Q&A has been exited, you'll need to create the macro in Write.

Special Custom Menu Syntax

With the addition of menu names, menu items, macro names, and so forth, custom menu macros will look different in the ASCII macro file than their unadorned simple **<Alt><key>** or **<Ctrl><key>** counterparts.

Your custom macro menus display on the Type/Edit screen looking something like this:

```
*
<begdef><nokey><name>"menu  name"<vidoff><menu>"menu
title,FAN:on escape menu/item 1,macro1/item2,macro2/
item3,macro3/...  itemn,macron/"<enddef>
*
```

The macro was created by complying with the following rules:

- The macro begins with **<begdef>** as must all Q&A macros.

- There are no keystrokes (key identifier) associated with invoking a macro menu, so the code **<nokey>** is the second item in the menu macro.

- The tag **<name>** tells Q&A that a macro name follows. Every menu must have a name.

- The "menu name" can be up to 31 characters long. It cannot contain quotation marks, but is *enclosed* in quote marks. This is the name Q&A uses to call the menu, not necessarily the name that appears at the top of the displayed menu (the menu Title). If an asterisk is part of the menu name, such as in "*menu name," it means that this is the menu that Q&A should display when the macro is finished running.

- The **<vidoff>** code indicates that the display is off while the macro calling the menu is working. The **<vidon>** command displays any intermediate screens.

- The tag **<menu>** tells Q&A that a menu definition follows.

- The opening quote mark starts the menu definition.

- Then comes the menu's title followed by a comma, the three-letter code that indicates display, status, and menu returns followed by a colon, and the name of the "on escape menu," if any. **FAN** is a three-letter code that means the display is set to Full screen, the menu status is set to Active, and the Menu Returns is set to No — options that were selected for this menu at the Macro menu Options screen. These three elements are then followed by the slash character.

- You then have the first item on the menu, which corresponds to Item 1 on the Macro menu Options screen, followed by a comma.

- Next comes the macro for item 1, followed by the slash character.

- You then have the second item and its corresponding macro name, then the third item name and its macro name, and so forth. Each item/macro combination is separated by **/** (slash). A menu macro can contain up to nine item/macro combinations and be up to 255 characters in length. No spaces or carriage returns are allowed anywhere within the structure.

- The entire menu definition is then finished by close quote marks, and the macro is ended by the usual **<enddef>**.

Since these menu macros are more complex then ordinary macros, edit them whenever possible using the Macro menu Options screen (following essentially the same procedure you used to design them originally). Although you *can* edit menu macros in Write, a single typographical error or missing quote mark there could cause you a great deal of trouble — a pain to track down and correct.

The macros in Figure 8-11 are shown as each appears in the macro file when viewed on the Type/Edit screen. The collection includes all the macros related to the File Search menu created at the Macro menu Options screen in Figure 8-9 and then shown, along with several other custom menus, in Figure 8-10. Here you see the Q&A Main menu macro that calls the custom menu; the macros that constitute the selections on that custom menu, and the macro that defines the complete structure of the custom menu.

More Custom Menu Ideas

Tip: As you've probably gathered, custom menus open the door to a vast range of time- and work-saving possibilities. You certainly don't have to go as far as replacing Q&A's menu system with your own in order to take full advantage of the benefits tailored menus can bring to your Q&A sessions.

```
<begdef><alts><name>"<caps,>alts<caps.>"<vidoff><menu>"*File<sp>
Search<sp>Menu"<enddef>
```

Figure 8-11a: The `<Alt><S>` Macro (S - Search Menu). Installed on the Q&A Main menu in Figure 8-10, it calls the custom File Search menu. The asterisk preceding the menu name tells Q&A to display the menu that follows it when the macro is finished running. In this case a name was not assigned to the macro at the Macro Options box, so Q&A named the macro alts on its own.

```
<begdef><nokey><name>"search<sp>invoice"<vidoff><esc>fsinvoice
<enter><enddef>
*
<begdef><nokey><name>"search<sp>po"<vidoff><esc>fspo<enter>
<enddef>
*
<begdef><nokey><name>"search<sp>customer"<vidoff><esc>fscustomer
<enter><enddef>
*
<begdef><nokey><name>"search<sp>stock"<vidoff><esc>fsstock<enter>
<enddef>
*
<begdef><nokey><name>"search<sp>employee"<vidoff><esc>fsemployee
<enter><enddef>
*
<begdef><nokey><name>"search<sp>vendor"<vidoff><esc>fsvendor
<enter><enddef>
```

Figure 8-11b: The Six Macros Constituting the Six Selections Available from the Custom File Search Menu. Note that these macros do not contain key identifiers (they're all no-key macros), but they're all named. Note also the `<Esc>` command included in each macro, giving them a common starting point at the Q&A Main menu.

```
<begdef><nokey><name>"File<sp>Search<sp>Menu"<menu>"File<sp>
Search<sp>Menu,FAN:/Invoice<sp>Search,search<sp>invoice/PO
<sp>Search,search<sp>po/Customer<sp>Search,search<sp>customer/
Stock<sp>Search,search<sp>stock/Employee<sp>Search,search<sp>
employee/Vendor<sp>Search,search<sp>vendor/"<enddef>
```

Figure 8-11c: The Macro that Defines the Structure of the Custom File Search Menu. This macro was generated by Q&A when the Macro menu Options screen (see Figure 8-9) was filled out and saved. Note that the structure includes the item/macro combinations for the six macros in Figure 8-11b.

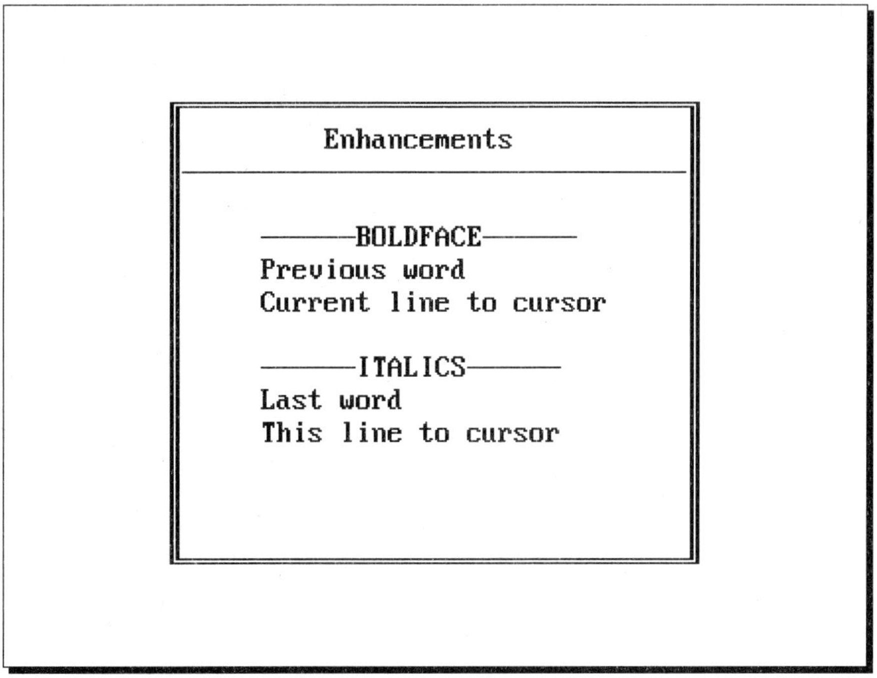

```
┌─────────────────────────────────────────────┐
│                                               │
│    ┌───────────────────────────────────┐     │
│    │            Enhancements            │     │
│    │    ───────────────────────────     │     │
│    │                                     │     │
│    │        ──────BOLDFACE──────         │     │
│    │        Previous word                │     │
│    │        Current line to cursor       │     │
│    │                                     │     │
│    │        ──────ITALICS──────          │     │
│    │        Last word                    │     │
│    │        This line to cursor          │     │
│    │                                     │     │
│    └───────────────────────────────────┘     │
│                                               │
└─────────────────────────────────────────────┘
```

Figure 8-12: A Custom Menu that Can Speed Up Your Work.

A custom menu that you call when working on a document in the word processor, for example, can help speed up your work significantly. Consider the custom menu in Figure 8-12.

This menu includes six items, although only four of the six items have corresponding macros. The two headings, "BOLDFACE" and "ITALICS," have no macros associated with them that Q&A can run — they are there, preceded and followed by ASCII 196 graphics characters, simply to differentiate between the two types of enhancements and dress up the menu a bit.

This custom menu can come in handy if, when composing your documents, you routinely need to embolden or italicize a word or line just typed.

To embolden a word just typed and then move the cursor into position for the start of the next word, you'd ordinarily have to perform these steps:

1. Press **<Shift><F6>** for the Enhancement menu.

2. Type **B** for boldface.

3. Press **<Ctrl><⊖>** to highlight the word just typed.

4. Press **<F10>** to enhance the word.

5. Press **<Ctrl><>>** or **<End>** to move the cursor back to the end of the word just enhanced.

6. Press the space bar or **<>>** to position the cursor for the start of the next word.

But with a custom menu and macro-driven enhancements as above, you can boldface the word just typed and position the cursor for the next word with these two steps alone:

1. Press **<Alt><E>** (or whatever identifier you've assigned) for your custom Enhancement menu.

2. Press **P** to boldface that previous word and position the cursor ready for the next word.

Your macro for this enhancement would *include* the six steps you'd otherwise have to carry out from the keyboard one at a time.

Notice that no two items (including the headings) on the custom menu shown above start with the same letter. This allows you to run any of the four macros simply by pressing the first letter of the item with the menu displayed. Additionally, you can use the four enhancement macros *without* having to call the menu. For example, if the macro that boldfaces the previous word is **<Alt><B>**, you can simply type the identifier **<Alt><B>** to run the macro. So whether you run the macro from the custom menu, or by typing its identifier, you've still saved enough keystrokes to make a real difference in your productivity.

With the menu, however, you won't have to remember the key identifiers that invoke the four enhancement macros.

You could add yet another macro to a menu like this — one containing a pause code, for example, that pauses until you highlight all the text you want to enhance and press **<Enter>**.

Similarly structured custom menus can be used to enhance productivity in the other Q&A modules as well.

To illustrate, suppose you routinely produce three different types of invoices — Retail, Trade, and Pro forma — all using the same database form. You could create a custom menu with these three selections, each of which would fill out those portions of the invoice with the values appropriate to the type of invoice you want to generate.

Descriptively naming a macro, while avoiding assigning a key identifier to it, makes the macro impossible to run *except* from the custom menu on which it's included and the List of Macro Names. If the menu or list isn't displayed, the macro isn't executable. This is a particularly important option to consider when recording macros that run mass update, posting, form copying, form removing, and other delicate operations which, if inappropriately run, can potentially harm your database. Naming such macros and placing them on menus removes them one significant step from inadvertent execution from the wrong location in the program or following a slip of the finger. In any case, batch operation macros such as these should always be recorded as if starting from the position of the Q&A Main menu.

To add even more insurance against accidental macro execution, store your "Big" macros in files that have to be scrupulously loaded into memory before they can be used. For example, if you run a series of macro-driven batch operations at the end of the day, week, or month, force the user to load the appropriate macro file before any of these "Big" macros are accessible. The few additional keystrokes needed to swap out alternate macro files is cheap insurance by any standard.

Protecting Macro Files

Q&A gives you the option of protecting entire macro files. When you encode a macro file, users are only allowed to run its macros. This permits the application designer to exercise an extraordinary degree of control over how Q&A is used, since the user won't be able to do anything involving macros except to run them — and, of course, any custom menus you create are macro-driven.

Warning: Once you encode a macro file you *cannot* uncode it, *so be sure to have a backup copy of the non-encoded version in case you later need to edit the file.*

Follow these steps to protect a macro file:

1. Select File, then Design a File, then Customize Application.

2. From the Customize Application menu choose Protect Macro File.

3. Enter the name of the macro file you want to protect. You can clear any entry on the filename line and press **<Enter>** for a list of files.

4. Enter the filename you want assigned to the protected macro file (don't use the original filename. You might want to use the DOS filename extension .MAC to avoid overwriting the original file) and then press **<Enter>**. The macro file is now encoded.

5. You can now configure your Q&A startup options to automatically load your protected macro file (see "Autoload Macro Files" earlier in this chapter).

Since the user is allowed to do nothing with an encoded macro file except *run* the macros in it, when he presses **<Shift><F2>** with the encoded file in memory he'll get only the list of macros to run. He won't be able to define a macro, get a new macro file, save a macro file, clear the macro file, or design or edit a menu. However, he will be able to edit your start-up options and have Q&A load a different macro file.

Macro file encryptions are stored in the QA.CFG file. This is the file that Q&A looks for on start-up for information on your computer's display, installed printers, alternate Main menu programs, and global options.

Q&A will load and run without the QA.CFG file. Normally, QA.CFG is created as you configure the program to your needs, usually during your first Q&A session. Conceivably, a user could delete the existing QA.CFG file and still be able to use Q&A, but not your custom menu macro file unless he knows the filename and how to load it. He would then of course be able to edit the file, design menus, and so forth. Because your custom menu structure (perhaps the entire application you've designed for the user) is in the macro file, and that file is protected by the QA.CFG file, be aware that this can happen.

Summary

In this chapter, you learned about Q&A's macro capabilities, including how to customize macros and menus to your applications.

The focus in the next chapter will be on utilities — converting documents into other formats, creating font description files, importing and exporting documents to other applications, and performing DOS "housekeeping" tasks without leaving Q&A.

Chapter 9
Utilities — The Q&A Toolkit

In this chapter you'll learn how to:

▶ Create and edit font description files.

▶ Launch other programs from the Q&A Main menu.

▶ Create alternate Q&A configurations.

▶ Import documents and data into Q&A from other popular software programs.

▶ Export your Q&A documents and data files to other programs.

▶ Perform DOS housekeeping chores without leaving Q&A.

▶ Use Q&A's List Manager to locate files.

▶ Give your data and document files longer, more descriptive names.

▶ Recover damaged documents and database files.

▶ Back up your files.

▶ Set up locks to protect your database file designs.

Overview

Utilities are tools you use to take care of special tasks that are outside the normal day-to-day word processing, database, and report work you do in Q&A.

You may need to convert your Q&A documents or database files into formats that can be recognized or used directly by other programs, or bring information from other programs into Q&A in a format that Q&A understands. Q&A provides outstanding import/export support.

As the number of your Q&A document and database files grows, you'll benefit by knowing how to easily locate and manage them more efficiently, perhaps giving them new names or longer, more descriptive names, copying them to other directories, or deleting them from your hard disk to make room for new files. Using Q&A's List Manager and DOS file facilities, make these "housekeeping" chores a breeze.

Documents and database files can become damaged by power fluctuations and failures. In most cases, however, they can be rescued in a matter of minutes using Q&A's excellent recovery utilities.

And should you need to tamper-proof your hard-won database designs or limit access to certain Q&A's features, Q&A provides a variety of options you can use to prevent anyone but yourself, and others you name, from making changes to your working designs and specifications.

All of these are considered to be *utilities* in Q&A and, like all of Q&A's features, are very easy to use.

Q&A provides three different utility modules — one specifically for document-related activities, which is available as a selection from the Write menu; one for database related activities, available from the File menu; and another, available as a selection from the Main menu.

Main Menu Utilities

The Main menu utilities focus on globally related tasks and are used to install your printer, modify font files, set global defaults, and specify alternate programs you can launch from Q&A's Main menu.

Figure 9-1 shows the Utilities menu reached by selecting **U** from the Q&A Main menu. I'll explore these utilities first, after which I'll look at the Write and then the File Utilities, followed by a discussion of Q&A's DOS file facilities. Some of the selections in these various utility menus have already been treated in previous chapters, and you'll be referred to those chapters where appropriate.

Install printer is the first selection on the main Utilities menu. You'll recall that we went through the printer installation procedure in Chapter 1, customizing Q&A for your brand of printer. Refer to the material there to install or un-install a printer and also to Appendix B for additional details on:

- Serial printer installation options.
- Using the Special Printer Options screen to define special printer setup options.
- Using the Intel Connection Coprocessor fax board with Q&A.

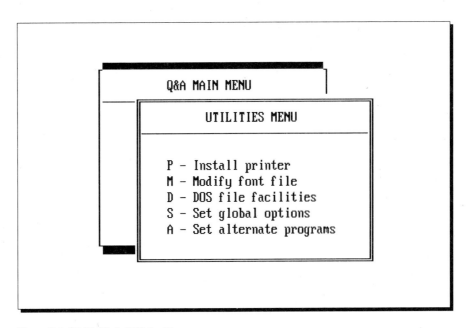

Figure 9-1: Q&A's Main Utilities Menu.

- Troubleshooting common printer problems.

- Troubleshooting font problems.

Modify font file enables you to delete, edit, and even create custom font descriptions for the fonts you want to use with Q&A.

DOS file facilities allows you to do DOS housekeeping chores such as searching, copying, renaming, and deleting files without having to leave Q&A. The Write module Utilities menu has its own DOS file facilities selection, but since these utilities work essentially the same throughout the product, I'll take up the DOS facilities as a whole later in the chapter.

Set global options enables you to specify default directories for your document, database, and Q&A's temporary files.

Set alternate programs provides the capability to launch other DOS programs and Q&A macros from the Q&A Main menu.

Modifying Font Description Files

With Q&A you can create the font descriptions you need or customize existing ones to suit your preferences. Before you begin, however, you should be familiar with your printer, its built-in capabilities, and the control codes needed to access those capabilities.

 Note: If you need to upgrade user-modified font description files from Q&A Write or earlier versions of Q&A, or convert HP LaserJet-compatible or PostScript soft font files to Q&A 4.0 format, see "Converting and Upgrading Font Files" later in this chapter.

If you're planning to create or modify a *proportionally* spaced font description (a more involved operation) you'll also need to know about ASCII characters and character width tables. This is all technical stuff, and your printer manual (and font package manual if you're using third-party fonts) is the place to find out about it. The way printers are controlled by application programs such as Q&A is an exact science, so be sure you know what you're doing before embarking on a font file creation odyssey. At least do yourself the favor of working with a *copy* of your font description file, not the original file.

During the course of this section you'll see references to both *font descriptions* and font description *files*, and you'll need to know the difference between the two.

- A *font description file* may contain dozens of individual *font descriptions* for a particular make and model of printer.

- A *font description* is a unified set of values and control codes that governs one particular printer feature such as boldfacing or a single font size.

Neither of the above contains *fonts*. You must supply your own fonts to use with Q&A.

When you send a document to the printer, Q&A looks to the font description file associated with that printer to find the information needed to properly "drive" the printer. If your document includes a text enhancement like a font change, for example, then Q&A must separate out of the entire font description file that *individual* font description containing the instructions about the font specified in the document, and send *that* information to the printer at the appropriate moment. This is how the printer, as it's printing the document, is able to turn on and then off again the enhancements you specified when creating your document.

To create a new font description file, or modify an existing one:

1. Select Utilities from the Q&A Main menu.

2. Select Modify Font File from the Utilities menu.

```
=============== MODIFY FONT DESCRIPTIONS ===============
Font name: Univers ItaMed                    Abbreviation: Univ
Printer name: HP LaserJet III/IIID Internal
On codes : ←(8U←(s1p*v1s0b4148T
Off codes: ←(10U←(s0p10h12v0s0b3T
Point size: S              (a number, Scalable, or Enhancement)
Characters per inch: P     (a number, Proportional, or Enhancement)

Printer resolution (dots per inch):  300

                Character   Code  Width (in dots)

                   space     32    346              PgUp - Previous
  ┌──────────────┐   !       33    346
  │ Complete for │   "       34    519        Ctrl PgUp - Top
  │ proportional │   #       35    653
  │ fonts only   │   $       36    653
  └──────────────┘   %       37   1037        Ctrl PgDn - Bottom
                     &       38    788
                     '       39    346              PgDn - Next


HPLASERJ.FNT                              Font 17   of 268

Esc-Exit   F1-Help   F3-Del   ↑F5-Copy  F8-Add  F9-Prev  F10-Next   ↑F10-Continue
```

Figure 9-2: Q&A's Modify Font Description Screen. This shows a font description for the HP LaserJet III/IIID internal Univers font. Note that this is font number 17 of 268 font descriptions in this font description file. If you're creating a new font description file, this screen will be blank.

3. When prompted for a font filename, type the name of the font description file with which you want to work, or the name of the new file you're about to create. If you're creating a new font file from scratch, name the file with a .FNT extension so both you and Q&A will always be able to identify it as a font file.

   If you don't remember the name of an existing font file you want to modify, leave the filename blank and press **<Enter>** to see a list of the font description files that have been installed in Q&A.

Note: If you're planning to modify an existing font description file, be sure you make a backup copy of it first. If the font file was supplied with Q&A and has not been modified, then you'll have it on one of the disks supplied with the Q&A program. Otherwise, make a backup copy of it now by pressing **<F5>** and saving it to disk. You should work with the copy, not the original file.

4. If you've entered an existing font filename, the first font description in the file will appear on the screen (see Figure 9-2). If this is a new font file altogether, the Modify Font Description screen will be blank.

5. If you're adding a new font description, press **\<F8\>** to get a blank Font Description screen.

   If you're adding a new font description that's similar to an existing one, get the existing one on screen with **\<F10\>** or **\<F9\>** and then press **\<Shift\>\<F5\>** to make a copy of it. You can then modify the copy (giving it a new font name). It'll save some work.

6. Fill in the top portion of the screen for all new fonts you're adding (see below for details).

7. The lower portion of the screen is filled in only for proportional (including scalable) fonts.

8. Press **\<F10\>** to add the new font definition to the current font description file and view the next font description in the file. Press **\<F9\>** to see the previous font description. **\<F3\>** deletes the displayed font description, and **\<Shift\>\<F10\>** saves the font description and returns you to the Utilities menu.

Summary of Function Keys Used on the Font Description Screen

- **\<F1\>** displays help on working with the Modify Font Descriptions screen.

- **\<F10\>** saves the displayed description and brings up the next font description in the file.

- **\<F9\>** saves the displayed description and brings up the previous font description in the file.

- **\<Shift\>\<F5\>** copies the displayed font description. You can now change the font name and edit the description. The original description won't be affected.

- **\<F8\>** displays a blank font description form for you to create your new font description from scratch.

- **\<Esc\>** cancels (after a warning) any modifications you've made to the displayed font description and return you to the Utilities menu.

- **\<F3\>** deletes the displayed font description after a warning message. If you continue by answering "Yes," the next font description will appear; otherwise, you'll be returned to the same one.

Fields on the Font Description Screen

Font name: The name of the font. It must be typed exactly the same way here as on the Font Assignments screen where you tell Q&A which fonts you want to have available for your documents. To avoid conflict with other font descriptions and confusion among those who may specify your custom font files, establish a naming convention and stick to it for all your created font files. Here's a suggested procedure for doing this:

1. Begin the name with any letters that refer to the cartridge (if this is a cartridge font) such as A, B, C, etc.

2. Use a descriptive font name such as "Courier" or "Helv" or "LnPtr."

3. Add the point or pitch size such as "10" or "12" or "24" unless the font is scalable. With scalable fonts you'll specify the point size later, at the Font Assignments screen.

4. Add the style of the font. You have four choices: Lit for Light, Med for Medium, Bld for Bold, and Ita for Italics.

   The end result should be a unique font name that describes what the font actually consists of. For example: "Courier 10 bld" or "A-Helv 24 bld" not only names the font, but tells you what it will look like when printed. You can use up to 27 character spaces.

Abbreviation: Type a four-character abbreviation here. The abbreviation will then appear on your Font Assignments screen when you press **<Ctrl><F9>**, on the Text Enhancements and Font menu when you press **<Shift><F6>** or select it from the Options menu, and on the status line when the cursor is on any text formatted with the font. Again, use a combination of any four characters that tells you something about the font. Four example, Courier 10 bold could be abbreviated "C10b."

Printer name: Type the name of the printer (up to 31 characters, including spaces) with which this font description will be used. In Figure 9-2 the Printer Name is "HP LaserJet III/IIID Internal."

Point size: Point size is a measurement of character height. There are 72 points to an inch. If this is a monospaced font with a fixed point size such as Courier (standard 10-pitch Courier is a 12-point font), enter that point size. For proportional fonts, use a number from 1 to 999. Enter the letter **E** if this is an Enhancement description, or the letter **S** for Scalable fonts. Scalable and Enhancement font descriptions don't have a corresponding point size.

Q&A uses the font's point size to calculate vertical spacing (known as *leading*) when printing the page, according to the following rules:

- For point sizes 1 to 14, set vertical spacing to 1 point.

- For point sizes 14.1 to 26, set vertical spacing to 2 points.

- For point sizes greater than 26, Q&A adds 1 point of line spacing for every additional 12-point increment.

On scalable fonts you can follow the **S** with the spacing value you want. Normally, a 16-point scalable font would print with 2 points of leading, but by specifying **S1** or even **S0** you can achieve what is called *tight leading*, and get more lines of type to a given vertical distance. Likewise, **S3**, **S4**, or even a higher value entered into the Point Size field will add more space between the lines of 16-point type.

When editing a font description for a scalable font, you need:

- An **S** in the Point Size field.

- An asterisk (*****) in the On code field that tells Q&A to replace the ***** with the point size at printing time.

On codes: Your printer or font manual will contain a list of the On and Off codes you'll need. These are the codes Q&A sends to your printer to turn fonts, enhancements, and other special effects on and off. Type the On code that turns on the font or enhancement.

LaserJet Series II On codes, for example, consist of seven elements: font symbol set, spacing (proportional or fixed), pitch, point size, style (Roman or italic), stroke weight (light, medium, or bold), and typeface (the type style, such as Times Roman, Helvetica, etc.).

The **Esc** (or **Ec**) code shown in the printer manual must be converted to its ASCII decimal equivalent before typing it in the On code field of the Modify Font Description screen. This decimal equivalent is **\027**. A small left arrow may appear at the beginning of some of the On code strings. This is equivalent to **\027**.

HP LaserJet III scalable font On codes are different in only one respect. Instead of the On code containing a point size, you enter an ***** preceding the **v** to indicate a scalable font.

Epson dot-matrix codes are different, and are all preceded by **27**, which, like the LaserJet II code, stands for Escape.

PostScript printers have their own On codes as well. The best way to define a new font description for a PostScript font is to display and then copy a font description that's close to the one you want, and then modify the copy.

Off codes: These are structured like the On codes, but tell the printer that a particular font or enhancement previously turned on should now be turned off. The LaserJet series Off code is usually:

```
\027(8U\027(s0p10h12v0s0b3t
```

And those are zeros, not the letter O. Be very careful when entering On and Off codes, because if the command is even one character off, your printer won't recognize it and you may have a heck of a time trying to track down the bug.

The On and Off control codes you send to your printer don't necessarily have to be font codes. By passing it the proper escape sequence, code, or code string you can turn on and off most any feature your printer is capable of producing. For example, if you set up a "font description" with On and Off codes for a change in line spacing, Q&A will send these codes to your printer when you select this "font" for your document as though the codes were embedded right inside the document.

If you're new to the world of printers and the ways in which they can be manipulated from inside software programs, take an evening to acquaint yourself with the command-mode capabilities of your printer. Every printer manual contains a section devoted exclusively to these particular product features, and often the printer's visible control panel provides no clue as to what sophisticated operations the device is actually capable of performing. You may be pleasantly surprised at the gymnastics your printer is capable of achieving, given the proper control codes and a smart package like Q&A to help you tap those features.

You have three options in Q&A for specifying the control codes to be sent your printer at printing time: embedding the codes inside your Write document at the locations where you want the feature turned on and off; at the Print Options screen where you can specify an On or an Off code, but not both; and using any Font Assignments screen.

Characters-per-inch: If this is a *monospaced* font (where all the characters are the same width), type the number of characters your font will occupy per inch of horizontal line space, and ignore the character spacing table in the lower section of the Modify Font Descriptions screen. In monospaced fonts, this characters-per-inch (cpi) measurement is often expressed in *pitch* (for example, a 12-pitch font prints at 12 cpi). If this is a double-wide (elongated) font based on a 10-pitch standard font, your character spacing would be set to 5 cpi.

For a *proportionally* spaced font (one in which the characters have varying widths), enter a **P** for proportional and then fill in the information fields in the lower portion of the screen (see below).

If the font you're editing is to be used only as an enhancement (such as color), type an **E** in the Characters-per-inch field and ignore the character spacing table.

Printer resolution: If this is to be a proportionally spaced font, you'll need to indicate the printer's resolution capability. For laser printers, inkjet printers, and dot-matrix printers, this is usually expressed in "dots per inch." Three hundred dots per inch is common for lasers, but some have a lower resolution, and some higher. Many 24-pin dot-matrix printers are capable of printing at a variety of dots per inch, some all the way up to 240 or even 360. Be sure to select the printing density you want for the font you are editing or creating. Consult your printer manual for information on resolution.

Character spacing table: Here's where you tell Q&A how much space to assign to each character you'll be using in a proportionally spaced font. Remember that you're creating or editing an actual font description in order to tell Q&A exactly how you want your custom font to print on the page. For any proportionally spaced font, including those available for dot-matrix, daisy wheel, inkjet, and laser printers, you'll need to:

- Determine how the spacing units for the font are expressed. They could be based on dots per inch (dpi), tenths of a space (decispace), twentieths of a point, or some other value. If your printer supports proportional printing, the manual will contain a proportional spacing table that shows the width assigned to each character in the character set. You can, of course, increase or decrease that spacing on a character-by-character basis.

- Specify the spacing for all the characters you want to be available in the font, including all the upper- and lowercase letters, numbers, punctuation marks, and any special symbols you want your printer to be able to print. If you fail to provide spacing information for one or more characters, Q&A won't be able to count the spacing needed for the line, and although the character may print, the line length may be off.

Don't confuse a *proportional font* with *justification*. Justification has to do with placing small variable spaces between words in order to make the lines in a document the same length, whereas when a font is proportional, it means the characters in the font have different widths.

Filling in the Width Table: Q&A supplies the 254 ASCII characters and codes, a portion of which you can see under the "Character" and "Code" columns in the Figure 9-2 Modify Font Descriptions screen. But when customizing a font description, you have to tell Q&A what widths to assign to each of these characters (at least the ones you plan to use with Q&A). These width values can be found in your printer or font manual. The "Character," "Code," and "Width" columns comprise a table that scrolls up and down in a window on the screen.

Here's the procedure for filling in the width portion of the table:

1. Type the width of the first character expressed in the units of measurement appropriate to your printer and font. The value must be a whole number from 0 to 65534.

2. Press **<Enter>** to move to the next character-width field, and type that particular character's width.

   - When you get to the bottom of the window, it will scroll up as you enter subsequent character widths.

   - Press **<PgUp>** to view the previous eight lines; **<PgDn>** to see the next eight lines; **<Ctrl><PgUp>** to move to the top of the table (ASCII 01); **<Ctrl><PgDn>** to move to the end of the table (ASCII 254).

   - Press **<Home>** twice to return to the upper area of the screen.

3. When you're finished describing your font, press:

   - **<F9>** or **<F10>** to save the current font description and view other font descriptions in the file.

   - **<F8>** to build a new font description from scratch.

   - **<Shift><F5>** to make a copy of the font description you just created.

   - **<Shift><F10>** to save the font and return to the Utilities menu.

If you've created a new font description file with a new filename, be sure to reinstall your printer and type the new filename at the Special Printer Options screen. See the section on troubleshooting font problems in Appendix B if you're having trouble getting your fonts to print properly or at all.

Support for PostScript Printers

Q&A supports PostScript laser printers with two PostScript font description files. The POST.FNT font description file includes approximately 70 standard PostScript fonts. Consult your printer's manual for information on the range of PostScript fonts supported. To modify a PostScript font description (change the point size, line spacing, density, etc.):

1. From the Utilities menu, select Modify Font Description and enter the name of the PostScript font file you wish to modify.

2. Press **<F9>** and **<F10>** until the font description you want to modify is displayed.

3. Press **<Shift><F5>** to make a duplicate of it.

4. Change the On code to reflect the point size, density (gray level), and line spacing for this custom font description. The On code format for a PostScript font description is: **FontName Pointsize Gn Ln**.

- **FontName** is the name by which your printer knows this font. The name must be entered exactly (and with the same upper- and lower-case letters) or your printer won't recognize it and will use the default font instead.

- **PointSize** indicates the height of the font and is expressed in PostScript in 72nds of an inch. You can use a digit or a decimal number. Entering the number 12 would give you a font 12 points (or 12/72nds of an inch) in height.

- **Gn** is an option that specifies the density or gray level of the font. The *n* value can range from 0 (white) to 1 (black), so you'd express this as a decimal number percentage of black. Omitting the **Gn** option defaults to a value of 1 (black).

- **Ln** is another option that specifies the font's line spacing or leading. The *n* value is the distance between lines in points (72nds of an inch). The default is **L12**, which would result in 6-lines-per-inch printing, Q&A's default line spacing. Books and magazines typically use an extra one to three points of leading between lines. You can experiment to see which leading value best suits your font's point size and page layout.

If you select a value other than the standard 12 and use the font in a document, you'll need to take this into account when specifying your page length at any Define Page screen. Q&A uses the default (regular) font line spacing to set the line spacing for the entire document. If this font will be brought into the document as a font enhancement (1 through 8), the **L**-value will be ignored.

5. Change both the font description name and its abbreviation to reflect the new point size. You'll probably want to change only the point size portion of the name and abbreviation to avoid confusion.

6. Press **<Shift><F10>** to save the new font file and return to the Utilities menu.

There are more advanced techniques for customizing Q&A to access PostScript's rich variety of features, but you must be familiar with the PostScript language before attempting to do so. PostScript is not a Symantec product, and Q&A tech support cannot give you any assistance in creating PostScript programs or using the PostScript "Makefont" command. If you're interested in further study, a number of excellent reference books on PostScript are available.

The following material is for those who possess a fair amount of PostScript know-how.

Three Ways to Print with PostScript Programs

You can employ various methods of utilizing PostScript in your documents. The best include:

- **Embed PostScript code into your text.** With Q&A's ***POST-SCRIPT*** command (abbreviated ***PS***) you can place lines of PostScript code directly in your document. You must start the command with the ***POSTSCRIPT** or ***PS**, follow it with the code, and end the command with another *****. If the command is on a line by itself, the printed output will not include the line. A PostScript command cannot be longer than one line.

- **Place a PostScript program file in your document.** Q&A supports a ***POSTFILE *filename**** command (abbreviated ***PF***) that you can insert in your text. The *filename* is the complete path, directory, and name of the file containing the PostScript program.

- **Download a PostScript file at printing time**. The path and file specifications of several PostScript files can be entered in the Printer Control Codes field of the Print Options screen (the screen displayed after you've pressed **<F2>** to print a document). Keep a space between each file specification. PostScript file specifications sent to the printer in this manner stay in the printer's memory throughout the printing of the entire document. PostScript's *save* and *restore* commands are used by Q&A to manage printer memory page by page, so any PostScript files embedded on a particular page are dumped when that page has been printed.

PostScript fonts can also be downloaded to the printer from the Printer Control Codes field of the Print Options screen. And you can define functions here that reference ***PS*** commands embedded in the document.

PostScript's Makefont Command

Q&A supports this command via the On code string of the font description in the font description file. The font's point size (following the font name) is used by Q&A to determine where lines will break, but the type is sized according to the specifications following the Makefont command. The syntax is **M xsize angle slant ysize xoffset yoffset** where:

M initiates the Makefont command

xsize is the font's width in points.

angle specifies the angle at which the line is printed.

slant is the font's oblique or italic characteristic. You slant a font x degrees by setting this specification to $y*\tan(x)$ where y is the font's point size.

ysize is the font's height in points.

xoffset controls the horizontal position from the current position, and is specified in points.

yoffset sets the vertical offset from the current position, and is expressed in points.

Defining IBM Accented Characters and Symbols

You can also use PostScript codes to replace IBM or non-IBM character codes in the following situations:

- Q&A can replace non-IBM character codes with PostScript codes that match the IBM character set as closely as possible when the parameters "**1 1**" are specified in the On code string. This action is turned off with "**1 0**."

- The "**S 1**" parameter substitutes symbol font characters to match the IBM character set as closely as possible. The action is turned off with "**S 0**."

- Downloading non-Adobe fonts to a PostScript printer requires that "**1 0**" and "**S 0**" be specified to avoid errors due to incompatibility with Adobe font conventions.

- PostScript code generated by Q&A can be examined by directing the printer to Print to File at the Port Selection screen displayed during printer installation.

Combining Font Files

If, in a single document, you find yourself wanting to use fonts from two or more different font description files, you can combine these files into a single font description file that contains all the font descriptions from both. This can be done in DOS using the copy command.

Suppose you had a font description file with the name IQSUPER.FNT, and another named HPIII.FNT, and you wanted to access the fonts from both of these files in a single document. The way to combine these files is to decide on a filename for the combined file (I'll use MYLASER.FNT) and, on the DOS command line (in this case, assuming the two font files are in the current directory), type the following:

```
COPY /B /V IQSUPER.FNT+HPIII.FNT MYLASER.FNT
```

This will create the combined font description file in binary mode and with the DOS verify option on. The two original files will remain unaffected.

If you do this be sure to install your new offspring by typing in its filename at the bottom of the Special Print Options screen, available via the Install Printer option at the Q&A Utilities menu.

You can combine soft font description files with cartridge font files in this manner, and have at your fingertips a huge variety of fonts to use in your documents. Keep in mind, however, that increasing the number of font descriptions in your driver files may slow down the printing operation. On the other end of the spectrum, some users delete from their font description files all the font descriptions they know they won't be using in their documents in order to speed up the printing process.

If you decide on this option, be sure you have a backup copy of your original driver so that, should you ever change your mind, you can easily reinstall the deleted descriptions.

Converting and Upgrading Font Files

If you plan to use font description files you've already customized in Q&A version 3.0 or Q&A Write, or need to convert HP-compatible or PostScript soft font files for use with Q&A 4.0, a font-conversion utility comes bundled with Q&A 4.0 for these purposes. It's called QAFONT.EXE; it extracts font descriptions from other files and converts them into a format compatible with Q&A 4.0.

QAFONT must be installed on your hard disk before you can use it. Refer to the installation procedure covered in Chapter 1. QAFONT is not built into Q&A — it must be run as a standalone program from the DOS prompt. You load QAFONT by exiting to DOS, changing to the directory where QAFONT is stored, typing **QAFONT** at the DOS prompt, and pressing **<Enter>**.

Upgrading Font Files for Use with Q&A 4.0

Font files from earlier versions of Q&A or Q&A Write that have been user-modified must be upgraded by QAFONT for use with Q&A 4.0. There's little point to upgrading *unmodified* Q&A 3.0 font description files — just use the 4.0 version of such files that were installed when you installed Q&A 4.0.

If you need to convert a customized Q&A font file to 4.0 format:

1. From the QAFONT Main menu, select Upgrade Font Description Files to Q&A 4.0 Format. The current drive and a list of .FNT files in the current subdirectory will display. Use your cursor keys to change to the drive or subdirectory that contains the font file you want to upgrade.

2. Tag the font file for upgrading by highlighting it and pressing the spacebar.

3. Press **<F10>** to convert the tagged file to Q&A 4.0 format with the same filename. QAFONT automatically renames the original font description *file*.BAK

To Create Q&A 4.0-compatible Font Descriptions from Soft Font Files

QAFONT works only with HP LaserJet-compatible soft font files. Check the documentation that came with your fonts to make sure they meet this requirement. To convert HP LaserJet-compatible soft fonts to Q&A-compatible font descriptions:

1. Select "Create Font Descriptions from Soft Font Files" from the QAFONT Main menu. The current drive along with a list of files from the current subdirectory will display. Use your cursor keys to change drives or subdirectories as necessary to locate the font file you wish to convert.

2. Highlight each file you want QAFONT to convert and press the spacebar to tag it. Press **<F10>** when you've tagged the files you want to convert.

3. Choose an existing font filename to hold the new font descriptions, or enter a new filename.

You can add converted font descriptions to an *existing* font description file (such as HPLASERJ.FNT). If you do this, Q&A will ask if you want the new descriptions added to the existing file or if you want the file overwritten — most likely you'll want to keep the existing file and add the new descriptions to it.

If you want the descriptions converted and stored under a *new* filename, select Create New File, press **<Enter>**, and then enter the path and new filename, using an .FNT filename extension to identify this as a font description file.

You can now use your converted soft fonts in Q&A 4.0 by (1) downloading them to your printer prior to starting Q&A, and (2) adding the font description file to your Font Assignments screen from inside Q&A, and assigning and then applying the fonts to your documents, forms, and/or reports, as discussed in Chapters 2, 3, and 6.

Creating Q&A 4.0-compatible Font Files from PostScript Files

PostScript soft font files have .AFM filename extensions. You can use QAFONT to convert these files into Q&A 4.0-compatible font descriptions.

1. From the QAFONT Main menu, select "Create Font Descriptions from PostScript Files." The current drive and a list of files from the current directory will display. Use your cursor keys to select the drive or directory where the PostScript file you want to convert is stored.

2. Highlight the PostScript file you want to convert for use by Q&A 4.0, press the spacebar to tag it, and press **<F10>**.

3. Choose the name of an existing Q&A 4.0 font description file, such as POST.FNT, to contain the converted font descriptions, or select Create a New File, and press **<Enter>**.

If you opt to use an existing filename for the converted descriptions, you'll be asked to confirm whether you want the descriptions added to the file or the file overwritten — you'll probably want to *add* the descriptions to the end of the existing file. To create a *new* filename for the converted descriptions, specify the complete path and filename.

To use the new fonts, they must be downloaded to your printer, and then properly installed on your Font Assignments screen as discussed in Chapter 2.

Set Global Options

In you'd like to have Q&A help you maintain separate directories on your hard disk for document and database files, you can create those directories in DOS, and then establish them as default directories at the Set Global Options screen (see Figure 9-3). When you do this, Q&A will always know where to search for your created files first, and it will save you from typing the directory name when you want to retrieve a document or database file.

Other options are available at the Set Global Options screen as well, including automatic execution for Q&A menu selections and setting your network ID if you're running Q&A on a network.

Setting Default Directories

Creating a subdirectory for your Q&A document files and another for your data files makes good sense. First of all, doing so tells Q&A which directory to check first when you want to retrieve a file. Second, it will make it easier to locate a file using the List Manager, because you'll know beforehand where the two different types of files are located. The third benefit (mainly for networked applications) is that it allows you to place your Q&A files in a "read-only" directory so they can be viewed by users, but not modified.

It's the addition of the *temporary files* option with Q&A 4.0 that makes this third benefit possible. When Q&A is sorting and merging, for example, it creates temporary files on your hard disk to hold information that it needs in order to complete the operation.

If the drive you use to store your Q&A files is cramped for room to the point where Q&A can't find a place for its temporary files, you'll get an error message and the sorting or merging operation will come to a grinding halt. So the option of being able to assign another, roomier drive partition and directory that Q&A can use has a clear advantage.

Your hard drive may be partitioned into more than one *logical drive* — for example, drive C: and drive D:. If your C: drive is becoming overcrowded, use

```
                        SET GLOBAL OPTIONS
                        ══════════════════

        Type the Drive and, optionally, the Path where the following
        kinds of files will be stored.  This will save you extra typing
        because Q&A will always know where to look first for these files:

                Q&A Document files : C:\QA\DOCS\
                Q&A Database files : C:\QA\DATA\
                Q&A Temporary files: D:\QA\TEMP\
        ─────────────────────────────────────────────────────────────
        You can make the program execute menu items as soon as you type the
        first letter of the selection.  (If you select this option, you may
        have to re-record macros that expect ENTER after the letter.)

                Automatic Execution:  ▶Yes◀  No
        ─────────────────────────────────────────────────────────────
        Type your name and phone number for network identification purposes:

                Network ID........: Network id not set
        ─────────────────────────────────────────────────────────────


        Esc-Exit                                          F10-Continue
```

Figure 9-3: The Set Global Options Screen. You can establish the default path and directory for your Q&A files, set Q&A menus for automatic execution, and enter your network ID.

the Global Options screen to tell Q&A to use the D: drive for its temporary files.

When setting the drive and path for your Q&A files at this screen, be sure that you've created the necessary subdirectories in DOS (this was covered in detail in Chapter 1). You can't very well store your database files in a C:\QA\DATA directory if the DATA subdirectory doesn't exist. You'll need to exit Q&A to the DOS operating system and create the subdirectory to branch off from the QA directory using the DOS **MD** (Make Directory) command. See Chapter 1 on how to do this. And if you're creating these new directories *after* you've created document and database files, you'll need to copy these files over to their new directories as specified on this screen. You can do this from inside Q&A, as you'll see when you get to the section "DOS File Facilities."

To set your default directories, type the drive and directory you want Q&A to use when storing and retrieving document and database files, and optionally enter the drive and path you want to assign to Q&A for its temporary files.

Note that you can store your document and database files anywhere DOS will permit them to be stored. These are simply *default* directories.

Automatic Execution

Q&A comes out of the box with its menu selections preset to require the **<Enter>** key. But you can change that default so all you'll need to do to activate a menu item is either press the letter of the item or the number that corresponds to its relative position on the menu. Setting up your menus for Automatic Execution can save keystrokes, help you move around the menu system faster, and simplify macro recording and editing.

To change from manual to automatic, or from automatic back to manual, use the cursor keys to highlight the appropriate setting. Keep in mind that changing the setting may affect existing macros. For example, if macros containing menu transactions were recorded when your menus were set to Manual Execution, they will contain the **<Enter>** key following the menu letter or number. You'll need to edit these **<Enter>** keystrokes out of such macros because Automatic Execution makes pressing **<Enter>** at a Q&A menu obsolete. Some macros, however, may contain a valid **<Enter>** keypress in other places, such as when the selected item was the first one on the menu.

Network ID

If your computer is on a network, your network administrator may require that your name and phone or extension number be typed in this field on the Global Options screen. If you're not using Q&A on a network, you don't need a Network ID.

Alternate Main Menu Programs

You can install up to six DOS programs on the Q&A Main menu, launch them from inside Q&A, and be returned to Q&A when you've exited them. This turns your Q&A Main menu into a program control center. Launch your communications program, your backup utility, or any DOS application program, run it, and then be returned to Q&A when you've finished.

You can also launch Q&A macros from the Main menu, a topic covered in the previous chapter.

Figure 9-4 shows the Alternate Program menu which you reach by selecting Set Alternate Programs from the Utilities menu.

To install alternate Main menu programs:

1. Select Set Alternate Programs from the Utilities menu. Q&A displays the Alternate Programs screen in Figure 9-4.

2. On the first available Alternate Program line type the complete drive, path, and filename of the program. The last item on the line must be the name of the file that executes the program. These files usually have .COM or .EXE filename extensions. You don't have to type the extension.

```
                        ALTERNATE PROGRAMS
                        ═══════════════════

        You can install up to six alternate programs for the Main Menu.
        You can then execute those programs by selecting them at that menu.
        When you exit from these programs, you will return automatically
        to the Main Menu.

              Alternate program 1: C:\PARADOX\PARADOX3
              Menu selection.....: Paradox
              Alternate program 2: D:\LOTUS\123
              Menu selection.....: Lotus 1-2-3
              Alternate program 3: C:\FLASHLNK\FL
              Menu selection.....: Flashlink
              Alternate program 4: E:\UTILS\SPINRITE\SPINRITE
              Menu selection.....: SpinRite
              Alternate program 5: E:\UTILS\FULLBACK\FULLBACK
              Menu selection.....: Backup
              Alternate program 6:
              Menu selection.....:
        ────────────────────────────────────────────────────────────────


        Esc-Cancel                                         F10-Continue
```

Figure 9-4: The Alternate Program Menu. Put alternate DOS programs on the Q&A Main Menu by entering their drive, path, and filename here.

3. Enter the program name or a description that identifies it on the menu Selection line (this is what will appear on the Main menu). You can enter up to 11 characters.

Note: Q&A uses *the first character* of this entry as the character that launches the program from the Main menu. If your Q&A menus are set to "automatic execution," you cannot use an initial character in your description here that duplicates any other initial character on the Main menu.

4. When you've entered your Alternate Program paths and menu Selections, press **<F10>** to save the screen and return to the Utilities menu.

Figure 9-5 shows what the Q&A Main menu now looks like with the alternate programs in Figure 9-4 installed.

Alternate Q&A Configurations

There's another trick you can do with the Alternate Programs feature that makes it possible to have several different configurations of Q&A available.

QA.CFG is a special file that Q&A creates and maintains, and then consults whenever you use the Q&A program. QA.CFG contains the specifications

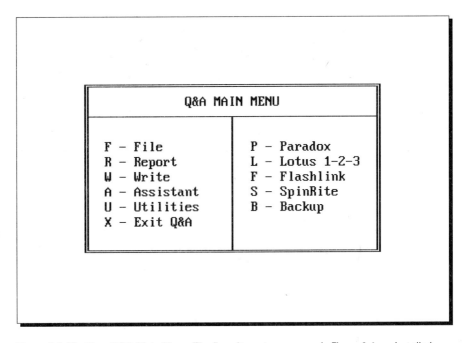

```
┌─────────────────────────────────────────────┐
│              Q&A MAIN MENU                    │
├────────────────────────┬──────────────────────┤
│                        │                       │
│  F - File              │  P - Paradox          │
│  R - Report            │  L - Lotus 1-2-3      │
│  W - Write             │  F - Flashlink        │
│  A - Assistant         │  S - SpinRite         │
│  U - Utilities         │  B - Backup           │
│  X - Exit Q&A          │                       │
│                        │                       │
└────────────────────────┴──────────────────────┘
```

Figure 9-5: The New Q&A Main Menu. The five alternate programs in Figure 9-4 are installed.

which you've established and which Q&A, in turn, uses to configure itself to your preferences. Included in these specifications are the following:

- Display switch for the type of monitor.

- User-defined macro buffer.

- File, Report, Write, and other Global Default settings.

- Alternate programs and macros installed on the Main menu.

- Document, database, and temporary files directories.

- Autoload default macro file.

- Macro file encryption information.

Some of these settings are established during your first session with Q&A, while others become part of the QA.CFG file as you work with and further customize the program. Changes to any of the above cause the QA.CFG file to be updated.

Depending on your needs you may want to create alternate, reusable Q&A configurations. For example:

- Configuration One could provide six Main menu alternate program or macro selections and Configuration Two of the Main menu could provide six *different* alternate programs or macros.

- One configuration could have five HP LaserJet modes available from any Print Options screen, and the other configuration could have several dot-matrix modes for forms printing, and even a couple of different fax modes.

- Your primary Q&A configuration could load the default QAMACRO.ASC macro file, while your alternate configuration could be set up to load a different macro file.

You can have any number of reusable Q&A configurations. Here's a sample procedure for creating a second configuration file which includes using the Alternate Programs feature to change Q&A configurations from inside the program. This procedure will not affect your current configuration:

1. Load Q&A from the DOS prompt.

2. Using Q&A's DOS file facilities (see this section further ahead in the chapter) copy QA.CFG to a different name, such as QA1.CFG, and then delete the original QA.CFG file.

3. Exit to DOS and reload Q&A, and customize this new Q&A configuration to your liking (changing your global defaults, installed printers or printer modes, or alternate Main menu selections, for example). These changes, as you save them, will now become the new QA.CFG file that Q&A will load on start-up.

4. Using the DOS file facilities in this second Q&A configuration, copy the current QA.CFG file to a new name, such as QA2.CFG, and then delete QA.CFG.

5. Now copy QA1.CFG to QA.CFG, and you'll have your original QA.CFG and its duplicate, QA1.CFG, along with QA2.CFG — two different Q&A configurations.

6. Now use the Write word processor to create a DOS batch file that copies the QA.CFG file you do *not* want to use to the other name, and copies the configuration file you *do* want to use to QA.CFG. Here's a sample DOS batch filenamed OTHER.BAT that will do the trick. The parameters in OTHER.BAT require that it reside in the same directory as the configuration files (this will likely be the QA directory).

```
ECHO OFF
ECHO SELECTING %2
COPY QA.CFG %1
COPY %2 QA.CFG
```

7. Press **<Enter>** after typing each line of the batch file. When you've finished, press **<Ctrl><F8>** to save it in ASCII format to the name OTHER.BAT.

8. Exit and reload Q&A to get the first configuration back. Enter the path and command that will execute the batch file (swapping out Configuration One for Configuration Two) as a selection at the Alternate Programs screen, as shown in the following example:

   Alternate program 6: C:\QA\OTHER.BAT QA1.CFG QA2.CFG
   Menu selection.....: Other Config2

9. Return to the Q&A Main menu and select "Other Config2." The batch file will execute outside of Q&A as an alternate program, swapping the configuration files, and loading the second configuration.

10. Now, with that second Q&A configuration loaded, enter the path and command that will execute the batch file (this time swapping out Configuration Two for Configuration One) as a selection at the Alternate Programs screen, as shown below:

    Alternate program 6: C:\QA\OTHER.BAT QA2.CFG QA1.CFG
    Menu selection.....: Other Config1

You can now alternate between the two different Q&A configurations simply by pressing the letter "O" from either of the two Q&A Main menus. With either configuration running you can still, at any time, change any settings that affect the QA.CFG file for that configuration of Q&A. You can even make the second configuration an entirely different application program with its own set of custom menus.

Keep in mind that the configuration you exit from when you press **X – Exit** from the Q&A Main menu is the configuration that will be loaded the next time you start Q&A. So you may want to return to your primary Q&A configuration before finally quitting Q&A and returning to DOS or your DOS shell program.

Write Utilities

Figure 9-6 shows the Write Utilities menu branching off from the Write menu. In Chapter 2 we covered all the Write Global Options. In a later section of this chapter I'll focus on the DOS Facilities. In this section I'll cover the other three

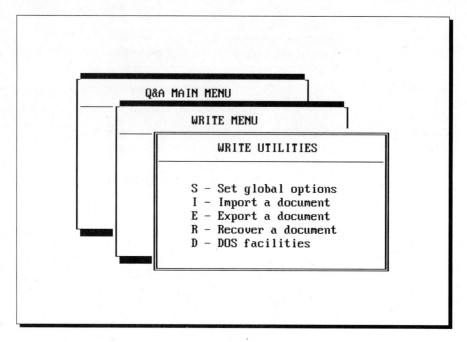

Figure 9-6: The Write Utilities Menu. It is strictly for document-related tasks.

selections on the Write Utilities menu: Import a Document, Export a Document, and Recover a Document.

The Write Import and Export menus

Q&A supports import conversion from a number of other popular word processing programs such as Wordstar, WordPerfect, Microsoft Word, MultiMate, and Professional Write. You can also import ASCII, DCA, and Macintosh ASCII documents into Q&A Write.

Export conversion is supported to the same word processing programs and standard document formats. Table 9-1 contains a summary of the Q&A-supported document formats for both import and export.

When you're ready to import a document from one of these other formats, choose Import a Document from the Write Utilities menu. Q&A will display the Write Import menu shown in Figure 9-7.

The process of converting a document from any of these formats and importing it into Q&A is straightforward. Q&A will convert the document with

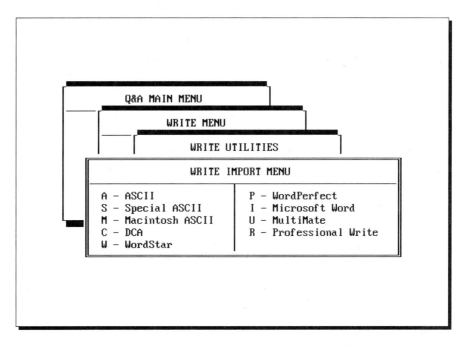

```
                    Q&A MAIN MENU

                     WRITE MENU

                    WRITE UTILITIES

                   WRITE IMPORT MENU

        A - ASCII              P - WordPerfect
        S - Special ASCII      I - Microsoft Word
        M - Macintosh ASCII    U - MultiMate
        C - DCA                R - Professional Write
        W - WordStar
```

Figure 9-7: Write's Import Menu. When you select a word processing format to import, a submenu may display prompting you to select the version of the program in which the document was created and saved. Q&A won't display this import menu if you've specified a **Default Import Type** at the Set Editing Options screen.

all formatting codes such as line spacing, margins, and enhancements fully intact. You will then be able to work with the document as you would any Q&A document.

If you've specified Default Import Type on the Set Editing Options screen (see the section on setting global options in Chapter 2), Q&A assumes the document you want is in that format when you choose Import a Document from the Write Utilities menu.

Otherwise, Q&A displays the Write Import menu, and you simply choose the appropriate word processor or document format. If you're importing a document created in a commercial word processing program, Q&A will ask you to choose the version of the selected program in which the document was created and saved. Q&A then prompts you for both the name of the source document (the one you want to import) and the name you want to give the document when it's brought into Q&A.

Table 9-1
Versions of Popular Word Processing Software Packages

These packages, along with standard document formats, are supported by Q&A 4.0 with the Spring 1991 release. You can import any of these into Q&A, and also export Q&A documents to any of these formats.

Word Processor Import/Export	Versions supported for Q&A
WordPerfect	5.0, 5.1
Microsoft Word	3.0, 3.1, 4.0, 5.0
Wordstar	3.3, 3.31, 3.45, 4.0, 5.0, 5.5
MultiMate	3.3, 4.0, Advantage 3.6, II 3.7
Professional Write	1.0, 2.0, 2.1, PFS:Write C, PFS FirstChoice 1.0 and 2.0
ASCII	With the ASCII standard CR/LF (Carriage Return/Line Feed) characters at the end of each line
Special ASCII	With ASCII standard CR/LF at the end of each blank line or paragraph only. Also known as Document ASCII
Macintosh ASCII	Imports documents saved as Macintosh ASCII
DCA	(Document Content Architecture)

Be sure to specify the drive and full path in addition to the source document's name. Otherwise Q&A may not be able to find it. When Q&A prompts you for the Q&A filename of the converted document, it will presume you want to save it to your default directory for Write documents. You can, of course, select a different directory by typing the new pathname over the default.

Keep in mind that new versions of these word processing programs, like any software product, are released from time to time. As of this writing, Q&A supported up to the latest versions. Table 9-1 lists the versions of the various word processing packages supported by Q&A version 4.0 as of Spring 1991.

Q&A can also export your Q&A documents to any of these other word processing formats. When you want to export a Q&A document, select Export a Document from the Write Utilities menu. Q&A will then display the Write Export menu. Select the appropriate export format, and then enter the filename of the Q&A document you want to export, along with the filename to be assigned to the document once it has been converted. That's all there is to it.

Q&A Write and Lotus 1-2-3

Q&A integrates tightly with Lotus 1-2-3 in both the Write and File modules. You can bring Lotus graphs into your Q&A documents at printing time, import Lotus 1-2-3 or Symphony spreadsheets into your Q&A documents where you can edit them, and import data from Lotus or Symphony spreadsheets into a Q&A database. The database import aspect is discussed later in this chapter. Q&A 4.0 supports Lotus 1-2-3 version 2.2 and earlier versions.

Q&A has a "Spreadsheet" command that you use to insert a Lotus or Symphony spreadsheet (or portion of a spreadsheet) into your Q&A document. The spreadsheet will appear in the printed document as it appears inside either 1-2-3 or Symphony. The procedure to import a Lotus or Symphony spreadsheet into a Q&A document when preparing to print is as follows:

1. Bring the Q&A document onto the Type/Edit screen, making sure your line length will be long enough to accommodate the worksheet (this can be done before or after the import).

2. Place the cursor where you want the worksheet to be inserted and at the beginning of a blank line.

3. Type ***SPREADSHEET fn, range*** where *fn* is the DOS path and filename of the spreadsheet, and *range* is the range or the top left and bottom right cells of a rectangular portion of the spreadsheet. The **SPREADSHEET** command can be abbreviated to **SS**. Be sure to type the asterisks immediately before and after the command, and separate the filename from the range with a comma. Separate a range of cells in the spreadsheet with a hyphen.

4. Repeat steps 2 and 3 for as many Lotus or Symphony spreadsheets as you want to import into your document.

Editing a Lotus or Symphony Spreadsheet in Q&A Write

In addition to printing a Lotus/Symphony spreadsheet in a Q&A document, you can bring it into the editor where you can edit and enhance it with the usual Q&A Write features.

To import a spreadsheet for this purpose:

1. Get the document and move the cursor to where you want the spreadsheet to be inserted.

2. Press **<F8>** for the Options menu.

3. Select **D** for Document.

4. Select **I** for Import a Document and Q&A will prompt for the filename.

5. Type the path and spreadsheet name and press **<Enter>.** The Import Document menu will be displayed.

6. Select Lotus 1-2-3 or Symphony. Q&A will display the Lotus range spec where you specify the spreadsheet range. Enter the column/row coordinates or type the name of the range and press **<F10>.** (If you don't indicate the range, Q&A will import the entire spreadsheet.)

7. Q&A will import the specified portion of the spreadsheet with a hard carriage return at the end of each row.

Inserting a Graph in Your Document

Q&A's **GRAPH** command enables you to bring a Lotus graph, PFS:Graph picture file, or other picture file into your Write document at printing time. You'll need to have a printer that supports graphics printing in order for this to work properly.

To integrate a graph into your document:

1. Bring the Q&A host document into the editor, and move the cursor to the line and column where you want the graph to be inserted.

2. Type: ***GRAPH fn density*** where *fn* is a valid DOS path and filename, and *density* is the letter **S**, **D**, or **Q** (for Single, Double or Quadruple density). Q&A uses single density if you don't specify one. **GRAPH** can be abbreviated simply as **G**.

3. Repeat the above procedure for as many graphs as you want inserted into the document.

Q&A will allocate space in the document for the graph at printing time. If it won't fit on the specified page, a new page will be started before the graph is printed. The graph will appear in the column in your document where you typed the first asterisk, and you can reposition the graph by indenting the command.

Q&A can also print Lotus 1-2-3 or Symphony .PIC files from inside Q&A by specifying the Lotus graph fonts, graph size, and graph rotation. The GRAPH command would look like this:

```
*GRAPH fs, density, font1, font2, width, height, rotation*
```

The command explanations are:

> **font1** is a DOS file specification and path for a Lotus font file. "BLOCK1" is the default. Don't forget the file extension.

> **font2** is also a valid DOS file specification. The default is whatever you specified as Font1.

> **width** is the decimal number for width in inches. The default is 6.5.

> **height** is the decimal number for height in inches. The default is 4.7.

> **rotation** is the number of degrees to rotate the graph counter-clockwise: 0, 90, 180, or 270 only. The default is 0.

If your other graphics programs allow you to save graph or picture files with the same format as files created with the BASIC **BSAVE** command, you can print these from Q&A also.

Document Recovery

The Write Utilities menu includes a utility to help you recover a damaged document file created in, or successfully upgraded to, Q&A version 4.0. A document can become damaged when open during power surges or outages.

 Warning: Before attempting to recover a damaged document, first make a backup copy of it, *and don't back it up by overwriting any existing good copy of the document.*

The procedure for recovering a document is simple. You select Recover a Document from the Write Utilities menu, type the name of the document, and press **<F10>**. Q&A displays the recovery progress indicator, returns you to the Write Utilities menu after recovery, and lets you know if the recovery was successful. If the document is severely damaged, recovery may not be possible.

You can't cancel a recovery operation once it's in process. But why would you want to?

File Utilities

Q&A's File utilities enable you to import data (or entire databases) from other popular database and spreadsheet products, export data from Q&A data files to these other programs, make backup copies of selected database files, and even recover a Q&A database that has been damaged by a power surge or power failure.

Importing Data into a Q&A Database

Q&A supports import conversion from a number of popular database and spreadsheet package formats, including PFS/Professional File, IBM Filing Assistant, Lotus 1-2-3 and Symphony, dBASE, and Paradox. You can also import data in DIF, Fixed ASCII, and Standard ASCII formats. If Q&A cannot directly import a particular format, the chances are very good that you can convert that database format to a format that Q&A *can* import.

Figure 9-8 shows the File Utilities menu, along with its Import submenu. You reach the Import menu by choosing File from the Q&A Main menu, Utilities from the File menu, and then Import Data from the File Utilities menu.

You'll notice that the first item on the File Utilities menu in Figure 9-8 is the "Link-to-SQL" selection. This is a highly specialized import activity — Q&A allows you to connect with Gupta SQLBase and Oracle SQL database servers and import the data from their tables into Q&A database files. The discussion of importing data, however, will start with the Import menu and its various selections. At the end of this section I'll cover the more specialized business of SQL importation.

When you import data from other programs, certain special conditions may apply if the database from which you're importing has:

- More than 10 pages per form/record.
- A zero-length field (a colon followed by something other than a space).

If any of these are present in the file you wish to import, that file will have to be modified before Q&A will accept it.

To import a database file into Q&A, choose the type of file from the File Import menu. When prompted, type the name of the source file (the path and name of the file to be imported), and then the name of the destination file — the Q&A file that will receive the imported data.

The next steps depend on the *kind* of file you're bringing in to Q&A. Each type of source file, along with any special steps you must perform to prepare for importation, will be described in the following pages.

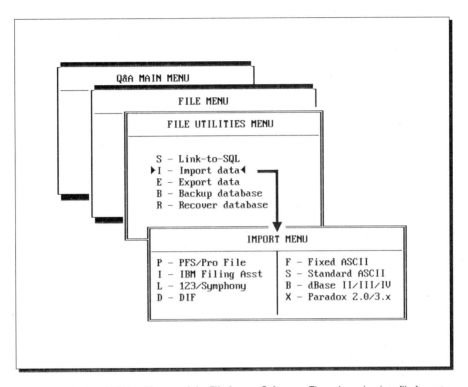

Figure 9-8: The File Utilities Menu and the File Import Submenu. They show the data file formats that can be directly imported into Q&A.

The following points apply regardless of the format of the data you're importing into Q&A:

- When Q&A imports data from another program (the *source* data), no calculations on the data can be performed during the process.

- Q&A does not change the original source database. The import process simply creates a copy of the selected data and converts it to Q&A database format. The imported data can now be accessed as if it were a Q&A database.

- During importation to an existing Q&A database, only the Field Template Spec changes (reformats) incoming data. Data being converted to Q&A format is unaffected by the Program Spec, Format Spec, Restrict Values Spec, Initial Values Spec, and all other Q&A specs.

- When Q&A imports data to an existing Q&A database that contains records, the imported records are appended to the end of the database.

Tips and Ideas when Importing Data into Q&A

These tips and ideas are generally not mentioned in Q&A's documentation. Reviewing them before you try to import data may save you a considerable amount of time and energy.

- If Q&A doesn't support conversion from the source file data format, first export the source file to a format that *is* importable by Q&A, and then have Q&A import the converted file. For example, you may have a database product whose files Q&A can't import, but whose files can be exported to dBASE format. From inside that product, export the relevant file to dBASE format, then load Q&A and import the dBASE format file. The vast majority of software products that store their information in a database format can export to dBASE. If not dBASE, then almost certainly ASCII.

- A great benefit of importing a data file stored in a commercial database format (non-ASCII) is that the conversion process preserves the correct information types of the fields (such as money, number, or text).

- Where possible, familiarize yourself with the data file you're about to import into Q&A. The more you know about the source file the better the job you can do importing it, and the more certain you will be of the results.

- If possible, have a graphic representation of the structure of the source file with the fields clearly labeled as to what kind of data they contain, and the field lengths noted. This can only help when designing a destination file in Q&A and when filling out a Merge Spec to tell Q&A which fields in the destination file correspond to the field positions in the source file. In many cases, however, you can have Q&A create the destination file for you "on-the-fly," and you won't need a Merge Spec.

- When importing to an existing Q&A database, fill out the Merge Spec carefully so that Q&A will know which value from the source file goes to what field in the Q&A destination file. If you import to an existing Q&A database with a blank Merge Spec, the value from the first field of the source file will appear in the first field of the destination file, the second in the second, and so on. And unless the two files have identical structures, you could wind up with a mess in the destination file.

- If you *do* wind up with a destination file mess, and the entire file is worthless, you can go to the DOS file facilities inside Q&A and send the file to the Great Beyond with a few keystrokes.

But first figure out what went wrong so you won't make the same mistake twice.

- You can save and then reuse Merge Specs — this is handy if you're routinely importing from the same source file into the same destination file. You can also create macros to take care of data importation for you.

- If you're concerned about importing records whose information may already exist in the destination file, you can use Q&A's Remove Duplicate Records feature to weed out the duplicates later. This is especially useful when renting lists of prospects or customers to use in mass-mailing purposes. It's referred to as merge/purge.

- When you plan to append imported records to an existing Q&A database, you may want to first mark those source file records (using a mass update procedure from within the source file software package) so that once they're in Q&A they can be easily identified and retrieved for updating, if necessary. You'll need an extra field designed into both files for this purpose. This field will be blank in the original Q&A records.

- Another trick that affords a measure of insurance when importing records to an existing Q&A database is to copy the design of the Q&A destination file and then import the records to the *duplicate* database. This way the original file is unaffected. You can then view the imported records in the duplicate file, and if the conversion was 100 percent successful you can then copy them over to the original file using the Copy Selected Forms command.

- If you're not sure what information fields are in the source file, don't import the file to an existing Q&A database that contains records. Instead, let Q&A create the database automatically. Then, once you're able to look over the imported records from inside Q&A, you can decide which fields to include in the records you'll append to the Q&A database. You can use the Copy Selected Forms command, along with appropriate Retrieve and Merge Specs.

- When Q&A creates the destination file on-the-fly, it makes the first field in the source file the first field in the destination file, and so on. In the destination file, Q&A places the fields in a column down the left side of the screen, one field per line, and then begins a second column if the number of fields exceeds 210.

- If Q&A has created the database design automatically during the import process, you can follow up by redesigning the form, moving the fields around (using the Options menu block copy feature), adding fields, changing labels, and enhancing the form's appearance with line draw. You may also want to add other custom features such as speeding-up fields, setting initial values, adding field templates, custom help screens, field programming, and so forth. These procedures are covered in Chapters 3 and 4.

- Pay attention when importing database records that contain name and address fields. If the source file has separate fields for title, first name, middle initial, last name, and suffix, or multiple address fields with separate fields for city, state, and zip code, your Q&A database will need the same fields. Of course, if you're allowing Q&A to create the destination file for you (which in many cases you can), this won't be a concern.

- After you've imported a file into Q&A, it's a good practice to scan through a sampling of records to make sure that date fields contain dates, number fields contain only numbers, the customer name field contains a name, and so forth. This will help you avoid problems when you start actually *using* the database for important work.

- You can use Q&A's Table View to rapidly scan through imported records and easily spot any errors that appear to be consistent from record to record.

Importing from PFS/Pro File

You can append PFS/Pro File data to an existing Q&A database, create a new form design for the incoming data, or import the file without a Q&A form design and let Q&A duplicate the source form's design.

When importing from PFS/Pro File, Q&A also imports Sort Specs, Retrieve Specs, Print Specs, and Report Specs, along with any calculated field formulas. When the import process has been completed, be sure to verify that any field formulas have been properly converted. If not, you can correct them with Q&A programming statements.

To have Q&A import the file data into an existing Q&A database, select PFS/Pro File from the Import menu, type the name of the selected source file, and then enter the Q&A destination filename.

If you want Q&A to *create* the destination database, enter a nonexisting Q&A destination filename, and a Format Spec will be displayed showing the form's design. Here you'll specify the information types for the fields, and can enter field formatting codes. When you've finished filling out the screen, press **<F10>**, and the Merge Spec for that database will be displayed.

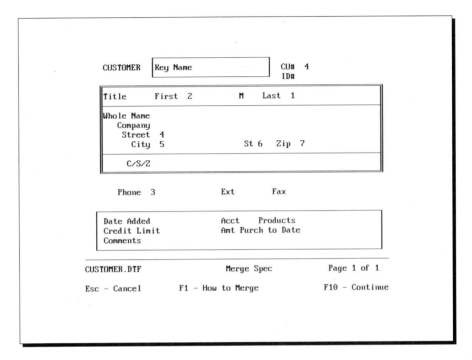

Figure 9-9: Merge Spec for the Customer (Destination) Database. The field numbered 1 tells Q&A to put the contents of the first field in the source database here; the field numbered 2 says put the contents of second field in the source database here, and so forth. If you press <F10> from a blank Merge Spec, the value from the first field in the source file will wind up in the first field of the Q&A destination file, and so on.

At the Merge Spec, type a number into each field that is to receive data from the source database; The numbers you type correspond to the location of the fields on the PFS/Professional File form. The order of the fields is top-left to bottom-right in the source file. For example, typing **4** in the first Merge Spec field tells Q&A to take the fourth field from the imported file and put the value here, in the *first* field in the Q&A form. Any PFS/Professional File fields not specified at the Merge Spec will be ignored unless you leave the Merge Spec completely blank (see Figure 9-9).

If you press **<F10>** from a blank Merge Spec, Q&A will place the contents of the first source file field into the first field of the Q&A database, the second source file field into the second Q&A database field, and so forth. If there are more fields in the source database than the Q&A database, Q&A will ignore the additional source file fields.

Importing PFS/Pro File with attachment fields requires a modified procedure, as follows:

1. Let Q&A create the form design for the destination file if you haven't created one already.

2. When the Format Spec appears, press **<Esc>** a few times to get to the File menu.

3. Select Design a File, and then Redesign a File. Type the name of the new Q&A database you entered previously.

4. With the form design on screen, add a **>** to where the multiline fields should end. Because line lengths in PFS/Pro File are slightly longer than Q&A's, you should add an additional line to your multiline fields in Q&A. If you have attachment fields, press **<PgDn>** for a blank form page and type **Attachment:** (include the colon) at the top of the page. Now move the cursor down to the bottom of the page and type the **>** end of field delimiter. Press **<F10>** when you're done. The number of attachment fields you can have is subject to the same limitation as any other field: 2,045 total fields and 64K of data per record.

5. At the Format Spec, enter the appropriate information types and press **<F10>**.

6. Now go back to the File Import menu and select PFS/Pro File, and once again enter the names of the source and destination files.

7. At the Merge Spec tell Q&A which fields in the Q&A database are to receive the data from the PFS/Pro File database, or press **<F10>** from a blank Retrieve Spec to have field 1 in the Q&A destination file receive the value from field 1 in the source field, field 2 from field 2, and so on. (See Figure 9-9.)

After the file has been imported, you should go to the Q&A Program Spec and verify that any calculated field formulas have been correctly imported.

Importing IBM Filing Assistant Files

You can append IBM Filing Assistant forms to the end of an existing Q&A database, or have Q&A create the destination database for you. Either way, the procedure is the same as outlined above for importing a PFS/Pro File database. Attachment fields are handled in the same way also. Don't forget to fill out the Merge Spec so Q&A will know what fields in the source database correspond to what fields in the Q&A destination database (see Figure 9-9).

Importing Lotus 1-2-3 and Symphony Files into Database Format

Q&A can import files from most versions of Lotus 1-2-3 and Symphony, except 1-2-3 version 3.0 files. If you don't already have a database in which to import the Lotus or Symphony file, you'll need to create one in advance — Q&A cannot create the target file for you.

When Q&A imports a spreadsheet file, each row in the spreadsheet is treated as a Q&A record, and each column cell as a field. If you're not familiar with spreadsheet formats, you can get a rough idea by looking at a Q&A database in Table View where the records are displayed in horizontal rows and the fields in columns. In a spreadsheet, the points where the rows and columns intersect are referred to as *cells*.

If the spreadsheet contains 50 columns and you're going to import them all, then you'll need to design a Q&A database with at least 50 fields to hold the information. And you'll need to make sure that your fields are wide enough to contain the corresponding spreadsheet cells. Otherwise, Q&A will be forced to truncate the imported values to make them fit.

To import a Lotus or Symphony spreadsheet, select **L** from the File Import menu. Enter the path and filename for the source file, and then the *existing* Q&A database name. The Define Range screen will be displayed.

You can either name the range to be imported, or specify the range by entering *from* column and row, and *to* column and row coordinates. If you don't indicate the range, the whole spreadsheet file will be imported. Don't include any nondata column headings or notes. If any are embedded in the range, edit them out — you can always save your edited version under another name so the original one will remain intact.

Since a Q&A database form can hold 2,045 fields, a large number of rows and columns in the spreadsheet file will present no problem. Any fields in the Q&A database over and above the number of spreadsheet columns will be left empty. If there are more spreadsheet columns than Q&A database fields, the rest of each row will be discarded.

Once you specify the range and press **<F10>**, Q&A begins importing. Data from the first column of the selected cell range will go to the first field of the Q&A database, data from the second column of the selected range will go to the second field, and so forth.

Optionally, you can press **<F8>** from the Range screen to go to the Merge Spec where you can indicate, by numbering the fields, which fields in the Q&A database are to receive information from the spreadsheet. Enter the number 1 in the Merge Spec field that is to receive the data from the first column of the spreadsheet range you specified earlier. Enter the number 2 in the Q&A Merge Spec field that is to contain the data from column 2 of the spreadsheet, and so forth (see Figure 9-9). Press **<F10>** when the Merge Spec is complete and you're ready to start importing.

Note that the Merge Spec works with the Lotus/Symphony *range* you selected at the Define Range screen, and considers *that* range to be the entire spreadsheet.

Printing a Spreadsheet or Lotus Graph File was covered earlier in this chapter under Write Utilities.

Importing DIF Files

Any file not directly supported for import can be imported into Q&A by first converting it to ASCII (Fixed or Standard) or DIF format. Most databases can be converted to one or more of these formats and the manual for the product will tell you how to do it.

In DIF (Data Interchange Format) files, a "vector" corresponds to a Q&A field, and a "tuple" corresponds to a Q&A form or record. A DIF import requires that you first create the destination database in Q&A. If the database already exists, then you can append DIF "tuples" to it.

It's a straightforward process. Simply select DIF from the File Import menu, provide Q&A with the filename of the DIF database and then the destination Q&A database. Fill out the Merge Spec in the usual way so Q&A knows where the contents of the source fields are to be placed in the Q&A forms (see Figure 9-9). Press **<F10>** from the Merge Spec to begin importing. You'll see each form displayed as it's information is imported to the Q&A database.

Importing Fixed ASCII Files

Most databases can be exported to ASCII format (American Standard Code for Information Exchange), and then imported by most any other database. The manual for the software product tells you how to do this. Two types of ASCII files are commonly used — Fixed ASCII and Standard ASCII. In Fixed ASCII files, each record is displayed on its own line, and there is one line per record or form; each field begins in the same character column from record to record.

Fixed ASCII records are delimited by a carriage return and line feed at the end of each line (record).

If you're not sure whether you've got a Fixed or Standard ASCII file on your hands, you can bring it onto the Type/Edit screen in the Write module to have a look.

You'll need an existing database to import the file into Q&A. A look at the file in the Write module will show you the information the records contain, and you can build your form with the fields you plan to import in mind.

As soon as you enter the name of the Q&A destination file, the Merge Spec will be displayed. But instead of typing only a single number into each field you want to import from the ASCII file, you'll need to type *two numbers*.

- The first number is the *column* number in the Fixed ASCII file where the field value to be imported starts.

- You follow this first number with a comma and then type the value's length in characters.

If you want the contents of the second column in the Fixed ASCII file to be imported into the first field in the Q&A form, and that second column begins at column 15 and is 10 characters long, type **15,10** in the first field at the Merge Spec.

Importing Standard ASCII Files

The requirements and procedure are the same for importing a Standard ASCII data file into Q&A as they are for importing a Fixed ASCII file — with one exception.

At the Merge Spec, instead of typing two numbers in the fields to indicate the field you want to bring in from the source file (as you're required to do with Fixed ASCII) you only need to type a single number for each field (see Figure 9-9). The number corresponds to the ordinal position of the field in the imported record. Again, unless you fill out the Merge Spec, the first field of the source file will be placed into the first field of the destination file, the second into the second, and so forth. But before the actual importation begins, Q&A will display the special ASCII Options screen shown in Figure 9-10.

ASCII Options

The defaults shown in Figure 9-10 will probably be fine for your imported ASCII file, but some ASCII files can be delimited by spaces, semicolons, or other characters. It's best to take a look at any ASCII file in Write before importing it to your Q&A database. If it's delimited differently than the usual double quotes around text and commas separating the fields, you'll need to select the appropriate options here before pressing **<F10>** to continue.

Importing dBASE II, III, and IV Files

Records from a dBASE II, III, or IV file can be imported into an existing Q&A database and appended to the end of the file. You can optionally create a new Q&A database design to hold the data, or you can have Q&A create the database for you as part of the import process.

```
                              ASCII OPTIONS


     Most ASCII files are formatted with quotes around text values (but
     not numbers), and commas separating field values.  Does your
     ASCII file have a different format?  If YES, make the appropriate
     selections below.  If NO, just press F10 to continue.


     Quotes around text..:      ▶Yes◀   No

     Field delimiter.....:       return   semicolon  ▶comma◀  space


     NOTE: All records must be delimited by carriage returns.
```

Figure 9-10: The ASCII Options Screen.

To have Q&A create the file, simply enter the new filename after you've entered the dBASE filename. Q&A will then take the form design directly from the dBASE file and present you with a Format Spec to assign your information types and any formatting codes.

After you've filled out the Format Spec, the Merge Spec will be displayed. Here you'll tell Q&A which fields in the source file correspond to the fields in the destination Q&A database (see Figure 9-9).

If you're importing to an existing Q&A database, you'll get the Merge Spec as soon as you type the destination filename and press **<Enter>**.

Q&A can handle a maximum of 32K from a dBASE memo field. If the corresponding dBASE field is longer, Q&A will truncate the value. Also, Q&A truncates numbers of more than seven decimal places.

Q&A has the capability to XLOOKUP dBASE fields directly and retrieve their values into your Q&A database during data entry. For information on how to do this, see the section on "Lookup Commands" in Chapter 4.

Importing Paradox 2.0/3.0/3.5 Files

You can import Paradox 2.0, 3.0, and 3.5 files into an existing Q&A database, or let Q&A create one for you as part of the import process.

If you choose to have Q&A create the destination file, you'll be presented with a Format Spec so you can assign the information types and formatting codes to the fields. Fill out the Merge Spec in the usual way to tell Q&A which Paradox field values go where in the Q&A database form (see Figure 9-9).

Importing SQL Databases

SQL, or Structured Query Language, is becoming increasing popular because it allows micro-computer users to access the resources of large mainframe computers. Q&A version 4.0 supports the importation of data from two SQL database servers: Gupta SQLBase, and Oracle.

You can create a destination database design, let Q&A create one for you automatically, or append downloaded data to an existing Q&A database.

When you select Link-to-SQL from the File Utilities menu, Q&A displays the Link-to-SQL submenu for you to make your choice between Gupta and Oracle. When importing data from an SQL table, Q&A gives you the opportunity to fill out a Retrieve Spec, allowing you to import only those records you want. Each record can contain up to 255 fields.

Note: An SQL server needs its own SQL driver to link with Q&A, and the driver needs to be located in the Q&A program files directory. If the driver you need doesn't appear on the Link-to-SQL menu, see your network administrator. SQL drivers can be ordered from Symantec, and they come with their own *Link-to-SQL Guide*.

Here's the procedure for importing data from an SQL database:

1. Load your SQL workstation software, and then load Q&A.

2. Select Link-to-SQL from the File Utilities menu.

3. From the Link-to-SQL submenu, choose the SQL driver you want (you may need to see your network administrator to obtain access to these drivers). Q&A will display a box for you to enter the required information. Use your cursor keys to move between the fields. The dialogue box in Figure 9-11 gives you an idea of the kind of information you'll be expected to enter.

4. Enter the information requested by the SQL driver and press **<F10>**.

5. Q&A attempts to connect to the database by presenting the user ID, password, and any other information required by the server. If there are no error messages, and Q&A prompts you for the name of a table you have access to, it means that the connection is successful.

   You will get an error message, and an opportunity to correct the situation (if possible), where:

   • There is no database with the name you specified.

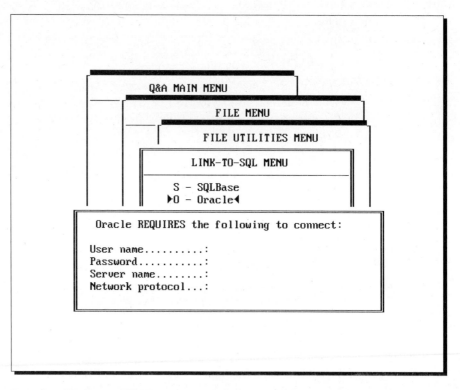

Figure 9-11: The Link-to-SQL Menu. Q&A prompts you to enter the information required to connect to the SQL table you want.

- You supplied an invalid user-ID or password.

- Your workstation or server software isn't running.

- Your workstation runs out of memory.

6. Type the name of the table you want to access and press **<Enter>**. You can press **<Enter>** with the field blank to view a list of tables you can access. See your database administrator if the table you want isn't there.

7. Enter in the name of the destination Q&A database, or press **<Enter>** from a blank field to view the list of Q&A databases. When you've specified the destination database:

- A Retrieve Spec representing the SQL database will display. You can fill it out like any Q&A Retrieve Spec, except that you cannot use Retrieve Spec formulas.

- You can press **<F8>** to create a Sort Spec. If you used MIN at the Retrieve Spec, that field becomes the primary ascending sort field; if you used MAX, that field becomes the primary descending sort field.

- If the Q&A destination file is new, you'll be presented with a Format Spec where you can enter in the appropriate information types.

- Q&A displays the Merge Spec for you to specify which fields in the source database correspond to the fields in the Q&A destination file (see Figure 9-9). Most SQL engines can handle up to 255 fields.

- If you don't have a destination file design and Q&A builds the database for you, the field values will be placed on the form based on their order in the SQL table. You can, of course, redesign the form later and place the fields where you want them.

8. Press **<F10>** to start downloading.

Exporting Data from Q&A Files

You can export your Q&A database files to a variety of formats acceptable to other database packages. Figure 9-12 shows the File Utilities menu and the Export menu that branches off from it.

The procedure for exporting a Q&A database file to another format amounts to no more than simply naming the files involved in the transaction, selecting the records, and telling Q&A which fields in those selected records to export to the corresponding fields of the destination file. In all cases, Q&A will create the export file and then pass the data into it.

When you export a file from Q&A, a *new* file is always created — your original database is unaffected. Exporting from Q&A means that the Q&A file is the *source* file, and the new converted file is the *destination* file.

The destination file can be placed anywhere DOS will allow it. Thus you can specify that the converted Q&A file be located in the subdirectory of the export program where all of its data files are stored.

When you export from Q&A you can always select the records to be exported. Q&A exports up to its maximum 32K field contents, and truncates values where necessary to fit the field lengths of the corresponding destination file fields.

To export a Q&A database file:

1. Select the export format you want from the Export menu.

2. Enter the name of the Q&A file you want to export.

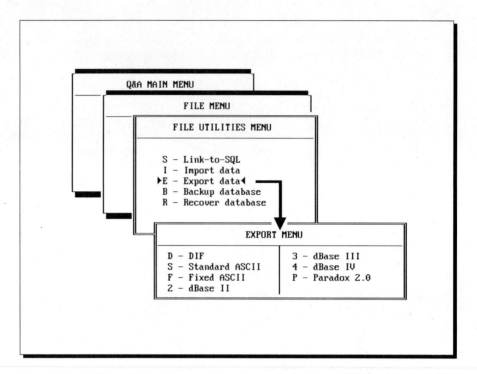

Figure 9-12: The File Utilities Menu and the Export Menu that Branches Off from It.

3. Type the name of the file you want to export the data to (including the drive and path where appropriate) making sure to use the proper extension for the type of file you're exporting. Press **<Enter>**.

4. At the Retrieve Spec, type the parameters that tell Q&A which records you want exported and press **<F10>**. You can optionally press **<F8>** to enter Sort criteria if you want the records in the export file to wind up in a particular order.

5. At the Merge Spec, specify what fields in the Q&A database you want exported to the destination file. If you press **<F10>** from a blank Merge Spec, Q&A will export all the fields in the same order (upper left to lower right) they're on your form.

For all types of exports except destination files in Fixed ASCII format, type **1** in the field whose contents you want exported to the first field of the destination file, type **2** in the field you want exported to the second destination file field, and so on.

```
                      ASCII OPTIONS
                      ============

Most ASCII files are formatted with quotes around text values (but
not numbers), and commas separating field values.  If you plan on
importing this back into a Q&A database, set NO templates.  Does
your ASCII file have a different format?  If YES, make the appropriate
selections below.  If NO, just press F10 to continue.

Quotes around text.....:      ▶Yes◀   No

Field delimiter........:      return   semicolon  ▶comma◀  space

Export field template..:      Yes    ▶No◀

NOTE: All records must be delimited by carriage returns.
```

Figure 9-13: ASCII Options. When exporting to Standard ASCII format, the ASCII Options screen displays. Most ASCII files use quotes around characters, commas as field delimiters, and carriage return/linefeed combinations at the ends of individual records.

For Fixed ASCII format export, your Merge Spec will require *two* numbers to be entered in each export field:

- The first number is the column number in the external file where the export value will begin.

- The second number is the length of the field in characters.

Be sure to allow enough spaces for field contents. If the export value is short, Q&A will add spaces, but if the export value is too long for the field length specified, it will be truncated to fit.

Note: Paradox can handle only up to 255 fields. Any export fields exceeding this limit will be dropped.

6. When you've finished filling out the Merge Spec, press **<F10>**. For all export formats except Standard ASCII, Q&A goes immediately to work exporting the data. If you're exporting a Standard ASCII file, the ASCII Options screen as shown in Figure 9-13 displays.

If the ASCII Options screen in Figure 9-13 displays, change the settings as necessary and press **<F10>** to begin exporting. If you've set the Export Field

Template line to "Yes," Q&A exports the template structure as well as the data. So if you plan on importing this file back into Q&A at some point, you'll probably want to set this line to "No."

Backing Up a Database

Back up your database files frequently. Power surges, power outages, hard disk crashes, and other unforeseen problems can cause you no end of misery if you don't have a recently made copy of your database in the drawer. When you back up a database file from inside Q&A, Q&A makes a copy of both the data file and its associated .IDX file. To make a backup:

1. Choose Backup Database from the File Utilities menu.

2. Enter the name of the database you want Q&A to back up for you. You can press **<Enter>** from a blank line to see a list of files, highlight the one you want to back up, and press **<Enter>**.

3. Enter the name of the target backup file. For example, if you're backing up CUSTOMER.DTF, you can name the backup file CUSTBACK. By default, Q&A places the backup copy on your hard disk, but you can tell Q&A to back up to any drive and/or directory.

If your target disk doesn't have enough space to contain the whole file, Q&A will tell you. Databases can grow rapidly to the point where they'll no longer fit on a single empty floppy disk. In this case you might consider using the QABACKUP utility that comes bundled with Q&A. QABACKUP lets you back up a single file, or any number of files, onto a series of floppy disks. Its use is fully covered in Appendix G.

You can also back up a file from the DOS File Facilities by highlighting the file at the List Manager screen, and pressing **<F5>** to have Q&A make a copy of it.

If your databases are quite large, you might consider a whole backup subsystem — a tape drive that installs in or connects to your computer and comes with special software to make backup of extremely large files — as well as entire directories or disks — fast and easy.

Whenever you back up a data file from outside Q&A, be sure you back up *both* the .DTF and its associated .IDX file. One isn't much good to you without the other. QABACKUP, fortunately, takes care of this for you automatically.

Recovering a Database

Any computer file you're working on can become damaged during a power interruption. Somebody might trip over the cord that connects the computer to the wall socket; a truck might crash into a power pole down the street; lightning may strike; *someone might inadvertently turn off the computer without properly exiting Q&A!* When this happens and a Q&A database file sustains damage, you'll get a message from Q&A telling you that something is wrong with the file. In most cases you can repair any damage by using the Recover Database option available from the File Utilities menu.

This utility can also be used to help optimize disk performance. After you've searched, sorted, added, and deleted records in a database over time, files can become fragmented on your hard disk and spread out all over the place. As this condition worsens, it can take Q&A longer to find and retrieve your records. Running the Recovery operation on the database recovers those wayward bits and compacts the file to optimize disk space and performance.

When you select Recover a Database, you'll be prompted to enter the name of the data file. Before proceeding with the recovery operation, Q&A will display a warning screen urging you first to make a backup copy of the file (which you most definitely should!), and informing you that this procedure *must not* be used to recover data files from an earlier version of Q&A that have not been successfully upgraded for use with version 4.0.

If you proceed with the recovery, Q&A will keep you informed of the progress. Large databases with thousands of records and lots of indexed fields can take some time, and you can't cancel the process once it has begun.

When the operation has been completed, the Utilities menu will redisplay with a message letting you know whether or not the recovery was successful. If it was *not* successful, and you don't know how to proceed from there, a call to Q&A Technical Support will be necessary.

- Always back up a database before attempting to recover it. Back it up to a different disk.

- Whenever you back up a damaged database file before recovering it, *don't* back it up over a previously saved *good* copy of the file. If the file has been too severely damaged to recover, that good backup may save your hide.

- Any time Q&A displays a warning message indicating that something is wrong with a database, it will provide an internal error code. *Write down the code exactly as Q&A displays it. Q&A tech support may need it to help you recover the database by other means.*

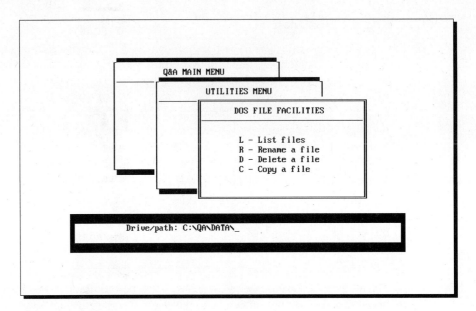

Figure 9-14: The DOS File Facilities Menu.

DOS File Facilities

Using the DOS file facilities utilities you can perform a number of common DOS operations from right inside Q&A. You can view all the files in any directory on your hard disk with the List Files command, remove files for which you no longer have any use, rename your files, or copy them to a backup disk or another directory. You can even create descriptions for your files of up to 70 characters in length — no more wondering whether SALES1.DOC, SALES2.DOC, or REPSALES.DOC is the one you really need. Figure 9-14 shows the DOS File Facilities menu.

List files shows you a list of all the files in the current directory. When you select List Files, you can type the drive and path of any directory on your hard disk and get an alphabetical listing of all the files.

Rename a file lets you change the name of any DOS file.

Delete a file lets you delete old, useless or duplicate files. You'll be asked for confirmation before the file is deleted. And once you delete it, there is no way to get it back through Q&A or DOS. Special commercial utility programs are available to help you recover accidentally deleted files, but it's better to be safe than sorry. When in doubt, don't delete — at least move the file or files to a floppy disk.

Copy a file can be used to make fast backups or move files to other locations on the hard disk.

```
                    LIST OF FILES IN C:\QA\DATA\*.*

  \..               EXPENSES.DTF      INVOICE.IDX      STOCK.DTF       UPS.IDX
  \CLIENTS          EXPENSES.IDX      LETTERS.DTF      STOCK.IDX       U.DTF
  \HASBEENS         FINANCES.DTF      LETTERS.IDX      SUM.DTF         U.IDX
  C.DTF             FINANCES.IDX      PO.DTF           SUM.IDX         ZIPLKUP.DTF
  C.IDX             FRIENDS.DTF       PO.IDX           TEMP.DTF        ZIPLKUP.IDX
  CREDMEMO.DTF      FRIENDS.IDX       POTEMP.DTF       TEMP.IDX
  CREDMEMO.IDX      I.DTF             POTEMP.IDX       TEST.DTF
  CUSTOMER.DTF      I.IDX             REMINDER.DTF     TEST.IDX
  CUSTOMER.IDX      INU-TM.DTF        REMINDER.IDX     U.DTF
  EMPLOYEE.DTF      INU-TM.IDX        S.DTF            U.IDX
  EMPLOYEE.IDX      INVOICE.DTF       S.IDX            UPS.DTF


            File name: C:\QA\DATA\


  Esc-Cancel  F1-Info  F3-Delete   F5-Copy   F7-Search   F8-Rename   F10-Continue
```

Figure 9-15: Q&A's List Manager. It shows you the list of files in any directory on your hard drive. Here we see a list of database files in the Data subdirectory. The path of all the files shown on this screen is C:\QA\DATA\.

The steps for these operations are essentially the same. After you've selected the action from the DOS File Facilities menu, Q&A prompts you for the filename. In the case of List Files, you're prompted to enter the drive and path, or you can press **<Enter>** to see the list of files in the current directory.

If you choose Rename a File, you'll be prompted to enter the old name and then the new one. When you select Copy a File, Q&A will need the name of the file you want to copy and the new filename specifications.

You can also carry out the Rename, Delete, and Copy operations with special function key assignment available at any List Files screen. Figure 9-15 shows the files in the directory C:\QA\DATA.

Q&A databases are stored together as two separate files: the data file (.DTF) and its associated index file (.IDX). If you were renaming, copying, or deleting these files in DOS, you'd have to treat them as individual files. When you do these actions from the List Manager, though, whatever you do with one will be done with the other. Q&A knows that they must be copied, renamed, or deleted as a pair because one isn't much good without the other.

When you open the List Manager and the files in the directory are displayed, the highlight bar will be positioned at the top left of the screen on a blank line. The parent directory (if any) will be first item on the list (in Figure 9-15 this is the **\..** entry).

Should there be one or more subdirectories below the current directory (the directory whose files are displayed), they will appear next on the list preceded by the \ symbol, which DOS uses to separate directories from other directories and files. In Figure 9-15, the two directories \CLIENTS and \HASBEENS are subdirectories of the DATA directory. If you want an alphabetical list of the files in one of the other directories, press <↓> to highlight the name of the directory and press **<Enter>**.

You'll notice in Figure 9-15 that three of the function keys are assigned to the same operations as those on the DOS file facilities menu: the **<F3>** Delete key, the **<F5>** Copy key, and the **<F8>** Rename key. Using your cursor keys you can highlight any file shown, and perform the operation simply by pressing the appropriate function key.

You can use the **<F7>** key to search for a file or files in a long directory listing. Q&A wildcard characters (..) can be used to search — you don't have to type the complete filename. Examples of using the Q&A wildcard characters are:

P..	Locates and highlights the first file in the directory that begins with the letter P.
..X	Finds and highlights the first file in the directory that ends with the letter X.
..STA..	Locates and highlights the first file in the directory that contains the three letters STA within it.
...PAT	Finds and highlights the first file in the directory with the DOS filename extension .PAT.

When using Q&A's wildcard symbol to search for a file in the current directory, enter the search parameter on the filename line at the List Manager screen and then press **<F7>**. Q&A will locate and highlight the first occurrence. You can then press **<F7>** again to find the second occurrence, and so on.

You can also use the DOS wildcard characters ***** and **?** at any List Manager screen to have Q&A create a subset (a separate listing) of files. For example, the command ***.PRO** would locate all the files in the current directory with a .PRO filename extension and display them in a separate list. When using DOS wildcard characters to display a subset of files, press **<Enter>** rather than **<F7>** after you've typed the search criteria.

Report, Retrieve, Sort, Posting, and other Q&A specs that have been named and saved are not DOS files, and cannot be searched or subsetted in this manner. You can similarly locate, copy, delete, and rename such specs, however, you have to do so at the List of Specs for the particular type of spec.

```
                    LIST OF FILES IN D:\QA\DATA\*.*

\..
\OLDCUST
C
C         Enter a description for CUSTOMER.DTF:
E
E  Client activity file for Bill Smith from 8/1/88 to 9/30/90
I
I          Press F10 when finished
S
STOCK.IDX




         File name: D:\QA\DATA\CUSTOMER.DTF


CUST.DTF      Size: 19,456      Date edited: 09/22/90      Time edited: 19:34

Esc-Cancel   F1-Info   F3-Delete   F5-Copy   F7-Search   F8-Rename   F10-Continue
```

Figure 9-16: File Descriptions. Give your data and document files more meaningful names. Just highlight the file, press **<F6>** for the Description Box, and type a few words that will help you remember what's in the file. Press **<F10>** to save the description and close the box. Now, when you highlight the file its extended description will display just above the function key assignments line at the bottom of the screen.

For example, if you want to rename a Report Spec in the Customer database, you'll need to go to the "List of Reports in Database" screen for the Customer database.

Long Filename Descriptions

With a maximum of 11 characters for the length of a filename in the DOS world, it can be hard to choose names that are both unique and meaningful. In Q&A, however, you can assign descriptions to your files of up to 70 characters, helping you to remember what's actually in the files when working with them inside Q&A. These extended filenames are for user-created Q&A files only — you can't use this feature with non-Q&A files or Q&A program files, and DOS doesn't recognize them. If you work with many documents, these long file description tags can be especially useful. Figure 9-16 shows the description box for composing extended names for your files. In this case a description is being assigned to a customer database file.

To write an extended description for a file, simply highlight the appropriate file from inside the List Manager and press **<F6>**. Enter your description of up to 70 characters, and when you're finished press **<F10>**. Now whenever you highlight that file, the extended description will display on the Status line just above the function key assignments line.

Should you wish to edit a description, simply highlight the file, press **<F6>** to bring up the box, make your changes, and then press **<F10>** to save the edited version.

Using the List Manager to Select Files

DOS facilities and the List Manager are also available from the Write module Write Utilities menu. If you've specified a directory for document files at the Set Global Options screen, Q&A will propose that directory when you access the List Manager to search for, rename, delete, or copy a file.

When you choose Get from the Write menu, and press **<Enter>** with no filename specified, Q&A shows you the list of files in the current directory (the "DOCS" directory, for example). You can then simply highlight the document file you want, and press **<Enter>** to bring it onto the Type/Edit screen.

If you're not in the Write module, and you've specified a directory for your database files at the Set Global Options screen, Q&A proposes, for example, the "DATA" directory when you access the List Manager. You can backspace over the default directory and type any directory whose files you want to see.

You can press **<Shift><F4>** to blank any "Drive/Path" or "Filename" line entirely, and type the one you want from scratch. Or, you can press **<Home>** at any filename prompt, in which case the first character you type will cause the "Drive/Path" or "Filename" specification already on the line to disappear.

Locking a Database

Once your database is up and running, you can prevent others from tampering with it by setting locks on any or all of the features one could use to change the character of the file. Access to this feature is not available from the Utilities menu, but it's included in this chapter since it qualifies as a utility. Figure 9-17 shows the Database Lock Options screen.

To reach the Database Lock screen from the Q&A Main menu, choose File, then Design File, then Customize Application, and then Lock Database. Type the name of the database whose design you want to lock, and press **<Enter>**.

When setting locks on *any* of the various items, it makes sense to assign a password that only you and those permitted to modify the database design will

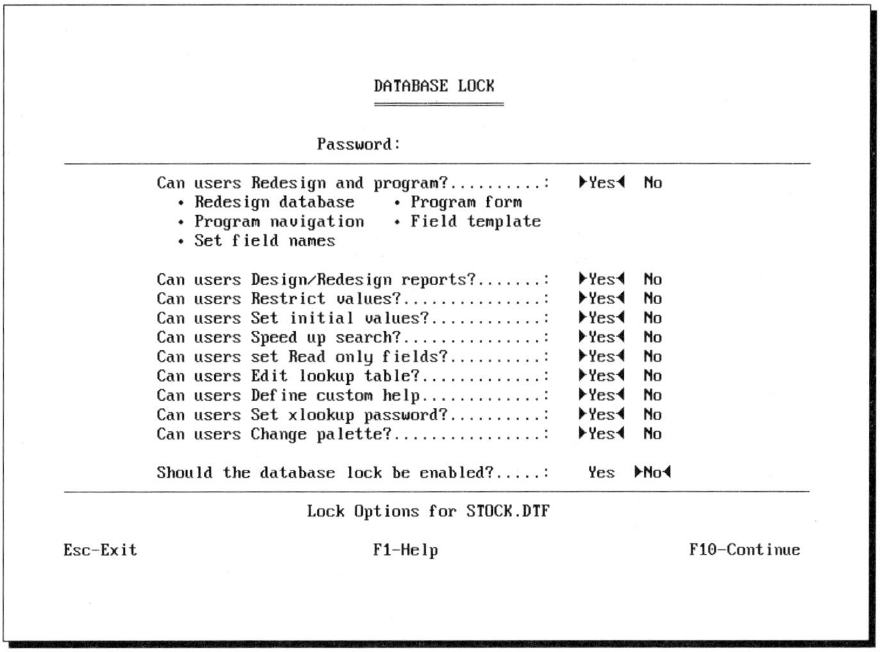

```
                          DATABASE LOCK
                          ============

                   Password:
_____
     Can users Redesign and program?..........:   ▶Yes◀  No
        • Redesign database     • Program form
        • Program navigation    • Field template
        • Set field names

     Can users Design/Redesign reports?.......:   ▶Yes◀  No
     Can users Restrict values?...............:   ▶Yes◀  No
     Can users Set initial values?...........:   ▶Yes◀  No
     Can users Speed up search?...............:   ▶Yes◀  No
     Can users set Read only fields?..........:   ▶Yes◀  No
     Can users Edit lookup table?.............:   ▶Yes◀  No
     Can users Define custom help.............:   ▶Yes◀  No
     Can users Set xlookup password?..........:   ▶Yes◀  No
     Can users Change palette?................:   ▶Yes◀  No

     Should the database lock be enabled?.....:   Yes  ▶No◀
_____
                   Lock Options for STOCK.DTF

  Esc-Exit                F1-Help                  F10-Continue
```

Figure 9-17: The Database Lock Options Screen.

know. Otherwise, anyone can undo your security measures. Type your password at the very top of the Lock Options screen, and record it someplace where you'll be able to find it should it slip your mind.

You're setting locks only on the database whose name you entered to reach this screen.

The most important locks on the database are likely to be the Redesign and Program and Speed-up Searches options, for any unauthorized tampering with these can wreak havoc on an application involving XLOOKUPs and Posting Specs.

Locking Design/Redesign Reports also prevents users from creating or changing Print Specs in the database.

Once you've set your individual feature locks, you'll also need to change the last line, "Should the database lock be enabled?" to Yes. Otherwise Q&A won't place your selected restrictions on the file and your locks will have no effect.

When you've placed your restrictions, enabled the lock, and assigned a password, press **<F10>** to save your settings and exit. If you later need to perform a locked operation, you can return to this screen via your password, disable the lock, finish your work on the database, and then reenable the lock.

There are other ways to secure Q&A database files, such as creating user groups and assigning access rights to them, adding field-level security to hide fields or make them read-only, and setting XLOOKUP passwords. These security measures are normally associated with shared databases in network applications, although they can be used in nonnetwork environments as well, for example, when several people use the same computer. I'll explore these other security features in Chapter 13.

Summary

In this chapter, you learned about the three utility modules offered by Q&A that let you perform DOS housekeeping chores and import and export text documents and databases.

In Chapter 10, you'll learn how to integrate your databases to make them more useful to you.

Chapter 10
Business Applications in Q&A

In this chapter you'll learn how to:

▶ Set up the invoice, customer, and stock databases to work interactively.

▶ Create purchase order, vendor, and supplementary databases to add power and flexibility to your order processing system.

▶ Take advantage of Q&A's macro and posting facilities to keep the information in your system up-to-date.

▶ Add custom features to your new integrated system to improve performance.

▶ Use time-saving advanced tips and tricks to increase all-around productivity.

This chapter will help you set up your databases to work together to increase your productivity.

The first part of the chapter covers redesigning your stock database and creating a purchase order database. The second part includes adding more power to the invoice database with a UPS rates database.

Overview

In Chapter 3 we created sample customer, inventory, and employee databases. In Chapter 4 we designed and then fully programmed an invoice database. Then in Chapter 5 we added some custom programming to the customer database in order to take full advantage of Q&A's powerful mail-merge capabilities.

To illustrate the dynamics of Q&A's report, mail-merge, macro, Intelligent Assistant, and Query Guide facilities, we illustrated practical examples of various processing and information needs that a company can meet by using these product features. For example, we designed a number of informative reports in Chapter 6, developed sample mail-merge applications in Chapter 5, and used the IA and Query Guide in Chapter 7 to retrieve information from our files using ordinary English-language commands.

You now know how to design, customize, and program databases in Q&A. You know how to enter, retrieve, update, and print information, as well as manipulate the records in your files using Q&A's copy, remove, and posting features. What's more, you now possess the savvy to create reports that reveal what's in your files, to develop sophisticated mail-merge applications, and to use macros to boost your productivity.

You've explored all the basics of using Q&A. College is over and you've got your bachelor's degree. It's time to move on to grad school. This and the following chapter will tie these various components together into an interactive system, and show you a variety of advanced procedures and techniques that you'll find useful for this or any other Q&A application.

Toward an Integrated Business System

You can view an *application* in at least two ways: an application can be as elementary as a stand-alone database that helps with one aspect of your business, or as sophisticated as a complete interactive order processing system utilizing several databases supported by other Q&A features (such as custom menus, macros, reports, and posting) to give your company the automation power and flexibility it needs. It's this second way of looking at an application that I'll focus on in this and the subsequent chapter.

An automated business system consists of component parts (databases) that are configured to interact with one another. Designing the databases to store all the information you want to keep track of is one thing. The trick is to enhance the application so that the files can pass information back and forth. You want your system's information to be up-to-date, with Q&A and your computer doing as much of the work as possible.

When you need to retrieve values from external file fields into fields in the current file, you use the XLOOKUP programming commands. To batch-copy data from specified fields in File A to related target fields in File B, you design a Posting specification, a process that requires no programming.

Macros and other Q&A features can also be incorporated into the system to automate procedures not otherwise available directly through software commands.

The business application we've been working toward in this book is an order-processing system. But we don't have the actual *system* yet because we haven't tied the various components together into a working whole.

Here are the features we need to build into our application before we have an intelligent and easy-to-use *system*:

- A way to update the customer's record from the invoice. Our application requires that there be a record for the customer in CUSTOMER.DTF before we can enter an invoice for that customer. When we create an invoice to fill a customer's order, we'll be able to update the customer's record with that invoice number, and add the invoice amount to the amount that customer has purchased from us to date.

- A method for updating our invoices with the date shipped once the items on the invoice have actually gone out the door. Then, should the customer call about his order, he can be told when his order was processed, whether it has been shipped, and, if so, by what method. A macro for accomplishing this operation was discussed in detail in Chapter 8 but we'll use a Posting Spec in this chapter.

- A way to update the records daily in STOCK.DTF from the invoices entered that day. We want to keep a running inventory balance on each product we sell, as well as maintain totals on how many have been sold month to date, year to date, and since time immemorial.

- A way to update the STOCK.DTF records from the purchase orders entered that day. We want our inventory records to reflect not only what's currently on hand, but also what's on order — for the sake of predictability.

- A procedure for updating the STOCK.DTF records when ordered items have been received. If we've placed a purchase order with a supplier for 20 of Item X last month, we'll want to close that purchase order and add those 20 to the on-hand quantity when our receiving department receives them.

- The capability to design and routinely run reports to keep us abreast of activities within the company, answer management questions, and facilitate appropriate decision-making. For example:

    What kind of volume has our ad campaign brought in? Should we run the ad again?

    What is the dollar total invoiced today? Last week? This month to date? Are orders falling off?

What is the dollar total shipped yesterday?

Which orders are overdue to be shipped? Is there a problem in the shipping department? Too many backorders?

How many new customers this week, and who are they? Let's send them a thank-you (mail-merge) letter.

Which customers have past due invoices? Call them, or send them a monthly statement of open invoices.

Which purchase orders are still open after three weeks? Let's follow up with those suppliers.

Which stock numbers are below the reorder level? Place purchase orders for them.

What's the value of our entire inventory at cost? At retail?

- To add standardization and speed to our system, we'll want to be able to launch our daily batch posting operations and routine reports from handy custom menus.

We'll tackle all of these requirements here and in the following chapter.

Understand that we're not designing a formal accounting system here, but one that automates the processing and tracking of incoming orders, maintains up-to-date information about customers, inventory, vendors, and employees, and provides fast and accurate feedback so that informed decisions can be made and the business runs smoothly as a result.

This is not to say that accounting applications can't be designed in Q&A. I've seen accounts payable, receivable, and even payroll applications in Q&A that did the job quite nicely. Moreover, many of the components of an order-processing system can be made to fill accounting-related needs.

For example, in Chapter 6 you learned how to design an accounts receivable aging report, as well as an inventory valuation report. With suitable invoice and purchase order reports you have standard business transaction summary information (such as income and expenditures) at hand, and there's nothing to prevent you from designing an application that will give you sophisticated month-end statements to send to your customers, or help you automate your routine payroll and associated reporting. We'll create an advanced billing application in Chapter 12.

The point is that I'm not talking about charts of accounts, journals, general ledgers, income statements, and balance sheets here. If you want a full-blown accounting system, buy one — there are plenty of specialty accounting software packages out there. Data integrity is absolutely crucial in accounting, and *rollback* features (automatically maintained transaction logs) are built into most accounting packages, enabling file operations to be undone or backed out by reversing the effects of the operations. *Rollback* permits changed records to be restored automatically — this feature is not possible in any database package without complex and extensive programming on the part of either the maker or the buyer.

On the other hand, if you're familiar with standard accounting practices, and want to tackle such an application in Q&A from scratch, go ahead — but be prepared to invest some time.

This book focuses on supporting the dynamic side of business operations rather than on the bookkeeping end of things. Nevertheless, given Q&A's export capabilities and the import features of many accounting packages, you should be able to configure your databases to satisfy virtually any additional accounting requirement. With version 4.0's posting feature, for example, it's a snap to post data from detailed transaction records (invoices, for example) to summary records (other databases); and the totals in those summary records can then be ported to your accounting package in ASCII or any one of a number of other formats.

After all, it's just data.

Preparing Databases for Interaction

These are the five main databases that will be integrated into the order processing system: Invoice, Purchase Order, Customer, Stock, and Vendor. Along with these will be three supplementary databases that you haven't seen yet, but that will be created during the course of this chapter:

- RECEIVER.DTF for information relating to goods received from vendors on our purchase orders. The data in this file will be posted daily to STOCK.DTF to help keep inventory up-to-date.

- SHIPDATE.DTF to record the invoice numbers and shipping dates of shipped orders. Information from this file will be posted daily to INVOICE.DTF so that our invoices will show the actual shipping date, a valuable customer service tool.

- UPSRATES.DTF as a lookup file to calculate invoice shipping charges for orders shipped by ground, second-day express, or overnight express.

In addition to these eight databases, we have the EMPLOYEE.DTF file designed in Chapter 3. This is a stand-alone application containing personnel records, however, and won't play a part in our order processing system.

All of the databases, as modified or designed from scratch in this chapter, can be found on the Applications disk supplied with this book.

You've seen the design of our invoice file and the rationale behind it in Chapter 4 — it's at the heart of the system. In order to automate invoice data entry, we programmed specific fields to look up customer information from the customer file and product information from the stock database. We'll do the same later in this chapter with the purchase order file, except that this database uses vendor information, not customer information. We'll design that vendor database, too.

We'll also modify the design of our stock (products) database form. We originally designed this one in Chapter 3 around a realistic company that distributes books, videos, and audio cassettes — we used it to illustrate a variety of meaningful reports, queries, and so forth. But since it's unlikely that you're in that same type of business, our database of product information should be more flexibly structured to meet a wider range of products and processing needs.

So the database design and redesign work we'll accomplish in this chapter will make these files more generic, more useful across a broader range of business types and practices.

Let's design a vendor database first — this is a relatively easy one with virtually no programming required.

Designing a Vendor Database

VENDOR.DTF is not a transaction file like INVOICE.DTF. It's simply a file that contains information about the companies from whom you purchase items, along with their addresses, principal contacts, phone numbers, terms of payment, and so forth. The information you'll need to enter into your records in VENDOR.DTF is likely to be contained in invoices you've received from these suppliers, and from your own purchase orders.

Figure 10-1 shows the form design of VENDOR.DTF. Don't be concerned if it doesn't contain all the information you'd like to maintain on your vendors; the form has plenty of room for more fields even though it's only a single screen page in length.

```
                                    VENDOR

              Key                            Vendor#


             Company
                Addr1
                Addr2
                Addr3


       Phone                   Ext       FAX
       Contact1                            Contact2

       Acct#               Manufacturer?   Distributor?   Terms

       Stock Numbers
       Notes:



VENDOR.DTF        New Form 1      of 1        Total Forms: 0      Page 1  of 1

Esc—Exit   F1—Help      F3—Delete form    F7—Search    F8—Calc   F10—Continue
```

Figure 10-1: Sample VENDOR.DTF Form. It can be used to keep track of information on your suppliers. The form design is shown here in Add Data.

VENDOR.DTF is designed to provide information on companies from whom you purchase products for your own inventory — products that you generally resell in the same form as you receive them, or after you've added some value to them. One of the purposes of the file is to provide lookup information for the purchase order part of the system we'll develop further on in this chapter. The borders around the VENDOR.DTF screen were created using ASCII graphic character 177 across the top and bottom, and ASCII 221 and 222 down the left and right sides of the form.

An explanation of the fields follows, as well as tips on how to format and customize them.

Key: This is the abbreviated name of the supplier or vendor. For example, the typist enters **Brookhurst** in this field where the name of the company is Brookhurst Supply, Inc. The Key field *identifies* the supplier and is used at the Retrieve Spec to locate the record.

It's also useful in reports, because it allows a smaller column width than the full company name. A practical width for the field is 15 to 20 characters. Make it Speedy and Unique to facilitate fast searches and to avoid duplication. Format it as a text field with all uppercase letters.

Vendor#: This is the number you assign to each of your vendors. You can specify @NUMBER in this field at the Initial Values Spec if you want Q&A to incrementally number each vendor as you enter the record for the first time. The field is formatted as a number. Make it Speedy and Unique, since it will be the external key field for looking up vendor information to include in purchase orders. You can also make it a Read-only field because it will likely never need to be changed.

Company: Make this a 30- to 35-character text field to contain the full name of the company. Format it for initial caps or all uppercase to save your typist from having to capitalize the parts of the name.

Address: The three address fields (text) should accommodate the longest addresses easily. Specific street address, city, state, and zip code fields aren't likely to be needed since you probably won't be using this file in mail-merge applications. If you have a great many vendors, however, and need to sort them by city or zip, you can include separate fields for the address components.

Phone: Text fields are included for the supplier's phone number, buyer's extension, if any, and the FAX number. Make telephone number fields 15 characters wide, and create field templates for them to reduce data entry keystrokes and force telephone format conformity.

Contact: The Contact1 field is for the name of your primary contact at the supplier, usually the salesman with whom you deal. A second name can be entered in the Contact2 field, perhaps the name of your customer service representative. These are text fields, 25 to 30 characters in length.

Acct#: This field is for the account number the supplier has assigned to your company. You'll want Q&A to pick it up and place it on your printed purchase orders so your vendor's order desk will recognize you immediately as having an account with the company.

Manufacturer? Distributor?: These are one-character Yes/No fields. It may be useful for you to be able to differentiate between suppliers who manufacture the products you buy from them and those that merely distribute products manufactured by others.

Terms: This text field contains the trade or payment terms extended to your company by the supplier, such as net 30 days, COD, and so forth.

Stock Numbers: If you have your own stock numbers for products purchased from vendors, make this a one-line keyword field to contain those stock numbers. It will serve to connect the source of the items with your own inventory and product lists.

Notes: Use this text field to enter notes or comments about the supplier, such as quantity price breaks or other special terms. You can include two additional single line fields directly below this one for extended notes, or use the **<F6>** Field Editor during data entry. The vertical border down the right-hand side of the form prevents multiline fields on the form. Erase the border and appropriately position your end-of-field delimiter (**>**) to make the Notes field a multiline field.

You can create more room on the form for additional fields by placing the Company and Addr1 fields on one screen line, the Addr2 and Addr3 fields on another line, and eliminating the double-line box. Or you can simply use another screen page.

As the form stands in Figure 10-1, it's unlikely that you'll need to bother with any real programming. You may want to program *on field entry* @MSG messages to display when adding new forms, so the operator will know what to type into the fields. And custom help screens are always recommended, especially for green data entry personnel who need a more detailed explanation of what's required in the fields.

Now let's proceed to a redesign of our stock database form. Both VENDOR.DTF and STOCK.DTF are important lookup files for our purchase order application to follow. So once we've got STOCK.DTF redesigned to accommodate a wide variety of product types, we can then lay out and program our purchase order form and get the three databases working together smoothly.

Redesigning STOCK.DTF

The STOCK.DTF form we've been using until now was designed for a particular product line and type of business activity — a distributor of books and tapes. It included fields for such values as the book's or tape's title, author, subject codes, whether it was a hardbound or paperback book, an audio tape or video tape, and so forth. I wanted to provide you with realistic sample reports, queries, and the like, and so I designed the form to suit a company that deals with specific types of products.

But now you're at the point where we can — and should — discard that narrow product-related design in favor of a STOCK.DTF design better suited to a broader range of products and applications. STOCK.DTF reborn, you could call it. It's shown in Figure 10-2 and is structured the same way on your Applications disk.

```
                        ▓▓▓▓▓▓▓▓▓▓▓▓▓ STOCK ITEM ▓▓▓▓▓▓▓▓▓▓▓▓▓

     ┌─────────────────────────────────────────────────────────────────┐
     │ Stk# #15    Description #20                        Type #25       │
     └─────────────────────────────────────────────────────────────────┘

     Cost #30     List #35      Disc #40      Status #45     Date Added #50

     Source #55                 Vendor# #60  Weight #65    Case Qty #70 Case Wgt #75
     Vendor Stk# #80
                                ┌──────── Product Notes ────────┐
     ┌─────────────────────────────────────────────────────────────────┐
     │  #85                                                              │
     │  #90                                                              │
     │  #95                                                              │
     └─────────────────────────────────────────────────────────────────┘

       Physical Count #100    Date Counted #105        Shelf Location #110

     ┌────────────────┐ ┌────────────────┐ ┌──────────────┐ ┌────────────────┐
     │ On Hand #115   │ │ On Order #120  │ │ Recd #125    │ │ Reord Lvl #130 │
     └────────────────┘ └────────────────┘ └──────────────┘ └────────────────┘

     ┌────────────────┐ ┌────────────────┐ ┌──────────────┐ ┌────────────────┐
     │ Sold Today #135│ │ Sold MTD #140  │ │ Sold YTD #145│ │ Total Sold #150│
     └────────────────┘ └────────────────┘ └──────────────┘ └────────────────┘
```

Figure 10-2: The New STOCK.DTF Form. The redesigned form is better suited to a wider range of products and applications, shown here with Field ID numbers.

If you're familiar with the original STOCK.DTF form we created in Chapter 3, you'll recognize many of the fields in the redesigned form in Figure 10-2. I'll deal with the purposes of the fields here one by one, and point out any special formatting requirements.

Stk#: This is the part number or stock number assigned to the product. It can be numeric or alphanumeric. Ours is formatted as a text field, and the operator is required to enter a unique value that has been assigned to the item. Using the @NUMBER and @STR functions you can have Q&A return an incremented stock number concatenated with a text value, such as PN-0033HB. The procedure for doing this was explained in Chapter 6.

Description: This 30-character field contains a description of the product. It should be no wider than the corresponding description field widths in your invoice and purchase order databases, or the values may overflow into the Field Editor when retrieved into these forms as a result of external lookup commands.

Type: Does this stock item fall within a particular class, category, or style of item? This field contains a prescribed value that identifies the item's type by characteristics such as size or color.

Cost: The price you pay your vendor for the item — a money field.

List: Your list or retail price for the item — a money field.

Disc: The maximum or standard discount allowed on the item — a number field. The contents of this field will display in a window during invoice entry so the operator will be aware of the maximum discount that can be extended to your best customers.

Status: A status code that identifies whether the item is on hold for some reason, OK to ship, or whatever.

Date Added: A date field set to @DATE at the Initial Values Spec. Records the date this item was added to your product inventory.

Source: Who you get the item from. The abbreviated company name entered here should match the Key field in VENDOR.DTF.

Vendor#: The vendor number that matches the corresponding field in VENDOR.DTF. You can program the field to look up the number so long as you have a VENDOR.DTF record with a Key field that matches the Source field in this file.

Weight: The weight of one unit of this item — a number field. The invoice form retrieves and uses this value to calculate the shipping weight of an order. See the section in Chapter 4 where we programmed the invoice form, as well as the section on calculating UPS charges further ahead in this chapter.

Case Qty: If you ever ship by the case, it may come in handy to know how many of the item are in one. This is a number field.

Case Wgt: This field is filled in automatically once the Weight and Case Qty fields contain values. If the Weight field value is in ounces, your programming statement for the Case Wgt field could be:

```
<#75=(#65*#70)/16;goto  #80
```

The statement multiplies the Weight by the Case Qty, divides the product by 16 (to get pounds), and places the result in the Case Wgt field.

Vendor Stk#: Your purchase orders may need to call out your *vendor's* part number for the item. Where a purchase order line item references the supplier's *and* the customer's item number, both parties know exactly what's being ordered, and the likelihood of a misinterpretation is lessened.

Product Notes: This isn't a field, but a heading for a section of the form that includes three unlabeled fields directly below it. You can turn the three individual fields into a single multiline field in Redesign by typing a colon where you want the field to start, and then typing the **>** end-field delimiter at the tag end of the field. There's more on how to do this in Chapter 3.

Physical Count: Use this number field for the item's count at physical inventory time.

Date Counted: A date field that contains the date the physical count was done.

Shelf Location: The code that indicates where the item can be found in the warehouse — a shelf or bin, for example.

The data entry values that will be entered in the above STOCK.DTF fields are unlikely to be frequently updated; they're relatively fixed values that describe characteristics about the item. As the form stands, little if any programming is required, except that you may want to add *on field entry* @MSG messages to help a novice operator along when entering new stock item records.

For the Source field, for example, you could add the programming statement:

```
<#55: If @add then @Msg("Enter the supplier name
contained in the KEY field in the Vendor file")
```

The operator would have handy a printout of the vendor Key field names. You can add similar messages to the other fields.

With a custom help screen behind each field — only the **<F1>** key away — your instructions can be more detailed, of course.

The STOCK.DTF Quantity Fields

Now we're looking at the dynamic quantity fields at the bottom of the STOCK.DTF form. The values in these fields, except for Reord Lvl (reorder level), will be updated frequently.

After the day's invoices have been entered, a predefined Posting Spec (that we'll design in a moment) will post the quantities of each stock number sold on those invoices to their respective STOCK.DTF records. Five fields in the stock records will be updated during this process. The Posting Spec will post the quantity sold figure to the Sold Today field, and then execute the programming statement in that field that will update the On Hand, Sold MTD (Month to date), Sold YTD (Year to date), and Total Sold fields.

The programming statement for the Sold Today field is:

```
#135: If @Update then {#140=#114+#135; #145=#145+#135;
#150=#150+#135;  #115=#115-#135;#135=""x}
```

Refer to the Field ID numbers shown in Figure 10-2 to see what this statement accomplishes when executed during posting:

- The Sold MTD, Sold YTD, and Total Sold fields are *increased* by the quantity posted to the Sold Today field.

- The On Hand field is *decreased* by the same quantity (the units sold must be deducted from inventory as they are now committed).

- The Sold Today field is then set to blank (empty), awaiting the next day's posted value of units invoiced (sold).

It may have occurred to you that fields #135 through #150 should be Read-only to avoid the possibility of inadvertently altering them during routine Search/Update.

You can indeed make these fields Read-only, but only *after* you've entered your initial load of new STOCK.DTF records (the cursor can't be moved into Read-only fields). The same goes for fields #115, #120, and #130. These can be made Read-only after your initial load of records has been added to the file. Making them Read-only will prevent them from being altered by the operator during updates to other portions of the records.

On Order: When a purchase order is placed with a vendor for stock items, we'll want that activity reflected in the corresponding STOCK.DTF records.

If you'll recall our INVOICE.DTF programming in Chapter 4, we programmed our Stk# fields to look up and display the On Order quantity so the order entry operator would know if more of a low stock item was on the way from the supplier. This is valuable information for an order entry operator to have, especially if an order is being taken over the phone and you want the customer to be advised of a temporary out-of-stock condition.

The On Order field will be updated from purchase orders by a Posting Spec which we'll create later on.

Recd: When the company receives inventory items into stock from an outside vendor, this field will be used to record those quantities and automatically update the related On Hand and On Order fields. The quantity of the received items will need to be deducted from the On Order quantity (since they're now in stock and no longer on order) and added to the On Hand quantity. The operation to do this will involve a Posting Spec (more on this topic later). The programming statement for this field is:

```
#125: If @Update then {#120=#120
#125;#115=#115+#125;#125=""}
```

Reord Lvl: Use this field for the minimum quantity of the item you want kept in stock. When the On Hand quantity reaches the Reord Lvl or dips below it, a report we'll design will flag the item, telling whoever is responsible to get more of the item into stock, and thus avert a potential backorder condition that could have your customers at your throat.

Physical Inventory

You'll use the Physical Count and Date Counted fields to enter the values from your physical inventory. Because a physical inventory involves an update to *all* the records in the database, you'll need a fast method of getting these values into the records. Here's how to do it:

1. Create a double-spaced report, sorted on the stock number field, that provides an underlined space for personnel to write in the item counts as they're proceeding through the physical inventory in the warehouse. See the section on underlining blank fields in a report in Chapter 6 for tips on how to do this.

2. Mass update the Date Counted field with the date the physical inventory was taken. Include all the records in your Retrieve Spec. If you're posting the counts on the same day the inventory was taken, your Update Spec in the Date Counted field will be **#1=@date**.

3. Use a sorted Table View of your forms in Search/Update to enter the item counts into the Physical Count field. To do this:

   a. Select Search/Update from the File menu, and enter the name of the database, STOCK.DTF.

   b. At the Retrieve Spec press **<F8>** for the Sort Spec, and type **1AS** in the Stk# field to sort your table by ascending stock number. Press **<F10>**.

   c. When the first form displays press **<Shift><F6>** to define your table view. Each field on the form will contain a unique number. Leave the Stk# field at **10** and the Description field at **20,** and type **21** in the Physical Count field. Press **<F10>** for a sorted, editable table view.

   d. You can now enter your physical inventory item counts swiftly, record by record, because you have the Physical Count fields all in a neat column with the stock number and description immediately to the left, and the records are in the same order as the report used by your personnel to count the items in the warehouse.

If you want to keep a history of order activity and physical inventories on your stock items, you can place fields on the second screen page of STOCK.DTF for this purpose.

You have the existing Physical Count and Date Counted fields to contain information from a physical inventory, typically done once each year. If your current system doesn't maintain running inventory balances, or if those balances may not be entirely accurate, you'll surely need to conduct a physical count of your stock items prior to entering your initial load of STOCK.DTF records.

The most recent count and date can be entered in the above two fields as you're adding each stock number to the data file. Should you want to maintain a history of each physical inventory, place fields like the following on the second page of the STOCK.DTF form:

```
Count1<     > CountDate1<          >

Count2<     > CountDate2<          >

Count3<     > CountDate3<          >
```

Then, when you do your *next* physical inventory, you can use Mass Update to move the previous physical inventory quantity and date values to the Count1 and CountDate1 fields, and then blank out the Physical Count and Date Counted fields on the first screen page, readying them to receive the current physical inventory information.

If, on the other hand, you want to keep your STOCK.DTF form trim and fast — and confined to a single screen page — you can create another database to which you can post your physical inventory date and count values from STOCK.DTF.

The third alternative is to simply print out your forms or run a report after the physical inventory data has been entered, and keep these hard copies in a file for future reference.

Sales History

You may also want to maintain a month-by-month and year-by-year history of sales activity for your products. You can do this by running a report on the last day of each month and on the last day of the year, showing the Sold MTD or Sold YTD figures, and then keeping the report in a folder with the previous months' (or years') reports.

You can optionally record the sales history figures right on the form — on the next available screen page. To do this, place number fields on the page for the months of the year — your field labels would be Jan, Feb, Mar, Apr, and so forth — and also place number fields labeled 1991, 1992, etc. You can then use Mass Update to move the values from the current fields to these new history fields.

On the last business day of June, 1991, for example, you'd run a mass update on STOCK.DTF as follows:

1. Set the Jun field equal to the Sold MTD field.

2. Set the Sold MTD field to blank.

On the last business day of 1991, another mass update would carry out these actions:

1. Set the Dec field equal to the Sold MTD field.

2. Set the Sold MTD field to blank.

3. Set the 1991 field equal to the Sold YTD field.

4. Set the Sold YTD field to blank.

Now that screen page of your STOCK.DTF form will show a month-by-month history of sales of your products for the year 1991, and also the year's total. Since you're now in a new year, the next time you perform a mass update for January's sales (on the last day of January, 1992), the previous year's January figure will be overwritten by the current year's January figure, and so on, month after month.

At the end of each year, after running the mass update, simply design a report that includes all of these history fields. Or, you can just print the forms using File Print. Either way, you'll have the records for future reference.

If you want to keep the *entire* history right there on the STOCK.DTF form, you can do that, too, by adding these fields to the form:

Jan91<	>	Jan92<	>	Jan93<	>	Jan94<	>
Feb91<	>	Feb92<	>	Feb93<	>	Feb94<	>
Mar91<	>	Mar92<	>	Mar93<	>	Mar94<	>
etc.		etc.		etc.		etc.	
1991<	>	1992<	>	1993<	>	1994<	>

Another method of maintaining a computer-accessible product sales history is to create a new database that contains only the stock numbers and the months and years fields, keeping these history fields off the STOCK.DTF form altogether.

The advantage to this method is that it keeps STOCK.DTF trim and thus faster when your lookup statements in INVOICE.DTF and PO.DTF need to access the file in order to retrieve information (the larger the records, the longer it takes Q&A to retrieve them).

The disadvantage is that whenever you add a new stock number to STOCK.DTF, You'll also need to add a new record to your history database.

To create and use a new sales history database:

1. Design the new form with a field for the stock number and fields to contain the quantities for the months and years, along the lines suggested above. Make the Stk# field Speedy and Unique.

2. Choose Copy Selected Records from the Copy menu, retrieving all the forms in STOCK.DTF.

3. At the Merge Spec, select only the Stk# field to copy to the new database's matching Stk# field. When this is done, you'll have a record in the new database for every record in STOCK.DTF.

4. At the end of each month:

   • Use a Posting Spec to post the Sold MTD figure from STOCK.DTF to the appropriate month's field in the sales history file.

   • Use Mass Update to blank out the Sold MTD field in STOCK.DTF, readying it for the next month.

5. At the end of each year:

   • Use a Posting Spec to post the Sold YTD figure from STOCK.DTF to the appropriate year's field in the sales history file.

   • Use Mass Update to blank out the Sold YTD field in STOCK.DTF, readying it for the following year.

A Posting Spec: INVOICE.DTF to STOCK.DTF

Q&A Power Feature: Now that we've got our INVOICE.DTF and STOCK.DTF forms ready for action, we want to take advantage of Q&A 4.0's powerful posting feature to update the inventory from sales. In other words, we've recorded the total sales of 10 of Item A, 15 of Item B, and 20 of Item C on today's batch of invoices, and we want to post these transactions to the respective STOCK.DTF records.

Once we've created and saved our Posting Spec, we can simply execute the post at the end of each business day and the stock records will be updated.

Here's the procedure for creating the Posting Spec we'll need to update the STOCK.DTF records from the day's invoices:

1. From the File menu select **T - Post**. Type **INVOICE.DTF** as the file to post *from*, press **<Enter>**, and then type **STOCK.DTF** as the file to post *to*, and press **<Enter>**.

2. At the Retrieve Spec, move to the Date field and type **{@Date}** to retrieve only the current day's batch of invoices. Press **<Shift><F8>**

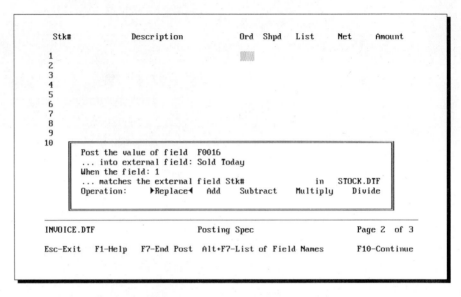

```
        Stk#                Description           Ord  Shpd  List     Net     Amount
         1                                        ░░░░
         2
         3
         4
         5
         6
         7
         8
         9
        10
        ┌────────────────────────────────────────────────────────────────────┐
        │ Post the value of field  F0016                                      │
        │ ... into external field: Sold Today                                 │
        │ When the field: 1                                                   │
        │ ... matches the external field Stk#              in   STOCK.DTF     │
        │ Operation:      ▶Replace◀   Add      Subtract   Multiply   Divide   │
        └────────────────────────────────────────────────────────────────────┘

        INVOICE.DTF                       Posting Spec              Page 2  of 3

        Esc-Exit   F1-Help   F7-End Post  Alt+F7-List of Field Names    F10-Continue
```

Figure 10-3: The Posting Spec Screen. The Ord (Quantity Ordered) column field on the first invoice line is highlighted, and Q&A prompts you to fill in the Posting box for this field.

and save this Retrieve Spec under a descriptive name such as *Daily Invoice Post to Stock*. Press **<Enter>** to save the Retrieve Spec under this name, and then press **<F10>**.

3. At the Posting Spec screen Q&A displays the invoice form. Press **<Tab>** until the highlight is in the first Ord column field in the invoice, as shown in Figure 10-3, and then press **<F7>** to open the Posting box.

The question arises as to whether we want to use the Ord (Quantity Ordered) or the Shpd (Quantity Shipped) column fields as our source post fields.

Look at it this way: If the customer orders 10 units of Item A, but you only have eight in stock, isn't it likely that you'll ship the eight and place the other two on back order. In such a case, won't you want to take all 10 off inventory — even if it means showing a Qty on Hand of -2?

If you use the Shpd column fields as your source post fields, you'll then be deducting from inventory *only the eight units you're shipping right away*. When you get more of the item in and ship the two back-ordered units to the customer, *how will you then deduct these two from inventory?*

How you post deductions from inventory depends on how you do business, your procedure for handling backorders, and how you prefer to maintain your records. Most companies I've dealt with prefer to deduct any backordered quantities from inventory right away so their stock item records reflect the actual situation.

For example, if 25 of Item A are backordered to various customers, the boss wants to see a -25 in the Qty on Hand field in the Item A record. This is like a red flag which, in a weekly stock condition report, says "DO SOMETHING — OUR CUSTOMERS ARE WAITING!"

Continuing with the design of our Posting Spec:

4. With the first Ord field highlighted and the Posting box open, fill in the Posting box as shown in Figure 10-3.

- In this example, **F0016** is the source file field whose value you want to post to the destination file target field. **F0016** is the default field name Q&A assigned to this unlabeled field — it means it's the 16th unlabeled field on the form. (You can give these Ord fields more descriptive names such as Ord1, Ord2, or Ord3 at the Set Field Names Spec. See this feature in Chapter 4.)

- **Sold Today** is the destination file *post-to* (target) field.

- **1** is the field label of the first invoice line item whose value matches the external field Stk#.

- **STOCK.DTF** is the destination filename.

- **Replace** is the operation you want performed.

Here's what you've done so far in a nutshell: You're linking the quantity of invoice line item 1 to the stock number on that same line, and telling Q&A to post that quantity to the target field when the stock numbers in the two files match.

5. When you've filled out the Posting box for the first line item Ord field, press **<F7>** to close the box and press the down arrow to move to the *second* invoice line item Ord column field.

6. You now fill in the Posting box as in step 4 above, except that your source file match field is now **2** instead of **1**.

7. Continue with this procedure until all 10 invoice line item Ord fields are included in the Batch Posting Spec. Your source file match fields will be 3, 4, 5, and so on respectively through the 10 invoice lines.

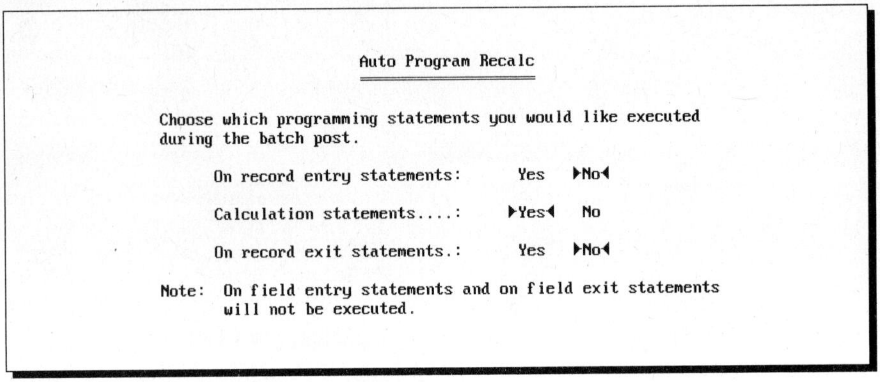

```
                        Auto Program Recalc
                        ═══════════════════

        Choose which programming statements you would like executed
        during the batch post.

            On record entry statements:      Yes   ►No◄

            Calculation statements....:    ►Yes◄   No

            On record exit statements.:      Yes   ►No◄

        Note:  On field entry statements and on field exit statements
               will not be executed.
```

Figure 10-4: The Auto Program Recalc Screen. It displays when you press <F8> from the Batch Posting Spec. You can select the types of programming statements you want Q&A to execute during the batch posting operation. Note: On-field-exit and on-field-entry statements (those preceded by "<" or ">") cannot be executed during posts.

8. After you've filled in the Posting Box from your last invoice line Ord column field, press <F8> for the Auto Program Recalc screen shown in Figure 10-4, and set Calculation Statements to Yes. This ensures that the On Hand, Sold MTD, Sold YTD, and Total Sold fields are updated by the value posted to the Sold Today field (recall the programming statement we wrote for this STOCK.DTF field earlier). Press <F9> to return to the Posting Spec.

9. When you've finished the Batch Posting Spec, press <F8>, type the name for this spec, *Daily Invoice Post to Stock*, and press <Enter>. Now press <F10> and Q&A will want to know if you want to execute the post now. Answer No unless you're ready to run it.

You'll want to thoroughly test your new Posting Spec on a few dummy invoices and stock records before incorporating it with confidence into your order processing system. Be sure to verify that all the Ord column fields in the invoice are posting properly, and that the fields in STOCK.DTF are showing the correct updated figures. Manually add up the quantities from the invoices and then check them against the relevant stock records.

To run this posting operation daily, then, you'll simply follow these steps after all your invoices have been input:

1. Select Post from the File menu.

2. Enter the names of the *Post-from* and *Post-to* files.

3. Press **<Alt><F8>** from the Retrieve Spec, highlight "Daily Invoice Post to Stock" from the List of Retrieve Specs screen, and press **<Enter>**. Press **<F10>** to confirm.

4. At the Posting Screen, press **<Alt><F8>**, highlight "Daily Invoice Post to Stock" from the List of Posting Specs, and press **<Enter>**. Press **<F10>** to confirm.

5. Answer Yes when Q&A asks if you want to run the post now.

Don't forget your Retrieve Spec, however. If you've specified **{@Date}** in the invoice date field at the posting Retrieve Spec, any new invoices entered the same day *after* the posting operation has been run will not get posted to the STOCK.DTF records. Those invoices will be a day old when tomorrow's Retrieve Spec for tomorrow's posting fetches only the current day's invoices.

Since *Daily Invoice Post to Stock* is a routine operation, you can fully automate it in a macro and install it on the Q&A Main menu as an alternate program or on a custom menu.

A Bridge from INVOICE.DTF to CUSTOMER.DTF

For those times during invoice entry when the customer is discovered to be new, you'll need a handy tool to take you from the invoice file to the customer file in order to add the new customer.

Recalling our invoice design in Chapter 4, we programmed two options for retrieving the customer's name, address, and other particulars into the invoice form. The order entry operator can enter the Customer number in the CU# field — the second field on the invoice form, or, if the CU# is unknown, the Customer ID# — consisting of the first five letters of the customer's last name (or company name) and the five digits of the zip code — can be entered.

If this latter shot at pulling up the customer's information fails, it's likely that you have a first-time buyer here, and a customer record will need to be created before the invoice for his order can be processed.

In such a case, a pair of simple macros can be used, one to take you directly to Add Data in CUSTOMER.DTF, and the other to return you from CUSTOMER.DTF to Add Data in INVOICE.DTF.

From INVOICE.DTF to CUSTOMER.DTF

Record your invoice-to-customer file macro starting from a displayed invoice form in Add Data with the following steps. The actual macro keystrokes are shown in boldface.

1. Define your macro.

2. With the recorder on, press **<Esc>** from the invoice form on the screen.

3. Answer **Y** to confirm that you want to exit without saving. You'll exit to the File menu.

4. Type **A** for Add Data.

5. Type **CUSTOMER** (or the complete path) to specify the file you want to open.

6. Press **<Enter>** to bring up a fresh, blank customer form.

7. End your recording and save the macro.

 Note: A note here concerning network applications and @NUMBER, since our invoice numbers are generated by the @NUMBER command at the Initial Values Spec.

Q&A assigns the @NUMBER as soon as a new form is displayed (if specified at the Initial Values Spec), or when a programming statement assigning the @NUMBER is executed. In a single-user environment Q&A *reuses* the same number if the form is abandoned before saving it.

In a network environment, however, several people may be entering new records in a shared database at the same time, so once the next @NUMBER in sequence is displayed on a form, that number cannot be reused.

If your database is shared, and you're @NUMBERing your forms, you might consider doing so with an on-record-exit programming statement, or at least a command that assigns the @NUMBER after the operator has gone past the point where the record is likely to be abandoned.

From CUSTOMER.DTF Back to INVOICE.DTF

When the new customer record has been filled in, the second macro is invoked, automating the following steps. Again, the macro keystrokes are shown in boldface:

1. Define the macro.

2. Press **<Shift><F10>** to save the new customer record and exit to the File menu.

3. Type **A** to select Add Data.

4. Type **INVOICE** (or the complete path) to specify the file.

5. Press **<Enter>** to bring up a fresh invoice form.

6. End your recording and save the macro.

The operator can now enter the new CU#, or press **<Tab>** and enter the Customer ID string, and the new customer's name, address, and so forth will be retrieved into the appropriate fields in the invoice.

Posting Invoice Numbers to Customer Records

You may want your system set up so that the invoice number is posted to the customer's record, and the record is updated with the customer's total dollar purchases to date. Having this information in the customer database can prove valuable in a number of ways:

- You'll know at a glance what your customers have spent with you without having to design a report totaling up their invoice dollar amounts.

- Having the last invoice number in the customer record will identify the customer's most recently processed order (invoice), which can then be looked up to answer a "where's my order?" query.

- The last invoice number for the customer reveals how recently he bought from you. Those who haven't patronized you for months can be sent a friendly personalized mail-merge letter ("Hello! — are you still there?") with a special inducement to buy. Those who don't respond can then be justifiably deleted from the file.

Our CUSTOMER.DTF form design already includes the two fields you'll need: Amt Purch to Date, and Last Inv#. To get this data from the invoices over to the customer records, you can design a Posting Spec along the following lines:

- Your Post-from (source) file is INVOICE.DTF. Your Post-to (destination) file is CUSTOMER.DTF. The Match Field in the destination file is the CU# (Customer number). Your Retrieve Spec is today's invoices only (you'll run this Post daily).

- When the fields in the two files match:

1. Post the Invoice Number from INVOICE.DTF to the Last Inv# field of the CUSTOMER.DTF record, *replacing* any existing value in the target field.

2. Post the value from the Total Invoice field in INVOICE.DTF to the Amt Purch to Date field in the destination record, *adding* the value to the existing value in the target file.

- Run the post on a daily basis, after all the invoices have been entered. Be sure to test it first on a few dummy records to make sure it's working properly.

You can create a macro to run the post for you with a single keystroke combination. You can then edit the macro file to have this macro called by a previous macro — the one that runs the *Daily Invoice Post to Stock*, for example.

In fact, you can string all your day-end batch operation macros together, having the first one call the second, the second one call the third, and so forth. Storing these kinds of macros in a macro file of their own — other than QAMACRO.ASC, so they have to be loaded into memory before launching — will help prevent their being accidentally triggered by an operator with slippery fingers.

A Purchase Order Database

The role of PO.DTF as a component in our order-processing system is to generate purchase orders for stock items that we sell, not for office supplies. You can, of course, design a general-purpose purchase order database for office consumables like pens and paper clips, or easily adapt the one we'll design here, but it won't integrate with the larger application we're tackling in this and the following chapter.

What we want PO.DTF to do in particular is to provide a fully automated method of preparing purchase orders for our stock items. And since purchase order activity relates to inventory, we want our inventory records to reflect the quantities of any stock items placed on order through purchase orders, and have those On Order quantities added to the On Hand quantities once the ordered items have been received into stock.

We'll be designing a Posting Spec around PO.DTF just as we did with INVOICE.DTF above. PO.DTF uses both STOCK.DTF and VENDOR.DTF as lookup files, and the workability of both the lookups and the Posting Specs will depend on the designs of the three forms as they've been structured in this chapter. Once you understand how the purchase order form works — especially the lookup commands programmed into it — and the design of our Posting Spec, you'll be in better shape to customize this end of the system to your own liking.

Looking over the PO.DTF form in Figure 10-5 (this database, fully programmed as follows, is included on your Applications disk) notice that it contains fields for the information you'll want on file about your purchase orders, and also what the supplier is likely to need to know in order to process and deliver your order to you.

```
━━━━━━━━ PURCHASE ORDER ━━━━━━━

┌──────────────────────────────────────────┐
│ PO Number: #5    Date: #10               │
│ [ →]Mail-in  [ →]Call-in  [ →]FAX-in     │
│ Acct#: #30       Buyer: #35              │
└──────────────────────────────────────────┘
                                    ┌──────── BILL TO ────────┐
                                    │ #40                      │
                                    │ #45                      │
                                    │ #50                      │
Vendor# #55                         └──────────────────────────┘
                                    ┌──────── SHIP TO ────────┐
                    Attn Sales      │ #60                      │
                                    │ #65                      │
┌──────────────────────┐           │ #70                      │
│ #75                   │           └──────────────────────────┘
│ #80                   │
│ #85                   │           ─────── SHIP VIA ───────
│ #90                   │           #95
└──────────────────────┘           #100
```

Please supply these items. Any prices shown are our estimates

	Our Stk#	Your Number		Description	Price	Qty	Amount
1	#101	#102	#103		#104	#105	#106
2	#201	#202	#203		#205	#205	#206
3	#301	#302	#303		#305	#305	#306
4	#401	#402	#403		#405	#405	#406
5	#501	#502	#503		#505	#505	#506
6	#601	#602	#603		#605	#605	#606
7	#701	#702	#703		#705	#705	#706
8	#801	#802	#803		#805	#805	#806

#900
Remarks— #905

All items are for resale (California Resale Permit No. SR AL 12-722-344).
Please extend your most favorable trade terms.

Backorders and partial shipments accepted, but please advise buyer at
213-123-4567 Ext 233, or by FAX at 212-321-7654 of any shipment delays.

Trade references available on request. Pro-forma invoices acceptable if
required for first order.

(Optional) [] Our check no._____in the amount of $_____ is enclosed.
Please bill any additional charges, or issue credit for overpayment.

```
┌──────────────────── Office use only ────────────────────┐
│ Estimated arrival date │ #910 │  Actual arrival date │ #915 │
│                                                          │
│    Do received items match PO? [ → ]   All contents undamaged? [ → ] │
│       —Explain below any discrepancies and handling done—            │
│ #930                                                     │
│ #935                                                     │
│ #940                                                     │
│ Invoice# #945                                            │
│ PO Value #950                                            │
│ Pay Code #955      │ Date PO Closed #960                 │
└──────────────────────────────────────────────────────────┘
```

Figure 10-5: The PO.DTF Form. It is shown here with the Program Spec Field ID numbers in place. The form is three screen pages long, enabling it to fit on a standard 8½-by-11-inch page.

- "PURCHASE ORDER," accentuated with ASCII graphics characters, appears right at the very top of the form — and the form itself appears on screen as it appears when printed out on paper.

- The box in the upper-left-hand corner of the form displays the purchase order number, the date it was cut, how it was forwarded to the vendor, your account number with the vendor, and your buyer's name.

- Separate areas are included for billing and shipping addresses, and there's a field to specify the desired shipping method.

- Fields #75 through #90 are for the supplier's name and address, positioned on the form so that when printed on 8½-by-11-inch paper the purchase order can be letter-folded and inserted into a standard #10 window envelope with the address exposed. You won't need to type an envelope.

- The purchase order can accommodate up to eight line items, with fields for your stock number, the supplier's stock number, the description, price, quantity, and amount.

- A multiline field is placed directly beneath the line items box for any special instructions you may want to pass on to the vendor about the order.

- The body of text on the form directly below the Remarks field tells the supplier a little about your company and what you expect from him. It's there to give you a few ideas. You supply whatever text you need for this area of the form.

- At the bottom of the form, in the Office Use Only area, you see fields for entering the estimated and actual arrival dates (of the ordered items), fields where any problems or discrepancies can be noted, and a few additional fields that I'll discuss in more detail below.

This area of the form is designed to serve as a receiver. When you print out the purchase order, a copy goes to the Receiving Department. Then, when the shipment arrives, your receiving clerk checks the shipment against the ordered items and hands the form in to the office with any discrepancies noted.

While the PO.DTF form in Figure 10-5 may appear imposing at this stage, you'll find that it's extremely fast and easy to use. It practically fills itself in — and even inexperienced operators get the hang of it after entering only a few

```
Field Label    ID#          Width   Formatting      Additional Requirements

PO Number      #5           6       N,JR       @NUMBER at Initial Values Spec,
Date           #10          12      D          @DATE at Initial Values Spec, Re
                                               You'll sort or retrieve often on
Mail-in        #15          1       T,U        These three fields don't actuall
Call-in        #20          1       T,U        simply types X in the one that i
Fax-in         #25          1       T,U        being forwarded to the vendor, b
Acct#          #30          10      T,U        Your account number with the ven
                                               automatically.
Buyer          #35          15      T,I        The name of the person placing t
None           #40-#50      35      T,U        The three BILL TO name and addre
Vendor#        #55          5       N          The vendor number assigned to th
                                               automatically.
None           #60-#70      35      T,U        The three SHIP TO name and addre
None           #75-#90      35      T,U        The four vendor name and address
None           #95          35      T,U        The operator enters a code to sp
                                               Filled-in automatically.
None           #100         35      T          A message field to enforce entry
```

Figure 10-6: Field Requirements for Top Ares of PO Form.

purchase orders. You'll see what I mean as we define the fields below, and then add our programming afterward.

Requirements for fields at the top of the purchase order form are illustrated in Figure 10-6 and discussed on the pages that follow.

Line Item Fields

The purchase order contains enough fields for eight line items (lines 1 through 8 in Figure 10-5). Each line of the purchase order has six fields across. The only fields that will contain any programming are the eight fields under the Our Stk# column and the eight fields under the Amount column. We'll program the Our Stk# fields to look up the vendor's stock number, the description, and price (vendor's price) when a valid stock number has been entered. The fields under the Amount column will be programmed to place the product of the Price times the Qty in the Amount fields and move on to the next line item.

- The eight fields under Our Stk# in the purchase order are 6-character text fields. Their field labels are 1, 2, 3, etc.

- The eight fields under Your Number are 10-character text fields. These will contain the vendor's part numbers looked up from the matching STOCK.DTF records.

- The eight fields under the Description heading are 30-character text fields to contain the descriptions of the items being ordered, retrieved from the matching STOCK.DTF records.

- The eight fields under the Price heading are 8-character money fields containing the costs of the items (the vendor's prices) retrieved from the matching STOCK.DTF records.

- The eight Qty fields are 4-character number fields containing the quantities of the items being ordered.

- The eight Amount fields are 4-character money fields that will be filled in by programming statements that multiply the Price field by the Quantity field.

Receiver Area Fields

The bottom of the purchase order form as shown in Figure 10-5 (Office Use Only) is for your use, not the supplier's. The text in this area of the form is self-explanatory.

When the purchase order is created, the operator can enter an Estimated Arrival Date (field #910) that can become the basis for follow-up reports on outstanding or overdue purchase orders. When the goods arrive and the operator has the written receiving report (from the copy of the purchase order used by the receiving department), the Actual Arrival Date field can be filled in, along with fields #920 through #960, making this area of the form a sort of permanent mini-receiving report for the purchase order.

If having the hard copy of the receiving report is enough, you may not want to bother entering the details in the database when the items are received from the vendor. But in any case you'll want to enter the date the purchase order was closed in the very last field on the form. Otherwise, when you pull open purchase order reports you won't be able to tell Q&A how to differentiate between purchase orders that are closed and those that are still open.

- Fields #910 and #915 are 12-character date fields.

- Fields #920 and #925 (both containing the →symbol in Figure 10-5) are 1-character Yes/No fields.

- Fields #930, #935, and #940 are 70-character text fields designed to contain any discrepancies in the received items, along with what was done to rectify the problem.

- Field #945 contains the vendor's invoice number so the vendor's billing can be matched against the appropriate purchase order.

- Field #950, a 10-character money field, will be filled in by a programming statement that totals the Amount fields.

- Field #955 can contain a code that authorizes payment of the vendor's invoice when all the items have been received in good condition and the purchase order is satisfied.

- Field #960 is a date field containing the date the purchase order was closed.

Entering a New Purchase Order

The following procedure explains how our sample purchase order is designed to work during data entry. Once you've got the flow of it, we'll move on to the programming details.

1. The PO Number and Date fields are filled in automatically using the @NUMBER and @DATE features at the Initial Values Spec, so the first field under the operator's control is the Mail-in field.

2. At the Mail-in field, a help screen pops-up instructing the operator to type **X** into either the Mail-in, Call-in, or Fax-in field. When this is done, the cursor moves to the Buyer field where the buyer's name is entered. The cursor then moves to the BILL TO area of the form.

3. At the first line of the BILL TO area the operator is prompted to enter a code (A, B, or C) that retrieves the BILL TO name and address information from the lookup table. Alternately, unique BILL TO information can be manually entered. The cursor moves to the SHIP TO area of the form.

4. At the first line of the SHIP TO area the operator is prompted to enter a code (A, B, or C) to pull up the SHIP TO name and address information from the lookup table. Alternately, the operator can enter unique SHIP TO information manually, or simply press **<Enter>** from the blank field to enter **Same**. The cursor moves to the SHIP VIA area of the form.

5. At the SHIP VIA field, the operator is prompted to enter a code (1-9) that corresponds to the preferred shipping method. Once a valid code has been entered, the cursor moves to the first Our Stk# field.

6. If an invalid stock number is entered, an error message is displayed in field #900 and the cursor will remain in field #101. When a valid stock number is entered, the programming will retrieve the vendor number for that stock number, place it in field #55, and then pull up the vendor's name and address and place this information in fields #75 through #90. The purchase order is now properly addressed and is locked into this particular vendor (one purchase order cannot go to two different vendors).

The programming in field #101 also retrieves the Vendor Stk#, Description, and Price for the valid stock number, and the operator is prompted to enter the Quantity. Once the Quantity has been entered, the Amount field for that line is calculated and the cursor moves to the next Our Stk# field.

7. The operator now enters the second stock number. If this item is not supplied by the current vendor, an error message displays in field #900 and the cursor doesn't move. When a valid stock number is entered, the Vendor Stk#, Description, and Price are retrieved as above and the operator is prompted for the quantity. If the operator exits a blank stock number field, the programming assumes that there are no more items to enter and the cursor is moved to the Remarks field (#905).

8. Any special instructions to the vendor are entered in the Remarks field and the cursor is moved to the Estimated Arrival Date field where the operator is prompted to enter a date and then press **<F10>** to save the form.

Updating an Existing Purchase Order

The following is what happens when the operator updates a purchase order that's already in the file.

1. When the purchase order is retrieved onto the display, a pop-up help screen provides brief update instructions. The operator can use the cursor and **<PgDn>** key to get to the appropriate area of the form to make the necessary changes.

2. If the purchase order is being retrieved in order to enter receiving information, the operator presses **<PgDn>** three times to get to the bottom of the form where the appropriate receiving information is entered. If the purchase order is being retrieved to change line item information (add another item, change a quantity, etc.), the operator presses **<PgDn>** twice to get to *that* area of the form.

3. When the changes have been made, the operator presses **<F10>** to save the updated form, or **<Shift><F10>** to save the form and exit to the File menu.

Now that you understand the flow of the form during data entry, let's look at the programming that makes it possible for the form to work this way.

Programming the PO Form

Since most of the fields on the purchase order have no labels, I'll refer only to the field ID numbers in the programming statements below. Use Figure 10-5 as your reference. You can also have Q&A running on your computer with the Program Spec for PO.DTF displayed, and go back and forth from the Program Spec to Add Data to get a feel for how the programming works when entering a new record.

Where any of the programming statements below contain GOTO commands, you should enter these cursor moves at the Field Navigation Spec also, especially if this database will be shared on a network that includes Macintosh computers. Field navigation programming is discussed in Chapter 4.

`<#15: If @add then @help(#15) else @help(#5)`

When adding a new form, this statement pops up the help screen for field #15 with instructions on how to fill in one of the three fields: Mail-in, Call-in, or Fax-in. When updating the form, the help screen for field #5 displays giving update-specific instructions.

`<#20:If #15<>"" then goto #35`

When the cursor enters the Call-in field, if the preceding field isn't blank the cursor is moved to the Buyer field.

`<#25:If #15<>"" or #20<>"" then goto #35`

When the cursor enters the Fax-in field, if either of the preceding two fields contain a value, the cursor is moved to the Buyer field.

`<#35: If #15="" and #20="" and #25="" then goto #15 else @msg("Enter buyer's name")`

When the cursor enters the Buyer field, if all the fields on the line above are blank, the cursor is moved back to field #15, and the help screen redisplays. Otherwise, the operator is prompted to enter the buyer's name.

`<#40:@help(#40)`

When the cursor enters the first line of the BILL TO area, the help screen for field #40 displays informing the operator of the available choices.

`<#45: If #40="A" or #40="B" or #40="C" then {lookup(#40,3,#50); lookup(#40,2,#45);lookup(#40,1,#40); goto #60}; If #40="" then goto #40`

When the cursor enters field #45 (the second BILL TO field), if the operator has entered **A, B,** or **C** in the field above, a series of three lookup commands is executed, retrieving the name and address for company A, B, or C from the lookup table, and the cursor is moved to the SHIP TO area of the form. If the operator entered something else in field #40, the lookups won't execute on the assumption that some different company name and address is to be entered. The cursor is returned to field #40 if it was left blank, and the help screen for that field redisplays.

The lookup table here contains **A, B,** and **C** in the Key column, the company names in column 1, the street addresses in column 2, and the cities, states, and zips in column 3.

```
>#50: goto #60
```

When the cursor leaves the third and final BILL TO field (in the case of manually entered BILL TO information) we want the cursor to move to the SHIP TO area of the form.

```
<#60:@help(#60)
```

When the cursor enters the first SHIP TO field, the help screen for that field displays giving the operator the options.

```
<#65:If #60="" then {#60 = "SAME"; goto #95};
If #60="A" or #60="B" or #60="C"then {lookup(#60,3,#70);
lookup(#60,2,#65); lookup (#60, 1,#60);goto #95}
```

When the cursor enters the second SHIP TO line, if the preceding field has been left blank the programming assumes the SHIP TO information is the same as the BILL TO information, places **Same** in field #60, and moves the cursor to field #95. But if **A, B,** or **C** has been entered in field #60, the programming picks up the appropriate information from the lookup table, places it in the SHIP TO fields, and then moves the cursor to field #95.

```
<#95: @help(#95)
```

When the cursor enters field #95, the help screen for that field pops up instructing the operator to enter a shipping method code. The help screen shows the valid codes along with descriptions of what they stand for (parcel post or UPS Ground, for example).

```
<#100:lookup(#95,1,#95);If #95="" then {#100 =
"You must enter a shipping code"; goto #95} else
{#100="";goto #101}
```

When the cursor enters the field directly below the shipping method field, the programming consults the Lookup Table, matches the code with the Key column in the table, and retrieves the shipping method into field #95. If field #95 has been left blank, field #100 displays the message: "You must enter a shipping code," returns the cursor to field #95, and the shipping code help screen redisplays.

If a valid shipping code has been entered (use the Restrict Values Spec to allow any number 1 through 9), the message field (#100) is blanked, and the cursor is moved to field #101 where the operator enters the first stock number.

```
>#101: Xlookup("stock",#101,"stk#","vendor#",#55);
If#55="" then {#900 = "Vendor Number missing for this
Stock Number Record. Press <F1>";goto #101};#900="";
Xlookup("Vendor",#55,"Vendor#","acct#",#30,"Company",
#75,"Addr1",#80,"Addr2",#85,"Addr3",#90);
Xlookup(`stock"",#101,"stk#", "VendorStk#",#102,
"description", #103,"cost",#104); goto #105
```

We're now into the line items area of the purchase order. The operator enters the first stock number and presses **<Tab>** or **<Enter>**. A valid stock number retrieves the Vendor# from the matching STOCK.DTF record, and places this number in field #55. If no Vendor# can be returned from this stock number, the message above displays in field #900 prompting the operator to press **<F1>** for more help, and the cursor is returned to field #101. This is an important step since the vendor's name and address is dependent on the value entered in the Vendor# field.

Once the Vendor# has been retrieved into field #55, the next part of the statement returns the vendor's name and address (from VENDOR.DTF) to the appropriate fields on the purchase order (fields #75-#90) from a match on the Vendor#. Once this has occurred, this purchase order cannot be used to order stock numbers from another vendor — only one vendor per purchase order.

The final portion of the statement now executes, retrieving the Vendor Stk#, the Description, and the Cost from the STOCK.DTF record that matches the stock number entered in field #101, and the cursor is moved to the first Qty field, prompting the operator to enter the quantity of the item that's being ordered.

```
<#106=#104*#105;goto  #201
```

When the cursor enters this first Amount field, the Price field is multiplied by the Qty field, the result is placed in the Amount field, and the cursor is moved to the next stock number field for entry of the second purchase order line item.

```
>#201:If #201=""then goto #905; If @xlookup ("stock",
#201,"stk#", "vendor#") <>#55 then {#900="Invalid Stock
Number for this Vendor. Try again""; goto #201} else
{#900=""; xlookup("stock", #201, "stk#","vendor
stk#",#202,"description",#203,"cost",#204); goto #205}
```

The programming in field #201 is similar to that of field #101, except that since the Vendor#, name, and address has already been established, we simply need to validate that the stock number entered in field #201 connects with the current vendor. If it doesn't, the warning message displays, and the cursor is returned to field #201.

If the stock number entered for this vendor is correct, then the Vendor Stk#, Description, and Cost information is retrieved from the matching STOCK.DTF record and the cursor is moved to the Qty field on that same line. If the stock number field is left blank, the programming assumes there are no more entries for this purchase order, and the cursor is moved to field #905.

Amount fields #206, #306, #406, #506, #606, and #706 are programmed exactly like #106 except for the field ID# references. These change from line to line as you can see in Figure 10-5.

Our Stk# fields #301, #401, #501, #601, #701, and #801 are programmed exactly like field #201 except for the different field ID# references. For example, wherever a field ID number starts with **2** in the programming for field #201, this **2** would be changed to a **3** in the programming for field #301, and so forth for the 4th, 5th, 6th, 7th, and 8th line item lines of the purchase order.

```
<#806=#804*#805; goto #905
```

This is the last field of the last line item line of the purchase order. So the cursor is now moved to field #905.

```
<#905:  #950=#106+#206+#306+#406+#506+#606+#706+#806;
@help(#905)
```

When the cursor enters field #905 (Remarks), the Amount fields are totaled and the result placed in field #950 (PO Value) at the bottom of the form. The help screen for field #905 then displays, prompting the operator to enter any instructions for the vendor with regard to this purchase order.

```
<#910: If @add then @help(#910) else goto #915
```

In Add Data, the operator gets a help screen prompting the operator to enter an estimated arrival date, and then press **<F10>** to save the form. If updating the form, the cursor is moved to the next field.

```
<#915: If @update then @help(#915)
```

If updating the purchase order (such as closing it out after the items have been received), a help screen pops up with brief instructions on how to fill out the receiver portion of the form and then save it to disk.

This is all the programming that's necessary to construct a friendly, quick, and relatively error-proof purchase order form. Depending on your needs you can, of course, customize the form even further, particularly the custom help screens. You've got your vendor information in VENDOR.DTF and your product information in STOCK.DTF, and you're making extensive use of Q&A's XLOOKUP feature to tap into these external files and help the operator complete the purchase order swiftly. Create your lookup table along the lines suggested above, automate your cursor moves to your best advantage, add help and other messages where a new operator is likely to need them, and you have a powerful tool that makes short work of your routine purchase orders, whether you're generating one a day or 500 a month.

Posting Purchase Order Data to the STOCK.DTF Records

At the end of the day you'll want to post your purchase order information to your STOCK.DTF records.

The STOCK.DTF records will then reflect what's been placed on order with your vendors. When the operator is entering an invoice, he or she will be able to see not only the quantity of the items that are in stock, but also the quantities on order. If the invoice In Stock window shows only three of Item X on hand when the operator is entering an order for 10, he or she will then know if more are on the way and can act accordingly. If the situation is critical, someone can always look up the purchase order and follow up with the vendor to find out when the order will be delivered.

Having the STOCK.DTF records reflect any quantities on order will serve the additional purpose of a management information tool. You can pull a report at any time showing a list of products, quantities on hand, quantities on order, minimum reorder level, and how many of each item you've sold so far during the current month. The information can help you better manage your inventory and purchase-ordering activities.

Posting ordered quantities from PO.DTF to the matching records in STOCK.DTF is similar to posting invoiced quantities from INVOICE.DTF to STOCK.DTF. Figure 10-2 shows the STOCK.DTF form. The field you're concerned with in STOCK.DTF is On Order — that's your posting target field. Here are the steps you'll need to take to get your information from PO.DTF over to STOCK.DTF at the end of each day:

1. From the File menu select **T - Post,** type **PO.DTF** as the file to post *from*, press **<Enter>**, and type **STOCK.DTF** as the file to post *to*, and press **<Enter>**.

2. Q&A now displays the Retrieve Spec for the source file PO.DTF. Move to the Date field and type **{@Date}**. This function returns the current date

(meaning that it retrieves only the current day's purchase orders). Enter any other retrieve criteria to select only those purchase orders whose values you want to post to STOCK.DTF. Press **<Shift><F8>** and save your Retrieve Spec as *Daily PO Post to Stock*, then press **<Enter>** to save the spec, and then press **<F10>** to continue.

3. At the Posting Spec screen for *Daily PO Post to Stock*, Q&A displays the purchase order form. Press **<Tab>** until the highlight is in the first Qty field.

4. Press **<F7>** and fill in the displayed Posting box as follows:

```
Post the value of field F0016 into external field:
On Order
When the field: 1 matches the external field Stk#
in STOCK.DTF
Operation: Add
```

- **F0016** is the source file field whose value you want to post to the destination file target field. (You can name these fields at the Field Names spec.)

- **On Order** is the destination file post-to (target) field.

- **1** is the field label of the first purchase order line item whose value matches the external field Stk#.

- **Add** is the operation you want performed. (We're using **Add** rather than **Replace** in case another purchase order is currently open for any particular stock number and that previously ordered quantity is already in the On Order field.)

5. When you've filled out the Posting box for the first line item Qty field, press **<F7>** to close the Posting Block, and press the down arrow key to move to the *second* purchase order line item Qty field.

6. You now fill in the Posting box as in step 4 above, except that your source match field is now **2** instead of **1**.

7. Continue with this procedure until all eight purchase order line items are included in the Batch Posting Spec. Your source file match fields will be 3, 4, 5, 6, 7, and 8, through the eight purchase order lines.

8. After you've filled in the Posting box from your last purchase order Ord column field, press **<F8>** for the Auto Program Recalc screen shown in Figure 10-4, and be sure Calculation Statements are set to No — no STOCK.DTF calculations are necessary during this posting operation.

9. When you've finished the Batch Posting Spec, press **<Shift><F8>** and save it to *Daily PO Post to Stock*. When you've pressed **<Enter>** and **<F10>**, Q&A will and ask if you want to execute the Post now. Answer No unless you've entered some purchase orders today and are ready to run the post.

You'll want to thoroughly test your new Posting Spec on a few dummy purchase orders and stock records before incorporating it with confidence into your order-processing system. Be sure to verify that all Qty fields in the purchase order are posting properly, and that the fields in the corresponding STOCK.DTF records are showing the correct figures.

On a daily basis, then, you can execute your *Daily PO Post to Stock* just like your *Daily Invoice Post to Stock*.

Now we need a way to update our STOCK.DTF records when items on order from our vendors have been received. This can be tricky for the following two reasons:

- You may have placed a purchase order for five different products from the same vendor, but only the first three of those products have been delivered to you. Do you want to wait until the other two products arrive before updating all five STOCK.DTF records? Probably not, because the information in your system wouldn't be consistent with the state of your actual available inventory.

- You may have ordered ten of Item X, but the vendor has shipped you only six, back ordering the other four. You'll want your system to reflect that you now have the additional six of Item X on hand, and that four are still on order from the vendor.

There are a number of ways to handle these situations. If every vendor delivered the correct quantity of each item on your purchase order — and all the items on the PO arrived at the same time — the task would be far easier. But that's not always going to be the case. So we need a method to *selectively* post quantities received to the STOCK.DTF records. In other words, when six of Item X have arrived, we want to be able to deduct those six from the On Order field in the Item X STOCK.DTF record (leaving the other four still on order), and also add the six received to the On Hand field. Then, when all the items ordered on the purchase order have been received in good order, and the purchase order is satisfied, we can then close the purchase order and file it away.

The one thing we *don't* want to have to do is manually Search/Update the relevant STOCK.DTF records one at a time as the items are received. Since

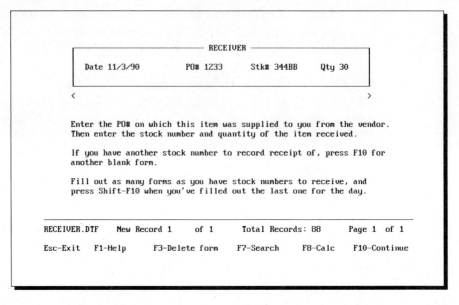

```
                          ─────── RECEIVER ───────
          ┌──────────────────────────────────────────────────────────────┐
          │  Date 11/3/90        PO# 1233      Stk# 344BB      Qty 30      │
          │                                                                │
          └──────────────────────────────────────────────────────────────┘

           <                                                             >


          Enter the PO# on which this item was supplied to you from the vendor.
          Then enter the stock number and quantity of the item received.

          If you have another stock number to record receipt of, press F10 for
          another blank form.

          Fill out as many forms as you have stock numbers to receive, and
          press Shift-F10 when you've filled out the last one for the day.


        ─────────────────────────────────────────────────────────────────

        RECEIVER.DTF    New Record 1      of 1      Total Records: 88      Page 1  of 1

        Esc-Exit    F1-Help       F3-Delete form     F7-Search     F8-Calc    F10-Continue
```

Figure 10-7: The RECEIVER.DTF Form. It is shown in Add Data mode with values entered for the stock number, quantity, current date, and purchase order number. You fill out one form for each stock number received during the day and, at the end of the day, post the quantities from the current day's forms to the Recd field of STOCK.DTF.

we're obliged to inform our system when any stock items have arrived, we expect to do *some* input, but we want to automate the procedure to make it as painless as possible.

Posting Received Items to STOCK.DTF

Because of the variables involved in receiving items from vendors on purchase orders (for example, when a purchase order stays open for weeks because the vendor ships your order to you in partials), you'll want an update tool for your STOCK.DTF records that's both fast and flexible. A Posting Spec can supply the ideal solution.

You've ordered 20 of Item X on purchase order Number 1022, but the vendor ships you only 15, telling you the rest will be shipped in another two weeks. Or you've ordered 20 each of Item X, Item Y, and Item Z on the same P.O., but you receive only Item X. Items Y and Z will be along later.

In both cases, you can't close the purchase order — it hasn't yet been satisfied — but you'll want your system to reflect that the items that *have* arrived are now available to fill orders from *your* customers.

Posting Received Items with a Supplementary Database

One approach you can use to update your stock records with quantities received involves the use of a simple supplementary database and a Posting Spec, both of which are included on your Applications disk.

Your database, RECEIVER.DTF, should contain fields for the stock number, quantity, current date (@DATE at the Initial Values Spec), and purchase order number (see Figure 10-7). You simply fill out a record for each stock number received during the day, and at the end of the day run a predefined batch post that adds the quantities received today to the matching STOCK.DTF records, and executes the programming statement in the STOCK.DTF Recd field that updates the corresponding On Order and On Hand fields as above.

This method has its advantages. First of all, it yields a computer record of what was received and when. Secondly, you can run reports from RECEIVER.DTF sorted by purchase order number, compare the information with your purchase orders, and spot which purchase orders should be closed (because all the items on them have been received).

Follow these steps to create and use a RECEIVER.DTF database:

1. Design the form along the lines shown in Figure 10-7, placing a large text field immediately below the box (as shown by the **<** and **>** field delimiter symbols) for error messages.

2. Specify information types for the fields as follows: Date=**D,** PO#=**N,** Stk#=**TU,** and Qty=**N,** and format the large message field as text, justified center (**T, JR**).

3. Set the Date field to **@Date** at the Initial Values Spec, and make it Read-only.

4. At the Program Spec, program the form as follows:

```
Date: #2 (no programming)

PO#: >#4: If @xlookup("PO",#4,""PO Number","PO
Number") =#4 then {#10="; goto #6} else
{#10="In  valid PO Number — No such PO Number on
File"; goto #4}
```

This statement checks the purchase order number entered to see if it exists. If there is no such purchase order number, the "Invalid PO..."

message is displayed and the cursor is returned to the field. Otherwise, the cursor is moved to the next field.

```
Stk#: >#6: If @xlookup("Stock",#6,"Stk#","Stk")=#6
then {#10="";goto #8} else {#10="Invalid Stock
Number — No such Stock Number on File"; goto #6}
```

The statement checks the validity of the stock number entered against the STOCK.DTF file. If there is no such record, the error message displays and the cursor is returned to the field.

```
Qty: #8 (no programming)
```

5. Once the form design is complete, create and save a Posting Spec that designates the destination file as STOCK.DTF, the matching key field as Stk# (in both files), the source post field as Qty, and the target file post-to field as Recd. Be sure to specify, at the Programming Executions Options screen, that you want the calculation statements in STOCK.DTF executed during the post. Press **<F8>** from the Posting Spec to reach this screen.

Your Retrieve Spec for the Posting Spec should be **{@Date}** in the Date field. This way, when you run the post, only the current date's forms in RECEIVER.DTF will be included in the post. Save and name both the Retrieve and Posting Specs with **<Shift><F8>**, and run the post at the end of any day where you've received purchase order items ordered from your suppliers.

Closing Off Purchase Orders

When all the items on a purchase order have been received, you'll want to close that purchase order by entering the current date in the Date PO Closed field in PO.DTF. Failure to do this will result in all your purchase orders appearing to be open, and you won't be able to pull a report on open purchase orders only.

You can automate the procedure for closing purchase orders by creating a Mass Update Spec, by using a macro, or by defining a table view of your open purchase orders with the purchase order number in column 1 and the Date PO Closed field in column 2. If you're only going to be closing a few purchase orders a week, however, you might as well just call up the appropriate purchase orders one at a time, move the cursor down to the Date PO Closed field manually, press **<Ctrl><F5>** to auto-type the current date, and then press **<Shift><F10>** to save the updated record and exit back to the File menu.

If you use a Mass Update Spec, its Retrieve Spec will include the numbers of the purchase orders you want to close off, entered in the PO Number field, with each number separated by a semicolon. Your Update Spec will be as follows:

Date PO Closed: #1=@date

You can automate even this simple procedure with a macro that pauses at the PO.DTF Retrieve Spec PO Number field for you to enter the relevant purchase order numbers. Then, when you press **<Enter>**, the macro will continue to play back with your saved Update Spec (as above) now closing those purchase orders off for you automatically.

If you want to avoid a mass update, and do the procedure entirely by macro, have the macro pause at the PO.DTF Retrieve Spec for you to enter the appropriate purchase order number, pull up that purchase order, move the cursor down to the Date PO Closed field, and auto-type the current date. You can make the macro repeat itself using the technique described in the section on the nested macro application in Chapter 8, allowing you to close off several purchase orders quickly, simply by entering the purchase order number each time the macro pauses for operator input.

Should you prefer to use an editable table view of your open purchase orders to close them, you can create a macro which, when invoked, takes you directly to that view with the cursor already in the Date PO Closed column. From there you can quite easily navigate to the appropriate records and press **<Ctrl><F5>** to plug in the current date.

Adding More Power to INVOICE.DTF

The invoice database is at the very heart of our order-processing system, for here we have the most data to enter on a daily basis, the largest variety of variables, and a veritable treasuretrove of management information.

I designed and programmed the invoice form in Chapter 4 with the accent on making data entry as fully automated as possible, and a promise was made that I'd explore a way to have UPS shipping charges automatically calculated during invoice data entry. You'll find out how to do that in this section.

Also, you may recall that we placed a date field at the top of the invoice form (the third field) when we designed it in Chapter 4 and that the purpose of this field was to contain the actual shipping date of the order. We want to record this information so should the customer call about his order he can be told when and how it was shipped (if it was actually shipped) simply by retrieving the invoice in question. So further ahead in this section we'll also create a supplementary database where we can record invoice numbers and shipping dates, and from which we can post this information to the invoices once a day.

Both of these components of the application, by the way, are provided with the relevant files in your Applications disk.

UPS Shipping Charges Displayed During Invoice Input

There are distinct advantages to having shipping charges automatically calculated and displayed during invoice entry — the major one being that these charges can then be added to the invoice right then and there, without the order having to first be weighed.

Of course, determining the shipment's weight with programming will result in an approximation; the exact weight can't be known with certainty until the shipment is packaged up and placed on the scales. But if you know your packaging materials, and if the item weights in the Weight fields in STOCK.DTF are accurate, you can obtain a figure that's awfully close to the actual shipping cost, if not dead-on.

To have your invoices calculate UPS shipping charges you'll need the following elements:

- UPS rate charts for your zip code area for both ground and air shipments. We'll limit this portion of our application to UPS *domestic* shipments only.

- A lookup table for INVOICE.DTF that contains the range of zip code prefixes in the Key column, and the corresponding ground, second-day air, and next-day air zones in columns 1, 2, and 3.

- A supplementary database containing the UPS rates, by zone, for each weight value from 1 to 70 pounds (70 pounds is the heaviest single parcel UPS will handle).

- Programming in INVOICE.DTF that will calculate the weight of the order, use the UPS zip code prefix and type of service to find the appropriate zone, look up the charges from the external rates database based on the weight and zone, and display those charges on the invoice. This programming is spelled out in Chapter 4, and is included in INVOICE.DTF on your Apps disk.

Note: A complete UPS Manifesting system for Q&A 4.0 is covered in detail in Chapter 12.

Assuming you have the UPS rate charts for your area, let's start with the lookup table we'll need to find the proper UPS zone based on the customer's zip code prefix and type of service specified on the invoice.

UPS Zone Lookup Table for INVOICE.DTF

UPS uses the first three digits of the destination zip code along with the type of service desired to determine what it calls the *UPS Service Zone.* This is no problem because our invoices contain the type of UPS service when UPS is specified, and our programming in INVOICE.DTF looks up the zip code.

The zip code prefix can be obtained by a programming statement that removes the last two digits from the customer's five-digit ship-to zip code. The type of service is specified in the Ship Via field of the invoice, and where that value is either **UPS Ground**, **UPS Second Day**, or **UPS Next Day**, the programming will be able to retrieve and display the correct rate for the calculated weight of the invoice.

UPS supplies two rate charts: one for surface shipments, and the other for air shipments. In the case of surface (ground) shipments, zones are determined by *zip code prefix ranges.* For example, prefixes 300 to 399 (representing zip code 30000 at the lower end of the range, and 39999 at the upper end) may be zone 6, while prefixes 400 through 485 may be zone 7. It all depends on where you're shipping *from.*

As a result, you need to structure your lookup table so that the Key column contains each prefix that represents the starting or *lower* value in the range for any particular zone. Using the sample prefixes above, type **300** in the Key column of your lookup table, and **6** in the corresponding column 1, and then **400** below the **300** in the Key column, and 7 in its corresponding column 1. We'll be using the range lookup command, "LOOKUPR," to return the next lowest value from the lookup table if an exact match cannot be found.

Figure 10-8 shows the first page of a lookup table for a shipper located in the Newport Beach area of Southern California.

Notice that in Figure 10-8 the first two lines of the lookup table are already taken up by entries used in INVOICE.DTF to return the company name. Type your UPS prefixes starting on the next available blank line.

Column 1 of the table contains the UPS surface zones, column 2 contains the second-day air zones, and column 3 contains the next-day air zones. Notice in the Key column for prefix 006 that the corresponding surface zone is No. This

KEY	1	2	3	4
A	Company A Name	12324 Company →	Company A City→	
B	Company B Name	34567 Company →	Company B City→	
004	8	12	22	
006	NO	15	25	
010	8	12	22	
324	8	12	22	
325	7	12	22	
326	8	12	22	
342	8	12	22	
350	7	12	22	
360	8	12	22	
364	7	12	22	
368	8	12	22	
369	7	12	22	
373	7	12	22	
375	8	12	22	
376	7	12	22	

INVOICE.DTF   Lookup Table   Page 1 of 1

Esc-Exit   F6-Expand   PgUp-Previous page   PgDn-Next page   F10-Continue

Figure 10-8: Sample Lookup Table (Page 1) for a UPS Shipper Located in Southern California. UPS zone prefixes start on line 3 of the table.

is because the 006 prefix is Puerto Rico, and no ground (truck) service is available to this location.

Notice also that the second-day air and next-day air zones are all 12 and 22 respectively on this page of the table, except for the 006 prefix whose air zones are 15 and 25.

Let's focus on the two Key column entries, 342, and the one directly below it, 350. If the zip code prefix on the invoice is 342, and ground shipment has been specified, our LOOKUPR programming statement will return zone 8 because an exact match has been found in the lookup table. If the prefix is anywhere *between* 342 and 350 inclusive, the programming will *also* return zone 8 because 342 is the next lowest value in the Key column when an exact match cannot be found. But if the prefix is 350 through 359, zone 7 will be returned to the selected field on the invoice form.

If this is bit hard to comprehend, you'll understand more clearly how the LOOKUPR statement works when we add our related programming to the invoice form.

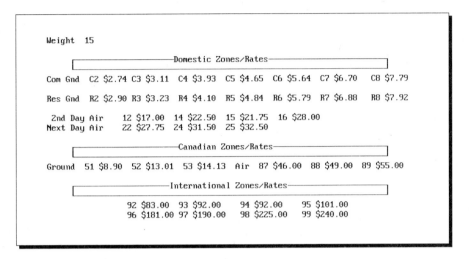

```
Weight   15

┌─────────────────────Domestic Zones/Rates──────────────────────┐
│                                                                 │
Com Gnd   C2 $2.74 C3 $3.11  C4 $3.93   C5 $4.65   C6 $5.64  C7 $6.70    C8 $7.79

Res Gnd   R2 $2.90 R3 $3.23  R4 $4.10   R5 $4.84   R6 $5.79  R7 $6.88    R8 $7.92

 2nd Day Air      12 $17.00  14 $22.50  15 $21.75   16 $28.00
 Next Day Air     22 $27.75  24 $31.50  25 $32.50

┌─────────────────────Canadian Zones/Rates──────────────────────┐
│                                                                 │
Ground   51 $8.90  52 $13.01  53 $14.13  Air  87 $46.00  88 $49.00  89 $55.00

┌───────────────────International Zones/Rates───────────────────┐
│                                                                 │
          92 $83.00  93 $92.00   94 $92.00   95 $101.00
          96 $181.00 97 $190.00  98 $225.00  99 $240.00
```

Figure 10-9: The UPSRATES.DTF Record for 15 Pounds. Rates for the "Com Gnd" (Commercial Ground) and "Res Gnd" (Residential Ground) zones require special field labels because although UPS considers these the same zones, the rates differ depending on whether the delivery address is a residence or a business.

A UPS Rates Database

Once we've established the weight and the proper UPS zone, we can then use XLOOKUP to get the rate in an external database created solely for this purpose. Figure 10-9 shows a sample filled-in record from UPSRATES.DTF. The records are keyed to the weight, not the zone, and the form requires no programming. When you've finished entering all your records, you'll have 70 of them, one for each weight value from 1 to 70 lbs.

The sample form in Figure 10-9 shows all the UPS zones as field labels, including Canadian and other international zones. For our invoice application, however, we'll be using only the domestic zones (through zone 25). The UPSRATES database template on your Applications diskette contains fields corresponding to *all* the UPS service zones as of this writing — as shown in Figure 10-9 — but you'll need to enter the rates unique to your own area. Here's the design rationale behind this lookup database, and a few tips on adding records to it:

- The UPS Ground zone fields (C2 through C8, and R2 through R8) have been placed on separate lines, and the Second Day Air zones

(12 through 16) and Next Day Air zones (22 through 25) also on their own lines. This helps you keep your place on the form when entering the rates from the UPS rate chart.

- The Weight field two characters wide, and the other are fields seven characters wide.

- Format the Weight field for numbers, and make it Speedy and Unique (SU) at the Speed-up Spec.

- All the other fields are formatted for money values.

- When entering your records in Add Data, start with the 1-pound form. Enter **1** in the Weight field, and then, with your UPS rate chart to hand, fill in the rates that correspond to the zones at that 1-pound level. When the record is finished, press **<F10>** to save it, and then do the 2-pound form, and so forth.

- When you've finished with all 70 forms (one for each pound), run a report with column 1 containing the weights, and subsequent columns containing the rates that correspond to the zones 2 through 25. You can use compressed print to fit all the columns across a single 8½-by-11-inch page. Have someone check the rates in the printed report against UPS's own rate charts, just to make sure they're all correct. Any errors can be corrected by updating the offending record(s).

Programming to Calculate and Display UPS Charges

Now that we've got a lookup table to give us the proper UPS service zone, and our external UPSRATES.DTF database to return the UPS charges based on the weight and zone, we need to add the programming statements to INVOICE.DTF to make it all happen smoothly and automatically during invoice input.

Figure 10-10 shows screen page 3 of the invoice form we designed in Chapter 4. Fields #850 and #852, and #890 through #899 are where all the action will take place.

Immediately above the "Backorder Will Ship" area of the form (as seen in Figure 10-10) is the multiline Remarks field, where the cursor is moved when there are no more line items to be entered in the invoice.

From the Remarks field or from the "Backorder Will Ship" area — depending on whether or not there are backordered items to be entered — the cursor is moved to field #848 where the cost of goods sold on the invoice is calculated, and from there the cursor is then moved onto field #850.

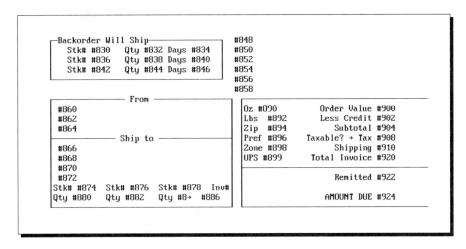

Figure 10-10: Screen Page 3 of the INVOICE.DTF Form at the Program Spec, with Field ID Numbers in Place.

The programming in this field #850 begins the series of events that will ultimately lead to the UPS charges displaying in the UPS field (#899). Here are the relevant programming statements:

```
<#850:   #890=(@xlu("stock",#101,"stk#","weight")*#401)
+(@xlu("stock",#102,"stk#","weight")*#402)
+(@xlu("stock",#103,"stk#","weight")*#403)
+(@xlu("stock",#104,"stk#","weight")*#404)
+(@xlu("stock",#105,"stk#","weight")*#405)
+(@xlu("stock",#106,"stk#","weight")*#406)
+(@xlu("stock",#107,"stk#","weight")*#407)
+(@xlu("stock",#108,"stk#","weight")*#408)
+(@xlu("stock",#109,"stk#","weight")*#409)
+(@xlu("stock",#110,"stk#","weight")*#410);
#892=@round(#890/16*1.05,0);  goto  #852
```

There are three parts to this programming expression. First, the weights for each stock number line item are looked up and multiplied by their corresponding line item quantities; these results are added together and placed into field #890 (the Oz field). @XLU is the abbreviation for @XLOOKUP.

Next, the value just placed in field #890, which is in ounces, is divided by 16 (to get the equivalent pounds), and then multiplied by a factor of 1.05 to add in a little extra weight for packaging materials (experience will determine the appropriate factor for your own business). This result, rounded to the nearest integer, is then placed in field #892 (Lbs).

Finally, the cursor is moved to field #852 where the following programming statements are executed.

```
<#852:  #894=@Xlookup("Customer",#4,"CU#","zip");
#896=@left(#894,3); If #42="UPS Ground" then
{lur(#896,1,#898);  #898="C"+@str(#898);
#899=@xlu("Upsrates",  #892,"Weight",#898)};
If #42="UPS Second Day" then {lur(#896,2,#898);
#899=@xlu("Upsrates",#892,"Weight",#898)};
If #42="UPS Next Day" then {lur(#896,3,#898);
#899=@xlu("Upsrates",#892,  "Weight",#898)};  goto #900
```

The preceding complex expression is the heart and soul of the UPS charges computation. It's a series of statements that carries out the following actions:

1. The programming first looks up the zip code from the customer file and places it in field #894. (Note: you can modify this portion of the expression to pull the zip code directly from the "Ship to" area of the invoice if your customers' shipping address zips frequently differ from their Billing zips.)

2. Next, the @LEFT function is used to get the first three digits of the zip code from field #894 and place the new value in the Pref field. Field #896 now contains the zip code prefix which can be used to lookup the zone.

3. Now a series of If/Then statements are brought into play. The programming looks to the Ship Via field (#42) and, depending on whether that field contains UPS Ground, UPS Second Day, or UPS Next Day, and also utilizing the zip code prefix in field #896, the appropriate zone is retrieved from the lookup table and placed into the Zone field (#898). Note that if it's a UPS Ground shipment, the letter **C** is tacked onto the zone. This zone, in conjunction with the weight value in the Lbs field (#892), is used to @XLOOKUP the charges in UPSRATES.DTF and return the value to the UPS field (#899).

The *commercial* delivery ground zone rate is returned in all cases where UPS Ground is specified (refer to the different ground zone destination rates in Figure 10-9). If your UPS deliveries are to *residential* addresses, then you'll need to change the **C** in the expression to an **R**. Or, you can modify the application so that the variable destination type (C or R) can be specified in some manner.

Note: where the Ship Via field in the invoice contains something other than one of the three UPS services (spelled precisely as contained in the programming statements) none of the lookups will execute; the cursor will be moved to the Order Value field (#900), in any case.

Notice also that the fourth argument in each of the three @XLOOKUP functions is a reference to the Zone field in the *current* database. This is a handy shortcut in applications such as this where the external lookup field specified in the function depends on a variable field value in the current record.

By the way, LUR is an abbreviation of LOOKUPR, the range lookup statement we referred to earlier. It returns the next lowest value from the lookup table if an exact match cannot be found. Also, the Zip, Pref, and Zone fields are formatted as text information types, and the UPS field is formatted as a number field with two decimal places so that no dollar signs display in this "workspace" area of the form.

Using the remaining space in your lookup table, along with external databases, you can include a variety of rate calculations for a number of different shipping methods. You can plug in U.S. Postal fourth-class book-rate calculations based on the shipping weight, priority mail, parcel post, Federal Express, or others. And should you run into conflict with duplicate values in the Key column of your lookup table, use external databases instead, or use the @STR function to tack a one-letter prefix onto the value you want looked up.

For example, the U.S. Post Office's priority mail rate chart uses zip code prefixes and zones just like UPS. In order to avoid Key column duplicate entries, you could leave your UPS prefixes as they are, and add the letter **P** to your priority mail prefixes. Lookup table entries are treated as text, and a "346" zone prefix will be seen by any lookup programming as completely different from a "P346" zone prefix.

With the UPS rate now displayed on the invoice form during data entry, the operator has the option of using it as the value to enter into the Shipping field where it will be added to the invoice total. You could add the programming to have the value placed in the Shipping field automatically if that would better suit your preferences.

If you use this feature of the application, you should check the calculated shipping charges on a batch of invoices against the *actual* shipping charges of the weighed packages. If your invoice charges are coming up a bit too low, you can adjust the 1.05 multiplication factor in the field #850 programming statement to 1.07 or 1.1. Or you can reduce the factor if your calculated shipping charges are greater than the actual UPS charges.

```
                                            ■■■■■  SHIPPING DATES  ■■■■■
        Date Shipped 11/3/90

        01 1211     11/3/90      02 1232    11/3/90      03 1243    11/3/90
        03 1222     11/3/90      04 1224    11/3/90      05 1210    11/3/90
        06 1235     11/3/90      07 1236    11/3/90      08 1237    11/3/90
        09 1238     11/3/90      10 1240    11/3/90      11
        12                       13                      14
        15                       16                      17
        18                       19                      20
        21                       22                      23
        24                       25                      26
        27                       28                      29
        30                       31                      32
        33                       34                      35
        36                       37                      38
        39                       40                      41

          Press Shift-F10 when all invoices have been entered, and run your Shipping
                     Date Post from the Daily Posting Menu.
```

Figure 10-11: A SHIPDATE.DTF Record. It is shown in Add Data mode with values entered.

Q&A has everything you need to develop an entire integrated UPS Manifest application, complete with all the required reports and shipper labels. See Chapter 12 for details. I've installed several such systems for clients who ship routinely via UPS, and they're just nuts about them.

Posting Shipping Dates to Your Invoices

The last database we'll design in this chapter (also included on your free disk) is SHIPDATE.DTF. Figure 10-11 shows it. The purpose of this file is to provide you with a fast and easy method to record the shipping dates of your orders, and get them posted to their corresponding invoices.

The design of this database is straightforward. The Date Shipped field at the top is 12 characters in length and formatted as a date field. When the cursor enters the field during Add Data, the current date is displayed along with a custom help screen. Here is the required programming:

```
<#2: If @add then {#2=@date;@help(#2)}
```

The custom help screen is automatically displayed to remind the operator to verify that the invoice numbers that are about to be entered are invoices that were in fact shipped today. If you'll be routinely entering invoice numbers that were shipped the *previous* working day, you can work out a programming

```
If the date shown is the actual shipping date of the
invoices you are about to enter, press <Tab> or <Enter>.

Note: the DATE SHIPPED shown is today's date. You can enter
a different date—the actual date this batch of invoices
you are about to enter was actually shipped. If it takes
more than one form to enter all the invoices shipped in one
day, be sure additional forms show the same date.
```

Figure 10-12: A Custom Help Screen for Field #2.

statement that will give you data you'll need. The custom help screen that displays this is shown in Figure 10-12.

As you might infer from looking at Figure 10-11, the first column of SHIPDATE.DTF relates to the second column, the third to the fourth, and the fifth to the sixth. The invoice numbers are entered into the first, third, and fifth columns, and their corresponding ship dates are automatically entered into the corresponding date columns. The field labels run from 01 through 42, so you can enter 42 shipped orders per form.

Make the invoice number fields long enough to accommodate your invoice numbers, and make the date fields in the second, fourth, and sixth columns about 12 characters wide. You don't need labels for these date fields.

At the Program Spec, assign field ID #2 to the Date Shipped field at the very top of the form, #10 to the field named 01, and number your fields across the page by ones, so that the field named 03 gets #16, and the last field on the form winds up getting #93.

Now you can add a short programming statement to all the date fields on the form (those with no field labels in the second, fourth, and sixth columns) as follows:

```
<#11=#2
```

This statement tells Q&A "when the cursor enters this field, copy to it the value in field #2." The statement is necessary because we need a date in every field that follows an invoice number in order to create a Posting Spec. These dates must be the same as those shown at the top of the forms in the Date Shipped field.

Now, at the Field Navigation Spec for SHIPDATE.DTF, enter the following navigation command in all the date fields except the Date Shipped field at the top of the form (you won't need to assign any field ID numbers for this operation):

```
< cnext
```

With these programming and navigation commands, when the operator enters an invoice number, the master date from the Date Shipped field will be copied into the subsequent field, and the cursor will move to the next invoice number field.

When you're programming a database like this one, you can use macros to help speed things up. For example, if you needed to enter the **< CNEXT** navigational command into all date fields, you could define a macro that would type the command and use the **<Tab>** key to move to the next date field automatically, saving you a lot of keystrokes.

A Posting Spec for Updating the Invoices

Now a Posting Spec is needed to get the ship dates posted to the invoices. The spec should contain the following parameters:

- The Post-from file is SHIPDATE.DTF. The Post-to file is INVOICE.DTF.

- At the Retrieve Spec, be sure to select only that form (or forms) in SHIPDATE.DTF that contain the invoice numbers you want to have posted. Remember, you're not selecting invoices here — you've already done that by entering the invoice numbers in the SHIPDATE.DTF record or records you created. Use the Date Shipped field to specify the forms in SHIPDATE.DTF you want posted to the invoices (this is likely to be **{@Date}**). Save your spec with **<Shift><F8>**.

- At the Posting Spec screen, move the cursor to the first date field that follows the first invoice number, and enter the criteria into the Posting box. The highlighted field will be named F0001 by default, because it's the first field on the form with no label and hasn't been assigned a different name at the Set Field Names Spec. You'll want to post the value of this field into the corresponding invoice's field designed to contain the shipping date. Figure 10-13 shows how the Posting box should look when filled out at the first date field in SHIPDATE.DTF.

- Continue filling out Posting boxes for all the date fields on the form. All of the elements of the Posting box will be the same except "Post the value of field..." and "When the field...," which will change from date field to date field.

```
Post the value of field  F0001
... into external field: F0001
When the field: 01
... matches the external field Invoice No        in  INVOICE.DTF

Operation:       ▶Replace◀   Add     Subtract      Multiply      Divide
```

Figure 10-13: The Posting Box at the First Date Field in SHIPDATE.DTF. In this example, F0001 just happens to be the default Field Name of the shipping date field in INVOICE.DTF.

- When you've finished filling out all the Posting boxes, press **<F10>** and save the spec under a descriptive name such as "Shipdates Post to Invoices."

Temporary Databases

INVOICE.DTF is no minor data file. Because it is three screen pages long, loaded with fields and data, and heavy with programming, you may experience storage problems as the volume of invoices increases.

You can always archive old invoices to another hard drive partition or to floppies. Available data compression utilities, and even add-in boards that interface with your hard drive controller, can shrink files down to half their normal size.

A dearth of storage may cause another more serious inconvenience, however. As the invoice file grows to contain thousands of records, virtually everything you do with it will take more time to complete. For example, when adding new forms and during Search/Update, you may have to wait while Q&A updates the indexes or searches through the swollen file for the forms you want to retrieve.

Sure, you can index the fields normally included in your Retrieve Spec parameters to speed up the record filtering process for reports, postings, copy operations, and single-record Search/Update. But that will result in perceptible delays when adding new and updated forms to the file.

Removing the indexes on fields, on the other hand, enables Q&A to add new and updated records to the file faster, but also slows down the record retrieval process.

You can overcome this catch-22 and have the best of both worlds by creating a *temporary* database for your invoices.

Using a temporary file to hold only one day's worth of invoices will reap the following benefits:

- New invoices will be added to the file swiftly.

- Any operations performed on a day's worth of invoices — such as batch posting, printing, and daily reports — will run much faster.

- Macros that perform operations on the file will execute more quickly.

There's another advantage to using temporary files. If you have INVOICE.DTF and PO.DTF set up for data entry in temporary files, you can add a feature to your system that will prevent an accidental double posting.

INVOICE.DTF and PO.DTF are your transaction files — the files you routinely post important information *from*. Suppose at the end of each day you run all your batch posting operations with a single chain of macros (each macro calling the next one), posting sales from INVOICE.DTF to STOCK.DTF, invoice numbers and amounts from INVOICE.DTF to CUSTOMER.DTF, and stock item orders from PO.DTF to STOCK.DTF. After these operations have been completed, if another series of chained macros is automatically called to copy the day's invoices and purchase orders from their temporary files to their master files, removing these same forms from the temporary files means that they cannot be accidentally posted *again* because there won't be any forms in the temporary files to meet the Posting Spec's Retrieve Spec. The day's invoices and purchase orders will be gone from the specified source file.

Here are the steps involved in creating and using a temporary database for your daily invoice input. The procedure applies to creating and using any temporary file.

1. Copy your invoice design to a new filename — INVTEMP.DTF, for example.

2. Enter each day's invoices into INVTEMP.DTF rather than INVOICE.DTF. In other words, let INVOICE.DTF be the "mother" file containing all the invoices, and have INVTEMP.DTF hold only the current day's invoices.

3. Run your daily postings and daily summary reports from INVTEMP.DTF rather than INVOICE.DTF.

4. At the end of each day, use "Copy Selected Forms" to append the day's INVTEMP.DTF records to the end of the INVOICE.DTF file. Your Retrieve Spec will be the invoices with the current date.

5. Use "Remove Selected Forms" (with the same Retrieve Spec as in step 4 above) to delete all the invoices in INVTEMP.DTF now that they've been copied over. INVTEMP.DTF now contains no records.

You can create a macro to fully automate steps 3 and 4 above. This macro can be the macro called by the last macro in the chain that runs your batch posting operations. Then, when you invoke the master posting macro, you'll get this result:

- The quantities sold on today's invoices in INVTEMP.DTF are posted to the corresponding STOCK.DTF records.

- The INVTEMP.DTF records are copied to INVOICE.DTF.

- The INVTEMP.DTF records are then removed.

Should you use this temporary database option, be careful not to redesign the form layout of either INVTEMP.DTF or INVOICE.DTF without redesigning the other in exactly the same manner. Otherwise, you could have a mess on your hands. As long as the forms are identical in layout (having the same number of fields in the same positions on the form), you can rest assured that the values from all the fields in INVTEMP.DTF will copy over to INVOICE.DTF without a hitch, and without requiring you to fiddle with a Merge Spec.

Summary

In this chapter we've further customized our database forms, created several new databases, demonstrated a variety of techniques for making our files interactive, and established the elements of a productive, integrated order-processing system.

In the following chapter I'll show how to fine-tune the system as a whole by creating a few custom Applications menus and making the best use of the files included on the Applications disk supplied with this book. I'll also describe the reports and Posting Specs supplied on the disk and show you how these can help you meet the day-to-day information and processing needs of your business.

Chapter 11
Using & Customizing Your Free Disk Applications

In this chapter you'll:

▶ Familiarize yourself with the files included on the Applications Disk supplied with this book.

▶ Copy the files from the disk to your hard disk.

▶ Find out about the predesigned reports and Posting Specifications.

▶ Begin using the applications right away.

▶ Tailor the databases, menus, reports, and other specifications to your own needs.

In this chapter I'll focus on the free Applications Disk supplied with this book, which I'll refer to as the "Apps Disk."

First I'll get the files on the disk copied over to your computer's hard drive so you can view and use them with Q&A. Then I'll walk you through the various databases one by one, showing you how they work during data entry and how you might want to modify them where necessary to suit your preferences.

Where there are predesigned reports or Posting Specifications connected to a database, I'll also cover these. Finally, I'll turn our attention to the custom menu system supplied in a macro file included on the Apps Disk.

About the Apps Disk Files

The files contained on your free disk constitute an interactive order processing and management information system. At the heart of this system are the database files, the structure and programming of each of which were covered in detail elsewhere in the book.

The supplied posting and report specs, along with the custom menu macros, are all tied to the names and designs of the databases. So if you change the name of your Apps Disk databases — or add, subtract, move, or otherwise modify any of their fields — the posting and report specifications and menus connected with those databases may no longer function as designed. I say "may," because it depends on *what* you modify.

Since there are a million and one ways you can change a data file — from simply renaming it, all the way to modifying its underlying structure — I can't possibly go into those ways here. This is why I strongly encourage you to work with the databases as supplied on the Apps Disk *before* modifying them.

Where appropriate, the databases are supplied with several records each. If you practice using the INVOICE database, for example, with the supplied records in the CUSTOMER and STOCK data files, you'll quickly get a feel for its features and capabilities and will be in a much better position to intelligently redesign it if necessary. Once the sample records are no longer of any use, you can delete them using the Remove command available on the File menu.

Predesigned Reports

You should also run any predesigned reports and Posting Specs connected to the Apps Disk databases before modifying them to observe how they work and the results they produce. For example, a Posting Spec is included that posts the quantities of items sold on your invoices to the STOCK file records. Enter a few invoices and then run this Posting Spec to see what it does *before* modifying either the Posting Spec or the databases associated with it.

Some of the supplied reports are too wide for printing at 10 cpi on standard paper, so they've been designed to print at Q&A's maximum 17 cpi. If you receive a "Too Wide" message, but can only print on $8^{1}/_{2}$-by-11-inch paper, change the settings at the report's Define Page screen for a wider page and try printing again. If you have a laser printer with the landscape mode installed in Q&A, try using that mode. You can always print the report to screen no matter how wide it is.

The best way to print the reports is to start by selecting Print a Report from the Report menu, choosing the report you want, and answering Yes to make temporary changes. You can then change the settings on your Print Options and Define Page screens to accommodate your particular printer or printer mode.

Keeping Your Apps Disk Files Separate

If you already have a number of Q&A databases set up and running, keep all the Apps Disk files in a separate directory and experiment with them from there. Then, when you have your entire system fine-tuned and ready to go, you can copy the files into the working directory where you normally store your other data files.

All this is said not to discourage you from tailoring the databases and specs to fit your needs — because that's what you *should* do — but simply to make you aware that sometimes when you change one element in a system, that alteration can unexpectedly affect a number of other elements in that same system.

At any rate, a brief tutorial will be presented along with the more complex databases (especially INVOICE and PO), walking you through them a step at a time. The success of these tutorials will depend on the integrity of the external files that hold the values returned into the current databases. So, at the very least, read this entire chapter before embarking on a redesign odyssey. And if you do redesign an Apps Disk database, report, or Posting Spec, for heaven's sake make a copy of the original and hack away at the copy, not the original. You'll then have the original design to fall back on if you need it.

Finally, if you're not conversant with Q&A or the material in previous chapters of this book, you may have a difficult time trying to understand much of what follows. You should be familiar, at the very least, with the material in Chapters 3, 4, 6, 8, and 10 before proceeding with the job of reconfiguring these Apps Disk files to accommodate your own application ideas. Even though the system — whose components *are* the Apps Disk files — is designed to be used "right out of the box" (or out of the book, in this case), you should expect that some tweaking here and there, at the very least, will be required.

I designed the system to work according to what I consider a practical application for such a system. If you need to modify any of the system components — and you likely will — you've first got to know what you're doing. And the best way to know that is to have read the book up to this point and to have made sure you understand what you have read.

Before You Copy the Files from the Apps Disk

Before you copy the Apps Disk files to your computer's hard disk and begin using them, you should understand the nature of the files you're dealing with and the fact that they interact with one another to form an automated system.

First, the Apps Disk files are in compressed format, so you cannot simply place the disk in drive A: and expect to start using the databases. You have to first follow the procedure below to "unpack" or "unzip" the files in a subdirectory on your hard disk. Once the files are unpacked, they are then available for use.

But even after the files are ready to be used, you'll need to understand which of the files interact with which other files, and what kind of interaction takes place, which is the subject of this chapter.

For example, you cannot effectively use the INVOICE file as it comes off the Apps Disk unless the CUSTOMER and STOCK files are also available. INVOICE.DTF is programmed to look up information from these other two files, and that information must exist before invoices can be entered.

Table 11-1 lists the files on the Apps Disk and indicates which other files, if any, they interact with. Some of these database files also contain predesigned reports and Posting Specs. Reports will be discussed along with the applicable database, while the Posting Specs — since each one involves two databases — will be treated in their own section further on in the chapter.

I'll look at the files in Table 11-1 one at a time in the following pages, showing you how you can use them "as is" and providing tips on how you can customize them to meet your own particular needs. As I take up each file, you'll be referred to the chapter in this book where they were designed and discussed in detail.

Copying the Files to Your Hard Disk

The first thing you should do is peruse the README.DOC included on the Apps Disk. It may contain information about the disk, or the files on it, that was written after this book went to press.

To access the README.DOC:

1. Load Q&A.

2. Place the Apps Disk in drive A: (or drive B:, if that's your 5¼-inch floppy drive) and close the drive door.

3. Select Write from the Main menu and then choose Get from the Write menu.

4. Press **<Shift><F4>** to erase whatever drive and path appears on the document filename line.

Table 11-1
Files on the Applications Disk

They are compressed in a single file named APPSDISK.ZIP. All database files listed include related .IDX index files. Any external database lookup programming presumes external file is named as shown and located in the same directory.

Filename	Description
README.DOC	Special instructions in ASCII document format on installing and using the Apps Disk.
MENUMCRO.ASC	ASCII macro file containing custom menu structures and menu items macros.

Business Transaction Databases. The data entry forms are designed to be printed and utilized as commercial documents.

INVOICE.DTF	Records and generates formal invoices you can send to customers. Retrieves information from external databases CUSTOMER.DTF, STOCK.DTF, and UPSRATES.DTF.
PO.DTF	Records and generates formal purchase orders you can send to suppliers for stock items. Retrieves information from external databases VENDOR.DTF and STOCK.DTF.

Business Records Databases — strictly for in-house information storage and retrieval.

CUSTOMER.DTF	Records and maintains customer-related information such as name, address, phone, and credit limit.
VENDOR.DTF	Records and maintains supplier-related information such as company name, address, phone, salesperson, products supplied, and terms.
STOCK.DTF	Records and maintains product-related information such as stock numbers, descriptions, costs, prices, and quantities on hand. Uses VENDOR.DTF as lookup file.

Table 11-1 *(continued)*

EMPLOYEE.DTF	Records and maintains employee-related information such as name, address, position, hire data, pay rate, tax status code, emergency contact, and vacation and sick days.

Support Databases — secondary or "servo" files used to enter transactions to be posted to other files.

RECEIVER.DTF	Records the receipt of stock items delivered from outside vendors, which are then posted to STOCK.DTF and PO.DTF. Uses both PO.DTF and STOCK.DTF to verify that PO number and stock number entered are valid.
SHIPDATE.DTF	Records actual date order was shipped. Dates are then posted to INVOICE.DTF.
REMIT.DTF	Where remittances received in payment of invoices are entered. They are then posted daily to INVOICE.DTF. Uses INVOICE.DTF as lookup file to validate invoice number entered.

Rates Database — functions as a lookup file only.

UPSRATES.DTF	Functions as a dummy UPS shipping rates database. INVOICE.DTF programming retrieves UPS shipping charges from this file based on shipping point, delivery zone, and calculated total weight of items on invoice.

5. Type in **A:\README.DOC** (or **B:\README.DOC**, if that's where you placed the disk) and press **<Enter>**. The document is in ASCII format, so Q&A will ask you to confirm the import format. Confirm that it's in ASCII format, and Q&A will retrieve it from the A: (or B:) drive and then display it on the Type/Edit screen.

6. You can now read through the document for any additional information about the Apps Disk or the files included on it. You can also press

<F2><F10> to print the document, assuming your printer is installed in Q&A and is on-line.

7. When you've finished reading the document, press **<Escape>** to get to the Main menu and exit Q&A using the normal **X** command.

You're now ready to copy the compressed file on your Apps Disk to your hard drive. But just before you do so, you should create a new subdirectory branching off of the directory where your Q&A program files are stored. The reason to copy the Apps Disk files to a special subdirectory is so that, when the file is uncompressed, the extracted files will not overwrite any existing files of the same name.

You'll need about a megabyte of available disk space to unpack the files. The unpacking procedure requires temporary space equal to approximately twice the size of the file that's being unpacked. Once the files are unpacked, they will take up only about 600K, a little over half a megabyte. You can then work with the files in this new directory from inside Q&A, or selectively copy the files from this subdirectory into the directory you normally use when running Q&A.

Creating the New Subdirectory and Copying the Files

A Quick-Start procedure is provided below for advanced users, followed by more detailed instructions if you need them:

Quick-Start Copy and Uncompress Procedure

1. Create a subdirectory to copy, unpack, and temporarily store the files on the Apps Disk.

2. Copy the Apps Disk file to that new subdirectory.

3. In the new subdirectory, at the DOS prompt, type:

   PKUNZIP APPSFILE.ZIP

   and press **<Enter>** to extract the Q&A files from the larger compressed file.

Detailed Copy and Uncompress Procedure

1. In DOS, go to the directory where your Q&A program files are stored. We'll assume this to be the directory called QA on the C: drive. If your Q&A program files are stored on a different drive or in a different directory, modify the procedure that follows, substituting your own drive and directory.

2. At the DOS prompt in the directory where your Q&A program files are stored, type **MD APPSDISK** and press **<Enter>** to create a subdirectory called "APPSDISK."

3. Now type **CD APPSDISK** and press **<Enter>** to change to your new "APPSDISK" subdirectory.

4. Place the Apps Disk in drive A: (or drive B:, if that's your 5¼-inch floppy drive) and close the drive door.

5. Assuming that the Apps Disk is in drive A:, type the following command to copy the file on the disk to your new "APPSDISK" subdirectory:

```
COPY A:\*.*
```

and press **<Enter>**. This may take a moment or two. Don't do anything until DOS confirms that the file has been copied.

6. From the new "APPSDISK" subdirectory, type the following command to unpack the files:

```
PKUNZIP APPSFILE.ZIP
```

and press **<Enter>**. The smaller files will be unpacked from the larger file. When the process is finished, you should see the files in Table 11-1 (plus the associated database .IDX files) all present in the directory. While still in the "APPSDISK" subdirectory, you can type **DIR** and press **<Enter>** from the DOS prompt to see the list of extracted files. The files can now be used by Q&A, and, if you like, you can copy the database files into the directory where you normally store your Q&A data files from inside Q&A at any DOS file facilities screen.

If you already have Q&A database files with the same names, be careful not to overwrite them by copying the Apps Disk files to the same directory.

Also, whenever you use DOS to copy a Q&A file with a .DTF (database file) extension, be sure you also copy its related .IDX file. One file is no good without the other. When you copy a database file from *inside* Q&A, the .IDX and .DTF files are copied together because Q&A knows that wherever one goes so must the other. Moreover, Q&A warns you — DOS doesn't — if you're about to overwrite an existing file of the same name.

After you've copied the files into the directory where you'll want to store them, you can delete them from your "APPSDISK" subdirectory, either from DOS or from inside Q&A at any DOS file facilities screen.

And once you no longer need or want the "APPSDISK" subdirectory, you can delete that, too, using the DOS **RMDIR** (ReMove DIRectory) command. But DOS won't let you delete a subdirectory unless it's empty (that is, contains no files).

To delete the "APPSDISK" subdirectory:

1. From the DOS prompt in the "APPSDISK" subdirectory, type:

```
DEL  C:\QA\APPSDISK\*.*
```

press **\<Enter\>** and then type **Y** to confirm. This command presumes that "APPSDISK" is a subdirectory of the QA directory on the C: drive. Substitute your own parameters as necessary. If you're certain you're in the "APPSDISK" subdirectory, you can simply type **DEL *.*** and press **\<Enter\>**, but if you're in the wrong directory when you enter this command you'll lose all the files in that directory. When you're deleting a group of files with the DOS delete command, it's always wise to include the drive and pathname parameters in the command.

2. With all the files in the "APPSDISK" subdirectory now deleted, you can delete the subdirectory. Assuming the "APPSDISK" subdirectory branches off from the QA directory, type **CD\QA** and press **\<Enter\>** to get into the QA directory.

3. Now type **RMDIR APPSDISK** and press **\<Enter\>** to remove the "APPSDISK" subdirectory.

4. You can now reload Q&A and begin working with your new files.

The Applications Disk Database Files _____

From this point on it will be presumed that you have your Apps Disk files available to work with inside Q&A. As I spotlight each database, I'll briefly review the role of the file in the application, refer you to the chapter where the file was designed, indicate if any sample records are supplied with the file, and give you a few recommendations as to how to proceed with data entry, along with some ideas on how you can customize the file to better accommodate your needs.

Some of the Apps Disk database files will have reports and Posting Specs connected to them. To view a list of reports in a database, simply choose Print a Report from the Report menu and enter the name of the file to see the list of predesigned reports for that database. You can either print the reports using the sample records provided with the database, enter some records on your own, or step through the various screens (such as Retrieve Spec, Column/Sort Spec) simply to see the make-up of the report. You can also, of course, modify the report designs as you wish.

Where there are Posting Specs connected to a database, I'll tell you how to access them and what they're designed to do.

At the end of the chapter I'll look at the predesigned custom menu system on the Apps Disk that you can use (or modify) to tie the various components in the system into a convenient whole.

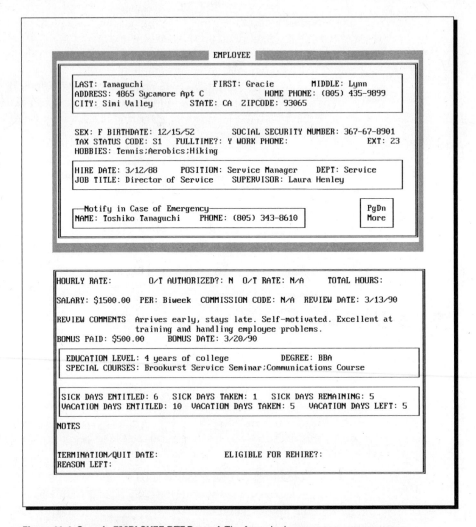

Figure 11-1: Sample EMPLOYEE.DTF Record. The form design uses two screen pages.

The Employee Database

Name: EMPLOYEE.DTF

Purpose: Maintains company personnel information

Lookup interaction with other files: None

Predesigned reports: Two

Posting Specs: None

The Employee file is a stand-alone database designed in Chapter 3. It contains no programming statements. Since it does not interact with any of the other files, you can redesign it to your heart's content without concern for the rest of the system (see Figure 11-1).

You may want to password-protect the file, even hiding sensitive fields with a Field Restriction Spec (Chapter 13), and further customize it with Restricted Values for the Dept, Supervisor, Tax Status Code, and other fields. If you have scores of employees, you can make the Last Name field Speedy for fast searches.

Reports included with EMPLOYEE.DTF are:

Employees by Last Name: Lists employees by last name, first name, home address, home phone, hire date, birthdate, emergency phone, and emergency contact.

Employees by Department: Lists employees by department, and then by last name. Includes employee's first name, position, supervisor, current rate, and phone extension.

Ten sample records are supplied with the Employee file. Use Search/Update to browse through them with **<F10>** and **<F9>** to see how the records are filled out.

The Customer File

Name: CUSTOMER.DTF

Purpose: Maintains customer information

Lookup interaction with other files: Used as a lookup file for INVOICE.DTF

Predesigned reports: Three

Posting Specs: Target posting file for last invoice number and invoice amount, which updates the Amt Purch to Date field.

CUSTOMER.DTF was originally designed in Chapter 3 and then redesigned and programmed in Chapter 5. Ten sample records are included with the file, which you can browse in Search/Update to see how they're filled out (see Figure 11-2).

The Customer file has the elements of a good mail-merge file because the name and address components are in separate fields and then combined by programming statements into single fields (Chapter 5). The name and address fields are formatted for initial capitals, which you can change at the Format Spec.

```
        CUSTOMER    Key Name CORELLI            CU# 2
                                                ID# COREL48543

       Title Ms.  First Lucille      M    Last Bagerstrom

       Whole Name Ms. Lucille Bagerstrom
          Company Corelli Manufacturing Co.
           Street 3455 Wakefield Dr.
             City Rochester                State MI   Zip 48543

            C/S/Z Rochester MI 48543


          Phone (313) 344-8977  Ext 32    FAX (313) 344-8999


       Date Added 1/6/91       Acct Type W      Products 234BD;482HB
       Credit Limit $5000.00   Amt Purch to Date $1875.55   Last Inv# 1205
       Comments
```

Figure 11-2: Sample CUSTOMER.DTF Form.

The file contains three fields conducive to fast and reliable search: The Key Name field, which is the most significant part of the customer's name; a customer CU# (Customer Number) field, which is incremented by @Number with each new customer record added; and a customer ID# field, a string value comprised of the first five letters of the Key Name field and the five-digit zip code. The customer's name, address, and account type can be retrieved into an invoice by using either the ID# or the CU#. A customer record must exist before an invoice can be generated for that customer.

After you've removed the sample records, you may want to reset the @Number to a new starting number. For example, if you want the first customer record you enter to be number 1,000, reset your @Number to 999. A description of the @Number function and the procedure for resetting the @Number are in Chapter 4.

CUSTOMER.DTF accommodates both company names and names of individuals as customers or buyers. You may want to make the CU#, ID#, Whole Name, C/S/Z, Amt Purch to Date, and Last Inv# fields Read-only fields so they can be changed only by programming statements or posting operations.

Predesigned reports included with the Customer file are:

Customers by Key Name: A list of customers sorted on the Key Name field, including the buyer's name, phone number, fax number, credit limit, and amount purchased to date.

Customers by Amt Purch: A report is generated by the amount purchased to date, including key name, buyer's name, phone, fax, and products.

Customers by Product: A Keyword report sorted by product code. Lists the key name, buyer's name, phone, fax, last invoice number, and amount purchased to date.

The Inventory File

Name: STOCK.DTF

Purpose: Maintains information on product inventory

Lookup interaction with other files: A lookup file for INVOICE.DTF, PO.DTF, and RECEIVER.DTF

Predesigned reports: Five

Posting Specs: A target file for posting from invoices, purchase orders, and receivers

STOCK.DTF (designed in Chapter 3 and redesigned in Chapter 10) keeps track of the products in your inventory. It maintains information about each product such as where you got it, how much it cost, its price and discount, and when it was added to the file. The file also includes fields to reflect the current on-hand count, show any quantity on order from a supplier, and how many of the item have been sold in the current month and the current year, along with the grand total (see Figure 11-3).

Warning: Since STOCK.DTF is an important lookup file for a number of other databases, as well as a crucial target file for Posting Specs supplied on the Apps Disk, you should not redesign it or change any of the field names until you're thoroughly familiar with its role in the system.

If you need to add some fields right away, place them on the blank second screen page. Chapter 10, in the discussion on this file, offers a few suggestions on what you can do to further customize the file for your own needs.

Fields included in STOCK.DTF which are lookup fields for other databases are: Stk#, Description, Cost, List, Disc, Status, On Hand, On Order, Vendor#, and Weight.

The target post-to fields are: Sold Today, On Order, and Recd. The other fields in the small boxes at the bottom of the form are calculated fields, meaning that they are updated when either invoice, purchase order, or receiver quantity information is posted to this file.

```
                    ▓▓▓▓▓▓▓▓▓▓▓▓  STOCK ITEM  ▓▓▓▓▓▓▓▓▓▓▓▓

    ┌──────────────────────────────────────────────────────────────┐
    │ Stk# 521GX  Description SHELF GRAY 12 X 18        Type 120     │
    └──────────────────────────────────────────────────────────────┘

    Cost $3.44   List $15.95  Disc 20%     Status OK     Date Added 1/6/90

    Source WESTERN        Vendor# 3   Weight 44.2  Case Qty 3   Case Wgt 8.3
    Vendor Stk# 8766
                         ──────Product Notes──────
    ┌──────────────────────────────────────────────────────────────┐
    │  Fits cabinet units 398XX, 403BR, 414XT. Same shelf also available │
    │  in black (521GB) and tan (521GT). Comes with mounting kit and │
    │  instructions. Packaged 3 to a carton. Price is per shelf.     │
    └──────────────────────────────────────────────────────────────┘

    Physical Count 9      Date Counted 10/31/90    Shelf Location E7

    ┌──────────────┐ ┌──────────────┐ ┌──────────────┐ ┌──────────────┐
    │ On Hand 12   │ │ On Order 10  │ │ Recd         │ │ Reord Lvl 20 │
    └──────────────┘ └──────────────┘ └──────────────┘ └──────────────┘

    ┌──────────────┐ ┌──────────────┐ ┌──────────────┐ ┌──────────────┐
    │ Sold Today   │ │ Sold MTD 8   │ │ Sold YTD 48  │ │ Total Sold 344 │
    └──────────────┘ └──────────────┘ └──────────────┘ └──────────────┘
```

Figure 11-3: STOCK.DTF.

All of these boxed fields, except perhaps Reord Lvl, should be protected by read-only status once you've entered your initial data load. Sold Today and Recd hold posted values used to recalculate related fields. For example, when you post invoices to this file, the Sold Today field holds the quantity sold in the current batch of invoices only until the other fields are recalculated. The Sold Today value is then deleted to make way for the next posting.

@Msg messages are programmed into the database to guide data entry. If you modify the design, be sure to revise these as well where appropriate.

The program forces the entry of a valid Source for the product and looks to the Vendor file Key field to return the Vendor#. Also, the Weight field is programmed for ounces, which are then converted to pounds in the Case Wgt field. You can change or disable these statements at the Program Spec.

STOCK.DTF includes these five predesigned reports:

Stock Items: Lists all products in ascending stock number order, along with description, cost, list price, source, discount, status, and quantity on hand.

Physical Count: This report lists all inventory items in shelf location order. The report shows the location, stock number, item description, category, and on-hand count and provides an underlined blank "count" column where the person counting the item can write in the actual count, which is great for counting items during physical inventories.

Physical Inventory Evaluation: A report sorted by stock number that shows the cost, shelf location, physical count, value at cost, list price, and value at retail. You'd run this report after having done your physical inventory and entered the physical count record by record. To update the Physical Count fields after an inventory, get your stock records in a Table View, sorted in the same order as the entries on the count sheets. You can then quickly move down the Physical Count column, entering the count for each item. The date of the physical inventory can be entered in the Date Counted field of all the records using Mass Update.

Low Stock Analysis: A report that flags all products where the on-hand count is less than five units more than the reorder level. Time to cut some purchase orders!

Top Selling Products: A report sorted by descending Sold YTD values. Shows the quantity sold year-to-date, the stock number, description, date added to the file, the quantity sold month-to-date, and total sold.

The UPS Rates File

Name: UPSRATES.DTF

Purpose: Provides United Parcel Service rates

Lookup interaction with other files: A lookup file used during invoice entry to calculate UPS shipping charges for the order

Predesigned reports: None

Posting Specs: None

UPSRATES.DTF is a dummy rates database (see Figure 11-4). The rates in it are not valid because UPS shipping rates differ from area to area. The file is included, along with programming in the Invoice file, to demonstrate that your invoice can calculate the cost of shipping an order via UPS based on (1) the calculated total weight of all the items on the invoice plus a little extra for packaging weight, (2) the type of UPS service desired, (3) the UPS rate chart for the shipping point, and (4) the UPS zone of the delivery point.

If you wish to use the UPS rate calculation feature built into the Invoice file, you'll need to get the UPS rate charts and plug the appropriate charges into the UPSRATES database. The rates will be unique for your area. You'll also need to fill out the Invoice Lookup Table with the zip code prefixes and corresponding Ground, Second Day Air, and Next Day Air zones. Chapter 12 provides more details on building a complete UPS Manifesting application into your system.

If you don't wish to use the UPS feature built into the Invoice, you can disable the appropriate programming statement in INVOICE.DTF. See the following section.

The Invoice File

Name: INVOICE.DTF

Purpose: Order entry

Lookup interaction with other files: Uses CUSTOMER.DTF, STOCK.DTF, and UPSRATES.DTF as lookup files

Predesigned reports: Three

Posting Specs: Source post file for updating Customer and Stock records; target post file for shipping dates and payments received

INVOICE.DTF is at the heart of the order-processing system and was given thorough treatment in Chapter 4. It's the most heavily programmed and sophisticated database on the Apps Disk and the one you'll most likely to want to further customize to suit your own order entry preferences. If you process a lot of orders, there is nothing quite so useful as an invoice design tailor-made to your particular business (see Figure 11-5).

If you plan to modify INVOICE.DTF, be sure you know what you're doing. If you want to use the same basic layout and program the form from scratch, copy its design to another name, and then, at the Program Spec, press **<F3>** to delete all the programming statements. But before you do anything, create a few new invoices following the procedure outlined below to get a feel for how the form flows and its programming action.

Ten sample completed invoices are available for you to browse in Search/Update. Be sure to remove these records and reset your @Number before you begin entering actual invoices for your company. Cursor moves are controlled by programming statements and differ depending on whether you're in Search/Update or Add Data mode. See Chapter 4 for the programming statements, or print the Program Spec and use it as a reference as you enter a few dummy invoices.

Let's walk though the process of entering a new invoice. Here's the procedure:

1. With a blank invoice on screen, type an **A** or **B** into the first field to retrieve the invoicing company's name and address from the Lookup Table. If you don't need the two-company feature, you can delete this field in Redesign or leave the field there and change its programming statement to some suitable alternative. In any case, you'll need to get

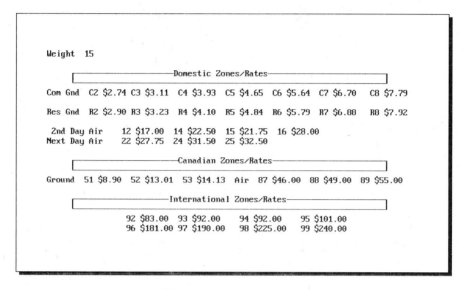

```
Weight  15

         ┌─────────────────Domestic Zones/Rates─────────────────┐

Com Gnd  C2 $2.74 C3 $3.11  C4 $3.93  C5 $4.65  C6 $5.64  C7 $6.70   C8 $7.79

Res Gnd  R2 $2.90 R3 $3.23  R4 $4.10  R5 $4.84  R6 $5.79  R7 $6.88   R8 $7.92

 2nd Day Air    12 $17.00  14 $22.50  15 $21.75  16 $28.00
Next Day Air    22 $27.75  24 $31.50  25 $32.50

         ┌─────────────────Canadian Zones/Rates─────────────────┐

Ground  51 $8.90  52 $13.01  53 $14.13  Air  87 $46.00  88 $49.00  89 $55.00

         ┌───────────────International Zones/Rates───────────────┐

            92 $83.00  93 $92.00    94 $92.00    95 $101.00
            96 $181.00 97 $190.00   98 $225.00   99 $240.00
```

Figure 11-4: UPSRATES.DTF. This is the record for a 15-pound package. The other fields represent UPS service zones and contain the UPS charges for shipping a 15-pound package to each of the zones. The database contains 70 records, 1 pound through 70 pounds.

your own company's actual name and address into the invoice, which you can do later by editing the Lookup Table, by making the name and address part of the form's design, or by entering the information at the Initial Values Spec.

2. Enter the customer's CU# so the programming can retrieve the full name and address from the Customer file. The sample records in CUSTOMER.DTF have CU#'s ranging from 1 to 10, so type any number from 1 to 10 and press **<Enter>**.

   If you press **<Enter>** from a blank CU# field, you'll be given the opportunity to retrieve the customer's CU# by entering the customer's ID#. The following ID#'s are valid for the sample records in the customer file. They are concatenations of the first five letters of the abbreviated customer name and the zip code:

   ANDYS90505, BADLA58333, BARDA90234, BARDL10033, CATSK60633, COREL48543, FUTUR50544, MARTI30533, PORKM20003, and VOLTA92655.

   Once the CU# field contains a value, you can then press **<Enter>** to retrieve the name and address. An invalid or blank CU# prevents you from proceeding with the invoice on the idea that a record for the customer should be present in CUSTOMER.DTF before an invoice can be

```
  ■■■■ PURCHASE ORDER ■■■■

 PO Number: #5    Date: #10
 [ →]Mail-in  [ →]Call-in  [ →]FAX-in          ─── BILL TO ───
 Acct#: #30     Buyer: #35                    #40
                                              #45
                                              #50

 Vendor# #55                                  ─── SHIP TO ───
                            Attn Sales        #60
                                              #65
  #75                                         #70
  #80
  #85                                         ─── SHIP VIA ───
  #90                                        #95
                                             #100


       Please supply these items. Any prices shown are our estimates

  Our Stk#   Your Number      Description        Price   Qty   Amount

 1 #101  #102    #103                            #104   #105  #106
 2 #201  #202    #203                            #205   #205  #206
 3 #301  #302    #303                            #305   #305  #306
 4 #401  #402    #403                            #405   #405  #406
 5 #501  #502    #503                            #505   #505  #506
 6 #601  #602    #603                            #605   #605  #606
 7 #701  #702    #703                            #705   #705  #706
 8 #801  #802    #803                            #805   #805  #806

 #900
 Remarks— #905


 All items are for resale (California Resale Permit No. SR AL 12-722-344).
 Please extend your most favorable trade terms.

 Backorders and partial shipments accepted, but please advise buyer at
 213-123-4567 Ext 233, or by FAX at 212-321-7654 of any shipment delays.

 Trade references available on request. Pro-forma invoices acceptable if
 required for first order.

 (Optional) [] Our check no.____in the amount of $_____ is enclosed.
 Please bill any additional charges, or issue credit for overpayment.

 ──────── Office use only ────────

 Estimated arrival date │ #910 │    Actual arrival date │ #915 │

    Do received items match PO? [ → ]   All contents undamaged? [ → ]
      —Explain below any discrepancies and handling done—
  #930
  #935
  #940
 Invoice# #945
 PO Value #950
 Pay Code #955                      │ Date PO Closed #960 │
```

Figure 11-5: Completed Sample INVOICE.DTF Form.

generated for that customer. See Chapter 12 for a method you can use to view a list of all customers on file without leaving the invoice.

3. With the Sold To box filled in with the customer's name and address, you can press **<Enter>** from the first Ship To field to duplicate the Sold To values, or you can enter unique Ship To information.

4. At the Ref field, enter the customer's PO number or some other reference that connects this invoice with the customer's order. If the order is prepaid, enter the check number in the Chk# field.

5. In the Terms and Via fields, press **<F1>** for a list of the valid entries and codes that retrieve them into the form for you. In the Pro field, enter a special promotion code, if you have one, that connects this order with a special advertising campaign, and then type your initials into the By field.

6. At the first Stk# field, enter a product stock number. The valid sample stock numbers in STOCK.DTF are: 243BD, 344BB, 345TT, 347BB, 420CB, 420CX, 482HB, 514BR, 521GX, and 588GF. When you type in a valid Stk#, the programming retrieves the Description, List Price, In Stock, Status, On Order, and Discount information. If you press **<Enter>** from any but the first Stk# field, the cursor will move to the large multiline Remarks field at the bottom of the screen page, on the assumption that there are no more items on the order.

7. Enter the quantity ordered in the first Ord field, and the quantity to ship in the corresponding Shpd field. The cursor will then move to the first Net field where you can enter a discounted price, or simply press **<Tab>** or **<Enter>** to copy the value from the preceding List field. The programming then calculates the Amount and moves the cursor to the second Stk# field.

8. Enter a few line items and then press **<Enter>** from a blank Stk# field. The cursor moves to the Remarks field, where you can type in a special message (e.g., "Thanks for your order!").

When you exit the cursor from this field, the programming adds up all the Ord quantities and compares the sum with the sum of the Shpd quantities. If a greater total quantity was ordered than is specified to ship, the cursor moves to the Backorder Will Ship box where you can advise the customer how long it will be before you can ship whatever items are back ordered.

After this, a series of programming statements are executed that:

- Calculate the total weight of all the items on the invoice.
- Calculate the cost of goods sold on the invoice.

- Determine the UPS zone and look up the shipping rate.

- Fill in the extra shipping label at the bottom left of the form.

- Calculate the total Order Value.

- Move the cursor to the Less Credit field.

You then enter any credit amount, and type a **Y** or **N** into the Taxable? field. (Be sure to incorporate your local sales tax rate into the sales tax calculation formula at the Program Spec — it's preset to 6.5 percent.) Next, enter the Shipping charge and any amount Remitted. The Amount Due will then be calculated, and you can either print and then save the invoice, save it for printing later, or go back and edit whatever needs changing.

The Remitted field, incidentally, contains an automatic-mode calculation statement (the only one in the file) that subtracts the Remitted value from the Total Invoice value and places the difference in the Amount Due field. This type of calculation statement is necessary because when posting payments to invoices, you want the amount of the payment added to the Remitted field value and the Amount Due field updated accordingly, but Q&A can't execute on-field-entry or on-field-exit statements (preceded by a "**<**" or "**>**" symbol) during a post.

See "The Remittance File" section below for posting payments received to invoices.

The predesigned reports included in the INVOICE.DTF file are:

Invoice Margins: Lists — by invoice — the invoice number, date, customer number, invoice order value, cost of goods sold, and gross margin per invoice, with totals for count, order value, cost of goods sold, and gross margin.

Amounts Due Over 45 Days: Lists — by oldest invoice date — the invoice number, amount due, number of days after invoice date, customer name, and phone number.

Customers Over 30 Days: Lists — by customer number — those customers who have outstanding balances due on invoices over 30 days old. Shows invoice number, date, amount due (with total), customer name, address, and phone number.

Chapter 6 includes a procedure for creating rudimentary monthly billing statements in the Report module. A more sophisticated billing statement application is presented in Chapter 12.

```
                                        ▬▬▬ SHIPPING DATES ▬▬▬
        Date Shipped 1/18/91

        01 1021    1/18/91      02 1033   1/18/91      03 1011   1/18/91
        04 1001    1/18/91      05 1022   1/18/91      06 1019   1/18/91
        07 1003    1/18/91      08 1004   1/18/91      09 1005   1/18/91
        10 1012    1/18/91      11 1034   1/18/91      12 1035   1/18/91
        13 998     1/18/91      14 1000   1/18/91      15 1017   1/18/91
        16 1021    1/18/91      17                     18
        19                      20                     21
        22                      23                     24
        25                      26                     27
        28                      29                     30
        31                      32                     33
        34                      35                     36
        37                      38                     39
        40                      41                     42

        Press Shift-F10 when all invoices have been entered and run your Shipping
                       Date Post from Daily Posting Menu.
```

Figure 11-6: Sample SHIPDATE.DTF Form. The operator enters the invoice numbers that were shipped during the day and posts the dates to the respective invoices.

The Shipping Date File

Name: SHIPDATE.DTF

Purpose: Records the shipping date of customer orders to help answer customer service inquiries

Lookup interaction with other files: None

Predesigned Reports: None

Posting Specs: Source post file. Posts actual ship dates to invoices

Figure 11-6 shows the SHIPDATE.DTF form designed and discussed in Chapter 10. It's a support file insofar as it's used solely to record the dates that orders (invoice numbers) have been shipped out the door to customers.

When a blank form is first displayed in Add Data, a help screen pops up, reminding you that if the date shown (the current date) is not correct for the batch of invoice numbers about to be entered, the actual shipping date should be entered.

You can then proceed to type in the invoice numbers of the orders that were shipped on that date. As each invoice number is entered, the program copies the date at the top of the form into the field adjacent to the invoice number, and then advances the cursor to the next invoice number field. If the shipping date of an invoice is different, you simply press **<Shift><Tab>** and enter the correct date for that invoice number.

When all the shipped invoice numbers have been entered, the form is saved and the dates are then posted to the corresponding invoices in INVOICE.DTF. Each invoice whose number was on the day's SHIPDATE.DTF form will then contain the actual shipping date, which is valuable information for busy customer service departments receiving frequent phone calls concerning order status.

The Remittance File

Name: REMIT.DTF

Purpose: Provides a means to update amounts due on invoices with payments received

Lookup interaction with other files: Uses INVOICE.DTF as lookup file

Predesigned Reports: None

Posting Specs: Source post file for INVOICE.DTF

REMIT.DTF is another support file. Its use is limited to recording checks received in payment of invoices, and that information is then posted to the corresponding open invoices. Figure 11-7 shows the form, along with several check numbers, amounts, and invoice numbers entered.

Where a check is received for payment of *several* invoices, you will need to know the portions of the payment to apply to each of the outstanding invoices, but this is typically answered by copies of the invoices, or statement, the customer has enclosed with the check.

Depending on your needs, you may want to redesign REMIT.DTF to look up and display the Amount Due as each invoice number is entered. You could position such a field adjacent to each invoice number field, or add a single field to each screen page that displays the Amount Due on the invoice number entered. Your lookup statement would use the invoice number as the matching key field in both files. This way, a payment on several invoices could be more readily apportioned.

Another solution would be to run an Open Invoice report at the beginning of each day, showing, by customer, the open invoice numbers, dates, and the amount due on each one. This report could be printed to disk and could then be "called up" from inside the REMIT.DTF form using the procedure described

```
                        INVOICE PAYMENTS RECEIVED

       Date Posted 1/18/91
                                                          Enter the Invoice
      ┌──────────────────┬─────────────────┬──────────────┐ Number the check is
      │  Invoice Number  │ Amount Received │ Check Number │ paying, the amount
      ├──────────────────┼─────────────────┼──────────────┤ of the check, and
      │  1    866        │    $122.15      │    34544     │ the check number.
      │  2    854        │    $1022.50     │    490       │
      │  3    902        │    $9.50        │    1022      │ Post to Invoice file
      │  4    919        │    $129.00      │    784       │ once each day to
      │  5   1001        │    $3255.88     │    34544     │ record payments on
      │  6               │                 │              │ the actual invoices.
      │  7               │                 │              │
      │  8               │                 │              │
      │  9               │                 │              │
      │ 10               │                 │              │  ┌──────────────┐
      │ 11               │                 │              │  │    PgDn       │
      │ 12               │                 │              │  │  More fields  │
      │ 13               │                 │              │  └──────────────┘
      └──────────────────┴─────────────────┴──────────────┘
```

Figure 11-7: Screen Page 1 of REMIT.DTF Record. The operator enters each check received in partial or full payment of an invoice, along with the check number and invoice number to which the payment applies.

in Chapter 12. With all the customer's open invoices thus displayed, there would be no doubt as to how to apportion a blanket payment. The oldest invoice could be settled first, followed by the next oldest, and so on.

REMIT.DTF programming validates each invoice number as it is entered, meaning that it looks to INVOICE.DTF to be sure the invoice number exists in the lookup file. The error message, "This Invoice Number is not in the file. Please check," is displayed whenever an invalid invoice number is entered.

There are dozens of ways to place further restrictions on the entry of payments recorded against open invoices, and you may wish to do so depending on your needs. You may want to make it impossible to enter a payment against an invoice that's already paid or prevent the recording of a payment greater than the amount due remaining on the invoice. You could also force the entry of a customer number *first* to help ensure that payments are at least credited to the proper customer's invoice or invoices. Considerable sophistication can be added to this part of the application to tightly control how payments are credited.

Of course if the check bounces you'll then have to redebit the customer by reversing out the credits to his invoices. Again, how you do this depends on your accounting practices. But if such cases aren't common, your best bet is probably simply to update the applicable invoice by deleting the check number and adjusting the amount due.

The Vendor File

Name: VENDOR.DTF

Purpose: To maintain information on vendors supplying stock items you resell

Lookup interaction with other files: Lookup file for PO.DTF

Predesigned Reports: One

Posting Specs: None

VENDOR.DTF, designed and explained in Chapter 10 and shown in Figure 11-8, is for maintaining information on those suppliers from whom you purchase your stock items. The form can be adapted for other types of vendors, such as those who supply you with products or services that your company consumes but doesn't resell. You can also extend the form onto two or more screen pages if you need space for more information.

Three vendor records are supplied with the database; use Search/Update to view them. When entering your initial load of vendor records, you'll want to have handy copies of any recent invoices or other paperwork from your suppliers that contain the information you need to fill out the records. The more thorough the job you do now, the more accurate and useful this file will be to you later on.

The @Number feature at the Initial Values Spec automatically assigns each new vendor the next number in sequence (Vendor#). When you're adding a vendor, use the Key field for the principal portion of the vendor name. For example, the Key field in Figure 11-8 contains "BANDER," although the full company name is "BANDER MANUFACTURING." This enables you to quickly retrieve any supplier's record.

The rest of the form is straightforward. Simply move from field to field, typing in the appropriate information and pressing **<F10>** when finished to add the next vendor. The programming in the form does nothing more than call help screens and display @Msg messages, which you can delete by pressing **<F3>** at the VENDOR.DTF Program Spec.

One predesigned report is supplied with the database:

Vendor List: A list of vendors with vendor number, address, phone, fax, names of contacts, and stock numbers supplied, sorted on the Key field.

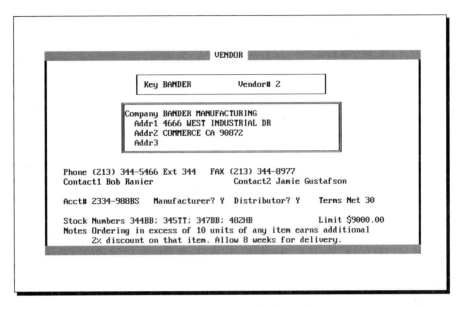

```
                    ▓▓▓▓▓▓▓ VENDOR ▓▓▓▓▓

        ┌──────────────────────────────────────────┐
        │ Key BANDER            Vendor# 2           │
        └──────────────────────────────────────────┘
          ┌────────────────────────────────────────┐
          │Company BANDER MANUFACTURING             │
          │  Addr1 4666 WEST INDUSTRIAL DR          │
          │  Addr2 COMMERCE CA 90872                │
          │  Addr3                                  │
          └────────────────────────────────────────┘

    Phone (213) 344-5466 Ext 344   FAX (213) 344-8977
    Contact1 Bob Ranier                 Contact2 Jamie Gustafson

    Acct# 2334-988BS   Manufacturer? Y  Distributor? Y    Terms Net 30

    Stock Numbers 344BB; 345TT; 347BB; 482HB         Limit $9000.00
    Notes Ordering in excess of 10 units of any item earns additional
          2% discount on that item. Allow 8 weeks for delivery.
```

Figure 11-8: Sample VENDOR.DTF Form with Information Entered.

If you need a report showing vendor by stock number, you can use the predesigned Stock Items report supplied with the STOCK.DTF database.

The Purchase Order File

Name: PO.DTF

Purpose: Purchase Order Entry

Lookup interaction with other files: VENDOR.DTF, STOCK.DTF

Predesigned Reports: Several

Posting Specs: Source post file for updating STOCK.DTF

PO.DTF is your purchase order entry and maintenance file, the design and use of which we covered thoroughly in Chapter 10.

The PO file interacts with both VENDOR.DTF and STOCK.DTF. It uses the vendor file to retrieve the supplier's name and address based on the entry of an initial stock number. In other words, the Lookup command utilizes the first stock number you've entered in the purchase order to retrieve the vendor number from the matching stock record. With the vendor number the programming can then proceed to retrieve the supplier's name and address information.

```
                    ▰▰▰ PURCHASE ORDER ▰▰▰
     ┌─────────────────────────────────────┐
     │ PO Number: 4      Date: 1/19/91      │         ┌──────── BILL TO ────────┐
     │ [ X]Mail-in  [  ]Call-in  [  ]FAX-in │         │ COMPANY A NAME          │
     │ Acct#: 2334-988  Buyer: BILL JONES   │         │ 12345 COMPANY A STREET  │
     └─────────────────────────────────────┘         │ WHATEVERTOWN A, STATE ZIP│
                                                      └─────────────────────────┘

     Vendor#                                          ┌──────── SHIP TO ────────┐
                                 Attn Sales           │ COMPANY A NAME          │
     ┌─────────────────────────────────────┐         │ 34223 COMPANY A STREET  │
     │ BANDER MANUFACTURING                 │         │ WHATEVERTOWN A, STATE ZIP│
     │ 4666 WEST INDUSTRIAL DR              │         └─────────────────────────┘
     │ COMMERCE CA 90872                    │
     └─────────────────────────────────────┘          ──────── SHIP VIA ────────
                                                              UPS Ground
```

Please supply these items. Any prices shown are our estimates

	Our Stk#	Your Number	Description	Price	Qty	Amount
1	344BB	123X33	UTILITY TABLE 12 INCH	$8.45	20	$169.00
2	345TT	X345BX	BENCH BROWN 36 INCH	$44.00	30	$1320.00
3	347BB	3X44B5	UTILITY TABLE 24 INCH	$14.55	50	$727.50
4	482HB	0XDE44	BENCH BLACK 36 INCH	$27.50	10	$272.00
5						
6						
7						
8						

Remarks— Call buyer at Ext 233 when ready to ship.

All items are for resale (California Resale Permit No. SR AL 12-722-344).
Please extend your most favorable trade terms.

Backorders and partial shipments accepted, but please advise buyer at
213-123-4567 Ext. 233, or by FAX at 213-123-5678 of any shipment delays.

Trade references available on request. Pro-forma invoices acceptable if

(Optional) [ ] Our check No._____in the amount of $_____is enclosed.
Please bill any additional charges, or issue credit for overpayment.

```
 ──────────────────────── Office use only ────────────────────────
 ┌─────────────────────────────────────────────────────────────┐
 │ Estimated arrival date │ 2/30/91 │  Actual arrival date │    │ │
 │                                                               │
 │    Do received items match PO? [  ]    All contents undamaged? [  ] │
 │      ── Explain below any discrepancies and handling done ──  │
 │                                                               │
 │                                                               │
 │ Invoice#                                                      │
 │ PO Value $2488.50                                             │
 │ Pay Code                        │ Date PO Closed              │
 └─────────────────────────────────────────────────────────────┘
```

Figure 11-9: Sample Purchase Order Filled Out and Ready to Be Mailed to Supplier.

At the same time, entry of a stock number retrieves the vendor's stock number, description, and cost from STOCK.DTF. Figure 11-9 shows a sample PO.DTF record.

Although you can adapt the form for any type of purchase ordering, its design and programming make it particularly suitable for ordering stock items — products you sell which are also in your STOCK.DTF file.

If you plan to modify PO.DTF — other than changing or deleting the text under the multiline Remarks field, which you can do in Redesign — be sure you know what you're doing. If you want to use the same basic layout and program the form from scratch, copy its design to another name, and then, at the Program Spec for the copy, press **<F3>** to delete all the programming statements. But before you do anything, enter a few new POs following the procedure outlined below to get a feel for how the form flows and its programming action.

Several sample completed purchase orders are included with the database for you to browse in Search/Update. Don't forget to remove these records and reset your @Number before you begin entering actual POs for your company. Cursor moves are controlled by programming statements and differ depending on whether you're in Search/Update or Add Data mode. See Chapter 10 for the programming statements, or print the Program Spec out and use it as a reference as you enter a dummy purchase order or two yourself.

Let's walk though the process of entering a new PO. Here's the procedure:

1. When the blank PO form displays, the PO Number and Date will already be entered courtesy of the Initial Values Spec. So the first thing you need to do is type an **X** into either the Mail-in, Call-in, or FAX-in field to indicate how the PO is being transmitted to the supplier. The cursor the moves to the Buyer field where you type in the buyer's name.

2. At the first field in the Bill To box, enter the letter **A**, **B**, or **C** depending on the name and address of the company you want retrieved from the Lookup Table. You'll want to add your own company's name and address to the Lookup Table (Chapter 4), and you can revise the programming to fill out both the Bill To and Ship To boxes without the cursor ever moving to them. You can even set the names and addresses at the Initial Values Spec and revise your programming to bypass this area of the form altogether.

3. At the Ship To box, you once again enter the letter **A**, **B**, or **C** that corresponds to the correct shipping information in the Lookup Table. If you press **<Tab>** or **<Enter>** from the first Ship To field, leaving it blank, the program enters the word "SAME." The cursor then moves to

the Ship Via area of the form and the help screen lists a variety of different shipping methods, any one of which you can specify by entering a one-digit code. If you need other shipping methods, revise both the help screen and the programming statement for the first Ship Via field.

4. At the first stock number (Stk#) field, enter a valid stock number. The stock number records supplied with STOCK.DTF are: 234BD, 344BB, 345TT, 347BB, 420CB, 420CX, 482HB, 514BR, 521GX, and 588GF. When you type in the initial stock number and press **<Tab>** or **<Enter>**, the programming (1) retrieves the vendor's corresponding part number, the item description and cost, and also (2) retrieves the Vendor#, your Acct# with the vendor, and the vendor name and address. The fields in the second step will be filled in automatically, but you won't see them as they are located on the previous screen page. (You can press **<PgUp>**, however, to take a look at them.)

You should now enter the quantity of the item you're ordering and press **<Tab>** or **<Enter>**. The corresponding amount field will be calculated and the cursor will move to the second stock number field.

If the second (and any subsequent) stock numbers entered are not available from the vendor supplying the *first* stock number, the programming displays an error message, prompting for the entry of a stock number that *is* valid for this vendor. This prevents a purchase order going to a supplier who doesn't sell the item.

5. When there are no more stock numbers to enter, press **<Tab>** or **<Enter>** from a blank stock number field and the cursor will move to the Remarks field where you can type in any special instructions for the supplier. Upon leaving the Remarks field the cursor moves to the Estimated Arrival Date field for the entry of the date you expect to receive the items on this purchase order. After entering this date (or nothing), you can press **<Home>** three times to return to the top of the form, or simply press **<F2><F10>** to print out the PO, or **<F10>** to add it to the file.

When retrieving an existing PO you can press **<PgDn>** twice to move to the first stock number field, or **<PgDn>** three times to move to the Actual Arrival Date field. In this final section of the form you can enter receiving information and formally close the PO by entering the date in the Date PO Closed field. Optionally, you can enter the vendor's invoice number for the order and a pay code if applicable.

There are two predesigned reports with this database:

Open POs: A report of open purchase orders — sorted by date — that shows the PO number, buyer, vendor name, contact, account number, and phone number.

On Order: A report — sorted by PO number — that shows PO date, vendor name, stock number, and quantity of each item on order.

 Note: This report can be used in conjunction with Daily Receiving Report (see next section) to determine which POs are *partially* closed because only some of the items on the PO having been received.

The Receiver File

Name: RECEIVER.DTF

Purpose: For the entry of items received into stock, whose quantities are then posted to the appropriate STOCK.DTF records

Lookup interaction with other files: Uses PO.DTF to validate PO number entered, and STOCK.DTF to validate stock number entered

Predesigned Reports: Several

Posting Specs: Source file for posting quantities received to STOCK.DTF records

Days or weeks after you place a purchase order with a supplier the ordered items are bound to arrive. When they do, the normal procedure is to receive them against a copy of the PO on which they were ordered. Once unpacked, checked for condition, and counted, the receiving information is then entered into the system. RECEIVER.DTF, designed and discussed in Chapter 10 and shown in Figure 11-10, serves this purpose.

Using RECEIVER.DTF is a matter of typing in the applicable purchase order number, the stock number, and the quantity received. The date is set at the Initial Values Spec, and the form's programming prevents the entry of invalid PO numbers ("No such PO number in PO.DTF") and stock numbers ("No such stock number in STOCK.DTF").

As receivers are transmitted to the front office from whomever is checking and counting arriving shipments (the lower portion of the purchase order form is designed to serve as a receiving form), the operator creates a RECEIVER.DTF record for each stock number so received. If the PO included six different items, and they're all received at once, the operator creates six new receiver records.

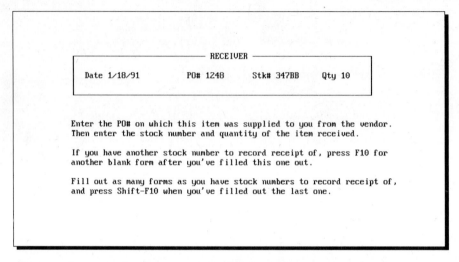

Figure 11-10: A Sample RECEIVER.DTF Record with Date, PO Number, Stock Number, and Quantity Entered.

Once each day, then, the quantities in the day's receiver records are posted to the corresponding records in STOCK.DTF, which updates the quantities on hand. Several procedures for closing off the POs (once all the items ordered on them have been received) are discussed in Chapter 10.

Two predesigned reports are included with the RECEIVER.DTF file:

Daily Receiving Report: Lists — by stock number — the quantity received and the PO number on which the item was ordered.

30-Day Receiving Report: Lists — by purchase order number — the stock numbers and quantities received and the date received. Included are all items received over the past 30 days. Since the report is sorted by PO number, it can be used to confirm that all items ordered on a PO have been received, and any POs that have been satisfied can then be closed.

About Supplementary Files

These supplementary databases (REMIT.DTF, SHIPDATE.DTF, and RECEIVER.DTF) can be considered temporary support files, and there's little to be gained by letting them stack up on your hard disk month after month. What you can do is periodically archive the records in these files to a floppy disk and then remove the same records from your hard disk, thus freeing up the space. Before doing so, however, you may want to print out the forms or at least print the data in a report format so you'll have a hard copy to refer to if needed.

The Posting Specs _____

Now that we've covered the various databases and reports supplied on the Apps Disk, let's take a look at the predesigned Posting Specs. These specs are what enable you to update the records in one file from the data in another file.

These Posting Specs are all designed for once-a-day posting operations. You can, of course, modify any of them to suit your needs or create new specs to add to the list of existing ones.

How a Posting Spec actually works was covered thoroughly in Chapter 4, and again in Chapter 10, so I won't go into detail here about how to create one. I'll simply list the names of the source and target post files, the names of the Retrieve and Batch Posting Specs, and briefly mention what each of the posting operations does. The six Posting Specs supplied on the Apps Disk and discussed below are all executable from a special "Posting menu" that's included with the custom menu system on the Apps Disk. The last section of this chapter will be devoted to these custom menus and the MENUMCRO.ASC file that contains their structures and macros.

Posting INVOICE.DTF Data to STOCK.DTF Records

Custom Posting menu selection: Invoices → Stock

Source Post File: INVOICE.DTF

Source Post Fields: The quantity fields in the Ord column of the invoice

Target Post File: STOCK.DTF

Target Post Field: Sold Today in STOCK.DTF

Match Fields: The stock number fields in the Stk# column of the invoice and the Stk# field in STOCK.DTF

Operation: Posts the quantities ordered on the day's invoices to the corresponding inventory records. Each invoice line item quantity is posted to the Sold Today field of the corresponding STOCK.DTF record. The Calculation Statements option at the Auto Program Recalc screen is set to Yes, so that once the quantity is posted, the calculation statement in STOCK.DTF will execute, reducing On Hand by the quantity sold and increasing Sold MTD, Sold YTD, and Total Sold by the same amount.

Retrieve Spec Name: Daily Invoice Post to Stock

Posting Spec Name: Daily Invoice Post to Stock

Posting Frequency: Once each day, after all invoicing is done

Posting INVOICE.DTF Data to CUSTOMER.DTF Records

Custom Posting menu selection: Invoices → Customer

Source Post File: INVOICE.DTF

Source Post Fields: Invoice Number and Order Value

Target Post File: CUSTOMER.DTF

Target Post Fields: Last Inv# and Amt Purch to Date

Match Field: CU#

Operation: Updates customer record with the invoice number entered for that customer during the day, and adds the order value of the invoice to the cumulative amount the customer has purchased since added to the customer database.

Retrieve Spec Name: Daily Invoice Post to Customer

Posting Spec Name: Daily Invoice Post to Customer

Posting Frequency: Once each day, after all invoicing is done

Posting Purchase Orders to Inventory

Custom Posting menu selection: POs → Stock

Source Post File: PO.DTF

Source Post Fields: The quantity fields in the Qty column of the purchase order

Target Post File: STOCK.DTF

Target Post Field: The On Order field in STOCK.DTF

Match Fields: The stock number fields in the Our Stk# column of the purchase order and the Stk# field in STOCK.DTF

Operation: Updates the matching inventory records by posting the quantities of items placed on order with suppliers.

Retrieve Spec Name: Daily PO Post to Stock

Posting Spec Name: Daily PO Post to Stock

Posting Frequency: Once each day, after all POs have been entered

Posting Received Items to Inventory Records

Custom Posting menu selection: Receivers → Stock

Source Post File: RECEIVER.DTF

Source Post Field: Qty

Target Post File: STOCK.DTF

Target Post Field: Recd

Match Fields: Stk# in RECEIVER.DTF and Stk# in STOCK.DTF

Operation: Updates matching inventory records with quantities of PO items actually received. The Calculation Statements option at the Auto Program Recalc screen is set to Yes, so that once the quantity is posted to the Recd field, the calculation statement in STOCK.DTF will execute, increasing On Hand by the quantity received and reducing On Order by the same amount.

Retrieve Spec Name: Daily Receiver Post to Stock

Posting Spec Name: Daily Receiver Post to Stock

Posting Frequency: Once each day, after all receiving information has been added to RECEIVER.DTF

Posting Shipping Dates to Invoices

Custom Posting menu selection: Shipdates → Invoices

Source Post File: SHIPDATE.DTF

Source Post Fields: All date fields

Target Post File: INVOICE.DTF

Target Post Field: Shipdate

Match Fields: The invoice number fields in SHIPDATE.DTF and the Invoice No field in INVOICE.DTF

Operation: Updates invoices (orders) that have been shipped with the actual shipping date.

Retrieve Spec Name: Daily Shipdate Post to Invoice

Posting Spec Name: Daily Shipdate Post to Invoice

Posting Frequency: Once each day, after all shipped invoices have been entered in one or more SHIPDATE.DTF records.

Posting Invoice Payments to Invoices

Custom Posting menu selection: Remits → Invoices

Source Post File: REMIT.DTF

Source Post Fields: Entries in the Amount Received and Check Number columns

Target Post File: INVOICE.DTF

Target Post Fields: Chk# (corresponds to Check Number column entry in source file) and Remitted (corresponds to Amount Received column entry in source file)

Match Fields: Entries in Invoice Number column of REMIT.DTF and Invoice No in INVOICE.DTF

Operation: Updates Invoice Amount Due field. The value from REMIT.DTF is posted (added) to the invoice Remitted field. The Calculation Statements options at the Auto Program Recalc screen is set to Yes, so that once the amount is posted (added to whatever amount is already in the Remitted field), the statement executes, updating the Amount Due field. Thus periodic payments on an invoice increase the Remitted field value and reduce the Amount Due. The Posting Spec also posts the customer's most recent check number, overwriting any value that the Chk# field in INVOICE.DTF already contains.

Retrieve Spec Name: Daily Remit Post to Invoice

Posting Spec Name: Daily Remit Post to Invoice

Posting Frequency: Once each day, when all checks received have been entered in one or more REMIT.DTF records.

Posting Caveats

There's one thing you'll need to be acutely aware of if you plan on running the supplied posting procedures with macros: their saved Retrieve Specs.

The Retrieve Spec portion of a Posting Spec is what tells Q&A which forms to post information *from*. Posting operation Retrieve Specs included on the Apps Disk are all preset to @DATE in the date field of the pertinent database. This means that whenever you run a post, the records selected from the source (post *from*) file are *the current date's records*.

So, if you enter 20 invoices on June 15, but decide to post these on June 16 with @DATE in the invoice date field at the Retrieve Spec, it isn't going to work. Why? Because Q&A will select only the *current* date's invoices, not yesterday's.

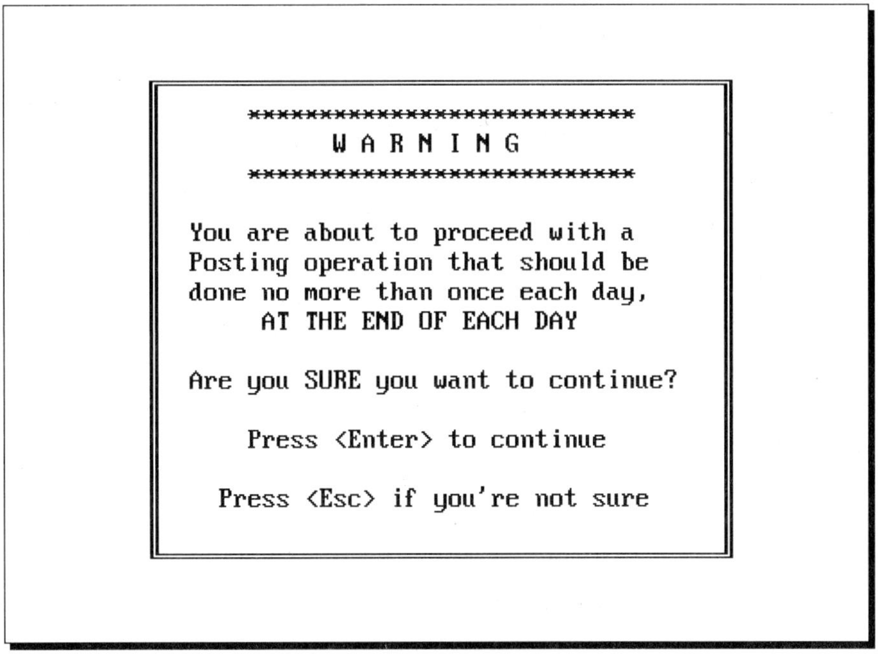

```
            ********************************
                   W A R N I N G
            ********************************

            You are about to proceed with a
            Posting operation that should be
            done no more than once each day,
               AT THE END OF EACH DAY

            Are you SURE you want to continue?

               Press <Enter> to continue

            Press <Esc> if you're not sure
```

Figure 11-11: A Suggested Warning Screen. You can create this in Write and incorporate it into your posting macros to help prevent inappropriate posts being run.

This applies to all the posting Retrieve Specs included on the Apps Disk. If you find that you can't always do your posting at the end of the day, edit your posting macros to pause at the Retrieve Spec so you can enter whatever parameters you need to run the post properly.

And remember this, too. Just because a batch of records has been posted doesn't prevent that same batch from being posted again. You'll want to have measures in place to prevent this from happening. One of the best safeguards is simply to get into the habit of running all necessary posts during the same time, and in the same manner, each and every day.

Another safety device you can use is a Write document screen such as the one shown in Figure 11-11. After creating and saving this document, you can edit your posting macros to bring it onto the Type/Edit screen with a pause code, giving the operator an opportunity to think twice before pressing **<Enter>** to execute the post. If the operator chooses to proceed by pressing **<Enter>**, the macro continues by escaping from the document (with a **Y** after the **<Esc>** to proceed without saving any inadvertent changes to the document), returning to the Main menu, and then executing the posting operation from there.

A more foolproof method of preventing a duplicate post is to mark the source post records and then use the *absence* of such marks as a Retrieve Spec parameter. You can set up such a scheme along the following lines:

1. Add a special Read-only field to the designs of your source (post-*from*) databases.

2. Have the macro that drives the posting operation perform a mass update on this special field with an **X** (or any character) immediately after the post has been completed.

3. Include a Retrieve Spec parameter in the posting procedure that requires that this special field be blank (empty). Since records that have already been posted will also have been mass updated with the **X**, these same records will not meet the additional Retrieve Spec constraint and will be excluded from an accidental duplicate post.

For databases that are the source files for *two separate* posting operations (such as invoices, where one posting updates inventory records, and another posting updates customer records), use two special Read-only fields, one that's marked by mass update after the first post, and the other that's marked after the second post. Then, in your posts from these files, use Retrieve Spec parameters that will exclude the marked records.

The Custom Menu System and Macros

Your Apps Disk contains a file named MENUMCRO.ASC. It's an ASCII macro file that includes:

1. Menu structures for four custom menus: File Data Entry menu, File Search menu, Posting menu, and a Canned Reports menu.

2. The macros — which are menu selections — that run when selected leading you to, or executing, the operation you want to perform.

The File Data Entry and File Search menus open the selected database in Add Data or Search/Update mode.

Choosing a database from the File Data Entry menu displays a fresh, blank form for that file, ready for you to enter a new record, while choosing a file from the File Search menu takes you to the Retrieve Spec for that database. In contrast to these two menus, selections on the Posting menu actually execute the posting operations as discussed in the previous section.

There is also a Canned Reports menu whose preassigned selections lead to the List of Reports screens for the various data files, via the Print a Report selection on the standard Q&A Report menu. You may wish to create several custom submenus from which you can select specific reports to run. For example, you might want a "Customer File Reports" submenu, a "Stock File Reports" submenu, an "Invoice File Reports" submenu, and so forth — each a selection on the Canned Reports menu. It's up to you to create these submenus and decide which reports to add to them, following the custom menu-creating procedures discussed in Chapter 8.

Figure 11-12 shows the Q&A Main menu set up so as to enable you to reach any of the supplied custom menus with a keystroke.

Using the MENUMCRO.ASC File

Because it contains the structures for the four custom menus shown in Figure 11-12, in addition to the macros that call the menus and those that run the menu selections, the MENUMCRO.ASC file is too large to fit into Q&A's standard 3K macro buffer. This means that if you're going to load this macro file you'll have to increase your macro buffer size to about 7K. But an additional 4K of memory doesn't seem like all that much to add when it will give you access to a custom menu system that will make your work with Q&A easier and more productive.

To set the default macro buffer size to 7K, simply load Q&A as follows:

QA –b7000

If you want to start Q&A and load MENUMCRO.ASC instead of the default QAMACRO.ASC file, use this autoload command at the DOS prompt:

QA –b7000 –alMENUMCRO.ASC

Note that this command assumes that the MENUMCRO.ASC file is in the QA directory. If the file is in a different directory, you'll need to also specify the path to the file. For example, if MENUMCRO.ASC is located in the "APPSDISK" subdirectory of the QA directory, the DOS command would be:

QA –b7000 –al \QA\APPSDISK\MENUMCRO.ASC

If you wish the MENUMCRO.ASC macro file to *always* load with Q&A, the following Autoload Default switch specifies it as the default macro file:

QA –adMENUMCRO.ASC

To set the macro buffer to 7K *and* make MENUMCRO.ASC the default macro file that Q&A loads on startup, use the following command at the DOS prompt:

QA –b7000 –adMENUMCRO.ASC

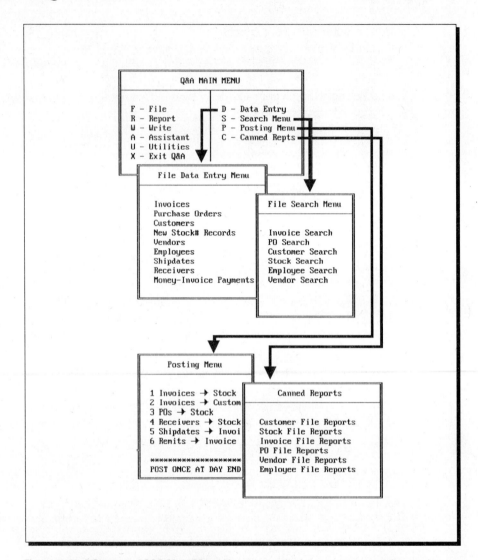

Figure 11-12: A Suggested Q&A Main Menu. You can see the four custom menus that can be called from it.

Of course, you can make life simpler by *combining* your existing QAMACRO.ASC file (if you're using it) with MENUMCRO.ASC into a single macro file named QAMACRO.ASC. As Q&A, by default, loads QAMACRO.ASC on startup, you can retain and use your existing macros while reaping the benefits of the custom menu system contained in MENUMCRO.ASC.

Combining Your Macro Files

The only macros in MENUMCRO.ASC that have key identifiers connected to them are those that call the custom menus from the Q&A Main menu (Figure 11-12): **<Alt-D>** for the custom Data Entry menu, **<Alt-S>** for the custom Search menu, **<Alt-P>** for the custom Posting menu, and **<Alt-C>** for the Canned Reports menu. All other macros in MENUMCRO.ASC are "nokey" macros, meaning that they have no key identifiers.

Before attempting to combine the two macro files, you'll need to make sure that your QAMACRO.ASC file does not contain macros that are called by any of the four key identifiers indicated above. You must also make a backup copy of your QAMACRO.ASC file just in case something should go wrong.

If you have one or more macros in your existing QAMACRO.ASC file with the same key identifiers, you can assign different key identifiers to them by editing them on the Type/Edit screen in the Write module. (See "Editing Macro Files in Write" in Chapter 8.)

Also, be aware that combining the two macro files may result in a new macro file that is now larger than your default macro buffer size. For example, if MENUMCRO.ASC is 6,500 bytes and your QAMACRO.ASC file is 2,130 bytes, combining them will produce a file that's 8,630 bytes, so you'll need to increase your macro buffer size to around 9,000 bytes to make enough room to record another few macros without running out of memory.

Of course, if you don't have a QAMACRO.ASC file and you want to make MENUMCRO.ASC your default macro file, simply change its name to QAMACRO.ASC. This way you won't have to go to the trouble of specifying it at the DOS prompt when starting Q&A.

To combine your existing QAMACRO.ASC file with the MENUMCRO.ASC file:

1. Make a backup copy of QAMACRO.ASC if the file exists.

2. Determine the sizes — in bytes — of the two files and add these values together.

3. If necessary, exit and then reload QA, specifying a macro buffer size that will accommodate the number of bytes in the combined files.

4. Bring QAMACRO.ASC into the editor in Write. (See the section entitled "Editing Macro Files in Write" in Chapter 8, if you need help here.)

5. Move the cursor to the first column position on the empty line immediately after the final macro, type *, and press **<Enter>**.

6. Press **<F8>** for the Options menu, select Documents and choose Insert a Document from the submenu.

7. When prompted for the document name, type in **MENUMCRO**.**ASC**, being sure to include the path to the file, such as **C:\QA\APPSDISK\MENUMCRO.ASC**, and press **<Enter>**.

8. Check to make sure the transition is correct between the two macro definitions at the point where MENUMCRO.ASC was inserted. There should be the usual asterisk and no blank lines.

9. When you're satisfied that your new macro file is all right and proper, press **<Ctrl><F8>** and save the file to QAMACRO.ASC.

10. Press **<Shift><F2>** and choose Get Macros. QAMACRO.ASC should be on the filename line. Press **<Enter>** to load the new, combined macro file into memory.

If you get the error message, "There's a bad macro definition near macro (*number*)," you'll have to pinpoint and edit the offending definition and then save and reload the macro file according to steps 8 and 9 above.

If you get the message, "Ran out of memory after getting macro (*number*)," it means you didn't set your macro buffer large enough when you started Q&A. Exit Q&A and reload the program with an increased macro buffer size.

Setting Up the Q&A Main Menu

If you're going to include the custom menus as selections on the Q&A Main menu, you'll now need to install, as alternate Main menu programs, the macros that call the custom menus. The procedure for installing macros as alternate programs on the Main menu is covered in detail in Chapter 8. Here's the procedure as it applies to the four menu-calling macros supplied on the Apps Disk:

1. Select Utilities from the Main menu.

2. Choose Set Alternate Programs from the Utilities menu.

3. At the first available Alternate Program line, type in **AltD**, the identifier of the macro that calls the custom Data Entry menu. On the Menu Selection line below it, type in **Data Entry Menu**.

4. On the next Alternate Program line, type in **AltS**, the identifier of the macro that calls the custom Search menu. On the Menu Selection line below it, type in **Search Menu**.

5. On the next Alternate Program line, type in **AltP**, the identifier of the macro that calls the custom Posting menu. On the Menu Selection line below it, type in **Posting Menu**.

6. On the next Alternate Program line, type in **AltC**, the identifier of the macro that calls the custom Canned Reports menu. On the Menu Selection line below it, type in **Canned Reports**.

7. Press **<F10>** to save your new Main menu alternate selections and **<Esc>** to the Main menu to view them.

If your menus are set to Automatic Execution, you should now be able to press the letter that corresponds to the custom menu selection on the Main menu and that custom menu will display. Pressing **<Esc>** from any of the four custom menus supplied should return you to the Q&A Main menu.

To get a taste for how the menus work, choose **D - Data Entry** from the Main menu and then press the letter **C** from the custom File Data Entry menu to display a blank CUSTOMER.DTF form ready for input.

Summary

In this chapter I've covered the procedures for installing and using the files included on the free Applications Disk. What you do now to utilize or modify the databases and reports, or tailor the custom menu system to your own needs, is up to you. The procedures on how to create, redesign, program, and use a database; design reports, posting procedures, and other specs; employ macros; and develop custom menus and menu systems are all covered in detail in the preceding chapters. And you should refer to these chapters whenever you're unsure about your next step.

What endears me to Q&A — and I hope you, too — is its tremendous capacity to accommodate one's particular application requirements and preferences. And it's this same remarkable power of flexibility that you can tap and use to your total advantage no matter what you need Q&A to do for you.

Explore Q&A's many features, and don't be afraid to experiment. As with most everything in life, you learn best — and fastest — by doing.

Chapter 12
Application Power Tools

In this chapter you'll learn about:

▶ Viewing lists and reports from external files without leaving the current record.

▶ Generating attractive open-invoice monthly billing statements with aged subtotals.

▶ Creating a complete, commercial-quality UPS computer manifest system in Q&A.

▶ Separating whole name fields into component parts.

▶ Validating states and zip codes during data entry.

In this chapter, you'll see Q&A solve problems that go beyond what people generally think Q&A is capable of doing. In fact, it goes beyond what most people need.

Overview

How you use Q&A to meet business and personal needs depends on your familiarity with the product and your own imagination.

Even a high level of expertise with an application program such as Q&A isn't always enough. You may have a clear idea of your objective, but the solution isn't so readily apparent. When what you require seems beyond the capability of Q&A to provide directly, you have to consider tackling the problem indirectly or in the form of a trick or workaround.

Reading through the book will have given you a good idea of what you can do with Q&A. You've seen examples of its programming power, its capability to manipulate data files and documents, its macro and custom menu-creating capabilities, and report-generating prowess.

In this chapter I'll show you at several fairly sophisticated application requirements that called for extraordinary solutions. The purpose in doing this is to get you thinking creatively, so that when you can't seem to get what you want from Q&A in a straightforward manner, you'll see that you can often combine and manipulate features to come up with the fix you need.

For example:

- You can't program Q&A to display pop-up scrollable windows containing live data from external files. But by using the Report module, the Field Editor, a macro, and several other features, you can, during order entry, call up from any text-formatted field a scrollable list of every one of the 500 items in your inventory, including their stock numbers, descriptions, prices, sizes, costs, discounts, and quantity on hand. This technique can be used in a variety of ways.

- Designing an application in Q&A that generates professional-looking open invoice billing statements for your customers requires extensive know-how. Considering the elements involved in monthly statements — sorted multiple invoice numbers, their dates and amounts with aged totals, and a statement total; the customer's name, address, and account number; your company's name and address; and all packaged in an attractive, readable document format — you may not quite know where to begin. I'll show you one approach.

- If you ship via United Parcel Service, perhaps you'd like to have a complete automated UPS Manifesting System in Q&A that will meet UPS's stringent approval standards. You can! And you can make it so fast and slick that all you'll need to do is type in the invoice numbers and weights for the parcels you want to include on the day's manifest, and then press a hot-key to print out your manifest and summary reports, ready for the UPS driver.

- Smaller companies, when starting out with automation, often rush to design a file for their customer data without giving much thought to how such a file can be used in other business areas as well. A common mistake is to put a customer's entire name — including the title (such as Mr., Mrs., and Dr.), given name, middle initial, surname, and suffix (such as Ph.D. and M.D.) — all in a single database field. Novice users often put the address — city, state, and zip code — in a single field, too. They find out later that they can't address a customer in a personalized mail-merge letter with "Dear Robert" or "Dear Mrs. Smith," or can't sort their customers by state or zip code. But Q&A has the tools to remedy such problems, as you'll see.

- Erroneous U.S. state abbreviations and zip codes in an address database can cause trouble and expense. But Q&A provides a number of tools to help ensure that your address components are entered into the file correctly the first time. In the final section of this appendix you'll find out what these tools are and how to use them effectively.

The beauty of Q&A is that you can start out simple and familiarize yourself with its more powerful features only as you need them. We'll tap more of Q&A's unexpected power with a variety of application examples, on the assumption that by now you're familiar enough with Q&A to handle the level of sophistication involved.

Q&A Does Windows?

A *window*, in software parlance, is typically a rectangular on-screen frame through which you can view a document, database record, or even another application. Microsoft Windows and DESQview have gained popularity because of their capability to let the user view and even run multiple applications simultaneously in windows. While this type of windowing environment is not a Q&A feature, you can design into your Q&A applications window-like displays that can greatly assist an operator with key information needed during data entry.

Q&A comes ready with a several types of displays that overlay the screen.

- You can create a "pick list" of restricted values to pop up during data entry when you press **<Alt><F7>**. An example of this was covered in Chapter 4.

- When creating a merge document, pressing **<Alt><F7>** displays a window-like list of field names in the merge file which you can grab and bring into your document.

- When you want to run a macro you can press **<Alt><F2>** to pop up the list of macros in memory, highlight the one you want, and press **<Enter>** to execute it.

- You can design and then display custom menus from which you can then select the menu item that's appropriate to what you're doing at the time.

- You can design custom help screens. And with programming statements you can cause your help screens or special messages to display in order to guide data entry.

These features are window-like in their appearance. They can be displayed when you need them, they normally overlay whatever is on the screen, and they allow you to view a particular assembly of information that's pertinent and in fact would be difficult to come by in any other way.

But what if you need a window through which you can view, for example, an entire compiled report or special list during data entry? Or a window you can pop up to answer a phone inquiry — an inquiry you'd like to handle without having to save and exit from the half-finished record you're working on to get to the other database that contains the information you need?

Well, that's possible too, using the Field Editor. It creates a window of sorts, through which you can view another file. That other file must be an ASCII text file, rather than a Q&A database file, which means we've got to come up with a workaround. Read on!

Much More Than an XLOOKUP

I'll illustrate the concept with an order-entry application you're developing for Jeannie and Jim down in customer service. Jeannie and Jim do all the order entry and also answer frequent phone calls from customers who want to find out the price and availability of this or that item, when their order was shipped, or what their current account balance is.

Now picture Jeannie — she's right in the middle of a detailed invoice when Bart Weatherspoon from Custom Micro calls. He'll be needing another 15 of those X344BB Half Slot Parallel Cards. He wants to know if you've got them in stock, what his price is, if his order of last week has been shipped, and if so, how, and what the balance of his account is with you. If you keep this information current in your Q&A databases and if you know how to "do windows" in Q&A, Jeannie may very well be able to answer all of Mr. Weatherspoon's questions without even leaving the invoice she's working on or having to run off in search of the information.

Here's how it can be done:

On a routine basis you run a macro that prints a variety of specially designed customer service reports to disk. For example, the macro prints the Stock Report that lists each product description, stock number, price, allowable discount, and quantity on hand. The same macro then runs the Receivables Report that shows who owes what, then the report that lists all the invoices that have been shipped in the last two weeks, showing the customer name, the date shipped, the method of shipment, and what have you. With your up-to-date reports in ASCII form on disk, you can then bring them into the Field Editor from any database field that's formatted for text.

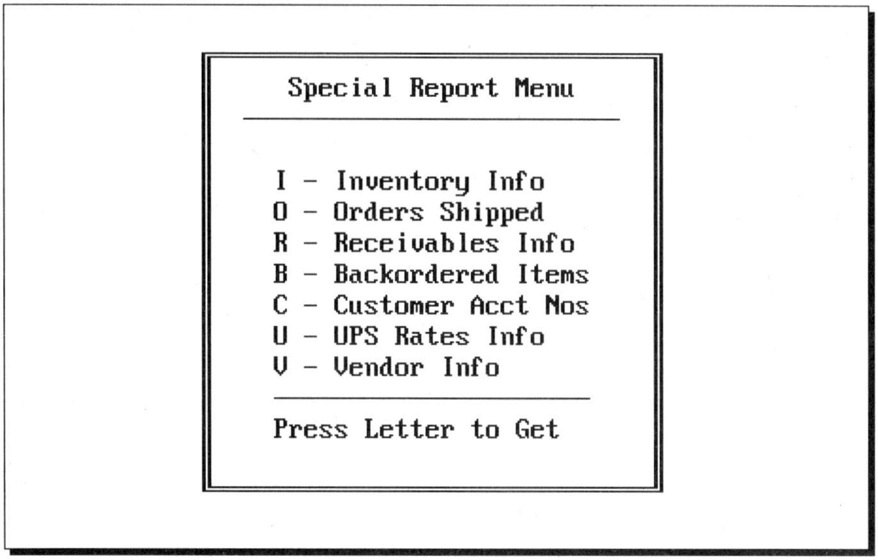

```
┌─────────────────────────────────────────┐
│   ┌───────────────────────────────┐      │
│   │       Special Report Menu     │      │
│   │   ─────────────────────────   │      │
│   │                               │      │
│   │   I - Inventory Info          │      │
│   │   O - Orders Shipped          │      │
│   │   R - Receivables Info        │      │
│   │   B - Backordered Items       │      │
│   │   C - Customer Acct Nos       │      │
│   │   U - UPS Rates Info          │      │
│   │   V - Vendor Info             │      │
│   │   ─────────────────────────   │      │
│   │   Press Letter to Get         │      │
│   └───────────────────────────────┘      │
│                                           │
└─────────────────────────────────────────┘
```

Figure 12-1: A Special Report Custom Menu.

A Sample Application Design Procedure

Here's a sample application along with a procedure you can use to display needed information in a window-like format. The particular style of this application would make it useful not only when dealing with customer service calls, but also as an information source to help with data entry as well. I'll use an order-entry environment to illustrate the application. Here's the procedure for bringing a sample report into the Field Editor.

1. Create a custom menu designed to be called from any field in any database, as long as the field is formatted for text or keywords. During data entry, the operator can press, for example, **<Alt><M>** to display the menu. The menu could include selections like those shown in Figure 12-1.

   Each menu selection calls an up-to-date report — a report printed to disk earlier that day (overwriting the file containing the previous day's report). To select a report or list, the operator simply presses **<Alt><M>** for the menu and then presses the first letter of the menu item to invoke that selection.

2. Define the macro that brings the first report ("Inventory Info") into the Field Editor. To show you the power available to you, let's assume the

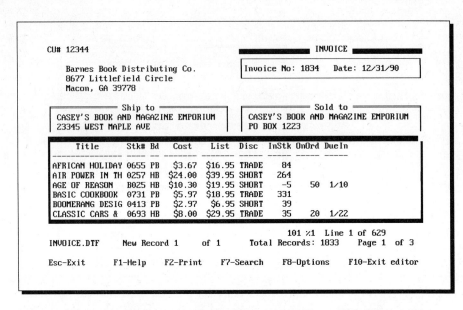

```
CU# 12344                                              ┃━━━━━ INVOICE ━━━━━┃

        Barnes Book Distributing Co.          ┃ Invoice No: 1834   Date: 12/31/90 ┃
        8677 Littlefield Circle
        Macon, GA 39778

     ┃━━━━━ Ship to ━━━━━┃              ┃━━━━━ Sold to ━━━━━┃
     ┃ CASEY'S BOOK AND MAGAZINE EMPORIUM ┃  ┃ CASEY'S BOOK AND MAGAZINE EMPORIUM ┃
     ┃ 23345 WEST MAPLE AVE               ┃  ┃ PO BOX 1223                        ┃

        Title       Stk# Bd   Cost    List  Disc  InStk OnOrd DueIn
        ─────       ──── ──   ────    ────  ────  ───── ───── ─────
     AFRICAN HOLIDAY 0655 PB   $3.67 $16.95 TRADE    84
     AIR POWER IN TH 0257 HB  $24.00 $39.95 SHORT   264
     AGE OF REASON   B025 HB  $10.30 $19.95 SHORT    -5    50  1/10
     BASIC COOKBOOK  0731 PB   $5.97 $18.95 TRADE   331
     BOOMERANG DESIG 0413 PB   $2.97  $6.95 SHORT    39
     CLASSIC CARS &  0693 HB   $8.00 $29.95 TRADE    35    20  1/22

                                        101 %1  Line 1 of 629
     INVOICE.DTF    New Record 1    of 1    Total Records: 1833    Page 1  of 3

     Esc-Exit    F1-Help    F2-Print    F7-Search    F8-Options   F10-Exit editor
```

Figure 12-2: Pressing I With the Special Report Menu Displayed Inserts the "Inventory Info" Report into the Field Editor. The report shows product descriptions in alphabetical order, with their stock numbers and other details. This "pop-up" report can be used for data entry or to answer a sales inquiry.

first column of the report is sorted alphabetically by product description and that there are 500 lines in the report. It doesn't matter if the operator is in Add Data or Search/Update mode, so long as the cursor is in a field formatted for text or keywords. The macro when invoked by a menu selection:

a. Presses **<F6>** to open the Field Editor.

b. Presses **<F8>** to display the Options menu.

c. Presses **D** for Documents and **I** to Insert a Document.

d. Types in **INVINFO** (if that's the name of the document that is actually the "Inventory Info Report") and presses **<Enter>**.

e. Presses **<Enter>** to confirm that it's an IBM ASCII document.

Q&A now retrieves the document/report into the Field Editor, and the operator can simply scroll down the list using the cursor keys — **<PgUp>**, **<PgDn>**, **<Home>**, and **<End>** — to locate the desired information. Figure 12-2 shows an example of how this might look inside an invoice.

But you can take it even further, by having that same macro:

f. Press **<F7>** to open the Search/Replace box.

g. Pause at the "Search for" line for the operator to enter a word, string, or partial string (such as the part number or a key word from the product description) for Q&A to search on.

h. Perform the search when the operator presses **<Enter>** to resume macro playback and place the cursor on the target item.

i. Pause again, and when the operator presses **<Enter>** to resume playback, the macro presses **<Esc>** to close the editor and **Y** (for Yes) to confirm that the data in the editor is to be abandoned. The operator is now back at the form to continue data entry or select another report to display in the editor.

You don't want the operator, after getting the needed information, to press **<F10>** or **<F6>**, as this would deposit the entire report (as long as it's 32K or less) into the field and close the editor. (This won't be disastrous if data already in the field is not upset. The Field Editor can be opened again and the expanded value block deleted.) You work out your macros here so that the final **<Enter>** (or any keystroke you designate to resume macro playback) discards the text in the editor and returns the operator to the form.

3. When you've got the macro working as you want it, add it to your custom Special Report menu.

4. Now define the macros for your other custom menu report selections by using the same procedure, adding them to the menu in turn until you've got the menu and its macros all working properly.

When you're finished you've got a fast-access customer service/order-entry information system, updated once or even several times a day (by generating new reports to replace those currently on disk) that can be called from any text field in any database.

Jim, who is busy updating a customer address change, takes a call from a customer about a shipment. He presses **<Alt><M>**, presses **O** for the "Orders Shipped Info" report, tells the customer his order went out on Wednesday via UPS, and goes right back to the customer record he never had to leave.

Jeannie, in the middle of a sales order, gets a call from the boss on the intercom. He wants to know how much Weatherspoon over at Custom Micro owes. Jeannie hot-keys the "Receivables Info" report, tells the boss "$576.48. . . and $320.19 of it is overdue! Give him hell!" and goes right back to her sales order still on screen.

During order entry, a report that lists the customer names alphabetically along with their corresponding customer numbers can be called. The operator gets the customer number and enters it into the field, and the form's programming returns the full name, address, city, state, zip, and any other particulars to the form. You get the idea. It's a time- and keystroke-saver.

A Few Tips to Guide You Along

The Field Editor has a 78-character line length, so limit your reports to that many, or fewer, character columns. You can set the space between report columns to as little as 1 at the Set Format Options screen under the Report Global Options menu. If you need to stuff a lot of information into the report, you can create derived columns to force an address, for example, to print under a name, instead of across the report. You should also set your report page length to a value higher than the number of lines in the report to avoid page breaks. Q&A's maximum report page length is 32,750.

The maximum amount of data Q&A will allow you to enter into a text or keyword field is 32K, but the Field Editor may hold a bit more than that depending on available memory. So the document/report you insert into the editor could conceivably be larger than 32K. If you get a "Not Enough Memory" message, try trimming a column or two out of the report (or truncating some of the longer entries where possible) until you've got a document size that works.

32K, incidentally, works out to about 16 pages, or around 1,000 lines. If your reports are only 20 character-columns wide, then you may be able to get three or four times as many lines into the editor. If worst comes to worst, divide your report in half in some sensible manner and save the two parts to different files. For example, print to disk a report of customers or products A-K to one file and L-Z to another, and give the user a choice between the two on your custom menu.

The document/report is editable while it's in the editor. But any inadvertent changes vanish when the editor is closed, so they won't appear in the report the next time it's called.

If you're concerned about a macro opening the editor and flowing in lots of text from the wrong place on the form, add a special field to the form and have your menu-calling macro take the cursor to that field before displaying the menu. For example, the special field could be the last field on the form, and the macro could include **<end><end><end>** as its first three actions.

Keep the display off (Show Screen = No at the Macro Options box) when running these macros in applications. It just looks cleaner.

If you like, you can have the macros on your custom menu display the same menu when they're finished running. Your operator can then call another list or report with a single keystroke, or press **<Esc>** to put the menu away and return to data entry.

I know of no way to select-out and transfer portions of text — a stock number, for example — from the editor into a field. A TSR macro utility with cut-and-paste features such as Borland's SuperKey will do it, but the mechanics may be too much to contend with unless you always run Q&A with such a utility resident. If you want a point-and-shoot "pick list" that lets you bring an item from a list into the field, you might be able to work something out using the Restrict Spec, as explained in Chapter 4.

Any macros on a custom menu in an application such as this should be named (with no key identifiers) in order to decrease the likelihood of their being invoked except from your custom menu.

As your documents are in ASCII, you can set your default import type to ASCII so Q&A won't have to stop to ask you what the format is. This step could then be eliminated from the macros that bring each document into the Field Editor.

By the way, you could create a series of documents with brief advertising pitches and select them from a custom menu, as above. During order entry, for example, and perhaps depending on what the customer's interests are, your operator could flow a pitch into the editor and place it into a multiline field in the invoice. Then when the customer sees your invoice, he also sees your special limited-time offer.

Now let's tackle another challenge and see how clever use of Q&A can solve it for us.

An Open-invoice Billing Statement Application

Monthly statements. Everyone knows them. You get them from your bank, for your credit cards, and your company gets them from its vendors and probably sends them to its customers as well. If your company records sales transactions on invoices, monthly statements provide a sensible way to let your customers know what invoices remain open and to remind them that you're expecting payment.

For example, a customer may place several orders with you during the month, and you routinely send him an invoice after each of his orders has been shipped. That customer may have also placed several orders with you last month and even perhaps the previous month. Each order generates an invoice, and you hope that the customer pays your invoices according to your standard terms (for example, 30 days).

But customers don't always pay according to terms, and you may wind up having to send another copy of the original invoice with PAST DUE stamped on it each time an invoice is overdue for payment.

Well, that's one way. But think of the work involved where you've got dozens of customers and hundreds of invoices a month to account for. Even if most of your invoices are paid within 30 days, you're still bound to have a number of customers who need the gentle reminder that a monthly billing statement can provide.

Why an Open-invoice Statement Is a Tough Application

When contemplating a monthly billing application in Q&A you can become overwhelmed by the sheer mechanics of it. For one thing, you've got to get all those open invoices separated out by customer. You then need those invoices in sorted order, each with its corresponding date and amount due.

This isn't difficult in the Report module (we designed a rudimentary billing statement in Chapter 6, using strictly a report format), but you may prefer to send your customers attractive, professional-looking statements rather than reports. And you may also want to "age" the invoice amounts, so your statements show the current amount, the amount over 30 days, over 60 days, and so forth, which is *not* so easy to do, even in the report module.

Even if you've handled this end of things, you still have to design the statement document itself; this is a job for the Write word processor. But how do you merge a report, along with customer name and address information, into a Write document so you can add graphic and text enhancements, and then have Q&A print out one of these for each and every customer who has one or more open invoices?

And the kicker: how do you get Q&A to do all this work for you automatically?

There are a number of ways to approach the application. The approach I'll explore here uses the following Q&A files and product features: your invoice and customer databases; a specially designed invoice summary database; a report printed to disk; a bag of search/replace tricks in Write; a data import procedure; a mass update; and a sophisticated merge document that will serve as the actual billing statement you can mail to your customers each month. The whole operation from start to finish will be handled by a macro. In other words, at the end of each month — or whenever you want to run your statements — you tap a few keys, and in a moment or two your printer is whirring and here come the statements — mighty good-looking ones, too.

Application Design Elements

This application can be adapted to accommodate virtually any printer and paper size or type. Ours will be designed with a LaserJet and standard 8½-by-11-inch paper in mind. You can run off your statements on company letterhead, have your local printer run off a stock of specially designed forms, or even buy preprinted statement forms on continuous feed, multipart paper that you load when preparing to print your statements. You can design your statements to look however you want them to look. The important thing is that they include the elements of a presentable and sensible statement from which your customers can and will pay.

Your Customer Database

This application assumes you maintain a customer file that includes the company name, address, city, state, and zip code for each of the firms with which you do business. We'll call ours CUST.DTF. I'll also proceed on the assumption that you've assigned some kind of customer number or account number to your customers (CU#, for example), so that each record contains at least the following fields, shown here with sample values entered:

```
CU#: 14322
Company: Banning Hardware
Street: 123 Westmoreland Ave.
City: Torrance
State: CA
Zip: 90505
```

These are the only elements required from your customer file. The customer number/account number is important for this application only insofar as we'll be sorting on it and using it as a key value in our merge document lookup commands.

```
CU#        >
    Inv1 #101        Date1 #201        Amt1 #301    >
    Inv2 #102        Date2 #202        Amt2 #302    >
    Inv3 #103        Date3 #203        Amt3 #303    >
    Inv4 #104        Date4 #204        Amt4 #304    >
    Inv5 #105        Date5 #205        Amt5 #305    >
    Inv6 #106        Date6 #206        Amt6 #306    >
    Inv7 #107        Date7 #207        Amt7 #307    >
    Inv8 #108        Date8 #208        Amt8 #308    >
    Inv9 #109        Date9 #209        Amt9 #309    >
    Inv10 #110       Date10 #210       Amt10 #310   >
    Inv11 #111       Date11 #211       Amt11 #311   >
    Inv12 #112       Date12 #212       Amt12 #312   >
    Inv13 #113       Date13 #213       Amt13 #313   >
    Inv14 #114       Date14 #214       Amt14 #314   >
    Inv15 #115       Date15 #215       Amt15 #315   >        Current #501    >
    Inv16 #116       Date16 #216       Amt16 #316   >     31-60 Days #502    >
    Inv17 #117       Date17 #217       Amt17 #317   >     61-90 Days #503    >
    Inv18 #118       Date18 #218       Amt18 #318   > Over 90 Days #504    >
    Inv19 #119       Date19 #219       Amt19 #319   >
    Inv20 #120       Date20 #220       Amt20 #320   >        TOTAL #505    >

INVSUM.DTF                       Program Spec                    Page 1  of 1
```

Figure 12-3: INVSUM.DTF Form Design. It is shown here with Field ID numbers entered at the Program Spec. The key field is the customer number field (CU#). The form includes 20 invoice number fields with corresponding invoice date and amount fields. Fields are also included for aged invoice subtotals and a grand total of all the open invoices.

Your Invoice Database

No matter what kind of Q&A invoice form design you're using, you'll need the following fields, shown with sample values entered. The date field can be any of Q&A's 20 date formats. If your field labels are different, you'll need to take this into account when writing your XLOOKUP statements later on.

CU#: 14322
Invoice No: 18745
Date: 6/15/90
Amount Due: $845.96

The presumptions are that your invoice numbers are incremented in an orderly ascending manner and the Amount Due shown on your invoices is the actual amount payable by the customer (but not necessarily due) at the time you run the monthly statements.

The Invoice Summary Database

The key to the application is the invoice summary database, which I'll call INVSUM.DTF, and the objective is to wind up with one record in INVSUM.DTF for each customer number with an open invoice.

INVSUM.DTF, as designed and shown in Figure 12-3, limits the application to a maximum of 20 open invoices per customer. (You could, of course, modify it to accommodate more if you needed to.)

The CU# and Invoice Number fields (Inv1 through Inv20) can be formatted for text. Format the date fields (Date1 through Date20) for dates, and the rest of the fields for money values. Make CU# Speedy and Unique at the Speed-up Spec. Be sure to make all your fields wide enough to accommodate the longest values they might be called upon to contain.

Programming INVSUM.DTF

We will not be entering data directly into INVSUM.DTF — the file will receive its data via an import process and from there be mass updated with calculation statement execution set to Yes.

Only fields #301 through #320 and field #505 contain programming statements. Use the standard manual calc statement format so that all the statements execute only when the **<F8>** calc key is pressed.

Before you write your programming statements, however, let's take advantage of a short-cut that will save us time later on when creating the Mass Update Spec we'll need. At the Program Spec:

1. Assign field IDs #101 through #120 to fields Inv1 through Inv20; #201 through #220 to fields Date1 through Date20; and #301 through #320 to fields Amt1 through Amt20. Do not yet type in field ID numbers for the other fields.

2. Press **<F10>** to save this portion of the Program Spec.

3. Choose Mass Update for the same database, and press **<F10>** at the Retrieve Spec.

4. At the Update Spec, press **<Shift><F5>** to copy the field ID numbers from the Program Spec to the Update Spec.

5. Press **<Shift><F8>** to save the Update Spec field ID numbers, naming the spec "Lookup Dates and Amounts."

6. Press **<Esc>** to leave the Mass Update Spec and reenter the Program Spec for INVSUM.DTF.

Now write your programming statements for the database. Program field #301 as follows:

```
#301: #501=""; #502=""; #503="";#504=""; #505=""; If
#201 >= (@date-30) then #501=#301 else if #201 < (@date-
30) and #201 > (@date-61) then #502=#301 else if #201 <
(@date-60) and #201 > (@date-91) then #503=#301 else
#504=#301.
```

The statement first of all blanks out the aged subtotal and total fields. This really isn't required since the application is designed to execute the calc statements only during the mass update, but it's included to ensure proper totals in the event the form is used in Add Data or Search/Update.

The long If/Then/Else statement evaluates the date field and, based on the date the invoice was created, adds the corresponding amount to the appropriate aged subtotal field. If the date is 30 days or less old, the Current field gets the amount. If the date is more than 30 days old but less than 61 days old, the 31-60 Days field gets the value. If the date is more than 60 days old but less than 91 days old, the 61-90 Days field gets the value. And if none of these conditions are true, the Over 90 Days field will get the amount value.

The statement for the next amount field (#302) is slightly different. Q&A executes calc statements in field ID number order, so we want to make sure, beginning with #302, that the amount value is added to whatever value any of the aged subtotal fields may already contain. Here's the statement for #302:

```
#302: If #202 >= (@date-30) then #501=#501 + #302 else
if #202 < (@date-30) and #202 > (@date-61) then
#502=#502+#302 else if #202 < (@date-60) and #202 >
(@date-91) then #503=#503+#302 else #504=#504+#302
```

Fields #303 through #320 are programmed exactly like #302 except for the variable field references. The fastest way to program this form is to record your programming statement for #302 in a macro with pause codes for the variable field references. You can then simply open the Program Field Editor for each subsequent amount field, invoke the macro, and type the appropriate field references when prompted.

When you're done programming the amount fields, number the aged subtotal and total fields as shown in Figure 12-3 and add the following statement to the TOTAL field (#505):

```
#505=@sum(#501..#504)
```

Test the form's programming in Add Data by entering a series of invoice numbers, dates, and amounts on a blank form. After you've entered the amount of the last invoice, press **<F8>** to calculate the aged subtotal and total fields. Now check the amounts by invoice age against the aged subtotals to verify that the aging resulted in the correct values. When everything is working OK, remove any test forms in the database so the file contains no records.

You'll now need a Mass Update Spec that retrieves the dates and amounts corresponding to the invoice numbers and executes the calc statements in INVSUM.DTF that age and total the invoice amounts.

INVSUM.DTF Mass Update

Your Mass Update Retrieve Spec for INVSUM.DTF will be all the forms in the database.

At the Update Spec, press **<Alt><F8>**, highlight the Lookup Dates and Amounts Spec, and press **<Enter>**. This spec, as you'll recall, contains the field ID numbers from the Program Spec.

At the first invoice number field (#101), enter the following programming statement:

```
#101:  xlu("Invoice",#101,"invoice  no","date",#201,"
amount  due",#301)
```

This XLOOKUP statement — when executed during the mass update — will use the value in the Update Spec field #101 (Inv1) to retrieve the invoice date and amount from the matching invoice in INVOICE.DTF and place them in the adjacent Date1 and Amt1 fields.

Write the same XLOOKUP statement for all the invoice number fields (#102 through #120), substituting the appropriate field references. For example, the programming statement for the second invoice number field (#102) is:

```
#102:  xlu("Invoice",#102,"invoice  no","date",#202,"
amount  due",#302)
```

Record and use a macro with pause codes to help speed the process of entering the statements. When you've entered all the Update Spec programming statements, press **<Shift><F8>** and save the spec under the same name, "Lookup Dates and Amounts."

With this end of the procedure now done, you can slip over into the Write module and create your merge document.

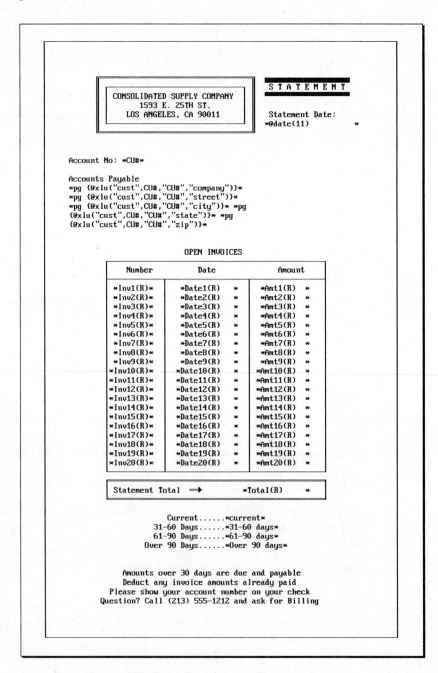

Figure 12-4: A Sample Write Module Merge Document.

The Billing Statement Merge Document

The form's design is entirely up to you. Figure 12-4 shows a sample form containing the basics, as well as a few graphics and text enhancements that add to the form's appearance and readability.

The sample statement shown in Figure 12-4 is designed for a standard page with 1-inch margins and a 10-cpi monospaced font, and includes your company's name and address inside a graphic box made with the Line Draw feature. The word STATEMENT stands out prominently by adding a space between each letter, enhancing it with boldface, and adding a thick black line above (ASCII 220) and below (ASCII 223) it. Date format #11 for the Statement Date was selected for its more formal appearance.

You can, of course, use fonts, shading (other ASCII graphics characters), different lines and boxes, and whatever else you like. Keep in mind, however, that proportional fonts can be tricky when it comes to aligning columns.

Two merge files are used in this document. The primary merge file is INVSUM.DTF, while the secondary merge file is CUST.DTF (your customer file). This is perhaps the opposite of what you'd expect, but the bulk of our merge fields are coming from the invoice summary file, not the customer file. See Chapter 5 for more information on creating and programming merge documents.

The first merge field (CU#) in the statement is a *primary* merge file field — the value is merged from INVSUM.DTF, not CUST.DTF. The series of @XLU (@XLOOKUP abbreviated) programming expressions use this CU# to retrieve the address block information — company name, street, city, state, and zip — from the matching customer record in CUST.DTF (the secondary merge file). All other merge fields on the statement are from INVSUM.DTF. You can see in Figure 12-4 how they're positioned in the document.

When you've finished creating the document, save it with **<Shift><F8>** to your default document directory under the name STATEMNT.DOC. You're now ready to design the report that will compile all the open invoices in INVOICE.DTF by customer number.

The Open Invoices Report

The approach we're using requires a standard columnar report in order to compile the open invoice numbers, in sorted order, by customer number.

Since we'll be printing this report to disk in standard ASCII and will need to bring it into the word processor in order to reformat it, you'll want to set your default import document type to ASCII so Q&A won't have to bother asking you for the format. You do this by choosing Write Utilities, then Set Global Options, and then Set Editing Options, and change Default Import Type to ASCII (*not* Special ASCII).

When you design the report, name it "Statements" so you can readily connect it with the application. The database is INVOICE.DTF, and here are design parameters for the Statements report:

Report global options: At the Set Format Options screen, set the number of spaces between columns to 1, and specify a line to be skipped at each column break. Press **<F10>** to save your new defaults, and choose Design/Redesign a Report.

Retrieve Spec: Include all the invoices on which the Amount Due is greater than the minimum value you want included on your statements. For example, if you want to include only those invoices on which the Amount Due is at least $3.00, then type **>$2.99** in the Amount Due field at the Retrieve Spec.

Column/Sort Spec: The report includes values from only two INVOICE.DTF fields and no derived columns. Type these parameters into the two fields at the Column/Sort Spec:

```
CU#: 1,AS,H(5:)
```

```
Invoice No: 2,AS,CS,H(5:)
```

The spec sorts on the customer number field and then on the invoice number field, with subcalculations canceled (CS) so we won't get a column break following each invoice number. Use the **H** command to limit the width of the report columns to the longest value each column may contain. The widths of the above two columns have been restricted to five characters. If your longest customer numbers or invoice numbers contain more or fewer characters, limit your column widths accordingly. You'll see why later on.

The Define Page screen: Set your left and top page margins to 0 (zero).

The Print Options screen: Use your regular print options, but be sure the following settings are specified:

```
Print to: DISK
```

```
Justify report body: Left
```

```
Line Spacing: Single
```

Assuming you have a few invoices in the file that meet your Retrieve Spec, go ahead and run the report, saving it to disk under the name STATEMNT.ASC (the "ASC" is for ASCII).

You'll now need to import this file into the Write word processor. But before you do this, be sure Write's import document page defaults are as follows: Left, Top, and Bottom margins and Page length set to **0** (zero), and Right margin and Page width set to **240**. You need the widest page you can get with no limit on page length.

Go to Write Utilities, to Set Global Options, and to Change Import Defaults; bring up the Define Page for Imported Documents screen, and reset the defaults, if necessary, as above.

Now go to the Write module and bring STATEMNT.ASC onto the Type/Edit screen. The report should display in the following format, with the customer numbers up against the left edge of the screen, the column headings at the very top of the screen, and a blank line at each break in the customer number:

```
CU#      Invoi

-----    -----

12333    18745
         18790
         18802
         18899
         18915
         19027
         19065
         19089

15244    17843
         17922
         18309

18647    18319
         18512
    etc.
```

Reformatting the Report in the Word Processor

We now need to reformat this report so it can be used as a source file whose data can be imported into INVSUM.DTF — the invoice summary database we designed earlier. If we just leave the report formatted as it was printed to disk and try to import the customer numbers and invoice numbers into the database, the first record created in the target file will get only the values from the first line of the report, and the second record will get only the next report line's values.

Why? Because the import-from-ASCII process uses a carriage return to define the end of a record, and our report was printed to disk in ASCII with a carriage return inserted after the last character of each line (row).

So we need to strip out those carriage returns we don't want while leaving in a carriage return at the end of the last record for each customer. In other words, we want to wind up with a single row (one line) per record. We can do this now with a macro to be called at the right moment by the macro that's running the larger statement-generating procedure.

Here's the STATEMNT.ASC reformatting sequence:

1. With the report on screen, start the macro recorder — I'll call this macro **<Alt><R>** for Reformat.

2. Press **<Shift><F4>** twice to delete the two lines containing the report column headings and the separator dashes.

3. Press **<F7>** for the Search Options box and enter these criteria:

   Search for: @cr@cr
   Replace with: *
   Method: Fast Automatic

Press **<F10>** to perform the search/replace. This process locates the double carriage returns at each break in the customer number, and replaces them with a single asterisk. Now press **<F7>** again and enter these new criteria:

   Search for: @cr
   Replace with: \

Press **<F10>** to perform the search/replace. Write replaces all carriage returns with a space. Now press **<F7>** one last time to enter these final search/replace criteria:

   Search for: *
   Replace with: @cr

This replaces the asterisks with a single carriage return and your document should now be reformatted so that the first value on each line is a customer number, followed on the same line by all the invoice numbers that belong to that customer number. The extra spaces between each value don't matter. Later, when our master macro invokes the reformat macro and then imports the STATEMNT.ASC values into INVSUM.DTF, we'll get one record for each customer number (CU#), with each record containing all the open invoice numbers (up to 20) for that customer.

Keep in mind that your page width is 240 character columns. This means that in order for this part of the application to work, a single record (including the customer number, invoice numbers, and empty spaces) cannot exceed 240 characters. Should the record exceed 240 character columns, Q&A will wrap the line and the ASCII data won't import properly to INVSUM.DTF.

We now have all the elements of the application ready to roll: the three databases (INVOICE, CUST, and INVSUM), the Statements report, our document reformatting macro, the Mass Update Spec for INVSUM.DTF, and the merge document (STATEMNT.DOC). We can now move on to recording the macro that drives the entire application and generates the statements.

Printing the Monthly Billing Statements

Although the following procedure will be macro-driven, you should step through it from beginning to end before actually recording it in a macro. This gives you the opportunity to see each element of the process in action, consider my remarks attached to several of the steps below, and verify that all is working properly before committing everything to a master macro.

Be sure your printer is on-line with the correct paper loaded and that you have at least a few open invoices in INVOICE.DTF so you can see the printed results.

1. Select Print a Report from the Report menu. Type in **INVOICE** as the name of the database, and press **<Enter>**.

2. At the List of Reports in Database, type in **Statements**, and press **<Enter>**. Press **<Enter>** again to signify no temporary changes. Q&A will compile your report.

3. When the Disk Print menu displays, press **<Enter>** to print the report in ASCII format, and type in **STATEMNT.ASC** (with the proper path, as necessary) as the name of the file. Press **<Enter>**.

4. When the warning screen displays, press **Y** to tell Q&A to overwrite the existing report of the same name. (Don't bypass this step. Be sure there *is* a document of the same name to overwrite.)

5. Press **<Esc>** to return to the Main menu. Select Write, then Get, and type in **STATEMNT.ASC** (with the correct path) if Q&A doesn't offer it to you. Press **<Enter>**.

6. With the report on the Type/Edit screen, press **<Alt><R>** to invoke the reformatting macro recorded earlier. (This step will work only if the **<Alt><R>** macro is currently in memory.)

7. When the macro has reformatted the document, press **<Ctrl><F8>** and then **<Enter>** to save the ASCII document to the same name.

8. Press **<Esc>** twice to return to the Main menu. Select File and then Utilities from the File menu.

9. Choose Import Data and then select Standard ASCII from the Import menu. On the ASCII File Name line, press **<Shift><F4>** to clear the proposed path and type in the full path of STATEMNT.ASC. Press **<Enter>**. On the Q&A File Name line, type in **INVSUM** (preceded by the proper path) and press **<Enter>**.

10. At the Merge Spec, type the number **1** in the CU# field and number the invoice number fields **2** through **21**. Press **<Shift><F8>** to save the spec under the name *Customer and Invoice Numbers*. (Later, when you record this step in your master macro, simply have it press **<Alt><F8>** for the List of Merge Specs in the Database, type in **Customer and Invoice Numbers** and press **<F10>**.) Press **<F10>** again for the ASCII Options screen. Set "Quotes around text" to No, and "Field delimiter" to Space. Press **<F10>** to begin the import process.

11. Press **<Esc>** for the File menu and select Mass Update. Type in **INVSUM** (with its path, if necessary) as the name of the database, and press **<Enter>**.

12. At the Mass Update Retrieve Spec, press **<F10>**.

13. At the Update Spec, press **<Alt><F8>** and type in **Lookup Dates and Amounts**, the name of the Update Spec we created earlier. Press **<F10>**.

14. Press **<F8>** for the Auto Program Recalc screen and set Calculation Statements to Yes. Press **<F10>** to continue.

15. When the mass update warning screen displays, select **N** to tell Q&A you don't wish to confirm each update manually.

16. When the mass update is finished, press **<Esc>** for the Main menu. Choose Write, then Get, and type in **STATEMNT.DOC**, your Q&A merge document. Press **<Enter>**.

17. With the merge document on screen, press **<F2>** for the Print Options screen. Verify that the name of the merge file is INVSUM.DTF and that your other print options are set correctly. Type a **2** in the Number of Copies field if you want an extra copy of each printed statement. Press **<F10>** to confirm the merge.

18. At the Retrieve Spec for INVSUM.DTF, press **<F10>**. Q&A will confirm the number of records to be merged, and you can press **<Enter>** to begin printing.

19. You should now use the Remove command on the File menu to remove all the INVSUM.DTF records. Or, you can make this the first step in your master macro, so the records will be available until the next time you run statements.

 Note: Before removing the INVSUM.DTF records, you may want to take advantage of them to run an accounts receivable aging analysis. Using INVSUM.DTF as the data file, you can pull a "Totals Only" report to reveal the totals for current receivables and those over 30, 60, and 90 days. Or, you can pull a detail report with aged subtotals by customer, using the customer number in a derived column formula to XLOOKUP the name and phone number from your customer file. Mail the statements, wait a few days, and then use the report to phone customers with past-due amounts.

A sample of a printed statement whose layout and programming was shown in Figure 12-4 is shown in Figure 12-5.

The macro it takes to run this procedure is rather lengthy. So you may first want to clear your everyday macro file from memory, then record the master macro, saving it to its own macro file which you load only when ready to run statements. Be sure the **<Alt><R>** Reformat macro is included in the same file.

Once you've got this application fully installed and fine-tuned to meet your needs, you'll have your billing statements each month with no effort at all. Just be sure the statements are printing out 100 percent in agreement with your invoices before giving the system your final stamp of approval.

Our next application is one that will show Q&A 4.0's power to the maximum: We will design a full-fledged UPS manifesting system, one so complete and functional that at one point I was seriously planning to release it as commercial software.

Tips and Tricks for a Powerful UPS Manifesting System

You can develop a super-efficient UPS manifesting system in Q&A and avoid the inflexibilities, high costs, steep learning curves, and long-term hardware commitments associated with commercially available third-party manifesting systems.

```
                                           ┌─────────────────┐
                                           │ S T A T E M E N T │
   ┌─────────────────────────────────┐     └─────────────────┘
   │  CONSOLIDATED SUPPLY COMPANY     │      Statement Date:
   │         1593 E. 25TH ST.         │      January 26, 1991
   │       LOS ANGELES, CA 90011      │
   └─────────────────────────────────┘


   Account No: 12333

   Accounts Payable
   Banning Hardware
   123 Westmoreland Ave.
   Torrance CA 90505


                        OPEN INVOICES

         ┌──────────────────────────────────────────────┐
         │   Number        Date           Amount         │
         │ ────────────────────────────────────────────  │
         │   18745        10/8/90         $234.55         │
         │   18790        10/15/90        $103.87         │
         │   18802        10/30/90        $2113.98        │
         │   18822        11/10/90        $98.55          │
         │   18899        11/20/90        $88.15          │
         │   18915        11/30/90        $24.66          │
         │   18937        12/5/90         $113.73         │
         │   18945        12/9/90         $13.73          │
         │   18966        12/27/90        $122.57         │
         │   18999        1/3/91          $228.32         │
         │   19027        1/12/91         $318.09         │
         │   19065        1/19/91         $18.09          │
         │   19089        1/22/91         $104.04         │
         │                                               │
         └──────────────────────────────────────────────┘

         ┌──────────────────────────────────────────────┐
         │  Statement Total  ⟶          $3582.33         │
         └──────────────────────────────────────────────┘

                    Current......$791.11
                    31-60 Days......$152.12
                    61-90 Days......$2300.68
                    Over 90 Days......$338.42


              Amounts over 30 days are due and payable
              Deduct any invoice amounts already paid
              Please show your account number on your check
              Question? Call (213) 432-3456 and ask for Billing
```

Figure 12-5: A Sample Printed Statement that Looks Good, Is Clear and Informative, and Encourages Prompt Payment. The position of the customer's name and address block shown here enables the statements to be letter-folded for standard #10 business window envelopes, eliminating the need for separately typed envelopes.

UPS doesn't openly encourage shippers to design their own manifest applications, but it will make available to you its illustrated *Guidelines for UPS Computer Manifest Systems* publication, which you can use in designing your application in Q&A. What UPS will be looking for in evaluating your home-grown application boils down to output. So the trick is to tap the database and reporting power of Q&A so that what comes out of your printer at the end of the day conforms to UPS's own specifications. After all, the UPS billing office must be able to read your manifest and bill you from it, and you must have an accurate record of what was shipped and when. So the requirements are there for your convenience and protection, as well as UPS's.

It would take another small book to go into detail on shipping and manifest terminology, service zones, parcel restrictions, classifications, and procedures. These are all covered in UPS's own publication. What I'll do in this section is presume that you're familiar with these requirements and, from there, take you through the design of an automated UPS manifest system that should easily win UPS approval.

The essential requirements of a UPS-approvable manifest system are:

- **Manifest Report** or **Shipping Manifest** which lists — by package ID number (typically the invoice number) or transaction number — each consignee's name and address, the UPS shipping zone, parcel weight, and charges, along with any COD amount, Declared Value amount (for extra insurance), AOD (Acknowledgement of Delivery), and oversize parcel notation. The Manifest Report must also show the shipper's name and address, UPS shipper number, Pickup record number, date shipped, and page number at the top of each page.

- The **Manifest Summary Reports**, which include a report of ground shipments with the total number of parcels, weights, and charges broken down by zone; the same report for air shipments; parcel totals for Next Day Air, Air Letters, and Second Day Air; and additional summary reports that show counts and total charges for parcels involving CODs, AODs, Call Tag transactions, Excess Value units (extra insurance), and total UPS revenue for the day's manifest.

- **UPS Shipper Labels** that your system prints and which you affix to each parcel. The label shows both your shipper number and the package identification number (PKG ID#). These labels are in addition to the delivery address labels affixed to the parcels, although you can design and print a combination label that includes the consignee's name and address along with your UPS shipper number and PKG ID#.

A tremendous time-saver in the long run is to incorporate your shipper number and PKG ID# into your Q&A invoice design and use the printed invoice itself as (1) your company's return address label, (2) the destination name and address label, (3) the UPS Shipper Label with your shipper number and PKG ID#, and (4) the packing slip. The shipping department packs and seals the parcel, folds the invoice to expose the above elements, and inserts the folded invoice into a clear plastic sleeve which is then affixed to the parcel.

The UPS *Guidelines* publication gives you the framework within which you can design your application to suit your particular shipping and information needs. Don't attempt to second-guess the UPS specs. Get a copy of the *Guidelines* from your local UPS rep and study it carefully, along with the Service Guides and other UPS publications.

In the following pages I'll show you the building blocks of a workable UPS manifesting application in Q&A. Using Q&A databases, standard columnar reports, and Write's mailing label facility, we'll develop a system that requires absolute minimal keystrokes to enter each parcel on the manifest, along with a macro engine that compiles and prints all the required reports and shipper labels in one fell swoop.

This approach assumes an existing customer invoice database which serves as a lookup file for the consignee's name and address, the invoice number (the PKG ID#), the type of UPS service specified, and the invoice amount (reflecting the insurable value of your UPS parcels).

Our output device will be any Q&A-supported printer that prints at 12 or more characters-per-inch, and I'll further assume that your shipping department each afternoon furnishes you with a list of invoice numbers packaged for UPS shipment, along with the weight of each parcel. Your setup will differ from this, of course, but you know Q&A well enough by this point to tailor the application to accommodate your own office procedures.

The Rates Database

Our UPS rates database will contain all the UPS service zones along with the charges that pertain to parcels shipped to those zones, including:

- Domestic residential and commercial destination Ground zone rates.

- Domestic Next Day Air, Second Day Air, and Air Letter rates.

- Canadian Ground, Air Parcel, and Air Letter rates.

- International Air Letter and Air Parcel rates.

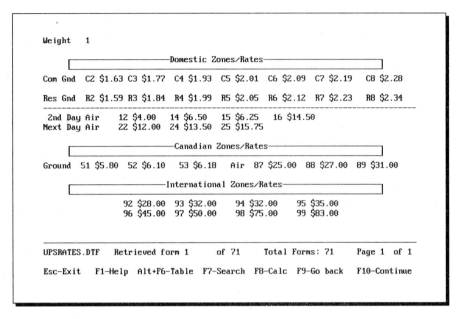

```
Weight    1

        ┌─────────────────Domestic Zones/Rates─────────────────┐

 Com Gnd  C2 $1.63 C3 $1.77  C4 $1.93  C5 $2.01  C6 $2.09  C7 $2.19   C8 $2.28

 Res Gnd  R2 $1.59 R3 $1.84  R4 $1.99  R5 $2.05  R6 $2.12  R7 $2.23   R8 $2.34
 ─────────────────────────────────────────────────────────────────────────
  2nd Day Air     12 $4.00   14 $6.50   15 $6.25    16 $14.50
  Next Day Air    22 $12.00  24 $13.50  25 $15.75
                    ┌──────────────Canadian Zones/Rates──────────────┐

  Ground   51 $5.80  52 $6.10   53 $6.18   Air  87 $25.00  88 $27.00  89 $31.00

                 ┌───────────────International Zones/Rates───────────────┐

             92 $28.00  93 $32.00    94 $32.00    95 $35.00
             96 $45.00  97 $50.00    98 $75.00    99 $83.00


 ─────────────────────────────────────────────────────────────────────────
 UPSRATES.DTF   Retrieved form 1      of 71      Total Forms: 71     Page 1  of 1

 Esc-Exit   F1-Help  Alt+F6-Table  F7-Search  F8-Calc  F9-Go back   F10-Continue
```

Figure 12-6: Sample UPSRATES Form Design. Rates are entered for a 1-pound parcel. Note that separate fields are included for domestic ground commercial rates and domestic ground residential rates. All other rates fields use the UPS Service Zone as their field label. UPSRATES.DTF is supplied on the Applications disk.

The UPS parcel weight limit is 70 lbs, so you'll create one record in your UPSRATES.DTF database for each pound (1 through 70) and another record for Air Letters, since these have their own rates. Figure 12-6 shows the UPSRATES.DTF form design.

The following tips will guide you in designing your rates database and entering your rates. UPSRATES.DTF is simply a lookup file of rates. No programming is required.

If you prefer to limit your system to accommodate domestic shipments only, you can leave out the Canadian and/or international zones and rates. UPS will have you sign a statement certifying that you won't be shipping to these destinations.

Leave at least two spaces between any nonlabel text and the beginning of the adjacent field label. This prevents Q&A from thinking that the descriptive text is part of the field label.

Make your rates fields wide enough to hold the longest rate value for the zone, remembering to include a space for the **$** sign. Make the Weight field three characters wide to accommodate the "LTR" record for UPS Air Letters.

Format your Weight field for numbers and all other fields for money.

 Note: You'll need one record where the Weight field contains "LTR" (for Air Letter). Format the field temporarily for text, create the "LTR" record, and then change the information type of the field back to numeric. The Weight field is both Speedy and Unique.

Once the form design is done, you'll need the current UPS rate charts (available from your nearest United Parcel Service office) for Domestic Ground and Air Service, Canadian Ground and Air Service, and International Air Service.

Enter the rates in Add Data, starting with the 1-pound form. Type the number **1** into the Weight field, and then type the 1-pound rates, zone by zone, into the other fields on the form. Then fill out the 2-pound record in the same manner, the 3-pound record, and so forth, until you have a record for all weights from 1 to 70 pounds. The 71st record in the database will be the "LTR" form. With this one, be sure to type rates only into those fields that correspond to actual Air Letter zones.

When you've finished creating all 71 forms with all the rates entered, your UPSRATES.DTF database is complete, and you can proceed to the design of your parcel entry database.

The Parcel Entry Database

The parcel entry database, which we'll call UPS.DTF, is the focal point of the application because that's where you'll enter your UPS parcel particulars on a daily basis.

Figure 12-7 shows the sample UPS.DTF form design with field ID numbers entered at the Program Spec. This database is heavily programmed to automate data entry as completely as possible. For a common, no-frills domestic ground parcel, for example, you'll need to type in only the invoice number and the parcel weight. And if most of your parcels are regular UPS Ground, inputting 50 or more of them on a daily basis shouldn't take more than a few minutes.

The form is designed not just for data-entry speed, but also to provide the fields and values you'll need for the required Manifest and Summary reports.

Once you've designed your form, you'll have to customize it, program it, and create a Lookup Table to handle the postal code-to-zone conversion. Let's discuss the Lookup Table first.

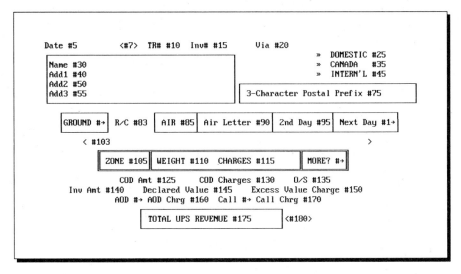

Figure 12-7: Sample UPS Parcel Entry Form. The field ID numbers are in place at the Program Spec. UPS.DTF is the transaction file with one record created for each parcel on the day's manifest.

The Postal Code-to-Zone Lookup Table

The Lookup Table for UPS.DTF contains the postal code prefixes in the Key column, their corresponding Ground Zones in column 1, Second Day Air Zones in column 2, and Next Day Air Zones in column 3. Air Letter zones are the same as Next Day Air zones. The postal code prefix is the first three digits of the zip code, or, in the case of Canadian addresses, the first three characters of the postal code.

Looking at the UPS Domestic Ground Service Zone Chart for your area, you'll see that the zones correspond to zip code prefixes. Note that almost every Ground zone corresponds to a spread, or range, of zip code prefixes. In the case of Second Day Air parcels, all 48 contiguous states are zone 12, with additional zones for Alaska, Hawaii, and Puerto Rico. Similarly, zone 22 applies to all Next Day Air parcels within the contiguous 48 states, with different zones for Alaska/Hawaii and Puerto Rico.

Your Lookup Table should contain domestic and Canadian postal code prefixes and their related zones, but not international zones. There are simply too many international destinations to try to get each and every one of them into the table. If you're shipping a parcel to a destination other than the U.S. or Canada, you can simply look up the proper zone in the UPS International Service Guide and type it in during parcel entry.

Starting with the smallest U.S. zip code prefix, type in the prefix in the Key column of the Lookup Table and its corresponding Ground zone in Column 1. There's a trick to this, however. The programming in the parcel entry form uses the *@LOOKUPR* function, which finds the next lowest value if the Key column doesn't contain an exact match. Therefore, your Key column will contain each of the lowest zip code prefixes that correspond to the zones that are valid to the end of each prefix range.

To illustrate, suppose your UPS Ground Zone Chart shows that zip code prefixes 320 through 355 (representing zips 32000 through 35599) are zone 6. This means that 320 should be a Key column value, with 356 as the value in the next Key column row. This way, if the @LOOKUPR function is searching the Key column for any prefix from 320 through 355, it will return the value from the specified column on the 320 row.

The UPS-supplied Ground Zone Charts for the U.S. and Canada will show all the lowest prefixes for each range along with their corresponding zones.

When filling out the table, remember that some U.S. and Canadian destinations do not have ground service and that Canadian Air shipments are not broken down by Second Day and Next Day Air; they're simply Air. When typing Canadian Air Zones into the table, type the same zone in columns 2 and 3, so the @LOOKUPR function will return the proper Canadian zone whether Second Day or Next Day Air is specified for a Canadian Air shipment during parcel entry. Figure 12-8 shows portions of a sample Lookup Table with several prefixes and their corresponding zones, giving you an idea of how the table is filled out and used by the @LOOKUPR function we'll program later into the database.

Programming the Parcel Entry Form

Table 12-1 contains design and customize parameters you can use, along with suggested programming statements and, in some cases, a brief explanation of the programming. Consult Figure 12-7 for the Program Spec field ID numbers.

Here's how the user moves through the form — and what happens — during parcel entry in Add Data.

1. The blank form comes up with the date and other initial values displayed. The incremental transaction number (@Number) is returned unless this is the first parcel of the day, in which case your help screen displays telling the user to press **<Alt><0>** which resets the @Number to 0, enters **1** in the TR# field, and moves the cursor to the Inv# field (you'll need an **<Alt><0>** macro to do this).

```
                                             Next Day Air,
                              2nd Day Air,     Air Letter,
        U.S./Canada    48 States/Canada  and Canada    and Canada
        Postal Prefixes  Ground Zones    Air Zones     Air Zones
```

KEY	1	2	3	4
004	8	12	22	
006	NO	15	25	
010	8	12	22	
100	8	12	22	
200	8	12	22	
300	8	12	22	
324	8	12	22	
325	7	12	22	
936	3	12	22	
940	4	12	22	
967	NO	14	24	
G0A	53	88	88	
G0B	53	89	89	
G0S	53	88	88	

Figure 12-8: Partial Lookup Table. It will enable Q&A to return the appropriate UPS Zone based on the postal code prefix. In the columns where that type of UPS service is not available from your shipping area (such as Ground service to Puerto Rico and the Maritime Provinces of Canada when shipping from California) use a No, or some other code that prevents the lookup from returning a valid zone. Or, simply leave the cell blank.

2. A valid invoice number is entered, which returns the information for the name/address block, the Via field, and the Inv Amt field. The invoice number serves as the Package ID Number. Maintain and use a series of numbers outside your invoice number range for noninvoice-related parcels. In such cases the lookup will fail and you can fill in the name/address block manually.

3. Domestic, Canada, or International shipment is specified, and the three-character postal code is typed in.

4. The type of service is selected (Ground, type of Ground, Air, type of Air). In the case of domestic and Canadian shipments, the Zone is returned from the Lookup Table.

5. The parcel weight is entered, and the charges are retrieved from the external UPSRATES.DTF file.

6. If that's all there is for the current parcel, the Total UPS Revenue is calculated and the user can save the record with **<F10>** and fill out the

Table 12 -1
Customized Reference Table for UPS.DTF

Cursor moves may be entered at the Navigation Spec.

Label, ID#, Width, Format	Initial Value	Restrict Spec	Programming and Comments
Date, #5, 13, D	@Date	!	<#5: If @add then goto #7
			[Comments: This is a Speedy field, but is not Unique.]
None, #7, 1, N	1	n/a	<#7:If @xlookup("UPS",#5,"date","date") <>#5 then @help(#7) else goto #10
			[Comments: When the first parcel of the day is about to be entered, your custom help screen pops up, instructing the user to press <Alt><0> (to reset the @Number to 0 and move the cursor to the TR# field). The field contains a "1" as its Initial Value, a trick that comes into play in the Summary Reports to get a total count of parcels by zone by specifying "Total" rather than "Count," saving a line at each break in the zone (see Summary Reports below). Make the field Read-only so it can't be altered during input.]
TR#, #10, 3, N	n/a	!	<#10:If @add then {#10=@number; goto #15}
			[Comments: The parcel transaction number is assigned here.]
Inv#, #15, 6, N	N	!	>#15:If@add then {xlookup("Invoice",#15, "Invoice No","Via",#20,"name", #30,"add1", #40,"add2",#50,"add3",#55, "Order Value", #140); goto #25}
			[Comments: This series of Lookups fills in the type of UPS service, the name/address block, and the order value from the matching INVOICE.DTF record. Also serves as the Package ID Number. Make this field Speedy and Unique.]
Via, #20, 10, T	n/a	n/a	No programming
Domestic, #25, 1, YU	Y	!	>#25: If #25="N" then goto #35;If #25="Y" and #30="" then goto #30 else goto #75
			[Comments: Allows user to manually fill out empty name/address block, or moves cursor to prefix field.]

(continued)

Table 12-1 *(continued)*

Label, ID#, Width, Format	Initial Value	Restrict Spec	Programming and Comments
Canada, #35,1, YU	N	!	>#35:If #35="N" then {#45="Y";goto #45};If #35="Y" and #30="" then goto #30 else goto #75
			[Comments: Allows user to fill out empty name/address block; if field contains "N," international shipment is presumed.]
Intern'l, #45, 1, YU	N	!	<#45:#103="YOU'VE SELECTED AN INTERNATIONAL SHIPMENT. AIR IS MANDATORY";If #30="" then goto #30 else {#80="N";goto #85}
			[Comments: Displays message; allows user to fill out empty name/address block; sets Ground field to "N" and moves cursor to Air field.]
Name, #30, 30, TU	n/a	!	>#30:goto #40
Add1, #40, 30, TU	n/a	!	>#40:goto #50
Add2, #50, 30, TU	n/a	!	>#50:goto #55
Add3, #55, 30, TU	n/a	n/a	No programming
Prefix, #75, 3, TU	n/a	n/a	>#75:If #25="Y" or #35="Y" and #75="" then {#103="DOMESTIC AND CANADIAN SHIPMENTS REQUIRE A 3-CHARACTER PREFIX"; goto #75}
			[Comments: Displays message and requires entry of a prefix for domestic or Canadian shipment. You can program this field to return the prefix from the postal code in the address block, as long as its position in the block is predictable.]
Ground, #80, 1, YU	Y	!	>#80:If#80="Y" and #25="Y" then goto #83; If #80="Y" and #35="Y" then goto #105 else goto #85
			[Comments: If it's a domestic ground shipment, the user is prompted to specify Residential ("R") or Commercial ("C") in the next field; if it's a Canadian Ground, the cursor is moved to the Zone field; if it's not a Ground shipment, the cursor moves to the Air field.]

(continued)

Table 12-1 (continued)

Label, ID#, Width, Format	Initial Value	Restrict Spec	Programming and Comments
R/C, #83, 1, TU	n/a	R;C	>#83: If #25="Y" and #80="Y" and #83="" then {#103="Enter R for Residential or C for Commercial Delivery"; goto #83} else goto #105 *[Comments: Displays message and forces entry of "R" or "C" if it's a domestic ground parcel.]*
Air, #85, 1, YU	N	!	<#85:If #80="N" then {#85="Y"; goto #90} *[Comments: Sets field to "Y" if Ground field is "N".]*
Air Letter, #90, 1, YU	N	!	>#90:If #90="N" then goto #95;If #90="Y" then {#110="LTR"; goto #105} *[Comments: If not Air Letter, cursor moves to next field; If Air Letter, Weight field gets "LTR," and cursor is moved to Zone field.]*
2nd Day, #95, 1, YU	N	!	>#95:If #95="Y" then goto #105 else goto #100
Next Day, #100, 1, YU	N	!	<#100:If #85="Y" and #90="N" and #95="N" then {#100="Y";goto #105}
None, #103, 78, TU	n/a	n/a	No programming
Zone, #105, 2, N	n/a	!	<#105:If#25= "Y" or #35 = "Y" and #80="Y" then {#105=@lookupr(#75,1); goto#110}; If #25="Y" or #35="Y" and #90="Y" then {#105=@lookupr(#75,3);goto#115}; If #25= "Y" or #35="Y" and #100="Y" then {#105=@lookupr(#75,3); goto #110}; If#25="Y" or #35="Y" and #95="Y" then {#105=@lookupr(#75,2); goto #110} else @help(#105) *[Comments: These are the lookup commands that return the zone from the Lookup Table based on the Prefix; international shipments are flagged and your help screen for #105 tells the user to look up the zone in the UPS Service Guide.]*
Weight, #110, 3, N	n/a	!	<#110:#103="»»»»Do NOT Press <F10> Yet. Form not Complete «««";If #105<2 then @help(#105);If #25="N" and #85="Y" and #105 < 87 then @help(#105); If #45="Y" and #105 < 92 then @help(#105); If#90="Y" then goto #115; *[Comments: Message warns user form not complete; calls your custom help screen for #105 if Zone value out of range for type of shipment; bypasses field if it's a "LTR".]*

Table 12-1 *(continued)*

Label, ID#, Width, Format	Initial Value	Restrict Spec	Programming and Comments
Charges, #115, 7, N2	n/a	!	<#115:If #110 > 70 then {@help(#110);goto#110} else#115=@xlookup("upsrates",#110,"weight",#83+@str(#105)); goto #120
			[Comments: Checks Weight, and if over 70 lbs. displays your custom help screen for #110; otherwise gets the charges from the UPSRATES database. The @STR function ensures distinction between Residential and Commercial domestic ground rates in the external file.]
More, #120, 1, YU	N	!	>#120:If #120="N" and #175="" then goto #175
			[Comments: If the field is left at the default "N," and the Total Revenue field is blank, the cursor moves there and the Total Revenue is calculated.]
COD Amt, #125, 8, N2	n/a	n/a	>#125:If #25="N" and #125>0 then{@help(#125); If #25="Y" and #125>0 then #130=3.75; goto#135}
			[Comments: If the user attempts to ship a nondomestic COD, your custom help screen displays; If COD is valid, the fee is placed in #130, and the cursor moves to the O/S field.]
COD Chrg, #130, 4, N2	n/a	n/a	No programming
O/S, #135, 1, TU	n/a	X;=	>#135:If #135<>"X" and #135<>"" then {@help(#135); If #135="X" and #110 < 25 then {#110=25; goto #115} else goto #145
			[Comments: Oversize parcel field. Enforces an "X" or nothing in the field along with your help screen; charges the minimum 25 lb rate for an oversize package.]
Inv Amt, #140, 5, N0	n/a	n/a	No Programming
Declared Value, #145, 5, N0	n/a	n/a	<#145:If #140>150 then {#145=#140*.75; goto #150}
			[Comments: If the Invoice Amount is greater than $150, the Declared Value is 75% of the amount. Use a formula that reflects your own average margins. UPS insures free to $100 value.]

(continued)

Table 12-1 *(continued)*

Label, ID#, Width, Format	Initial Value	Restrict Spec	Programming and Comments
Excess Val Chrg, #150, 6, N2	n/a	n/a	<#150:If @len(#145)=3 then {#150 =@left(#145,1)*.30};If @len(#145)=4 then {#150=@left (#145,2)*.30};If @len (#145)=5 then {#150=@left(#145,3) *.30};If #120="N" then goto #175 else goto #155
			[Comments: Excess Value is a Declared Value over $100, at 30 cents per each additional $100 or fraction thereof. The programming works for Declared Values up to $99999.]
AOD, #155, 1, TU	n/a	X;=	>#155:If #25="N" and #155="X" then @help(#155); If #155<>"X" and #155<>"" then @help(#155);If #85="Y" and #145>25000 then @help(#145);If #155="X" then {#160=.50; goto #165}
			[Comments: Acknowledgement of Delivery available on Domestic parcels only. Programming also traps an illegal Declared Value (max. $25000 on Air shipments). Your AOD rate may differ from the 50 cents shown here.]
AOD Chrg, #160, 4, N2	n/a	n/a	No programming
Call, #165, 1, TU	n/a	X;=	>#165:If #25="N" and #165="X" then @help(#165); If #165<>"X" and #165<>"" then @help(#165); If #165="X" and #80="Y" then {#170=1.50;goto #175};If #165="" then goto #175 else @help(#165)
			[Comments: Enforces an "X" or nothing in the field along with your help screen. Flags nondomestic call tag requests.]
Call Chrg, #170, 4 N2	n/a	n/a	No programming
Total UPS Revenue, #175, 8, N2	n/a	!	<#175=#115+#130+#160+#170+#150;#103=""; goto #180
			[Comments: totals up the charges and blanks any message in #103.]

(continued)

Table 12-1 *(continued)*

Label, ID#, Width, Format	Initial Value	Restrict Spec	Programming and Comments
None, #180, 1, T	n/a	n/a	<#180:If #5="" or #10="" or #15="" or #30="" or #40="" or #50="" or #105="" or #115="" or #175="" then @help(#180) else #103="IF THIS FORM IS FINISHED PRESS <F10> TO ADD IT TO TODAY'S MANIFEST";#120="N";goto #120 *[Comments: Checks the key fields to be sure they contain values. Displays your help screen if any are blank. Otherwise, displays an "okay to press <F10>" message, sets the More? field to "N," and moves the cursor there.]*

next one. Otherwise, the user fills out the information for the additional services desired, after which the Total Revenue is calculated and the form is saved.

Test your parcel entry form nine ways to Sunday, entering a wide variety of domestic, Canadian, and international parcels, and specifying different types of services. You may need to make programming adjustments based on current UPS optional services and rates, and your particular data entry needs and preferences.

The Required Reports

You'll need to design the series of required manifest reports which your macro will compile and print in sequence on a daily basis. When you've got the entire application installed, you'll enter the day's parcels and then simply invoke the macro to print the manifest that the UPS driver picks up along with the parcels.

The Manifest Report

Our standard columnar reports will be designed to print on 8½-by-11-inch paper in 12 pitch characters. Almost any printer will do — even a laser — but you'll need to take your particular make and model into consideration and perhaps experiment a bit to get optimum output. Consult UPS's *Guidelines for*

```
FREEMONT SUPPLY CO                 UPS SHIPPING              UPS SHIPPE
18734 MAIN STREET                    MANIFEST                PICKUP RECO
GLENDALE CA 93689               By Transaction No.      Date Shipped: 2/


                                                                   COD
        Invoice TR#    Consignee Name/Address    Zone Lbs Charges COD Amt Chrgs O/
        ------- ---    ---------------------     ---- --- ------- ------- ----- --

        21260  1    DAVID MICHAEL MERRIMER         7   4   3.40
                    988 DUNBAR AVENUE
                    BAY ST LOUIS MS 39521
        21261  2    ROBERT MC DONLEVY             12  25  26.50  323.44  3.75  X
                    2990 E CLARENDON
                    PHOENIX AZ 85016
        21262  3    ROBERTO CACCIANO               2   5   1.95
                    875 E LAUREL AVE
                    SIERRA MADRE CA 91024
        21304  4    JUDITH GORTURA                53   5   8.45
                    PO BOX 877 SUCC BROSSARD
                    BROSSARD QUEBEC J4X 1J3
                    CANADA
        21270  5    RICHARD FRANLERITI            22  LTR  9.75
                    5454 CANNON ROAD
                    TWINSBURG OH 44087
        21275  6    ERNEST BREENMAN               22  LTR  9.75
                    341 KNEELAND AVE
                    YONKERS NY 10705
        21277  7    MARY BILLINGER                22   2  13.00
                    RR #1 BOX 88
                    RUSKIN NE 68974
        21285  8    STANLY SAWALSKI                7   6   3.77
                    5325 S MENARD
                    CHICAGO IL 60638
        21289  9    LEE CARL FENTRIS              87   4  31.00
                    23266 72ND AVE RR 4
                    LANGLEY BC V3A 4P7
                    CANADA
        ~~~~~~~~~~~~~~~~~~~~~~~~~~~~~~~~~~~~~~~~~~~~~~~~~~~~~~~~~~~~~~~~~~
        ~~~~~~~~~~~~~~~~~~~~~~~~~~~~~~~~~~~~~~~~~~~~~~~~~~~~~~~~~~~~~~~~~~
        21327  19   WILLIAM FERNRATIN             92   3  38.00
                    35 LES BOULEZ RUE
                    VICHY 03200
                    FRANCE
        21344  20   MARK RICHARDS                  8   6   4.23
                    PO BOX 88 JERSEY AVE
                    GREENWOOD LAKE NY 10925
        21356  21   GUY CANLIN                     8   2   2.90
                    6833 VINE ST
                    PHILADELPHIA PA 19139
        21369  22   ELLIOTT BAY BOOK COMPANY       5   6   2.93
                    101 SOUTH MAIN STREET
                    SEATTLE WA 98104
        21372  23   ASSOC STUDENT BOOKSTORE        4   5   2.62
                    2ND AND ORANGE STREETS
                    CHICO CA 95929
        21352  24   BERNDT HELMUT SPITZER          7   4   3.40
                    6515 N MARMORA AVE
                    CHICAGO IL 60630
        21269  25   GERALD RIVIERA                 8   5   4.10
                    489 ELMWOOD AVE #12
                    BUFFALO NY 14222
        ======= ===  ============================  ==== === ======= ======= ===== ==
        Count:  25
```

Figure 12-9: The UPS Manifest Report (Partially Shown).

UPS Manifest Systems. Your reports can be different from those shown and still meet UPS requirements (final approval, by the way, is based on the output produced by your system and comes from the UPS corporate offices).

Before designing any of your manifest reports, set your Columnar Report Global Format Options for UPS.DTF as follows:

```
# of spaces between columns    1
Default to repeating value     No
Action on blank value          Leave blank
Action on column break         Don't skip line
```

Name your report UPS Manifest. Use the **{@Date}** formula in the Date field at the Retrieve Spec. This will ensure each time you run the report that only the current day's parcel records are selected for inclusion in the report.

The sample report design shown in Figure 12-9 produces 18 transactions per 8½-by-11 page. It's not the only possible design, but it provides plenty of room for all the columns at 12-cpi printing.

The Column/Sort Spec for *UPS Manifest* is the key to having your manifest columns fit comfortably across the page with appropriate column headings printed in boldface. You'll also need a couple of derived columns to force the name and address fields from the parcel entry form to wrap under the same column. Without these, you'll be hard-pressed to fit all the columns across the page, no matter how small a printing pitch you use.

Here are the Column/Sort Spec field names and specifications to get the Figure 12-9 report. The portions of text shown in boldface, when applied at the spec, will embolden your column headings and transaction numbers. Refer back to Figure 12-7 for a review of how the form is laid out.

```
TR#:  2,AS,F(JC),C
Inv#:  1,H(7:Invoice#)
Name:  4,I
Add1:  5,I
Add2:  6,I
Add3:  7,I
ZONE:  10,H(4:Zone)
WEIGHT:  11,H(3:Lbs)
CHARGES:  12,H(7:Charges)
COD Amt:  13,H(7:COD Amt)
COD Charges:  14,H(5:COD!Chrgs)
O/S:  15,H(3:O/S),F(JC)
Declared Value:  16,H(6:Decl!Value)
AOD:  17,H(1:A!O!D!)
Call:  18,H(1:C!L!L)
```

```
                              DEFINE PAGE


            Page width.: 96          Page length..: 66

            Left margin: 0           Right margin.: 96

            Top margin.: 4           Bottom margin: 0

            Characters per inch:    10  ▶12◀  15    17

 ─────────────────────────────── HEADER ───────────────────────────
 1: FREEMONT SUPPLY CO↑UPS SHIPPING↑UPS SHIPPER NO. CA X88-143
 2: 18734 MAIN STREET↑MANIFEST↑PICKUP RECORD NO. 123456789
 3: GLENDALE CA 93689↑By Transaction No.↑Date Shipped: @Date(3)  Page No. #
```

Figure 12-10: The Define Page screen for the UPS Manifest Report. The three header lines are enhanced with boldface, and the third line is underlined. When recording your macro to run the manifest, be sure to have it pause at the Pickup Record No. so you can enter this number which changes from day to day.

Derived Columns

Heading:
Formula: @text(30," ")
Column Spec: 8,I
Heading: 30: Consignee Name/Address
Formula: #4+#8+#5+#8+#6+#8+#7
Column Spec: 9

The @Text formula in the first derived column, when that column is referenced in the second derived column's formula, forces the name and address information to wrap so it can all be confined to a single column. When your derived columns are finished, press **<F10>** for the Print Options screen.

At the Print Options screen, select your printer and type of paper feed, and be sure to set Print Totals Only to No, Line Spacing to Single, and Split Records to No. Set up your Define Page screen to look like Figure 12-10. Run the manifest report with a few dummy records, redesigning it as necessary until you've got everything just right.

The Summary Reports

The UPS *Guidelines* are clear on the Summary Reports requirements, but not, of course, on how to get these reports from Q&A. Depending on your report designs and the particular information each summary report includes, you may be able to get away with as few as five reports. But we'll meet the requirements with six Summary Reports.

The Summary Reports, unlike the all-inclusive Manifest Report, are simply summaries or totals of the day's transactions. UPS will want a report showing the number of pieces, aggregate weight, and charges, with totals sorted by zone for both common carrier (ground) and air service.

UPS will also likely want a report showing the count of air parcels broken down by type of air service. It will want to see a summary report of the grand total number of pieces, the total weight, and charges. And it also requires a report showing the number of COD's and COD charges, a report of the number of AOD's and AOD charges, and finally, a report of the total UPS revenue for the day.

The difficulty lies not so much in designing Q&A reports to fulfill these requirements, but in deciding how to print them out in an acceptable fashion. The reports, after all, are just summaries, and you don't want to wind up printing out six pages, one page for each short Summary Report.

The object, rather, is to have all the Summary Reports print on a single page, which you can do by carefully designing each of the reports, printing them to disk when the time comes, and then using a Write merge document with a ***JOIN*** command for each of the reports to be included on the page. Once all the elements are in place, the daily process of compiling and printing the Summary Report page, like the Manifest Report, will be entirely macro-driven.

Figure 12-11 shows a sample summary page that includes all six Summary Reports. We'll design the reports one by one and then create the master merge document that prints them in this concise format.

The Common Carrier and Air Shipment Reports

Since we're limited by the amount of vertical space on the standard 8½-by-11 page, we don't want our Common Carrier and Air Shipment reports formatted in the usual columnar style with a column break and subtotal each time the UPS zone changes. If ten different Ground zones are included in the report, for example, this would mean an additional 20 or so lines required, making just this one report up to 30 lines long. Add this to the vertical space required by a similarly formatted Air Shipments report, and you'd be lucky to contain just these two reports in 60 lines. So we'll use a trick or two that results in these reports being printed with the absolute minimum number of lines.

```
FREEMONT SUPPLY CO            UPS MANIFEST SUMMARY        UPS SHIPPER NO. CA X88-143
18734 MAIN STREET                  SUMMARY               PICKUP RECORD NO. 123456789
GLENDALE CA 93689                                             DATE SHIPPED 2/3/91


                                 COMMON CARRIER
                        UPS Zone Pieces Weight Charges
                        -------- ------ ------ -------
                           2       2      4      3.35
                           4       1      2      2.16
                           5       2      7      5.13
                           6       2     12      6.69
                           7       4     80     42.13
                           8       6     69     47.87
                          53       2     10     16.90
                        ======== ====== ====== =======
                        Total:    19    184    124.23



                                  AIR SHIPMENTS
                        UPS Zone Pieces Weight Charges
                        -------- ------ ------ -------
                          12       2     31     34.50
                          14       1      6     12.50
                          22       2      2     14.25
                          92       1      3     38.00
                        ======== ====== ====== =======
                        Total:     6     42     99.25




                        NEXT DAY AIR   AIR LTRS   2ND DAY AIR
                        -------------  --------   -----------
                        =============  ========   ===========
            Total:            1           2            3


               GRAND TOTAL PIECES    GRAND TOTAL WEIGHT   GRAND TOTAL CHARGES
               ------------------    ------------------   -------------------
               ==================    ==================   ===================
      Total:          25                   226                  223.58


        NO. CALL TAGS  CALL TAG CHARGS  EXCESS VALUE UNITS  EXCESS VAL CHARGES
        -------------  ---------------  -----------------   ------------------
        =============  ===============  =================   ==================
Total:                      0.00               2                  0.60
Count:       0


        NO. OF AOD'S   AOD CHARGES   NO. OF COD'S   COD CHARGES   TOTAL UPS REVENUE
        ------------   -----------   ------------   -----------   -----------------
        ============   ===========   ============   ===========   =================
Total:                      0.50                        3.75             228.43
Count:       1                            1
```

Figure 12-11: The Summary Report Page. This is a Write merge document that contains a *JOIN* command for each report. All Summary Reports use the UPS.DTF database file.

Use the {@Date} function in the Date field at the Retrieve Spec for the Common Carrier report, additionally specifying a **Y** in the Ground field to select only those records from the database that include the current date and specify surface shipment. At the Column/Sort Spec for the Common Carrier report, number and code your columns as follows:

```
ZONE:  1,AS,H(8:UPS Zone),F(JC)
WEIGHT:  6,I
CHARGES:  8,I
```

Also, type **4,I** into the small labelless field just to the right of the Date field (this is the field that contains the Initial Value "1" during parcel entry).

Press **<F8>** for the Derived Column screen and create these four derived columns:

```
Heading:
Formula:  #1
Column Spec:  50,I

Heading:  Pieces
Formula:  @text((#1<>#50),@str(@total(#4,#1)))
Column Spec:  5,T,F(N0,JC)

Heading:  Weight
Formula:   @text((#1<>#50),@str(@total(#6,#1)))
Column Spec:  7,T,F(N0,JC)

Heading:  Charges
Formula:   @text((#1<>#50),@str(@total(#8,#1)))
Column Spec:  9,T,F(N2,JC)
```

At the Print Options screen, choose Print to Disk, set Print Totals Only to No, and center the report body on the page.

Set up your Define Page screen as follows:

```
Page width:  96     Page length:  16
Left margin:  0      Right margin:  96
Top margin:  1       Bottom margin:  1
Characters per inch:  12
```

Type **!COMMON CARRIER!** on the first header line, and boldface the text.

These specs will give you the Common Carrier report as shown in Figure 12-11.

Your Column/Sort Spec, Derived Columns, Print Options, and Define Page parameters for the Air Shipments report are exactly the same as the Common Carrier report with the following exceptions:

1. Your Retrieve Spec for the Air Shipments report is `{@Date}` in the Date field, and a **Y** in the Air field.

2. At the Define Page screen, type **!AIR SHIPMENTS!** into the first header line and boldface the text.

To design the Air Shipments report, simply make a copy of the Common Carrier report, naming it Air Shipments, and edit your Retrieve Spec and Define Page header as above.

The Other Four Summary Reports

Air Totals: The Air Totals report provides a *count* of the Next Day Air, Air Letter, and Second Day Air parcels on the day's manifest. Your only Retrieve Spec parameter for this report is the {@Date} function in the Date field. Fill out your Column/Sort Spec as follows:

```
Air Letter: 2,T,H(8:AIR LTRS),F(N,JC)
2nd Day: 3,T,H(12:2ND DAY AIR),F(N,JC)
Next Day: 1,T,H(12:NEXT DAY AIR),F(N,JC)
```

Select Print Report to Disk, Totals Only, and Justify Center at the Print Options screen. At the Define Page screen make your Page Width and Right Margin 96, your Page Length 6, your other margins 0, and your cpi 12.

Grand Totals: This report shows the grand total number of pieces on the day's manifest, the grand total weight, and grand total charges (not including any optional UPS services such as AOD, COD, extra insurance, or Call Tags). Again, your Retrieve Spec is `{@Date}` in the Date field. Your Column/Sort Spec is filled out as follows:

```
WEIGHT: 2,T,H(20:GRAND TOTAL WEIGHT),F(JC)
CHARGES: 3,T,H(20:GRAND TOTAL CHARGES),F(JC)
```

In the small labelless field just to the right of the Date field, type in:

```
1,T,H(20:GRAND TOTAL PIECES),F(N0,JC)
```

Your Print Options and Define Page settings are exactly the same as the preceding Air Totals report.

Call Tags/Excess Value: This report, shown in Figure 12-11 along with the other Summary Reports, shows the total number of Call Tags and Call Tag Charges, and the number of Excess Value Units and corresponding Excess Value charges.

Your Retrieve Spec for this report is simply **{@Date}** in the Date field. At the Column/Sort Spec, use these specifications:

```
Excess Value Charge: 4,T,H(18:EXCESS VAL CHARGES),F(JC)
Call: 1,C,H(15:NO. CALL TAGS),F(JC)
Call Chrg: 2,T,H(15:CALL TAG CHARGES),F(JC)
```

With the following Derived Column:

```
Heading: EXCESS VALUE UNITS
Formula: #4/.3
Column Spec: 3,T,F(JC)
```

Your Print Options and Define Page settings for this report are exactly the same as the Air Totals report above.

AOD/COD/TOT REV: The last item of information on your final Summary Report should be the UPS Total Revenue from all the parcel charges and optional service charges on the day's manifest. But instead of having one report for the AOD and COD totals and another for the total revenue, you can combine them into a single report. Your Retrieve Spec is **{@Date}** in the Date field. Type in the following column specs at your Column/Sort Spec:

```
COD Amt: 3,C,H(12:NO. OF COD'S),F(JC)
COD Charges: 4,T,H(12:COD CHARGES),F(JC)
AOD: 1,C,H(NO. OF AOD'S),F(JC)
AOD Chrg: 2,T,H(12:AOD CHARGES),F(JC)
Total UPS Revenue: 5,T,H(17:TOTAL UPS REVENUE),F(JC)
```

Your Print Options and Define Page settings for this final report are the same as the Air Totals report above.

With the designs of your six Manifest Summary Reports now completed and saved, you can create your Write merge document that will print them all out on a single page.

The Summary Report Merge Document

When you print each of your six Summary Reports to disk, give them DOS filenames that are as descriptive as possible and save them to your Q&A documents directory. You'll then specify these filenames in your merge document ***JOIN*** commands so Write can join them into the master document at printing time.

Figure 12-12 shows the construction of the merge document with a sample document heading in place (it's not a header) and the six ***JOIN*** commands and the document files they specify.

```
FREEMONT SUPPLY CO        UPS MANIFEST SUMMARY      UPS SHIPPER NO. CA X88-143
18734 MAIN STREET              SUMMARY             PICKUP RECORD NO.
GLENDALE CA 93689                                    DATE SHIPPED *@DATE(3)

*JOIN GROUND.DOC*       (The Common Carrier report)

*JOIN AIR.DOC*          (The Air Shipments report)

*JOIN AIRTOTLS.DOC*     (The Air Totals report)
*JOIN GRANTOTS.DOC*     (The Grand Totals report)
*JOIN CALLINS.DOC*      (The Call Tags Excess Value report)
*JOIN AODCOD.DOC*       (The AOD/COD/Tot Rev report)




[LLLLTLLLLTLLLLTLLLLTLLLLTLLLLTLLLLTLLLLTLLLL5LLLLLLLLL6LLLLLLLLL7LLLLLLLL8
SUMMARY.DOC                              0% Line 1 of Page 1 of 1

Esc-Exit  F1-Info  F2-Print  Ctrl+F6-Define Pg  F7-Search  F8-Options  ↑F8-Save
```

Figure 12-12: The Master Summary Report Merge Document. It has the required page heading information in place and the *JOIN* commands that will insert the reports in the document at printing time.

Notice in Figure 12-12 that the Pickup Record Number hasn't been typed in. This is because the number will change each day and you'll have to type it in manually when the macro pauses for you to do so. So when you've finished creating the merge document, be sure to save it with the cursor positioned where the first digit of the Pickup Record Number will be typed in later. This way, when Q&A brings the page onto the Type/Edit screen (in overtype mode), the cursor will be exactly where you want it.

Your page dimensions for the SUMMARY.DOC merge document are:

Left margin: 0   **Right margin:** 96
Top margin: 0   **Bottom margin:** 0
Page Width: 96   **Page Length:** 66 (or whatever your printer needs to properly print a standard page length)
Characters-per-inch: 12

Use the appropriate Print Options screen settings, single-spacing the document, setting justification to No, and leaving the Name of Merge File line blank.

The final component of the application — just before recording the macro that drives the procedure — is the shipper labels you'll need to affix to your UPS parcels. The UPS *Guidelines* publication gives you a variety of acceptable label formats.

You can, of course, integrate your UPS Shipper Label with an address label, or even an invoice or packing slip which folds into a clear plastic sleeve affixed to the carton. Assuming you're going to run shipper labels as a separate item, simply select a Write mailing label size that works with your printer and that meets UPS requirements, copy it to a new name, such as UPS Shipper Label, and add your text and single merge field along the following lines:

> UPS SHIPPER NO.
> CA X88-143
> PKG ID# *Inv#*

Replace the shipper number in the above example with your own UPS Shipper Number. The package ID number is actually the invoice number which is merged during printing from the Inv# field on the UPS.DTF parcel entry form. You can use Line Draw to create a box around the label text.

Your Retrieve Spec for the labels will be the **{@Date}** function in the Date field of the UPS.DTF form. You may also want to fill out a Sort Spec so the labels print out in invoice number or some other useful sequence. Be sure to save the specs so you can have your macro call them when the time comes.

Recording the Macro

You should now have a number of dummy Ground and Air parcel entry forms (with the current date) filled out, your Manifest and Summary Reports designs should be finalized, your SUMMARY.DOC merge document should be ready to roll, and your Shipper Label design fine-tuned to produce the labels you need. A sample of each Summary Report should already have been printed to disk as your macro will need to overwrite these with the current reports.

The macro you'll need isn't unduly lengthy, but you may still wish to save it to its own file rather than to the default QAMACRO.ASC file. You can then load your special UPS.MAC file into memory as the initial step in running your daily manifest.

I won't enumerate each and every macro keystroke here but rather will summarize what the macro needs to accomplish in order to produce the complete computer manifest and labels.

1. Starting from the Q&A Main menu, the macro selects Report and then Print a Report, and types in **UPS.DTF** preceded by its proper path. At the List of Reports, it types in **UPS Manifest**, and answers Yes to temporary changes. The macro then pauses at the Define Page screen for you to type in the variable Pickup Record Number. Pressing **<Enter>** resumes the macro, which compiles and prints out the shipping manifest.

2. The macro then prints to disk, in turn, each of the six Manifest Summary Reports. For each report, the macro selects Print a Report, types in the report name at the List of Reports, and answers No to temporary changes. IBM ASCII is selected for the format at the Disk Print menu, the filename to print the report to is specified, and (except in the case of the Common Carrier and Air Shipments reports — see step 5 below) the macro answers **Y** to overwrite the previous report/document of the same name.

Note: Be sure to include an extra **N** keystroke following the final **N** or **<Enter>** (at the Temporary Changes? screen) for the Common Carrier and Air Shipments reports. This is essential when there are Ground but no Air parcels (or vice versa) on the day's manifest. The additional **N**, in such a case, immediately routes the macro back to the Report menu for the next Summary Report. You can edit the macro file in Write, inserting the keystroke at both locations in the macro.

3. When the Summary Reports are all printed to disk, the macro then gets the SUMMARY.DOC merge document on screen and pauses at the exact location for you to type in the Pickup Record Number. Pressing **<Enter>** resumes the macro, joins the individual Summary Reports to the document, prints out the document, and then escapes to the Write menu, answering **Y** to continue without saving the edits to the document.

4. The macro now specifies **UPS Shipper Label** in the Mailing Label module, calls the saved Retrieve and Sort Specs, pauses for you to load your labels and, with your **<Enter>** keypress, prints out the labels.

5. The final macro step is to delete from disk the Common Carrier and the Air Shipments reports/documents (GROUND.DOC and AIR.DOC), an essential step in case the next day's manifest includes either no Ground or no Air parcels. If you don't delete AIR.DOC, for example, and the next day's manifest includes no air parcels, the Air Shipments report/document from the previous day will be joined with SUMMARY.DOC because it will not have been overwritten.

Along with a sample manifest and manifest summary, the UPS representative will want your system to produce a complete rate chart printout along with a printout of your ground zone chart.

The Ground Zone "chart" is your Lookup Table for UPS.DTF and can't be printed out in a way that is likely to make sense to whomever at UPS is reviewing your output for approval. The way to handle this is to compose a Write document with the starting and ending zip code prefixes for each zone. Whatever it is you wind up with merely needs to show UPS officials that your system will return the appropriate Ground Zone based on the prefix.

As for the complete rate chart printout, you'll need to design a report for UPSRATES.DTF that prints the zones, in ascending order, as column headings, and the weights, starting with "LTR," in ascending order, down the page as report rows. At each intersection of a weight and zone, the chart must show the correct UPS rate for your area.

Your report will need two sets of Ground Zones and rates — one for Commercial deliveries and one for Residential — and since this means a 35-column report (with the other zones included) it's unlikely you'll be able to get all these columns across a single page even on a wide-carriage printer with 17-cpi characters. The solution is to select "Split report across pages" when you get the "Report too Wide" message.

There may be additional performance demands placed on your Q&A manifest application by the local or corporate UPS office; their own *Guidelines* state that requirements are subject to change. Talk to your UPS representative at the outset and find out what, if anything, your system will have to produce that isn't specifically called for in the *Guidelines*. It could save you from having to repeat your efforts later on.

And that concludes our UPS rate base application. As you saw, each step along the way we applied a careful analysis of the results we must have to the surprisingly broad capabilities of Q&A. While the analysis was challenging, implementing the application isn't particularly hard.

Parsing Whole Name and Other Text Files

When you parse the value in a database field, you're breaking down or separating it into component parts in order to use those parts for some purpose. For example, if the Name field in your database looks like this:

Name: Gerald K. Morgan

you can't easily use this field in a personalized merge letter that you want to address "Dear Gerald" or "Dear Mr. Morgan."

Furthermore, since there is no indication, other than the apparent gender of the first name, that this is a Mr., Miss, or Mrs., you wouldn't be able to address your merge letters with a proper title such as "Mr. Gerald K. Morgan," unless you were willing to risk offending someone.

There's another problem with having the whole name in a single field: How do you sort on the last name?

Novice database designers also frequently put the city, state, and zip code in the same field, making it difficult later on to sort the records on the state or zip code.

If you have a database that includes what are rightfully two or more values in a single field, you can use a programming statement at the Mass Update Spec to separate them and place the component parts in their own fields.

Suppose you've been entering your customer names as whole names in a single field, as in the example above, and you now want to separate them. Here are the steps:

1. Back up the file you are about to mass update.

2. Redesign the form, adding first, middle, and last name fields. Format them as text fields, and make them each wide enough to accommodate the longest value they'll contain. These fields can be anywhere on the form for now. You can redesign the form again later and place them right where you want.

3. Select Mass Update from the File menu. At the Retrieve Spec, press **<F10>** to select all the forms. At the Update Spec, enter the following:

```
Whole Name: #1: If @instr(#1," ")>0 then {#2=@left(#1,
(@instr (#1," ")-1)); #3=@mid(#1,@instr(#1," ")+1,25);
#4=@mid(#3, @instr(#3," ")+1,25); #3 = @left(#3,
(@instr(#3," ")-1))}
```

```
First: #2    Middle: #3    Last: #4
```

This mass update will work where there are no middle names, where there are middle initials, and also where the last name contains one or more spaces, such as in "Van Buren" or "Van de Kamp." The procedure would work equally well to parse a field containing a city, state, and zip code.

You can also use this same formula at the Program Spec to parse a whole name into separate fields during data entry. The only difference is that you'd want the cursor to move to a field other than #2, #3, or #4 upon exiting from the whole name field.

Once the forms have been updated and you've verified that the new name fields are correct, you can redesign the form if you like, removing the whole name field and positioning the other name fields where you want them. Entering a person's name from this point forward, then, would entail typing in the first, middle, and last names in their own separate fields.

If your whole name field currently contains titles such as "Mr." or "Mrs." and/ or suffixes such as "Ph.D." or "M.D." after the name, you'll have to modify the above formula as well as add the extra fields to account for these components. What the above formula does is locate spaces in the field, using their positions to separate the parts of the name.

If you need to build a whole name from component parts (the opposite of what we've done above), see the programming statement written for this purpose for the customer database in Chapter 5. Whole name fields are sometimes more practical than component name fields for form letters when looked up for inclusion in invoices and other files, and when specified in reports for name and address lists and such. The process of bringing several values together to create single field value is called concatenation.

If your work includes frequently creating personalized merge letters in conjunction with a name and address database, having a whole name field and a combination city, state, zip field — as well as separate fields for the components — can speed your work along and still enable you to construct your salutation and sort your form letters any way you want.

Any time you mass update a file involving crucial information such as people's names and addresses, you should run a report — or at least pull a Table View — to verify that the operation produced the desired results in each and every record. And do this before you delete any fields you may think are no longer needed.

Validating State and Zip Code Entries _____

The entry of incorrect U.S. zip codes and erroneous two-letter state abbreviations in databases containing addresses can wreak havoc on your otherwise well-constructed mailing application. But with a little restriction programming, a Lookup Table, and @Help, there is much you can do to minimize errors along these lines.

The simplest thing you can do is plug the two-letter state abbreviations into the zip field at the Restrict Spec. The user then has available during input a handy pop-up list of valid state abbreviations. This won't help much when it comes to zip codes, however, as there are just too many of them. So you may wish to try a more comprehensive approach to validating state and zip code entries.

KEY	1	2	3	4
AK	AK	995	999	
AL	AL	350	369	
AR	AR	716	729	
AZ	AZ	850	865	
CA	CA	900	966	

Figure 12-13: Lookup Table Entries for Alaska, Alabama, Arkansas, Arizona, and California.
Note that the Key column state abbreviations are duplicated in column 1.

You can create a Lookup Table for the database, entering the valid two-letter state abbreviations in the Key column and again in column 1. Then enter the first three digits of the beginning zip code range for the corresponding state in column 2, and the first three digits of the ending zip code range in column 3. Figure 12-13 shows a portion of the Lookup Table (the first five entries).

Figure 12-14 shows listing of all the U.S. state and territory abbreviations, their full state names, and corresponding beginning and ending zip code prefixes.

Once your Lookup Table is finished, proceed to the Program Spec for the same database. For the sake of illustration, we'll assign field ID #19 to our State field, field ID #20 to our Zip field (the Zip field usually follows the State field in any name/addresses database) and field #21 to the field that follows the Zip field. Your field ID numbers will probably be different. Here are the programming statements to enter:

```
State: >#19:If @lookup(#19,1) <> #19 or #19="" then
{@help(#19); goto #19}
```

When the cursor leaves the State field, the statement checks the abbreviation entered against the values in the Lookup Table. If there is no matching abbreviation, or if the field has been left blank, a help screen will pop up and the cursor will be returned to the field.

Note: This programming will not catch an error such as MA entered for the state of Montana (which is MT). All it does is check to see that the abbreviation is in the table.

```
Zip:>#20: If @left(#20,3) >= @lookup(#19,2) and
@left(#20,3) <= @lookup(#19,3) then goto #21 else
{@help(#20); goto #20}
```

AK	Alaska	995	999	MO	Missouri		630
AL	Alabama	350	369	MS	Mississippi		386
AR	Arkansas	716	729	MT	Montana		590
AZ	Arizona	850	865	NC	North Carolina		270
CA	California	900	966	ND	North Dakota		580
CO	Colorado	800	816	NE	Nebraska		680
CT	Connecticut	060	069	NH	New Hampshire	030	038
DC	Dist. of Columbia	200	205	NJ	New Jersey		070
DE	Delaware	197	199	NM	New Mexico		870
FL	Florida	320	349	NV	Nevada		889
GA	Georgia	300	319	NY	New York		100
GU	Guam	969	969	OH	Ohio		430
HI	Hawaii	967	968	OK	Oklahoma		730
IA	Iowa	500	528	OR	Oregon		970
ID	Idaho	832	838	PA	Pennsylvania		150
IL	Illinois	600	629	PR	Puerto Rico		006
IN	Indiana	460	479	RI	Rhode Island		028
KS	Kansas	660	679	SC	South Carolina		290
KY	Kentucky	400	427	SD	South Dakota		570
LA	Louisiana	700	714	TN	Tennessee		370
MA	Massachusetts	010	027	TX	Texas		750
MD	Maryland	206	219	UT	Utah		840
ME	Maine	039	049	VA	Virginia		220
MI	Michigan	480	499	VT	Vermont		050
MN	Minnesota	550	567	WA	Washington		980
				WI	Wisconsin		530
				WV	West Virginia	247	268
				WY	Wyoming		820

Figure 12-14: U.S. State and Territory Abbreviations with Starting and Ending Zip Code Prefixes.

When the cursor leaves the Zip field, Q&A takes the first three digits of the zip code entered (via the @Left function) and, using the state abbreviation entered previously, checks to see if these three digits are within the beginning and ending ranges in columns 2 and 3 of the matching line of the Lookup Table. If the lookup checks out OK, the cursor moves to the next field. Otherwise, the help screen for field #20 pops up and the cursor is returned to the field.

It should be noted here that if your Lookup Table for the database is already filled, you can create an external database to serve the same purpose. If you do, you'll use @XLOOKUP syntax rather than @LOOKUP in your programming expressions.

Figure 12-15 shows the suggested help screens for fields #19 and #20. You can use @Msg messages instead, but these are often hard for an operator to spot, especially on monochrome monitors.

```
      NOT A VALID STATE ABBREVIATION OR STATE FIELD EMPTY

    Enter a two-character state abbreviation or consult your
    zipcode book for the correct state abbreviations. Press
    <Alt><F7> for a list of valid abbreviations.


           Press <Esc> to return to the form...
```

```
       THIS ZIPCODE IS NOT VALID FOR THE STATE ENTERED

    Have you entered the correct state abbreviation?

    Please check the zipcode and reenter.


           Press <Esc> to return to the form...
```

Figure 12-15: (Top) Help Screen for Field #19, (Bottom) Help Screen for Field #20.

If you already have help screens defined for these two fields, you can define a couple of unused help screens for two other fields and then reference these in your programming statements. If all your help screens are spoken for, position two new invisible fields (using the **< >** characters in File Design) on the form (perhaps on blank screen page), define their help screens along the lines of Figure 12-15 and then reference *these* in your programming statements.

If your input operator is hearing the state over the phone (as opposed to reading it off a document), you can add another measure of guidance in the following way:

1. Using the **< >** field delimiter characters, place a new labelless text field strategically close to the State field on the form. Make it wide enough to accommodate the longest full state name.

2. Add the full state names to column 4 of your Lookup Table, making sure they correspond to the abbreviations in the Key column.

3. Include in your programming statement for field #19 the additional command to return the full state name from the Lookup Table to the new text field you just created.

4. Include in your programming statement for field #20 the additional command to blank out the contents of the new field.

This supplementary help tool will work as follows: If the operator hears Arizona and, thinking the abbreviation for Arizona is AR (which it's not), enters AR, the additional text field will display Arkansas (the full state name), and they'll know at that point that AR isn't the correct abbreviation for Arizona and can back up and try again before entering the zip code.

With the tips in this section you can:

1. Trap state abbreviations that don't exist.

2. Display the full state name for any valid abbreviation entered.

3. Catch a zip code that falls outside the range for any state.

4. Guide your operator toward the entry of correct values.

5. Keep your address data more accurate so the Post Office won't become even more confused and so your customers will get your mailings.

Of course, a chart of state abbreviations posted close to the PC can also help prevent the entry of incorrect values.

Note that your Zip field should be formatted as a text field. Lookup Table values are always regarded by Q&A as text. The restrictions we've discussed here are *hard* restrictions, in that the operator cannot get past the relevant fields until the restrictions are satisfied. You can make the restrictions soft ones (requests, rather than requirements) by, for example, simply entering the state abbreviations in the State field at Q&A's Restrict Values Spec (separating each abbreviation with a semicolon) and requiring that a value be entered in the Zip field. But since state and zip information can be crucial, I'd opt for the hard restrictions.

If you keep foreign addresses in your database you'll have to modify your form navigation, field count or placement, and/or your programming logic to turn these restrictions off when such an address is entered. Canadian addresses, for example, are typically accommodated by a three-character state field (for the province abbreviation) and a six-character field for the postal codes used up there.

The programming statements as shown above, however, will work on Zip+4 zip codes.

Summary

Using some of the tricks and techniques I've covered here, you can add speed, flexibility, and real power to your Q&A applications.

Chapter 13
Multiuser Systems & Database Security

In this chapter you'll learn how to:

▶ Recognize the advantages of using Q&A on a network.

▶ Set up Q&A databases for sharing in a multiuser environment.

▶ Upgrade Q&A with the Q&A Network Pack and fine-tune your system for optimum network performance.

▶ Set up different classes of user groups on the network.

▶ Assign passwords and restrictions to prevent unauthorized file access and activity.

▶ Use other security features to protect your databases.

The first part of this chapter deals with networking issues — terminology, Q&A installation, users' rights, and other networking concerns. The last part of this chapter tells you how to lock your database files to either restrict or prevent access by given users.

Overview

Companies are increasingly turning to microcomputer networking to enable individual users to have access to shared programs and data files.

In a typical DOS network environment, personal computers are connected to one another usually through a centrally located computer called a file server. When individual users need access to program and data files, they obtain it from the server, work with these files as permitted by the established password and security levels of the system, and put the files back when finished.

A local area network (LAN) offers a number of advantages over stand-alone PCs. For one thing, the necessity of swapping between machines is eliminated since files can be obtained directly from the server — or from the other PCs on the network — over the network lines. In other words, all users have access to the same data.

Second, a LAN allows a number of people to work on database maintenance at the same time. Suzie can be busily entering sales orders while Bill updates the customer files and Joan runs a report on last month's purchase orders. And if business is extremely brisk, Suzie, Bill, and Joan can crank out sales orders at the same time, each on their own PC.

Third, a LAN allows hardware resources — such as printers — to be shared. Each PC on the network can be configured to send output to its own printer, as well as use more expensive, centrally located peripherals, such as laser printers, that are shared by all users in the system.

Q&A 3.0 added full network support for the Q&A program files themselves, and Q&A 4.0 includes a host of new multiuser features that managers responsible for the network can use to control who is permitted to access Q&A data files and how those files can be manipulated.

Network Terminology

Certain definitions are useful when discussing aspects of multiuser systems. Here are the terms you'll need to be familiar with to understand the material covered in this chapter.

Local Area Network: The hardware and software installed and configured to permit a group of computers to share files and programs. The computers on LANs are normally located relatively close to each other, such as in the same building or on the same site.

Server: The central processing unit dedicated to storing the multiuser files and handing them out to network users on request. On some network systems the server can also be configured to function as a workstation. Some network systems do not require a central server since different multiuser files can be stored on the hard disks of the individual PCs in the network. Where the system does include a server, this unit should be the fastest and most powerful computer on the network.

Workstation: The individual PCs in a multiuser system connected to the file server by network cabling and network software. Although this term has other meanings in other contexts, when we use it here we are referring only to networked PCs.

Database administrator: The person who is responsible for maintaining database files and programs that are shared by users on the network. The database administrator's duties normally include assigning passwords and access rights, installing software upgrades, and creating the shared database structures.

Network administrator: The person charged with managing the network hardware and connections, who is usually also responsible for scheduling regular backups and overseeing network security.

Security: Processes and procedures established by the database or network administrator to ensure the integrity of the multiuser files. These include assigning user IDs, individual and group-level passwords, personal paths and directories, and assigned rights such as Read/Write privileges. Network security allows only those who are authorized to enter the system to do so and prevents certain users from changing information in the files.

Password: The confidential series of characters that you enter to access a network database. In addition to preventing unauthorized people from using the database, passwords also allow the database administrator to assign differ-ent levels of access to individual users, as well as to groups of users, on the network. One password may entitle you to change data in the file, while another permits the mere viewing of records.

User ID: The unique name that identifies you as a user on the network. User IDs are known to all users on the network. For example, Dave Smith's user ID might be DSmith, and everyone would know that.

Multiuser: Computer procedures that can be conducted by more than one person simultaneously. Application software like Q&A can be installed as a multiuser program. Databases and other files, when set up to be shared by several people at the same time, are said to be multiuser files.

User Group: A class of users in a multiuser system. For example, users in the personnel department might need access to employee records, including salaries, review comments, and bonus information, whereas other users on the network would typically be prevented from seeing or changing these sensitive files. Similarly, users who process orders would need access to customer, sales order, and invoice database files, while their coworkers in the personnel department would not. The database administrator establishes user groups based on what information they need to see and routinely change.

File Locking: A system capability that, under certain conditions, prevents access to a given database file by more than one user at a time. The first user to access the file secures rights to it, and any subsequent users are locked out of the file until the first user releases it.

Record Locking: A system capability at the individual form or record level that prevents two or more users from modifying the same record simultaneously. The first user to access a given record can modify the record, while other users can only look at the record until the first user releases it.

Program Files: These are the files on the Q&A master disks. You cannot change program files; they're what allow Q&A run on your computer. Filenames with .OVL, .COM, .EXE, or .DIS extensions are fixed. Filenames ending in .DCT, .CFG, and .ASC are modifiable, but only within specific parameters.

User-created Files: These are the database, document, and macro files created entirely by the people using Q&A. Users have full access to these files and can view and change the information in them subject to the network security measures in place.

Local Drive: A networked PC's own internal floppy and hard disk drives.

Network Drive: Typically the hard drive on the file server, usually designated as drive F:, G:, or H: for the individual workstations. In other words, a network PC's own local drive might be drive C:, whereas its network drive (located on the server) might be designated as drive G: (which could be the network server's local drive C:). Users need to know the network drive name so they can enter the correct pathname to get to network files.

Compatible Networks

Q&A program files and your databases can be used on a variety of different LANs. Q&A is compatible with all major networks that support MS-DOS 3.1 or PC-DOS 3.1 and later versions. Among the packages supported are 3Plus, NetWare, IBM PC Network, and IBM Token-Ring LAN on the higher performance and pricier end of the scale, and Lantastic, Invisible Software Net/30, and ReadyNet at the more economical end. Chances are that no matter which network product you're using, Q&A will support it.

On some networks the file server is "dedicated," which means it does not function as a workstation, but is used exclusively for storing data and handing it out to users on demand. Your network may have a nondedicated file server that is also used as a workstation. In distributed networks, the individual PCs can act both as file servers and workstations. Q&A works in any of these network environments.

The Q&A program itself requires 512K of RAM to run, so you'll need 640K of RAM to run it on a network. Moreover, if your network software requires more than 128K of RAM (such as NetWare), you may not be able to use Q&A on that network unless you have Extended or Expanded RAM available. Network packages generally eat up more server RAM than workstation RAM. Artisoft's Lantastic, for example, needs about 25K of RAM on the server, only about 11K on the workstations, and 34 to 38K of RAM if you configure your machine to operate both as a server and a workstation. Other packages require substantially more memory.

Two Ways to Use Q&A on a Network

Q&A can be configured to run on a multiuser system in either of two ways:

- Each workstation can have its own installed copy of Q&A and can access Q&A database and document files across the network. Network operations will run faster this way since the workstations won't have to get their program data from the server, and the server won't be tied up dealing with program file calls from the workstations. However, this may also be the most expensive alternative, since it requires the purchase of a copy of the single-user version of the software for each PC on the network.

- One copy of Q&A can be installed on the server, along with the Q&A Network Pack, facilitating the sharing of data files and the Q&A program files among all users on the network. Each Network Pack accommodates an additional three users. So with one Network Pack you have a total of four users (the original user and the Network Pack's three additional users); two Network Packs are required for five to seven users, and three Packs for eight to ten users, and so on. Even so, the Network Packs are substantially more economical than purchasing multiple copies of the single-user Q&A program.

You only need the Network Pack if you want to install the Q&A program itself on the network file server and allow several people to use the program simultaneously. The Network Pack converts your single-user copy of Q&A to a multiuser version.

You don't need the Network Pack to share data files (user-created files). Several users, each with a single-user copy of Q&A installed in their workstations, can simultaneously access Q&A database or document files stored on the server.

Also, you don't need the Network Pack to install Q&A on the network file server. Without the Pack the Q&A program can be made available to all users, but only one at a time.

In order to run Q&A on a network in either of the above configurations, the workstations and file server must be properly connected and appropriately configured for network operations. When you purchase a network package, you normally receive network interface adapters that you install in each machine; network cabling that connects the workstations to each other, to the server, or to a central hub; and network software that you install and use to configure the file server and the workstations to operate together as a multiuser system.

The Q&A Network Pack is not network software, per se. It simply allows you to convert your single-user copy of Q&A to a multiuser version so you can then use the Q&A program files on the network.

When Security Is Critical

You can use the data security and password capabilities of Q&A whether or not you're running in a multiuser environment. Even if yours is the only PC in the office, you can still password-protect databases, place read-only restrictions on fields, and prevent others from redesigning forms and reports and running mass updates.

Suppose you have a personnel database containing sensitive salary, review, and bonus information that only you should be able see and change. You can place the entire file off limits by requiring that a password be entered before access can be obtained. Or you could allow access to the file, but hide the fields that contain the sensitive information.

A third alternative would be to permit others to view the information, but not be able to change it.

Typically, database security and integrity considerations come into play when more than one person has routine access to database information. Security means keeping the data safe from loss, harm, or unauthorized changes. Integrity has to do with making sure the information in the database is valid.

One way Q&A helps ensure data integrity is to allow only one person at a time to edit a record or conduct certain database operations that might corrupt the data if two or more users were permitted access to the same operation simultaneously. To help ensure data security and integrity, the database administrator usually authorizes only certain people to add or change data, design reports, or delete forms, while any number of others are permitted to browse or read database information.

For example, the person in charge of updating customer files would be authorized to add new records to the database, change the information on existing records, and delete records that were no longer useful to the company.

In contrast to this, the people in customer service may only be authorized to search and view invoices and customer records, so that customers who call about their orders can be given the correct shipping and billing information.

The database or network administrator assigns passwords to individual users and establishes user groups to control who has access to the files and the kinds of operations that can be performed on them.

If you forget your password, the network administrator can issue you a new one. If you're the network administrator and you forget your own password, however, you'll have to send your database off to Symantec to have the password reset.

Send the database to:
Symantec Corp.
Customer Support, Password
10201 Torre Ave.
Cupertino, CA 95014

Follow these instructions to have Symantec reset the password:

1. On your company letterhead, authorize Symantec to reset your password. You must sign the document.

2. Enclose a check or money order for $50 for a two-week or less turn-around. Enclose $100 for return of the database within one working day.

3. If you want the original locked database returned, include an additional $15.

Always send a backup copy of your database to Symantec so the original file can be used (by those who still know their passwords) while the backup copy is being unlocked.

Accessing a Database _____

When any user attempts to access a restricted database or operation, Q&A checks the User ID and password entered to see what rights and restrictions apply to that user. These rights and restrictions, and how to assign them, will be discussed in more detail later in the chapter.

Once Q&A has your password, it remembers the information for the duration of the Q&A session. So long as you don't exit the program, reboot, or clear your password, you can access, leave, and then reaccess the same database or operation without having to reenter your password.

The database administrator normally assigns passwords and establishes and controls access rights and restrictions, since he or she is the person responsible for the security and integrity of the files.

Record Locking and File Locking

What happens when more than one person attempts to use the same database file depends on what is being done with the file.

Normally, several users can be adding or updating different records in the same database and there will be no problem. However, when one person is redesigning or customizing the file — that is, modifying the underlying structure of the database — all other users will be temporarily locked out.

There are a number of other operations in Q&A that only one person can do at a time and that automatically lock any other users out during the course of the operation. Tables 12-1, 12-2, and 12-3 summarize the operations normally open to all users, those open only to one user at a time, and those that lock all others out of the given file.

Where individual database records are concerned, the person who requests the record first will have read and write privileges, assuming he is entitled to them. The second and any subsequent users requesting the same record can only read the record. When the person with write privileges leaves the form, Q&A then unlocks it for updating by others.

Write module document files are handled somewhat differently. The first person requesting a document can both read and update it. No other users can even look at that particular document until the first user has finished with it.

If user IDs have been set up properly, Q&A will let you know who is working on the file when it has been locked. You can then call that person's extension to find out what's going on. Unfortunately, the only time Q&A will tell you who has "beaten you to it" is when that other user's activity is causing the entire file to be locked.

Other Restrictions

Only one person at a time can view or change a given Write document that's stored on the server. You can, however, save documents to your workstation's local drive by specifying the local drive path and filename. Or you can have

Table 12-1
Multiple Users can Perform the Following Operations on a Given Database Simultaneously

File	Search/Update
	Add Data
	Delete a record
	Table View
	Print forms
Report	Print a report
Assistant	Search/Update
	Add Data
	Print a report or forms
Query Guide	Build a query or report
	Print a report or forms
Write	Mail Merge
Utilities	Import/Export operations
Macros	All macro operations

Table 12-2
Single-User Functions on a Shared File

Only one user at a time can perform the following operations on a given database. These functions don't lock the file, but prevent others from performing the same operation on the same file.

File	Design a Print Spec
	Assign Password/Rights/File Security
	Naming and saving specs
Report	Design/Redesign a report
Assistant	Teach the Assistant
	Learn Values for Assistant
Query Guide	Teach Query Guide

Table 12-3
Single-User Functions on a Locked File

The following operations cannot be started until all other users are out of the file. Once commenced, other users are locked out of the file until the operation has been completed and the first user has returned to the Q&A Main menu.

File	File redesign
	Customize
	Copy database design/forms
	Mass Update
	Remove forms
	Posting
	Backup database
Assistant	Teach the Assistant
	Mass Update
Query Guide	Teach Query Guide
Utilities	Recover database
	DOS commands on database files

your network administrator create a personal path for you on the network drive where you can store your personal documents and other files (even databases), thereby placing them off limits to other network users. We will discuss this further later in the chapter.

Only one user at a time can teach the Intelligent Assistant or Query Guide. However, several users can use the IA or Query Guide simultaneously.

Macros can be recorded and used on a network the same as in a single-user environment. Where macros must access password-protected files or operations, save yourself from having them interrupted during playback by pressing **<F6>** at the Main menu and entering your User ID and Password immediately after Q&A loads. You can also load your personalized macros into memory from your workstation's local drive or from your personal path on the network drive. I'll discuss this later.

On the network Q&A treats macros as if the individual user were pressing the keystrokes. If a macro attempts a restricted operation, Q&A will halt it in progress and display the appropriate network message.

A printer that's shared by users on the network can still handle only one printing job at a time. Your network software takes care of competing requests for printing by queuing print jobs in a RAM cache or by temporarily spooling them to the network drive. When you send a job to a shared printer, the operation should be no different than a single-user print job except that you may have to wait a while as previous print jobs requested by others are run.

You can always, of course, configure your network set-up to print your output on your personal printer, thus avoiding network/printer bottlenecks.

When a network user sends a report, forms, mailing labels, or merge document from a shared database to a shared printer, there's always the possibility that others may change the data while the job is queued up for printing, or during the printing process itself. Q&A averts this potential problem by taking a "snapshot" of the records to be included in the printing job when the job is first sent over the network to the printer. This enables others — and you — to carry on adding data and changing the same records without affecting the printing job.

Network Messages

Special messages may be displayed by Q&A when you're using the product on a network. A summary of these messages is provided below.

Form is being edited by another user. You tried to modify a form already being edited by another. You'll have to wait until the form is released by the other user before you can update it.

This function is currently in use. Please try again later. Press ESC. You tried to perform a single-user operation, such as design a print spec while another user was doing the same thing. This doesn't prevent you from performing other functions, such as a Search/Update, using the IA or using the Query Guide.

This function cannot be used while others are using the database. Press Esc. You tried to perform a single-user operation while one or more other users were using the file. Operations that affect the underlying structure of the database — such as file redesign, customize operations, and mass update — lock all other users out of the file. And rightly so! If Q&A allowed you to run a mass update on a file that was in the middle of a redesign, you could wind up with one heck of a mess on your hands!

File is in use by (*network ID*). You tried to access a file that's been locked by another user who is performing a single-user operation. The Network ID tells you who is using the file.

Note: Network ID identifies you on the network when you're performing an operation that locks a file; it's the name you enter on the Set Global Options screen under the Q&A Utilities menu. This is not the same as your User ID, which is assigned by your network administrator and which identifies you to the database.

There are (x) current users out of (y) permitted under your license. Q&A displays this message when first loaded. It indicates how many people are using the multiuser version of Q&A, and how many users are permitted to use the version as currently configured. This message will not appear if you're on the network with your own single-user version of Q&A.

User ID: Q&A is requiring you to enter your assigned name or code that identifies you to the database. This is normally not the same as your password.

Password: Q&A is requiring you to enter your unique password in order to gain access to the database or to any protected or restricted operations or data. This prompt, along with a request for your User ID, appears in a password box automatically where required, or when you press **<F6>** from the Q&A Main menu.

Other messages may be displayed when you attempt to perform operations restricted by the database administrator. While these are not, technically, network messages, they usually relate to multiuser activities since, in those type of environments, restrictions are normally placed on users and user groups.

Setting Up the Network

After you've got the network hardware and software installed according to the directions supplied with the network product, you need to decide if you're going to share the Q&A program with users on the network or if each workstation will have its own single-user copy of Q&A installed.

The decision will probably boil down to one of cost vs. performance. Shared Q&A program files will slow down the server, and thus the system, because each workstation will have to go to the server for data files *and* program files.

If cost is no object and you want network speed at maximum, purchase single-user copies of Q&A and install one on each workstation. There are a number of other ways to improve network performance. We'll look at these alternatives in detail later on in the chapter.

The set-up procedure for sharing data files only is easy. I'll discuss that alternative first, followed by the more involved procedure for installing the Q&A program itself on the network.

No matter which alternative you use, your network may require that the DOS Share program be loaded at the server and at each workstation. Share is a memory resident utility included with DOS 3.1 and later that helps prevent data disasters by double-checking every DOS read and write operation. It uses about 5K of RAM. If the Share program is required by the system, but is not loaded, record locking may not be supported, and Q&A will not be able to protect your data.

Some network packages include Share and automatically load it for you. You should find out whether or not your LAN requires it to support record locking and what, if anything, you have to do to see that it's loaded before running Q&A or sharing your databases on a multiuser system.

If Share is required, your network administrator can include the utility in users' network logon procedures so it will be loaded automatically.

You can also load Share yourself by typing **share** and pressing **<Enter>** at the DOS prompt. DOS will tell you if Share is already in memory.

Sharing Database Files Only

So long as each workstation on the network has its own copy of Q&A installed, setting up your database to be shared by multiple users is simply a matter of setting your Network ID, declaring the sharing mode, and optionally assigning access rights and restrictions for individuals and user groups.

To set your Network ID:

1. Select Utilities from the Q&A Main menu.

2. Choose Set Global Options from the Utilities menu. The Set Global Options screen in Figure 13-1 will be displayed.

3. Move the cursor to the bottom of the screen, to the Network ID line.

4. Type in your name, or an abbreviation of your name, and optionally your phone number or extension.

5. Press **<F10>** to save the new information and return to the Utilities menu.

 Note: Your Network ID is not the same as your User ID or password. The only purpose of entering your Network ID is to tell other users that you have single-user control of a particular database when they try to access that same file.

```
                        SET DEFAULT DIRECTORIES
                        ========================

      Type the Drive and, optionally, the Path where the following
      kinds of files will be stored.  This will save you extra typing
      because Q&A will always know where to look first for these files:

           Q&A Document files : C:\QA\DOCS\
           Q&A Database files : C:\QA\DATA\
           Q&A Temporary files: D:\QA\JUNK\

      You can make the program execute menu items as soon as you type the
      first letter of the selection.  (If you select this option, you may
      have to re-record macros that expect ENTER after the letter.)

           Automatic Execution:  ▶Yes◀  No

      Type your name and phone number for network identification purposes:

           Network ID........: Jimmy G, Ext 344


   Esc-Exit                                              F10-Continue
```

Figure 13-1: The Set Global Options Screen. At the bottom of this screen type in your Network ID, which identifies you to other users on the system.

If database or network administration is your responsibility, make sure that all users understand that when they have a given record displayed on their workstation monitor, other users may not be able to update that record. Encourage your people to display a record only for the length of time necessary to view or update it and to release the record as soon as possible and return to one of the Q&A menus.

The Security Menu

New: Q&A 4.0 provides a Security menu that offers a number of options for protecting your database against unauthorized access. One method of controlling access to shared files is to assign each user a unique user ID and password. Unless these are then entered correctly, the user is denied access to specific network features, programs, or files.

Figure 13-2 shows the Security menu, which you reach by selecting File from the Main menu, Design File, and then Secure a File.

Allowing/Disallowing File Sharing

Before multiple users can share a database file, Q&A will need to know how you want it configured for sharing. This is the third selection on the Security

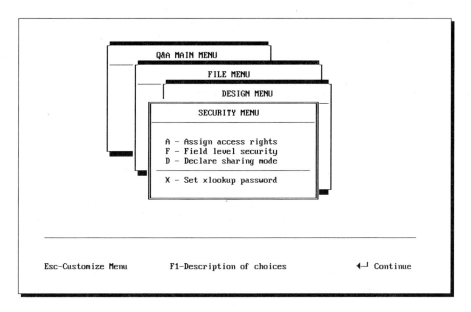

Figure 13-2: Q&A 4.0's Security Menu. Here you assign access rights to the database, establish field-level security, declare sharing mode, and assign passwords for external lookup operations.

menu shown in Figure 13-2. Choose Declare Sharing Mode from this menu to bring up the Declare Sharing Mode screen where you specify how Q&A is to manage requests for the file across the network.

Q&A handles contention for files automatically by determining whether files are being stored on a network server or on a local workstation. Files stored on a server are assumed to be shared files, and the default setting at the Declare Sharing Mode screen is "Automatic" since this is the correct selection for the majority of users.

For some applications, however, you may want to force "Allow" or "Disallow." For example, if you want to maintain a private database on the server, you can prevent others from accessing it by disallowing sharing at the Declare Sharing Mode screen. If the private file is on your local drive, sharing will be automatically disallowed unless you specify the "Allow" option.

In addition, if you want only one person at a time to have access to the database, choose Disallow. Other users will be prevented from opening the file until the first user closes it by returning to a Q&A menu.

If you're using a local drive as the network drive and "Automatic" is not working properly, select Allow to force Q&A to allow multiple users to share the database even though it's stored on a local drive.

Note: If the database sharing mode is set to "Allow," and you copy the file to a nonnetwork drive, you won't be able to open it unless you run the DOS Share program first.

"Allow" lets Q&A know that several users have access to the database even though it is stored on a local hard drive. Some network packages such as TOPS and Lantastic — which use a nondedicated or distributed network — require that Declare Sharing Mode be set to "Allow." Any database file that is the target of lookup functions should also be set to "Allow" if there's a chance that several users might look up data simultaneously.

Passwords and Access Rights

As the database administrator, you can select from four different types of database protection:

- **Access Rights.** By filling out Access Control forms you can control which users are able to access the database and what actions they are permitted to perform.

- **Restriction Groups.** You can assign users to groups and control field-by-field access to data at the group level.

- **Read-only Fields.** You can prevent all users from changing data in a field by making the field Read-only. Read-only fields can be filled in only by programming statements, posting operations, and initial values.

- **Application Locks.** You can lock users out of specific database operations and protect macro files. This form of security is independent of any access rights.

The first of these security alternatives we'll explore is the assignment of access rights.

Selecting Assign Access Rights from the Security menu brings up the List of Users/Groups screen. Here you type in the group names or User IDs — the names of the groups or individuals authorized to be on the network and have at least some degree of access to the database.

Assuming you're the database administrator, start off by typing in your own name. Let's call you "Fred Davies" for the time being. The name can be up to 31 characters.

After typing in **Fred Davies** at the List of Users/Groups screen, press **<F10>** to assign yourself a password and database access rights. Figure 13-3 shows the Access Control form for Fred Davies.

```
                         ACCESS CONTROL
                         ═════════════

         Initial Password:  PASSWORD

     Make the selections below to indicate what rights this person has:

         Can assign password rights?........:    ▶Yes◀  No

         Can change design and program?.....:    ▶Yes◀  No

         Can mass delete?...................:    ▶Yes◀  No

         Can delete individual records?.....:    ▶Yes◀  No

         Can run mass update?...............:    ▶Yes◀  No

         Can Design/Redesign reports?.......:    ▶Yes◀  No

         Can enter/edit data?...............:    ▶Yes◀  No
     ──────────────────────────────────────────────────────────────
     STOCK.DTF           Access Control Form for FRED DAVIES

       Esc-Exit                    F1-Help                  F10-Continue
```

Figure 13-3: An Access Control Form. Use this form to specify the level of database access for each user.

Notice in Figure 13-3 that the Initial Password line at the top of the form indicates PASSWORD, and that all the rights are set to "Yes." These are the defaults for new Access Control forms. If you leave this form as it stands and press <F10> to save it, you — Fred Davies — will be assigned the password "PASSWORD," and you'll have unrestricted administrative and other access rights to this database.

As the database administrator, you'll want to assign yourself a unique confidential password and establish yourself as the only user who can assign password rights. Otherwise, someone else could change your password and lock you out of the database. Therefore, the first Access Control form you create should be your own.

Here's a rundown on what the database rights options mean, as shown in Figure 13-3.

Can assign password rights? This is an administrative right. Without this right the user is not allowed to assign or change passwords, or create or change Field Restriction Groups. A user who is part of a field security spec cannot be given rights to assign passwords. (More on that later.) At least one user must have administrative rights, and this user is the only one who can teach the Intelligent Assistant.

Can change design and program? This is another administrative right, without which the user cannot secure the database, change the database design, customize the file, enter the Field Programming or Program Navigation Specs, or reset the @Number. Administrative rights normally mean that the person can assign password rights and change the database design.

Can mass delete? Without this right, the person is prevented from using Remove Selected Records or Remove Duplicate Records from the Remove menu.

Can delete individual records? Without this right, the user cannot delete single database records by pressing **<F3>** when viewing a form.

Can run mass update? Without this right, the user is locked out of the Mass Update selection on the File menu.

Can design/redesign reports? Without this right, the user cannot design or redesign a report in the database. The user can, however, print existing reports, including making temporary changes to them.

Can write data? Without this right, the user can't add data, or enter or edit any field in this database; all he can do is browse and view forms. If the user's job requires him to add or update data, you'll have to grant this right.

Once you've set up your own Access Control form, you'll need to create forms for the other users on the network. However, before you assign User IDs, passwords, and rights to the other users, you may want to establish, in advance, special user groups, and designate the field-level restrictions for these groups. Then, as you fill out each Access Control form, you can immediately assign the user to an established user group. See Specifying Field Restrictions below for details.

Here's the procedure for creating Access Control forms for all users who will be permitted to open the database for any reason:

1. Select Assign Access Rights from the Security menu.

2. At the List of Users screen, type in the User ID of the person, and press **<F10>** for an Access Control form with that person's User ID stamped on it.

3. Assign this user a password. Passwords do not necessarily have to be unique. All members of a particular user group, for example, can have the same password — but their User IDs will, of course, be different. The restrictions placed on the user at the Access Control form determine what rights the user has, and two users with the same password can have different privileges. Database security, however, is best ensured when each user is assigned a unique password.

4. Fill out the Access Control form, giving the user the appropriate rights. Press **<F10>**.

5. If the user does not have password and database redesign rights (i.e., does not have administrative rights), then he can be added to a Field Restriction Group, and the List of Field Restrictions will appear. (This will be discussed further on in the chapter.) If you want to add this user to a restricted user group, highlight the user group in which you want to place the user and press **<F10>**.

6. Repeat steps 2 through 5 for all other users who will have at least some access to the database, even if their only right is to view the data. Since creating even one Access Control Form password protects the database, users who are not assigned passwords (i.e., do not have Access Control forms) will not be able to open the file at all.

Once the Access Control forms are filled out, Q&A will regulate access to the restricted file by evaluating both the User ID and the password entered in the password box.

- If the User ID entered isn't valid, any password will be meaningless and Q&A will not open the file.

- If the User ID is correct, but the password entered doesn't match the one on the Access Control form for that user, no access to the file will be granted.

- If the User ID/password combination is valid, the user will be allowed to open the file and work with it subject to the restrictions placed on his user group and specified on his Access Control Form.

User IDs and Access Control forms can be edited by anyone who has administrative rights to these procedures. You simply go to the List of Users/ Groups screen when you want to delete, rename, or add a user. The function key assignments at the bottom of the screen indicate the operations that can be performed. When you want to edit an Access Control form, you simply highlight the user at the List of Users screen, press **<Enter>**, make your changes, and press **<F10>** to save the edited form.

Access Rights can be assigned whether or not the database is used on a network. Even if you have only one PC in the office being used by several people, you can still assign User IDs, passwords, and rights.

Some security measures, however, are less likely to be effective where only a single stand-alone PC is used. Suppose, for example, that you've restricted access to the employee file to yourself alone. Once you enter your User ID and password and open that file, anyone else can get into that file on that PC without being required to enter a User ID or password, so long as Q&A hasn't been exited, the computer hasn't been rebooted, or the password hasn't been cleared using **<Shift><F6>** at the Main menu.

But this is true of any network PC as well. If Betty enters a restricted database to do some work, exits back to the Main menu, and then goes off on a coffee break, Joe can come along and, on Betty's workstation, get into that same database (or any other restricted file that Betty opened during the current Q&A session), and enjoy all of Betty's rights and privileges with respect to that file.

How do you, as a database administrator, guard against this type of unauthorized access? The most practical method is to require that users return to the Q&A Main menu and press **<Shift><F6>** to clear their passwords before leaving their machines unattended.

Specifying Field Restrictions

As the database administrator, you may grant write privileges (via Access Control forms) to certain users because their jobs require that they be able to change information in the database. But you may want to place limits on which fields on the form they can edit, or even see. These considerations, and the practicality of assigning users to user groups, are the purposes behind creating Field Security Specs.

The second selection on the Security menu — Field Level Security — brings up the List of Field Security Specs. Q&A allows you to designate up to eight field security specs per database. Using these specs you can control, on a field by field basis, how users within user groups can view and work with the database. Field protection includes the following three options and their codes:

- **Read/Write privileges (W).** This is the default setting that allows users to both see and change data in the applicable field.

- **Read-only privileges (R).** The field can be seen but not edited.

- **No access (N).** The field can't even be seen — so of course it can't be edited.

You create a Field Restriction Spec by first typing in a name for the spec (typically a name that identifies the user group) at the List of Field Restrictions screen. When you press **<F10>**, Q&A displays the database form. Each field on the form contains the default **W** code — indicating that the field is unprotected — until you change the code to either **R** (read only) or **N** (no access).

To protect a field, move the cursor to it and simply type in the appropriate code. Then move to the next field you want to protect, and type in the protection code for that one. Repeat the procedure until you've entered the appropriate codes for all the fields you want to protect. Leave the **W** code in any fields that you don't want to protect.

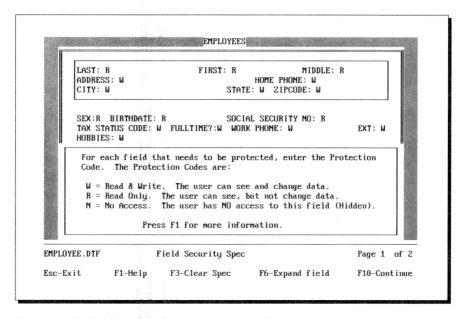

Figure 13-4: The Field Security Spec for the Employee File. Note that some of the fields — those that are not likely to change — contain the "R" code, making them read-only fields that cannot be edited by any person in this user group.

Figure 13-4 shows the employee database form at the Field Security Spec.

When you've finished typing in the protection codes, press **<F10>** to save the spec and display the User Selection screen. You now choose which users or groups from this list are to be linked with the Field Security Spec you just created. Enter the name of the user or group, or press **<Alt><F7>** for a list all available user or groups. (Users with administrative rights will not appear.) Choose a name or group and press **<Enter>** to place it in the next available slot on this list. You can now create an Access Control form for each user who will have access to this file, and assign each one to a user group.

To place a user in a user group, subject to the Field Security Spec you've just designed:

   1. Assign the user a User ID and fill out an Access Control form per the steps in the above section on Passwords and Access Rights. Press **<F10>**.

 Note: If an Access Control form has already been filled out for a particular user, and you wish to add this user to a field restriction group, highlight his User ID at the List of Users/Groups screen, press **<Enter>** to bring up his form, and press **<F10>**.

2. At the List of Field Restrictions, highlight the user group to which you want to assign this user and press **<Enter>**.

Now, whenever users open the database, what fields they can see and edit and what operations they can perform on the file will be subject to the rights granted on their Access Control form as well as the field restrictions placed on their user group.

Persons with administrative rights to the database can edit Field Security Specs, and delete, rename, add, and copy user groups from the List of Field Restrictions screen. You can create a maximum of eight Field Security Specs per database.

Because you can have up to 24 users per screen at the List of Users/Groups, and a total of four screens, you can thus link up to 96 users and groups to a single Field Security Spec. And with a maximum of eight Field Security Specs available per database, you can therefore have up to 768 users and groups linked with your Field Security specifications.

When do you need to protect fields? Well, you might want to prevent employees in the personnel department from seeing the fields that contain sensitive salary and bonus information, while allowing them to update employee addresses and other fields.

In an inventory database, you may want to make the stock number, description, and price information Read-only fields to protect them against accidental or deliberate modification.

Certain information on invoices and purchases orders can be made read-only for all users except the supervisors. Remember, read-only means that the field can be updated by programming statements, posting, and initial values.

Sensitive negotiation information in sales and contract files may need to be hidden from all users except certain authorized personnel.

Set Xlookup Password

The final selection on the Security menu — Set Xlookup Password — enables users to bypass restricted access to external databases so that XLOOKUP statements and functions can be executed.

The inventory file may be placed completely off limits to an order entry operator whose job is to type invoices. But the invoice database contains programming statements that retrieve needed information from the inventory file.

If this user is not given XLOOKUP access to the inventory file, execution of XLOOKUP statements to that file will be halted, and the user won't be able to retrieve the needed information for the invoice.

If you want to restrict access to a file, but allow XLOOKUPS on that file to be executed, select Set Xlookup Password from the Security menu, and at the Set Xlookup Password screen, type in the User ID and assign a password.

Once this is done, the next time an XLOOKUP statement to a restricted external database is executed, Q&A will prompt the user for the special XLOOKUP User ID and password. When these are entered correctly, XLOOKUPS will be allowed until the user quits Q&A, reboots, or clears the password with **<Shift><F6>** from the Main menu.

Entering a User ID and Password

There are only two times you can enter your User ID and password into Q&A:

- You can enter your User ID and password voluntarily at the Q&A Main menu by pressing **<F6>**. This isn't very practical, however, if you've been assigned different passwords for different databases. As a database administrator, you'll probably want to assign individual users the same User ID and password for all databases to which they've been granted access, even though specific rights for the given user may vary from file to file.

- You can wait until Q&A prompts you for your User ID and password. This will occur when you attempt to open a restricted file or perform a restricted operation.

The only exception to the above is the special XLOOKUP password box that appears when an XLOOKUP programming statement attempts to retrieve information from a restricted external database. Your password for this operation may be different from the password that enabled you to open and work in the current file.

Unless you have administrative rights, you cannot change your User ID or assign passwords. If you forget your password your database administrator can tell you what it is or assign a new one.

You can easily change your own password, however. When the first password dialogue box of the session is displayed, press **<F8>**, enter your User ID and current password, and then your new password. The new password becomes effective immediately.

If you're the only one who has administrative rights, and you forget your own password, you'll have to send a copy of the database to Symantec to have the password reset. The procedure for doing this was outlined at the beginning of the chapter.

Installing the Q&A Program on the Network

Earlier in this chapter we pointed out the two ways you can run Q&A on a network:

- Each workstation has a single-user copy of Q&A installed and only the data files are shared.

- The Q&A program itself, as well as the data files, are shared by all the users on the network.

This section shows you how to install a standard, single-user copy of Q&A on your network's file server and upgrade it to a multiuser copy with the Q&A Network Pack. Each Network Pack adds three users to your system.

From the perspective of a database administrator whose job it is to ensure database security and integrity, it makes no difference how the Q&A program itself runs on the network. Such tasks as assigning User IDs and passwords and establishing file restrictions, user groups, and field level security on a file-by-file basis will be the same whether or not the program files are being shared by users along with the data files.

Moreover, network particulars — such as file- and record-locking, declaring sharing mode, printing, and accessing a database as discussed above — work essentially the same because they pertain to user-created files rather than program files.

You'll see what differences there are between the two methods of running Q&A in a multiuser environment as you proceed through this section.

Installation Procedure

Follow these steps to install the Q&A program on the network:

1. If you own a standard single-user version of Q&A (versions earlier than 3.0 don't support shared program files), purchase a Q&A Network Pack to accommodate up to three additional users (for a total of four users).

2. Create a network directory following the instructions that came with your LAN package, and give full rights to that directory to all users who'll be using Q&A on the network. (Personal paths for individual users can be established. This will be discussed later. Full access rights are essential if there's a chance that anyone might use the program without a personal path.)

3. Install Q&A in your network directory, following the instructions in Chapter 1.

4. Place the copy-protected Q&A Network Pack disk into drive A, type **A:** and press **<Enter>**.

5. Type **ADDUSER** and press **<Enter>**.

6. When prompted, enter the drive and path to the network directory you created for Q&A. For example, if you created a directory called QA on network drive G: you'd type **G:\QA** at the prompt.

The upgraded single-user version of Q&A writes its serial number to the Network Pack diskette, and the Network Pack diskette, in turn, writes its serial number to the network copy of Q&A. Store the Network Pack diskette with the Q&A master diskettes as you may need them again to reinstall this copy of Q&A on the network.

Warning: Once you've upgraded a single-user copy of Q&A with the Network Pack disk, you can't use it with any other copy of Q&A.

And once you've upgraded Q&A to the multiuser version, you won't be able to use that same copy of Q&A on a local hard disk. If you need to use Q&A both ways, you'll have to buy another copy of the program.

Personal Paths

Once you've upgraded Q&A with the Network Pack, users can specify locations for personal preference files other than the Q&A home directory using a personal path command.

In a multiuser application where the program files are shared, Q&A maintains separate files for each individual user that contain information such as printing and page defaults, editing options, personal spelling dictionaries, and so forth. This prevents each user's personal preferences from constantly being overwritten by the other users.

Personal paths allow network users to customize Q&A to their individual preferences. Such paths can point to a subdirectory on the network drive or to the user's local hard drive. In fact, if each user's personal path directs Q&A to their own workstation hard drives, traffic over the lines can be substantially reduced, thus increasing overall network performance.

To invoke a personal path at your workstation when loading Q&A, type at the system prompt:

QA -P<Drivename:Pathname>

where **-P** (upper- or lowercase) is the command that tells Q&A to use the specified personal path, and **<Drivename:Pathname>** is the personal path.

For example, the command

```
QA -PC:\QAMINE
```

tells Q&A to use the directory QAMINE on local drive C: as the location of personal Q&A preference and temporary files. There's no space between the –P and the drive and path that follow it.

Your network administrator can create a public directory batch file for all users, saving them from having to enter personal path information at start-up. Such a batch file might look like this:

```
G:
CD\QA
QA %1 -PC:\
```

Assuming that all users have network drive G: and that's where the Q&A program files are stored, this batch file moves each user into the public directory, loads Q&A, and specifies each user's local C: drive as the location for preference and temporary files. The batch variable %1 gives the user the option of typing another command line of his own, perhaps to load a custom macro file.

Once Q&A is loaded at the workstation, the user can then customize it to his personal preferences. He or she can choose the various defaults, font assignments, editing options, and so on, without having to worry about them being overwritten by other users.

User Count

When the Q&A program is being shared on the network, you'll see the current user count displayed at the Main menu along with the number of users the system will support. When the user count is the same as the number of users permitted, no additional user can load Q&A until one of the current users exits the program properly.

Q&A increases the user count by one when a user loads the program and decreases it by one when a user exits Q&A. If a user does not exit the program by selecting **X - Exit** from the Main menu, the user count won't be decreased.

If you find that you have to reset the user count, all current users will need to exit the program properly. Then, when the first user starts Q&A, the user count will be reset to one automatically.

Incorrect user counts, which occur when people do not properly exit the program, are corrected for at least once a day, when the first user starts up Q&A in the morning.

Personal Paths and Disk Space

Q&A creates temporary files while performing certain operations such as sorting, producing complex reports, and teaching the Assistant. Sometimes these temporary files can grow quite large. A "Copy Selected Forms" operation, for example, can create temporary files nearly as big as the .DTF and .IDX files themselves. The point is, such operations can commandeer a rather large chunk of hard disk real estate, even if only for a few moments.

You can imagine what might happen if a number of users on the network proceeded to run sort or copy operations on large files at the same time; hard disks only have so much room.

You can head off this potential problem by encouraging users, wherever possible, to maintain personal paths that point to their own local hard drives. This way, any temporary files that Q&A needs to create to fulfill the user's command will be created on that user's hard disk, rather than on the network drive.

Personal paths that point to local hard drives increase network performance as well by reducing network traffic.

Workstation RAM Requirements

In order to run Q&A from a file server, each user needs at least 484K of free memory. You can check the amount of available ram in the PCs on the network by running the DOS Chkdsk utility at each workstation.

Q&A will load into a PC with less than 484K of free RAM, but operations requiring more memory will be aborted, accompanied by the message "Not enough memory to complete your request."

If DOS Chkdsk reveals that your PC doesn't have at least 484K of free RAM and you don't want to chance running out of memory, you may have to remove a memory-resident utility or two or have your network administrator see what can be done to reconfigure the network to consume less RAM at the workstations.

CONFIG.SYS and NetBIOS

Both the network software and Q&A require an adequate number of file handles. These are the number of open files that can access certain DOS system calls. Each user should have a CONFIG.SYS file on their machine that contains the statement **FILES=20**.

Q&A does not use NetBIOS. If your network supports DOS 3.1 or later networking calls — including the Share call — you should be able to run Q&A on it.

Network Performance Considerations

There's almost always a noticeable degradation in speed between a dedicated PC running off the network and that same PC running on the network as a workstation or file server.

When you move files to a central, shared resource like a server's hard disk, individual PC performance is bound to suffer, even if only somewhat. After all, each PC is competing not only for the same files, but also for the server's hard drive, RAM, and processor. Even where only one workstation is logged onto the network and operating, the fact that commands have to travel from that PC to the server, through the server's system, and then back again, is going to affect response time.

Add another three, five, or 20 active workstations to the system, and through-put degradation will be even more noticeable. You should expect the multiuser performance of Q&A to be slower than single-user performance. This doesn't mean, however, that you can't take steps to improve overall network perfor-mance. There is usually room for improvement on any system, and there are a number of options you can look into to make the network respond faster to individual workstation needs.

You can purchase a more efficient computer for use as your file server. Today's 386 and 486 PCs are fast and powerful, and as die-hard computer buffs are fond of saying, "You can never have too much memory or too much speed." A 25- or 33-megahertz 386 machine with 4MB of RAM and a large, fast hard drive, can be had for around $4,000 at today's street prices. These make excellent file servers for small-to intermediate-size networks. Even more efficient machines custom-configured as file servers are available at prices rising sharply to well up into the $10,000 range, some even as high as $30,000 when fully configured. But if network throughput is crucial, and your network serves 10 or more local computers, you may want to look into these.

You can also install a high performance disk drive on your network file server. Some hard drives have access times of 80 milliseconds or more, making them too sluggish for network operation. Today's high performance drives, especially those that feature SCSI and ESDI interface technology, have access times as low as 15 milliseconds and can increase throughput over a standard

RLL or MFM drive by up to 40 percent. These super-drives, even in the 150MB to 300MB range, are faster than blazes. But they don't come cheap. Expect to pay $800 to $1,200 for a 150MB ESDI drive with controller.

In addition, you can choose a network package that offers the performance you need. Many of the less expensive LAN packages offer nontechnical installation procedures and easy learning curves, but may come up too short on data transmission speed. A three- or four-megabit-per-second transmission rate may be enough for a small workgroup, but ten megabits per second or better will move the data through the network more than twice as fast.

You can also configure any extra RAM on the file server as a disk cache. This is an effective way to increase network speed.

You can set up the server as a server only and don't use it as a workstation. If you can afford it, a dedicated network file server will increase network efficiency.

Indexing database fields speeds up searches, but slows down the speed at which Q&A adds or updates records. To obtain the best network performance for all your users, index only those fields on which users most often need to search.

 Author's Tip: Once the Intelligent Assistant or Query Guide has been taught, they are updated each time you add or change records in that database. If you don't plan to use the Intelligent Assistant or Query Guide with a database, don't teach them. If the Intelligent Assistant or Query Guide were previously taught, but are no longer used, copy the design of the database to another filename, and follow that by copying the forms. You can then delete the old file and give the new file the original name. This is the only way to create a duplicate untaught database.

Additional memory installed in the server and local machines also reduces disk activity, thus improving network performance. The Virtual Memory Management feature in Q&A version 4.0 can make use of both extended and expanded memory.

Another option is to install a single-user copy of the program on each workstation, instead of sharing the Q&A program from the network file server. If you do run Q&A from a shared network drive, have users specify personal paths that point to their own local hard drives. Then temporary files won't have to go over the network, and the demands placed on the server's resources will be reduced.

Network Troubleshooting

Here are a few network problems and solutions not covered elsewhere in this chapter.

Records and functions stay locked when they shouldn't be. If a user doesn't exit Q&A properly, Q&A may continue to think that a record or function is still being used. If the user is the first to enter a database, Q&A automatically resets the locks, cleans out any deleted records, and performs other housekeeping chores. If the condition won't correct, have all users exit the database momentarily.

A user can't run Q&A from a shared directory. There may be several reasons:

- The user may not have full access rights to the directory.

- The user may be trying to run Q&A off a nonnetwork drive.

- The user may not be running Q&A from the directory he's actually in. Q&A cannot be placed in a search drive because it locates its files in what it assumes is the current directory. If you want users to be able to run the program from anywhere in their directory structures, write a batch file for the public search drive that changes the active directory to the one that QA.COM is in.

A user can't access a database on the network. Check the following:

- Does Q&A know it's on a network? Some networks don't fully support DOS 3.1 (or later) network calls.

- Try loading the DOS Share program into RAM before loading Q&A. Share provides some record-locking support that may be required.

- Make sure the user has full rights to the directory where the database is located. Network access rights are controlled by the network software, not by Q&A.

- Make sure the user is entering his User ID and password correctly.

- Make sure the database is set for concurrent use at the Declare Sharing Mode screen.

Backing Up Shared Files

Backing up files in a multiuser environment merits special consideration, particularly where information in large databases is needed routinely by multiple users.

At any given time of day several data files may be open simultaneously while users on the system view and update the information in them. A sudden power loss can wreak havoc on a network, not only by causing the system to crash, but also by damaging more than one data file and creating a situation where perhaps dozens of people must now sit idly by while the problems are corrected, even hours after the power has been restored.

Regularly scheduled backups of the data files by the network administrator are thus crucial. But backing up to floppy disks — as one might do in a single-user environment — is usually not only impractical, but downright impossible, as individual floppies don't have the capacity, and the process is too time consuming.

For such systems, a streaming tape backup subsystem could be purchased and installed in the network file server.

Combining a special internally or externally mounted tape drive with proprietary backup software, these add-on subsystems make short work of backing up even the largest files rapidly and reliably. Dozens of megabytes — even very large files — can be backed up from the network drive in a matter of minutes, and the tape can then be removed and locked away each night for safekeeping.

Such a product need not drain the company's financial resources. You can purchase 120MB backup systems for under $500, and they can usually be installed without any special hardware knowledge or other technical expertise.

Uninterruptible power supplies (UPS) are another way to protect data vital to your organization. These units provide a constant flow of regulated power to the server or to all machines attached to the UPS in the event of sudden brownouts or even total electrical failure.

While such emergency power may be sustainable only for a few minutes, enough time can be provided to get users off the network and the system properly shut down, thus turning the potential for serious file damage and consequent extended downtime into a relatively minor inconvenience that's over as soon as normal power is restored.

Backup tape drives and uninterruptible power supplies add a substantial measure of protection against data loss. Prices today for this equipment are

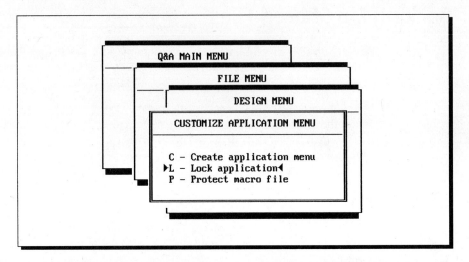

Figure 13-5: Selecting Lock Application on the Customize Application Menu. You can prevent users from tampering with your application by locking it. This protection is completely independent of any other type of password protection.

extremely reasonable in light of what can happen to a small or large organization's ability to rapidly recover and resume operations when disasters like power failures strike.

Placing Locks on the Database

In addition to, or in lieu of, controlling access to a given data file by creating access control forms, assigning passwords, and placing restrictions on fields, the database administrator or application developer can lock various application design features and functions, and thereby protect against any tampering with the underlying structure of the file.

Figure 13-5 shows the Customize Application menu with the Lock Application selection. You reach this menu through the Design menu, after entering the name of the database and, if required, your User ID and password.

The Customize Application menu includes two additional choices: Create Application Menu and Protect Macro File. These other selections, since they involve Q&A's macro facilities, are covered in Chapter 8.

If the database is password protected, you must have administrative rights to use the Lock Application feature. These rights are normally reserved for the database administrator.

```
                              DATABASE LOCK
                              ============

                    Password : ░░░░░░░░░░░░░░░░░░░░

_____

        Can users Redesign and program?..........:   ▸Yes◂  No
          • Redesign database      • Program form
          • Program navigation     • Field template
          • Set field names

        Can users Design/Redesign reports?.......:   ▸Yes◂  No
        Can users Restrict values?...............:   ▸Yes◂  No
        Can users Set initial values?...........:   ▸Yes◂  No
        Can users Speed up search?...............:   ▸Yes◂  No
        Can users set Read only fields?..........:   ▸Yes◂  No
        Can users Edit lookup table?.............:   ▸Yes◂  No
        Can users Define custom help.............:   ▸Yes◂  No
        Can users Set xlookup password?..........:   ▸Yes◂  No
        Can users Change palette?................:   ▸Yes◂  No

        Should the database lock be enabled?.....:    Yes  ▸No◂
_____

                    Lock Options for EMPLOYEE.DTF

    Esc-Exit                 F1-Help                  F10-Continue
```

Figure 13-6: At the Database Lock Options Screen. You can assign a password, select which database features you want to protect, and then enable the lock.

If yours is not a multiuser system, the file may have been locked by the applications developer or value added reseller from whom you purchased the application, in which case you'll need to contact that person for assistance.

The Database Lock Options screen is shown in Figure 13-6.

The Lock Options screen offers protection for virtually every feature of the database design, including report design and redesign. All selections except Should the database lock be enabled? default to "Yes." You lock the items by changing their default "Yes" to "No," and then turn on all the selected locks by enabling the lock.

When you lock the Redesign/Program item, you prevent users from redesigning or programming the database, including changing information types, format options, field templates, and field names.

Locking Design/Redesign Reports prevents users from changing or creating report designs, but still enables them to run reports with or without temporary changes.

As you go down the list of items that can be locked, you'll see that the database design can be made virtually, if not completely, impervious to any unauthorized modification.

Combine these locks with your defense arsenal of read-only and hidden fields, as well as other restrictions placed on users by virtue of their Access Control forms, and you'll have a foolproof database protection scheme in place.

To complete the Database Lock Options screen:

1. Assign yourself a password, and type in at the top of the screen. Make a note of it; if you forget your password and you're the only one who knows it, a copy of the file will have to be sent to Symantec to have the password reset.

2. Navigate to any item you want to protect and change the default "Yes" to "No."

3. When you've locked all the items you want to protect, move to the last line on the screen and change it from "No" to "Yes." If you fail to do this, none of the locks will be placed on the file.

4. Press **<F10>** to save your locks on the database and return to the Customize Application menu.

Later, if you need to perform a locked operation, simply return to the Database Lock screen, change the locked item from "No" to "Yes," and press **<F10>**.

If you want perform a number of locked operations, you can leave the individual locks set to "No" and simply disable them all by changing the last line of the Database Lock screen to "No," and pressing **<F10>** to save and exit.

Once you've finished your work on the database you'll need to return to the Database Lock screen and reenable the temporarily disabled locks. Otherwise, users will have access to access those operations.

Summary

In this chapter you've seen how you can set up and use Q&A in a multiuser environment, improve network performance, and add security measures to protect entire applications and the operations and procedures associated with them. Keep in mind that many of these security features can be used even in offices where only one PC is used by several people. In addition to Q&A's security features discussed here, even greater levels of security and control can be established by the developer by directing access to applications and procedures through a well-structured custom application menu system — see Chapter 8.

Appendix A
Summary of 4.0 Upgrade Features

A wealth of remarkable and useful new features has been incorporated into the 4.0 upgrade. However, many of these new features are primarily for the benefit of the more experienced Q&A user. Symantec made sure that the new Q&A didn't sacrifice a single thing where the product's familiar feel, friendly interface, or exceptional ease of use are concerned. So whether you're a first-timer to the world of computers and software or an automation veteran, Q&A is now better equipped than ever to help you tackle even your toughest word processing, mailing merging, reporting, and database applications.

Despite the added power, Q&A is easier than ever to use, and now vastly more versatile. A summary of these new features follows, along with descriptions of what they entail, under the heading of the Q&A module mainly affected by the enhancement (File, Write, Report, and so on). There are even more — often subtle — product enhancements than can be listed here. This is an overview of the major ones.

General (Nonmodule-specific)

Simplified program installation. Q&A 4.0 comes with an installation utility that practically installs the program for you. All you do is answer a few questions about where you want the program on your hard drive, what kind of printer you have, and other basic topics. See Chapter 1.

Simplified printer installation procedure. First select printer manufacturer and *then* select the printer model. User interaction with the Special Printer Options screen (now split into two screens) is an option rather than a necessity. Most users won't ever need to see it. See Chapter 1 and Appendix B.

Improved margin formatting. You'll get the page widths specified even when printing to a printer that has virtual margins. There is no user interaction, but improved WYSIWYG capabilities in margin formatting will be noticeable.

Direct cut-sheet feeder support. This features allows you to install printers and cut-sheet feeders attached to them without having to do anything else so long as the feeder information is in the printer driver. If not, the codes can be entered using the Special Printer Options screen during printer installation. See Appendix B.

Box character drawing. This feature eliminates dash character output and is supported for many printers that don't support the full IBM character set — such as some Epson, Hewlett-Packard, and PostScript printer models. See Appendix C.

Envelope printing enhancements. The standard 24-line envelope printing format was not valid for all types of printers and envelopes. Now you can set envelope page-length defaults at the Special Printer Options screen. This does not apply to laser printers that require a special printer driver for the envelope printing function.

Mouse support. Use a Microsoft-compatible mouse to select items from menus and lists, move through fields and forms, and choose operations from word processing menus. See Appendix F.

Microsoft Windows 3.0 compatibility. Q&A 4.0 can be run under Windows as a full-screen application only. Two files, QA.PIF and QA.ICO, included on the Q&A program disks, need to be installed in Windows for Q&A to run. See Appendix H for more on running Q&A under Windows.

Intel Connection Coprocessor and SatisFAXtion support. Send documents and reports as faxes from inside Q&A. See Appendix B.

File descriptions. Users can give word processing document and database files 70-character descriptions. Using Q&A's DOS File Facilities (List Manager) you can create, view, and/or edit these descriptions. Q&A program files and non-Q&A files, however, are off limits. When you go to the List Manager you highlight a filename and the description is shown on the status line. Pressing **<F6>** will bring up an editing box where changes to the description can be made. See Chapter 9.

Define Page screens. This feature offers characters-per-inch selections based on the capabilities of the printer. In version 3.0 the cpi line offered 10, 12, 15, and 17 characters-per-inch even if one or more of these was unsupported at the printer. Now, if the user has formatted his document for a particular cpi, then chooses another printer from the Print Options screen that doesn't support that cpi, the Define Page screen will show the closest match. In such cases Q&A will alter the formatting of the document to accommodate the printer's cpi capability, and a pop-up message will warn the user of the impending modification. See Chapter 2.

More help at Define Page. Page widths, margins, and characters-per-inch settings are all closely related — a difficult concept for many users to grasp. An additional help screen has been placed behind all Define Page screens in the form of a chart indicating maximum characters available per line (page width in characters) at various paper sizes and characters-per-inch settings. The screen applies only to mono-spaced fonts.

Expanded menus. Users upgrading from Q&A version 3.0 to 4.0 will immediately notice the appearance of this new feature. Several 3.0 single-column menus were changed to dual-column to support the added features. The File and Import menu selections have been increased, and there is now a Remove menu branching from the File menu, as well as a new Programming menu.

Specify location of temporary files. Q&A creates temporary files when sorting, merging, or performing other tasks, and as a result you may quickly run out of hard disk space. Version 4.0 allows you to specify the location of these temporary files, whether in another directory on the same drive, or on another drive altogether. A new line was added to the Global Options screen (accessed from the Utilities menu) where you can indicate where Q&A should place temporary files. Incidentally, this allows the Q&A program files to reside on a read-only drive, as long as all other files (including temporary files) are in a read/write directory/drive. See Chapter 1.

Custom application menus. You can create custom menus and place selections on them. These menus can be configured to bypass or even replace standard Q&A menus, allowing you to build complete stand-alone applications with their own modules and unique characteristics. See Chapter 8.

Named macros. Assign descriptive names to your macros and run them from lists and custom-designed menus. Eliminates the need to remember key identifiers such as **<Alt><C>**, and helps you control from where in Q&A your macros can be launched. See Chapter 8.

Encode macro files. Use this feature to protect custom application menus and macros from unauthorized changes. See Chapter 8.

Virtual memory manager. This feature improves Q&A's memory usage and allows you to create longer word processing documents and build more complex queries and reports.

Font Assignment screens and enhancement menus. In File and Report, enhance portions of forms and reports with boldface, italics, fonts, etc.

Case formatting. Assign text as all uppercase, lowercase, or initial capitals in the File and Write modules.

Write Module

Import/export support. Support has been added for the latest versions of WordPerfect, Microsoft Word, MultiMate, WordStar, and Professional Write.

Mail-merge programming. This feature allows you to specify programming expressions and calculations in the word processor for execution on the merge file during mail-merge operations. It also enables lookups to external databases to retrieve values for placement into the merge document and provides the capability to specify operations (such as **+**, **−**, *****, and **/**) on database values at merge time. Programming *statements* (for example, If/Then/Else), however, are not available for use in mail-merge programming. See Chapter 5.

More page characteristics on screen. See line spacing, tabs, carriage returns, and accurate line and page breaks for all types of fonts on the display screen. See Chapter 2.

Page preview. Get a WYSIWYG representation of the page layout before printing. Page Preview is available at most Print Options screens, including the Write, File, and Report modules. Zoom in and out and see facing pages. Change your document layout or reformat your report before wasting a single sheet of paper.

Built-in 660,000-word thesaurus. Look up and select synonyms. Available in the Write and File modules. See Chapter 2.

Multiple mailing-label printing. Run off dozens or hundreds of the same label. See Chapter 5.

Scalable fonts. This feature is supported throughout the product.

Text Enhancement menu. A handy pop-up menu lets you to select the enhancement or font you want with a single keystroke. This feature is available in Write, File, and Report. See Chapter 2.

Options menu. Press **<F8>** to display an Options menu from which you can select virtually any word processing-related operation, from laying out the page to blocking text and searching/replacing.

You can now choose to use the function keys, the Options menu, or a combination of both. See Chapter 2.

Search and replace across documents. Use the **JOIN** command to join a series of documents (chapters of a book, for example) and then perform search and replace operations across all of them at the same time. See Chapter 2.

Define Page for imported documents. Establish default page settings for imported documents only. Also, choose a document default import type so Q&A won't question you when you import a document in the selected format. See Chapter 2.

Justification options. You can specify the type of justification desired at print time: justification (micro-justification), space justification, or no justification. See Chapter 2.

More Avery label support. More than 50 Avery label formats are now supported, including special labels for audio cassettes and videotapes. See Chapter 5.

Document recovery. Recover documents damaged by power fluctuations. The utility rebuilds the document in ASCII format. See Chapter 9.

File Module

Posting. Post field values in one database to linked fields in another database. For example, you can post quantities of sold items from an invoice database to an inventory database. Mathematical operators can be used along with calculation options in the target file. See Chapters 4 and 10. In mass update and posting you have the option of posting the first few forms manually with **<Shift><F10>** and then pressing **<Alt><F10>** to have Q&A automatically update the remaining forms in the stack. See Chapter 4.

Editable Table View. View *and edit* your database records in a table format (records in rows and fields in columns). Use horizontal and vertical scroll to move around. Full record-locking is supported while editing in Table View in network environments. See Chapter 3.

Mass Update Auto Recalc. Specify which programming actions (On-Record-Entry, Calculation, and On-Record-Exit statements) should be executed during mass updates. On-Record-Entry statements are executed first, followed by Mass Update statements, Calc statements, and On-Record-Exit statements, in that order, but only as specified by the user at the Calculations Options screen. The same calculation options are available at the Posting Spec. See Chapter 4.

Field restrictions list. During data entry, press **<Alt><F7>** to display a list of restrictions for the field, highlight the value you want, and press **<Enter>** to retrieve it into the form. See Chapter 4.

New text options at Format Spec. Format a field for all uppercase text, all lowercase, or initial caps. Text already in the database will be displayed at the new setting. With the initial caps option, all data will be seen in lowercase except for the first character in the field and the first letter following a space. See Chapter 3.

Form printing enhancements. Define text enhancements such as bold, underline, font changes, and others on a field-by-field basis when printing forms. You can enhance fields, fields and their labels, or labels only. Up to nine fonts can be selected per form. In coordinate printing, rows and columns may now be specified in inches down and across the page in addition to the usual lines and character columns method. This is useful when printing in proportionally spaced typefaces. See Chapter 3.

Delete duplicate records. A Remove submenu allows users to remove selected records, duplicate records, or duplicate records with an ASCII database created to store any duplicate records found. This utility-like feature scans the database for records with duplicate fields specified by the user at the Duplicate Spec. See Chapter 4.

Field editor. During data entry, expand a field for the entry of long values by pressing **<F6>**. The editor holds approximately 16 pages of text. You can use it for sales call reports, employee review comments, product notes, and other needs. Most of the word processing functions are available when inside the editor. Closing the editor returns the user to the form to continue with data entry. See Chapter 3.

Program editor. Pressing **<F6>** (Expand Field) now pops up a word processor-like editor, instead of version 3.0's one-line, 240-character input line at the bottom of the screen. This editor, 78 columns by 8 lines, is available almost everywhere the Expand Field option is permitted and allows you to see up to 624 characters at a time by scrolling. The Program editor has the standard word processor features such as delete, copy, search, replace, export/import document, macro interface, and print, and eases the entry of long programming statements. See Chapter 4.

Field templates. Specify field attributes so that values entered into database fields will be formatted automatically. These templates are visible on screen during Add and Search/Update and are useful for forced formatting of phone numbers, Social Security numbers, and so forth. Use this feature to design and redesign templates or select predefined ones. See Chapter 4.

Save named specs. Version 3.0 enabled you to save Report Specs and File Print Specs. In 4.0 you can also name and save specs for Retrieve, Sort, Merge, Mass Update, Posting, Table View, and other activities. At any of these specs, the user can call up the list of predefined specs and select the one desired. The specs can be used as they are, or modified and resaved to disk. When a Mass Update or Posting Spec is saved, any calculation options associated with it are also saved. See Chapter 4.

XLOOKUP to multiple database fields. Standard XLOOKUP commands remain unchanged, but you can now specify a series of external database lookups in a single command. Previous to version 4.0 you wrote an XLOOKUP command for each field in the external database to be looked up. With one command, up to 17 fields can now be looked up and their values placed in the designated fields of the current form. The single XLOOKUP command specifies the external filename, the primary key field, and the external key field as usual. But now you can designate source fields and destination fields, one right after the other, in the same command. This feature works with XLOOKUP statements only. See Chapter 4.

XLOOKUP directly to dBASE files. You can accomplish this task from within a Q&A database simply by adding the .DBF extension to the filename in the command — a feature supported in both XLOOKUP statements and @XLOOKUP functions. See Chapter 4.

XLOOKUP passwords. Specify a special "surrogate" password for all external lookup statements in a database, regardless of the user's access rights, thus enabling external lookups to work where the user would not normally have the right to read that database or the restricted fields in it. See Chapter 13.

Required fields. This feature enables the database designer to absolutely *require* entry of data into specified fields, preventing the operator from otherwise bypassing the field or adding the form to the database with an out-of-range value entered. See Chapter 4.

Database locks. Easily password-protect access to database and report redesigns, and prevent access to Initial Values, Field Names, Speed-up, Restrict Values, and Read-only Specs. This feature also enables the designer to set locks on "Edit lookup table," "Define custom help," and "Change palette procedures." See Chapter 13.

Concurrent custom help. Data can be entered into fields as custom help screens remain displayed. When a help screen is displayed, moving to subsequent fields displays the custom help screens for those fields until you press **<Esc>** to put them away.

Field-level security. Assign a field read/write, read-only, or hidden status, altering a user's view of the form according to their access rights.

Clearing Specs. Pressing **<F3>** to clear any Q&A spec now results in a warning that the latest changes to the spec have not been saved. Accidentally pressing **<F3>** no longer automatically dumps spec changes, wasting the work associated with creating them.

Retrieve Spec programming. Allows you to enter valid programming expressions and calculation formulas at any Retrieve Spec. The usual search restrictions can be entered, or the user can opt to use the new programming capability (or a combination of both). @XLOOKUP functions are supported, enabling one to specify a retrieve criterion based on a match between a value in the current database and one in an external database, for example. Retrieve Specs can be named and saved to disk for future use.

Assign field names. With earlier versions of Q&A the user had the option of assigning field labels and logical field numbers (field ID#s). A third option in 4.0 creates default field names for no-name fields and allows the user to change these from the Field Names Spec available via the Programming menu. This gives users with labelless fields the ability to use the improved mail-merge capability. When pressing **<Alt><F7>** to merge database fields into a Q&A document, the field name will now appear in the list of database merge fields, making every field readily identifiable. Nonunique field labels have a suffix appended to them to make unique default field names. By default, no-name fields will be designated Field 0001, Field 0002, and so forth, but the user can change these. Field names, like field ID#s, must be unique and you can optionally reference field names — rather than field ID#s — in programming statements. See Chapter 4.

Abbreviated function names. Most Q&A function names have been abbreviated to make it easier on the programmer, who now has the choice of using the longer name or its abbreviated equivalent. @XLOOKUP, for example, can now be typed as @Xlu, @NUMBER as @Nmb. See Chapter 4 for a full list of abbreviations.

Print specification data. Print specification data from Retrieve, Sort, Program, and other specs. If the user is in the Program Editor, pressing **<F2>** will print only the contents of the current field. Otherwise the entire spec will print out with the user having the option (at the File Print Options screen) to print expanded values or only the portion of the values that are actually seen in the fields on screen. When selecting Print from the File menu of a database containing expanded values, the user specifies a free-form print spec to have the expanded values printed in their entirety, or may select which individual expanded fields are to be printed. In coordinate printing only the data visible in the fields will be printed, although multiple-line fields where all the data is visible on screen will print in their entirety as usual.

Indirection. This is a new Q&A programming function that references a specific field, written as @Field(expression) or simply @(expression). Q&A evaluates the expression and, if it's a field name (text) in the current database, the reference is to that field. If the expression is not text, or the field name is not found, the value of the expression is converted to an integer. If this integer is then equal to a logical field number (field ID#), the value having the matching logical field number is the reference. See Chapter 4.

Gosub/Return. A new programming feature allows users to create subroutine-like programming statements by temporarily passing control of the programming to the field given in the command. Control of the program is returned to the Gosub field that called it when the word "return" is encountered. An additional command, "Stop," is available to cancel all pending returns and halt program action. The programmer can use this in combination with conditional statements and/or an @MSG for the operator. See Chapter 4.

Other new built-in programming functions. @SELECT provides conditional logic for report-derived columns; @MOD returns the remainder from a divisor; @CLEAR clears a field or list of fields; @REPLACE replaces field values with different data; and typecast functions convert between different information types. See Chapter 4 for all the built-in functions available in Q&A 4.0.

Navigation programming. This capability provides an environment in which the user can (and is strongly encouraged to) program database fields in two layers — Field programming and Navigation programming — necessary for interoperability with other multiuser platforms. Navigation programming is strictly for controlling how the cursor moves on the form. The 3.0 programming style is still supported. See Chapter 4.

Read-only fields. This feature has been added to the new Programming menu, mainly for use with fields that have their values changed strictly by calculation statements or by Mass Update or Posting operations. A Read-only field is seen by the operator but cannot be edited. If such a field is the first field on the form, its programming will be executed but the field itself will be skipped by the cursor. See Chapter 4.

Link to SQL. Oracle and Gupta SQL servers are supported. From inside Q&A you can easily connect with SQL tables and import the data into Q&A where you can then manipulate, query, and use it in reports. Special SQL drivers are available from Symantec. See Chapter 9.

Report Module

Report enhancements. Multiline text values can now be kept in the same column on the same page (widow and orphan control); an option is available to indent the second and subsequent lines of multiline text values (hanging indent); double-line spacing is available in reports; you can specify Standard Deviation and Variance using a method that is similar to the way in which Total is specified in standard reports; enhanced printing is available in Report (bold, italic, underline, etc.) with font selection (in headers and footers, too); and report separator lines and label names for totals, subtotals, averages, and more are now user-definable. See Chapter 6.

Crosstab reports. Summarize information across three fields by specifying row, column, and summary fields (before version 4.0, only individual report columns could be specified, not rows). For example, you can ask Q&A for a report summarizing average salary by supervisory and hourly employee by department, and the report would print with an average salary column and a calculated average salary row as the final report line. The crosstab spec will compute summary values such as total, average, count, minimum, maximum, standard deviation, and variance depending on the data type of the fields involved. Predefined grouping functions have been added to make specifying groups easier. The usual report options are all still available for crosstab reports, including keyword reports, derived columns (referred to in crosstab reports as derived *fields*), special formatting, enhancements, etc. See Chapter 6.

Report preview. Get a WYSIWYG representation of how your columnar or crosstab report will look when printed, *before* you print. Zoom in and out and see subsequent pages. Shows fonts, headers, and footers, with all report characteristics in correct proportion. See Chapter 6.

Intelligent Assistant

Expanded vocabulary. The Assistant better understands your queries and commands the first time. Over 600 words are now included in the IA's built-in vocabulary. See Chapter 7.

Query Guide. Build your queries and reports a step at a time by selecting fragments of commands from lists. When you go to the Query Guide, you choose the type of operation you want to do, and you're then guided through each of the steps required to build the query or report. If you use a mouse, you can create even more complex reports without having to touch the keyboard. See Chapter 7.

Network

Automatic record-locking. Workgroup users simultaneously share the same database. See Chapter 13.

Instant screen update. Changes made to a database are reflected on all users' screens so that everyone using the file sees the most current data as they view and edit forms.

Expanded password protection. Up to seven levels of password protection can be attached to any database. User groups can be created and assigned access rights. The Field Security Spec allows selected fields to be assigned Hidden or Read-only status, placing them off-limits to selected user groups. See Chapter 13.

Field protection/restricted access. Database administrators can deny operator access to designated fields on a form. This is especially useful in multiuser environments. Fields can be "Hidden Read-only." By default a user has complete access to forms, reports, and other entities. The database administrator can assign individual users to groups (up to eight groups) and then restrict access to fields on a group basis. When displaying lists of specs and reports, version 4.0 excludes specs that contain fields that are off-limits to the user group (salaries and review information in a personnel database, for instance). See Chapter 13.

Utilities

More import/export support. Both dBASE IV and Paradox (2.0, 3.0, and 3.5) import and export are supported in Q&A version 4.0. Import of Professional File 2.0 is also supported, in addition to Lotus 1-2-3 2.2 spreadsheets, which can be imported into a Q&A database or into a Write document from where they can be dynamically printed along with Lotus graphs. See Chapter 9.

Database locks. Database administrators can protect against database redesign and changes to other database features and operations by selecting the "Lock database" option. A valid password is needed to unlock the database for redesign or to gain access to the "Customize menu" features that have been locked. One could lock "Define custom help" and "Define program form," for example, while leaving other customization features unlocked. See Chapter 9.

Diagnostic support information. To help Q&A Technical Support personnel, a dialogue screen is built into Q&A 4.0 that supplies important information about paths, directories, file dates, available and total memory, disk space, available drives and ports, video control cards, handles, switches, the DOS version, and so forth. The user can be directed to call up this screen when a tech support person needs the information to help the user with a problem. It's available from the Q&A Main menu by pressing **`<Ctrl><F3>`**.

Bundled utilities. Q&A comes packaged with a Microsoft expanded memory manager (HIMEM.SYS) that converts extended memory into expanded memory for use by Q&A (see Chapter 1); a font utility (QAFONT.EXE) that converts customized font description files and HP LaserJet- and PostScript-compatible soft font files for use by Q&A (see Chapter 9); and a handy backup utility (QABACKUP.EXE) that enables you to back up and restore files larger than a single floppy disk (see Appendix G). Q&A 4.0 also comes with two files (QA.PIF and QA.ICO) that enable you to run Q&A under Microsoft Windows 3.0 (see Chapter 1 and Appendix H).

Appendix B
Special Printer Installation and Troubleshooting

Installation and Printer Options

Using Q&A's Fax Capabilities

If your computer has an Intel Connection Coprocessor or SatisFAXtion board, you can use it and Q&A to send faxes to other fax machines or to remote computers also equipped with these boards. Your faxes can be individual letters, mail-merge letters, reports, forms, or answers from the Query Guide or Intelligent Assistant. Virtually anything you can print in Q&A you can send as a fax, subject to a few limitations.

Fonts, other enhancements (such as bold or italics), and the ***GRAPH*** command are not supported — they'll be stripped from the output during transmission preparation. Also, the maximum report width you can fax is 132 columns.

To set up Q&A to transmit faxes:

1. Choose "Install printer" from the Utilities menu.

2. At the Printer Selection screen highlight printer A, B, C, etc. (the one you want to install or change), and press **<Enter>**.

3. When Q&A prompts you to select the port, highlight FAX and press **<Enter>**. The Special Port Options screen in Figure B-1 displays.

4. Highlight the fax option you want.

   FAX1 produces your faxes with fine resolution (200 3 200 dots per inch) in an 80-column format.

   FAX2 gives you fine resolution in a 132-column format.

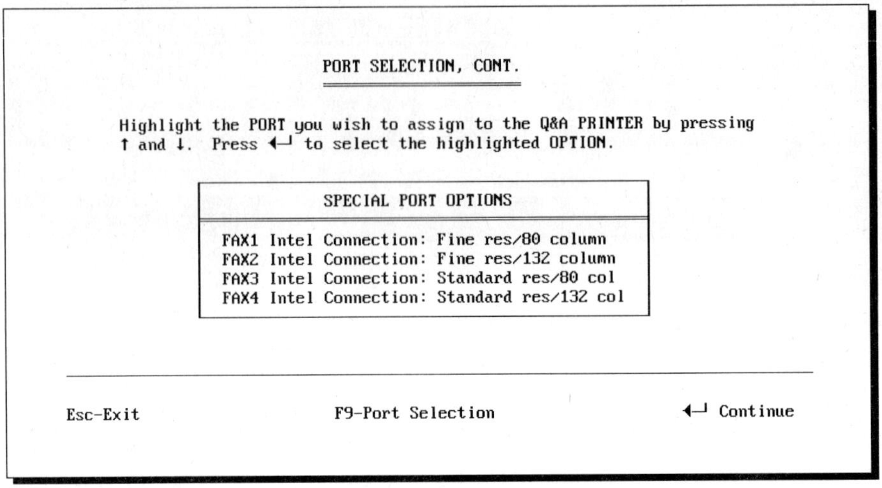

```
                           PORT SELECTION, CONT.
                           =====================

             Highlight the PORT you wish to assign to the Q&A PRINTER by pressing
             ↑ and ↓.  Press ↵ to select the highlighted OPTION.

                    ┌──────────────────────────────────────────┐
                    │            SPECIAL PORT OPTIONS            │
                    ├──────────────────────────────────────────┤
                    │  FAX1 Intel Connection: Fine res/80 column │
                    │  FAX2 Intel Connection: Fine res/132 column│
                    │  FAX3 Intel Connection: Standard res/80 col│
                    │  FAX4 Intel Connection: Standard res/132 col│
                    └──────────────────────────────────────────┘



      Esc-Exit                     F9-Port Selection              ↵ Continue
```

Figure B-1: The Fax Port Special Options Screen. Highlight the option you want and press
<Enter>.

FAX3 provides a standard 200 3 100 resolution in 80 columns.

FAX4 outputs your faxes with standard resolution in a 132-column format.

The 80-column format produces 10 characters-per-inch and a maximum
of 66 lines per page for letters, forms, and so forth. The 132-column
option produces compressed characters and 88 lines per page — ideal for
reports up to 132 columns wide.

5. Press **<Enter>.** Q&A confirms installation and asks if you'd like to install
   another printer.

Sending a fax couldn't be easier. When you come to the Print Options screen,
simply select the printer setup for fax transmission and press **<F10>.**

You can install more than one fax option for use at any Print Options screen,
as long as you have "printer" slots available at the Printer Selection screen.

If you're on a network, both Q&A and the fax board software must reside on
the same local hard disk.

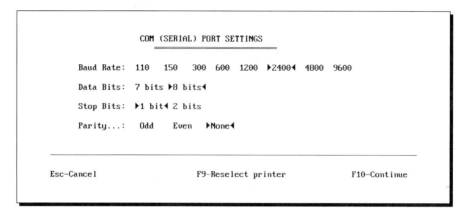

Figure B-2: Serial Printer Options.

COM (Serial) Port Settings

If you've selected a COM port for your printer, in addition you may want to choose a particular baud rate, data-bits setting, stop-bits setting, and parity. Figure B-2 shows the COM port screen with the most common preset values highlighted. Consult your serial printer's manual to find out which settings are optimum for your printer. Use the cursor navigation keys and space bar to move to your selection and press **<Enter>** when the highlight bar is over the value you wish to set. Press **<F10>** when finished, or **<F8>** for the Special Printer Options screen shown in Figure B-3.

Baud rate is the speed at which characters and codes are transmitted from Q&A to your printer. The default is 2400. If your printer has a large memory, it may be capable of handling a baud rate of up to 9600. Check your printer manual, and be sure the baud rate set here is the same as that set at your printer.

Data bits are the size of the character (in bits) that your printer expects to receive. Eight bits are required for graphics and special characters above ASCII 127, and is the correct setting for most serial printers.

Stop bits are the number of bits (1 or 2) your printer needs to understand a stop command.

Parity refers to the number of bits your printer may require during transmission to make the total number of bits odd or even for a given sequence or group of characters. Today's printers typically require no parity.

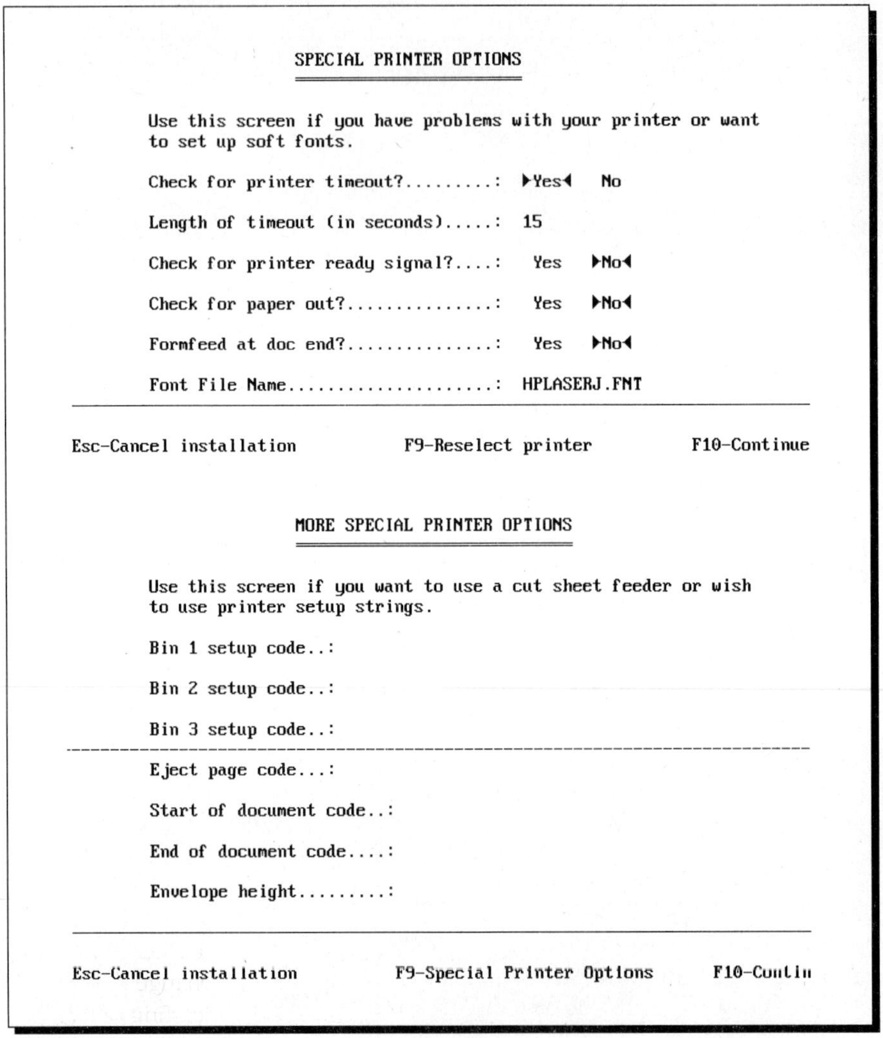

```
                    SPECIAL PRINTER OPTIONS
                    ═══════════════════════

          Use this screen if you have problems with your printer or want
          to set up soft fonts.

          Check for printer timeout?.........:  ▶Yes◀    No

          Length of timeout (in seconds).....:  15

          Check for printer ready signal?....:   Yes    ▶No◀

          Check for paper out?...............:   Yes    ▶No◀

          Formfeed at doc end?...............:   Yes    ▶No◀

          Font File Name.....................:  HPLASERJ.FNT
     ─────────────────────────────────────────────────────────────────

     Esc-Cancel installation       F9-Reselect printer       F10-Continue



                    MORE SPECIAL PRINTER OPTIONS
                    ════════════════════════════

          Use this screen if you want to use a cut sheet feeder or wish
          to use printer setup strings.

          Bin 1 setup code..:

          Bin 2 setup code..:

          Bin 3 setup code..:
     ─────────────────────────────────────────────────────────────────
          Eject page code...:

          Start of document code..:

          End of document code....:

          Envelope height........:
     ─────────────────────────────────────────────────────────────────

     Esc-Cancel installation      F9-Special Printer Options    F10-Continu
```

Figure B-3: The Special Printer Options and More Special Printer Options Screens. Default settings and LaserJet font file are shown. For most lasers, your bin setup codes will already be installed.

Special Printer Options

You can access Q&A's Special Printer Options screen by pressing **<F8>** after installing your printer. If you're doing a standard printer installation and don't need to set any options, you can press **<F10>** to continue. See Figure B-3 for a look at these two special options screens.

Enter your selections on the Special Printer Options screens to fine-tune the way you want Q&A to work with your printer. Use the cursor navigation keys to move to your choices and press **<Enter>** to confirm. If your printer uses a cut-sheet feeder you may have to specify the bin setup codes.

Check for Printer Timeout

Printer timeout is the length of time Q&A waits for your printer to respond to commands. The default setting is Yes, so that when the printer *doesn't* respond in the length of time specified, Q&A will tell you "Your printer is not responding" to let you know there's a problem.

You may get a "Printer not responding" message while your printer is happily printing away. This can happen when the printer requires a longer timeout period than the default eight seconds. If you're experiencing this you can increase the timeout period or set the "Check for printer timeout" line to No.

Length of Timeout

The default is 15 seconds. You can go as high as 999 seconds (more than 16 minutes). But if your "Check for printer timeout" is designated No, then Q&A will ignore the timeout length and assume it to be infinite.

Check for Printer Ready Signal

Select Yes if your printer sends a signal when it's ready to receive data to print. If you select Yes and your printer doesn't transmit a ready code, Q&A may tell you immediately that the printer is not responding when you press **<F10>** to begin a print job. If this occurs, set this line to No to tell Q&A not to wait around for the ready signal that will never come.

Check for Paper Out

Most printers send a signal to the software program when they run out of paper. Set this to Yes if yours does. If you get a "Printer not responding" message although there's paper in the machine, change this setting to No. Some cut-sheet feeder printers are in the habit of broadcasting out-of-paper signals even though there's plenty of paper in the bin.

Formfeed at End of Document

Some printers (usually lasers) won't eject a page unless there's another one to be printed behind it. Setting this option to Yes will force the formfeed. However, an *unnecessary* Yes setting may cause a blank sheet of paper to be fed and ejected after the last printed sheet.

Font Filename

This is the font description file Q&A is using for your particular printer make and model. If you selected a manufacturer and model from the lists supplied by Q&A earlier in the printer installation process, the filename should already be on this line when you access the Special Printer Options screen.

 Note: Setting all the options to No may cause your computer to lock up if no printer is connected.

Cut-sheet Feeders and Bin Setup

Cut-sheet feeders are attached to some printers to feed paper from one or more bins during printing operations. If your printer has bins, and the Q&A printer driver doesn't contain the bin information, then you'll need to specify the correct control codes so Q&A will know from which bins to tell the printer to feed paper. For standard brands of printers, however, this bin information will already be contained in the Q&A printer driver, and you won't need to worry about these special codes.

You can determine whether your feeder works with Q&A by printing a document of multiple pages with the "Type of paper feed" at the Print Options screen set to Continuous. If the paper feeds correctly for each page, then you don't need to do anything further and should definitely *not* enter any "Bin setup codes" at the Special Printer Options screen.

If, on the other hand, the paper *doesn't* feed the way it should, or if you want to print from more than one bin and the information on how to do this is not contained in Q&A's driver for your printer, then you can enter these codes at the Special Printer Options screen as explained below.

If you need to specify bin setup codes, first consult your printer manual for the special codes needed to activate the paper feed mechanism, and then enter these as a literal string (the decimal equivalent of the ASCII codes), separating the codes with commas. Your printer manual will tell you how to type out these codes.

When you specify control codes in the Special Printer Options screen, and select the appropriate type of paper feed on the various Print Options screens at printing time, Q&A will automatically know where to find the paper and will load it from the specified bins.

Bin 1 setup code: Enter the code that activates the paper feed from Bin 1. If your feeder has only one bin, and Q&A needs the code to make the paper feed properly, enter the code for it here. If you're using a letterhead paper feed ("Lhd" on the Print Options screen), enter the codes for both Bin 1 and Bin 2.

Bin 2 setup code: Enter the code that feeds paper from this bin. In the case of letterhead printing this will usually be the bin that feeds second and subsequent sheets.

Bin 3 setup code: Enter the code that activates paper feed from this bin.

Eject page code: If the last printed page isn't ejecting from the printer, enter the code your printer needs to ejects the page.

Other Document Codes

The "Start of document" code is sent by Q&A to indicate the first page of a printing job. This line can be used to tell a printer with a sheet feeder to load the first page.

Q&A sends an "End of document" code when the printing job is finished. A printer reset code can also be used on this line. Consult your printer manual for the code strings (if any) that should be entered on these lines.

Envelope Length

Q&A's default envelope height is 24 lines. However, some printers with built-in envelope feeders don't support 24-line envelope printing. On this line you can enter a number (usually 21 to 24 lines) to set the default height for your envelopes so that they'll print properly. Every laser printer requires a special driver that contains its own information for the envelope function. *Do not* place a value on this Envelope Length line if you're using a laser printer.

Types of Paper Feed

When it comes time to print out a document from the word processor, a report from the Report module, or a form from File, a Print Options screen is available for you to select from a variety of printing alternatives. These Print Options screens are somewhat different, depending on the module from which you're printing, and details on how to use these options are included in the relevant chapters. Chapter 2 includes considerable detail on using the Print Options screen. The following explanations should be helpful when deciding on the type of paper feed to specify at any Print Options screen:

Continuous: This is continuous form or sprocket-fed paper that comes with holes along the left and right edges. Often the margins where these holes are located are perforated so they can be removed after printing. Even some printers that feed paper in sheets from a tray or bin (LaserJets, in particular) will work fine when set to continuous feed at Print Options screens. Sheet-fed printers that will print on a continuous feed setting will select paper from the first bin.

Manual: This type of feed is for printing on stationery or other single sheets. After printing and ejecting a page, Q&A waits for you to load another sheet and press **<Enter>** before printing the next page. Today, many printers can handle both continuous and manual feed paper. For example, when continuous paper is loaded, it can be backed out temporarily from the printer while you insert and print a single sheet. In such cases manual feed should be selected at the Print Options screen so that Q&A knows to stand by between the printing of each manually loaded sheet.

Bin: If your printer feeds paper from more than one bin, Q&A will need to know which bins to use during a printing job. Typically, letterhead is loaded from Bin 1 and second sheets are loaded from Bin 2, so a letterhead printing job will take the first page (the letterhead) from Bin 1 and all subsequent pages from Bin 2. Letterhead printing jobs can be specified at Write's Print Options screen by selecting "Lhd" on the line that asks for "Type of paper feed."

Troubleshooting

Troubleshooting Common Printer Problems

Printer doesn't power up: Make sure it's plugged in, its fuse isn't blown, and it's turned on.

Power on but not printing: Be sure it's on-line and physically connected to the printer port you selected when you installed it in Q&A.

Printer won't go on-line: Is there paper in it?

Characters like P or D2 print at the top of the first page: This is usually an indication that you have the wrong printer installed in Q&A. This can also result when the printer is set up in an emulation mode using its own switches, but not installed in that same mode in Q&A.

The screen shows the text on page 1, but the printer prints the bottom of page 1 on another page: Your printer may have its own margins which, when added to the margins specified at the Define Page screen, prevent you from printing a page of text on a single sheet of paper. Set the top margin in Q&A to zero and the page length to 60. Check your printer manual to find out how many lines it is capable of printing on an 8½-by-11-inch sheet of paper.

Q&A's left margin is set at 10 characters or one inch, but the printer prints more than a one-inch left margin: Physically reposition the paper in the printer until the test document prints with the correct left margin. Then mark that spot on the printer for future reference.

When Q&A is set to print at 12 cpi, the document text is squeezed to the left: When you change the cpi, the margins and page width must also be changed. These settings are all closely related. Use the following guide to set your page dimensions at the Define Page screen in Q&A:

- **10 pitch:** (Pica) Set the left margin at 8 and the right margin at 75. Set the page width at 78.

- **12 pitch:** (Elite) Set the left margin at 8 and the right margin at 90. Set the page width at 95.

- **15 pitch:** (Condensed) Set the left margin at 10 and the right margin at 128. Set the page width at 130.

 Note: You can define your page margins in inches to get true margins irrespective of the pitch selected. When using proportional fonts, page margins should always be specified in inches.

An HP LaserJet II prints 15-pitch type when set for 12-pitch type in Q&A: The LaserJet Series II doesn't have a 12-pitch internal font. You'll need to purchase a soft font or font cartridge with a 12-cpi font, or use the LaserJet control code that forces the 10-cpi font to print 12 characters to the inch.

The printer won't print a solid line or box with Q&A's draw feature: Most printers need to be set up in IBM mode to be able to recognize and print the graphics character set. See your printer manual. LaserJets can be set using the printer control panel set to SYM SET-US.

Pressing <Shift><Prtscn> prints garbage: The printer isn't set up for IBM graphics mode. Check your printer manual.

The page won't feed on a LaserJet when pressing <Prtscn> or <Shift><Prtscn> although the cursor races down the screen: Take the printer off-line, press the form-feed button, put the printer back on-line, and the paper should feed.

I don't know how to type special graphics characters and symbols: To access the IBM graphics characters, hold down the **<Alt>** key and press the keys on the numeric keypad that correspond to the decimal code for the character you want. If this doesn't print the character on screen, hold down the **<Alt>** and **<F10>** keys while using the numeric keypad. See Appendix C for a table of the available characters and their corresponding keyboard decimal codes. The graphics characters will display properly on screen in Q&A, but remember that your printer must be set up to print them.

If your printer doesn't print from Q&A, here's a quick way to check if the problem is related to Q&A or not:

1. Exit Q&A to DOS.

2. At the DOS prompt, type **DIR>LPT1** and press **<Enter>**. Substitute for LPT1 the port your printer is physically connected to (LPT2, or COM1, for example). Your printer should print a directory.

   • If nothing is printed, the problem is with your computer and/or printer, not Q&A. Check all your cables, connections, switches; be sure the printer is on-line, and try the test again.

   • If the printer now prints properly, reload Q&A and print out a document or form.

   • If the printer still won't print from inside Q&A, change all the settings at the Special Print Options screen to No and try another print test from inside Q&A. If you're now getting results, experiment with the Special Print Options one at a time until you've isolated which setting is causing the problem. It's often a Paper Out or Printer Ready signal.

Troubleshooting Font Problems

You may experience difficulties when using fonts — especially after creating or modifying a font description at the Modify Font Descriptions screen. Here are a few things you can check:

   • Be sure the correct font is installed and available to Q&A. The printer or font cartridge may not have the font you assigned, or the cartridge may not be fully seated in the slot. If a selected soft font must be downloaded, be sure it has been downloaded following the manufacturer's recommended procedure. If a selected font is not available to Q&A, Q&A uses the regular font specified at the Font Assignments screen.

   • Verify that the font is on the Font Assignments screen and that you properly selected the font you wanted.

   • Check to be sure the font names on the Font Assignments screen match the font names in the font description file.

   • If the font is one you created or modified at the Modify Font De-scriptions screen, check the On code you entered against the On code for the font specified in the font or printer manual. Even a tiny typo here can prevent Q&A or your printer from understanding what's supposed to be done.

- Font On codes are used by Q&A to access the fonts available at your printer. For example, you can't create an italic version of a Helvetica font merely by changing the style in the font's On code to italic and then expect Q&A to print it properly if there's no italic font available.

- Verify that the font filename on the font Assignments screen matches the font filename on the Special Printer Options screen.

- Make sure you selected the correct printer at the Print Options screen.

Getting Font Support

If no font description file is available for the printer or fonts you own, here are some suggestions:

- Did you install the font file for your printer or fonts when you installed the Q&A program in Chapter 1? If you bypassed this step, you can do a selective installation for font files only. See "Installing Q&A" in Chapter 1.

- Are your font files in the \QA subdirectory along with the Q&A program files? They need to be. If they're in another directory, copy them to the \QA subdirectory.

- With a modem, you can use the Symantec Bulletin Board System (BBS) to download new font files as they become available (see Appendix D). You can likewise download font files from the Symantec forum on CompuServe. Or, you can call Q&A Technical Support to see if the font file you need is available. If it's available, your printer or font manufacturer may be able to supply a font description file for use with Q&A. And if all else fails, you can create your own font description file (see Chapter 9).

- Your printer may emulate another manufacturer's printer, in which case you can use the other printer's font description file to drive the built-in fonts in your model. This may require that you to set dip switches on a dot matrix printer. Consult the manual that came with the printer.

- You may be able to install your printer successfully as a "Basic Vanilla" printer. When you choose Basic Vanilla from the List of

Manufacturers screen during printer installation, Q&A displays the list of Basic Vanilla printers. You can then select from the following:

Non-Laser Printer
Laserprinter (Portrait)
Laserprinter (Port, Legal)
Laserprinter (Landscape)
Laserprinter (Land, Legal)
PostScript (Portrait)
PostScript (Portrait, Legal)
PostScript (Landscape)
PostScript (Landscape, Legal)

For a dot-matrix, daisywheel, or inkjet printer, select Non-Laser Printer.

If your printer is a non-PostScript laser, install the Laserprinter Portrait mode first. If a test printing turns out fine, you may be able to install additional Laserprinter modes as well, and select them at any Print Options screen.

For a PostScript printer, try the same experiment using a PostScript Basic Vanilla selection.

- You can upgrade a user-modified Q&A version 3.0 font description file so it can be used with version 4.0. The QAFONT.EXE utility program is supplied for this purpose. QAFONT.EXE should be in the directory where your Q&A program files are stored if, during 4.0 installation, you told Q&A to copy the utility files from the Master Program Diskettes to your hard drive. See Chapter 9 for information on using QAFONT.EXE.

Appendix C
The Extended Graphics Character Set

The IBM graphics set decimal numbers 176 through 223 are your best bets for drawing lines, borders, and boxes in Q&A Write, and when designing your database forms in the File module. Decimal numbers 128 through 159 access additional accented letters and international symbols. Q&A can display characters from number 33 on up. Consult your printer manual to see if your printer supports the printing of these special characters. Most dot matrix, laser, and ink-jet printers have a mode available for special ASCII graphics characters.

To display one of these literal characters on screen in Q&A, press **<Alt><F10>**, and then hold down the **<Alt>** key while typing the number of the character on the numeric keypad.

1	☺	18	↕	35	#	52	4		
2	●	19	‼	36	$	53	5		
3	♥	20	¶	37	%	54	6		
4	♦	21	§	38	&	55	7		
5	♣	22	▬	39	'	56	8		
6	♠	23	↨	40	(	57	9		
7	●	24	↑	41	)	58	:		
8	◘	25	↓	42	*	59	;		
9	○	26	→	43	+	60	<		
10	◙	27	←	44	,	61	=		
11	♂	28	∟	45	-	62	>		
12	♀	29	↔	46	.	63	?		
13	♪	30	▲	47	/	64	@		
14	♫	31	▼	48	0	65	A		
15	☼	32	blank	49	1	66	B		
16	►	33	!	50	2	67	C		
17	◄	34	"	51	3	68	D		

69	E	116	t	163	ú	210	
70	F	117	u	164	ñ	211	
71	G	118	v	165	Ñ	212	
72	H	119	w	166	ª	213	
73	I	120	x	167	º	214	
74	J	121	y	168	¿	215	
75	K	122	z	169	⌐	216	
76	L	123	{	170	¬	217	
77	M	124	|	171	½	218	
78	N	125	}	172	¼	219	
79	O	126	~	173	¡	220	
80	P	127	⌂	174	«	221	
81	Q	128	Ç	175	»	222	
82	R	129	ü	176	░	223	
83	S	130	é	177	▒	224	α
84	T	131	â	178	▓	225	ß
85	U	132	ä	179	│	226	Γ
86	V	133	à	180	┤	227	π
87	W	134	å	181	╡	228	Σ
88	X	135	ç	182	╢	229	σ
89	Y	136	ê	183	╖	230	μ
90	Z	137	ë	184	╕	231	τ
91	[	138	è	185	╣	232	Φ
92	\	139	ï	186	║	233	Θ
93	]	140	î	187	╗	234	Ω
94	^	141	ì	188	╝	235	δ
95	‾	142	Ä	189	╜	236	∞
96	`	143	Å	190	╛	237	φ
97	a	144	É	191	┐	238	∈
98	b	145	æ	192	└	239	∩
99	c	146	Æ	193	┴	240	≡
100	d	147	ô	194	┬	241	±
101	e	148	ö	195	├	242	≥
102	f	149	ò	196	─	243	≤
103	g	150	û	197	┼	244	⌠
104	h	151	ù	198	╞	245	⌡
105	i	152	ÿ	199	╟	246	÷
106	j	153	Ö	200	╚	247	≈
107	k	154	Ü	201	╔	248	°
108	l	155	¢	202	╩	249	·
109	m	156	£	203	╦	250	·
110	n	157	¥	204	╠	251	√
111	o	158	₧	205	═	252	ⁿ
112	p	159	ƒ	206	╬	253	²
113	q	160	á	207	╧	254	■
114	r	161	í	208	╨		
115	s	162	ó	209	╤		

Appendix D
The Symantec
Bulletin Board System

As a Q&A user, a tremendous amount of support is available to you courtesy of Symantec's free Bulletin Board System (BBS). Among the things you can do on the BBS are:

- Browse around.

- Leave messages for Q&A Technical Support and other BBS users, as well as receive answers.

- Check out the latest product information news from Symantec.

- Read posted messages and replies from other Q&A users.

- Read and download Q&A technical bulletins.

- Download Q&A utility programs, font files, ready-to-use Q&A databases, and shareware programs.

- Upload files.

- Chat with other users on-line.

- Place or read ads in the Classified section.

To use the BBS, your computer must be equipped with a 300, 1200, or 2400 baud modem and a communications software package whose features and operation you're familiar with. You must also configure your software to communicate with the Symantec BBS at full duplex, 8 data bits, no parity, and 1 stop bit (8N1), which usually involves entering the name of the BBS, the phone number, and these additional communications parameters on a screen provided for that purpose by your communications software package. Symantec's BBS, as of this writing, is serviced by four incoming lines at 408-973-9598.

When you dial up the BBS via your modem an opening screen welcomes you. You'll be prompted for your user-ID and password. If this is your first time on the BBS just follow the on-screen instructions. New users get a half-hour on-line time. Users with established accounts get an hour. The exception to this is if you're in the process of downloading or uploading a file. In such cases the BBS remains open to you until the file has been fully transmitted.

The BBS Main Menu

At the time of this writing the Symantec BBS was undergoing an upgrade. The Main menu, however, includes selections for the kinds of broad activities you can do on the BBS, and these aren't likely to change significantly. Here are the Main menu selections:

S	Special Interest Groups (SIGS)	Read/write support messages
F	File Libraries (LIBS)	Upload and download files
I	Information Center	Technical tips, virus updates, etc.
E	Electronic Mail	Read and write private mail
C	Comments for the Sysop	Leave a note for the System Operator
G	Goodbye	Log off the BBS
H	Help with the BBS	System information, how to download
T	Teleconferencing	Chat with users on-line
L	List users online	Show who's currently on-line
U	Upload a file	Send a file to Symantec.

If you're unfamiliar with how the BBS works, type **H** for Help at the Main menu, and press **<Enter>**; the next menu to display will offer you selections along the following lines:

1 .. All about the Symantec BBS
2 .. Help with the commands on the Symantec BBS
3 .. A tutorial on uploading and downloading files
4 .. What is Shareware?
5 .. How do I get Symantec Product Support online?
6 .. Common questions and answers about this system
7 .. System configuration — hardware and software
8 .. Your usage agreement and rights
9 .. What's new with the Symantec BBS?

I encourage you to find out what there is to know about using the BBS. The more familiar you are with its menu system, offerings, and commands, the faster you'll be able to locate what you need the next time.

The Q&A SIG

The BBS contains a Q&A SIG (Special Interest Group) consisting of a message database with attached files that you can download. You can browse through messages left by Q&A users, download files attached to these messages, leave a message, and even upload a file attached to your own message.

BBS messages left by your fellow Q&A users are sometimes quite interesting and informative. If you have a question about Q&A, you can leave it here in the form of a message, and you might be surprised to find that a day or two later several other users have answered you. Messages posted to SIGs are erased after 90 days.

The Q&A SIG Menu includes these selections:

S .. Select a new SIG
R .. Read messages
W .. Write a message
D .. Download a file attached to a message
U .. Upload a file for attachment to a message
T .. Teleconferencing
X .. Exit from SIGs

By selecting "Read messages" you can scan through the messages one at a time, view a list of the messages by date and topic a screenful at a time, do a keyword search for specific messages, or use the Quickscan menu for configuring how you want to conduct your search.

By scanning through all the messages in the SIG you can read dozens of informative Q&A-related questions, appeals for help, tips, tricks, and workarounds left by users on the BBS. Where a file has been attached to the message, or there's a reply from another user, you can download the file or read the reply.

You can choose to view a list of the messages whose topics will normally indicate their contents, and you can go back and read the entire message — along with any replies — should something pique your interest.

By selecting "Write a message" from the SIG menu you can address a message to an individual, Q&A tech support, or all Q&A SIG users. Questions directed to tech support are normally answered within 24 hours. A message open to all users may receive any number of replies — or none — depending on the interest it generates.

File Libraries

In the File section of the BBS you'll find the latest Q&A and Q&A Write printer drivers and font files, along with sample Q&A databases, MS-DOS utility programs, and other useful utilities and files. To select a file library from the menu, just type in its name and press **<Enter>**.

Almost all the files available for downloading have the .ZIP filename extension, indicating that they've been "zipped" or compressed. They'll download much faster in this format, but it also means that you'll have to uncompress them once you've got them safely copied to the receiving directory on your PC.

PKUNZIP.EXE is included in the Applications disk that accompanies this book, but it can also be downloaded from Symantec's BBS. You can "explode" the files by typing:

```
PKUNZIP filename
```

at the DOS prompt in the directory where these files are stored.

Some of the files available for downloading, although zipped, are still quite hefty, and may take a half hour or more to download even at 2400 baud. In addition, these files sometimes come with special usage instructions, so be on the lookout for .TXT, .DOC, and README files that may appear after you've uncompressed the main file.

Information Center

At the Information Center you have access to Symantec product information, Q&A technical tips and bulletins, Q&A consultant classified ads, and more. Selecting Q&A tech tips, for example, displays another menu you can use to home in on areas of particular interest:

A .. Index of all technical tips available
1 .. Programming and design tips
2 .. Advanced programming with Q&A
3 .. Q&A report tips
4 .. Write and mailing labels
5 .. Database recovery tips
6 .. Tutorial and MS DOS information
7 .. Documentation for Q&A Utilities
8 .. Miscellaneous application notes

From the File Library you can download all the Q&A technical bulletins in a single compressed file and peruse them at your leisure off-line.

The following choices are available in the consultant classified section:

S .. Scan or read ads
P .. Place an ad
M .. Modify an ad
D .. Delete an ad
C .. Check reader responses
G .. Get general information

Electronic Mail

The following E-mail services are available on the BBS:

R .. Read message(s)
W .. Write a message
M .. Modify a message already written
E .. Erase a message
X .. Exit from E-mail

To leave a private message, select "Write a message" from the E-mail menu, and you'll be prompted for the user-ID of the recipient (the person's name) and the topic. You can then type away (to a maximum of 1,920 characters). When you've finished typing your message, type OK on a blank line and press **<Enter>**. The Editor's Options menu will then display and you can:

- Save your message
- Append to the message
- Redisplay the message
- Change text
- Change the topic
- Retype a line
- Delete a line
- Insert one or more lines
- Start a new message
- Display a help screen

If an E-mail message has been left for you, the BBS will let you know as soon as you've logged on. Don't forget to erase any messages to or from you that are no longer of any use.

There is much more to the BBS than can be presented in this appendix. Symantec has a number of other software products, and these, of course, have their own SIGs and File Libraries, too. The thing to do is to get logged on, make use of the generous help facilities, and get to know what's on the BBS simply by looking around.

A **?** entered at any prompt displays a list of the commands you can use at that point, and entering **go help** at any prompt takes you directly to the BBS help menu.

Pressing the letter **X** at any prompt will always exit you from the current section and move you back to the previous menu. Once back at the Main menu you can press the letter **G** to say goodbye and log off. But you might first want to take just a moment or two to leave a comment for the Sysop, letting him or her know how you enjoyed the tour and appreciate the facilities the free BBS has to offer.

Appendix E
Files Supplied
With Q&A 4.0

Should a Q&A program file become damaged during a power outage, or a hard disk problem occur, it may become necessary for you to reinstall one or more files on the advice of Q&A Technical Support. The files listed below are supplied with Q&A 4.0; the list includes Q&A program files (those that are essential to the full operation of Q&A), as well as tutorial files, sample database files, and utility files. Q&A also comes with over 50 printer-driver files, which are not included in this listing. Special files containing SQL drivers may not be included with your copy of Q&A but are available from Symantec.

If it should become necessary to reinstall any of the files supplied with the program, you must use the installation utility that came with the program. The files are "packed" on the master program diskettes to conserve space, and the installation program is required to "unpack" them.

Filename	Description
• Program Files	
QA.DIS	Screen displays
QA.COM	The primary executable program file
QA1.EXE	The main Q&A program engine file
QADFONT.OVL	Page preview overlay file (overlay files allow the transfer of segments of the program from the disk into RAM. Such files are used to increase the apparent size of memory by keeping in RAM only the parts of the programs or data that are currently being accessed. The rest of the program is stored on disk until needed)

Filename	Description
QAFAX1.OVL	Fax driver overlay
QAFR.OVL	File/Report overlay
QAFRI.OVL	File/Report/Intelligent Assistant overlay
QANIA.OVL	Intelligent Assistant overlay part 0
QAIA1.OVL	Intelligent Assistant overlay part 1
QAIA2.OVL	Intelligent Assistant overlay part 2
QALABEL.OVL	Mailing label overlay
QAMAIN.DCT	Spelling dictionary
QAPRINT.CFG	Printer configuration file
QAPRNDRV.OVL	Printer driver overlay
QAQG.OVL	Query Guide overlay
QASPELL.OVL	Spell checker overlay
QATHES.OVL	Thesaurus overlay
QATHES.DCT	Thesaurus file
QAWP.OVL	Word processor overlay
QAW4W04F.EXE	Import from WordStar
QAW4W04T.EXE	Export to WordStar
QAW4W05F.EXE	Import from Microsoft Word
QAW4W05T.EXE	Export to Microsoft Word
QAW4W07F.EXE	Import from WordPerfect
QAW4W07T.EXE	Export to WordPerfect
QAW4W08F.EXE	Import from PFS
QAW4W08T.EXE	Export to PFS
QAW4W10F.EXE	Import from MultiMate
QAW4W10T.EXE	Export to MultiMate
QAW4W15F.EXE	Import from DCA
QAW4W15T.EXE	Export to DCA
QAW4W23F.EXE	Required for all non-ASCII exports
QAW4W23T.EXE	Required for all non-ASCII imports

Filename	Description
• Tutorial Files	
WRIGHT.DTF	Tutorial database file
WRIGHT.IDX	Tutorial database index file
INVITE.LTR	Tutorial document
• Sample Database Files *(ready to use)*	
CLIENT.DTF	Sample client database
CLIENT.DTF	Index file for client database
EMPLOYEE.DTF	Sample employee database file
EMPLOYEE.IDX	Index file for employee database
INVNTORY.DTF	Sample inventory database
INVNTORY.IDX	Index file for inventory database
MAILLIST.DTF	Sample mailing list database
MAILLIST.IDX	Index for mailing list database
PERSFIN.DTF	Sample personal finance database
PERSFIN.IDX	Index file for personal finance database
SALESORD.DTF	Sample invoice database
SALESORD.IDX	Index file for invoice database
• Utility Files	
ASC-CODE.ASC	ASCII document file that contains the ASCII decimal codes and graphics character set
BAR.PIC	Lotus bar graph file for import
BLOCK1.FNT	Lotus font driver
HIMEM.SYS	Extended memory driver
LINE-DOC.DOC	Document to assist in determining page layout
PTESTREL.DOC	Printer test document
QABACKUP.EXE	Database backup utility
QAFONT.EXE	Font conversion utility
SALES.PIC	PFS bar graph file for import

Appendix F
Using Q&A
With a Mouse

You can use a mouse or other pointing device with Q&A to choose items from menus, select function keys, move between fields on a database form or in Table View, or perform block operations. Mouse support is built into Q&A 4.0. You can also run Q&A 4.0 under Microsoft Windows 3 as a full-screen application. See Appendix H for details.

Q&A supports the Logitech Serial/Bus Mouse, the Microsoft Serial Mouse drivers, and compatibles. While no extra memory is required by Q&A to work with a mouse, the mouse driver provided by the mouse manufacturer will require some RAM — on the order of 10K to 20K. Two- or three-button mice can be used, and you can both "click," and "click and drag" your mouse depending on what you're doing in Q&A.

Once the mouse and driver are installed, you can turn off mouse operation by exiting Q&A to DOS, and reloading Q&A with the **QA -g** command, which turns off the mouse for the current session only.

With your mouse installed, its pointer — a small box — will appear on screen when you load Q&A. When you move the mouse, the pointer moves, and allows you to select function keys and items, block text, and so forth.

My personal opinion on using a pointing device with Q&A is this: If you already have a mouse installed in your computer and use it routinely in your work, then by all means click away with Q&A. But don't go out and buy a mouse just because Q&A supports it, unless what you're doing in Q&A are the kinds of activities where a mouse would prove more practical and productive than the keyboard. Your own experience will help you decide. This appendix is here to give you specifics on the kinds of activities in Q&A that can be performed with, and may be augmented by, the use of a pointing device.

Selecting a Menu Choice

With any menu displayed, you can place the pointer on your selection and click the mouse to execute it. This includes custom menus as well as standard Q&A menus. Clicking outside the menu is like pressing **<Esc>**.

Function Key Selection

No matter what you're doing in Q&A, you'll usually see a group of function key assignments along the bottom of the screen. These are the function keys you're most likely to use during the current activity. To "press" one of these function keys with the mouse, move the mouse so that its pointer is over the function key name (not the description), and click it. You can invoke the **<Esc>** or **<Enter>** commands in the same manner.

At the List Manager

When Q&A prompts you for a filename in any module, you can press **<Enter>** or click **<Enter>** to display the list of files in the current directory. Once the list is displayed, you can do any of the following actions with the mouse:

- Place the pointer on a filename and click to highlight the file, and then click **<Enter>** on the status line to retrieve it.

- Double-click the filename to highlight and retrieve it.

- Click a file to highlight it, and then click a function key at the bottom of the screen to perform some operation on the file.

- Click the **\..** symbol to display the list of files in the parent directory.

- Click a subdirectory, such as **\DATA** or **\DOCS**, to bring up the list of files for that directory.

Block Operations

Block operations are available in Write, File, and the Program and Field Editors. To block text:

1. Place the pointer at the beginning or end of the text you want to block.

2. Drag the mouse across the block of text to select it. The text is highlighted as you select it.

3. Click (or press) **<F8>** to open the Options menu. The "Block operations" submenu displays.

4. Choose from the available block operations.

In the File Module

During data entry you can use your mouse to move from field to field. Simply position the pointer in the field you want the cursor to move to, and click the mouse. Programming statements set to execute when the cursor leaves the field will be executed if your click causes the cursor to exit from such a field. For example, a navigation statement in the field might cause the cursor to move to a field other than the one you clicked. Any on-field-entry statement will be executed when the cursor arrives at the field you clicked, or at the field your click caused the cursor to move to.

In Table View, you can use the mouse to scroll vertically or horizontally to find the record or field you want.

When designing a database form you can click to bring the cursor to the position you want. You can also click and drag the cursor to select text blocks. To move through several screens, click and drag the mouse from the top or bottom of the screen, outside of any text. Click outside of any selected text to "unselect" it.

You can add or change a tab marker by clicking the mouse on the ruler line. Clicking the mouse repeatedly deletes the tab marker, or changes it to a **T** (Tab) or **D** (Decimal Tab).

In the Write Module

You can move the pointer around the Type/Edit screen and click it to position the cursor. Click and drag selects text on which you can then perform a block operation. Clicking outside of selected text "unselects" it. Scroll through screens by clicking and dragging across the top or bottom of the screen.

Click **<F8>** to bring up the Options menu for almost any word processing-related operation. Then click on the type of procedure you want to perform and then select the operation from the submenu.

Click on the ruler line to create or change a tab marker. Repeated clicks delete the tab marker, or change it to a regular tab or decimal tab.

With the Intelligent Assistant

Use your mouse in the Query Guide to make selections while building your query or report. If you've taught the Query Guide the values in your database, you may be able to build a complete query or report without ever having to touch the keyboard.

With Macros and Custom Menus

You can name a macro or custom menu after the Center or Right mouse button, and then click your mouse to execute the macro or call the menu. However, you can only assign these buttons once per file.

Until you assign a macro to a mouse button, the Run Macro screen will display by default when you click the right or center mouse button.

Appendix G
Using Q&A's Backup and Restore Utility

Backing up your data and document files routinely may be a minor inconvenience, but it's certainly cheap insurance. In days of yore only a major calamity like fire, theft, or a federal raid could claim your files.

Today, a flash of lightning, a traffic accident a mile away, too many air conditioners turned on simultaneously, or any number of other unexpected (and sometimes unnoticed) electrical or system glitches can wreak unimaginable havoc on your data.

Better to be safe than sorry. If you back up your important files daily, then the most you stand to lose is a day's work. Back up when you feel like it or have the time and you're courting disaster.

Q&A comes bundled with an easy-to-use backup/restore utility that you run, not from inside Q&A, but from the DOS prompt. It's called QABACKUP.

Unlike the "Backup database" selection on the File Utilities menu, QABACKUP lets you back up continuous file sets and files too large to fit on a single floppy disk. Like any commercial backup program, QABACKUP prompts you to insert the next diskette when the first one is full and offers to erase whatever files are on the diskette before backing up your selected files onto it.

What's more, QABACKUP contains a built-in compression utility that squeezes your files down to less than half their size. This means you'll be able to backup nearly three megabytes worth of data onto a single 1.2MB floppy. It also means that if you use QABACKUP to back up your Q&A data and/or document files, you'll have to use the same utility to restore those files should it ever become necessary.

The most convenient way to run QABACKUP is to add it to the Q&A Main menu as an "Alternate program" selection, or first create a DOS batch file that loads the program and then install the batch file as an "Alternate Main menu program." Assuming the second option and that the QABACKUP.EXE file is located in the C:\QA directory, here are the steps needed to do this:

1. Select Write from the Main menu and then choose Type/Edit from the Write menu.

2. Type the line: **QABACKUP**

3. Save the batch file to ASCII format by pressing **<Ctrl><F8>**, typing in **C:\QA\BACKUP.BAT**, and pressing **<Enter>**.

4. Now select Utilities from the Q&A Main menu, and choose "Set alternate programs" from the Utilities menu.

5. At the Set Alternate Programs screen, move the cursor to the "Alternate program 6" line and type in the lines shown here in boldface:

   Alternate program 6: **BACKUP.BAT**

   Menu selection: **Backup Files**

   If you already have a Main menu selection that begins with the letter "B," you'll have to think of a different name for the menu selection line, perhaps something like "Q&A Backup."

6. Press **<F10>** to save the screen and return to the Main menu. Your new selection will be displayed.

Now, with your Q&A menus set to Automatic Execution, you can simply press the letter **B** to exit Q&A, load QABACKUP, back up your selected files, and then be returned to Q&A when you exit from the backup program.

Backing Up with QABACKUP

The QABACKUP opening screen offers the following choices:

B – Backup Q&A Files

R – Restore Q&A Files

You can press **<Esc>** to exit from the utility (which reloads Q&A) or press **<Enter>** or **B** to back up files. Selecting Backup displays the Backup Q&A Files screen shown in Figure G-1.

The program takes a moment to scan your hard drive and then displays the drives in your computer, the directories, and subdirectories on the current drive, along with any Q&A files in the current directory. Only Q&A document and data files are displayed. The utility will not allow you to back up Q&A

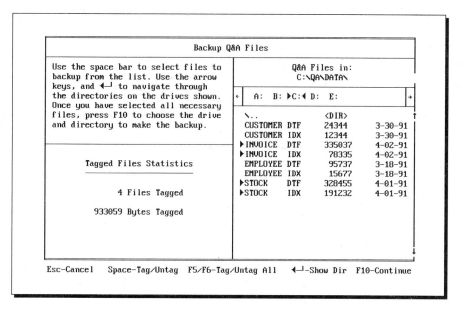

Figure G-1: The Backup Q&A Files Screen. This is where you select the drive and directory as well as tag the files you want to back up.

program or font files or, for that matter, any files belonging to a program other than Q&A.

Use the → and ← keys to highlight the drive where the Q&A files you want to back up are stored.

When you've highlighted the correct drive, use your cursor to highlight the QA directory (if that's where your Q&A files are stored) and press **<Enter>**. If your data and document files are stored in subdirectories of the QA directory (\DATA and \DOCS, for example), highlight the proper directory whose files you want displayed and press **<Enter>**.

With the files listed, navigate to the first file you want to back up and press the space bar to tag it. If it's a data file, both the .DTF and IDX. files will be tagged when you tag one or the other. Optionally, you can press **<F5>** to tag all the files in the directory.

Untag a tagged file by highlighting it and pressing the space bar again. Untag all tagged filed by pressing **<F6>**.

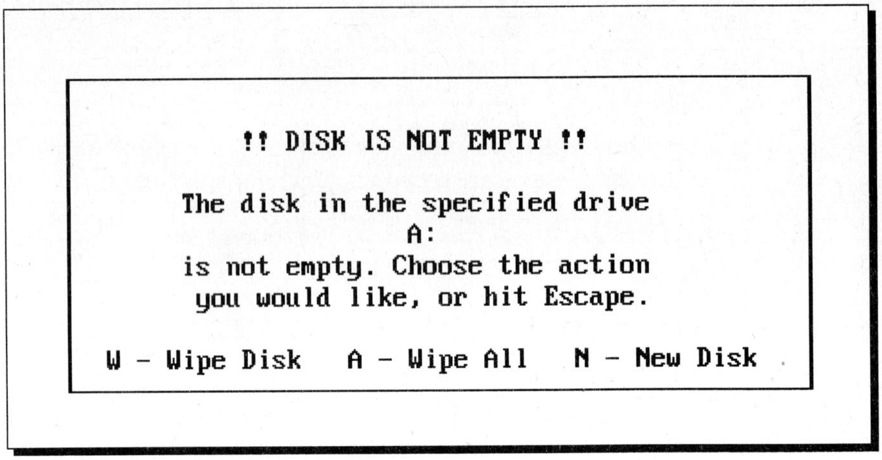

```
            !! DISK IS NOT EMPTY !!

        The disk in the specified drive
                      A:
        is not empty. Choose the action
          you would like, or hit Escape.

     W - Wipe Disk    A - Wipe All    N - New Disk
```

Figure G-2: The Disk Is Not Empty Warning Screen.

You can change drives and directories and tag additional Q&A data or document files. Files already tagged remain tagged.

The "Tagged files statistics" area in the lower left of the screen indicates how many files have been tagged so far, and the total number of bytes contained in those files, giving you a rough idea of the number of floppy disks you'll need to back up the set based on an approximate 2-to-1 compression.

When you've tagged all the files you want to back up, press **<F10>** to choose the destination drive and directory. Let's assume you're backing up to the A: drive.

1. Place a formatted floppy disk in the A: drive.

2. Use your cursor to highlight the A: drive.

3. Press **<F10>**. If the disk is not empty, the screen in Figure G-2 will be displayed:

Choose one of the following by pressing its letter or highlighting it with your cursor key and pressing **<Enter>**.

W – Wipe Disk: To erase all files on the destination diskette and commence the backup.

A – Wipe All: To erase all the files on this and any additional diskettes inserted to complete the current backup session. If you like, you can use the same set

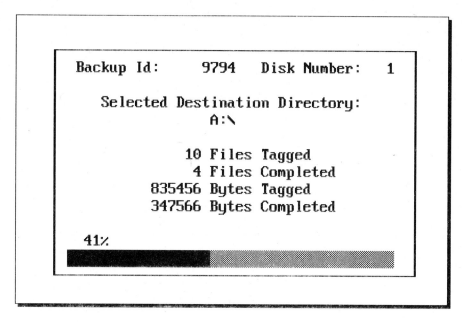

```
        Backup Id:        9794    Disk Number:    1

        Selected Destination Directory:
                         A:\

                    10 Files Tagged
                     4 Files Completed
                835456 Bytes Tagged
                347566 Bytes Completed

        41%
```

Figure G-3: QABACKUP Is Backing up Your Files and Keeping You Posted on How the Operation Is Progressing.

of backup diskettes each time you run a routine backup session on the same set of files.

N – New Disk: Prompts you to insert a different diskette in the destination drive. When you've done so, press **<Enter>** and the backup procedure will commence if the new diskette is empty.

As the tagged files are being backed up, the screen (shown in Figure G-3) displays the number of files and bytes tagged, along with the number of files and bytes completed (safely backed up). The meter at the bottom left of the screen indicates the percentage of the backup set completed.

As the backup operation proceeds, QABACKUP prompts you if additional diskettes are required. When all your tagged files have been backed up, you'll be prompted to reinsert disk #1 so the catalog file can be updated. The program then signals a successful completion and you can exit and return to Q&A.

Restoring Backed-up Files

When you make a backup, QABACKUP creates a catalog entry for the files in the backup set and places this on the first diskette in the set. The catalog is a DOS file with a byte count and the date of the backup. A typical catalog file might look like this: **9794_QAB.CAT   175   3-03-91**. This file will be displayed when you place the #1 diskette in drive A:, load the utility, select Restore from the opening menu, and choose the drive from which to restore.

To restore previously backed up files, use your cursor keys to highlight the drive from which to restore, and press **<F10>**.

The utility then gives you the option of restoring to the same directory from which the files came or to a new directory. When you've made your choice, press **<Enter>** and then press the space bar to tag the files you want to restore (press **<F5>** if you want to restore all the files). Press **<F10>** to begin the restore.

The restore operation is monitored much like the backup operation; you're prompted to insert a specified diskette if necessary and the progress indicators keep you posted. If your parameters will cause an existing file to be overwritten, the program first asks for confirmation.

Appendix H
Q&A Under Microsoft Windows 3.0

Q&A will work with most multitasking programs, including Microsoft Windows 3.0, provided your computer has sufficient memory.

 Warning: If there is any possibility that you will access the same database from two different windows in the multitasking program (in other words, you are running multiple sessions of Q&A by loading a copy of Q&A in each of two windows), you *must* load the DOS SHARE utility. Failure to do so can result in damage to your Q&A database files.

Q&A 4.0 can be run under Microsoft Windows 3.0 as a full-screen application only. It cannot be sized in a window. The Q&A program disks include two files you will need to have available in your Q&A program files directory for Q&A to run under Windows: QA.PIF (which tells Windows some basic facts it needs to know about Q&A) and QA.ICO (an icon for Windows to use to represent Q&A).

To install Q&A in Windows:

1. Be sure QA.PIF and QA.ICO are in your Q&A program files directory, and then start Windows.

2. At the Program Manager window, click on the window where you want to install Q&A. To create a new window, choose "New..." from the File menu, click Program Group, and then OK. Type the window description, type **C:\WINDOWS** for the Group File, and click OK.

3. Select "New..." from the File menu. At the New Program Object dialog box, click Program Item, and then OK.

4. At the Program Item Properties dialog box type the descriptive text you want to appear below your Q&A icon, such as "Q&A 4." For the Command Line, type **C:\QA\QA.PIF**, or the correct path to your Q&A program files directory.

5. Click Change Icon, and then type **C:\QA\QA.ICO** (or whatever is the correct path to your Q&A program files directory).

6. Click OK, and then OK again to exit.

You cannot use the Windows mouse driver when running Q&A under Windows — you'll need to load your own. You can have your mouse driver loaded automatically when you boot up by adding the command to your AUTOEXEC.BAT file. See the documentation that came with your mouse for information on how to do this. See also Appendix F for details on using Q&A with a mouse.

Index

IDG Books Worldwide Registration Card
PC World Q&A Bible, Version 4

Fill this out—and hear about updates to this book & other IDG Books Worldwide products!

Name _____

Company/Title _____

Address _____

City/State/Zip _____

What is the single most important reason you bought this book? _____

_____

Where did you buy this book?
- ❏ Bookstore (Name _____)
- ❏ Electronics/Software Store (Name _____)
- ❏ Advertisement (If magazine, which? _____)
- ❏ Mail Order (Name of catalog/mail order house _____)
- ❏ Other: _____

How did you hear about this book?
- ❏ Book review in: _____
- ❏ Advertisement in: _____
- ❏ Catalog
- ❏ Found in store
- ❏ Other: _____

How many computer books do you purchase a year?
- ❏ 1
- ❏ 2-5
- ❏ 6-10
- ❏ More than 10

How would you rate the overall content of this book?
- ❏ Very good
- ❏ Good
- ❏ Satisfactory
- ❏ Poor

Why? _____

What chapters did you find most valuable? _____

What did you find least useful? _____

What kind of chapter or topic would you add to future editions of this book? _____

_____

Please give us any additional comments. _____

_____

Thank you for your help!

❏ I liked this book! By checking this box, I give you permission to use my name and quote me in future IDG Books Worldwide promotional materials.

IDG
BOOKS

Fold Here

IDG Books Worldwide, Inc.
155 Bovet Road
Suite 730
San Mateo, CA 94402

Attn: Reader Response

DISCLAIMER AND COPYRIGHT NOTICE

NOTE

IDG Books Worldwide, Inc., warrants that the diskette that accompanies this book is free from defects in materials and workmanship for a period of 60 days from the date of purchase of this book. If IDG Books receives notification within the warranty period of defects in material or workmanship, IDG Books will replace the defective diskette. The remedy for the breach of this warranty will be limited to replacement and will not encompass any other damages, including but not limited to loss of profit, and special, incidental, consequential, or other claims.

3 ½ INCH DISK FORMAT AVAILABLE. The enclosed disk is in 360K 5 ¼ inch format. If you don't have a drive in that size or format, and cannot arrange to transfer the data to the disk size you need, you can obtain the code on 3 ½ inch 720K disks by writing: IDG Books Worldwide, Attn: Q&A Disks, c/o IDG Peterborough, 80 Elm Street, Peterborough, NH 03458. Or call 1-800-282-6657. Please allow 3 to 4 weeks for delivery.

IDG Books Worldwide, PCW Communications, and the author specifically disclaim all other warranties, express or implied, including but not limited to implied warranties of merchantability and fitness for a particular purpose with respect to defects in the diskette, the programs and source code contained therein, the program listings in the book, and/or the techniques described in the book, and in no event shall IDG Books Worldwide, Inc., PCW Communications, Inc., and/or the author be liable for any loss of profit or any other commercial damage, including but not limited to special, incidental, consequential, or other damages.

Licensing Agreement

Do not open the accompanying disk package until you have read and unless you agree with the terms of this licensing agreement. If you disagree and do not wish to be bound by the terms of this licensing agreement, return the book to the source from which you purchased it.

The entire contents of this disk are copyrighted and protected by both U.S. copyright law and international copyright treaty provisions. You may copy, modify for your own purposes, embed portions in your own code, and distribute the results for NONCOMMERCIAL PURPOSES ONLY the code from this disk, under the following limitations: First, as noted above, we make no warranties of any kind as to the merchantability or fitness of the code for any particular purpose; second, you assume full responsibility and liability for the resulting code, and the publishers and author shall in no event be liable for any damages or loss of profit or any other commercial damages, as noted in the paragraphs above, for the resulting code or for the portions of that code taken from this book or disk; and third, in all cases any distribution of any kind must include a copyright notice to wit: "Copyright ©1991 by IDG Books Worldwide, Inc." or "Portions copyright © 1991 by IDG Books Worldwide, Inc.," as appropriate. Absolutely none of the material on this disk or listed in this book may ever be distributed, in original or modified form, for commercial purposes.

QUALITY FIRST
3 MONTHS FREE

RECEIVE 15 MONTHLY ISSUES FOR THE PRICE OF 12 WHEN YOU SUBSCRIBE TO
THE QUICK ANSWER

*"**T**he Quick Answer has the expert application articles, shortcuts, tips, and tricks you'll need to get the most from Q&A. Whether you develop sophisticated interactive database applications for others, or are primarily concerned with maintaining basic business records or designing mail merge applications, **The Quick Answer** offers solutions you can use."*

—Tom Marcellus
Technical Editor
The Quick Answer